BLOOMSBURY GUIDES TO ENGLISH LITERATURE

The Renaissance

A Guide to English Renaissance Literature: 1500–1660
Edited by Marion Wynne-Davies

BLOOMSBURY

This edition published in 1992
by Bloomsbury Publishing Ltd
2 Soho Square, London W1V 5DE

The moral right of the authors has been asserted.

A copy of the CIP entry for this book is available from the British Library.

ISBN 0 7475 1261 2

Typeset by Hewer Text Composition Services, Edinburgh
Printed in England by Clays Ltd, St Ives plc

Contents

Acknowledgements

General Editor
Marion Wynne-Davies

Originator
Christopher Gillie

Editor
Marion Wynne-Davies, University of Keele

Contributors
John Drakakis (Critical theory), University of Stirling
Christopher Gillie (Historical Background), Homerton College, Cambridge
Lesley Johnson (Medieval literature), University of Leeds
John O'Brien (French literature), University of Liverpool
Valerie Pedlar (Context of literature), University of Liverpool
Jonathan Sawday (Renaissance poetry), University of Southampton
René Weis (Renaissance drama), University College, London
Marion Wynne-Davies (Renaissance literature), University of Keele

Editorial
Editorial Director Kathy Rooney
Project Editor Tracey Smith

General Editor's Preface

The Bloomsbury guides to English literature derive directly from *The Bloomsbury Guide to English Literature* (1989), and are intended for those readers who wish to look at a specific period or genre, rather than at the wide-ranging material offered in the original text. As such, the guides include material from the larger and earlier work, but they have been updated and supplemented in order to answer the requirements of their particular fields. Each individual editor has selected, edited and authored as the need arose. The acknowledgements appropriate for the individual volumes have been made in the respective editor's prefaces. As general editor I should like to thank all those who have been involved in the project, from its initial conception through to the innovative and scholarly volumes presented in this series.

Marion Wynne-Davies
University of Keele

Editor's Note

Cross References

A liberal use of cross references has been made. In both the essays and the reference entries, names, titles and topics are frequently marked with an arrow ($\triangleright$) to guide the reader to the appropriate entry in the reference section for a more detailed explanation. Cross-reference arrows appear both in the text and at the end of entries.

Dates

Dates after the names of people indicate their life spans, except when they follow the names of monarchs when they show the length of the reign.

Editor's Preface

Editing the *Bloomsbury Guide to English Renaissance Literature* has given me a solid grounding in the cultural and social aspects of the period, as well as the exciting experience of discovery as I searched for new authors to add to the alphabetical reference section. Considerable thanks are owed to Christopher Gillie, Jonathan Sawday and René Weis, who wrote the original essays and entries. Christopher Gillie's plot summaries are invaluable for rapid checking; Jonathan Sawday's knowledge and application of contemporary critical theory reveals texts and authors in a dramatically new light; and René Weis's scholarly approach to the drama, especially the plays of Shakespeare, provides the necessary background for a close study of the texts. My main contribution in the reference section has been to add women writers who although well known in their own time, have since become neglected.

My thanks are also due to John Drakakis for his lucid entries on critical theory, to Lesley Johnson for her informed work on the medieval period, and to Val Pedlar for the accuracy and detail of the references to classical and biblical material. I should also like to thank Richard Dutton for his careful reading of the manuscript and my husband Geoff Ward, both for his informed criticism and his loving support; would that I had their knowledge and insight. Any errors and omissions I freely acknowledge as my own. Finally, my thanks go to Kathy Rooney and Tracey Smith of Bloomsbury Publishing for their help in the production of this work.

Marion Wynne-Davies
University of Keele

Essay section

'By Any Other Name': Understanding Renaissance Literature

Marion Wynne-Davies

1

Introduction

When Juliet calls upon Romeo to reject his surname so that they will no longer owe allegiance to the warring Montague and Capulet families, she explains her argument through the metaphor of a rose:

> *What's in a name? That which we call a rose*
> *By any other word would smell as sweet.*
> (▷ *Romeo and Juliet*, II. ii. 43–4)

Juliet asserts that names are superfluities which may be discarded at will, since the substance of identity can never change – the material body of the rose will remain the same, whatever arrangement of letters or sounds we use to describe it. To a certain extent, Juliet's concerns prefigure the twentieth-century theory of semiotics, of which ▷ Ferdinand de Saussure was an important initiator. The difference between the two ideas – Juliet's simple poetic argument and de Saussure's complicated construction of a theory of language – lies in the character's insistence upon the material object and the theoretician's primary concern with the name. In other words, de Saussure pointed out that each name or 'sign' has two component parts: the sound or letters (signifier) and the concept or idea (signified). For Juliet we must take meaning a step further: to the 'referent', to the 'thing' which exists in the real world. What we are faced with as readers is the conflict between the name 'rose', which through previous cultural associations carries a romantic and beautiful signification, and the recognition of a practical argument about real objects – we must admit that if the same flower were called 'rhosyn' (Welsh for 'rose'), it would make no difference to the smell. But how do these arguments forward an understanding of what is meant by the name 'Renaissance'?

The word (and sound) 'Renaissance' is like any other signifier, a jumble of letters that may change to 'Rinascimento' in another language (Italian), or to 'renascence' when Matthew Arnold (1822–88) decided to alter the term to a more nationalistic form:

> *The great movement which goes by the name of the Renascence . . . I have ventured*
> *to give to the foreign word* Renaissance *an English form.*
> (*Culture and Anarchy*, 1869)

Indeed, the name in English does have a somewhat bastard origin in that it derives from the French verb 'renaître' (to be born again), and only began to be used commonly during the nineteenth century in scholarly tomes such as John Ruskin's *The Stones of Venice* (1851) and Walter Pater's *Studies in the History of the Renaissance* (1873). However, the name gradually developed a coherent concept (signified), which was grounded upon its original meaning of a rebirth of classical learning after the 'dark ages' of medieval scholarship. This denigration of the ▷ Middle Ages is today recognized as erroneous; in order to fashion itself, each age tends to denigrate the previous period.

Nevertheless, that there was a difference cannot be questioned. Apart from the rebirth of knowledge, the Renaissance encompasses the valorizing of the individual, the centralization of power systems and the primacy of gold, as well as discoveries in the realms of science and the New World. In this manner, we can perceive that further signifiers reverberate about the central name; ▷ humanism, neo-Platonism (▷ Platonism), alchemy, the prince and the courtier, are simply a few. Beyond this, pictorial signifiers emerge, images depicted in the most resplendent colours: the gold-clad figures of ▷ Henry VIII and ▷ Elizabeth I, the highly glazed paintings of Leonardo da Vinci, Michelangelo, Raphael and Titian, the statuesque characters from the literary works of ▷ Shakespeare and ▷ Milton, the figure of Columbus leaping ashore into a bright and vivid new world, and the rebellious ▷ Galileo confronting the Inquisition with proof that the earth moves around the sun. The complex interrelationships between these words and images – and each individual reader will be able to provide additional information – combine in various permutations to weld signifiers and signifieds into the meaning of the 'Renaissance'.

This general indeterminacy and widespread application of the term 'Renaissance' has led some critics to reject it altogether. For example, ▷ C. S. Lewis in his comprehensive *English Literature in the Sixteenth Century* (1954) complains that,

> *'The Renaissance' can hardly be defined except as 'an imaginary entity responsible for everything the speaker likes in the fifteenth and sixteenth centuries'.*

Moreover, if we take the European Renaissance as a whole into account, then we must extend the dates from the fourteenth-century Italian poet ▷ Petrarch, to mid-seventeenth-century English writers such as John Milton, ▷ Andrew Marvell and ▷ Katherine Philips. Despite Lewis's objections, however, it is both possible and necessary to draw certain margins. For example, we may accept that the Renaissance began in Italy and spread northwards and westwards, so that the English Renaissance occurred much later than the Italian. In England, we may use the commencement of the Tudor dynasty in 1495 and the end of the ▷ Interregnum in 1660 to limit the chronological extent of the Renaissance. This temporal enclosure exhibits a certain cultural and political uniformity; it begins with ▷ Henry VII's self-conscious attempts to create the court of a Renaissance prince with its panoply of entertainments and ▷ patronage, and ends with the Restoration of ▷ Charles II.

But what of Juliet's rose? For her, the names and ideas, which we so readily acknowledge, are meaningless. Instead, what is important is the material object, the referent. Juliet's understanding of the 'Renaissance' would not consist of discussing the word's etymology or of tracing the scholarly concepts which the letters imply, but would develop from discussion of the period itself, the cultural practices, the social and political events, the material circumstances of people's lives during that unique period. Although productive, we must also be aware that this approach can be unstable, since objective and timeless judgements of external reality cannot be achieved. If a text was produced in a period distant from our own, the instability is compounded. The rose is a case in point. The twentieth-century European image of a rose is most commonly the long, pointed, velvet-leafed hybrid tea, which was a development of nineteenth-century horticulture. The Renaissance rose had more in common with today's wild plants, being more globular in form and of trailing habit, with fewer petals and only two colours, red and white. The rose adopted by the Tudors as their emblem was the red version, the Rosa Gallica. Juliet's rose may be as equally romantic as those purchasable at Interflora today, but it was quite a different species. To understand the Renaissance, we too must combine historical investigation with a self-aware recognition of our own temporal distance.

Although the nineteenth century fixed the period's identity in scholarly terms, the name 'Renaissance' was probably first used by Giorgio Vasari in *The Lives of the most excellent Italian Architects, Painters and Sculptors* (1550 and 1568), where he argues that his contemporaries are not anonymous artisans like the painters of the previous period, but individualistic artists and creators. Vasari's understanding of the Renaissance subject lies at a substratum of the same seam excavated by the ▷ new historicist critic Stephen Greenblatt, with his focus upon 'self-fashioning'. Both highlight the marked increase of self-determination in Renaissance culture and society. Another twentieth-century commonplace of the Renaissance configuration, the concept of the rebirth of knowledge, was evident still earlier, when the Italian neo-Platonic philosopher Marsilio Ficino (1433–99) wrote:

> *This century, like a golden age, has restored to light the liberal arts ... achieving what had been honoured among the ancients, but almost forgotten since.*
>
> (*Theologia Platonica*, 1482)

It seems that Renaissance men and women carried convictions about their own age which remain current, and it is these areas of convergence that we must investigate. In the remainder of this essay I shall focus upon the rebirth of knowledge; the rise of individualism; political power and patronage; and the age of gold. However, this exploration is not intended to uncover a reflection of the fifteenth to seventeenth centuries in the writing of that time. Although referents are a necessary component of meaning, literary texts are not mimetic (▷ Mimesis), reproducing exactly an external reality. Nor are we able to receive the words and images without introducing our own twentieth-century interference. Instead, we must look for ways in which literature develops a dialogue with other ▷ discourses of both periods. For example, while Ficino alerts us to the idea of the Renaissance as a golden age, he simultaneously appears to be participating in a dialogue in which that notion has been contradicted. Note: he does not write that it *is* a golden age, but *like* one. Finally, we must simultaneously be aware of our own historical and cultural positioning. As the new historicist critic Louis A. Montrose writes:

> *Integral to ... historical criticism must be a realization and acknowledgement that our analyses and our understandings necessarily proceed from our own historically, socially and institutionally shaped vantage points; that the histories we reconstruct are the textual constructs of critics who are, ourselves, historical subjects.*
>
> ('Professing the Renaissance: The Poetics and Politics of Culture', 1987)

For example, the popularity of ▷ feminist criticism in the late twentieth century has focused readers' attention upon female authors, and several books (this guide included) have attempted to redress the gender imbalance in our canon by making contemporary readers aware of the large number of Renaissance women writers who have been neglected since the mid-seventeenth century. The recovery of authors like ▷ Lady Anne Clifford, ▷ Lady Eleanor Davies and ▷ Lady Elizabeth Cary is clearly an important historical contribution to our understanding of cultural productivity in the Renaissance. But at the same time we must not expect these women writers to have modern feminist values. ▷ Rachel Speght might well defend women against Joseph Swetnam's attack in his *Arraignment of Lewd, idle, forward, and unconstant women* (1615; ▷ *Querelle des Femmes*), but she also accepts women's inferiority to men, because they are the 'weaker vessel' (*A Mouzell for Malastomus*, 1617). Rather than condemn her out of hand, we should recognize that the increased number of women writers during the sixteenth century was partially a result of humanist edicts on education. For them, perhaps, the period was a 'naissance' and not a *re*birth of knowledge.

II

Pleasure Reconciled to Virtue

The rebirth of classical learning in the English Renaissance combined a moral and civic education of the individual together with an inspirational delight derived from the ideal beauty of words and images. Classical texts were revived not simply for their scholarly merit, but because they were in themselves pleasurable to read. Under the influence of humanism, these works were quickly absorbed by national grammar and local public schools, so that by the mid-sixteenth century writers and officials had a solid grounding in the 'classics'. One of the major influences on Renaissance poetry was ▷ Aristotle's *Poetics*, which emphasized the need for consistency; the unities of time and place may be found in Milton's ▷ *Samson Agonistes*. ▷ Homer and ▷ Virgil were seen to be the originators of the epic tradition, each celebrating his own nation and nobility for posterity; here ▷ Spenser's nationalistic epic dedicated to Elizabeth I, ▷ *The Faerie Queene*, followed their example. ▷ Seneca's drama was immensely influential upon ▷ revenge tragedy through its emphasis upon ▷ Stoical dignity and individual responsibility. Finally, the neo-Platonists replaced Aristotelian logic with ▷ Plato's rejection of the material world as transient and his belief in a higher, eternal realm in which opposites could be reconciled in an ideal and ultimate truth. This allowed writers such as ▷ Sidney to accept the poetic imagination as a powerful and mystical force for wisdom and virtue, rather than as a series of false tales or dreams (▷ *An Apologie for Poetrie*, 1595). Similarly, it facilitated the acceptance of pagan gods and goddesses into the dominant Christian ideology; ▷ Jonson relied upon classical material in much of his poetry and all of his ▷ masques, yet it is not used to contradict conventional spiritual beliefs.

Indeed, the title of this section is taken from one of Ben Jonson's masques, *Pleasure Reconciled to Virtue* (1618), which marked Prince Charles's (▷ Charles I) first court performance. In it the prince plays the classical hero, Hercules, who is faced with a choice between a life of delight, or one of toil ultimately leading to glory. The symbolic figures of Pleasure and Virtue, recalling the ▷ morality play tradition, appear on stage at the same time as Hercules, Mercury and Daedalus. A further idealized unification occurs when the two possible existences are seen to be reconcilable:

> Grace, laughter and discourse may meet,
> And yet the beauty not goless:
> For what is noble should be sweet,
> But not dissolved in wantonness.
> (II. 270–3)

Political expediency made it essential that Jonson should offer the prince a delightful vista – immediately, in the courtly dances that followed the speeches, as well as a happy life in the prolonged future. However, the masque could also be used to teach both the prince and the court the value of virtue and hard work, and the last speech appears to emphasize moral endeavour:

> There, there is Virtue's seat,
> Strive to keep her your own;
> 'Tis only she can make you great,
> Though place here make you known.
> (II. 304–7)

Although the masque is a highly mannered court entertainment, Jonson's educative agenda and his use of the classics draw us back to the tenets of humanism mentioned briefly at the beginning of this section.

The contribution of humanism to a greater awareness of classical literature cannot be questioned, but this was not its only contribution to Renaissance culture. The central force of humanism, from the Platonist versions of the fifteenth-century Italians Ficino and Pico della Mirandola to the evangelical Christian interpretations of ▷ More and ▷ Erasmus, was the essential dignity of mankind. The key text was Pico's *Oration on the Dignity of Man* (1486), where he asserts that men are capable of self-determination, being able to choose freely between good and evil. In the *Oration*, Pico composes a speech given by God to man:

> *You shall fix the limits of your own nature according to the free choice in whose power I have placed you. We have made you neither mortal nor immortal, so that with freedom and honour you should be your own sculptor and maker, to fashion your form as you choose.*

Within Christian humanism this emphasis upon self-determination was to lead finally to Erasmus's rejection of the ▷ Lutheran theory of grace in his work *On Free Will* (1524), where he asserts that man is capable of choosing moral virtue for himself.

During the discussion of humanism I have consistently used the word 'man' or the masculine pronoun, when I could have reworked the phraseology into 'woman and man' or 'she and he'. However, while the humanists professed a belief in the importance of educating women to the same standard as men (in theory in Erasmus's *The Abbot and the Learned Woman* (1516) and in practice in the programme of studies in the More household), they were far from advocating sexual equality. Although it is essential to consider the impact of humanism upon both genders, it is at the same time important not to imbue fifteenth-century philosophers with late twentieth-century notions of political correctness. Moreover, the humanist focus upon the individual's ability to choose freely did not remain closeted within a philosophical, or even a religious, discourse. The construction of individual identity may be seen as basic to further aspects of Renaissance culture.

III

The Renaissance subject: symbolism to individualism

The relationship of the individual to his of her world underwent a radical change in the Renaissance. Seemingly, in every area of human existence there was a shift of perspective. No longer was the world linear and hierarchical, arranged neatly along the ascending rungs of a ladder, but sliced through in a horizontal cross-sectioning, allowing each component part an unprecedented degree of attention and autonomy. While the humanists focused upon the individual's spirit and intellect, parallel developments occurred in other areas:

increased urbanization and freedom of the market allowed greater logistical and class mobility, and the discovery of the New World and the recognition of the earth's place in the solar system demanded that traditional religious theories about man's development be questioned. Perhaps the impact of this changing self-image may best be seen in the differences between medieval and Renaissance works of art. After all, as architecture has heralded the late twentieth-century discourse of post-modernism, so fine art appears to have encapsulated the vanguard of the Renaissance.

In medieval paintings figures are depicted in exact relation to their symbolic significance; so, in *The Wilton Diptych* (c 1400 at the National Gallery in London), for example, ▷ Richard II, as a worldly monarch, is smaller and less sumptuously arrayed than the holy figures of Saint John the Baptist, Saint Edward the Confessor and Saint Edmund who accompany him. In addition, the diptych's background makes no gesture towards naturalism; instead, its gold pattern confirms the wealth of its royal commissioner. Compare this ornate emblematic style with the meticulous secularization of ▷ Hans Holbein's pen-and-ink sketch of the More family (1527, at the Öffentliche Kunstsammlung in Basel). Here the figures are drawn in proportion to one another; their material positioning is of more importance than their relative status. Although the male heads of the household still sit centre-stage and the women stand or kneel about them, suggesting conventional gender hierarchies, these stances are simultaneously challenged by the varying gazes, foregroundings and exchanges of the family group. As Catherine Belsey writes in her article on the Holbein drawing:

> *There begins to be . . . an alternative meaning for the family in the sixteenth century . . . The home comes to be seen as a self-contained unit, a little world of retreat from the conflict of the market-place, and at the same time a seminary of good subjects, where the wife enters into partnership with her husband in the inculcation of love, courtesy and virtue in their children.*
>
> (*Disrupting Sexual Difference*, 1985)

Holbein's sketch represents the More family as a self-contained unit caught during one brief moment of activity, their books scattered upon the floor and the candle still alight upon the window-ledge. Each component of the work is given equal artistic care and imaginative value: who can judge between the delicate, inquisitive stare of Anne Cresacre and the solid triangular form of ▷ Margaret Roper?

Literary discourses echoed those of fine art. In drama the symbolic figures of the virtues and vices were replaced by the lively secularized types of the ▷ citizen comedies. Although the eponymous protagonist in Jonson's ▷ *Volpone* clearly represents the cunning fox whose greed and megalomania ultimately lead to his downfall, the audience is encouraged to admire the dexterity with which he plays upon characters who themselves can hardly be said to exemplify moral virtue. We respond automatically when Volpone begs for our approval at the end of the play:

> *Now, though the Fox be punished by the laws,*
> *He yet doth hope there is no suff'ring due*
> *For any fact which he hath done 'gainst you,*
> *If there be, censure him; here he doubtful stands.*
> *If not, fare jovially, and clap your hands.*
>
> (V. vii, 153–7)

The 'laws' may exact a moral and secular punishment upon Volpone, but the audience redeems him with their applause, forgiving and condoning a contravention of didactic virtue because of the pleasure awarded them. The public theatre with its fee-paying audience enabled the dramatists to evade the necessity of pleasing a single patron, whether noble or clerical. Instead, they foregrounded the concerns of other classes, challenged the validity of the law, questioned the absolutes of established religion and subverted conventional gender roles. Examples of these may be seen, firstly in *Arden of Faversham* where the central characters are the burgher Thomas Arden and his wife, Alice. Secondly, in the mode of revenge tragedy which allowed for the enactment of personal vengeance against the tenets of society and the church when both failed to see justice done. Finally, at the end of Shakespeare's comedy ▷ *As You Like It*, where the boy-actor playing Rosalind provokes homoerotic phobias when he/she offers to kiss the men in the audience:

> *If I were a woman I would kiss as many of you as had beards that pleas'd me,*
> *complexions that lik'd me, and breaths that I defied not; and, I am sure, as many*
> *as have good beards, or good faces, or sweet breaths, will, for my kind offer, when*
> *I make curtsy, bid me farewell.*
>
> (Epilogue)

The dynamic and vivid upsurgence of individualism, of a challenge to the dominant spiritual and secular ideologies, cannot but make the Renaissance appear like the paintings of Bruegel or Bosch, at once lively, comic, carnivalesque, grotesque and tortured.

Yet surely these elements of excess contradict the 'Renaissance' of classical rebirth discussed in Section II? A possible way of relating these opposite forces is provided by the theoretician ▷ Mikhail Bakhtin, who explained how the Renaissance both welcomed classical aesthetics and retained the bodily allegiances of the medieval period:

> *The new historic sense that penetrates them gives these images a new meaning but*
> *keeps intact their traditional contents: copulation, pregnancy, birth, growth, old*
> *age, disintegration, dismemberment ... they are contrary to the classic images of*
> *the finished, completed man, cleansed, as it were, of all the scoriae of birth and*
> *development.*
>
> (*Rabelais and His World*, 1965)

It is important to recognize that beliefs as disparate as classical idealism and grotesque superfluity – Michelangelo's *David* and Bosch's demons – could, and did, coexist in a perpetual dialogue with one another. But the nature of these uneasy relationships, these disquieting dialogues, needs to be examined more closely.

IV

The prince and the courtier: power and patronage

The previous two sections have identified several interconnecting and some-times contradictory discourses. However, in combination they open up a further line of debate, in that both humanist learning and the growth of individualism would seem to eradicate the feudal class structures of the medieval period. Yet the Renaissance was not a period of democratic liberty or of a utopian classless society. Indeed, its autocratic princes demanded absolute authority, punishing transgressions with death, rather then responding with enlightened understanding. A case in point is Sir Thomas More, the philosopher discussed earlier. More might have been one of the leading exponents of humanism, but that did not prevent Henry VIII from executing him because he would not recognize the king's divorce from his first wife, Katharine of Aragon, nor acknowledge the ▷ Act of Supremacy. Nevertheless, while the relationships between a Renaissance ruler and his noble servants could undoubtedly be fraught, their mutual dependency cannot be denied. These negotiations between governor and governed are the focus of two influential Renaissance texts, ▷ Machiavelli's *The Prince* (1513), and ▷ Castiglione's *The Courtier* (1528).

The Prince is simply one of Machiavelli's treatises on statecraft, but it best encapsulates the complex notion of an autocratic ruler who simultaneously recognizes his duty to the people. The work was not translated into English until 1640, so that it was the idea of Machiavellian power – diabolical and cunning – which carried sway in England. In ▷ Marlowe's tragedy ▷ *The Jew of Malta*, the Prologue is spoken by Machevill, who counts 'religion but a foolish toy' (l. 14) and states that,

> *Might first made kings, and laws were then most sure*
> *When, like the Draco's, they were writ in blood.*
>
> (20–1)

The immense and unconditional power of the monarch is evidenced, with or without tacit criticism, throughout Renaissance literature. Examples range from Spenser's idealized vision of Elizabeth I in *The Faerie Queene*, to Shakespeare's treatment of corrupt rule and deposed monarchy in ▷ *Richard II*, with whose eponymous protagonist the queen is said to have identified:

> *So her Majestie fell upon the reign of King Richard II, saying, 'I am Richard II, know ye not that?'*
>
> (William Lambarde, *Memorandum*, 1601)

Of all the English Renaissance monarchs, perhaps it was Elizabeth who most appreciated the fine line of conditional autocracy along which she must practise a skilful tracery. The queen's 'Golden Speech' to Parliament in 1601, when she repealed several unpopular monopolies, is remarkable for the way in which it reminds her subjects of a prince's God-given authority, while at the same time stressing their influence over her decisions:

> For myself, I was never so much enticed with the name of a King or royal authority of a Queen, as delighted that God hath made me His instrument to maintain His truth and glory, and to defend this Kingdom (as I said) from peril, dishonour, tyranny, and oppression.
>
> There will never Queen sit in my seat with more zeal to my country, care for my subjects, and that will sooner with willingness venture her life for your good and safety, than myself. For it is my desire to live nor reign no longer than my life and reign shall be for your good. And though you have had and may have many princes more mighty and wise sitting in this seat, yet you never had nor shall have any that will be more careful and loving.
>
> (Elizabeth I in *Women Writers of the Renaissance and Reformation*, ed. K. M. Wilson, 1987)

Power for Elizabeth is clearly the monarch's by right, but is exercised only with the compliance of his or her populace.

The negotiation of political power was similarly recognized by the Renaissance subject. In his book of instruction on the behaviour of the ideal nobleman and -woman, Castiglione writes that,

> the aim of the perfect Courtier . . . is so to win for himself, by the means of the accomplishments ascribed to him by these gentlemen, the favour and mind of the prince whom he serves that he may be able to tell him the truth about everything he needs to know, without fear or risk of displeasing him; and that when he sees the mind of his prince inclined to a wrong action, he may dare to oppose him and in a gentle manner avail himself of the favour acquired by his good accomplishments, so as to dissuade him of every evil intent and bring him to the path of virtue.
>
> (*The Courtier*, Book Four, 5.)

Writers, like courtiers, often depended upon patronage, and they were called upon to create pleasure for their wealthy patrons, even as they attempted to inculcate certain moral lessons in them. As in Ben Jonson's masque discussed at the beginning of section II, the bitter pill of didacticism had to be sugar-coated with flattery. A mutual relationship existed, but it was hardly even-handed.

V

The age of gold

The gilded self-fashioning of the Renaissance monarch and the glorious swirl of centrifugal power in the Renaissance court cannot be better exemplified

than in the meeting of Henry VIII and King Francis I of France at the
▷ Field of Cloth of Gold in 1520. The sobriquet derived from the lavish
decoration and ornamentation on the 'field' of chivalric combat, where the
two kings jousted with the flower of English and French knighthood. The
display was an affirmation of royal identity, a statement of personal worth,
and above all, a powerful assertion of wealth. The acquisition, show and even
attempted manufacture of gold provide the final glittering accoutrement of
Renaissance culture. It may be seen in the neo-Platonic aspects of alchemy,
in the carnivalesque power of the market-place, and in the political displays
of princes and courtiers alike. Morever, it was gold that provoked the fiercest
racial confrontations, from the stereotyping of Jews to the bloody massacres in
the New World. Colonization was as much the product of economic enterprise
as it was of the desire for discovery or of the need for glorification.

Shakespeare's play ▷ *The Merchant of Venice* is a comedy, a romantic play with
marriage at its conclusion, but the idealized action takes place in the ▷ pastoral
world of Belmont, while the remainder occurs in the city of Venice. The choice
of setting was not random. Renaissance Venice was the market-place of the
western world; its rich beauty, cosmopolitan splendour and naval superiority
gave it a pre-eminence. At the hub of the mercantile republic stood the Rialto
bridge; here, under the great wall map depicting Venice's major trading routes,
the merchants sold goods and bought shares, Europe's busiest money market
did business, and the government carefully guarded national interests. When
Shylock cites Antonio's business ventures, his words evoke a goal for London's
own mercantile classes:

> *he hath an argosy bound to Tripolis, another to the Indes; I understand moreover*
> *upon the Rialto, he hath a third at Mexico, a fourth for England.*
>
> (I. iii, 16–18)

England was increasingly a nation dependent upon its seaborne trade and
the strength of its navy, and Elizabeth's rule encouraged an international
economic expansionism similar to that of the governorship of the Doge in
Venice. Investments in foreign trade to Africa, the East and the New World
were central to both the Venetian and English economies, and it is especially
significant that in Shylock's speech the only European country given equal
weight with Venice is England. But the play also allows Antonio's diverse
investments to introduce a threatening aspect to the narrative, since when his
ships fail to return to port, his life becomes forfeit to Shylock, the moneylender.
Indeed, although Antonio's ventures ultimately prove successful, it is through
no action of his but by a 'strange accident' which he is not allowed to know
about (V. i, 273–8). Thus the play interacts with the dominant social valuation
of economic growth to reveal both its successes and its moral inadequacies.
After all, it is Shylock's equal estimation of his ducats and his daughter that is
condemned most strongly in the play. But Shakespeare also propels the audience
into a confrontation with racial stereotypes – the wicked Jew – that slides in
easily alongside the play's questioning of nationalist expansionism. Gold, race

and colonialism reverberate through the play without any satisfying outcome, their interactions with audience expectations as mutable as the earlier dialogues between classical rebirth and individualistic regeneration, and between the creation of an independent subject and the autocratic power of a prince.

VI

Conclusion

There are several ways of re-envisaging these Renaissance power relationships. It is possible to perceive the dominant political and religious groups as exerting absolute control, with any possible challenges being seen as futile and puny in comparison with the overwhelming might of the monarchy and the Church. Here we could cite the insurmountable feudal traditions facing humanism. Alternatively, we could stress the radical changes that did occur during the Renaissance: more women were educated and more published books than in the medieval period. We could, however, follow the new historicist trend, which portrays the radical subversion of some texts as ultimately contained and suppressed by official bodies. As Jonathan Dollimore writes:

> *Subversiveness may for example be apparent only, the dominant order not only containing it but, paradoxical as it may seem, actually producing it for its own ends.*
>
> (*Political Shakespeare*, Jonathan Dollimore and Alan Sinfield, 1985)

What Dollimore suggests is that authority needs some form of challenge so that it may assert itself and thus retain its sense of an empowered identity. Thus the courtier's never-ending and always-failing attempts to curb the prince's power might be exactly what the monarchy requires to sustain itself. Elizabeth I's magnanimity was called into existence mainly because of her necessary response to Parliament's questioning of her absolute power. Or we could return to Bakhtin's notion of a perpetual dialogue, each discourse interacting with others, so that literature is affected by social forces as well as empowered to change that which it condemns. In *The Merchant of Venice* Shakespeare mirrors a nationalistic desire for mercantile wealth, while at the same time offering the audience an altered self-image in which gold is seen as less valuable than lead. Each interpretation may be substantiated textually and critically, leaving the reader with a sense of transience and mutability; relationships shift in perpetuity, at one minute offering harmonious homogeneity, at another radical marginality. It seems, then, that names may not be distilled to essence as easily as Juliet would wish.

This essay began with a conventional Shakespearean heroine. To conclude, I shall turn to his most unconventional female character – Katharina in ▷ *The Taming of the Shrew*. The narrative and theme of this play turn upon the power relationship between men and women, more explicitly, between Katharina and Petruchio. During the 'taming' of his independent wife, Petruchio insists that she voluntarily accept his erroneous naming of the sun and moon. He does this to confirm overwhelmingly Katharina's total submission to his will. She responds with the tired resignation of the oppressed. Or does she?

> Petruchio. *Nay then you lie, it is the blessèd sun.*
> Katharina. *Then God be blessed, it is the blessèd sun.*
> *But sun it is not, when you say it is not,*
> *And the moon changes even as your mind.*
> *What you will have it named, even that it is,*
> *And so it shall be so for Katharine.*
>
> (IV. v, 18–22)

Meaning appears to be controlled by the dominant party, in this case a husband, but any of the social and religious leaders already established as conventional in this essay could easily be substituted for Petruchio. Katharina's submission to the necessity of changing meaning according to the demands of hierarchy – 'what you will have it named, even that it is' – directly refutes Juliet's innocent 'What's in a name?' Therefore, determining a meaning for the 'Renaissance' becomes a question of locating the various powerful discourses that lay claim to the definition. Classicism, humanism, autonomy, patronage, monarchy, wealth and colonization each file their petitions of ownership, engaging in an unceasing bargaining process about meaning.

But is Katharina totally submissive? When she responds to Petruchio's continual metamorphoses of meaning she appears to agree that the moon will become the sun whenever he so decides: 'And the moon changes even as your mind'. Yet she too has learnt to exploit verbal ambiguity, and with more subtlety than her husband, for this same line also suggests that Petruchio's mind is as inconstant as the moon, in other words, that he is mad – a lunatic. Katharina ceases to be an object upon whom meaning is imposed; instead she is presented as an independent subject, quite capable of making meaning for herself. So, when searching for the meaning of a 'rose', the 'Renaissance' or of any sign or text, simply recall how Katharina tamed Petruchio – remember that while meaning may appear to be already established and unchallengeable, it is in fact open to perpetual reinterpretation.

Reading Renaissance poetry   2

Jonathan Sawday

The concealed poet

> Is not this excuse for mere contraries
> Equally strong? Cannot both sides say so?
> That thou mayest rightly obey power, her bounds know;
> Those passed her nature and name is changed; to be
> Then humble to her is idolatry.
> As streams are, power is:
>
> (▷John Donne, Satire 3, 98–103)

We might begin this discussion of ▷ Renaissance poetry with an account of poetry as secrecy. In 1589, ▷ George Puttenham published *The Arte of English Poesie*, a work that was to have considerable influence on Renaissance writers. When, in Book III of this theoretical treatise, Puttenham came to consider 'Ornament' in language, the ornaments which decorate his own prose are metaphors of secrecy and duplicity. Figurative language, in this account, is inseparably caught up in a web of deceit and (to use Puttenham's word) 'doubleness'. So, the writer is:

> ... *occupied of purpose to deceive the ear and also the mind, drawing it from plainness and simplicity to a certain doubleness, whereby our talk is the more guileful and abusing* ...
>
> (III. ch. VII)

For Puttenham, such doubleness lay at the heart of the courtly aesthetic, and it is not difficult to understand how this awareness of poetic language as a concealing device could have a certain political efficacy. Puttenham continues:

> *And ye shall know that we dissemble, I mean speak otherwise than we think, in earnest as well as in sport, under covert and dark terms and in learned and apparent speeches, in short sentences and by long ambage and circumstance of words, and finally as well when we lie as when we tell the truth. To be short every speech wrested from his own natural signification to another not altogether so natural is a kind of dissimulation, because the words bear contrary countenance to the intent.*
>
> (III. ch. XVIII)

What Puttenham has observed here is crucial to our understanding of Renaissance writing. In trying to isolate the function of poetic language (an attempt whose result is not dissimilar to the discovery of 'defamiliarization' by the Russian ▷ formalist critics of the early twentieth century), he has focused attention not simply on the latent 'ambiguity' of all linguistic transactions but also on the struggle which takes place in all discourse. That struggle he expresses through a series of oppositions: speaking/thinking, serious/unserious, dark/apparent, lies/truths.

In reading Renaissance texts, this sense of doubleness, this possibility of concealment, and this understanding of poetic discourse as encompassing contradiction and struggle must be kept in mind. For ▷ Thomas Wyatt, courtier and diplomatic servant of ▷ Henry VIII, doubleness is itself a theme of his writing. 'What 'vaileth truth?' he asks in one of his poems, concluding:

> *True meaning heart is had in disdain.*
> *Against deceit and doubleness*
> *What 'vaileth truth?*

The opposition between truth and deceit here has implications for meaning itself. Wherein can 'meaning' lie if, as Puttenham was to observe some fifty years later, we 'speak otherwise than we think'? 'Meaning', too, becomes of significance in dealing with another of Puttenham's oppositions, that between what is 'dark' or concealed, and what is 'apparent' or open to interpretation. Wyatt's poem 'My galley charged with forgetfulness', itself a version of an earlier poem by ▷ Petrarch – *'Passa la nave mia colma d'obblio'* (*Rime* CLXXXIX) – displays the problem for us:

> *My galley charged with forgetfulness*
> *Thorough sharp seas in winter nights doth pass*
> *'Tween rock and rock, and eke mine enemy alas,*
> *That is my lord, steereth with cruelness,*
> *And every oar a thought in readiness,*
> *As though that death were light in such a case.*
> *An endless wind doth tear the sail apace,*
> *Of forced sighs and trusty fearfulness;*
> *A rain of tears, a cloud of dark disdain*
> *Hath done the wearied cords great hinderance,*
> *Wreathed with error, and eke with ignorance.*
> *The stars be hid that led me to this pain,*
> *Drowned is reason that should me comfort,*
> *And I remain despairing of the port.*
>
> (XXVIII)

Richard Tottel, the editor of the anthology in which this poem first appeared in published form in 1557, was in no doubt as to the meaning of the sonnet. 'The lover', he headed the poem, 'compareth his state to a shippe in perilous storme tossed on the sea' (▷ *Tottel's Miscellany*, sig. E3). Tottel is reminding the poem's sixteenth-century readers of the tradition of love poetry, stemming from Petrarch, which employs a conventional pattern of metaphors, images and formal metrical and rhythmical devices. Wyatt (together with ▷ Surrey, as has been often noted) was instrumental in importing these conventions into English verse. So, the storm-tossed lover might appear as a familiar figure to the Renaissance reader (see, for example, ▷ Edmund Spenser's ▷ *Amoretti* 63, 'After long stormes and tempests' sad assay'). We might compare Wyatt's sonnet to the 'original' (though the very question of originality is a concept to which we shall have to return):

> *My ship full of forgetful cargo sails*
> *Through rough seas at the midnight of a winter*
> *Between Charybdis and the Scylla reef,*
> *My master, no, my foe, is at the helm;*
>
> *At each oar sits a quick and insane thought*
> *That seems to scorn the storm and what it brings . . .*
>   (trans. Mark Musa)

Who are Petrarch's 'master' and Wyatt's 'lord'? The god of love, perhaps, and thus the enemy of reason. Yet, in Wyatt's version of the poem the character of this figure undergoes significant alterations. Where Petrarch suggests a certain unsureness as to the true nature of the helmsman ('My master, no, my foe'), Wyatt is unequivocal: at the helm is 'my enemy, alas,' who, inevitably, is also 'my lord'. And where, in Petrarch, the image was that of a blind and unreasoning steersman, rushing the ship headlong through the storm, in Wyatt he is possessed of intent – steering 'with cruelness'.

Reading Wyatt's sonnet against Petrarch's 'original' (as opposed to reading it in the way in which Richard Tottel asked his sixteenth-century contemporaries to read it) , we begin to sense that all is not quite as it appears. Once the 'code' located within conventional Petrarchan imagery has been identified, we might still feel that there is more than simply a generalized meditation on the pangs of despised love at work in the poem. At this point we might move away entirely from Petrarch and the overt conventions of sixteenth-century love poetry, to read the sonnet for what it might also be – a profoundly disturbing meditation, not on love, but on the very nature of existence within the ▷ Tudor polity. Wyatt, a diplomat, a justice of the peace, marshal of Calais, ambassador to Spain and to France, M.P. for Kent, and vice-admiral of the Fleet, would appear to represent (and to have gained) all that was most glittering in the establishment of the society in which he found himself. Yet, at the head of that society was a monarch – Henry VIII – with whom conversation, in Stephen Greenblatt's memorable phrase, 'must have been like small talk with Stalin' (*Renaissance Self-Fashioning*, 1980).

The other side of Wyatt's double existence (and the double existence of so many Renaissance writers) is what is represented in his ▷ sonnet 'My galley charged with forgetfulness'. That side – which involved, for Wyatt, imprisonment in 1534, further imprisonment and release on parole in 1536, the execution of his patron, ▷ Thomas Cromwell, in July 1540, and a final period of imprisonment in the Tower in 1541 – is one that might be drawn from any twentieth-century catalogue of existence under the conditions of absolute power. It is the realization of this existence which sends us back to the sonnet and to those key phrases – 'forgetfulness', 'mine enemy . . . my lord', 'cruelness', 'a thought in readiness', 'trusty fearfulness', 'wreathed with error', 'drowned is reason' – with a rather different sense of what this text may encode, and with an understanding, too, of the sonnet's ambiguous air of the sinister. To recall Puttenham again, we are in the presence of a text which possesses a certain 'doubleness'.

From writing to interpretation

For the poets of the ▷ Elizabethan and early ▷ Jacobean period, the contradictions involved in manoeuvring between the 'dark' and the 'apparent' produced, in turn, an awareness that the act of writing could itself be worth writing about. This self-conscious awareness of the writing process (which can be uncovered in the later parts of Petrarch's *Rime*) is the opening theme of ▷ Sir Philip Sidney's ▷ *Astrophil and Stella* (1591), and it was the status of writing, and the relationship *within* writing between meaning and truth, which was to fascinate the sonnet writers of the 1590s – ▷ Samuel Daniel, ▷ Michael Drayton, Edmund Spenser, ▷ Thomas Lodge and ▷ Shakespeare (to name but a very few). For Astrophil, in Sidney's sequence, the task is to uncover 'fit words' (I. 5) to 'entertaine' his female reader. But where are these words to be found? And once located, what process gives them utterance?

> *Thus great with child to speak, and helplesse in my throwes,*
> *Biting my trewand pen, beating my self for spite,*
> *'Foole' said my Muse to me, 'looke in thy heart and write.'*

This comic self-presentation of the poet conceals an important Renaissance theoretical problem associated with the act of writing. Sidney, here, abandons the conventional notion of male authorship 'begetting' his works upon the world (and we might recall the 'onlie begetter' of Shakespeare's sonnets here). Instead, writing is, once more, a struggle – a painful delivery rendering the author paradoxically helpless. At the same time, writing is a process by which that which was hidden within becomes manifest, and hence it entails an inward scrutiny, promoted by a voice ('my Muse') whose origin is also located within the writing self of the poet. But this inner search should not be understood as a quest for originality in the modern sense. What is at stake here is the Renaissance concept of ▷ 'imitation'. 'Imitation', as it was understood by the Renaissance writer, did not entail mere copying, but an assimilation of other voices into the unique voice of the individual poet. Writing, as ▷ Erasmus claimed in the *Ciceronianus* (1527), is therefore not an isolated utterance, but it is the product of other discourses, jostling in the mind. For the poet, working amidst these competing voices, the problem becomes one of establishing a position from which to speak, as Shakespeare's dramatic denial of other poetic voices in his sonnet 130, 'My mistress' eyes are nothing like the sun', evidences. Here, a series of Petrarchan motifs are summoned up, only to be dismissed as not answering to the reality of the woman he addresses. The paradox is, of course, that the very gesture of denial serves to evoke the competing voices of those other poetic discourses.

If writing is a proposition which involves the poet in a search for an authority with which to speak, what of reading? To the modern reader, what may be striking about Renaissance poetry is its determination both to create the reader and to control his or her response to what is read. We might understand this desire to forestall the reader's licence to interpret (for this is what it amounts to) as being a manifestation of a literary culture which is at once enclosed (in a social sense) and also profoundly anxious as to the results of unlicensed interpretive power. The freedom to interpret, as Elizabeth's ▷ Protestant divines were never tired of pointing out, could have unfortunate results. Protestant culture may, on the one hand, have championed the right to interpret scriptural texts when that interpretation seemed to support Protestant beliefs against the perceived threat of ▷ Roman Catholic ▷ Counter-Reformation, but that did not mean that the right to interpret should be invested in each and every reader. The ▷ Thirty-nine Articles, passed under Elizabeth at the Convocation of 1562, might be thought of, within this context, as an attempt at controlling the interpretation of key doctrinal issues. What the articles set out to establish was 'consent touching true religion' and the 'avoiding of diversities of opinions'. Their end, in other words, was to create a homogeneous reader.

Interpretation was understood as involving the assumption of power over the text and the experience inscribed within that text. Is this, then, the key to understanding the Renaissance poet's constant anxiety as to the way in which his secular verse is to be understood? Are the Stellas, Delias, Dianas, Licias, Zephiras, Fidessas and Chlorises (the antique names of imagined or real readers to whom sonnet collections are addressed, and whose names are inscribed in their titles) fierce interpretive presences before whom, in true Petrarchan style, the poet-writer trembled? Indeed, they are. But herein lies another paradox of Renaissance writing. In ▷ lyric poetry in particular, the relationship between the writer and the reader is above all sexual. But this sexual connection, though it involves (as we might expect) an active male author confronting a female reader (as the titles to countless sonnet sequences announce), does not position the female reader in a necessarily passive role, since she is not only a reader but an interpreter. As an interpreter she may be threatened, cajoled, persuaded, but never ignored. We can thus understand the female figure, within the dominant masculine codes of Renaissance writing, as one in whom there is invested a network of competing claims and counter-claims. She is the mainspring of the poet's invention, the object of sexual desire, the prize, the besieged fort, the source of religious or quasi-religious consolation or agony, and, most important of all, the reader and interpreter of his verses. So, Stella, in Sidney's *Astrophil and Stella*, is not only the object of Astrophil's verse (whilst his own sufferings and triumphs are the subject), she is also the final reader and interpreter of the verses laid before her. In Spenser's *Amoretti* (1595), the sequence of sonnets opens with an invocation of the reading-presence of his mistress, who is the final interpreter of what is to follow: 'Leaves, lines and rymes, seeke her to please alone, whom if ye please I care for other none' (I. 13–14).

'Politique Devotion'

It would be simple to dismiss this presence of the female reader as no more than a conventional trope of praise – a means of ensuring that the elaborate fiction of the intimacy of the lover's adoration of the beloved is sustained. Thus, the argument would continue, the true object of the sonnet-writer's fascination is himself, and the female subject is evoked only in order that she be marginalized. But to dismiss the importance attached to interpretation on the part of Renaissance poets is not only to dismiss the serious implications of interpretive power discerned by Elizabethan writers in general, but also to ignore the presence of the most important female interpreter of all – that of the queen herself.

It is almost impossible to over-estimate the awareness of late sixteenth-century poets of the abiding presence of the queen. The queen as head of state, head of the Church and ultimate source of patronage is a figure of real, not merely idealized, power. She is, moreover, a dominating presence in all forms of literary and artistic culture of the period. As such she is a protean figure, paradoxically subject herself to the transforming power of the very verses which sought to confirm her central position in the political hierarchy. But it is in the figure of the queen that the complete identification of aesthetic forms with political power is manifested. Her very name becomes an emblem of power, even whilst it is transformed, literally, through the devices of art:

E   urope, *the Earthes sweete Paradise:*
L   *et all thy Kings that would be wise,*
I   n Politique Devotion:
S   *ail hither to observe her eyes,*
A   *nd marke her heavenly motion.*

B   *rave Princes of this civill Age,*
E   *nter into this pilgrimage:*
T   *his Saints tongue is an oracle,*
H   *er eye hath made a Prince a Page,*
A   *nd workes each day a Miracle.*

R   *aise but your lookes to her, and see*
E   *ven the true beames of Majestie,*
G   *reat Princes, marke her duly;*
I   *f all the world you do survey,*
N   *o forehead spreades so bright a Ray,*
A   *nd notes a Prince so truly.*

These acrostic verses, written by ▷ Sir John Davies and entitled 'To all the princes of Europe', form part of a sequence entitled *Hymns of Astraea*, published in 1599. Elizabeth is addressed as the goddess Astraea, a title bestowed upon her not only by Davies, but by other poets including Spenser and ▷ George Peele. Astraea, associated with spring and with justice, is, in ▷ Ovid's *Metamorphoses* (an important source of poetic mythologizing in the period), a symbol of the former ▷ Golden Age when justice and prosperity ruled on earth, whilst in ▷ Virgil she is associated with a future Golden Age. The Golden Ages of the future and of the past thus meet in the figure of Elizabeth in the present.

To say of these verses that they are sycophantic or contrived is to miss the fundamental connection between art and political power which the poets and the queen herself sought to preserve. We might take Davies's poem as itself emblematic of the queen's presence within art. Her name and title function as the springboard for the poet – the place from which the lines themselves originate. Through her name, she is embedded within the poem – a poem which sets out to admire her, as Davies puts it, with 'Politique Devotion'. Devotional politics, indeed, are precisely what the poem produces. But the poem memorializes the queen in more than one role. Passively, she is the object of pilgrimage and devotion, moving as does the constellation Virgo (an alternative, and of course immediately appropriate name for Elizabeth/Astraea) above and beyond the earth. As an object she is, within the poem's structure of images and language, the recipient and bestower of glances and gazings. Her eyes, in a Petrarchan conceit, must be observed, her motion marked, looks raised to her. But her own glances have within them political force, and the Petrarchan conceit is itself transformed in a movement of appreciation of political reality: 'Her eye hath made a Prince a Page'.

For Sir John Davies, lawyer and aspiring politician, later (in 1603) solicitor-general to Ireland, the conjunction between the forms of art and the realities of political power meet in the multiple personae of the queen. Similarly, for the contemporaries of Davies, and as Elizabeth's reign drew to its close, the queen's continuing presence becomes itself the subject of ever-more elaborate poetic and artistic device. In ▷ Sir Walter Ralegh's poem of devotion 'The Book of the Ocean to Cynthia' (or 'The Ocean's Love to Cynthia'), a text of which only a fragment exists in manuscript form, the queen is Cynthia/Diana, goddess of the moon, hunting and chastity, whilst the poet is the ocean, subject to the moon's transforming power, a power which is absolute and, disturbingly, seemingly arbitrary:

> *No other power effecting wound or bliss,*
> *She gave, she took, she wounded, she appeased.*
> ('Ocean's Love', ll. 55–6)

What can we conclude from this assimilation within art of the realities of power? Reading the poetry of the late sixteenth century, we realize that at the very heart of the literary culture of the period lies the pervasive belief that art and the state must conspire together to affirm a vision of national identity. That it is a vision and not a reality is exemplified by the very urgency with which Renaissance writers pressed home the point that the country was a united whole. Late Elizabethan culture, rather than appearing 'monumental' (as it has been described) or as the product of a realized sense of national selfhood, begins to appear as a rather more anxious moment of history. That pressing need for unity – whether it be unity of religion, of social practices, of cultural forms, of political expression, or of interpretation (all of these being linked in any case) – like all such calls of national unity, indicates the awareness of what is potentially disuniting and positively disruptive. Within this context the 'monuments' of Renaissance culture, the poets of the late sixteenth century, begin to appear not only as poets but, at one and the same time, as ideologues of the first order. Their function was not only to adorn or beautify, but to affirm (sometimes, one feels, for the benefit of Elizabeth as well as her subjects) that the hierarchy was an established reality.

Nowhere is this awareness of the poetic text's power to sanction or authorize a sense of national selfhood more apparent than in what may appear, from the outside, to be the most monumental text of them all – Spenser's ▷ *The Faerie Queene*. Indeed, it is as a monument that the poem is approached in the first instance. On the dedicatory page of the 1596 edition of the poem appears this inscriptive address:

TO
THE MOST HIGH,
MIGHTIE
and
MAGNIFICENT
EMPRESSE, RENOW-
MED FOR PIETIE, VER-
TUE, AND ALL GRATIOUS
GOVERNMENT ELIZABETH BY
THE GRACE OF GOD QUEENE
OF ENGLAND FRAUNCE AND
IRELAND AND OF VIRGI-
NIA, DEFENDER OF THE
FAITH, &c. HER MOST
HUMBLE SERVAVNT
EDMUND SPENSER
DOTH IN ALL HU-
MILITIE DEDI
CATE, PRE-
SENT
AND CONSECRATE THESE
HIS LABOURS TO LIVE
WITH THE ETERNI-
TIE OF HER
FAME

The queen and her titles are inscribed (together with the poet's name) in the form of a memorial urn whose function is to preserve and consecrate the text which is to follow. The queen's titles, held under God (the teaching of whose works she sanctions as head of His Church in her realm), are titles of monarchy over three nations, and sovereignty over a new entity – the colony of Virginia. The poem that follows (and which will also serve to memorialize the queen and the nation, the two being, once more, inseparable) is thus approached through an elaborate token of royal power.

The Faerie Queene is, however, not only a monument to Elizabeth, but a legendary history of the nation over which she governs. It is important, here, to be fully aware of the circumstances of its composition. When Spenser embarked upon the poem (some time prior to October 1579), he was shortly to gain the position of private secretary to Lord Grey, the newly appointed lord deputy of Ireland. Ireland was to be Spenser's home throughout the period of composition and publication of *The Faerie Queene*, and it was as a diligent servant to the government in Ireland that Spenser was to fashion his own career.

The poem is, therefore, composed not close to the source of political patronage and power, but at the very margins of the Elizabethan polity. To Elizabethan authority, Ireland presented a continuing source of disruption. A Catholic and unruly nation (in the eyes of Elizabeth's government), it was not until the Battle of Kinsale (1601), where a combined Irish and Spanish force was defeated by the English under Lord Mountjoy, that the Protestant domination of the country was assured. Spenser, whose own colony of English settlers established on confiscated land was destroyed in 'Tyrone's Rebellion' (1598), was an active administrative cog in what is generally agreed to have been a brutalized (and brutalizing) regime. Indeed, Spenser was the author of two important 'policy documents' on Ireland written in the late 1590s. These works are important for what they tell us of the attitude of mind of Spenser and his contemporaries. Informing them is, above all, fear. Fear of the Irish, their alien religion, their customs, their language (which Spenser, though he lived in Ireland for nearly twenty years, never understood), and the threat which they represented to England, determines to a large extent his understanding of the country in which he found himself. They are, in short, documents of colonialism, some of the earliest we possess.

We can perceive this sense of threat, this awareness of an alien alternative to the 'civilizing' culture of the Protestant poet, at work throughout Spenser's text. In the poem we encounter an evocation of a brutal wilderness, a complex psychological state of 'otherness' which it is the task of Spenser's knights to banish from both the fantastic environment through which they move, and, more importantly, from themselves. This fear, or anxiety, which permeates the poem is, it is important to recognize, not simply a fear which can be dispelled through heroic endeavour. It is a fear, rather, of what is uncontrollable within the subject. If we need an analogy in more recent writing, then Joseph Conrad's Mr Kurtz in *Heart of Darkness* might serve. For Conrad's figure of colonial corruption, isolated from any 'civilized' values, it is the discovery that the darkness and horror lie within which is finally destructive of his own sense of integrated selfhood. So, in similar measure, with Spenser's knights. As they progress on their episodic forays into a world of alien values, their discovery of a struggle taking place within themselves is what the poem dramatizes. When, for example, at the climax of Book II (the legend of Guyon, or temperance), Guyon and his guide enter the 'Bower of Blisse' to confront a world of sensuous and artificial luxury (a world rich in images of frozen sexuality), their iconoclastic endeavour is simply to destroy the *representations* of sensuality with which they have been confronted. Yet they themselves are not untainted by what they encounter. Kurtz-like, they creep through the undergrowth to witness the strange rites from which they cannot draw their eyes. The object of their voyeuristic gaze is the enchantress Acrasia:

> Her snowy brest was bare to readie spoyle
>   Of hungry eies, which n'ote therewith be fild,
>   And yet through langour of her late sweet toyle,
>   Few drops, more clear then Nectar, forth distild,
>   That like pure Orient perles adowne it trild,
>   And her faire eyes sweet smyling in delight,
>   Moystened their fierie beames, with which she thrild
>   Fraile harts, yet quenched not; like starry light
> Which sparckling on the silent waues, does seeme more bright.
>
> (II. xii. 78)

What, and who is Acrasia? Like the queen, she is the object of a male gaze which is fascinated by what it has alighted upon. Unlike the queen (at least overtly) a world of sensual delight is promised. Acrasia, perceived in a moment of sexual passivity, is offered as a dual object of desire. There to be consumed by 'hungry eies', thrilling 'fraile harts', she is also a place of danger and destruction. Just as Ireland, or Virginia, or America itself were represented as female figures in need of mastery, so Acrasia must be captured and her Bower destroyed by the stern masculine (and Protestant) rigour of Spenser's knights.

In externalizing this inward struggle, Spenser's poem is truly a Protestant epic. ▷ Calvinism (the official doctrine of the Church of England under the Elizabethan 'settlement') served to draw attention to the adherent's inner state of mind and promoted a seemingly obsessive curiosity as to the inner health of the individual. But even once this awareness of the poem's Protestant roots has been grasped, we also need to be aware of it as a validating text. *The Faerie Queene* glances back to other epics (to ▷ Tasso and to Virgil in particular) not out of conservatism, or a desire to emulate what previous cultures had produced, but to authorize the present. Spenser himself, in the course of a letter to Ralegh written in 1589, termed the poem a 'darke conceit' – a text which is both apparent and concealed and which might remind us, once more, of Puttenham – but he also described his own method as being that of 'a poet historical'. Within this context, Spenser's epic can be understood as part of an important Elizabethan project. That project entailed nothing less than the active creation in imaginative culture of the nation state as an understandable entity.

Together with later texts such as Samuel Daniel's eight books of *The Civil Wars* (1609) and Michael Drayton's vast *Poly-Olbion* (1612–22), Spenser's epic looks back to the past (albeit in Spenser's case a legendary past) to uncover not only 'thinges forepast' but 'thinges to come'. The nation, in other words, must not only have its past created by its poets, but its future mapped out as well.

The deliberate creation of a mythopoeic past was to have enormous influence on the poets who followed Spenser. For one group in particular, the so-called 'Spenserian poets', Spenser's writing served as a model for their own attempts to creat a visionary sense of national and political identity. These writers, who include Michael Drayton, ▷ William Browne and ▷ Phineas Fletcher, discovered in Spenser's writing a readily adaptable means of expressing their own sense of both a mythical past and a wished-for future. The past which these poets created, however, was one governed by the forms and styles exploited by Spenser not only in *The Faerie Queene*, but in his autobiographical ▷ *Colin Clout's Come Home Again* (1595), and ▷ *The Shepherd's Calender* (1579). What Renaissance readers uncovered in these poems was a world determined by the conventions, inherited from ▷ classical and continental writers, of ▷ pastoral. It is important to understand that 'pastoral' poetry did not represent simply an idealized retreat into a mythic world of shepherds, shepherdesses and arcadian delight. But it did signal another form of retreat, and one that was predominantly political. The adoption of pastoral personae, the evocation of a vanished 'golden age' became, for the poets of the early seventeenth century, a means of registering their own sense of isolation under the changed conditions of the early Jacobean period. The sense of poetry occupying a central position within the political culture has begun to fragment. Instead, a new kind of poetry begins to emerge – one that we might begin to term 'oppositional'.

Pastoral has been described as an omnipresent metaphor in Renaissance writing rather than a strict genre in its own right. As such it could be endlessly adaptable, but still provide a framework which both the poet and the reader could recognize. For the poets of the seventeenth century (up to and including ▷ John Milton), pastoral forms allowed them a significant freedom. Phineas Fletcher's *The Purple Island* (written c 1614–15, but published in 1633), for example, indicates the adaptability of pastoral forms. This (to modern eyes) strangely incongruous poem – incongruous since its ostensible subject is the anatomized human body – indicates the uses to which pastoral could be put in the years after the death of Elizabeth and the accession of ▷ James I. Fletcher's twelve-canto poem is narrated by a shepherd-poet named Thirsil. Thirsil's task, to which he had been elected by his fellow-shepherds, is to become their poetic spokesman. But what is to be his subject? What role is now allotted to poetry? What kind of audience must the poet create? The answer to these questions involves Thirsil in a literary search for a subject in what he calls 'these iron daies/(Hard daies)' which 'afford nor matter nor reward' for the poet. On the surface, the theme upon which he alights is profoundly apolitical – six cantos of his poem are spent in celebrating the dissected human body. Yet we should remember Puttenham's distinction between the 'dark' and the 'apparent'. For the human body, in Fletcher's poem, is the setting for war. Just as *The Faerie*

Queene had dramatized the creation of an individual identity within an alien world of uncivilized values, so *The Purple Island* represents the struggle for the human subject to define itself within a religious and political sphere. The 'Island' of the poem can be understood as the individual (and it thus offers, through allegory, an answer to Donne's famous observation that 'No man is an island', for in Fletcher's alienated world everyone is an island) and, at the same time, the potentially saved island which is Protestant England. We can call this island *potentially* saved, since the poem's function is to serve as a warning to its readers that a state of continual armed vigilance against the encroaching forces of Catholic Europe has to be maintained. Poetry, in other words, has begun to stand outside the culture of the court, serving a different function – that of warning, rather than endorsing. It is also worth remarking, in this context, that the creation of the myth with which modern British readers are familiar, of Elizabethan culture as a 'golden age' of national unity to which subsequent generations are to look for political and national definition at moments of crisis, began almost before Elizabeth herself was in her grave.

Constructing identities

If national identity is an important theme in the poetry of the late sixteenth and early seventeenth centuries, what of individual identity? Here we might remember, once more, the figure of Acrasia from *The Faerie Queene*. Acrasia represents a dual object of desire promising both sexual delight and an abyss of destruction which culminates in the loss of masculine identity. For Spenser's contemporaries – those poets of the late sixteenth century who have been celebrated for their evocation of erotic love – the figure of Acrasia seems to return, though appropriately, always in different guises. The key to these texts is not their representation of unproblematic human sexual desire, but, rather, the possibility which they uncover of confusing the boundaries of sexual identity. Shakespeare's sonnets, first published in 1609, might come to mind in this context – poems whose fascinated, and playful, confusion of the boundaries of sexual identity have presented a disturbing problem for those critics and readers who prefer a more tidy, and sanitized, national poet. But Shakespeare was not alone in preferring the confusingly playful to the depressingly ordered. Both he and ▷ Christopher Marlowe were to explore the question of sexual identity in the form of the 'brief epic', which, in the late sixteenth century, emerged as a genre in its own right. Shakespeare's ▷ *Venus and Adonis* (1593), Marlowe's ▷ *Hero and Leander* (1598), and the now largely unread *Scilla's Metamorphosis* (1589) by Thomas Lodge are usually cited as representative of this short-lived genre. Informed by the eroticism derived from the understanding of Ovidian poetry, these texts seem constantly to play with the possibility of a duality of identity. In *Hero and Leander*, the opposition between male and female – expressed in the opening opposition of the two cities which are the homes of the lovers – forms a boundary that it is not only Leander's task to cross, but the text's endeavour to confuse. Thus, Hero is at once the chaste devotee of the rites of Venus, and the tutor of the unskilled Leander. But she is also (and here we might remember Acrasia) both the voyeuristically sought-for object of sexual longing, displayed in a world of sensual (and violent) artifice, and the bestower of glances and gazes charged with erotic power. At the same moment, Leander too becomes the focus of erotic longing – an object of male sexual devotion:

> *Some swore he was a maid in man's attire,*
> *For in his looks were all that men desire . . .*
>
> (I. 83–4)

This sense of confusion, which Shakespeare was to take continual delight in exploiting in the playhouse, is sustained throughout that portion of the poem written by Marlowe. But was a fascination with such sexual identities the sole preserve of the male poet? What of Renaissance women themselves?

We have seen that, in the poetry of the sixteenth century, the female presence can be discerned occupying an interpretive role, and as the focus for a conflicting series of messages based on poets' experiments with language, images and forms inherited from continental models, the most important of whom was Petrarch. But this fluid female presence is largely the creation of male poets. Women as patrons are, of course, familiar figures. Not only the queen, but others such as John Donne's patron ▷ Lucy Russell, Countess of Bedford, and (most famous of them all) ▷ Mary Sidney, Countess of Pembroke, were celebrated by writers as diverse as Sir Philip Sidney, ▷ Fulke Greville, ▷ Thomas Nashe, Edmund Spenser, ▷ Gabriel Harvey, Samuel Daniel, Michael Drayton, ▷ John Davies of Hereford and ▷ Ben Jonson. But the question of women's writing in the Renaissance period has increasingly become a subject of urgent debate. In England, the ▷ humanist endeavour of the early sixteenth century promised women a *theoretical* access to education, but whether such liberal sentiments affected any but a tiny elite is doubtful. The figure of the woman reading in the Renaissance period is one that is, as we have seen, constantly evoked. The figure of the woman writing is another matter. Elizabeth herself was, of course, a poet and scholar of some distinction. So, too, in the earlier period, was ▷ Margaret More Roper. Mary Sidney and her niece ▷ Mary Sidney Wroth (Lady Wroth) wrote not only poetry, but in the case of the latter, the first full-length work of fiction by an Englishwoman. But these were women whose access to the literary culture of the period was based on considerable fortune and political power in its own right. It is not until the turmoil of the revolutionary period of the 1640s and 1650s that a recognizably female presence begins to emerge to challenge the dominant voices of what is, by and large, an exclusively male preserve.

The question 'Did women have a Renaissance?' is an important one in this context. A powerful conclusion to this problem, on the part of contemporary ▷ feminist scholarship, is that not only was there no such thing as a 'Renaissance' for women, but that women's status and freedom actually declined in the period we are considering. Rather than looking for a female presence in the writing of the period, it is, with significant exceptions, more accurate to speak of a female absence. Absence, at a point when so much writing by men seems devoted to registering the continual presence of the female, alerts us to a further irony as we move from the period of Spenser into the very different world inhabited by the Jacobean and ▷ Stuart poets of the seventeenth century. No poet could be said to be more alive to the possible presence of the female in his writing than John Donne, but then no poet so determinedly ensures that she remains so absent when compared to the true centre of his poetry – the fascinating object of contemplation that the poet's own self presents:

> *Thou at this midnight seest mee, and as soone*
> *As that Sunne rises to mee, midnight's noone,*
> *All the world growes transparent, and I see*
> *Through all, both Church and State, in seeing thee;*
> *And I discerne by favour of this light,*
> *My selfe, the hardest object of the sight.*
> ('Obsequies to the Lord Harrington', ll. 25–30)

Thus Donne, in a meditation addressed to the soul of his dead friend (and brother of his patron, Lucy, Countess of Bedford) Thomas Harrington. These lines, though they speak in a different vein from the more familiar voices heard in the ▷ *Songs and Sonnets* or the *Holy Sonnets*, nevertheless alert us to a voice and a theme with which the reader of Donne's writing soon becomes familiar. Donne, at a moment of still quietness, contemplates the departed soul of his friend, and discovers . . . himself. The world and the poet, rendered transparent in the moment of meditation, merge together to present that 'hardest object' before the enquiring gaze of the imagination.

The urge to render things 'transparent', a desire to peer beyond surface representation, together with the triumphant discovery of the dramatic speaking voice in poetry, and the continual awareness of the poetic self as both the subject and object of his writing, combine to make Donne and Donne's poetry almost inseparable. But which Donne do we read? In an age of poetic self-creation, Donne seems to have been continuously alive to the possibility of re-creating versions of himself in his writing. Indeed, Donne's eight surviving portraits suggest an urge to record all of those different variants for the eye of posterity. Dramatically interjecting an image of himself before the reader's gaze, we must also be aware that this poetic Donne is in a state of almost continual flux and fluidity. 'Oh, to vex me, contraryes meet in one' he exclaims in his *Holy Sonnet* XIX, but the meeting of contraries was hardly a vexing possibility for the poet. In 'A valediction: of my name, in the window' Donne imagines himself to be metonymically reduced to a sign of his absence – his name, scratched in the glass of a window. But even that transparent reminder of Donne can be further reduced – the name itself is no more than a 'ruinous anatomy', waiting to be 'recompacted' at the moment of return to the mistress. In poem after poem, Donne signals his threatened absence from what is happening, imagining himself dead and waiting for dismemberment, or embarked upon a

journey which leaves behind both mistress and a unified sense of selfhood, only
to remind the reader that this unstable entity is, in its continuous instability, the
most constant object in this poetic universe. The multiplicity of 'John Donnes'
which first circulated in manuscript for the delight of his contemporaries, and
which were, for the most part, first inscribed on the printed page only after
his death in 1631 (itself, as ▷ Izaac Walton records, an act of controlled
self-presentation) constitute perhaps the most dramatic series of poetically
shifting presences of the period.

The language of God

In remarking upon this shifting poetic awareness of a created sense of selfhood,
I do not wish to imply that Donne's poetry can somehow be categorized as
constantly breaking across a simple binary divide – the 'religious' Donne, for
example, and the 'sensual' Donne. Sensual images and language are as much
to the fore in his overtly religious poetry as religious images are constantly
present in his secular verses. And this was true not only of Donne, but
of many of those poets of the seventeenth century who wrote on religious
themes. In the writings of ▷ Richard Crashaw, for example, sensuality and
eroticism combine to present a religious aesthetic which still possesses the
power, within the dominant Protestant culture of Anglo-American criticism,
to shock and disturb.

On the surface, Donne's contemporary ▷ George Herbert offers a rather
different set of poetic values. Herbert's English poetry, all of which is devoted
to religious themes, first appeared in printed form in 1633 (the same year
that Donne's poetry was published) in a volume entitled *The Temple*. Reading
Herbert's verses we appear to have left Puttenham's world of 'doubleness', the
conjunction between the 'dark' and the 'apparent', behind. Yet has it entirely
vanished to be replaced by the light of ▷ Baconian reason? Certainly, where
in an earlier period the Renaissance poet delighted in uncovering a poetic
language based on 'ornament', Herbert offers a manifesto for a different kind
of poetry:

> *Who says that fictions only and false hair*
> *Become a verse? Is there in truth no beauty?*
> *Is all good structure in a winding stair?*
> *May no lines pass, except they do their duty*
> *Not to a true, but a painted chair?*
>   ('Jordan I', ll. 1–5)

Fiction, falseness, a 'winding' structure (terms in which the contemporaries
of Puttenham would have delighted) are here denied. What is offered as
an alternative is 'truth' – a kind of poetry which will specifically transcend
the ▷ Platonist distinction between representation and object, figured in the
opposition between a 'true' and a 'painted' chair.

Yet, reading the complete collection of poems contained in Herbert's *The*

Temple (a collection which was to be of profound influence on Herbert's immediate contemporaries, especially Crashaw), we encounter an elaborate structure of metaphor and formal experiment. Take, for example, the careful 'patterning' of the collection as a whole. On the title-page of the 1633 edition we read a quotation from *Psalms*: 'In his temple doth every man speak of his honour', and as we move through the collection we become aware that, in an elaborate architectural conceit, we are indeed placed within a 'temple' where speech – the words of man to God and (more problematically) God to man – is dramatized. But 'speech' is not necessarily open to all. In the opening poem of the collection we read: 'All things are big with jest: nothing thats plain,/But may be wittie, if thou hast the vein' ('Perirrhanterium', ll. 239–40), a statement which not only appears to contradict that poetic manifesto quoted above, but alerts us to a playfully ironic awareness of the resources of interpretation. In other words, beyond the seemingly artless structure of Herbert's verse lies a dense web of poetic device.

However, Herbert's dualistic conception of language – where the seemingly 'plain' may yet conceal the riddlingly 'wittie' – was to echo throughout the later part of the seventeenth century and in contexts which, to modern eyes, seem curiously inappropriate. For example, long after Herbert's collection appeared, ▷ Thomas Hobbes was to argue for a reform of language in all areas of discourse, whilst in the 1660s ▷ the Royal Society was to promote language reform as one of its main objectives. Underpinnning those demands was a belief that it was possible to take control of the words we use, and to uncover the very nature of external reality which (so the argument ran) had been hitherto concealed in the metaphoric (▷ metaphor) labyrinths of poetry. The world, in other words, need no longer be understood as the product of a riddlingly (and fascinatingly) obscure God. Instead, what has been created is a God endowed not only with reason but (unlike Donne's God, and even on occasions, Milton's) reasonableness.

Retreat or engagement?

We do not, however, have to leap so far forward in time to uncover in poetry a desire to escape out of the world of brittle linguistic ornamentation. Ben Jonson, for example, in the celebration of aristocratic comfort which is depicted in his poem in praise of the Sidney family, 'To Penshurst' (published in 1616), calls for an aesthetic which is in direct contrast to that enshrined in the writings of an earlier generation. The house, Penshurst, which is the home of the family his poem celebrates, is not

> *. . . built to envious show*
> *Of touch or marble, nor canst boast a row*
> *Of polished pillars, or a roof of gold;*
> *Thou hast no lantern whereof tales are told,*
> *Or stair, or courts; but stand'st an ancient pile,*
> *And these grudged at, art reverenced the while.*

What is enacted here is just that revolution in taste which Herbert, in a very different context, had called for. And yet, what are the virtues of Penshurst? Essentially they are the virtues of an emergent bourgeois existence. Penshurst is a place of fruitful production, which extends outwards from its walls to embrace the surrounding countryside and its inhabitants. But Penshurst also stands in stark distinction to other houses, and other kinds of social relations, hinted at in the poem as places less benign than that which is contemplated in these verses. At the same time, as the verses quoted indicate, Penshurst represents a different set of aesthetic values. Those values might be characterized as artful without artifice, avoiding of structural complexity, at ease (as the poets of Spenser's generation plainly were not) with the history that surrounds the house and its inhabitants. 'Polished pillars', 'a roof of gold', a 'lantern whereof tales are told', the architectural equivalent, in other words, of the world of ornament and allegory which sixteenth-century poets set out to evoke, has been banished, to be replaced by a house which is 'ancient' in its own right, no longer needing the mythographic enterprises of Elizabethan culture. It is as though the frenzied *creation* of a past has finally triumphed, and Jonson's house and its inhabitants can relax in a history which has been secured.

Of course, 'To Penshurst' represents an idealized understanding of society and social relations. It is not the case that Jonson has somehow thrown off, in one swift move, the burden of creating identities and histories which Renaissance poets felt. 'To Penshurst' is, in fact, a brilliantly successful deception. It is a performance which manages to unite the present with a past discovered in Jonson's enormous reading and imitation (in the Renaissance sense) of classical literature. As such the poem manages to suggest an assimilated sense of past and present working in harmonious unity. But that Penshurst the place may be unique, and may, in fact, stand in complete isolation from the society in which it seems to rest so securely is hinted at throughout the poem.

At the same time, 'To Penshurst' signalled for the poets who came after Jonson a moment of retreat. Nestling in the idealized Kent countryside, Jonson's creation of a secure bourgeois existence was to serve as a place of pilgrimage for poets who in other respects seem very different to all that Jonson appeared to stand for in the realm of aesthetics. What these poets were retreating from was, of course, the political and ideological fragmentation of the period of the English ▷ Civil War. What they were retreating to (and whether such retreat was, in fact, possible) is open to question. On the surface, the poets of the late 1630s, 1640s and 1650s are searching for Jonson's idyll of Horatian retirement. Thus ▷ Andrew Marvell, a poet of avowedly republican sympathies (at least at certain moments), seeks a retirement from a world that appears to have fallen apart. Only behind the walls of the garden of Nun Appleton (the home of the Fairfax family, celebrated in Marvell's 'Upon Appleton House', composed c 1651) can Marvell discover 'more decent Order tame'. But is this order real, or is it an illusion? Can the world, with all its pressing engagements, in reality be fenced in behind (or outside, depending on your point of view) a garden wall? In Marvell's 'An Horatian Ode upon Cromwell's Return from Ireland' – a poem which memorializes the return of the lord protector to England in May 1650 after his bloody campaign against the Irish – the restless figure of ▷ Cromwell is imagined as being urged out of a moment of Horatian retreat into confrontation with political realities. The political reality with which it is Cromwell's task to engage is one in which the state, government, the nexus of social affiliations as a whole, would appear to have broken apart. What Marvell offers in his heroic depiction of Cromwell is an alternative and elemental figure of power – a refashioner not only of kingdoms and states, but of the very structures of thinking. It is an alternative, too (though Marvell could not have known it), to that other elemental image of power offered in the 1650s, the *Leviathan* of Thomas Hobbes. For Marvell, caught up in the turmoil of post-revolutionary thinking, any retreat into a world of disengagement is fraught with difficulties that cannot be negotiated. So, Marvell's figure of pastoral retreat – Damon the Mower – encounters in the fields not an idyll of rural innocence, but his own downfall:

> *While thus he threw his Elbow round,*
> *Depopulating all the Ground,*
> *And with his whistling Sythe, does cut*
> *Each stroke between the Earth and Root,*
> *The edged Stele by careless chance*
> *Did into his own Ankle glance;*
> *And there among the Grass fell down,*
> *By his own sythe, the Mower mown.*
> ('Damon the Mower', ll. 73–80)

It is not difficult to understand the self-mown mower as expressing a powerful (even if humorous) image of what seemed to many Englishmen to be the self-induced catastrophe of civil war. For Damon is a reflexive figure. He is both the victim of 'edged Stele' and the wielder of steel himself: an embodiment of death, lurking in the seemingly innocent fields, and one of death's victims.

The self-destructive double-figure of Damon can be met with again and again, in various guises, in the poetry of the Civil War period. But for other poets, other forms of retreat presented themselves. For the ▷ Cavalier poets (a misleading term since the poets who are usually denoted in the phrase were neither artistically nor politically homogeneous, though they all shared a general sense of the ultimate value of the rule of kings rather than parliaments or, worse, people), pastoralism, sensuality, drink or the mind itself offered alternatives. Thus ▷ Robert Herrick, in his volume of poetry entitled *Hesperides* (1648), evokes a world of minutely observed detail, which in its fetishistic attention to the elaborate codes of dress and food, offers a form of nostalgic sensuality to counter the breakdown in social structures. But was it possible to evade what Herrick himself in his opening poem of the collection ('The Argument of his Book') termed 'Times trans-shifting'?

For Herrick's close contemporary, ▷ Richard Lovelace, the heroic self-image of the soldier fleeing the 'nunnery' of the 'chaste breast and quiet mind' of his mistress to encounter a new 'faith' composed of 'a sword, a horse, a shield' ('To Lucasta, Going to the Wars'), breaks apart when confronted with his own form of the double-figure which Marvell's Damon seemed to represent. That figure appears most memorably in Lovelace's poem 'The Snail', a poem which, on the surface, appears to be no more than an exercise in contrived wit. Yet the poem's object of contemplation, the unlikely figure of the snail itself, is an ambiguously sinister figure – a confusion of geometric order, familial relationships, gender and questions of origin. If the snail is, as the poem claims at the opening, a 'Wise emblem of our pol'tic world', then this world is one which has become a 'deep riddle'. Fluidly mysterious, the world now conforms to no fixed model of social and political stability. By the end of the poem, the snail has dissolved into a jelly, its 'dark contemplation' of its own self no preservative against dissolution. In the directly political 'A Mock Song', Lovelace depicts the universe itself as dissolving, a response to the ultimate political cleavage of the 1640s, that which took place in Whitehall in the January of 1649:

> *Now the sun if unarmed,*
> *And the moon by us charmed,*
> *All the stars dissolved to a jelly;*
> *Now the thighs of the crown*
> *And the arms are lopped down,*
> *And the body is all but a belly.*
> ('A Mock Song', ll. 15–20)

Social dissolution, the collapse of the body politic, the transformation of an ordered world into an image of chaotic misrule – it is as if that uncivilized wilderness which Spenser and his contemporaries some fifty years earlier had struggled to keep at bay has intruded into the very heart of the culture in which Lovelace is writing.

'Recent liberty recovered'

To express the literary culture of the Civil War and post-Civil War years as a struggle against encroaching forms of social and political fragmentation is to understand the poets of the mid-seventeenth century as engaged in a desperate form of self-preservation. But to other writers (and Marvell comes to mind once more), working in an alternative political tradition – one that might be termed, broadly, republican – other problems seemed to emerge. What the short-lived experiment in a different form of government of the early 1650s represented was the possibility of engagement with a radically altered set of political co-ordinates. Within this new matrix, whose boundaries can be charted in the numberless ▷ pamphlets and broadsheets of the period, in popular songs, ▷ sermons, prophetic writings, political treatises and poems, and in the diaries and letters of ordinary men and women, we can locate the most dominant poetic figure of the seventeenth century – John Milton.

Milton's poetic career is one of linguistic and formal experiment. Almost no

poet since Spenser had traversed with such skill such a range of possible genres
– which included ▷ masque, sonnet, ▷ translation, ▷ elegy, sacred drama, and,
of course, ▷ epic. But in understanding Milton's poetic achievement we also
need to recognize the continual presence of Milton's political convictions –
though that is not to say that those convictions, in themselves, were somehow
set in rigid tablets of stone. But for Milton, read by his contemporaries as the
prose defender of the great experiment in new forms of government, poetry
and politics are inextricably interwoven.

At the centre of Milton's conception of political revolution stands his
awareness that language is the key to ordering and understanding the world
in which we live. What Milton's poetry represents, therefore, is a recognition
that the language in which he is writing – indebted as it is to the language of
prophecy and lyric encountered in the Old Testament, in the patristic authors,
and in the classics – is one that has to be recaptured from the determining
ideological structures of the moment. It is not, I think, coincidence that, at the
very point when a strangely familiar (to modern ears) language of technology
and utilitarian values is being demanded by the supporters of the Royal Society,
▷ *Paradise Lost* (1667) should appear. We can glimpse the revolutionary nature
of Milton's struggle on behalf of language in the 1668 preface to the poem,
where Milton offers the following justification of his writing:

> *The measure is English heroic verse without rhyme, as that of Homer in Greek
> and Virgil in Latin, rhyme being no necessary adjunct or true ornament of poem
> or good verse . . . but the invention of a barbarous age . . . This neglect then of
> rhyme so little is to be taken for a defect, though it may seem so perhaps to vulgar
> readers, that it rather is to be esteemed an example set, the first in English, of
> recent liberty recovered to heroic poem . . .*

This, it need hardly be said, is a revolutionary poetic manifesto. And in terming
it revolutionary, I have in mind the notion of a cyclical movement. Poetic form
and political engagement became linked in Milton's demand for 'a recent liberty
recovered'. For both poetry and political expression now seem to exist in an age
which is 'barbarous' to both.

Paradise Lost is, above all, the poem of recovered poetic liberty enacted in
its very language, and, just as importantly, in what the poem has to say about
language. For Adam, in the poem, is the discoverer of a language which not
only identifies for himself his position within the world, but initiates his own
quest for self-identity. Remembering his own creation, he recalls that without
language he did not know 'who I was, or where, or from what cause' (VIII.
270–1). His response is speech, and in discovering speech, he discovers not
only God but an identity and a world which can be named. Against this
Frankenstein-like fable is set the negative language of a 'barbarous age' –
the language of Babel and of Hell, linked, in the final moments of the poem,
to a 'jangling noise of words unknown', which is the language given by God
'in derision' to the followers of Nimrod: the type of human oppression. The
universal history lesson with which the poem closes endeavours to demonstrate

that the transgression of human and divine law involves the denial of political equality:

> ... *man over men*
> *He made not lord; such title to himself*
> *Reserving, human left from human free.*
>
> (XII. 69–71)

The link between language and identity, which lies at the heart of the experience of both Adam and Eve in the poem, alerts us to Milton's other great theme of *Paradise Lost* and one with which it would be appropriate to end this account of Renaissance poetry. In terming Milton the poet of 'recovered poetic liberty', what we must also acknowledge is that Milton is, at the same time, at one with his contemporaries in seeking to establish a coherent identity for the human subject. Paradoxically, that search for a unified sense of selfhood – the discovery of an identity which has been secured – is dramatized not only in the memories of creation possessed by Adam and Eve and in gender distinction, but in the figure of Satan who claims an autonomous position in God's creation. 'Who saw/when this creation was?' Satan asks, before offering his own version of separate identity:

> *We know no time when we were not as now;*
> *Know none before us, self-begot, self-raised*
> *By our own quick'ning power . . .*
>
> (V. 859–61)

Milton's demonic figure of self-creation – one that entranced that other great poetic visionary and revolutionary William Blake – stands alongside Marvell's lyrical figure of self-destruction found in the fields and meadows. We do not need, therefore, to place Satan in the simple role of grand adversary, or counter-hero. For Adam, Eve and Satan are bonded to one another in a triangular design which cannot be disrupted. Satan's spiritual home, from which he cannot be excluded by God (into which, indeed, God welcomes him), is neither Heaven, nor Hell, but, disturbingly, Eden. '*Et in Arcadia ego*' – that motto of Renaissance mortality – is also Satan's motto, as the ever-perceptive Eve acknowledges in questioning what kind of freedom Eden can represent. And in ▷ Arcadia Satan undergoes the same tormented search for identity that the human figures strive to discover rooted in one another, as, in the most famous exit in English literature, they leave Eden and the poem together, hand in hand.

This account of poetry in the Renaissance period began with Puttenham's description of a 'certain doubleness' which seemed, to the Elizabethan critic, to haunt the language of poetry. It has ended with a description of the creation of a figure of division – Milton's Satan. Doubleness, division and duplicity have become almost the themes of this essay. But I do not want to suggest, in deploying this alliterative trio, that there exists therefore a homogeneity in the writing we have been discussing. What I would argue instead is that in the enormous richness and diversity of literary forms and experience which have reached us in the twentieth century from the early modern period, we perceive a culture which is neither monumental, nor the product of a mythic golden age of national experience. The lines from Donne's satire on religion quoted at the start of this essay suggest a more complex set of possibilities. What Donne, in these lines, seems to be contemplating is the problematic status of the individual's identity within the boundaries determined by the power relationships in society. The 'nature and name' of power in fact defines, for Donne and for so many other Renaissance writers, the nature of identity itself. But Donne continues:

> . . . *those blest flowers that dwell*
> *At the rough streames calme head, thrive and do well,*
> *But having left their roots, and themselves given*
> *To the streames tyrannous rage, alas, are driven*
> *Through mills, and rockes, and woods, and at last, almost*
> *Consum'd in going, in the sea are lost:*
>
> (Satire 3, ll. 103–108)

Here is the Renaissance writer's dilemma. To obey, sometimes to celebrate, the nature and name of power is to risk that very loss of identity which so much of Renaissance poetry is designed to preserve.

Shakespeare and English Renaissance drama 3

René J. A. Weis

Sixteenth-century drama

Arguably the most productive period of English drama dates from the establishment of the first professional playhouse, The Theatre, outside the City of London in Shoreditch in 1576, and comes abruptly to an end in 1642 when Parliament decreed that 'publike Stage-Playes shall cease, and bee forborne'. The intervening 66 years and particularly the 40 years from the mid-1580s to the death of ▷ James I in 1625 produced some 20 playwrights of distinction and at least half a dozen major theatres. The 'Acte for the Punishment of Vacabondes' of 1572 forced players to constitute themselves into mostly shareholding companies under the protection of patrons such as the Earls of Essex, Oxford, Sussex, Warwick and ▷ Leicester. Leicester's influential patronage resulted in the granting of a royal patent to ▷ James Burbage's company, Leicester's Men. Burbage duly proceeded to invest in the building of The Theatre as the focus of his company's London activities. Burbage's theatre was succeeded by the Curtain (1577), then by ▷ the Rose (1587) and the Swan (1595) – both on the south side of the Thames in the 'Liberty of the Clink', beyond the bounds of the City and outside its control – the ▷ Globe (1599), built from the timbers of the dismantled Theatre, the Fortune (1600) and the Red Bull (1605), as well as the small Blackfriars theatre in which ▷ Shakespeare's company would eventually perform during the winter season.

Originally the Blackfriars had housed the Children of the Chapel Royal, who, with the boy players of St Paul's (▷ Paul's, Children of St), would regularly perform at Court alongside the adult companies. Unlike the professional theatre, the children's companies were less immediately vulnerable to the opposition of the City Fathers. The mostly Puritan-inspired antagonism to the theatre forced the professional drama to operate largely outside the City walls, except when companies played at Westminster or in the ▷ Inns of Court.

From its early years the history of the Elizabethan theatre is one of a continuous struggle against a hard core of ▷ Puritans who launched several colourful attacks on it, notably ▷ Stephen Gosson's *Playes Confuted in Five Actions* (1582) and ▷ Philip Stubbes's *The Anatomie of Abuses* (1583). In the end it was royal patronage that ensured both the survival and the continuity of the professional companies and theatres. Although the Puritans may well have begrudged the theatre its sheer fun and its ability to draw large crowds – the Globe accommodated nearly 3,000 people – they were also wary of its secular bias. The entertainments written by the first generation of Elizabethan dramatists were a long way from the medieval ▷ morality and miracle plays, although the morality form and its favourite character ▷ the 'Vice' endured throughout the period in plays like ▷ Marlowe's ▷ *Doctor Faustus* (?1592) and as late as ▷ Jonson's *The Devil is an Ass* (1616).

The earliest extant English comedy, Nicholas Udall's (1505–56) ▷ *Ralph Roister Doister* (1552), shows that the imaginative roots of drama were changing from primarily Christian and native to largely classical ones, in this case the ▷ New Comedy idiom of ▷ Plautus and ▷ Terence, focusing on domestic relationships and involving stereotyped figures such as the wily servant and the swaggering soldier. The impact of classical history, myth and drama through both Latin and contemporary European literature appears in the titles of some of the better-known plays of the 1560s such as Richard Edwards's *Damon and Pythias* (1565), Thomas Preston's *Cambyses* (1569), ▷ George Gascoigne's popular *Supposes* (1566) and George Whetstone's influential *Promos and Cassandra* (1578).

The imprint of the classics is palpable in the writings of the first significant playwright of the period, ▷ John Lyly (1554–1606), who wrote for the children's companies and, like several of his contemporaries, was university-educated. Although Lyly was best known in the sixteenth century as the author of two prose romances, ▷ *Euphues, or the Anatomy of Wit* (1578) and *Euphues and his England* (1580), which bequeathed the most admired and most often parodied style ('Euphuism') to the period, it is his plays that are now more highly regarded. The stylized sophistication of works such as *Alexander and Campaspe* (1584), *Sapho and Phao* (1584), ▷ *Gallathea* (1585), *Endimion* (1588) and *Midas* (1589) appeals to an audience steeped in ▷ Ovid and courtly allegory. In them Lyly reveals a remarkable dramatic tact and a unique rhetorical lucidity that owe much to the antithetically poised style of *Euphues*, as well as to the need to accommodate the limitations of boy-actors. *Gallathea* is Lyly's most accomplished play. Integrating native and classical strands in its ▷ pastoral, which is set in North Lincolnshire, it is coloured by ▷ Virgil's *Ecologues* and Ovid's ▷ *Metamorphoses*. The story of the two girls disguised by their father as boys to save them from a virgin sacrifice to Neptune derives from Ovid's tale of Iphis and Ianthe in *Metamorphoses IX*. The girls fall in love with each other and are granted a happy consummation of their love affair through a promise that Venus will transform one of them into a boy.

▷ George Peele (1556–96), ▷ Robert Greene (1558–92), ▷ Thomas Lodge (1558–1625) and ▷ Thomas Nashe (1567–1601) were all ▷ 'University Wits', like Lyly and Christopher Marlowe (1564–93). Nashe and Lodge are remembered mostly for their prose. Lodge's two plays, *A Looking Glass for London and England* (1594) and *The Wounds of Civil War* (1594), are now forgotten, whereas his pastoral prose romance *Rosalynde* (1590) is still read, not least because it provided the main source for ▷ Shakespeare's ▷ *As You Like It*. Nashe is the author of the ▷ picaresque and journalist narrative ▷ *The Unfortunate Traveller, or the Life of Jack Wilton* (1594), as well as of the satire *Pierce Penniless, His Supplication to the Devil* (1592) and the ironic 'pleasant comedy' *Summer's Last Will and Testament* (1592), which for all its poetic inventiveness and wit resembles a procession of seasonal allegorical figures more closely than the vibrant five-act plays of the professional theatre. Peele and Greene follow Lyly in writing romantic comedies; Peele's jewelled idiom, as well as his classical and mythological motifs and pastoral settings, reflect his enduring interest in pageantry without sacrificing dramatic plausibility altogether. The titles of his three best-known works, *The Arraignment of Paris* (?1584), *The Love of King David and Fair Bethsabe* (1587) and *The Old Wives' Tale* (1590), reflect their imaginative preoccupations with mythic, biblical and native pastoral themes, which, in his dramatization of the love affair of King David and the revolt of Absalom, fruitfully interact to produce an impressive and moving play.

Robert Greene is known among others for his scurrilous attack on Shakespeare in *Greene's Groatsworth of Wit bought with a Million of Repentance* (1592) and for the pastoral prose romance ▷ *Pandosto, The Triumph of Time* (1588), which Shakespeare used in ▷ *The Winter's Tale* (1610). But two of Greene's comedies deserve special attention and are still performed: ▷ *Friar Bacon and Friar Bungay* (1589) and *The Scottish History of James IV* (1590). The former dramatizes the medieval philosopher Roger Bacon's alleged experiment with a head of brass and interweaves this necromantic plot with a gentle romance narrative of the simultaneous wooing of a fair maid by the Prince of Wales and a nobleman. This early formal experiment in the use of double plot is reflected in the narrative perspective of *James IV*, which, through its framing device, anticipates the stylization of Shakespeare's ▷ *A Midsummer Night's Dream* (1595). Psychologically, Greene's drama displays a new realism in understanding human motivation and to that extent it foreshadows Shakespeare's comedies.

If English comedy was well established by the late 1580s, tragedy was in its fledgling stages when ▷ Thomas Kyd (1558–94) wrote ▷ *The Spanish Tragedy* (1587). It was to become the most popular play of the period and marks one of the first Elizabethan attempts at writing a tragedy after ▷ *Gorboduc* (1561), a play by Thomas Norton and ▷ Thomas Sackville which is an artistic failure 'notwithstanding . . . it is full of stately speeches and well-sounding phrases, climbing to the height of ▷ Seneca's style, and as full of notable morality' (▷ Sir Philip Sidney, ▷ *Apologie for Poetrie*, 1595). Like the earlier play, *The Spanish Tragedy* reflects a strong Senecan influence in its bloodthirsty plotting and declamatory rhetoric as its protagonist, Hieronimo, the Marshal of Spain, labours in vain for justice and has, in the end, to resort to revenge. Although *The Spanish Tragedy* was largely superseded by the more mature scrutiny of the ethics of crime and punishment in Shakespeare's ▷ *Hamlet*, it retains much of its rhetorical force and manifests a distinct awareness of the moral nefariousness of indiscriminate revenge and its consequences.

A very different note is sounded in the works of Kyd's contemporary and friend Christopher Marlowe, who was born the son of a cobbler in Canterbury, where he attended the King's School. Marlowe went up to Cambridge on a scholarship instituted by the former Archbishop of Canterbury, ▷ Matthew Parker (1504–75). His attendance was erratic, and rumours about his alleged Catholic as well as atheistic leanings were rife. These may have led to the university's decision at first to withhold his degree, but the Queen's Council intervened and overturned it on the basis of Marlowe's good service to the Crown. Marlowe was killed in what was allegedly a tavern brawl in Deptford on 30 May 1593, when he was 29 years old. During this short and turbulent life Marlowe wrote seven plays, translated Ovid's *Amores* and ▷ Lucan's *Pharsalia* and composed one of the most successful English narrative poems, ▷ *Hero and Leander*, as well as the famous lyric 'Come live with me . . .', the subject of several contemporary imitations and parodies. There is little agreement on the exact dates of the plays other than that they were written between 1585 and 1593, possibly in the following order: *Dido, Queen of Carthage*; ▷ *Tamburlaine the Great, Parts I and II; The Tragical History of Doctor Faustus*; ▷ *The Jew of Malta; Edward II; The Massacre at Paris*. It is on a handful of plays and on his one long poem that Marlowe's reputation as Shakespeare's most talented contemporary rests; and it is a measure of Marlowe's precocious achievement that, although he was born in the same year as Shakespeare, he was already dead when Shakespeare's first great play, *Richard III*, was performed.

Marlowe's choice of subject matter is revealing as much for its diversity as for its unifying vision. To a young man trained in the Elizabethan classical curriculum, his adaptation in *Dido* of the central episode from Virgil's epic poem the ▷ *Aeneid* must have seemed part of a natural process. Marlowe does not simply imitate Virgil's stirring account of Dido and Aeneas, but transforms it into a self-contained dramatic vehicle of which the Trojan imperial quest constitutes an ancillary if necessary part. Pyrrhus's spectacular killing of Priam in front of a pleading Hecuba provides Marlowe with an opportunity to indulge his taste for grotesque imagery. The inset narrative of Troy in an otherwise essentially 'romantic' work contains the shape of things to come. In his ruthless and measured calm ('So, leaning on his sword, he stood still,/Viewing the fire wherewith rich Illion burnt'), Pyrrhus anticipates Tamburlaine, the Guise (*The Massacre at Paris*), and, to a lesser extent, Barabas (*The Jew of Malta*) and Young Mortimer (*Edward II*). Equally enduring in the later plays is Marlowe's ability to pull out all the stops afforded by lyrical rhetoric and mythopoeia.

Ideologically, *Dido* holds out few challenges to established orthodoxies. Notwithstanding its rhetorical resourcefulness it is a light piece compared to *Tamburlaine* and *Doctor Faustus*, Marlowe's most controversial plays. As the Prologue to *Tamburlaine, Part I* boldly announces, the audience will be transported from the 'jigging veins of rhyming mother-wits/ And such conceits as clownage keeps in pay . . . to the stately tent of war'. Consequently, the play traces the emergence of Tamburlaine from obscurity to his victory over the Turks led by Bajazeth and the Egyptians under the Soldan, whose daughter Zenocrate Tamburlaine woos and eventually marries. From the beginning it is clear that *Tamburlaine, Part I* is not at all intended to be an exemplar work in the didactic > *Mirror for Magistrates* tradition in which hubristic aspirations become the means for exemplary punishments. In this play the overreacher is celebrated by the author, however reprehensible he appears. Tamburlaine explodes ordained hierarchy and received wisdom. As he tells us at his first appearance: 'I am a lord, for so my deeds shall prove,/ And yet a shepherd by my parentage'. Against such existentialist convictions, the calculated and coercive assertions of Tamburlaine's foes that he is a mere Scythian thief are of little avail. On the contrary, Tamburlaine claims to 'glory in the curses of my foes,/ Having the power from the empyreal heaven/ To turn them all upon their proper heads'. As if his self-appointed role as the scourge of God were not enough, Tamburlaine proclaims his desire to scale the heavens to 'become immortal like the gods'. The words 'will' and 'shall' best befit him, he claims, and in a moment of supreme confidence he professes to 'hold the Fates bound fast in iron chains,/ And with my hand turn Fortune's wheel about'. As Marlowe knew from the classics, not even Zeus controls the Fates. To convey the stature of Tamburlaine, Marlowe endows the character with the most grandiloquent and declamatory style of address. Like a colossus or a Phaeton at the reins of the chariot of the sun, Tamburlaine bestrides his play and in epic battles defeats the traditional enemies of Christendom, particularly the Turks, who had recently been overcome at Lepanto (1571). In spite of this partial concession – in that the enemies of Tamburlaine are the arch-enemies of every European Christian nation in the sixteenth century – Tamburlaine displays no sign of allegiance to any particular faith or political doctrine. He is relentless, ruthless and uncompromising, true only to himself and to his wife, Zenocrate. He exists in the public eye, and we are not invited to share his inner thoughts. Soliloquies are beneath Tamburlaine, because they recognize human complexity and the need for reflection, neither of which squares with the image of the man of action. Only once, after the massacre of the virgins of Damascus, does he pause to consider Zenocrate's pleas for her father's life, and momentarily grants us the briefest glimpse of a sensibility which is as responsive to physical beauty as it is to the lure of power. Tamburlaine is a titan whom Zeus is unable or unwilling to defeat, and he ends *Part I* victorious.

Marlowe would not again match the sustained intensity and clear-eyed achievement of *Tamburlaine, Part I*. *Doctor Faustus* and *The Jew of Malta* have, however, fared better in the theatre. An improved sense of dramatic timing and stage-action, as well as a more moderate and ironic imaginative vision, have superseded the earlier defiant rhetoric addressed to the audience. If the moralizing tenor of the chorus in the 'Epilogue' of *Doctor Faustus* is credited ('Cut is the branch that might have grown full straight . . .') as Marlowe's own work – the textual history of the play is very complex – *Doctor Faustus* would demand to be seen as a late sixteenth-century morality play. Marlowe's reworking of the medieval Faustbook contains all the natural and supernatural ingredients of a work tailored to commercial success.

If the admonitory tone of *Doctor Faustus* perfectly conterbalances *Tamburlaine*, the tone and structure of *The Jew of Malta* suggest that the Marlovian myth of the overreacher is becoming domesticated and socially accommodated. The famous prologue to the play is spoken by ▷ Machiavelli or 'Machevill' himself, but thereafter the work hardly concerns itself with dramatically disembodied reflections on the nature of power and of good and evil. The stereotyped villain of the piece is the greedy, scheming Jew, Barabas. Though he is not a Shylock, Barabas is not wholly undeserving of our sympathy, as he inhabits a virtually unreclaimed world in which Jew and Christian alike are corrupt. Barabas is flexible, inventive, resilient and witty to the point of virtually turning the play into a black farce. He finds his perfect match in the Thracian and Semitic slave, Ithamore. Both are capable of the most sublime rhetoric, both delight in mass murder. In its irreverence about religion and those who most profess it, like nuns and friars, *The Jew of Malta* reflects its author's alleged inconoclasm, as in a different way does *Edward II*, the most explicit ▷ homosexual play of the period, and the truncated *The Massacre at Paris*.

More than any dramatist of this period, Marlowe emancipated the theatre from the shackles of orthodoxy. His maverick, epic vision and distinct blank verse paved the way not only for Shakespeare but also for ▷ Ben Jonson and ultimately for ▷ John Milton.

Shakespeare and his contemporaries

From the death of Marlowe in 1593 to the ill-fated performance of Shakespeare's ▷ *Henry VIII* in 1613, during which the Globe Theatre burned to the ground, Shakespeare's plays and poems commanded an unchallenged allegiance from his public. In some 20 years of creative activity Shakespeare wrote over a dozen comedies, ten history plays, ten tragedies and four romances, as well as at least two long poems and a cycle of sonnets; and he almost certainly contributed to the work of others.

Of the 37 plays generally attributed to Shakespeare (1564–1616), all except ▷ *Pericles* – which is not wholly his – were printed in the First ▷ Folio of 1623 under the supervision of Heming and Condell, two of Shakespeare's fellow actors. This collection printed plays such as ▷ *Macbeth*, ▷ *Antony and Cleopatra*, ▷ *Coriolanus* and ▷ *The Tempest* for the first time and also provided important alternate texts for works that had appeared earlier in ▷ quarto form – *Hamlet* in 1603 and 1604 and ▷ *Othello* in 1622 – sometimes in longer or shorter versions. The qualitative distinctions formerly drawn by editors of Shakespeare between Quarto and Folio have recently been called into question, and the plays are increasingly perceived as essentially dynamic texts intended for theatrical performance. This challenging process of editorial realignment has occupied the centre stage of Shakespearean studies since the late 1970s, and all the signs are that it will endure as its focus in the closing years of the twentieth century. The textual radicalism pioneered under the auspices of the Oxford University Press, and particularly its championing of Shakespeare the reviser, has affected readings in ▷ *Henry IV, Part I*, ▷ *King Lear* and *Pericles*. The restoration in some modern editions of the name ▷ 'Oldcastle' for ▷ 'Falstaff' in *Henry IV, Part I*, and the establishing of a two-text *King Lear* are its most contentious conclusions.

The critical debate about Shakespeare continues vigorously. If ▷ structuralism and ▷ deconstruction have failed to make a major impact, ▷ feminism, on the other hand, has powerfully engaged with Shakespeare and has recently produced some of the most valuable Shakespearean criticism by tapping gender ambiguities deeply embedded in the plays and poetry themselves. Currently,

▷ new historicism, with its emphasis on *Zeitgeist* and its margins, is the most articulate heir to the traditions of ▷ humanist thinking about Shakespeare.

The 1590s mark the main period of Shakespeare's histories, comedies and poetry. The first tetralogy of ▷ history plays was written and performed by 1594, as well as three of the comedies based on models derived from Plautus (▷ *The Comedy of Errors*, 1592–3), Italian ▷ *commedia dell'arte* (▷ *The Taming of the Shrew*, 1593–4) and native and foreign romance narratives (▷ *Two Gentlemen of Verona*, 1593–4). The imaginative idiom of Shakespeare's early comedies testifies to a searching and essentially open intellect, eager to experiment with the demanding forms of classical comedy and the anarchic energy of sprawling prose texts. The latter had formed the staple theatrical diet throughout the Elizabethan period and had recently been legitimized in Sir Philip Sidney's *Old Arcadia*. Like the revised *New Arcadia* and ▷ Edmund Spenser's ▷ *The Faerie Queene*, it affords a rich seam which Shakespeare mined repeatedly.

The first tetralogy of history plays, and particularly ▷ *Richard III*, were popular successes for Shakespeare's company at their regular venue, The Theatre. They show him turning to English history through the chronicles of Edward Hall and ▷ Raphael Holinshed. In *Richard III*, the hunchbacked Yorkist usurper emerges as a fearsome challenger both to the legitimate powers of the state and to our sympathies. Unlike Marlowe's Tamburlaine, Richard Gloucester is mordantly funny in the chrysalis of evil explored in the last three plays of the tetralogy. In one of the longest soliloquies in the entire works, ▷ *Henry VI, Part III* (III.2, 124–95, 'Ay, Edward will use women honourably'), Richard promises to 'set the murderous Machiavel to school'. His superb plotting and his triumph against the odds in *Richard III* underline the measure of his intellect. The audience is always privy to Richard's schemes, as he evinces a pathological need to confide in us. His soliloquies and asides never convey the impression of true intimacy, but reflect a melodramatic and histrionic concept of stage-character derived from the Vice of the medieval morality play.

The cluster of plays written in the mid-1590s – ▷ *Love's Labour's Lost* (1594–5), ▷ *Romeo and Juliet* (1594–5), *A Midsummer Night's Dream* (1595–6), ▷ *Richard II* (1595–6), ▷ *King John* (1596–7) and ▷ *The Merchant of Venice* (1596–7) – and the writing of most of the sonnets as well as the narrative poems ▷ *Venus and Adonis* and *The Rape of Lucrece* just before the mid-decade, further confirm Shakespeare's position as the foremost lyrical poet of the age. The stirring language and evocative imagery of Clarence's dream vision in *Richard III* (I.4, 'Methoughts that I had broken from the Tower . . .') anticipate the tropes of *A Midsummer Night's Dream* and *Romeo and Juliet*, two plays which are equally stylized, despite their generic differences.

A Midsummer Night's Dream is often now judged to be one of Shakespeare's finest and most atmospheric achievements. The tribulations of the love-struck quartet of young Athenians temporarily at the mercy of the woodland fairies led by ▷ Oberon and ▷ Puck provide the mainspring of the play's action. Woven into this seemingly light and courtly rhetorical fabric is a searching exploration of the relationship between the unconscious world of dreams and the deluded controlling power of reason. The realist anchoring of the play's fiction through the robust comedy of the well-intentioned tradesmen and their burlesque of 'Pyramus and Thisbe' provides not only laughter but wonderment at the poet's skill and tact.

For its tender and generous portrayal of star-crossed young love, *Romeo and Juliet*, which is virtually contemporary with *A Midsummer Night's Dream*, remains a great favourite among the plays. It is Shakespeare's first attempt at writing a romantic tragedy. If in the end its verse does not always rise to the challenge of the tragic idiom, the comic parts of the play and its gallery of unforgettable characters such as ▷ Mercutio and Juliet amply vindicate its popularity. The more formally curtailed and less individuated mode of comedy proved easier for Shakespeare to manage at this point, as is evident from the control in *A Midsummer Night's Dream* and the play which precedes it, *Love's Labour's Lost*, an elegant and sophisticated comedy exploring the limits of the rhetoric of love in expressing true feeling in a mode inspired by the idiom of Lyly's plays.

But from *The Merchant of Venice* to the 'mature' comedies, *Much Ado About Nothing* (1598–9), *As You Like It* (1599–1600), *Twelfth Night* (1599–1600), and the ▷ 'problem plays', ▷ *Measure for Measure* (1600–1), ▷ *Troilus and Cressida* (1601–2) and ▷ *All's Well That Ends Well* (1602–3), Shakespeare increasingly questions the adequacy of the genre and its imaginative legitimacy. Shylock's angry question ('Hath not a Jew eyes?') cannot comfortably be reconciled to the fairy-tale world of Belmont. He leaves the play unreclaimed: 'I pray you, give me leave to go from hence;/ I am not well.' In this he anticipated several later characters who fail to be accommodated into the magic circle where lovers are happily matched to create a future world. The darker side of Shakespearean comedy, already intimated in the 12-month penance exacted from Berowne in *Love's Labour's Lost* and the near rape of Silvia by Proteus in *Two Gentlemen of Verona*, is developed further in *As You Like It* and *Twelfth Night*. The two plays engage with a world of threatened identities in which Rosalind and Viola, the plays' respective heroines, visibly have to disguise their femininity before they can actively involve themselves in their alternative societies. Rosalind quickly realizes the potential of her assumed maleness and buoyantly puts it to good use, whereas Viola becomes trapped by her androgyny in a version of the classic love triangle. Notwithstanding the mellow wistfulness of Illyria in *Twelfth Night* and Feste's melancholy songs, or the sheer resilience of the inhabitants of the wintry forest of Arden who are forever singing songs, doubts about the comic vision prevail in the inability of Jaques in *As You Like It* to leave Arden and in the vengeful exit of Malvolio in *Twelfth Night*.

Shakespeare's 'problem plays' almost certainly coincide with the period of the writing of *Hamlet* (1600–1). In *Measure for Measure*, the generic framework barely survives the onslaught of Angelo's treachery, Claudio's fear of death and Isabella's relentless and perhaps uncharitable morality. The moated grange in which, through a bed-trick, Mariana instead of Isabella gives herself to Angelo, is all that remains of the never-never land of the early and later comedies. The play is as rife with real and imaginary diseases and corruption as *Hamlet*, and in its moral probings it appears to be equally cognizant of complexity and despair. Questions about honour and death, crime and punishment are more easily resolved in the abstract than in concrete instances. In his disguise as a friar, the Duke eloquently persuades Claudio to 'be absolute for death' on the basis that life is too painful to bear and too prone to casual accidents to be worth living. Isabella argues with equal perception and greater passion that 'the sense of death is most in apprehension', and that Claudio, her brother, must not surrender to the temptation of asking her to sacrifice her virginity to Angelo to save his life. After initially concurring with the Duke and his sister, Claudio suddenly realizes the full horror of unnatural and premature death:

Claud.   *Death is a fearful thing.*
Isab.   *And shamed life a hateful.*
Claud.   *Ay, but to die, and go we know not where . . .*

(III.1, 118–33)

The resonance and poignancy of such plain language almost transcends the more poised rhetoric of *Hamlet* and properly belongs to the imaginative and rhetorical spheres of *Othello* and *Macbeth*.

Towards the end of the sixteenth century, Shakespeare completed his second English tetralogy of history plays, which cover the reigns of ▷ Richard II and those of his successors, ▷ Henry IV and ▷ Henry V (*Richard II, Henry IV, Parts I and II*, ▷ *Henry V*). *Henry IV, Part I* (1597–8) introduces one of the favourite characters of English drama, Sir John Falstaff, who will recur in *Henry IV, Part II* (1597–8) and, in a much diminished and domesticated form, in ▷ *The Merry Wives of Windsor* (1597). Through his corpulence and anarchic manner Falstaff, as the Lord of Misrule in Eastcheap, epitomizes the opposition to the rule of Bolingbroke at Westminster, and the seeming attachment of Hal, the Prince of Wales (and future Henry V), to the lawless *bon viveur* and his cronies fuels the plot of *Henry IV, Part I*. This play also features ▷ Hotspur ('By heaven, methinks it were an easy leap/ To pluck bright honour from the pale-fac'd moon . . .'), Hal's flamboyant counterpart who is said to put him to shame by his unquestioned military prowess.

This second tetralogy is partly a study in kingship as we witness Hal's progress from his conscious disowning of Falstaff (*Henry IV, Part I*, I.2, 187 ff.: 'I know you all, and will awhile uphold/ The unyok'd humour of your idleness') to his victory at Shrewsbury, and finally his coronation at the end of the second part of *Henry IV*. Reflections about the sacramental nature of kingship loom large in *Richard II*, providing the imaginative material for the great emblematic scene in the encounter between Hal and his dying father in *Henry IV, Part II* (IV.5) and emphasizing the importance of the play's presentation of the Lord Chief Justice in relation to Falstaff and the new king.

The promise of greatness is fulfilled in *Henry V* at the battle of Agincourt, and the play ends like a comedy in the happy marriage of France (Kate) and England (Henry). Yet the doubt expressed by Williams the Welshman about the 'cause' of the French wars (*Henry V*, IV.1, 132 ff.: 'But if the cause be not good, the King himself hath a heavy reckoning to make . . .') refuses to disappear and lingers on in spite of Henry's indignant reply about the nature of delegated responsibility and the hard condition of the king's being 'twin-born with greatness'.

A similar distrust of power enters Shakespeare's first great Roman play, ▷ *Julius Caesar* (1599–1600), written at about the same time as *Henry V*. In dramatizing one of the most famous stories of the classical world, Shakespeare pursues his interest in questions of politics and ethics in a Roman and republican context. The austere quality of the play's verse has at times been interpreted as corroborating politically revisionist readings of it in terms of the prevailing monarchical Tudor doctrine, which strongly condemned dissent from established power through its historiography and pamphlets. This is to underestimate the intelligence of Shakespeare's use of Plutarch's Rome, as well as his portrayal of Brutus. The idealist impulse of Brutus's soliloquy (II.1, 10 ff.: 'It must be by his death . . .'), when he attempts to justify to himself his share in the killing of his friend Caesar ('I know no personal cause to spurn him'), anticipates the *angst* of Hamlet. It is Brutus's moral integrity that causes him to conspire against Caesar, and which draws from Antony the tribute to Brutus's egalitarianism: 'only in a general honest thought/ And common good to all made one of them'.

Hamlet (1600–1) remains the most often quoted work of English literature and is Shakespeare's longest play. Its instant fame has not diminished in 400 years, even if its hero has recently been scrutinized more critically. Fewer readers and audiences now project their existential anxieties on to Hamlet, who after all causes at least five people to die. Because so much of the play's action is viewed through Hamlet's eyes, he naturally controls our sympathies, and his Oedipal fears and filial dilemmas have struck a particular chord in post-Freudian audiences, notwithstanding our scepticism about Hamlet's motives. If *Hamlet* thrives on its famous soul-searching soliloquies, it is also the case that their measured intellectual tone at times belies the pressing intensity of the character's emotion, which is why too often *Hamlet* has wrongly been read as a play about a young man who could not make up his mind. Rhetorically, *Hamlet* has proved one of the most prolifically inventive of English texts, as if Shakespeare needed to coin a new language to express the predicament of the first tragic hero on the European stage since the Hellenic tragedies of ▷ Aeschylus, ▷ Sophocles and ▷ Euripides. In the play the contemporary worlds of Renaissance and Reformation Europe (Hamlet is a student at Wittenberg University, the seat of the Lutheran breakaway movement) and the universal predicament of man fruitfully interact. The sheer scale of destruction in *Hamlet*, as well as its use of an inset playlet, reflect its indebtedness to earlier revenge dramas such as the lost *Ur-Hamlet*, which was probably by Thomas Kyd. *Hamlet* outstrips such narrow imaginative moulds by refusing to surrender its intimations of complexity to formulaic resolutions. To the extent that, like his lover Ophelia and her brother Laertes, the play's princely protagonist appears young – in spite of the enduring debate about Hamlet's exact age at the beginning of the play – *Hamlet* is a tragedy of adolescence and political intrigue.

Othello (1604–5) radically differs from *Hamlet*; the sprawling and even leisurely expanse of the earlier tragedy is sharply contracted in the focus on the deterioration of Othello's relationship with Desdemona. This primarily domestic tragedy moves at a precipitate pace, as the middle-aged and exotic Othello is increasingly dominated by his 28-year-old ensign, Iago. *Othello* is a brilliant exploration of obsessive erotic passion and its dangers. The Moor destroys the woman he loves, and audiences sympathize with his pathos-ridden predicament. But Othello is not a popular hero. Uniquely among Shakespeare's tragic protagonists, Othello is perceived mostly through the refractive eyes of his detractor. He is never allowed to stand apart from his ritualized action. Through its glamorous tropes and rhythms his intoxicating rhetoric blinds Othello to his more rational self, and as the play moves towards its ineluctable conclusion, the Moor increasingly regresses into the arcane image that Iago projects for him.

From the oppressive privacy of *Othello* Shakespeare moves to the apocalyptic dimensions of *King Lear* (1605–6). The play is set in a storm-swept Britain and relates the story of an old king abdicating most of his duties to his three daughters and their spouses. But the youngest, Cordelia, who is also his favourite, publicly humiliates him by refusing his invitation to flattery. The fairy-tale motif, which opens the play and casts the youngest daughter as a Cinderella figure, underlines its almost archetypal quality. As the country's king, Lear functions in a necessarily public role, which he retains and even reasserts in moments of supreme agony. There is no scope for royal soliloquies in the play, and there are none. Lear's ragings against the elements (III.2, 1 ff.: 'Blow, winds, and crack your cheeks; rage, blow . . .') suggest the enduring measure of his stature even after the trappings of kingship have been shed. More than any other Shakespearean text, *King Lear* is passionately committed to the imaginative mediation of profound moral convictions. This is strikingly evident in the encounter between Lear and Gloucester in Act IV Scene 6, when the crazed king lectures his fellow sufferer about the nature of empathy and the need for forgiveness. But such 'poetic' forgiveness as there is is not extended to Cordelia, whose integrity and selfless devotion to her father go unrewarded. The death of Cordelia more than any other aspect of the work proved unpalatable and in 1681 resulted in Nahum Tate's rewriting of the end of the play as a tragicomedy in which Lear and Cordelia survive to live happily ever after. *King Lear* has recently been the particular focus of editors and textual scholars because of the crucial differences between its quarto and folio texts, which suggest that Shakespeare rewrote it and shortened the original version. The implications for interpreting the play's pace and thematic patterning are significant, as the changes directly affect important characters like Edgar and Albany and long passages like the 'trial' in Act III Scene 6, or the entire scene reporting the French invasion in Act IV Scene 3.

The text of *Macbeth* (1605–6), Shakespeare's shortest tragedy, likewise shows signs of corruption, if not revision, through addition from a later work by ▷ Thomas Middleton. The play tells a story of temptation and damnation as its eponymous hero wrestles with his own better self and finally destroys it. In the process he commits every crime under the sun. Like Hamlet, Macbeth is a great soliloquizer and, like Richard III, he commits premeditated murder.

But Shakespeare has come a long way from the exhibitionist antics of Richard and his declamatory verse. *Macbeth* is the married tragedy of Macbeth and Lady Macbeth, and in this mutuality it anticipates *Antony and Cleopatra*. Macbeth retains much of our sympathy through his passionate soliloquies, as in his lines spoken in agony before his wife reaffirms his original decision to murder Duncan:

> *If it were done when 'tis done, then 'twere well*
> *It were done quickly.*
>
> (I.7, 1 ff.)

He is unable to name the deed. These famous reflections culminate in the apocalyptic images of Duncan's virtues in the form of divine children pleading

> *like angels, trumpet-tongu'd, against*
> *The deep damnation of his taking-off;*
> *And pity, like a naked new-born babe,*
> *Striding the blast, or heaven's cherubin, hors'd . . .*
>
> (I.7, 19–22)

Shakespeare's most guilty tragic hero discovers the roots of his moral being in a powerful poetic imagination which, like the play itself, revolves around child metaphors and similes. There is a grim poetic justice operating in the defeat of Macbeth, a childless husband, at the hands of Macduff, born by Caesarean section and the father of the children murdered by Macbeth. Even so, Shakespeare's Macbeth, unlike Holinshed's historical figure, revolts from his own evil at the last moment when he warns off Macduff by telling him, 'my soul is too much charg'd/ With blood of thine already'.

The astonishing metaphorical and symbolic depths of *Macbeth* are only matched by *Antony and Cleopatra* (1606–7). Before Shakespeare turned to his new subject matter in ▷ Sir Thomas North's translation of ▷ Plutarch's *Lives* of the Greek and Roman heroes, the story of Antony and Cleopatra had long been an exemplary tale of dotage and sexual folly, resulting in Antony's loss of the Roman empire for a whore, as ▷ Bacon noted in his essay 'Of Love'. But Plutarch had created a fascinating Cleopatra in the pages of 'The Life of Marcus Antonius', and Shakespeare responded to the challenge by turning his queen of Egypt into an even more mysterious creature inhabiting the realms of Isis on the banks of the River Nile. Far from being an exemplar of tragedy about the disgrace of Antony, *Antony and Cleopatra*, as its double title indicates, concentrates on an infinitely rich and varied mutuality. The geopolitical conflict of the play is indissolubly linked to its romantic interests. Its politics are now increasingly stripped of their moral momentum and are viewed as part of a wider patterning of the lovers whose aspirations, by their very stature as the eastern and western pillars of the classical world, are apocalyptic. As the play evolves, the lovers' separate male and female, Roman and Egyptian identities are increasingly blurred, as if Shakespeare were intent on exploring not only the dissolution of empire, but also, and above all, the merging of gender, thereby completing an imaginative movement initiated in the early comedies and in the sonnets. *Antony and Cleopatra* is the only Shakespearean tragedy that moves towards a resolution in a cosmic lovers' meeting beyond death. Its action and luminous Mediterranean setting contrast with the brooding darkness and chill winds of the other tragedies. Thematically, *Antony and Cleopatra* reaches out naturally to the romances, Shakespeare's 'last plays'. Yet *Coriolanus* and ▷ *Timon of Athens* intervene before *Pericles*, the first of the tragicomedies.

Coriolanus (1607–8) is rightly viewed as one of Shakespeare's most enigmatic works. Its eponymous protagonist appears stolid and uncharismatic. Whereas Hamlet insistently relates his fears and dilemmas to whichever audience he has, Coriolanus refuses to make us privy to his inner being. He fiercely insists on his ancient privilege to be a proud patrician and cannot accept a newfound political and social reality. His is the tragedy of archaic values tested and aborted in a world of intrigue and of government by delegation. Like its titan hero, *Coriolanus* is uncompromisingly spartan and yields few of the excitements and luxurious pleasures of *Antony and Cleopatra*. Its interweaving of unrelenting directness and seemingly effortless flexibility conveys a rare sense of Shakespeare's maturest verse.

A despairing vision prevails in *Timon of Athens* (1607–8), to such an extent that scholars have at times claimed to detect evidence of a nervous crisis in the play's author towards the end of the first decade of the new century. Shakespeare is now embarking on the last part of his creative work, the romances: *Pericles*, ▷ *Cymbeline*, *The Winter's Tale*, and *The Tempest*. They form the most unified body of works in the canon, even though the Folio of 1623 did not put them in a separate category, but classed *Cymbeline* as a tragedy and the others among the comedies. *The Winter's Tale* and *The Tempest* best illustrate the new and more sanguine direction in which Shakespeare was heading. They constitute the perfectly counterbalanced pair: on the one hand, the sprawling and anarchic pastoral, *The Winter's Tale*, whose action stretches over more than 16 years; on the other hand, the tightly structured and neo-classical *Tempest*, in which the playing time mimetically enacts the three hours of the dramatic action dictated by the magus Prospero.

The Winter's Tale (1610–11) shows a Shakespeare reaching back to the idiom of his younger days, particularly the lyricism of Spenser and the pastoral of Sidney. In structure and dialogue the play is more ritualized than the earlier romantic comedies, and its imaginative focus rests on parent-child relationships as much as on the youthful loves of a prince and a princess. The visual impact of the pregnant Hermione's presence on the stage during the first half of the play is without parallel and intimates the degree to which this neo-pastoral drama breaks new ground, not least in its theatrical iconography. The pacing of *The Winter's Tale* is leisurely, and enables Shakespeare almost nostalgically to explore traditional themes of innocence and experience.

Both *The Winter's Tale* and *The Tempest* emphasize the urgency of Shakespeare's growing concern with themes of spiritual and specifically Christian recovery:

The 'art gallery' of Paulina and the reconciliation of Leontes and Hermione in *The Winter's Tale* are echoed in Prospero's recognition that 'the rarer action is/ In virtue than in vengeance', and more somberly, in his retreat to a Milanese hermitage where every third thought will be his grave. After *The Tempest* Shakespeare wrote ▷ *Henry VIII* (1612–13) and contributed to ▷ *The Two Noble Kinsmen* (1612–13).

Jonson and his comedies

In 1616, the year of Shakespeare's death, Ben Jonson published a folio edition of his plays and called them *Works*, thereby indicating that he regarded his craft and its products with the utmost seriousness. Whereas Shakespeare has struck successive generations as 'the poet of nature . . . that holds up to his readers a faithful mirror of manners and of life' (Dr Johnson, *Preface* 1765), Ben Jonson conveys the impression of great artifice and immense learning. Unlike Marlowe's and Shakespeare's, Jonson's achievement has not gone unchallenged. In T. S. Eliot's words, Jonson's reputation

> has been of the most deadly kind that can be compelled upon the memory of a great poet; to be damned by the praise that quenches all desire to read the book; to be afflicted by the imputation of the virtues which excite the least pleasure; and to be read only by historians and antiquaries.
>
> (*Selected Essays*, 'Ben Jonson')

Among other things Eliot is alluding here to Jonson's self-appointed task of moral teacher in his works. But Jonson's didacticism is no easy matter. In ▷ *The Alchemist* (1610), for example, he builds up a conventional structure of moral expectation – that the returning master, Lovewit, will set right the abuses perpetrated in his house – only to invert it totally when Lovewit is unmasked as just as unscrupulous and rapacious as the other cozeners.

▷ *Volpone* (1605), ▷ *Epicoene, or the Silent Woman* (1609), *The Alchemist* (1610) and ▷ *Bartholomew Fair* (1614) remain Jonson's most highly regarded plays in prose and poetry and have all seen successful performances in the modern theatre. They best epitomize Johnson's shrewd sense of timing, his use of nomenclature to reflect his characters' essential 'humours', and his uncompromising commitment to portraying the contemporary scene in its local, mostly cockney, idiom. It may be this as much as the plays' moralism – of which it forms a part – which sometimes renders Jonson difficult for modern audiences. The sheer burgeoning in his plays of detailed physical description is not always easy to assimilate, nor are Jonson's many and pugnacious involvements in contemporary controversies, which are mirrored in the plays.

Jonson's robust idiom refuses to accommodate romantic love, hence the weakness of his female characters such as Dame Pliant in *The Alchemist* or Celia in *Volpone*. He has no Violas or Rosalinds, let alone Cleopatras or ▷ Vittoria Corombonas. But in his last works, which Dryden famously described as belonging to his 'dotage', Jonson seems to acknowledge the imaginative force of a more romantic idiom. This is true particularly of ▷ *The New Inn* (1629), which is increasingly acclaimed as a late Jonsonian masterpiece with a Shakespearean transsexual formula. Jonson's two dramatic works on Roman themes, ▷ *Sejanus* (1603) and ▷ *Catiline* (1611), show him experimenting in a new mode, as do the 25 ▷ masques he wrote between 1605 (*The Masque of Blackness*) and 1625, mostly in collaboration with ▷ Inigo Jones. Jonson is the greatest and most prolific English writer of masques. He was also an impressive critic, sometimes to the detriment of his art, as in the overly discursive and explanatory discussion of the laws of comedy in ▷ *Every Man out of his Humour* (1599). Jonson's most pungent pronouncements on the responsibilities of literary art are contained in his 'common place' book *Timber; or discoveries made upon Men and Matter* (1640) and in his reported *Conversations with William Drummond of Hawthornden* (1618, although not published in their entirety until 1833).

In the last act of Jonson's *The Poetaster* (1601) ▷ John Marston (1575–1634) is parodied as Crispinus, who, through the administration of emetic pills, is made to vomit up his bilious vocabulary. Marston's reputation as a savage satirist partly belies his genuine achievement, which includes his contribution to the politically foolhardy collaborative effort (with Jonson and ▷ George Chapman), ▷ *Eastward Hoe* (1605). In *Antonio and Mellida* (1600) and its sequel, *Antonio's Revenge* (1601), Marston wrote in a heavily derivative idiom about young love and its eventual destruction. There is a strong, if flawed, idealist strain in Marston's work. But unlike Jonson, who castigates to reform, Marston's energy is wholly curtailed by the vituperative strain in his writing. His most successful play is the tragicomedy ▷ *The Malcontent* (1604). Although it lacks the single-minded naturalism of the scatalogical *Dutch Courtesan* (1605), and the lyricism of *Sophonisba, Wonder of Women* (1605), *The Malcontent* exhibits a remarkable grasp on moral complexity, as the banished Duke of Genoa, Altofronto, assumes the disguise of a malcontent to wreak revenge on his successor. After a confrontation with true evil, as opposed to assumed mischief, the play ends happily in a recovery of conjugal relations.

Nothing could be more different from Marston's painful vision than the works of Beaumont and Fletcher. ▷ Sir Francis Beaumont (1584–1616) and ▷ John Fletcher (1579–1625) share with Shakespeare and Jonson the accolade of having the fruit of their famous ten-year-long collaboration published in a folio volume in 1679. Both also wrote plays independently. Beaumont's first play, *The Woman Hater* (1605), reflects the influence of Jonson, who in turn yoked Beaumont together with ▷ Chaucer and Spenser in his elegy to Shakespeare. Beaumont's burlesque ▷ *The Knight of the Burning Pestle* (1607) is his finest work and is still performed successfully today. It is simultaneously a flamboyant parody of chivalry and of ▷ citizen comedy. But interweaving a main plot with a play-within-the-play, the aspirations of a grocer's family and their apprentice, and a romance drama, Beaumont recovers in a Jacobean idiom some of the self-referential dimension of *A Midsummer Night's Dream*.

Fletcher succeeded Shakespeare as the main writer of the King's Men after collaborating with him on *Two Noble Kinsmen* and perhaps earlier on *Henry VIII*. He was prolific and is credited with over 15 plays on his own, as well as an equal number with Beaumont. Best known among his own works is ▷ *The Faithful Shepherdess* (1608), a pastoral imitation of Guarini's *Il Pastor Fido* (1589). Through its brief prologue, which defines the new mode of tragicomedy, *The Faithful Shepherdess* announces the advent in England of a new 'old' romance form. Shakespeare's late plays and Beaumont and Fletcher's joint efforts epitomize the incipient Elizabethan nostalgia which set in during the second decade of the seventeenth century. Three of their works in particular underline the extent to which they are in touch with both the old and the novel: ▷ *Philaster* (1611), *The Maid's Tragedy* (1610), and ▷ *A King and No King* (1611). In *Philaster* Beaumont and Fletcher explore the romantic motif of transvestism in a mode which borrows its sensibility from Shakespeare's *Twelfth Night*, while providing a paradigm similar to Jonson's *Epicoene* (an exactly contemporary play that is equally secretive to the audience about the true nature of the disguise). The so-called 'female-page' in *Philaster*, Bellario, who in reality is a young romantic girl, Euphrasia, is *not* rewarded with a husband, but is left to lead a chaste and solitary life. Similarly redolent of the imaginative world of Sidneian pastoral is *The Maid's Tragedy*, probably the greatest work in the Beaumont and Fletcher canon, whose erotic and psychological charge redeems the tragedy from its melodramatic plotting. Equally suggestive of the period is Beaumont and Fletcher's *A King and No King*, which flirts with incest, but allows its characters to resolve their dilemma through a *deus ex machina* intervention. If Beaumont and Fletcher have not lasted as well as they promised, this is partly due to the joint effects of romantic saturation and tortuous plotting in much of their work.

▷ Thomas Dekker (1570–1632), ▷ Thomas Heywood (1574–1641) and ▷ Cyril Tourneur (?1575–1626) are each remembered by one play. Although Dekker wrote, or collaborated on, over 50 plays, his reputation rests on ▷ *The Shoemaker's Holiday* (1600), a gentle and forgiving London romance of royal wooing in disguise which treats even its minor characters such as Jane Damport, the wife of a conscripted soldier, with affection and regard. Dekker's comedy straddles the century-divide and marks the accommodation of a romantic idiom to a city setting.

Thomas Heywood, whose comedies such as ▷ *The Fair Maid of the West* (1600 and 1630) and *The Four Prentices of London* (1600) were lampooned by Beaumont, displays a remarkable dramatic intelligence in his domestic tragedy *A Woman Killed with Kindness* (1603), which echoes the powerful anonymous play *The Tragedy of* ▷ *Arden of Faversham* (1592), sometimes ascribed to Shakespeare. The story of Frankford's torturing of his unfaithful wife Anne through banishment from her children and himself is presented by Heywood with poise and insight. On her deathbed Anne asks for forgiveness, which is granted. The climax of the play occurs after Frankford has discovered positive proof of Anne's fallibility. He is no Othello, but his agonized response to the shattering of his dreams is impressive:

> *O God, O God, that it were possible*
> *To undo things done, to call back yesterday;*
> *That Time could turn up his swift sandy glass,*
> *To untell the days, and to redeem these hours;*
> *Or that the Sun*
> *Could, rising from the west, draw his coach back-*
> *ward,*
> *. . . that I might take her*
> *As spotless as an angel in my arms.*

> (Sc. 13)

Jacobean tragedy

The reputation of Cyril Tourneur rests exclusively on ▷ *The Atheist's Tragedy* (1611), as ▷ *The Revenger's Tragedy*, formerly thought to be his, is now attributed to Thomas Middleton. The play invites comparison with Marlowe's *Doctor Faustus*, of which it seems at first a domesticated version, since for Faustus's aggressive Manichean creed it substitutes D'Amville's 'natural philosophy'. But the play quickly abandons its sub-Marlovian ambitions and becomes a story of sexual and material intrigue that results in the atheist's accidentally braining himself with the axe intended to kill his innocent nephew, Charlemont.

Whether or not Tourneur was indebted, as is sometimes argued, to George Chapman (?1559–?1634), and particularly to his play ▷ *The Tragedy of Bussy D'Ambois* (1604), the fact remains that Chapman was highly regarded by his contemporaries. The learned author of the complex poem *Ovid's Banquet of Sense* (1595) and of the equally demanding continuation of Marlowe's *Hero and Leander* (1598) also collaborated with other playwrights and wrote a number of comedies as well as tragedies. *The Tragedy of Bussy D'Ambois* tells the story of the meteoric ascendancy of its eponymous hero through a combination of patronage and stamina in a manner reminiscent of Tamburlaine. D'Ambois dies unrepentant and will be partly avenged by his brother Clermont in the sequel, *The Revenge of Bussy D'Ambois* (1610), a play which interestingly questions the notion of revenge. Chapman's tragédies are informed by a distinctly metaphysical sensibility. Partly for this reason his comedies work better than his tragedies. *May Day* (1611), for example, is contemporary with the second *Bussy* play, but easily transcends it aesthetically by its assured construction, controlled language and multiple ironies as its various characters head for a life-enhancing romantic consummation.

A harsher and more fraught vision informs ▷ *The White Devil* (1612) and ▷ *The Duchess of Malfi* (1613), which constitute the claim to fame of ▷ John Webster (1578–1632). In Vittoria Corombona, the 'white devil' of the play's title, Webster created a tragic female figure who exists unapologetically in her sexual immorality and who thrives on the machinations of her Machiavellian brother, Flamineo. In the play's most famous scene, 'The Arraignment of

Vittoria' (III.2), Vittoria Corombona is allowed a spirited defence against her accusers, whose ethics are hardly preferable to hers. Her refusal to bow to their sentence, and her courage in facing death at the end, leave us with an ambiguous response to her character.

The Duchess of Malfi dramatizes the story of an intelligent and generous widow, the duchess of the title, who secretly marries her steward, Antonio, in a secular ceremony of binding vows. She bears him several children. Whereas Vittoria's brother is her co-conspirator (Flamineo's role is here assumed by the malcontent ▷ Bosola), the duchess's brother Ferdinand is incestuously obsessed with his sister's sexuality. He cruelly dupes her with a dead man's hand and with waxen figures of her husband Antonio and their children. Although the good characters in the play are unable to overcome death, their quiet dignity and courage are summed up in the duchess's calm reply to Bosola before she is strangled: 'I am Duchess of Malfi still'. In spite of a sometimes baroque idiom and melodramatic stage-managing of plot, Webster's two great tragedies stand out in this period of ebullient dramatic activity.

Webster's achievement is often compared and contrasted with that of Thomas Middleton (1580–1627), not least because both dramatists share an interest in tragic female figures. Middleton ranks as one of the most successfully prolific writers of the period. Like Webster, he collaborated with several of his contemporaries, notably with ▷ William Rowley (1585–1637) on ▷ *The Changeling* (1622). His output is impressive. It includes *The Family of Love* (1602), *A Trick to Catch the Old One* (1604), *Michaelmas Term* (1605), *A Mad World, My Masters* (1606), ▷ *The Roaring Girl* (1606), ▷ *A Chaste Maid in Cheapside* (1613), ▷ *No Wit, No Help like a Woman* (1613), *A Fair Quarrel* (1614) ▷ *Women Beware Women* (1614) and the political, allegorical satire ▷ *A Game at Chess* (1624). Middleton's fascination with the psychology of illicit passion and intrigue manifests itself best in the main plot of *The Changeling*. Instructed by her father to marry Alonzo, a man whom she does not love, the 'heroine' employs the repellent servant ▷ De Flores to murder him so that she will be free to marry Alsemero, with whom she has fallen in love. De Flores then blackmails ▷ Beatrice-Joanna into a sexual relationship. She will have to hide the loss of her virginity from Alsemero through a bed-trick. The play ends with the exposure of the guilty couple, who commit suicide. As the main plot evolves, the increasing attraction of the romantic and flawed heroine to the satanic De Flores develops into her claim that he is 'a wondrous necessary man' who has both made and destroyed her. The unresolved pessimism that pervades Middleton's *The Changeling* and *Women Beware Women* is balanced by the sprightly energy of his comedies, as in *No Wit, No Help like a Woman*. The title refers to Kate Low-water, the play's disguised married heroine who at times proclaims her affinity with Middleton's own 'roaring girl', both in her courage and in her ultimate tenderness. Few lines better illustrate Middleton's restrained and lucid language than Kate's soliloquy on 'wit' and 'fate':

Since wit has pleasur'd me, I'll pleasure wit;
Scholars shall fare the better. O my blessing!
I feel a hand of mercy lift me up
Out of a world of waters, and now sets me
Upon a mountain, where the sun plays most,
To cheer my heart even as it dries my limbs.
What deeps I see beneath me . . .

(II.3, 250–67)

The four dramatists who see out the ▷ Stuart (1603–25) and ▷ Caroline (1625–42) period are ▷ Philip Massinger (1583–1640), ▷ John Ford (1586–?1640), ▷ Richard Brome (1590–1653) and ▷ James Shirley (1596–1666). Massinger took over from Fletcher as the King's Men's main dramatist after the latter's death in 1625. He had earlier collaborated with him on over a dozen plays, and his own writing reflects some of Fletcher's romanticism. His best comedies are ▷ *A New Way to Pay Old Debts* (1625) and ▷ *The City Madam* (1632), while among his tragedies *The Duke of Milan* (1621) and ▷ *The Roman Actor* (1626) are not without imaginative insight. Much of Massinger's work is lost, and his modern reputation rests primarily on the achievement of *A New Way to Pay Old Debts*. The play's popularity in the theatre has never waned. Although its plotting – the overthrow of the mean and cruel Sir Giles Overreach through wit, and his subsequent confinement to Bedlam – is reminiscent of Jonson's *Epicoene* and *Volpone*, Massinger's idiom characteristically reconciles romance with the economic nexus.

John Ford is famous primarily for his one impressive Caroline play, ▷ *'Tis Pity She's a Whore* (1632). Writing towards the end of an extraordinary period, Ford reflects many of its preoccupations, and his work shows the influence of Shakespeare, Beaumont and Fletcher, Greene and others. *'Tis Pity* is a play about taboos, particularly in its treatment of the incest between Giovanni and his sister Annabella, whom he makes pregnant. She marries a rich suitor, Soranzo, but refuses to reveal to him the identity of her child's father. The play ends with Giovanni killing his sister and then Soranzo, before he himself dies at the hands of the latter's servant. The subtle layering of the play's plot, its sympathetic portrayal of the foolish Bergetto, and its masterly control of the tender dialogue between the two lovers who refuse to accept the secular and Christian sanctions against their sin, vindicate the prominent place which *'Tis Pity* has long occupied in the history of English drama.

Richard Brome and James Shirley inhabit the twilight of the Caroline theatre, as the clouds were gathering of the political confrontation between the king and the ▷ Puritans that was to close the playhouses in 1642. Brome was a friend of Jonson's, and the latter's influence is evident in ▷ *The City Wit* (1629), but less so in *The Jovial Crew* (1640). *The City Wit* is an intensely theatrical comedy of manners which in its rapid plotting recalls *Epicoene* and *The Alchemist*, while anticipating the idiom of Restoration comedy. *The Jovial Crew*, on the other hand, is a rural romantic comedy, in the style of Sidney's pastoral, about fathers, daughters and prophecies. It is an attractive and big-hearted play, which extends its understanding to beggars and gypsies, a rare occurrence during the period.

James Shirley was the last writer of the King's Men. He was prolific and successful, and some of his works, such as *The Lady of Pleasure* (1631) and *The Cardinal* (1641), have stood the test of time. But they lack substance and, as ▷ C. S. Lewis pointed out, depend overly on 'variations' on one or two themes. Shirley was a professional whose craft reflects the influence of Jonsonian comedy, but never rises to its imaginative level. One suspects that the social conditions prevailing in the 1630s in London and at the Court of Queen Henrietta Maria, as mirrored in Shirley's writings, contributed materially to the decadence of the theatre just before it finally closed.

From the courtly Elizabethan theatre of the pre-Shakespeareans to the darker rhythms of the Jacobean period and the fossilization of both these strains in the Stuart plays, the achievement of English Renaissance drama is distinguished by its buoyancy. Few of the dramatists pursued an active interest in form, which, like their ethical intelligence, is often overridden by a predilection for spectacle, taboo and set speeches. Even if one excepts Lyly, Shakespeare, Jonson and others to a lesser extent, the fact remains that Elizabethan–Jacobean drama and its Stuart twilight show the symptoms of a rambling and creatively chaotic dramatic culture.

If the theatre was perceived by the City Fathers as spiritually subversive, its political critique was generally negligible. On the few occasions that a politically inspired play escaped the censor's notice, it was either by collusion, as in the case of Middleton's *A Game at Chess* (1624), or by mistake, as with *Eastward Hoe* (1605), which nearly ruined its authors, fairly mild though its lampooning of the Stuarts was. The most famous example of a play exploited for political capital and, ultimately, high treason, were the unlicensed and private performances of Shakespeare's *Richard II* in the period immediately preceding the Essex rebellion in 1601. That Shakespeare's finely honed balancing of Richard's neglect of his duties with the monarchical ambitions of Bolingbroke could lend itself to such distortions does not reflect on the play's politics. If anything *Richard II* is a conservative work. The point is that theatre was potentially a political weapon and one of socio-economic import.

In the best possible sense, the theatre was classless. In the large public London playhouses poor apprentices would hobnob with the lords and ladies of the court during afternoon performances, even though admission prices would stand and seat them in different parts of the buildings. The medium of live theatre ensured that the dramatists never lost touch with the public on whom they depended for their livelihood. Even so, the theatre did not degenerate into populist entertainment such as was on offer in the nearby bear gardens or gambling houses. Ben Jonson's strenuous attempts – not always successful – at educating his audience are as significant in this respect as the testimony provided by the long runs of Marlowe's and Shakespeare's plays. The English theatre would never again achieve the degree of social integration, economic success and imaginative integrity that it enjoyed in this period.

Renaissance Political History and Social Context 4

Christopher Gillie

I

1485–1603

The daughter of debate, that eke discord doth sow
Shall reap no gain where former rule hath taught still peace to grow

Elizabeth I

England was one of the first countries in Europe to feel the impact of nationalism, but by the sixteenth century France and Spain had also achieved unity and nationhood. They towered above England almost as the U.S.A. does today, and constituted a potential – at times an actual – threat to its very existence. Fortunately, they were often hostile to each other. Yet this was not a period of decline for England; its relative inferiority was due to the increase in stature of its neighbours, not to its own diminution. On the contrary, the sixteenth century was one in which the nation developed, consolidated its energies, and found a use for them overseas in seafaring activities. The century was indeed more fortunate for England than for France and Spain, for at the end of it England, unlike Spain, was still advancing economically, and unlike France it had lost none of its representative political institutions.

All this was thanks partly to the reigning family, the ▷ Tudors, the most gifted of the dynasties that have reigned over England. Elsewhere in Europe national solidarity had been gained by the consolidation of monarchic power, and in this England was no exception; the period is in fact sometimes described as that of the 'Tudor despotism'. Yet ▷ Henry VIII (1509–47), one of the most despotic of English sovereigns, has also been described by English historians as a great parliamentarian. This seeming paradox is explained by the fact that, whereas the other sovereigns of Europe relied on their professional armies for their authority, and abandoned, as forces of disunity, their representative institutions, the Tudors had no such armies, and, realizing that they could achieve little if they did not carry the nation with them, therefore found it necessary to keep Parliament alive. So it happened that the political institutions that eventually made for popular government survived in England while they decayed elsewhere. Their survival in this period accounts for the difference between the later history of England and that of the other, larger nations of Europe.

Although they found it wiser to respect and use Parliament while other European monarchs found it more convenient to relinquish institutions, the

Tudors nonetheless required other institutions of government that strengthened their power.

In the fifteenth century, Parliament, though it had by no means yet become the channel of national feeling, was already an instrument of opposition to the monarchy. The House of Lords was the meeting-place of the great nobles who had torn England apart in the Wars of the Roses, and they were able to use the House of Commons as their tool, for the townsmen and small landowners who composed it were not yet able to find an independent voice and leadership. To manage so dangerous a body, the Tudors relied upon the old Curia Regis (King's Council), which by this time was known as the Privy Council. The Privy Council had the acknowledged right to issue ordinances which had the force of law, and when the matter affected the nation too gravely for this to be a wise procedure, the Councillors took their seats in Parliament, much as modern ministers do, and directed the needed Bills through both Houses.

But the Privy Council was put to other purposes as well; subcommittees of it were used to expand the king's administration and justice, just as Henry II in the twelfth century had used the Curia Regis to expand his system of justice by imposing on the feudal nobles the rule of Common Law. The weaknesses of the Common Law courts in the sixteenth century were that their procedure was often slow, and that the juries employed in them could be bribed or intimidated by powerful influences, especially in the wild districts of the north, where the old feudal nobility was still strong, and in Wales. Thus new courts were shaped out of the Privy Council, such as the Council of the North, the Council of Wales, and, most famous of all, the Court of the Star Chamber, so called from the pattern of stars on the ceiling of the room in which it met. These new courts did not supersede the courts of Common Law; they even revived the prestige of the Common Law courts by restoring public faith in and respect for justice.

However, these new courts had two characteristics that eventually turned public opinion against them: they based their authority on royal prerogative, *ie* powers peculiar to the king; and they worked without juries. Hence when Parliament once more set itself against the king in the seventeenth century, it saw the courts no longer as instruments of justice but of tyranny, and abolished them. The Privy Council, on the other hand, survives today; it is no longer the central instrument of executive power (the Cabinet is that), but a body serving a variety of consultative purposes.

The time was well past when the kings depended on churchmen as the only men educated enough to be capable of the art of government; ▷ Cardinal Wolsey was the last priest-statesman in the tradition of Thomas à Becket. Country gentlemen, lawyers and merchants of the towns were now plentiful in the educated classes, and it was from among these that the Tudors chose their Privy Councillors and Ministers of State. This policy replenished the English aristocracy; not only were the new men of power different in kind from their predecessors, and from different families, but they used their power in a different way. They were politicians and administrators in the modern sense, and they established traditions within their families in such a way that the descendants of some of them, for instance the Cecils, the Russells and the Cavendishes, continue to play an important part in politics.

The former feudal nobility had battered themselves into relative weakness during the fifteenth-century Wars of the Roses, and the first Tudor, ▷ Henry VII, eliminated their private armies by fining heavily any nobleman who tried to keep one. The strongholds of this old nobility were in the economically backward north and west, and they did not give way without a struggle; the ▷ Pilgrimage of Grace in 1536 and the rebellion of the northern earls in 1569 were their principal endeavours to re-establish their prestige and the interests of their more conservative society. But the advancing society of the south-east was more numerous, and its interests were strengthened by the inter-relationship of the classes: landed gentry apprenticed their younger sons to merchants of London – at the end of the century already the largest city in Europe – and both intermarried with the great aristocracy.

The landed gentleman, high in prestige among his lesser farming neighbours who were often bound to him, not by feudal obligations, but as rent-paying tenants, was the successor to the medieval baron, and exerted comparable but very different powers as Justice of the Peace. As such he was responsible for the law and order of his neighbourhood, and if in this he was sometimes unduly mindful of his interests – especially the protection of his 'game', ie animals reserved for hunting on his land – he was too much in awe of the Privy Council who commissioned his authority to carry tyranny far. The Justices of the Peace, settled men in the upper-middle ranges of society, carried ideas of government and order from the professional administrators of the Privy Council into the intimate world of the village parishes, making justice and politics human, if not always humane.

Since 1066, Britain has never had a reigning family of purely English origins; the Tudors were a Welsh family, who in the fifteenth century connected themselves with the Lancastrian branch of the originally French Plantagenets. No other reigning family assimilated so powerfully English ways of thinking and feeling, and this is most apparent in their handling of the great crisis of the century – the crisis which absorbed into itself so many other crises of domestic and foreign concern – that of the religious ▷ Reformation. This movement, which divided Europe in ways that were to prove permanent, was common to most of the northern countries, but in England it took a peculiar form. As elsewhere, the English Reformation had two aspects, political and doctrinal; it also had three phases, corresponding to the reigns of Henry VIII (1509–47), of his son ▷ Edward VI (1547–53), and of his younger daughter ▷ Elizabeth I (1558–1603).

The Church of the Middle Ages had not only been a religious body; it had been a political and legal power as well. Its bishops and greater abbots owned extensive property, which gave them material importance in an age when ownership of land was the measure of influence. Their interests involved them in political games, the prizes of which rewarded the international Catholic Church as well as the English clergy. The Church had its own courts of law, which sometimes competed for authority with those of the Common Law. Taxes, often resented throughout society, were paid to the head of the Church – the Pope in Rome. Nor was the Pope the only international authority of the Church; the heads of the great monastic orders often lived in France or Italy, and the abbots of English monasteries owed obedience and financial contributions to them as well as to the English king. Thus the medieval kings were never full masters of their country, but it often suited them to accept the special position of the Church for the sake of its support against their own barons or some foreign prince, or because they needed churchmen in the running of their governments.

The circumstances that made the Church partly acceptable to the medieval kings no longer applied to the sixteenth-century monarchy. Henry VIII felt only exasperation at the Church's exercise of authority within English frontiers, at the draining away of money to Church authorities abroad, and at the lack of practical value of monasteries which had lost many of their social functions and (often) their spiritual vocations. He knew that public opinion was mainly behind him, and his 'Reformation Parliament' (1529–36) supported him in passing the necessary laws to separate the Church of England from Rome, and place it under the supremacy of the king himself. Yet Henry – whom the Pope had rewarded with the title 'Defender of the Faith' for writing against the German reformer ▷ Martin Luther – was conservative in his beliefs, and the Act of ▷ Six Articles (1539) reaffirmed the Catholic dogma of transubstantiation, and such conservative practices as the celibacy of the clergy and the duty of regular confession to and absolution by a priest.

'There are many opinions in England concerning religion', a Venetian ambassador had written early in the century; in the fourteenth century, ▷ John Wycliffe had been a radical reformer of doctrine, and he had died peacefully in his bed instead of being put to death like his contemporary, the Bohemian John Huss. Some of Henry's subjects were more Protestant than himself, and some were more Catholic; his Archbishop of Canterbury ▷ Thomas Cranmer was amongst the former. Cranmer led the Protestant movement in the next reign (Edward VI) with his ▷ Book of Common Prayer for use in all English churches; in the reign after, he was burnt alive in accordance with the ▷ Counter-Reformation policy of Henry's Catholic daughter, ▷ Mary I (1553–8), who brought England back to allegiance to Rome. Neither reign was popular with the English, perhaps as much for political reasons as religious ones. The Protestant reign of the boy-king Edward let loose upon the country the more rapaciously self-seeking of the new style of nobleman, and it upset conservative sentiment by the unnecessary destruction of time-honoured religious images in the churches. Mary I, however, was much worse hated for her public burnings of Protestants, and for opening the way to foreign influences by marrying 'His Most Catholic Majesty' Philip II of Spain – a much fiercer persecutor of Protestantism in his own dominions. ▷ Foxe's Book of Martyrs (1563) was revered next to the Bible in many English households for generations to come.

So Elizabeth I, last and considered to be the greatest of the Tudors, re-established the Anglican Church – again by Act of Parliament – in 1559, but, characteristically, she chose 'a middle way'. Her Settlement was so cautiously worded as to admit the possibility that good Catholics might feel they could combine their loyalty to the Pope with their allegiance to the queen, and their faith in Catholic dogmas with membership of the Anglican Church. It was not until 1571 that the Pope brought himself to excommunicate Elizabeth, and the Anglican opinion was that the Church of Rome 'seceded' from the Church of England, not the other way round.

The Elizabethan Settlement established the ▷ Church of England durably. It has remained largely what she meant it to be, a religious body elastic enough to include, to this day, Christians who are Catholic in all points except acknowledgement of the Pope, and Christians who are Protestant enough to resent all but the austerest religious ritual – the High Church and the Low Church, as the two extremes came to be called in the nineteenth century. It did not, indeed, do all that she meant: the Roman Catholics did not join it, and the more extreme Protestants – who were first given the name ▷ Puritans during her reign – remained discontented with it, until they were cast out a century later to make up those numerous dissenting denominations that caused the French writer Voltaire to describe England as the land of 'many religions and only one sauce'. It is often called the 'Elizabethan Compromise', but it was no mere compromise, as testified by the thinkers of great spiritual dignity it was to produce in the next hundred years: ▷ Richard Hooker, ▷ Lancelot Andrewes, ▷ Jeremy Taylor. Nor were they alone, for we have Anglican poets of the same period: ▷ George Herbert, ▷ John Donne and ▷ Henry Vaughan.

The ▷ Renaissance was Rebirth – Europe recovering its supposed origins in the cultures of ancient Greece and Rome. The Reformation was a product of it: first people became critical of the unexamined assumptions of the Middle Ages, and then – in northern Europe – they turned against the Church that seemed to embody them. They were disintegrating movements, but also liberating ones, and they were consistently related, by cause and by effect, to liberating movements in politics, commerce and society in every country.

The liberation of English national energies at the end of the century – in trade, seafaring, literature and music – was new; never before had the people cohered in the many-sided activities of nationhood. The English felt that they were experiencing *rebirth* as a nation. The glorious myth of ▷ King Arthur gave them an image of an ancient British golden age, with which the Tudors asserted an astute political connection. King Arthur had been an ancient Briton; the descendants of those Britons were the Welsh; the Tudors were Welsh – ▷ Henry VII called his eldest son Arthur – and like King Arthur, Henry had rescued the country from the darkness of civil war. With less reliance on myth, the English treasured the memory of an earlier Henry – Henry V, who had modelled himself on the pattern of an ideal Christian prince (like King Arthur himself) and had demonstrated the splendour of national unity by the glorious victory of Agincourt in 1415. Henry at Agincourt, with his inferior forces, was an image of the prince whose personal destiny was identified with the destiny of his people. Whatever the truth of this image, such identification of princely and national destinies seemed almost fact in the reign of Elizabeth.

The nation was committed to its own version of Protestantism, and so was the queen; to lose her was to lose Protestantism, and national independence as well. Elizabeth's position was vulnerable, for her mother, Anne Boleyn, had been the cause of Henry VIII's divorce from Katharine of Aragon, which had been the occasion for the separation of the Church of England from Rome. Good European Catholics were forced to regard Henry's divorce as illegal, since it had not been allowed by the Pope, and thus to consider Elizabeth an illegitimate child. Legitimacy, in that view, lay with the Catholic ▷ Mary Queen of Scots, and she had the support of the greatest European military power, ruled by Europe's most ardently Catholic sovereign, Philip II of Spain. His attempted invasion of England in order to depose Elizabeth was defeated in 1588, and England and Elizabeth were saved. The great outpouring of Elizabethan poetry came principally in the last 15 years of her reign, after the victory over the Spanish ▷ Armada. It was, no doubt, partly an expression of the release of national energies no longer inhibited by foreign menace, and much of it (notably ▷ Spenser's ▷ Faerie Queene) celebrated the glory of the queen who had become identified with national salvation. But some of this poetry, for instance the verse of ▷ Ralegh and the plays of ▷ Shakespeare written towards the end of the reign, had a more sombre tone, as though anticipating the darker mood of the nation in the period to come.

II

1603–1660

All order was confounded
John Bunyan

The theme of this period, which is as coherent as a drama, is the battle for supreme power between king and Parliament, and the eventual supremacy of the latter. How did this struggle arise? The causes were partly economic: the kings never had enough money to pay for government; consequently they went to Parliament – though sometimes they took other courses – to raise taxes. But Members of Parliament looked after their own interests; if they were to pay for government, they wished it to be conducted in accordance with these interests. And here we come to the social causes of the conflict. The centre of power in Parliament had shifted since the fifteenth century. No longer were the Commons the tool of the Lords – it was beginning to be the other way round. The House of Commons represented the merchants and the landed gentry, who were not definitely distinguishable, just as the gentry were not clearly distinguishable from the class represented in the Upper House: the sons of the Lords were usually 'commoners', and could and did sit in the House of Commons when they were elected to it. The opposition to the monarchy was more geographical than social; the south and east of England were economically the most developed, and were more conscious of disagreement with the policies of the king, who, when the ▷ Civil War eventually broke out in 1642, found that his supporters lived chiefly in the more conservative north and west.

Finally, there are the religious causes of the conflict. Religion, till the second half of the seventeenth century, still affected every department of life, and religious division corresponded to economic and social divisions as well. The more extreme kind of Protestantism known as Puritanism suited the mentality of the mercantile middle classes, and so the emotional fervour that led to the Civil War was religious fervour, even when the disagreements might in fact be practical issues of politics or economics.

After 1660, when the monarchy was restored, a major change began to affect political behaviour: religion influenced all aspects of experience less and less, and itself became a mere compartment of life. The Revolution of 1688 was indeed made on account of the Catholicism of James II – but chiefly because it was leading him into despotic practices. After 1688, men's ideas were increasingly cast in the mould of the tolerant and sceptical philosophy of John Locke, the thinker whose ideas were to dominate the eighteenth century.

The term 'Puritan' arose early in the reign of Elizabeth I, as an expression of impatient contempt for those militant Protestants who, discontented with the attempt of the Elizabethan Settlement of 1559 to solve the religious debate, wanted to carry the purification of what they regarded as Catholic abuses of religion to limits beyond compromise. Puritanism covered a wide variety of beliefs, but its outstanding characteristics can be summarized as follows. Firstly, Puritans rejected any spiritual authority save that of the Bible – 'the pure Word of God'. Secondly, they were opposed to the appointment of official Church authorities, such as bishops, regarding instead the government of the Church as a matter for those whom they considered to be the true believers, though they disagreed among themselves about what form this government should take. Thirdly, in keeping with this objection to temporal authorities imposed from above, they believed that the Voice of God spoke in each man's individual conscience, and that no priest or other intermediary could rightfully come between. Fourthly, they insisted on extreme austerity of worship, believing that images, ornaments, altars, ritual and embroidered surplices worn by priests were all no better than superstitions. Fifthly, in their insistence on nothing but the pure truth of religion, they tended to regard all fiction such as stage plays as deceiving vanities, tending to divert the minds of men from spiritual devotion, and they were also disapproving of costly clothing, long hair, and even amusements such as dancing.

Not all these characteristics applied to all Puritans: some, for example, were much less severe on worldly amusements than others; on the other hand, something of the Puritan austerity coloured people such as the Elizabethan poet Spenser who would not have described themselves as Puritans. Again, within the mentioned characteristics, there was plenty of room for disagreement, both in doctrine and in opinions about church organization. But the variations within Puritanism are less important to notice than the kinds of people who were attracted to it, for it was the adoption of its principles by whole classes of society that made it such a formidable political and cultural force.

Its austerity appealed to the businesslike, *ie* those who made work rather than pleasure their chief occupation; so did some of its doctrines, such as predestination, which declared that some people were irredeemably damned, and that a sign of Divine Grace being on a person's side was whether he or she prospered in his or her worldly pursuits. Also, the Puritan reliance on the individual conscience tended to encourage independence of political judgement, and Puritan belief in the supremacy of religion over all other considerations accorded with a desire to control the political machine, since Puritans were seldom in doubt that true religion was identical with what they happened to believe. It was thus the hard-working, practical, commercial and agricultural classes of south-eastern England that were attracted to Puritanism, and economically as well as religiously, in an age when governments were not yet predominantly commercial, they felt that they had to fight for their interests. When ▷ James I rejected the moderate Puritan appeals to him at the Hampton Court Conference of 1604 with the terse pronouncement 'No Bishop, no King', he was speaking prophetically out of his bitter previous experience as king of Puritanical Scotland; the English Puritans felt that war had been declared upon them.

The ▷ Stuarts had been kings of Scotland since the fourteenth century. When Elizabeth died, childless, James VI of Scotland, descended from a sister of Henry VIII, was heir to the English throne; he thus became king of both countries as James VI and I. He insisted on the Divine Right of kings to rule, but the sacredness of a crowned head, which was strong in people's imaginations, was the more respected the less it was proclaimed. He also called his judges 'lions beneath the throne', whereas the English assumption had long been that the king himself was subject to the law. He combined these tactless assertions of royal status with the incompatibility of a timid personality and an ambitious foreign policy which, moreover, since it involved coming to terms with the national enemy, Spain, in itself angered Parliament.

Charles I (1625–49) had equally unfortunate qualities, but very different ones. James had lacked personal dignity, whereas his son possessed it notably, and the royal court under James was scandalously conducted, while that of Charles was cultivated and fastidious. On the other hand, Charles was bigoted and unyielding in all his opinions. He quarrelled with his Parliaments by trying to raise taxes without their consent, using imprisonment without trial, and insisting on conformity to the rites of the Anglican Church. After he had tried and failed to rule without summoning Parliament, the breach between himself and the Puritans became too great to be mended. The Parliamentary Puritans (a majority of the House of Commons and a minority of the House of Lords) tried to impose on him a Puritan reformation of the Church of England. This finally divided the nation between Royalist ▷ Cavaliers (*ie* courtiers) and Puritan ▷ Roundheads (so called because they wore their hair short): between, that is to say, those who cared less for Parliamentary power than for the Anglican establishment on the one side, and those who saw in Parliament the only protector of religious truth on the other.

The fifteenth-century Civil Wars of the Roses had been fought with professional soldiers, newly released from the wars in France; the Civil Wars of the seventeenth century were fought by a nation that lacked professional armies, since it had grown accustomed to relying upon its navies for defence. Forseeably, victory came to the side that succeeded in professionalizing its army first. Thanks to the military genius of ▷ Oliver Cromwell, this was achieved, and the war was won, by Parliament. With Cromwell's Ironsides the English military tradition was renewed; the oldest regiment of the modern British army, the Coldstream Guards, is of Cromwellian origin.

King Charles I was executed in 1649. From that year until 1660 England was a republic, under the rule of the House of Commons and a Council of State until 1653, and then under Cromwell as Protector, a position resembling that of the modern President of the United States. The Protectorate, however, solved no problems; it only brought to light the reality of the English political predicament. This was not, fundamentally, a matter of religious or social differences, none of which were as final as the mismanagement by the first two Stuarts had made them seem; it was a problem of political machinery. Parliament had grown strong enough to insist that governmental policy should accord with its wishes, and the governments – whether of king or of protector – needed Parliament's financial support. The solution might seem to be that Parliament, the legislative or law-making power, should itself become the executive or policy-making power; but, as Cromwell and the nation discovered in the years 1649–53, a body of several hundred men is altogether too clumsy to devise and execute policy. The dilemma remained, until by slow experiment over the next century and a half the Cabinet system was evolved.

When the great Protector, Cromwell, died in 1658, after finding that he was unable as Charles I had been to rule either with or without Parliament, the nation recalled the Stuart dynasty. So came about the Restoration of the monarchy in 1660.

Reference section

Abergavenny, Frances Neville (?–d.1576)
Devotional writer. She wrote a collection
of prayers which were originally intended
for her daughter's personal use, but which
were published in the first and fifth parts
of Thomas Bentley's *Momument of Matrones*
(1582). The prayers are written about
essentially female experiences, such as
childbirth. Frances Neville's writing is
part of an expanding group of Renaissance
women's writing which may be read both as
an example of private devotion, as well as
for its more general account of how women
lived at that time.

Abigail
In the Bible (*I Samuel 25*), the wife of
King David. In addressing him, she calls
herself 'thine handmaid'. ▷ Beaumont
and ▷ Fletcher gave the name Abigail to
a 'waiting-gentlewoman' in their play *The
Scornful Lady*. From this, the name came to
be used generically in English for superior
woman servants.

Act
In politics: a law which has been passed
through both Houses of Parliament and
accepted by the monarch. Until this process is
completed, it is called a Bill.
    In drama: a division of a play. Acts are
sometimes subdivided into scenes. The
ancient Greeks did not use divisions into
acts; the practice was started by the Romans,
and the poet-critic Horace (1st century BC)
in his *Ars Poetica* laid down the principle that
the number of acts should be five. Since
the renaissance of classical learning in the
16th century, most dramatists have used act
divisions, and many have obeyed Horace's
precepts. All ▷ Shakespeare's plays are
divided into acts and scenes in modern
editions, but it is certain that he did not
write them in labelled scenes, and uncertain
whether he thought in terms of acts; some of
the first printed versions of his plays show act
divisions and some do not.

Acting, the profession of
Acting began to achieve recognition as a
profession in the reign of ▷ Elizabeth I. The
important date is the building of The Theatre
– the first theatre in England – by ▷ James
Burbage in 1576. It was followed by many
others in London, and theatres soon became
big business. Previously, actors had performed
where they could, especially in inn yards and
the halls of palaces, mansions and colleges.

They continued to do so, but the existence
of theatres gave them a base and (though
they still required an official licence) the
independence they badly needed in order to
win social recognition.
    Until the mid-16th century, acting was
practised by many kinds of people: ordinary
townsmen at festivals, wandering entertainers,
boys and men from the choirs of the great
churches, and members of the staffs of royal
or aristocratic households. It was from these
last that the professional actors emerged.
They still wore the liveries – uniforms and
badges – of the great households, but the
connection was now loose (good performers
could transfer from one household to another)
and was chiefly a means of procuring a licence
to perform. This licence was essential because
the City of London, around which dramatic
activity concentrated, feared the theatre as
providing centres of infection for the recurrent
▷ plague epidemics (which from time to time
sent the companies away on tour) and disliked
acting as a morally harmful and anomalous
way of life. Moreover, the royal court, which
favoured the stage, was nonetheless on guard
against it as a potential source of sedition.
▷ Censorship and licensing, however, had the
advantage of helping to distinguish the serious
performers from the vulgar entertainers.
    By the time of Elizabeth's death two
great companies were dominant: the ▷ Lord
Chamberlain's Men, for whom ▷ Shakespeare
wrote, and the ▷ Lord Admiral's Men,
headed by the leading actor of the day,
▷ Edward Alleyn. Women did not perform;
their parts were taken by boys who enlisted
as apprentices. Companies of boy actors
from the choirs of St Paul's and the Chapels
Royal also had prestige (see ▷ *Hamlet* II.2.),
especially in the 1570s. The establishment of
the profession owed most to the dramatists,
but much to the energy of actor-managers
and theatre proprietors such as ▷ Philip
Henslowe, Edward Alleyn, James Burbage,
and his son ▷ Richard.
    Actresses were allowed to perform after the
Restoration of the monarchy (1660).
    ▷ Paul's, Children of St; Puritanism;
Theatres.
Bib: Bradbrook, M. C., *The Rise of the Common
Player*; Bentley, G. E., *The Profession of a
Player in Shakespeare's Time*.

Admiral's Men, The Lord
A company of Elizabethan actors under the
protection of Lord Howard of Effingham, who
became Lord Admiral in 1585. They are first
heard of in 1574, and were at their height

in the 1590s, when they were led by one of the two chief actors of the time, ▷ Edward Alleyn, and when their only rivals were the ▷ Lord Chamberlain's Men, who were led by the other, ▷ Richard Burbage. As Burbage was ▷ Shakespeare's leading actor, so Alleyn and the Admiral's Men were associated with ▷ Christopher Marlowe. The chief financial management of the company was under Alleyn himself and his father-in-law, ▷ Philip Henslowe, a financier. In the reign of ▷ James I (1603–25) the company came under the patronage of his eldest son, ▷ Prince Henry; and on his death under that of James's son-in-law, the Elector of the Palatinate. The company came to an end in 1628.

Adonis

A supremely beautiful youth in Greek myth. Beloved by Aphrodite, he was cured of a mortal wound by Persephone on condition that he spent half the year with the latter in the underworld and half with the former on earth. The myth thus symbolized the change from winter to summer; images of Adonis were surrounded by gardens of flowers; hence the Garden of Adonis in, *eg*, ▷ Spenser's ▷ *Faerie Queene*, Bk. III. The myth is also comically inverted in ▷ Shakespeare's ▷ *Venus and Adonis*, where the youth displays an effeminate reticence, and the goddess adopts the masculine role of ardent wooer.

Advancement of Learning, The (1605)

A philosophical treatise by ▷ Francis Bacon published in 1605 in English, and expanded in a Latin version entitled *De Augmentis Scientiarium* published in 1623.

The purpose of the book is to suggest ways in which the pursuit of knowledge can be encouraged, and the methods of observation and recording of both natural and human phenomena improved. To this end, Bacon's work proposes nothing less than a taxonomy of all knowledge, a proposition strikingly familiar to that advanced by the French Encyclopaedists of the 16th century.

Perhaps the most influential aspect of *The Advancement* is the methodology that Bacon employs. In surveying all fields of knowledge Bacon offers a form of catalogue of existing fields of enquiry. This attempt at classification, whereby branches of knowledge are grouped together under common headings, relies on a system of particularization. In each subject considered, Bacon argues that the first step is the fresh observation of the detail of the phenomena. Once the detail, or particularities, had

been assimilated it would become possible, through the process of induction, to assert the general propositions under which groups of phenomena could be considered. This method signalled both a break from what Bacon considered to be the traditional methods of enquiry (which involved deduction from generalized propositions) and the re-examination of observable phenomena through the process of experimentation.

As a theorist of scientific method (rather than as an experimenter in his own right) Bacon was to have considerable influence on the early founders of ▷ The Royal Society, particularly in the area of language reform. On the question of language, and the idea of an appropriate language for scientific discourse, *The Advancement of Learning* is a key text. At the same time, the importance of language to Bacon's project necessitated an exploration of poetic language which was to be influential for poets of the later 17th century, in particular ▷ Abraham Cowley.

▷ Dissociation of Sensibility.

Aeneas

Hero of the Latin ▷ epic the ▷ *Aeneid* by ▷ Virgil. Traditions about him existed long before Virgil's poem. He was the son of Anchises and the goddess Aphrodite, and the son-in-law of Priam, king of Troy. In ▷ Homer's ▷ *Iliad* (v) he is represented as the chief of the Trojans and one of the most formidable defenders of Troy against the Greeks. Other records stated that after the fall of Troy, he set out to seek a new kingdom with some of the surviving Trojans, and eventually settled in central Italy. By Virgil's time, the Romans were already worshipping Aeneas as the father of their race.

▷ Tudor myth.

Aeneid

An ▷ epic poem by the Roman poet ▷ Virgil (70–19 BC). The poem tells the story of ▷ Aeneas, from his flight from Troy during the confusion of its destruction by the Greeks to his establishment as king of the Latins in central Italy and his death in battle with the Etruscans. The poem thus begins at a point near where ▷ Homer left off in the ▷ *Iliad*, and its description of the wanderings of Aeneas is parallel to the description of the wanderings of ▷ Odysseus in Homer's *Odyssey*. It is divided into 12 books, of which the second, fourth and sixth are the most famous: the second describes the destruction of Troy; the fourth gives the tragedy of Queen Dido of Carthage, who dies for love of Aeneas; the sixth shows his descent to the underworld and the prophetic visions of those who are to build the greatness of Rome.

Virgil wished to relate the Rome he knew, a settled and luxurious civilization which threatened to degenerate into complacent mediocrity, to her heroic past, and to inspire her with a sense of her great destiny in world history. The *Aeneid* is thus a central document for Roman culture, and inasmuch as Roman culture is the basis of the culture of Western Europe, it has remained a central document for European culture too.

The most notable English translations of the *Aeneid* are those by the Scottish poet ▷ Gavin Douglas (1553) and by John Dryden (1631–1700; 1697). Henry Howard, ▷ Earl of Surrey translated Books II and III into the earliest example of English blank verse.

▷ Tudor myth.

Aeolian

From Aeolus, god of the winds in ancient Greek myth. An Aeolian harp is a stringed instrument placed across a window or outside a house so that the wind causes the strings to vibrate and make music. ▷ Shakespeare's ▷ *Cymbeline* makes reference to and use of an instrument of this kind.

Aeschylus (525–456 BC)

With ▷ Sophocles and ▷ Euripides, one of the three great tragic poets of ancient Greece. Only seven of his 70 plays survive; of these the best known are *Agamemnon*, *Choephori* and *Eumenides*, making up the *Oresteia* trilogy. Aeschylus is the great starting point of all European tragedy, but it was the derivative tragedy of the Latin poet ▷ Seneca which influenced the great period of English tragedy between 1590 and 1630. Reacting against this, ▷ Milton deliberately based his tragedy ▷ *Samson Agonistes* (1671) on the Greek pattern.

▷ Tragedy.

Ages, Golden, Silver, etc.

The Greek poet Hesiod (8th century BC) in *Works and Days* writes of an ideal golden age in the past, comparable to the Garden of Eden; from this period, he considered that there had been a progressive decline through the silver, bronze and heroic ages until his own time. His classification has been adapted by other writers to describe cycles of history. The terms have also been applied more or less loosely: so one speaks, for example, of the ▷ Elizabethan period as being the golden age of English drama.

Agincourt (1415)

A battle in the Hundred Years' War, in which the English king ▷ Henry V defeated a much larger French army. The victory was the more inspiring because it was especially a victory for English yeoman archers – humble foot-soldiers – over the aristocratic French cavalry. This allowed ▷ Shakespeare to make use of the battle as part of his creation of the myth of nationhood in his play ▷ *Henry V*: in this Henry is represented as the leader of a whole people, not merely of an aristocracy. The early modern period, in which the play was written, saw the rise of the great nation states and the development of a system of representation that would reinforce a sense of political unity within them. Agincourt became a useful symbol in that project. Another famous account of the battle is ▷ Michael Drayton's *Ballad of Agincourt* (1606–19).

Alchemist, The (1610)

A comedy by ▷ Ben Jonson. The scene is a house in London during a visitation of the plague; its master, Lovewit, has taken refuge in the country, leaving his servant, Face, in charge. Face introduces two rogues: Subtle, a charlatan alchemist, and Dol Common, a whore. Together they collaborate in turning the house into a centre for the practice of alchemy in the expectation of attracting credulous clients who will believe that alchemical magic can bring them their heart's desire. Their expectations are realized, and their dupes are representative social types. Sir Epicure Mammon dreams of limitless luxury and the satisfaction of his lust; the Puritans, Ananias and Tribulation Wholesome, hope to enrich their sect; Drugger, a tobacco merchant, wants prosperity for his business; Dapper, a lawyer's clerk, seeks a spirit to guarantee him success in gambling; Kastril, a young country squire, desires a rich husband for his sister (Dame Pliant) and knowledge of the secret of fashionable quarrelling. Only Pertinax Surly, a friend of Mammon, sees the fraudulence of the enterprise, but Face and his colleagues manage to turn the clients against him and he is routed. Each of the clients has to be deceived by a separate technique, depending on his peculiar brand of social credulity, and this requires swift changes of role by the cheats, especially Subtle. They are equal to all emergencies until Lovewit suddenly returns – a crisis which only Face survives. He expels Subtle and Common, and then wins over his master, who admires his ingenuity and is satisfied with the plunder, which includes Dame Pliant. The play is one of Jonson's best; it has energetic wit and extraordinary theatrical ingenuity. Moreover the characterization has behind it the force of Jonson's conviction that human folly is limitless and can be cured only by exposure and castigation.

Alexander, Sir William, Earl of Stirling (1567–1640)

Poet, dramatist, statesman, colonialist. Alexander's chief literary work was a collection of sonnets entitled *Aurora*, published in 1603. In addition to the composition of dramatic works (*The Tragedy of Darius* appeared in 1603), he accepted positions as tutor to ▷ Prince Henry, and Secretary of State for Scotland under ▷ Charles I. Alexander was also an early enthusiast for the foundation of colonies. In 1624 he published a work entitled *Encouragement to Colonies*, which was followed, in 1630, by *The Map and Description of New England*.

Alexander the Great (356–323 BC)

He succeeded to the throne of Macedon in 336 BC after the assassination of his father, Philip II. Alexander began by consolidating his father's hegemony. Then he embarked on a rapid career of conquest which took his armies as far as the valley of the Indus in north-west India. In the ▷ Renaissance, Alexander always figures among ▷ the 'Nine Worthies'.

Alexandrine

A 12-syllable line of verse, possibly owing its name to the French medieval work the *Roman d'Alexandre*. It is common in French poetry, particularly of the classical period, but unusual in English, where the commonest line length is ten syllables. ▷ Michael Drayton used it in his long poem *Poly-Olbion* (1613–22), but its most famous use is in the last line of the ▷ Spenserian stanza, invented by ▷ Edmund Spenser for his ▷ *Faerie Queene*.

Allegory

From the Greek, meaning 'speaking in other terms'. A way of representing thought and experience through images, by means of which (1) complex ideas may be simplified, or (2) abstract, spiritual or mysterious ideas and experiences may be made immediate (but not necessarily simpler) by dramatization in fiction.

In the Renaissance, however, explicit allegory, though still pervasive, was greatly

complicated by the break-up of the dominant Catholic framework; various Christian doctrines competed with one another and with non-Christian ones such as ▷ neo-Platonism, and also with political theories. Thus, in a work like ▷ Spenser's ▷ *Faerie Queene*, religious, political and Platonic allegories are all employed, but intermittently and not with artistic coherence.

Since the 17th century deliberate and consistent allegory has continued to decline; yet the greatest of all English allegories, ▷ *The Pilgrim's Progress* by ▷ John Bunyan, is a 17th-century work. The paradox is explained by Bunyan's contact with the literature of the village sermon, which apparently continued to be conducted by a simple allegorical method with very little influence from the ▷ Reformation.
Bib: Murrin, M., *The Veil of Allegory*.

Allegro, L' (c 1631)

A poem by ▷ John Milton, published in 1645 though composed c 1631. The poem is a companion piece to ▷ *Il Penseroso*, and the title can be translated from the Italian as signifying the cheerful or happy individual. The poem's theme celebrates the active life of engagement with the world, as opposed to the reflective life depicted in *Il Penseroso*.

Alleyn, Edward (1566–1626)

Son of an innkeeper, Alleyn rose to become one of the two foremost tragic actors of the great age of English drama. In 1586 he was performing for Lord Worcester's Men; in 1592 he married the stepdaughter of the financier ▷ Philip Henslowe, and together they built up the prosperity of the ▷ Lord Admiral's Men. In this company he was celebrated for his performances of ▷ Christopher Marlowe's heroes: ▷ Tamburlaine, Faustus (▷ *Doctor Faustus*) and Barabas. He became the main owner of the ▷ Rose and the Fortune theatres, and a wealthy man by his speculation in land. He founded Dulwich College, to this day a leading public school. After the death of his first wife, he married the daughter of ▷ John Donne, the poet and Dean of St Paul's. His acting was highly praised by contemporary dramatists and other writers – ▷ Thomas Nashe, ▷ Thomas Heywood, and ▷ Ben Jonson among them – and was likened to that of the Roman actor ▷ Roscius.
   ▷ Acting, the profession of; Theatres.
Bib: Hosking, G. L., *Life and Times of Edward Alleyn*.

All's Well that Ends Well (1602–3)
A play by ▷ Shakespeare in which the
heroine, Helena de Narbon, pursues Bertram,
Count of Rousillon, whom she loves but
who seeks to elude her. He is misled by a
dishonourable young courtier, Parolles; she
eventually ensnares him by a trick. The plot
is taken from Painter's ▷ *Palace of Pleasure*
(1566–7) but the play is difficult to date
precisely owing to its mixture of styles. ▷ Sir
Edmund Chambers dates it 1602–3. This
agrees with the kind of difficulty with which it
faces critics: uncertainty about Shakespeare's
intention; the play seems to be a romantic
comedy, but the treatment of the subject is
often unromantic and the comedy is often
harsh. Thus *All's Well* resembles other
▷ problem plays of Shakespeare written
between 1600 and 1604: ▷ *Hamlet*, ▷ *Measure
for Measure*, ▷ *Troilus and Cressida*.

Althusser, Louis (1918–90)
One of the most influential French ▷ Marxist
philosophers of the 1960s, whose work
began to appear in English translation from
1965 onwards: *For Marx* (1965), *Reading
Capital* (with Etienne Balibar; 1968), and
Lenin and Philosophy (1971). Althusser's
ideas have been influential in the area of
Renaissance literary criticism, where his
particular brand of structural Marxism has
led to a radical rethinking of society and
the place of the human subject within it.
His essay 'Ideology and Ideological State
Apparatuses' (*Lenin and Philosophy*) lays the
foundation for a reconsideration of literature
and its relationship to ▷ ideology. Althusser's
work has had a major impact on ▷ new
historicism and ▷ cultural materialism, both
theoretical approaches which have dominated
Renaissance criticism in the last 15 years.

Amaryllis
A name used for a shepherdess in Greek and
Latin pastoral poetry, *eg* by ▷ Theocritus,
▷ Virgil and ▷ Ovid, and borrowed by
English pastoralists such as ▷ Spenser.

Amoretti (1595)
A sequence of 89 sonnets by ▷ Edmund
Spenser, first published, together with the
wedding-song ▷ *Epithalamion*, in 1595. The
title of the sequence is derived from the term
applied to Italian love songs which take the
exploits of Cupid as their subject. *Amoretti*
is unusual amongst the ▷ sonnet sequences
of the period in that it moves towards an
evocation of sexual love within a Christian
context, which has, as its end, the sacrament
of marriage. Though much of the language
and many of the ideas in the sequence
are derived from ▷ Petrarch, Spenser
nevertheless developed the Petrarchan model
in introducing a carefully organized structure
to the work. Thus, the events described in
Amoretti follow the course of the Christian
year, while the work as a whole evokes the
progress of the seasons. It has long been
assumed that the sonnets were addressed to
Spenser's second wife, Elizabeth Boyle, whom
he married in 1594.

Anatomy of Melancholy, The (1621–51)
A treatise by ▷ Robert Burton (1577–1640)
on a topic which was of enduring interest,
in particular to Elizabethan and Jacobean
playwrights. It was first published in 1621,
but by the time the sixth (posthumous) edition
of 1651 appeared, Burton had expanded the
original book of approximately 860 pages
by about one-third. Though its ostensible
theme is an enquiry into the 'symptoms,
prognostickes and severall cures' of the
psychological disorder of melancholy, it is
also a wide-ranging exposition of the role and
function of the human being in the natural
order of the universe (▷ humanism). Not the
least of the work's concerns is the principle
of ordering and classification itself, and it
thus bears comparison to ▷ Francis Bacon's
▷ *Advancement of Learning* and the work of
later scientists associated with ▷ The Royal
Society. But in its digressive and allusive
pursuit of curious forms of knowledge, and
in its stylistic delight in the piling up of
quotation, modification and qualification,
it stands as a work without any immediate
precursors or later emulators.
▷ Humour.
Bib: Vicari, E. P., *The View from Minerva's
Tower*.

Andrewes, Lancelot (1555–1626)
A bishop and leader of the ▷ Church of
England during the most formative century
(1550–1650) of its thought. His ▷ sermons
were famous in an age when preaching
was a high art; their prose was vivid and
condensed, and an important contribution to
the development of English prose. He took
part in the translation of the King James
Bible. Andrewes is compared to ▷ John
Donne, poet and Dean of St Paul's, whose
prose comes near his own poetry. As an
intellectual defender of the Anglican religious
position, Andrewes was the successor of
▷ Richard Hooker; but whereas Hooker was

mainly concerned to defend Anglicanism against the ▷ Puritans, Andrewes defended it against the Catholics. Both he and Hooker are representatives of Anglicanism as the *via media* between the two.
Bib: Eliot, T. S., 'Lancelot Andrewes' in *Selected Essays*; Higham, F., *Lancelot Andrewes*; Welsby, P. A., *Lancelot Andrewes*.

Anger, Jane (fl. 1588)

Tract-writer. Pseudonym for the author of a proto-feminist pamphlet, *Jane Anger, Her Protection for Women* (1588–9). There is no indication as to the true identity of the writer. This work is a polemical contribution to the ▷ *Querelle des Femmes* in which Anger attacks men for the way they slander women, and praises her own sex for their grace, wisdom and 'true fidelity'. It was uncommon for a woman to write for publication at this time, which perhaps explains the need to conceal her true name. However, Anger explicitly calls attention to the fact that women have been denied a public hearing and stresses that this unfair treatment has led to her own 'angry' response. Jane Anger's pamphlet is published in *Half Humankind: Contexts and Texts of the Controversy about Women in England*, 1540–1640, ed. K. U. Henderson and B. F. McManus (1985).
▷ Munda, Constantia; Sowernam, Ester; Speght, Rachel.

Anne of Denmark, Queen of Great Britain (1574–1619)

Patron. ▷ King James I's consort is often attacked as being light-minded and pleasure-loving. The latter is certainly true, but it is important to bear in mind that the courtly entertainments which she encouraged were not simply childlike amusements, but important pieces of political propaganda. These ▷ masques allowed Anne to participate in the public sphere, an arena that would otherwise have been denied her by the misogynous king. Numerous arguments occurred between her and James over which ambassadors should be invited to the masques, which suggests the powerful diplomatic significance of these events. Her son ▷ Henry, Prince of Wales, similarly recognized the value of court shows. Moreover, Queen Anne's commissioning of masques allowed her a certain input into the contents of the pieces and her involvement is detailed by ▷ Ben Jonson in his annotations and prefaces to various works.
Bib: Williams, E. C., *Anne of Denmark*.

Anthology

A collection of short works in verse or prose, or selected passages from longer works, by various authors. Some anthologies lay claim to authority as representing the best written in a given period, *eg* the Oxford Books (of Sixteenth-Century Verse, etc.), and others are standard examples of taste at the time of compiling, *eg* ▷ *Tottel's Miscellany* and ▷ *A Mirror for Magistrates*. An influential anthology of women's writing was Thomas Bentley's *The Monument of Matrones* (1582), which included the works of ▷ Elizabeth I, ▷ Katherine Parr, ▷ Lady Jane Grey, ▷ Frances Abergavenny and ▷ Elizabeth Tyrwhit.

Antonio and Mellida (1600)

A play in two parts by ▷ John Marston. Part I is a transvestite, stylized and Italianate comedy about the loves of its eponymous protagonists. Part II, usually known as *Antonio's Revenge*, protrays the savage destruction of the same characters in the idiom of an Elizabethan blood tragedy.
▷ Revenge tragedy.

Antony and Cleopatra (1606–7)

A tragedy by ▷ Shakespeare, probably written in 1606–7, and first printed in the First Folio edition of his collected plays in 1623. The source is ▷ Sir Thomas North's translation (1587 edition) of ▷ Plutarch's *Lives*.
    Mark Antony, with Octavius Caesar and Lepidus, is one of the 'triumvirate' (43–31 BC) which rules Rome and its empire, and he is Rome's most famous living soldier. At the opening of the play, he is the lover of ▷ Cleopatra, Queen of Egypt, and, to the disgust of his officers, is neglecting Rome and his political and military duties. All the same, he cannot ignore Rome, and from time to time he reacts strongly against Cleopatra when he remembers his public position and his reputation. His strained relations with Octavius Caesar are temporarily mended when he marries Caesar's sister, Octavia, but he soon abandons her and returns to Cleopatra. Caesar is enraged, and is in any case anxious to secure sole power over the empire for himself. Open war breaks out between them, and Antony is defeated at the sea battle of Actium, largely owing to Cleopatra's attempt to participate personally in the campaign. After Antony's final defeat on land, he attempts to kill himself, and eventually dies of his wounds in the arms of Cleopatra, who has taken refuge in her 'monument'. This is a mausoleum which she had built so that she and Antony could

lie together in death; it serves as a kind of miniature fortress. After Antony's death, she makes a bid for survival by pitting her wits against Caesar's. When she sees that she has failed, she takes her own life. The two death scenes, her own and Antony's, are amongst the most famous scenes in Shakespeare's work.

One of the ironies of the tragedy is that Cleopatra loves Antony just because he is a great Roman hero, and yet, in order to get full possession of him, she has to destroy this part of him. At a deeper level, Rome and Egypt are set in dramatic contrast: Rome stands for the political world, with its ruthless and calculating manoeuvring for power; Egypt stands for the heat and colour of passion, tending always to dissolution and corruption. The play belongs to Shakespeare's maturest period. As in his other 'Roman' plays, ▷ *Julius Caesar* and ▷ *Coriolanus*, Shakespeare shows an awareness of writing about the pre-Christian era, in which the hero represents the highest human type, instead of the saint.

John Dryden's (1631–1700) *All for Love* is also a tragedy about Antony and Cleopatra; a comparison of the two plays is instructive in showing the changes that came about in English verse in the intervening period.

Apollyon
In the Bible, *Revelation* 9:11, Apollyon is 'the angel of the bottomless pit'. He is chiefly famous in English literature for his appearance in ▷ Bunyan's ▷ *Pilgrim's Progress*, where he is identifiable with Satan. Apollyon means 'destroying'.

Apologia, Apology
In ordinary speech, *apology* has the sense of an expression of regret for offensive conduct, but as a literary term it commonly has the older meaning still conveyed by *apologia*: defence, *eg* ▷ Sir Philip Sidney's ▷ *Apologie for Poetrie*.

Apologie for Poetrie, An (1595)
A critical essay by ▷ Sir Philip Sidney, the *Apologie* appeared in 1595, when it was also published under the alternative title *The Defence of Poesie*. Though it has long been assumed that Sidney's treatise was designed to function as a reply to a ▷ pamphlet by ▷ Stephen Gosson entitled *The Schoole of Abuse* (1579), the *Apologie* undertakes to defend imaginative writing from more general objections than those propounded by Gosson. Instead, the *Apologie* undertakes to define the role of both the artist and the literary text in respect of the society and the competing forms of alternative discourses in which they operate and are read. To this end, the *Apologie* explores the classical concept of imaginative writing, arguing that the poet can be considered as a 'creator' or 'maker' rather than a sterile copier of forms located in the real world. The autonomy of the artist is guaranteed against the competing claims of philosophical and historical writing, and, at the same time, Sidney offers a refutation of ▷ Plato's famous condemnation of poetry in his ▷ *Republic*. The essay concludes with a survey of contemporary English writing.

The importance of Sidney's work is that it provides a clear statement of several important themes of Renaissance poetics. In particular, it deals at length with the idea of imitation and with the Platonic objection to poetry – that it is morally questionable, and that the poet is, in producing works of fiction, little better than a liar. In producing a range of arguments to deal with these two points, Sidney offers a synthesis of ▷ humanistic arguments derived from his readings in the classics and in the works of continental critics. At the same time, the *Apologie* stands as an example of the ▷ Renaissance use of the art of ▷ rhetoric, which determines the work's careful structure. For all its rootedness in late 16th-century debates on poetics, Sidney's treatise was to become, in the 17th century and later, an important statement in its own right on the nature and value of poetic discourse.

▷ *Poetics*.
Bib: Shepherd, G. (ed.), *An Apology for Poetry*.

Apprenticeship
A system of training undergone by youths entering on a trade or craft. The apprentice was indentured to a master in the craft, *ie* entered into a contract with him, to serve him in return for maintenance and instruction for seven years, usually between the ages of 16 and 23. The apprentice was a member of the master's household and the master was responsible for his behaviour before the law. Thus apprenticeship provided social control, as well as a form of education, and tended to maintain standards in manufacture and professional conduct. It also had the social advantage of mixing the classes and ensuring that the landed classes retained an interest in trade, for the smaller landed gentry commonly indentured their younger sons, who had no land to inherit, to master craftsmen, especially in London. Until the 18th century (when the gentry, grown richer, tended to despise trade) this mixture of classes, as well as their large numbers, made the London apprentices a

formidable body of public opinion not only politically, but, for instance, in the Elizabethan theatre. Apprenticeship was systematized by law under the Statute of Artificers, 1563. It had its beginnings in the ▷ Middle Ages. Usually women were not permitted to be apprenticed; in this way they were excluded from skilled paid work, although wives, daughters and sisters often helped in the work of their male relatives. Until the 17th century, apprenticeship was the only way to enter most trades and professions.

Arcades (c 1633)

A short ▷ masque by ▷ John Milton written c 1633. Like all masques, the title of the work indicates the occasion of its production: 'Part of an Entertainment presented to the countess dowager of Derby at Harefield by some noble persons of her family'. The work – an exercise in the ▷ pastoral – is so short that it hardly warrants the description of 'masque', being really little more than a dramatized form of brief tribute. Music for the work was composed by ▷ Henry Lawes, who was to write the music for Milton's more elaborate masque, ▷ *Comus*, when it was performed in 1634.

Arcadia

A mountainous district in Greece, with a pastoral economy, and in ancient times the centre of the worship of Pan. The country was idealized by ▷ Virgil in his *Eclogues*, and again in the Renaissance in ▷ pastoral works, notably in ▷ Sir Philip Sidney's ▷ *Arcadia*. By this time Arcadia was thought of purely as an ideal country of the imagination, uncorrupted by the sophistications of civilization.

Arcadia, The (1578 and 1590)

▷ Sir Philip Sidney's ▷ pastoral romance *The Arcadia* exists in two distinct versions. The 'old' *Arcadia* was begun c 1578, and circulated widely in manuscript form before Sidney undertook to revise it in 1584 – a task interrupted by his death in 1586. This revised (though incomplete) version – the 'new' *Arcadia* – was published in 1590. In 1593 Sidney's sister, Mary Herbert, Countess of Pembroke (▷ Mary Sidney), to whom the work had been dedicated, undertook to publish a composite version of the text, which combined the two versions in existence together with her own (substantial) emendations. Thus *The Arcadia*, which enjoyed enormous popularity in the 16th and for much of the 17th century, was a curious hybrid.

In its original version the work was a mixture of love and intrigue, but in its revised form, Sidney broadened the scope of his undertaking. The episodic narrative of lovers, derived from Sidney's reading in late Greek romance, was transformed into what Sidney termed 'an absolute heroical poem', the purpose of which, in accordance with the critical precepts that had been established in ▷ *An Apologie for Poetrie*, was to instil 'delightful teaching'. From the first appearance of the work, critical opinion has been divided as to its seriousness. Some of Sidney's contemporaries understood *The Arcadia* as a profound meditation on morals and politics. For other writers, in particular ▷ John Milton, the work was no more than an exercise in escapist fantasy.

Bib: Editions include: Evans, M. (ed.), *The Countess of Pembroke's Arcadia*; Duncan Jones, K. (ed.), *The Old Arcadia*.

Archaeology

This term is commonly used to describe the scientific study of the remains of prehistoric times. However, in the 20th century the French philosopher ▷ Michel Foucault has sought to redefine it in such a way that the focus of attention becomes not objects, or documents, but the very ▷ discourses through which they come to have meaning. In other words, 'archaeology' does not designate the process of returning to some sort of 'origin' or basis which has an existence outside or beyond language (*ie* the bottom layer of a 'dig'); rather it concerns itself with what Foucault describes as 'the systematic description of a discourse-object' (*The Archaeology of Knowledge*, 1972). Foucault contends that knowledge is produced within social contexts where questions of power, politics, economics and morality intersect. It is the purpose of archaeology to rediscover discursive formations in all their complexity as indices of the ways in which society is organized and it is therefore interdisciplinary in its historical concerns. This form of analysis is to be distinguished from a more traditional 'history of ideas' which privileges evolution and development.

Bib: Foucault, M., *The Archaeology of Knowledge* (1969; translated into English, 1972).

Archery

The invention of gunpowder and the spread of muskets and pistols in the 16th century gradually made the longbow obsolete, although 16th-century governments continued to enforce or at least to encourage the practice of archery. The military importance of the longbow, however, was past by 1500; ▷ Roger Ascham's *Toxophilus* (1545) is a defence of archery.

Arden, Forest of
Formerly an extensive forest in the neighbourhood of Stratford. It gave its name to the important landed family of Arden; ▷ Shakespeare's mother, Mary Arden, may have belonged to a junior branch. The Forest of Arden in Shakespeare's ▷ *As You Like It* is the forest of the Ardennes, but Shakespeare may have had the English forest in mind as well when he used the name.
▷ *Arden of Faversham, The Tragedy of.*

Arden of Faversham, The Tragedy of (1592)
An anonymous Elizabethan tragedy which is sometimes attributed to ▷ Shakespeare and occupies pride of place in the 'Shakespeare Apocrypha'. The play is almost unique in the period in dealing with recent history. Its subject-matter – the murder in Faversham in 1551 of Thomas Arden by his wife Alice and her accomplices – is related in ▷ Holinshed and vividly dramatized in this early domestic tragedy about criminal passion and greed.
Bib: Belsey, C., *The Subject of Tragedy.*

Areopagitica (1644)
Title of a ▷ pamphlet, published on 28 November 1644, written by ▷ John Milton. In June 1643 Parliament had passed an ordinance which attempted to license the press – in effect it was designed as a form of covert political ▷ censorship that allowed officers of Parliament to search for, and confiscate, unlicensed books. Milton's *Areopagitica* was offered as a powerful statement on behalf of liberty of the press. In arguing for such liberty, Milton was aligning himself with radicals such as William Walwyn and Richard Overton, and entering a forceful plea for the free dissemination of information and ideas without which, in his opinion, it was impossible for individuals to make genuine political choices. In discussing this question of choice, *Areopagitica* can be thought of as being a precursor of one of the major themes of Milton's ▷ *Paradise Lost.* The title itself implicitly compares the Parliament of England, to whom Milton was addressing his comments, to the Supreme Court of ancient Athens which met on the hill Areopagos, situated to the west of the Acropolis.

▷ Levellers, The.

Aretino, Pietro (1492–1556)
Italian writer, the author of tragedies such as *Orazio* (1546) and comedies such as *La Cortigiana* (1525) – the latter containing his infamous creation, Alvigia, a bawd whose speeches are a combination of the obscene and Latin orations. He also wrote an ▷ anti-Petrarchan ▷ sonnet sequence that transmutes the conventional idealized love into eroticism and pornography. Aretino enjoyed a considerable reputation in England in the late 16th and early 17th centuries, ▷ Thomas Nashe proclaiming himself a particular admirer.
▷ Italian influence on English literature.
Bib: Lawner, L. (trans.), *Sonetti Lussuriosi.*

Ariosto, Ludovico (1474–1533)
Italian author of comedies, ▷ satires, and, most famously, the romantic ▷ epic ▷ *Orlando Furioso* (1532). Ariosto's comedies include *I suppositi* (1509), which was translated by ▷ George Gascoigne in 1572 and used by ▷ Shakespeare in the composition of ▷ *The Taming of the Shrew.* His satires owe much to ▷ Horace, but it was *Orlando* which was to have the greatest influence on English writers, in particular ▷ Edmund Spenser.
▷ Italian influence on English literature.
Bib: Rich, T., *Harington and Ariosto: a study in Elizabethan verse translation.*

Aristophanes (c 448–c 380 BC)
The greatest of the Attic comic poets and the most important writer of Old Comedy, which is distinguished by its aggressive, bawdy satire and personalized attacks. Aristophanes' plays evolve against the background of contemporary political, philosophical and literary concerns, such as the Peloponnesian war between Athens and Sparta (*Lysistrata*), or the rivalry between the Greek tragedians (*The Frogs*). His influence on English drama is reflected in ▷ Ben Jonson's comedies, particularly in ▷ *Bartholomew Fair*, although Jonson and his contemporaries are far more dependent on the formal and thematic properties of the ▷ New Comedy idiom of ▷ Plautus and ▷ Terence.

Aristotle (384–322 BC)
A Greek philosopher, born at Stageira, and so sometimes called the Stagirite. He was first a pupil of ▷ Plato, later developing his thought on principles opposed to those of his master. He was tutor to the young ▷ Alexander (the Great). His thought covered varied fields of

knowledge, in most of which he has been influential. His best-known works are his *Ethics*, *Politics* and ▷ *Poetics*.

The difference between Aristotle and Plato has been described as follows: Plato makes us think in the first place of an ideal and supernatural world by turning our minds to ideal forms that are the truth in terms of which imperfect earthly things can be known and judged; Aristotle turns us towards the natural world where things are what they are, perfect or imperfect, so that knowledge comes through study and classification of them in the actual world. It can thus be seen that whilst Plato leads in the direction of mysticism, Aristotle leads towards science.

The *Poetics* is based on the study of imaginative literature in Greek from which Italian critics of the 16th century constructed a system of rules. ▷ Sidney knew Aristotle chiefly through the Italians, who had derived from Aristotle some rules not to be found in him – notably the unities of time and place.

Armada, The (Spanish), 1588
The fleet dispatched by Philip II of Spain to transport a Spanish army from Flanders to land in and conquer England. The attempt was deafeated by the English fleet under Lord Howard of Effingham and his sea-captains, some of whom were already famous for other exploits, such as ▷ Drake, Hawkins, Frobisher. It was written up as part of the nationalist myth of both countries involved and, in consequence, contrasting accounts of it are given in Spanish and English history. For Philip II of Spain it was a holy war against the heretical English who had abandoned Rome and recently put the Catholic ▷ Mary Queen of Scots to death; under Franco the Armada was said to illustrate the Christian fortitude of Philip II and the need for stoicism in adversity. At the time the English represented it as a national triumph, a personal triumph for the queen and an inspiration for the whole people. It did have far-reaching cultural effects both for Europe and for the non-European world that Europe was about to expand into. England was the most important country to have renounced papal authority; her defeat might have been disastrous to the ▷ Protestant side in its struggle against the ▷ Catholic powers, of which Spain was then the chief. Instead, the English victory meant a decisive check to the formidable (▷ Counter-Reformation) attempt of Catholicism to recover the northern countries of Europe. The English victory was a milestone in the shift

of power from the Mediterranean region to the Atlantic powers of England, France and Holland, which henceforth increasingly led the European expansion over the globe.
Bib: Martin, C. and Parker, G., *The Spanish Armada*.

Arthur, King
King Arthur became an important feature of the English literary and historical landscape, and Arthurian narrative was constantly open in the course of its development for appropriation as a means of expressing and exploring different kinds of political and cultural ideals. ▷ Spenser's epic, ▷ *The Faerie Queene*, has the figure of Prince Arthur as its central protagonist, and later writers such as ▷ Ben Jonson and ▷ Milton appropriated Arthurian material for their own purposes.
Bib: Merryman, J. D., *The Flower of Kings*.

Ascham, Roger (1515–68)
Humanist, educationalist, tutor to ▷ Elizabeth I and secretary to ▷ Mary I. In 1538 he was made Greek reader at St John's College, Cambridge, and later, in 1546, public orator of the university. His two major works are *Toxophilus* (1545) and *The Schoolmaster* (1570). The latter is an educational manual, addressed to the prospective tutors of the children of the social elite, which sets out the ▷ humanist ideal of creating the harmonious individual. His *Toxophilus* is a dialogue in praise of the sport of ▷ archery.
Bib: Ryan, L. V., *Roger Ascham*.

Askew, Anne (1520–46)
Protestant martyr and writer of an ▷ autobiographical account of her spiritual beliefs. She was married in her early twenties to a Catholic squire, but was expelled from his household after becoming a Protestant. She resumed her maiden name and travelled to London where she came under the protection of ▷ Queen Katherine Parr. Askew was then arrested for heresy – she believed that the Mass was a religious metaphor – and tortured. It is likely that the Lord Chancellor and his fellow nobles wished to incriminate Katherine Parr to the ageing ▷ King Henry VIII, thereby lessening her power and increasing their own. She refused to confess, however, or to incriminate any others, and was eventually burned at the stake. Her accounts were published as the *First and Lattre examinacyon of Anne Askewe, latelye martyred in Smythfelde* (1546–7). Her bravery later gained recognition in ▷ John Foxe's *Acts and Monuments* (1563) and excerpts from her work may be

found in *The Paradise of Women, Writings by Englishwomen of the Renaissance*, ed. Betty Travitsky.

Astrophil and Stella (1581–3)

A sequence of 108 ▷ sonnets and 11 songs written by ▷ Sir Philip Sidney and composed c 1581–3. The collection was first published (in a pirated edition) in 1591. While early texts give the title name as 'Astrophel', the modernized 'Astrophil' is almost certainly right. The sonnets as a whole take the form of a series of poetic addresses from Astrophil (star-lover) to Stella (star), though it is not difficult to pierce this fiction and associate Astrophil with Sidney himself and Stella with Penelope Devereux, daughter of the first ▷ Earl of Essex and sister to the second. The sequence should not, however, be taken as a simple disguised ▷ autobiographical record. Instead, the sonnets are an investigation of an obsession, a complex depiction of a psychological impasse. Adopting many of the conventions of ▷ Petrarch's poetry, they catalogue not only the cumulative progress of a love affair, but raise important theoretical questions concerning the act of writing and recording a state of mind, whilst also questioning the conventions by which writer and reader are tied to one another. Though sonnet sequences were published before Sidney's collection appeared, *Astrophil and Stella* set the standard by which later sequences were to be judged.

▷ Daniel, Samuel.

As You Like It

A comedy by ▷ Shakespeare. Produced about 1599, and first printed in the ▷ folio of 1623. Its source is ▷ Thomas Lodge's romance, *Rosalynde*.

The story is romantic and ▷ pastoral. A Duke, the father of the heroine, Rosalind, has been turned off his throne by his ruthless brother, the father of Rosalind's devoted friend, Celia. He has taken refuge with a few loyal courtiers in the neighbouring ▷ Forest of Arden. An orphan son, Orlando, is tyrannized by his wicked elder brother, Oliver. Orlando and Rosalind fall in love. Rosalind is banished from court, and goes to the forest in male disguise, calling herself Ganymede; Celia goes with her as Rosalind/Ganymede's sister, Aliena, and they are also accompanied by the court jester, Touchstone. Orlando follows them. He does not discover Rosalind's disguise, however, when, as Ganymede, she makes him 'play-act' courtship with her, episodes which are used by Shakespeare as light satires on the conventions of romantic love. Another pair of lovers in the forest are the shepherd and shepherdess Silvius and Phebe, a couple who are drawn from the most artificial pastoral mode. Phebe (true to her convention) disdains Silvius, but falls embarrassingly in love with Rosalind (in her disguise) at first sight, and in spite of Rosalind's rudeness to her. Touchstone engages the affections of an unromantic and realistic village girl, Audrey, and thus frustrates her unromantic village lover, William. There is also Jaques, a fashionable and affected young man in the Elizabethan style, attached to the court of the exiled Duke. Rosalind, who is extremely plain-spoken except when she remembers that she is in love, exposes his affectations. In the end the couples are sorted out appropriately, and Rosalind's father regains his dukedom.

Shakespeare thus plays off real life against literary convention. The play is bright, satirical and romantic, all in one. Together with ▷ *Twelfth Night* it is his best work in the style of romantic comedy.

Atheism

Disbelief in God. In the ▷ Middle Ages and the 16th and 17th centuries, atheism was abhorrent; it was equivalent to a denial of conscience – an attitude shown in the play ▷ *The Atheist's Tragedy* (1611) by ▷ Cyril Tourneur. There were some who were suspected of having adopted this position and of effectively challenging the power of organized religion. For example, ▷ Christopher Marlowe came under suspicion in 1593. Nevertheless, atheism at this period was different from the systematic belief that man's reason suffices for his welfare.

Atheist's Tragedy, The (1611)

The only extant tragedy confidently attributed to ▷ Cyril Tourneur, formerly thought to be the author also of ▷ *The Revenger's Tragedy*. The play dramatizes the evil plotting of D'Amville, the atheist, to advance his wealth through marital intrigue, and ends in a grotesque manner with the involuntary suicide of the villain and the safeguarding of true love.

Atlantis

A legendary mid-Atlantic island, described by the Greek philosopher ▷ Plato in his dialogue *Timaeus*. It is said to have had immense power and prosperity until it was submerged by the sea. Its existence was believed in during the ▷ Middle Ages, partly owing to legends about other mysterious western lands such as Avalon in Arthurian legend. Such places were imagined as earthly paradises, and in the ▷ Renaissance the myths were used to demonstrate ideal governments and countries, in the Platonic style. Hence *The New Atlantis* (1626) by ▷ Francis Bacon.

Aubrey, John (1626–97)
Biographer and antiquary. Aubrey was a man of endlessly fascinated speculation on every aspect of the world in which he found himself. Entirely without any form of method, he nevertheless produced (though never published) an invaluable record of people, events and happenings of the period in which he lived. Frequently the record of personalities preserved by Aubrey is highly untrustworthy in terms of its factual content, and yet his *Brief Lives* is still an important document not least because of its often penetrating assessment of his subjects' lives and works. If nothing else, Aubrey has preserved a critical running commentary on many of the figures from the 17th century whose works are read in the 20th century.
    ▷ Biography.
Bib: Dick, O. L. (ed.), *Aubrey's Brief Lives*.

Authorized Version of the Bible
    ▷ Bible in England.

Autobiography
The word came into English at the very end of the 18th century and by the 19th and 20th centuries the writing of the story of one's own life had become a common literary activity. However, the practice already had an ancient history, and English autobiography may be divided into three overlapping historical segments: 1 the spiritual confession; 2 the memoir; 3 the autobiographical novel.
    1 The spiritual confession has as its basic type the Confessions of St Augustine of Hippo (345–430) who described his conversion to Christianity. Such records of the inner life existed in the English ▷ Middle Ages, but the great age for them was the 17th century, when the ▷ Puritans, depending

on the Word of God in the Bible and the inner light of their own consciences, made a practice of intensive self-examination. By far the best known of these records is ▷ Bunyan's ▷ *Grace Abounding to the Chief of Sinners* (1666). However, the greater freedom accorded to women under Puritan principles allowed several women to write spiritual autobiographies, including ▷ Margaret Fell and ▷ Alice Sutcliffe. It is characteristic of such works that they contain detailed accounts of the emotional life, but little factual description of events.
    2 The memoir, on the other hand, of French derivation, originates largely in the 17th century and owes much to the practice of extensive ▷ letter-writing which then developed, *eg* the letters of Madame de Sévigné (1626–96). An unusual early example of this class is the autobiography of the musician Thomas Whythorne (1528–96), published in 1964 and entitled *A Book of Songs and Sonnets*. One of the earliest and most interesting of such secular autobiographies written by a woman was that of ▷ Lady Anne Clifford.
    3 Although the autobiographical novel developed a formal identity in the 18th and 19th centuries, a prototype may be found in the mock-autobiographies of ▷ Elizabethan novels, such as ▷ Thomas Nashe's ▷ *Unfortunate Traveller* (1594).

Autolycus
A character in ▷ *The Winter's Tale* who is one of ▷ Shakespeare's most resourceful rogues. He 'haunts wakes, fairs, and bear-baitings' in search of victims to fleece.

Avon
The river of ▷ Shakespeare's birthplace, Stratford-on-Avon, from which he is called the 'Swan of Avon' by ▷ Ben Jonson in his poem *To the Memory of Shakespeare*. The word derives from Celtic *afon* = 'river'; three other rivers with the same name exist in England.

Ayre
    ▷ Madrigal.

Babes in the Wood
▷ *Children in the Wood*.

Bacon, Ann (1528–1610)
Translator. Famed for her translation from
Latin into English of Bishop Jewel's *Apology*
(1564), and for the letters she wrote to her
sons, one of whom was ▷ Francis Bacon,
the Lord Chancellor. Ann Bacon was the
daughter of Sir Anthony Cooke and was,
with her sister Mildred (wife of William Cecil
(▷ Burghley)), reputed to be amongst the most
highly educated women of their age. She was
a staunch ▷ Puritan and is said to have been
one of ▷ Edward VI's tutors. Her relationship
with her own sons was very intense and she
maintained a vigorous correspondence with
both. Indeed, Francis Bacon left instructions
in his will that he should be buried with his
mother.
Bib: Travitsky, B. (ed.), *The Paradise of
Women*.

**Bacon, Francis, 1st Baron Verulam and
    Viscount St Albans (1561–1626)**
Politician, philosopher and essayist, Francis
Bacon rose to the rank of lord chancellor,
before being dismissed from that office
in the same year in which he attained it –
1621. Bacon's offence was, technically, his
conviction for accepting bribes whilst a judge
in chancery suits. The cause of his conviction,
however, was the ascendency of political
enemies he had made in the course of his
ambitious career.

It is, however, as an essayist, and, more
importantly, as one of the earliest theoreticians
of scientific methodology for which Bacon was
to become famous. A series of works – which
included ▷ *The Advancement of Learning* (1605
expanded into *De Augmentis Scientiarum* in
1623), *De sapientia veterum* (1609, translated
as *The Wisdom of the Ancients* in 1619) and
the incomplete ▷ *Novum Organum* (1620) –
established his claims to philosophical and
methodological pre-eminence amongst his
contemporaries. The *De Augmentis* and the
Novum Organum formed the first two parts
of his enormous project, gathered under the
title ▷ *Instauratio Magna*, which remained
unfinished but which proposed nothing less
than a reordering of all fields of human
enquiry. In addition Bacon wrote a history of
the reign of ▷ Henry VIII (published in 1622),
a collection of anecdotal stories (1625) and a
▷ utopian work, based on the new scientific
endeavours of the age – ▷ *The New Atlantis*
(1626). His major philosophical works were
written in addition to his contribution to the
law and his *Essays*, which were first published
in 1597 and issued in a final form (much
expanded) in 1625.

Until recently, Bacon's reputation tended
to rest on his *Essays*, which represent a series
of terse observations in the style of ▷ Seneca
rather than the more fluid meditations to
be found in the writings of ▷ Montaigne,
who is credited with originating the essay
as a distinctly modern form. More and
more attention is, however, being paid to
his theoretical work in the general area of
scientific methodology and taxonomy. It was
Bacon who was to be celebrated in the later
17th century as the true progenitor of the
▷ 'New Science', not least because of his
intense interest in the language of science,
and in the forms of discourse appropriate
to different rhetorical and methodological
projects. As a scientist in the modern sense,
his contribution to knowledge was negligible.
But as the author of a series of 'manifestos'
which set out to establish the basis for
inductive or experimental philosophy, his
influence on later generations of English
philosophers was to be incalculable. The
'Baconian' method – an adherence, that is, to
the importance of observation and definition
of the particular, rather than a delight in
deduction from the general – was to be
the legacy of his work and the basis for his
reputation in later periods.
  ▷Bacon, Ann.
Bib: Spedding, J., Ellis, R. L., and Heath
D. D. (eds.), *Works of Francis Bacon* (7 vols.);
Rossi, P., *Francis Bacon: From Magic to Science*
(trans.) S. Rabinovitch; Vickers, B. (ed.),
Essential Articles for the Study of Francis Bacon.

Bakhtin, Mikhail (1895–1975)
Bakhtin's first major work was *Problems in
Dostoevsky's Poetics* (1929), but his most famous
work, *Rabelais and His World*, did not appear
until 1965. Two books, *Freudianism: a Marxist
Critique* (1927) and *Marxism and the Philosophy
of Language* (1930), were published under
the name of V. N. Volosinov, and a third,
The Formal Method in Literary Scholarship
(1928), appeared under the name of his
colleague P. N. Medvedev. Bakhtin's concern
throughout is to show how ▷ ideology
functions in the process of the production of
the linguistic sign and to develop and identify
the concept of 'dialogism' as it operates in
literary texts. In Bakhtin's words, 'In dialogue
a person not only shows himself outwardly,
but he becomes for the first time that which
he is, not only for others but himself as well.
To be means to communicate dialogically.'

His work has in recent years enjoyed a revival, particularly among critics. Especially important is the way in which he theorizes and politicizes the concepts of festivity and carnival. The notion of carnival or misrule is discussed in *Rabelais* and deals with changing traditions from the ▷ Middle Ages to the ▷ Renaissance. As such, Bakhtin's work is gaining precedence in Renaissance literary criticism, especially concerning playwrights such as ▷ Ben Jonson. Also one of his concerns is to identify the dialectical relationship between those various 'texts' of which any one literary work is comprised. This notion of ▷ 'intertextuality' is currently used within areas such as ▷ feminism and ▷ deconstruction. Much of Bakhtin's work was suppressed during his lifetime and not published until after his death.

　▷ Rabelais.

Bale, John (1495–1563)

Bishop of Ossory, dramatist and literary historian. A staunch ▷ Protestant, Bale came under the ▷ patronage of ▷ Thomas Cromwell and wrote several anti-Catholic (▷ Catholicism) plays before the downfall of his patron. Bale himself was imprisoned for treason by ▷ Mary I and released on a fine of £300; he finally returned to Britain when ▷ Elizabeth I came to the throne. He is best known for his play *King John* (c 1540), which is acknowledged to be the first drama to bridge the gap between the ▷ morality plays of the medieval period and the history plays of the Renaissance, such as those of ▷ Shakespeare and ▷ Marlowe. The play combines moral analysis with historical representation. Bale also compiled the notes of John Leland, which led to an immensely useful index of 1,400 English writers.

Bib: Blatt, T. B., *The Plays of John Bale*.

Ballad

Traditionally the ballad has been considered a folkloric verse narrative which has strong associations with communal dancing, and support for that link has been found in the derivation of the word 'ballad' itself (from the late Latin verb *ballare* – to dance). More recently scholars have viewed the association between ballads and dance forms rather more sceptically. Generally, the term is used of a narrative poem which uses an elliptical and highly stylized mode of narration, in which the technique of repetition with variation may play an important part. Often ballads contain repeated choral refrains but this is not a universal feature.

The so-called ▷ broadside ballads, sold in Elizabethan times, were narrative poems on a wide range of subjects printed on a single side of a broadsheet.

Bib: Bold, A., *The Ballad*.

Ballet

　▷ Madrigal.

Bankside

The south bank of the Thames in London. It was famous in ▷ Shakespeare's day for its theatres. The City of London refused to allow public theatres within its bounds; hence famous theatres such as the ▷ Globe and the ▷ Rose had to be built in Southwark on Bankside.

　▷ Theatres.

Baptists

An important sect of Nonconformist Protestants; originally one of the three principal branches of English ▷ Puritanism, the other two being the Independents (▷ Congregationalists), and the ▷ Presbyterians (Calvinists). Their especial doctrine is to maintain that the rite of baptism must be administered to adults, and not to infants. They began as an offshoot of the Independents in the first decade of the 17th century, and made rapid progress between 1640 and 1660 – the period of the ▷ Civil War and the ▷ Interregnum, when the Puritans usurped the position of the ▷ Church of England. One of the foremost exponents of the Baptist Church in the second half of the 17th century was ▷ John Bunyan (1628–88).

　▷ Protestantism; Parr, Susanna.

Barabas

In the ▷ Bible, the robber whom the Roman governor Pilate released at the demand of the Jews, instead of Jesus (*Matthew* 27). Barabas is the Jew of Malta in Marlowe's play of that name.

　▷ Race.

Bard

A member of the privileged caste of poets among the ancient Celtic peoples, driven by the Romans and then the Anglo-Saxons into Wales and ▷ Ireland and, legend has it, exterminated in Wales by Edward I. The term became known to later English writers from references in Latin literature. Poets such as ▷ Shakespeare and ▷ John Milton have since been termed 'bard' as a form of high praise.

Barnes, Barnabe (c 1559–1609)
Poet and dramatist. Barnes's life seems
to have been as adventurous and dark as
his dramatic writing; he fought alongside
▷ Essex in 1591 and was called before the
Star Chamber when he tried to poison the
recorder of Berwick (1598). Barnes came
through both events unscathed and is known
today chiefly for his lyrical ▷ sonnet sequence
Parthenophil and Parthenope (1593). Another
collection of sonnets, *A Divine Century of
Spiritual Sonnets*, appeared in 1595, and
a prose work, *Four Bookes of Offices*, in
1606. Barnes's only surviving drama, *The
Devil's Charter* (1607), is an anti-Catholic
(▷ Catholicism) account of poisoning, magic,
subterfuge and evil, which is thought to
have been performed before ▷ James I. His
patron was Henry Wriothesley, ▷ Earl of
Southampton, and as such Barnes is one of
the contenders for the role of rival poet in
▷ Shakespeare's sonnets.
Bib: Sisson, C. J., *Thomas Lodge and Other
Elizabethans.*

Barnfield, Richard (1574–1627)
Poet. Barnfield wrote almost all his poetry
before 1600, when he gave up writing to
become a prosperous Shropshire landowner.
Barnfield published three volumes of poetry,
in 1594, 1595 and 1598. Of these volumes,
*The Affectionate Shepherd, Containing the Love
of Daphnis for the Love of Gannymede*, which
appeared first, is an exercise in ▷ pastoral.
The second volume, entitled *Cynthia, with
Certain Sonnets and the Legend of Cassandra*,
claims to imitate ▷ Edmund Spenser's ▷ *The
Faerie Queene*. The third and final collection
contains ▷ satire, pastoral elegy and a 'debate'
entitled 'The Combat Between Conscience
and Covetessnesse'. In this final collection can
be found two poems by Barnfield ('If music
and sweet poetrie agree' and 'As it fell upon a
day') which were published in the anthology
▷ *Passionate Pilgrim* (1599) and were not
recognized as being the work of Barnfield.
Bib: Klawitter, G. (ed.), *The Complete Poems of
Richard Barnfield.*

Baroque
A term mainly applied to the visual arts,
particularly architecture, and (with a
somewhat different meaning) to music, but
now increasingly used in literary contexts
also. It derives from the Italian word *barocco*
meaning rough and unpolished, and was
originally used to denote extravagance
or excessiveness in the visual arts. The
epithet 'baroque' has recently come to be
used in literary contexts by analogy with
its use in relation to the other arts. Thus
the extravagant Italianate conceits of the
Catholic poet ▷ Richard Crashaw who ended
his life in Rome, can be called 'baroque'.
In music the term denotes the new, more
public, expressive and dramatic style,
characterized by free recitative, and most
typically seen in the new genre of opera,
originating in the Italy of Monteverdi in the
late 16th century. It is closely associated with
the introduction of new, more expressive
and louder instruments, ideal for public
performance, such as the transverse flute, the
violin and the harpsichord, which at this time
began to supplant the softer recorder, viol
and virginals, suitable for the intimate, often
amateur, music-making of the ▷ Renaissance.
The term is now applied to all music between
this time and the onset of classicism and
romanticism with Haydn and Mozart in the
later 18th century.

Bartholomew Fair (1614)
A vigorous prose comedy of London life by
▷ Ben Jonson. The scene is that of a famous
fair held annually in Smithfield, London, from
the 12th century till 1855. The cast includes
traders, showmen, dupes, criminals, a gambler
and a hypocritical ▷ Puritan – the best-known
character, called Zeal-of-the-land Busy. It has
very lively surface entertainment, and some
of Jonson's characteristic force of satire; the
vicious pursue their vices with eloquence
but such extravagance they they overreach
themselves, and not only produce their own
doom but bring ridicule on their own heads by
self-caricature.

▷ Humours, Comedy of; Bakhtin, Mikhail.

Basset, Mary (c 1522–72)
A translator of religious material, Basset
came from the learned More family. Her
mother was ▷ Margaret Roper, herself an
accomplished translator, and her grandfather
was ▷ Sir Thomas More, whose *History of
the Passion* she translated into English (1566).
She also translated the first five books of
Eusebius's *Ecclesiastical History* from Greek
into English and presented it to Mary Tudor
(▷ Mary I), in return for which she obtained a
position at court.
Bib: Hallett, P. E. (ed.), *The Works of Sir
Thomas More.*

Bastard
A bastard is born out of wedlock, *ie* has no
legal parents; in law, he is *filius nullius* =

the son of no one. When land, and with it, status, were derived from the legal father, the bastard could inherit nothing by his own right. In early medieval times an exception was sometimes made for bastards in ruling families; thus William I of England (1266–87) took the appellation William the Bastard. But in general a bastard was by law something of a social outcast. Hence Edmund in ▷ Shakespeare's ▷ *King Lear* (I.ii) 'Why brand they us/With base? with baseness? bastardy? base, base?' However, a bastard could in exceptional circumstances acquire a position in society, acquiring land, marrying legally and bequeathing his property – all depended on his natural worth, abilities and energies. This is more apparent in the bastard Philip of Shakespeare's ▷ *King John* than in Edmund.

Baxter, Richard (1615–91)

Theologian, religious writer and autobiographer. Baxter was one of the dominating figures in the period of the English ▷ Civil War. A chaplain to ▷ Oliver Cromwell's army, Baxter served after the Restoration as chaplain to ▷ Charles II, but he soon fell out with the king on religio-political grounds. Though an initial supporter of the Parliamentarian cause in the Civil War, Baxter's experiences in the New Model Army, in particular his exposure to the thinking of the ▷ Levellers, Seekers, ▷ Quakers and Behmenists, led him to adopt rather more conservative postures. In the 1650s his position changed once more and he emerged as a strong supporter of the Protectorate, dedicating his *Key for Catholics* (1659) to Richard Cromwell. Baxter's stance on religious issues has been defined as one of the earliest examples of ecumenicism or, as he put it in his *A Third Defence of the Cause of Peace* (1681): 'You could not have truelier called me than an *Episcopal – Presbyterian – Independent.*' A prolific writer, Baxter composed over 100 works on religious topics, including *The Saints Everlasting Rest* (1650) and *Call to the Unconverted* (1657). His major work, however, has come to be recognized as his spiritual autobiography, *Reliquiae Baxterianae* (1696). This 800-page ▷ folio volume is one of the most important of 17th-century ▷ autobiographies.
Bib: Schlatter, R. B., *Richard Baxter and Puritan Politics*; Keeble, N. H. (ed.), *The Autobiography of Richard Baxter*; Webber, Joan, *The Eloquent 'I': Style and Self in Seventeenth-century Prose*.

Bear-baiting, Bull-baiting

In the ▷ Middle Ages and the 16th century a popular pastime, in which a bull or a bear was tied to a stake and then attacked by bulldogs or mastiffs. Bull-baiting continued longer and these 'sports' were only made illegal in 1835. In Elizabethan times, bear-baiting was an alternative amusement to drama; 'bear gardens' (notably the Paris Garden) were situated in the same region as the theatres – Southwark, on the south bank of the Thames. The theatres themselves were used for the purpose. It is possible that the bear which appears in ▷ Shakespeare's ▷ *The Winter's Tale* could have come from one of the Southwark bear gardens. Earlier in the century, ▷ Erasmus speaks of herds of bears being kept in the country to supply the bear gardens. The ▷ Puritans disliked the meetings as scenes likely to lead to disorder, and condemned bear-baiting alongside theatrical performances.

Beatrice and Benedick

Two characters in ▷ Shakespeare's comedy ▷ *Much Ado About Nothing*. They hate each other and engage in witty exchanges of repartee. The hatred is only apparent, however, and they are brought together in love by a trick. Their witty interchanges may owe more to the convention of courtly discourse (▷ *Euphues*) than to a naturalistic portrayal of character.

Beatrice-Joanna

The deeply divided female protagonist of ▷ Middleton's and ▷ Rowley's tragedy ▷ *The Changeling*, whose refusal to marry her father's choice of a husband leads to murder and ultimately delivers her into the arms of the repellent ▷ De Flores. The combination of sexual desire and madness in Beatrice's character allows for interesting interpretations from ▷ feminist and ▷ psychoanalytical criticisms.

Beaumont, Francis (1584–1616)

Dramatic poet and collaborator with ▷ John Fletcher. They wrote comedies (*eg The Coxcomb*); tragedies (*eg The Maid's Tragedy*); romantic dramas (*eg A King and No King* and ▷ *Philaster*). Fletcher also collaborated with other writers – ▷ Shakespeare, ▷ Massinger – and wrote plays on his own, but the general superiority of those he wrote with Beaumont has suggested to modern critics that Beaumont may have been the more talented partner. Their plays were immensely popular in the 17th century, and having undergone

a decline are now being reintroduced into the theatrical canon. The tragicomedies (*Philaster* and *The Maid's Tragedy*) have been critically reassessed, revealing that the move towards self-destruction and anticlimax at the end of the plays represents a reluctance to contemplate a world in which all humanity has been lost.
Bib: Macaulay, G. G., *Beaumont: a critical study*; Appleton, W. W., *Beaumont and Fletcher: a critical study*; Finkelpearl, P. J., *Court and Country Politics in the Plays of Beaumont and Fletcher*.

Bedford, Countess of
▷ Russell, Lucy.

Beggars, Sturdy
An expression used in the 16th century for the able-bodied poor who were unemployed and lived by begging. Unemployment was a serious social problem throughout the 16th century for a succession of causes. ▷ Henry VII (1485–1509) disbanded the private armies of the nobles; ▷ Henry VIII (1509–47) dissolved the monasteries, and threw into unemployment the numerous servants and craftsmen who had served them; the nobles enclosed extensive tracts of arable land for sheep-farming, which required less labour, or simply to surround their great houses with ornamental parks; prices rose, and periods of inflation sometimes made it impossible for poor men to support themselves without begging. The beggars were regarded as a serious social threat, since they often moved about in bands and took to robbery with violence. In the reign of ▷ Elizabeth I (1558–1603), the government made serious and fairly successful attempts to deal with the problem: they instituted a succession of ▷ Poor Laws, culminating in the Great Poor Law of 1601, in accordance with which the aged, sick and crippled were given financial relief by the parishes, but the 'sturdy beggars' were forcibly set to work. Not all the 'sturdy beggars' were from the poorer classes; in an age of enthusiastic financial speculation, richer men were sometimes suddenly ruined, and forced to take to the roads. Indeed, ▷ Orlando and Adam in ▷ Shakespeare's ▷ *As You Like It* distinctly display the plight of the sturdy beggars.
Bib: Beier, A. L., *Masterless Men: The Vagrancy Problem in England* 1560–1640.

Belphoebe
A character in Edmund Spenser's ▷ *The Faerie Queene* (1596). Belphoebe, described at

some length (Book II, canto iii, stanzas 21–4), is one of the symbolic representations of ▷ Elizabeth I in the poem. Etymologically, her name signifies both beauty and, through the association with Phoebe, the moon, chastity and hunting.

Benedick
▷ Beatrice and Benedick.

Beulah, The Land of
In the ▷ Bible, *Isaiah* 62:4. A Hebrew word = 'married'. In ▷ Bunyan's ▷ *Pilgrim's Progress* it lies in sight of the Heavenly City and beyond the reach of Giant Despair. It signifies the state in which the soul is 'married' to God.

Bevis of Hampton
A popular metrical romance translated into English sometime in the late 13th/early 14th centuries. The story-type is one that is found in versions across Europe. Bevis's father has been murdered by his mother's lover, Sir Murdour. Bevis is sold as a slave and has many adventures with his horse Arundel and his sword Morglay before the happy ending with Bevis married to Josiane. The story was circulated in the ▷ chapbooks of the 16th century and is retold in ▷ Michael Drayton's *Poly-Olbion*.

Bible in England
In the ▷ Middle Ages the only version of the Bible authorized by the Church was the ▷ Vulgate, *ie* the translation into Latin by St Jerome, completed in 405. Partial translations were made into Old English before the 11th century. From the 14th century translations were made by reformers, who believed that men without Latin should have the means of seeking guidance from divine scripture without dependence on Church authority. The main translators were these: Wycliffe (14th century); ▷ Tyndale, and Coverdale (16th century). The last-named was the producer of the *Great Bible* (also called ▷ Cranmer's Bible after the Archbishop of the time), but ▷ Henry VIII, concerned for his intermediate position between Catholics and Protestants, ended by restricting its use. Under the Catholic ▷ Mary I (1553–8) English reformers produced the *Geneva Bible* abroad, with annotations suited to ▷ Puritan ▷ Calvinist opinion; and in 1568 the so-called *Bishops' Bible* was issued by the restored Anglicans to counteract Puritan influence. Finally, in 1611 the Authorized Version was produced with the approval of ▷ James I

(1603–25). For three centuries it was to be the only one in general use, and it is still the prevailing version. Indeed, in spite of various other translations, Catholic and Protestant, in the 19th and 20th centuries, the Authorized Version is by far the most important for its literary and social influence. It was based on previous translations, especially that of Tyndale, so that the cast of its prose is characteristically more 16th than early 17th century in style. Nonetheless much of it is of supreme eloquence, *eg* the book of *Job*, and the last 15 chapters of *Isaiah*. It was for many people in the 17th and 18th centuries the only book that was constantly read, and it was familiar to all from its use in church and education. The musical cadence of Authorized Version prose can be often heard in the prose of English writers, whether or not professing Christians, for example it is conspicuous in ▷ John Bunyan's ▷ *Pilgrim's Progress*.
Bib: Daiches, D., *The King James' Version of the Bible*.

Biography

The chief source of inspiration for English biographers was the Greek ▷ Plutarch (1st century AD), whose *Parallel Lives* of Greek and Roman heroes was translated into English by ▷ Sir Thomas North in 1579 and was widely read. Biography had been practised before in England; there had been the lives of the saints in the ▷ Middle Ages, and in the 16th century Cavendish's life of the statesman ▷ Cardinal Wolsey had appeared. The regular practice of biography, however, starts with the 17th century, not merely owing to the influence of North's translation of Plutarch, but as part of the outward-turning, increasingly scientific interest in many kinds of people (not merely saints and rulers) that in the 18th century was to give rise to the novel. Biography is a branch of history, and the art of historical writing advanced with biography: Edward Hyde, ▷ Earl of Clarendon included fine biographical portraits in his history of the Great Rebellion, written between 1646 and 1670. ▷ Izaak Walton's lives of ▷ John Donne (1640), ▷ Sir Henry Wotton (1651), ▷ Richard Hooker (1665), ▷ George Herbert (1670) and Bishop Sanderson (1678) are closer to our modern idea of biography. Women writers of the period also excelled at biography: the royalist ▷ Margaret Cavendish wrote a biography of her husband William Cavendish, Duke of Newcastle; ▷ Lady Ann Fanshawe wrote an account of the life she and her husband led during the ▷ Interregnum as exiles; and ▷ Lucy Hutchinson wrote a

poignant record of the life and death of her Parliamentarian husband, Colonel John Hutchinson.
Bib: Gittings, R., *The Nature of Biography*.

Black Friars (Blackfriars)

Dominican ▷ friars, called 'Black' in England owing to the colour of their robes. Their convent in London was dissolved by ▷ Henry VIII (1509–47), but the district has continued to bear their name. Part of the old convent was adapted into two distinct theatres, although they were in the same building. The first Blackfriars theatre was in the hands of boy actors – the Children of the Chapel – during the 1570s and 1580s. The second Blackfriars theatre was built by ▷ James Burbage in 1596 and initially used by the Children of the Chapel, then by the King's Men, which the Lord ▷ Chamberlain's Company had become. It was a 'private' theatre with a more affluent and probably more educated kind of audience than frequented the public theatres such as the ▷ Globe. The change of audience encouraged a change in the mode of drama. Never again would the theatre serve the whole society: its present status in this country as an entertainment for the relatively privileged is derived from the move from 'public' to 'private' theatres.
▷ Theatres.

Blank verse

Verse which is unrhymed, and composed of lines which normally contain ten syllables and have the stress on every second syllable, as in the classical iambic pentameter.
The first user of the iambic pentameter in English was ▷ Chaucer and he used it in rhyming couplets, *eg The Prologue* to ▷ *The Canterbury Tales*. The first user of blank verse was Henry Howard, ▷ Earl of Surrey (?1517–47), who adopted it for a translation of the second and third books of ▷ Virgil's ▷ *Aeneid* in order to get closer to the effect of the metrically regular but unrhymed Latin hexameter. The effect in Surrey is that Chaucer's measure is being used but without rhyme:

> They whisted all, with fixèd face attent,
> When prince Aeneas from the royal seat
> Thus gan to speak.

The dramatist ▷ Christopher Marlowe (1564–93) first gave blank verse its distinctive quality. In his plays, he combined the rhythm of the verse with the normal rhythm and syntax of the sentence, so that the effect begins to be like natural speech expressed with unusual music:

Hell hath no limits, nor is circumscrib'd
In one self place: for where we are is hell,
And where hell is, there must we ever be . . .
                                    (*Dr Faustus*)

Blank verse as used by Marlowe was carried on by ▷ Shakespeare, who employed it with steadily increasing flexibility and power. His contemporaries did the same, but in his immediate successors' work great freedoms are taken with the metre, and the rhythm of the sentence begins to dominate over that of the line, so that the effect is of rhythmic paragraphs of speech.

The next phase is the epic use of blank verse by ▷ Milton in ▷ *Paradise Lost* (1667), who gave the weight of Latin syntax to the long sentences and accordingly moved away from speech rhythms.

Blood, Tragedy of
▷ Revenge tragedy.

Boadicea (d AD 61)
A Celtic queen (also Bonduca, Boudicea) who is a national heroine because of her rising against the Roman occupying forces. Her people were the Iceni of what is now the county of Norfolk; she was defeated by Suetonius Paulinus and killed herself. She has been celebrated in the tragedy *Bonduca* by ▷ John Fletcher.

Boccaccio, Giovanni (?1313–75)
Italian ▷ humanist scholar and writer, born near Florence. His literary studies began in Naples, where he wrote his first works, but he later returned to Florence and was employed on diplomatic missions for the Florentine state. He publicly lectured on ▷ Dante's ▷ *Divine Comedy*, was a friend of ▷ Petrarch and the centre of a circle of humanist learning and literary activity. His works included a wide range of courtly narratives, a vernacular imitation of classical ▷ epic and a number of important encyclopaedic works in Latin which occupied the last years of his life.

Boccaccio's collection of brief tragic-narratives in Latin (*De Casibus Virorum Illustrium*) was reworked in English by ▷ Lydgate in the 15th century and provided much material for the Elizabethan compilation of short tragic-narratives, the ▷ *Mirror for Magistrates*. Tales from the *Decameron* were included in William Painter's anthology ▷ *The Palace of Pleasure*, and many Elizabethan dramatists, including ▷ Shakespeare, quarried plots from either Painter's collection or from the *Decameron* itself.
Bib: Chubb, T. C., *The Life of Giovanni Boccaccio*; Wright, H. G., *Boccaccio in England from Chaucer to Tennyson*.

Boiardo, Matteomaria (?1441–94)
Italian poet who reworked the legends of ▷ King Arthur and ▷ Charlemagne. His principal work was the unfinished *Orlando Innamorato*. ▷ Ludivico Ariosto produced a sequel ▷ *Orlando Furioso*.

Bosola
A hired assassin in ▷ John Webster's play ▷ *The Duchess of Malfi* who belatedly discovers the stirrings of conscience in himself and assumes the role of revenger.

Bottom, Nick
A comic character in ▷ Shakespeare's ▷ *A Midsummer Night's Dream*. He is a weaver, and the most prominent of the 'Athenian artisans'.

Bradley, A. C. (Andrew Cecil) (1851–1935)
Professor of Poetry at Oxford whose books on ▷ Shakespeare, *Shakespearean Tragedy* (1904) and *Oxford Lectures on Poetry* (1909), were inspired by 19th-century idealism and had a considerable influence on the study of character in Shakespeare.

Bradstreet, Anne (1612–72)
Poet. Bradstreet's poetic writings are noteworthy not only because she was a woman writing at a time when female authorship was actively discouraged, but also because she was one of the first poets, of either sex, to write in America. Hence, her work is included in collections of 17th-century women poets (*Kissing the Rod*, ed. G. Greer (1988)), as well as amongst 'The Poets of America' (*The World Split Open*, ed. L. Bernikow (1984)). She was born into the strongly ▷ Puritan Dudley family and for the first 18 years of her life lived in England. She received a thorough education, reading the works of ▷ Edmund Spenser and ▷ Sir Philip Sidney, and at 16 married Simon Bradstreet. The persecution of radical Puritanism determined Bradstreet's father, Thomas Dudley, to emigrate to the New World, where he, with many others of his sect, hoped to practise their religion freely. In March 1630 the family set sail on the *Arbella* and in June landed in

Massachusetts. Like many of the settlers, the
Dudleys and Bradstreets were dogged with
ill health and economic hardship, and Anne
herself probably suffered from tuberculosis.
Yet in spite of bouts of sickness, having eight
children, and several moves to increasingly
remote settlements, she constantly wrote
poetry. At first her work was ▷ epic in nature,
focusing upon political events such as the
▷ Civil War, or on spiritual concerns such
as the Second Coming of Christ. The latter
theme occurs in *The Four Monarchies*, which
is loosely based upon ▷ Sir Walter Ralegh's
The History of the World. The Four Ages of Man
is another 'quaternion' and follows Joshua
Sylvester's translations of ▷ Du Bartas. Both
are included in *The Tenth Muse Lately Sprung
up in America* (1650), which was published in
London, without Bradstreet's knowledge, by
her brother-in-law, John Woodbridge. After
the death of her father and the birth of her
last child (c 1652) Bradstreet's poems take
on a more personal and contemplative tone,
and these are the poems by which she is best
known today. They are beautiful ▷ lyrics
which address the problems of piety, marital
love and parental duty; they also include
accounts of actual events in her life. These
later poems were published posthumously,
together with a second edition of *The Tenth
Muse*, as *Several Poems* (1678).

Brandon, Katherine (1520–80)
Letter-writer. Katherine Brandon, Duchess
of Suffolk is notable both for her own
letters (which may be seen in the Public
Record Office, London) and for her role
as a ▷ patron. The letters are personal and
colloquial, covering concerns of faith as well
as the duties of parents to their children;
she believed, for example, that young people
should be allowed to marry for love. As part
of ▷ Katherine Parr's ▷ Puritan circle she
came under threat during the trial of ▷ Anne
Askew, and she lived on the continent during
▷ Queen Mary's reign.
Bib: Prior, M. (ed.), *Women in English Society,
1500–1800*.

Brownists
A ▷ Puritan religious sect founded by
Robert Browne (?1550–?1633); from about
1640 they were known as Independents,
and since the 18th century they have been
▷ Congregationalists. Their best-known
doctrine is that on the evidence of the New
Testament each religious congregation should
be self-governing, so that there should be no
overriding Church, *eg* no government through

bishops under a central figure such as the
Pope or, in the Anglican system, the Crown.
    ▷ Italian influence on English literature.

Bryan, Sir Francis (d1550)
Poet and diplomat. Bryan was one of the
few courtiers to maintain close and cordial
relationships with ▷ Henry VIII and was chief
mourner at the king's funeral. Perhaps this
unusual fact may be accounted for by his
readiness to acquiesce to any of his monarch's
desires, however pernicious. For example,
even though he was related to the Boleyn
family, Bryan faked a quarrel with George
Boleyn and aided the king to condemn Queen
Anne Boleyn to death. For his services Bryan
accepted a pension from Henry that had
belonged to one of the men he had helped
execute. These actions, together with his
scarred appearance (he had lost one eye while
jousting) led to his being called 'the vicar
of hell', a name ▷ John Milton refers to in
▷ *Areopagitica*. Bryan was also the Master of
Entertainments at court, a friend of ▷ Sir
Thomas Wyatt and a poet; his work was
included in ▷ *Tottel's Miscellany*.

Breton, Nicholas (?1545–?1626)
Poet, miscellanist, pamphleteer. Little is
known of the life of Nicholas Breton – a
curious irony in that he was one of the most
prolific writers of the ▷ Renaissance period.
Still, we do know that he was the son of a
wealthy London merchant, but that on his
father's death his mother married ▷ George
Gascoigne, who quickly spent Breton's
inheritance. Between 1575 and his death
he published over 30 individual collections
of verse, three prose fictions and at least 25
▷ pamphlets and miscellaneous works. From
the evidence of the number of times certain
of his works were reprinted (in particular
his *A Post with a Mad Packet of Letters*, first
published in 1602) there is the suggestion
that, on occasions, he was able to secure an
audience. Indeed, although he never received
the court preferment he desired, he did obtain
▷ patronage from ▷ Mary Sidney.
Bib: Robertson, J., *Poems by Breton*.

Bridges-Adams, William (1889–1965)
Director of the Shakespeare Memorial
Theatre in Stratford-on-Avon from 1919
to 1934, during which time he directed 29
of ▷ Shakespeare's plays. His productions
were influenced by the work of Harley
Granville Barker. Unlike his predecessor,
Frank Benson, he did not act in his own
productions and aimed for: 'The virtues of the

Elizabethan theatre without its vices, and its freedom without its fetters: scenic splendour where helpful, but . . . the play to be given as written: the text unmutilated whether in the interests of the stage carpenter or the leading man.'

Broadside Ballads
Popular ▷ ballads, printed on ▷ folio sheets. They formed a cheap method of publishing songs on topical subjects. The term 'broadside' meant that only one side of the paper was printed. They were a means of issuing news items, political propaganda, religious controversy, travellers' tales, attacks on (or defences of) women, the last words of condemned criminals, etc. Often decorated with wood-cut prints, they were a major source of information in the 16th and 17th centuries. The British Library possesses a unique collection of broadsides amongst the 'Thomason Tracts'.
Bib: Reay, B., *Popular Culture in Seventeenth-Century England*.

Brome, Richard (1590–1653)
The author of two popular ▷ Caroline comedies, ▷ *The City Wit* (1629) and *The Jovial Crew* (1640). His work reflects the influence of ▷ John Fletcher, but is indebted particularly to ▷ Ben Jonson in whose service Brome spent some time, perhaps as Jonson's secretary.
Bib: Kaufman, R. J., *Richard Brome, Caroline Playwright*.

Browne, Sir Thomas (1605-82)
Physician and author. Sir Thomas Browne studied medicine at Montpellier, Padua and Leiden, and began practising medicine in 1633, before moving in 1637 to Norwich, where he was to spend the rest of his life. Browne's most influential work was ▷ *Religio Medici* (1642, reissued in an authorized edition in 1643), a title which can be translated as *The Religion of a Physician*. The conjunction between religious meditation and an enduring fascination with the observation of the most minute details of the physical world informs the *Religio*, which stands as both a determined act of creation of an authorial persona, and as a disquisition which attempts to reconcile scepticism and belief.

In some ways, Browne can be thought of as a ▷ Baconian in his adherence to the principles of observation, and his determination to refute ideas commonly entertained by the credulous. But his Baconianism is tempered by a vein of

mysticism. The two tendencies in his thought are displayed in his later works – *Pseudodoxica Epidemica*, or *Vulgar Errors* (1646); *Hydriotaphia*, or ▷ *Urn Burial* (1658); and ▷ *The Garden of Cyrus* (1658).
Bib: Keynes, Sir G. (ed.), *Works*, 4 vols.; Bennett, J., *Sir Thomas Browne*; Post, J., *Sir Thomas Browne*.

Browne, William (1591–1643)
One of the 'Spenserian' poets, Browne wrote mainly ▷ pastoral verse, and was tutor to the family of ▷ William Herbert. He contributed seven eclogues to *The Shepherd's Pipe* (1614), a work written in collaboration with ▷ George Wither. Browne also composed a ▷ masque, produced in 1614, entitled *The Inner Temple Masque* – a title which was changed to *Ulysses and Circe* when the work was staged again in 1615. In 1613 appeared the first part of Browne's *Britannia's Pastorals*, poetic accounts of familiar pastoral stories derived from Browne's reading in ▷ Edmund Spenser, ▷ Torquato Tasso and ▷ John Fletcher, and placed within an English landscape, itself a reworking of Spenser's descriptions. Subsequent parts of the work were published in 1616 and (as a Percy Society edition) in 1852. In 1613, in collaboration with ▷ Fulke Greville, Browne published *Two Elegies*, works commemorating the death of ▷ Henry, Prince of Wales.
Bib: Grundy, J., *The Spenserian Poets*.

Buc, Sir George (d 1623)
▷ Master of the Revels, 1608–22. Educated at the ▷ Inns of Court, Buc pursued a political career under the auspices of ▷ Sir Francis Walsingham and Sir Robert Cecil. He was at the Cadiz expedition and later served as a Member of Parliament and an envoy. He is best remembered for his post as deputy master, and later Master of the Revels. Buc's influence on ▷ Jacobean drama was cut short, however, when he became mentally unstable. Although most of his papers were destroyed in a fire, several works survive: a history of ▷ Richard III, an ▷ eclogue (*Daphnis Polystephanos*, 1604), and a treatise arguing that London should have a university in addition to those at Oxford and Cambridge (*The Third Universitie of England*, 1615).

Buchanan, George (1506–82)
Scottish poet, classicist, educationalist. George Buchanan's life was a curious mixture of high scholarly endeavour and political intrigue. In this, he can be thought of as representing that ability, described by ▷ Thomas Browne, to

live in 'divided and distinguished worlds'. As an educationalist and a classicist he was tutor to ▷ Mary Queen of Scots and James VI (later ▷ James I of England). His most illustrious pupil, however, was the French essayist ▷ Montaigne, whom Buchanan taught after fleeing to Bordeaux to escape punishment for writing ▷ satires against the Franciscans. On returning to Scotland he helped prosecute his former pupil Mary Queen of Scots for high treason, and later, under James VI, he held high office in the Scottish government. The great majority of his works were written in Latin, and included love poems, ▷ tragedies, legal works and a history of Scotland.
Bib: Ford, P. J., *George Buchanan: Prince of Poets.*

Buckingham, George Villiers, first Duke of (1592–1628)
Courtier and favourite of ▷ James I. After the death of his astute principal minister, Robert Cecil, Earl of Salisbury, in 1612, the king turned for affection and advice to handsome young courtiers, the most prominent of whom was George Villiers. James's ▷ homosexual fascination with Buckingham allowed the younger man considerable political influence, while the king lavished wealth upon his 'sweet Steenie'. As the king's power faded, however, Buckingham transferred his affections to ▷ Prince Charles, the heir to the throne. When he acceded to the throne, Charles allowed Buckingham to lead him into a series of dangerous quarrels with Parliament and to almost complete dependence upon the Duke after the king's alienation from his wife, ▷ Henrietta Maria, in 1626. Buckingham's powerful influence over the British crown was brought to an abrupt end in 1628 when he was assassinated.
Bib: Lockyer, R., *Buckingham.*

Bulstrode, Cecily (1584–1609)
A writer of light prose ▷ satires, which categorized women as good or bad solely in accordance with their ability to please men, often in a sexual manner. However, she was part of the small group of women who congregated about ▷ Queen Anne, many of whom were more supportive of their own sex, such as ▷ Lady Anne Clifford and ▷ Lady Frances Southwell. Bulstrode is named as the author of 'Newes of my Morning worke', which was published with other ▷ Theophrastian character sketches in the second edition of ▷ Sir Thomas Overbury's *The Wife* (1614 and 1622). ▷ Ben Jonson wrote a scathing attack of her literary ability and sexual morality in 'An Epigram on the Court Pucell', but he, ▷ Donne and ▷ Edward Herbert all wrote commendatory elegies for Bulstrode at her death.
Bib: Savage, J. E. (ed.), *Overbury's Characters.*

Bunyan, John (1628–88)
Born at Elstow, near Bedford, Bunyan was the son of a tinsmith, educated at the village school. Of ▷ Baptist sympathies, he fought in the ▷ Civil War, although little is known of his military activities. With the persecution of the ▷ Puritans which followed the Restoration of Charles II, Bunyan's Nonconformist beliefs came under severe censure, and in 1660 he was arrested for preaching without a licence.

For most of the next 12 years Bunyan was imprisoned in Bedford jail, where he began to write. His spiritual ▷ autobiography, ▷ *Grace Abounding to the Chief of Sinners,* appeared in 1666, and the first part of his major work, ▷ *The Pilgrim's Progress,* was published in 1678. *The Pilgrim's Progress* was largely written during this period of imprisonment, though it is probable that Bunyan completed Part I during a second spell in jail in 1676; the full text, with the addition of Part II, was published in 1684. A spiritual ▷ allegory strongly in the ▷ Puritan tradition, it tells of the pilgrimage of Christian to reach the state of grace. Bunyan's other major works, *The Life and Death of Mr Badman* (1680) and ▷ *The Holy War* (1682), are also spiritual allegories.
Bib: Collmer, R. G. (ed.), *Bunyan in our Time.*

Burbage, James (d 1597)
Actor and theatre manager. Originally a carpenter, in 1576 he built the first English ▷ theatre, called simply The Theatre, in London's Shoreditch. In 1596 he opened the ▷ Blackfriars Theatre, where the Children of the Chapel performed.
Bib: Levi, P., *The Life and Times of William Shakespeare.*

Burbage, Richard (?1567–1619)
Son of ▷ James Burbage. On his father's death, he dismantled The Theatre and rebuilt it as the ▷ Globe on the south bank of the Thames. As a shareholder in the ▷ Lord Chamberlain's Men he took the leading part in plays by ▷ Shakespeare, ▷ Jonson, ▷ Fletcher and others, using the Globe and (after 1608) the ▷ Blackfriars Theatre. He and ▷ Edward Alleyn were the most well-known actors of the time.
Bib: Levi, P., *The Life and Times of William Shakespeare.*

Burghley, William Cecil, Lord (1520–98)
Lord treasurer. Cecil had a successful and
prolonged political career; he was secretary of
state (1550–3), was employed by ▷ Mary I,
and became ▷ Elizabeth I's lord treasurer and
her chief minister and adviser.
Bib: Read, C., *Lord Burghley and Queen
Elizabeth*.

Burgundy, Duchy of
A province in the south-east of France, with
which it was united in 1477. In the phase
of the Hundred Years' War associated with
▷ Henry V of England (1413–22) Burgundy
was for the time an important ally of England
against France.
  The early ▷ Renaissance Burgundian
court had a considerable artistic and cultural
influence upon portraiture and court
entertainments in England during the reign of
▷ Henry VII.
  ▷ Masque.
Bib: Kipling, G., *The Triumph of Honour*.

Burton, Robert (1577–1640)
Oxford scholar and author. Burton was
born in Leicestershire, and in 1593 entered
Brasenose College, Oxford, where he
was to remain. Besides the anti-Catholic
Latin comedy *Philosophaster* (acted in
1618), Burton's one major project was the
publication of his ▷ *Anatomy of Melancholy*, a
project which occupied him for the majority
of his life. He wrote under the pseudonym
of 'Democritus Junior', thus emulating the
Greek philosopher of the 5th century BC,
Democritus.
Bib: Babb, L., *Sanity in Bedlam*; Keissling,
N. K., *The Library of Robert Burton*.

Bussy d'Ambois, The Tragedy of (1604)
The best-known tragedy by ▷ George
Chapman, which dramatizes the rise and fall
of Bussy d'Ambois at the court of Henri III of
France. The play's complex rhetoric reflects
the philosophic, particularly neo-Platonic
(▷ Platonism) bent of the author's mind and
sometimes inhibits its imaginative flow.

Butler, Samuel (1612–80)
Poet. The son of a Worcestershire farmer, he
became the friend of ▷ Thomas Hobbes and
▷ Sir William D'Avenant. His mock-heroic
(▷ Heroic, mock) satire on ▷ Puritanism,
▷ *Hudibras*, employs deliberately rough-
and-ready tetrameter couplets, which were
frequently imitated by later poets and became
known as 'hudibrasticks'. Butler's other
works were neglected and most of them,
including the ▷ Theophrastian *Characters*
and the satire on ▷ The Royal Society, *The
Elephant in the Moon* (it is actually a mouse
trapped in the telescope), were not published
until 1759, when his *Genuine Remains*
appeared.
Bib: Johnson, S., in *Lives of the Poets*; Jack, I.,
Augustan Satire.

Byrd, William (1540–1623)
Composer. Most well-known of all Elizabethan
composers, Byrd is chiefly remembered for
two innovative collections, *Psalmes, Sonets and
Songs* (1588) and *Psalmes, Songs and Sonnets*
(1611). Although these are often considered
to be ▷ madrigals, they are not influenced
to any great extent by these Italian imports,
and Byrd was more indebted to the writing
and composition of his youth. He wrote a vast
amount of music, including both sacred pieces
and vocal parts for secular performance. He
was a pupil of Thomas Tallis, with whom he
held a monopoly on music publishing from
1575, and he also held the post of Organist
of the Chapel Royal. However, although Byrd
conformed to the ▷ Protestant state religion,
he was a recusant and was excommunicated in
1598 for his ▷ Catholic practices. He chose,
therefore, to live outside London so as not to
attract attention, and this must certainly have
hindered his efforts to attain valuable political
patronage.

C

Caesar, Augustus (Gaius Julius Caesar Octavianus) (63 BC–AD 14)
Great-nephew of ▷ Julius Caesar, and his adopted son. He adopted the surname Caesar and was awarded the title of Augustus by the Roman Senate. He overcame the political enemies and assassins of his uncle, and after defeating his other rivals (notably Mark Antony) he achieved complete power and became first Emperor of Rome. ▷ Horace, ▷ Virgil, ▷ Ovid, Propertius, Tibullus and Livy were his contemporaries; in consequence, 'an Augustan age' has become a term to describe a high peak of literary achievement in any culture, whenever such achievement shows similar qualities of elegance, restraint and eloquence. In these qualities, France in the 17th century and England in the 18th century consciously emulated the Augustan age of Rome.

Octavius Caesar, in ▷ Shakepeare's ▷ *Antony and Cleopatra*, is a portrait (based on ▷ Plutarch) of Augustus during his struggle with Antony.

▷ French literature in England.

Caesar, Gaius Julius (?102–44 BC)
Roman general, statesman and writer. He conquered Gaul (*ie* modern France) and in 55 and 54 BC undertook two expeditions to Britain. He described these wars in *De Bello Gallico*, a work long and widely used in English education for instruction in Latin. His victories led to civil war against his chief political rival, Gneius Pompeius, generally known in English as Pompey, whom he defeated. He then became dictator in Rome, but was assassinated by other patricians, led by Marcus Brutus, for overthrowing Roman republican institutions. For the ▷ Middle Ages, Julius Caesar represented all that was great in Rome. His life was described by the Greek biographer ▷ Plutarch and this along with Plutarch's other biographies was translated into English by ▷ Sir Thomas North. ▷ Shakespeare used it as the basis of his play ▷ *Julius Caesar*.

Caliban
A character in ▷ Shakespeare's play ▷ *The Tempest*. The word is almost an anagram for 'cannibal', and in part Caliban represents man at his most primitive as reported by travellers of the day. He is also an unnatural monster, child of the witch Sycorax, and as much animal as human. Shakespeare also seems to have intended him to symbolize the body, untouched by any spark of spirit. Unlike his counterpart Ariel, who is composed purely

of the element of air, Caliban represents the earth. Both of them are slaves of the magician Prospero, who dominates the play.

▷ Colonialism.

Calvin, John (1509–1604)
French religious reformer and author of the *Institutes of the Christian Religion* (1535). He settled in Geneva, which was to become, under his influence, an important centre of one of the most disciplined and militant branches of ▷ Protestantism.

Calvin's teachings were widely influential in England, Scotland, France and Switzerland in the 17th century and later. Out of the *Institutes* and his book on predestination (published in 1552) emerged the five chief points of Calvinism, namely its belief in: (1) 'predestination', which holds that God has determined in advance who shall be 'elected' to 'eternal life' and who shall be condemned to everlasting damnation; (2) 'particular redemption', or the choosing of a certain predetermined number of souls redeemed by Christ's death; (3) 'original sin', which holds that the infant enters the world in a state of sinfulness, carrying with it the burden of Adam's fall; (4) 'irresistible grace', which argues that those chosen to be of the 'elect' have no means of resisting that choice; and (5) the final perseverance or triumph of the 'elect'.

Taken with Calvin's views on church government and the relation between state and ecclesiastical power, Calvinism was to be of enormous influence on the ▷ Church of England in the 16th and 17th centuries. From the early 17th century onwards his doctrines became those of the established church. Calvin's *Institutes* became a recognized textbook in the universities, and it was not until the rise of Arminianism under ▷ Archbishop William Laud in the pre-Civil War (▷ Civil Wars) years that an effective opposition to Calvin's influence was mounted. **Bib:** Knappen, M. M., *Tudor Puritanism*; Dickens, A. G., *The English Reformation*.

Cambridge Platonists
▷ Platonists, The Cambridge.

Camden, William (1551–1623)
Historian and antiquary. Camden was educated at Oxford and was appointed headmaster of Westminster School in 1593, where ▷ Ben Jonson was one of his pupils. His main works are *Britannia* (1586; an enlarged sixth edition appeared in 1607)

and *Annales* (1615 and 1625), both of which were translated from the original Latin into English between 1610 and 1635 (*Britannia* was translated by Philemon Holland in 1610). All were scrupulously researched – for example, he made a tour of Britain while writing *Britannia* – and he is recognized as one of the first modern historians who demanded authenticity in his sources, rather than relying upon mythology (▷ Tudor myth). He founded a chair of history at Oxford in 1621 and was buried in Westminster Abbey.
Bib: Trevor-Roper, H. R., *Queen Elizabeth's First Historian: William Camden and the Beginnings of English Civil History*.

Campion, Edmund (1540–81)
English ▷ Catholic. After becoming a fellow of St John's College, Oxford in 1557, Campion enjoyed the patronage of the ▷ Earl of Leicester before fleeing to Rome in 1572 as a suspected Catholic. In Rome he joined the ▷ Jesuit order in 1573, before being ordained a priest in 1578 and being chosen to return to England as a priest in 1580. In England he distributed anti-Protestant material (specifically the *Decem Rationes* in 1581) and was arrested, sent to the Tower, tortured and finally executed in 1581. His death was said to have been the cause of many former ▷ Protestants in England returning to Catholicism. He was the subject of a hagiographic biography, Evelyn Waugh's *Edmund Campion*.
Bib: Kavanagh, J., *Edmund Campion and the Elizabethan Government*.

Campion, Thomas (1567–1620)
English lyric poet and musician. He wrote and composed when the art of English song was at its height; the words do not exist merely as a pretext for the music, but are so composed that the music brings out their expressiveness. This led naturally to metrical experiment, and the resulting increase of rhythmic flexibility no doubt influenced the playwrights in the great range of expression which they achieved in ▷ blank verse. Campion wrote ayres, ▷ madrigals and ▷ masques. Despite his fine command of the rhymed ▷ lyric, he wrote an essay against the use of rhyme, *Observations in the Art of English Poetry* (1602). This provoked a reply in one of the more important Elizabethan critical essays, ▷ Samuel Daniel's *Defence of Ryme*.

Campion's reputation suffered in the early part of this century due to the championing of ▷ Donne and 'metaphysical' poetry (▷ Metaphysical poets) by critics such as

T. S. Eliot (1888–1965). But his reputation has always fluctuated considerably – his contemporaries ▷ Ben Jonson and Daniel both attacked him in print. The chief difference between a poet such as Campion and the styles developed by Donne is that Campion is concerned with the auditory effects of poetry rather than concentrating on the striking effects of images. However, recent ▷ materialist criticism has highlighted Campion's awareness of the changing political situation and has suggested that his poetry and masques are more critical of the court than the previous emphasis on oral play would suggest.
Bib: Colles, H. C., *Voice and Verse*; Kastendieck, M. M., *Thomas Campion, England's Musical Poet*; Lindley, D., *Thomas Campion*; Mellers, W., *Music and Poetry*; Pattison, B., *Music and Poetry of the English Renaissance*; Warlock, P., *The English Ayre*; Smith, H., *Elizabethan Poetry*; Fellows, E. H., *English School of Lutenist Song Writers*.

Canterbury Tales, The
A famed story-collection by ▷ Geoffrey Chaucer, begun sometime in the late 1380s. The General Prologue gives details of the occasion for the story-telling, relating how a group of pilgrims, bound for the shrine of St Thomas Becket at Canterbury, meet up at the Tabard Inn in Southwark. The pilgrims are introduced in a sequence of portraits that focus on the professional activities of the company (who number 31 in all). The material for these portraits derives partly from a long-standing literary tradition of social analysis and ▷ satire, but Chaucer enlarges the scope of the cross-section of society on the pilgrimage by including a broader range of bourgeois professionals in the group. The varied format and style of the descriptive cameos (in which details of dress, character or professional habits are mentioned seemingly at random) enhances the impression of the individuality of the pilgrims, who are introduced by a pilgrim-narrator whose stance is that of a reporter of events.

The list of portraits begins with that of the Knight, a representative of the higher levels of the social elite, who is travelling with his son, the Squire, and their Yeoman. The focus then shifts to the description of members of the clerical elite on the trip, including a Prioress, a Monk and a Friar. There is no clear-cut ordering principle in the sequence of portraits that follows (other than perhaps a broad downward movement through the social scale), describing a Merchant, a Clerk of Oxford, a Lawyer, a Franklin, a group of five Guild members, their wives and their Cook, a Shipman, a Physician, a Wife of Bath, a Parson and his brother, a Ploughman, a Miller, a Manciple, a Reeve and, finally, a Summoner and a Pardoner who pair up as travelling companions. The pilgrim-narrator is described in more detail by the Host later in the journey. The General Prologue concludes with an account of how the Host of the Tabard Inn, Harry Bailey, devises a story-telling competition to take place on the round trip to Canterbury. The pilgrims agree to tell two stories each on the forward and return journeys; Harry Bailey plans to accompany the pilgrims, act as games-master and reward the pilgrim providing the best story with a meal on return to Southwark.

Diversity seems to be the organizing principle of the collection. *The Canterbury Tales* includes an extraordinarily wide range of material in verse (in rhymed decasyllabic couplets, rhyme royal verse) and prose, covering a wide range of literary genres and forms: romances, fabliaux, an animal fable, saints' lives, exemplary narratives, a moral treatise, a prose treatise on the process of penitence (which concludes the game). The relationship between 'earnest' and 'game', between serious and playful literary material, is one of the running topics of debate within and between the tales.

Judging from the condition of the extant manuscript copies of the *Canterbury Tales*, the project outlined by Harry Bailey in the General Prologue was never completed by Chaucer. The *Canterbury Tales* has the status of a 'work in progress', comprising a series of fragmentary tale-telling sequences, some of which are linked by dramatic interactions between the pilgrims and Harry Bailey, some of which begin and end without any contextual framing, and some of which show signs of being linked to other tellers at an earlier stage in the process of compilation. However, the opening and closing sequences of the *Tales* are provided and from these it seems that the literary plan was designed to change *en route* from a round journey to a one-way trip. The last tale of the sequence, the Parson's prose treatise on penitence, signals not only the end of the journey to Canterbury, but also the end of story-telling altogether, and is followed in most manuscripts by Chaucer's literary Retraction.

None of the 82 manuscripts of the *Tales* was copied during Chaucer's lifetime, and variations in form, style and tale-teller linkage are apparent. Some of the variations seem to reflect the attempts of later scribes and editors to tidy up some of the loose ends of the story-collection and provide more cohesive links for the series of fragmentary sequences left by Chaucer. Modern editions of the *Canterbury Tales* are based on two important early-15th-century manuscripts: the Ellesmere manuscript (E) and the Hengwrt manuscript (H). The form and arrangement of the text in E have provided the basis for the most accessible editions of the *Tales* (by F. N. Robinson, revised and updated by Larry Benson et al.). In E, 22 of the pilgrims mentioned in the Prologue produce a tale, beginning with the Knight, followed by the Miller, the Reeve, the Cook, the Man of Law, the Wife of Bath, the Friar, the Summoner, the Clerk, the Merchant, the Squire, the Franklin, the Physician, the Pardoner, the Shipman, the Prioress, the pilgrim/narrator (who tells two tales, *Sir Thopas*, which is rejected by the Host, and *Melibeus*), the Monk, the Nun's Priest, the Second Nun, the Canon's Yeoman (who joins the pilgrimage *en route*), the Manciple and finally the Parson. It is now generally accepted that the E text has been quite extensively edited by Chaucer's literary executors and represents a later, tidied-up version of the text represented in H, and more recently the Hengwrt manuscript has been used as the basis for new editions of the *Canterbury Tales* (by N. Blake, by Paul Ruggiers and David Baker). The differences between the two versions are mainly in the ordering and linking of the tales: the E text has more connected sequences of stories and contains the *Canon's Yeoman's Prologue and Tale*, which is not in H.

Since its publication by Chaucer's literary executors, the *Canterbury Tales* has had an active 'afterlife'. Some new tales were added to the collection by 15th-century editors (notably Gamelyn), an attempt was made to continue the narrative after the arrival at Canterbury (in the *Tale of Beryn*), and ▷ John Lydgate, the prolific court writer of the 15th century, wrote himself into the literary event of the *Tales* in his work *The Siege of Thebes*, which opens with a description of Lydgate himself joining the pilgrimage and then contributing his Theban story to the competition. The attention given to the *Canterbury Tales*, in relation to the rest of the Chaucerian canon, has varied according to the critical temper and tastes of the time, but the enormous attention given by modern scholars and critics to the phenomenon of the *Tales* is only the most recent stage in the long history of their critical reception. The

Canterbury Tales continues to be a work in progress.
Bib: Benson, L., et al. (eds.), *The Riverside Chaucer*; Boitani, P., and Mann, J. (eds.), *The Cambridge Chaucer Companion*; Cooper, H., *The Structure of the Canterbury Tales*; Howard, D. D. R., *The Idea of the Canterbury Tales*; Pearsall, D., *The Canterbury Tales*.

Capitalism

The system by which the means of production is owned privately. Production is for private profit and productive enterprise is made possible by large-scale loans of money rewarded by the payment of interest.

The rapid growth of capitalism in the 17th century was aided by the ▷ Reformation, since certain of the ▷ Puritan sects – notably the Calvinist Presbyterians (▷ Calvin, John) – found that religious individualism gave support to and was supported by economic individualism. The dramatists of the period of English drama 1580–1640 found the Puritans to be against them, and they (*eg* ▷ Ben Jonson, ▷ Thomas Middleton, ▷ Philip Massinger) tended to satirize the money-loving, socially ambitious middle classes, among whom the Puritans had their main strength. By the end of the 17th century, however, Puritanism was losing its ferocity but the traditional non-economic bonds of community were by then gravely weakened.

While every age seems to reveal signs of capitalism, this area has been highlighted in ▷ Renaissance criticism with the advent of ▷ new historicism and ▷ cultural materialism.

Capulet

In ▷ Shakespeare's ▷ *Romeo and Juliet* the name of the family to which Juliet belongs. The inveterate hostility between the Capulets and the ▷ Montagues, the family to which Romeo belongs, causes the tragedy.

Carew, Thomas (1594–1640)

Poet. In the 1630s Carew was a member of the court of ▷ Charles I, and his association with the court and the group of poets moving either within or on the fringe of court circles in the pre-Civil War years, has led him to be grouped as one of the ▷ 'Cavalier' poets. His first important work was his elegy on the death of ▷ John Donne, which appeared in the first edition of Donne's poems in 1633. In 1634 his ▷ masque *Coelum Britannicum* was performed by the king and his gentlemen. His *Poems* were published in 1640 with further editions in 1642 and 1651.

Carew's poetry is remarkable for its combination of eroticism, wit and logical demonstration. His elegy on Donne, as well as representing a tribute to the dead poet, also offers itself as a critical statement in its own right, and is an important commentary on the type of verse which came to be known as ▷ 'metaphysical'.
Bib: Miner, E., *The Cavalier Mode from Jonson to Cotton.*

Carey, Mary (c 1610–80)

Poet and devotional writer. Carey began her spiritual life at the age of 18 when she recovered from a serious illness, and began collecting together her meditations in verse and prose c 1653. Although these may be found in manuscript form at the Bodleian Library, Oxford, selections are published in *Kissing the Rod*, ed. G. Greer (1988). She was married twice, the second time to George Payler, a Parliamentarian paymaster whose occupation ensured that Carey was continually moving about the country from garrison to garrison. Her poems are dedicated to Payler and a number of her works, which are usually in the form of a dialogue, appear as conversations with him. She also includes exchanges with God and Satan, as well as the conventional dialogue poem between body and soul (▷ Andrew Marvell). Her tone is always modest and pious, although she often questions God as to why her babies were allowed to die.
Bib: Blain, V. et al (eds.), *The Feminist Companion to Literature in English.*

Carol

A hymn of praise, especially associated with Christmas. The origin of the carol may have been pagan, and connected with New Year and spring festivals. Dancing and singing in early medieval churches was common, for instance round the Christmas 'crib' or model of the Christ-child's birthplace in the stable at Bethlehem. English Christmas carols, like those of other nations, are freer of the restricted sentiment of Church piety than other hymns. Examples dating from the 15th century are 'Joseph was an old man' and 'I saw three ships come sailing in'. The earliest collection in English is by ▷ Wynkyn de Worde in 1521.

Caroline Period, The

Term given to the period of the reign of ▷ Charles I and ▷ Henrietta Maria (from the Latin *Carolus* = Charles). The 'Caroline

poets' (eg ▷ Thomas Carew, ▷ Sir John
Suckling, ▷ Richard Lovelace) and the
'Caroline divines' (eg ▷ William Laud) are all
associated with the court culture of the period.
The term is thus something of a misnomer,
since it represents not so much a period,
but rather an ideological and cultural stance
which stands in opposition to the popular and
emergent republican culture.
    ▷ Cavalier Poets.
Bib: Sharpe, K., *Criticism and Compliment*.

Cary, Anne (1615–1671)

Biographer. Anne Cary was one of the
younger daughters of the prophetess
▷ Elizabeth Cary, whose ▷ biography she
wrote. Anne and her three sisters escaped
their father's ▷ Protestant household to
live with their Catholic mother, and in time
they too converted and became nuns. They
also helped their two younger brothers to
escape. It is most likely that Anne, later Dame
Clementia, wrote the biography, although
there is a slight possibility that it was another
daughter, Mary, since both joined the
Benedictine convent at Cambrai where the
work was composed. The manuscript work
remains with the nuns, but was published in
1861 as *The Lady Falkland, her Life from a ms
in the Imperial Archives at Lisle*, ed. Richard
Simpson.
    ▷ Catholicism.

Cary, Lady Elizabeth (1585–1639)

Dramatist and translator. At 15 she was
married to Henry Cary, Lord Falkland and
until 1626 she tried to please her husband
in all things, presenting herself as the ideal
Renaissance woman – 'chaste, silent and
obedient'. During this period she wrote her
most well-known work, *The Tragedie of Mariam*
(pub. 1613), which is the first original drama
in English written by an Englishwoman.
Written in the ▷ Senecan mode, it recounts
the story of King Herod's wife, Mariam,
who is eventually executed on his orders, and
the plot closely follows Cary's source text,
Josephus's *Antiquities*. However, the female
characters are subtly changed so that the
central issue of the play becomes how an
independent woman is caught between the
public and political demands of queenship and
her personal emotions. In the play it becomes
impossible to balance these differing demands
and tragedy inevitably ensues. Cary also wrote
an unfinished play, *The History of King Edward
II* (1627), which shows a major development
in her skill at handling lengthy plot sequences
and many diverse characters. This latter

play was erroneously published under her
husband's name in 1680. The crisis in
Elizabeth Cary's own attempts to reconcile
her public duty to her husband and her
private religious convictions occurred in 1626
when she converted to ▷ Catholicism. She
became estranged from her husband, who
removed their children from her care and
reduced her to poverty, but she continued
to write. Cary's major scholarly achievement
at this time was the translation of the
complete works of Jacques Davy, Cardinal
Du Perron, which remained unpublished
with the exception of Du Perron's reply to
James I's attack on his works. This was issued
in 1630 with a dedication to ▷ Henrietta
Maria, in which she clearly takes pride in
her female authorship. Few copies survive,
as it was ordered to be burned. Later she
became reconciled to her husband and was
with him at his death in 1633. One of her
daughters, probably ▷ Anne Cary, wrote her
biography.
    ▷ Lumley, Lady Joanna; Sidney, Mary.
Bib: Beilin, E.V., *Redeeming Eve*; Travitsky, B.
(ed.), *The Paradise of Women*.

Castiglione, Baldassare (1478–1529)

Italian ▷ humanist and author of *Il Cortegiano*
(1528), translated as *The Courtier* by ▷ Sir
Thomas Hoby in 1561. *Il Cortegiano* is
based on Castiglione's years spent as a
courtier at Urbino under Guidobaldo da
Montefeltro, and takes the form of a debate
on what features should be possessed by
the perfect courtier. Those qualifications
include: swordsmanship, nobility, military
understanding, skill in virile sports (hunting,
swimming, running and riding), dancing,
grace, skill at repartee and telling of stories
and anecdotes; the possession of the virtues of
prudence, justice, temperance, and fortitude;
adaptability, literary knowledge, the ability to
write prose and verse, musical proficiency,
and the gift of charm.
    The two important features of Castiglione's
book, and the ones that were to become most
influential in England in the ▷ Renaissance
period, were his description of *sprezzatura*
and his ▷ neo-Platonic conception of love
and harmony. *Sprezzatura* implies an ease
of manner, a suggestion that what has
been done has been achieved effortlessly
and without art. Qualities such as these
were to play an important role in the
definition of courtly behaviour in the late
16th century in England. The neo-Platonic
elements (to be found in Book IV of
the work) elevate beauty, together with

human and divine love, into an ideal of harmony.

Castiglione was to be of enormous importance to contemporary readers of his work in introducing the idea that individuals can create an identity and a personality for themselves. It is this idea which lies, for example, at the heart of ▷ Edmund Spenser's *The Faerie Queene*, and in the poetry, in the earlier period, of ▷ Sir Thomas Wyatt. **Bib:** Greenblatt, S., *Renaisssance Self-Fashioning*.

Catholicism (Roman) in English literature
Until the ▷ Act of Supremacy (1534) by which ▷ King Henry VIII separated the English Church from Roman authority, and the more violent revolution in Scotland a little later, both countries had belonged to the European community of Catholic Christendom. This community was a genuine culture, allowing great unity of belief and feeling together with great variety of attitude. In the 16th century this community of cultures broke up, owing not only to the ▷ Protestant rebellions but also to the increase of national self-consciousness, the influence of non-Christian currents (especially ▷ Platonism), and the gradual release of various fields of activity – political, commercial, philosophical – from religious doctrine. ▷ The Counter-Reformation after the Catholic Council of Trent (1545–63), even more than the ▷ Reformation, tended to define Roman Catholicism in contrast to Protestantism. Thus, although the dramatists and lyric poets in England from 1560 to 1640 show a plentiful survival of medieval assumptions about the nature of man and his place in the universe in conflict with newer tendencies of thought and feeling, the Roman Catholic writer in the same period begins to show himself as something distinct from his non-Catholic colleagues. Two clear examples in the 17th century are the poet ▷ Richard Crashaw and the dramatist and translator ▷ Lady Elizabeth Cary. ▷ Milton's epic of the creation of the world, ▷ *Paradise Lost*, is in many ways highly traditional, but the feeling that inspires it is entirely post-Reformation.

Catiline (1611)
A tragedy by ▷ Ben Jonson, about the attempt by Lucius Sergius Catilana to overthrow the government of the Republic of Rome in the 1st century BC. It is an example of Jonson's finest classical scholarship, and was, perhaps, one of the most admired plays in the scholarly and critical circles of the 17th century. Subsequently, *Catiline* has had a more chequered career: early 20th-century criticism suggested that Jonson's overt scholarship impeded the dramatic impact of the tragedy instead of enhancing it, as in the case of his other Roman tragedy, ▷ *Sejanus*. However, late 20th-century rereadings of the play have perceived more value in the political material and in Jonson's ability to present subtle challenges to dominant authority.

Catullus, Gaius Valerius (?84–54 BC)
A Roman lyrical poet, famous especially for his Lesbia cycle of love poems. He was one of the Latin poets who had an extensive influence over English ▷ lyric poets in the 16th and 17th centuries. For instance, ▷ John Skelton's *Book of Philip Sparrow* (1503–7) echoes Catullus on Lesbia and the sparrow; ▷ Ben Jonson's *Song to Celia* is modelled on Catullus, and so is ▷ Andrew Marvell's *To his Coy Mistress*. Jonson, with his sensitive and profound Latin scholarship, was the most important English follower of Catullus and he transmitted the strength and delicacy of the Latin poet to the ▷ 'Cavalier' lyricists and to Marvell. The most important period for Catullus's influence on English poetry was therefore 1600–50.

Cavalier
A word, meaning 'horseman', which was used for the supporters of ▷ Charles I in the ▷ Civil War. It was first used as a term of reproach against them by their opponents, the supporters of Parliament (▷ Roundheads); in this sense it meant an arrogant and frivolous man of the court. Soon, however, it was accepted with pride by the Royalists themselves. It is a mistake, however, to think of the Cavaliers merely as members of the court and of the aristocracy; many of the aristocracy supported Parliament and many of the Cavaliers were fairly modest country gentlemen who never came near the court. The Cavalier Parliament sat from 1661 to 1678 after the Restoration of ▷ Charles II and was so called because the king's supporters won most of the seats.
▷ Cavalier Poets.

Cavalier Poets
An unhelpful critical term used to encompass the group of poets associated with the court of ▷ Charles I (in particular ▷ Thomas Carew, ▷ Sir John Suckling and ▷ Richard Lovelace), often known as the ▷ Caroline poets. The term is suggestive of a homogeneity amongst this

group of poets, and also contains a romanticized implication of their soldierly and martial prowess.

Cavendish, Lady Jane (1621–69) and Lady Elizabeth (1626–63)

Poets and dramatists, devotional and autobiographical writers. The two sisters were the daughters of William Cavendish, Duke of Newcastle, and their stepmother was ▷ Margaret Cavendish, herself an acclaimed author. Although the writings of both women never attain scholarly heights or reveal any individualistic imagination, their work is bold, lively, sometimes satirical and often intimate. The first body of work was composed in unison during their occupation of Welbeck Castle in the ▷ Civil War period; their father was absent, mother dead, and the house passed back and forth between Royalists and Parliamentarians. To occupy their time, and possibly as a future present for their father, they wrote *Poems, Songs and a Pastoral* (1643–5) – to which they added 'a Play' – now in manuscript at the Bodleian Library, Oxford. Their linguistic and grammatical capabilities are virtually nonexistent, but the political ▷ allegory (including an unflattering portrait of their father's new wife, Margaret), the colloquial language and the proto-feminist theme (the two heroines train their suitors to desire equality with, and not domination over, their future wives) make this an important document. Excerpts are available in *Kissing the Rod*, ed. G. Greer (1988), and the play, *The Concealed Fansyes*, was published in 1931, ed. N. C. Starr. Both sisters married, Jane to Charles Cheyne in 1654, and Elizabeth to John Egerton, Earl of Bridgewater. Both continued to write. What we know of Jane's work amounts to several letters and poems, but a large canon did exist and may still be traceable. Elizabeth's devotional writings and her ▷ autobiography were collected by her husband after her death as 'True Coppies of Certaine Loose Papers Left by the Right Honorable ELIZABETH Countesse of BRIDGEWATER' (1663), which is deposited at the British Library. These writings are more sober than those written before their marriages, but still reveal an emotional and intellectual closeness between the women despite the changes in their lives.
Bib: Travitsky, B. (ed.), *The Renaissance Englishwoman in Print.*

Cavendish, Margaret Duchess of Newcastle (1623–73)

Prolific author. Margaret Cavendish wrote poetry, drama, natural philosophy, ▷ biography, orations, letters, science fiction and ▷ autobiography. She was both admired and ridiculed in her lifetime, but seems not to have cared much for either opinion. While appearing modest in her writings, she simultaneously reveals an overwhelming desire for earthly fame. A woman of contradictions and controversy, Cavendish began her life as a tongue-tied lady-in-waiting to ▷ Henrietta Maria, and she followed the queen to exile in France. There she met her husband, William Cavendish (the father of ▷ Jane and Elizabeth Cavendish by his first marriage), whose biography she was later to write. During the ▷ Interregnum, Newcastle's estates were sequestered by Parliament and Margaret was forced to visit Britain in an attempt to raise finances. It was during this stay that she wrote her first book, *Poems and Fancies* (1653), which already showed signs of her later scientific interests; for example, there is a poem on the theory of atoms. After their return to Britain during the Restoration, Margaret continued to write in several genres, covering issues such as women's oppression. Though she was lavishly entertained by the ▷ Royal Society in 1667, it was never suggested that she be elected to a Fellowship. She also wrote an autobiography, *A True Relation of My Birth Breeding and Life*, which was published with *Natures Pictures* (1656). Despite the fact that she was considered eccentric her tombstone at Westminster Abbey provides a fitting epitaph; 'wise, witty and learned lady'.
Bib: Graham, E. et al. (eds.), *Her Own Life*; Hobby, E., *Virtue of Necessity*; Greer, G. (ed.), *Kissing the Rod*; Jones, K., *A Glorious Fame*; Meyer, G. D., *The Scientific Lady in England 1650–1760.*

Caxton, William (?1422–91)

The first English printer. He established his press in Westminster in 1476, and in the years 1477–91 he issued nearly 80 books, many of them translations from the French and many of these made by himself. Of English works that he printed, some of the most important are ▷ Chaucer's ▷ *Canterbury Tales, House of Fame* and ▷ *Troilus and Criseyde*, and ▷ Sir Thomas Malory's ▷ *Morte D'Arthur*.

Caxton was a good ▷ translator, and has his place in the development of English prose. No great writer had set a standard for prose as Chaucer had for poetry. The language was in a fluid state, with no accepted standards of spelling, grammar or style. Caxton had to fix these for himself, not only as a printer but as a publisher aiming to be intelligible to the

widest possible public. With few English prose works available for printing he had to fall back on producing his own by translation.
Bib: Awner, N. S., *Caxton: A Study of the Literature of the First English Press*; Bennett, H. S., *English Books and Readers, 1475–1557*.

Celestial City
The name by which Heaven is denoted in ▷ John Bunyan's ▷ *Pilgrim's Progress*. It is contrasted with the ▷ City of Destruction, a typical earthly town standing for worldliness, from which Christian flees on hearing that it is doomed.

Censorship and English literature
Systematic censorship has never been an important restriction on English writing except in times of war, but English writers have certainly not always been entirely free.

Until 1640 the monarch exercised undefined powers by the Royal Prerogative. Early in her reign, ▷ Elizabeth I ordered dramatists not to meddle with politics, though this did not prevent Norton and ▷ Sackville's ▷ *Gorboduc*, with its warnings on national disorder. However, Ben Jonson, ▷ Chapman and ▷ Marston found themselves in prison for *Eastward Hoe* (1605) because it offended the Scots friends of ▷ James I. In the reign of ▷ Charles I the term Crop-ears was used for opponents of the king who lost their ears as a penalty for criticizing the political or religious authorities. Moreover, printing was monopolized by the ▷ Stationers' Company, whose charter might be withdrawn by the Crown, so that the monopoly would cease.

In the ▷ Civil War, Parliament was in control of London, and issued an edict that the publication of any book had to be licensed, and it was during the ▷ Interregnum that censorship became most important. The edict provoked ▷ John Milton's ▷ *Areopagitica*, an appeal for freedom of expression. Its influence was not immediate; after the Restoration of the monarchy, Parliament issued a similar edict in the Licensing Act of 1663. The Act was only for a period, however, and in 1696 it was not renewed. The lapsing of the Licensing Act was the starting-point of British freedom of the press, except for emergency edicts in times of war in the 20th century.
Bib: Clare, J., *'Art Made Tongue-tied by Authority': Elizabethan and Jacobean Dramatic Censorship*; Potter, L., *Secret Rites and Secret Writing*; Patterson, A., *Censorship and Interpretation: The Conditions of Reading and Writing in Early Modern England*; Dutton, R., *Mastering the Revels: The Regulation and Censorship of English Renaissance Drama*.

Chamberlain's Men, The Lord
The more important of the two leading companies of actors in the reigns of ▷ Elizabeth I and ▷ James I, and the one to which ▷ Shakespeare belonged as both actor and playwright. All companies of actors had to have licences in order to perform, and this meant they had to have the patronage of some leading nobleman, or be attached to the royal household. The Lord Chamberlain's Men seems to have been formed in 1594 by a regrouping of various companies depleted by a plague epidemic. Its patron was Lord Hunsdon who held the office of Lord Chamberlain at the royal court. After the accession of James I, the king himself became its patron, and the company was known as 'the King's Men'. It played at court, and at a number of theatres in London, but its most lasting homes were at the ▷ Globe on the south bank of the Thames, and at the ▷ Blackfriars on the north bank. No doubt it was the popularity of Shakespeare's plays, both at court and among the general public, which gave the company its commanding position, though the quality of ▷ Richard Burbage's acting must also have counted. Its rival was ▷ Edward Alleyn's ▷ Lord Admiral's Men. The King's Men retained its supremacy among the acting companies until the closing of the theatres by Parliament in 1642.
▷ Acting, the Profession of.

Chambers, Sir Edmund (1866–1954)
Scholar. The exceptional breadth and exactness of his work on English literature make his books indispensable reference works for students of English literature in the medieval and Elizabethan periods. His best-known works are: *The Medieval Stage* (1903); *The Elizabethan Stage* (1923); *William Shakespeare* (1930).

Changeling, The (1622)
A poetic tragedy by ▷ Thomas Middleton and ▷ William Rowley. Rowley seems in fact to have been responsible for the comic subplot, the value of which is contested; the play is sometimes produced without it, since the connection between the two plots has in the past been considered loose. The main plot, by Middleton, concerns the murder by ▷ Beatrice-Joanna of her prospective husband, Alonso de Piracquo, so that she can marry another man. To execute the

murder she employs one of her admirers, the servant ▷ De Flores, a man who physically revolts her, as if by employing such a man she could herself remain free of the guilt and horror of the crime. Instead, De Flores insists that they are now partners and equals in the sin of bloodshed, and blackmails her into becoming his mistress. The play is one of the most imaginative and individualistic in English after ▷ Shakespeare; it is written in sober, forceful ▷ blank verse that is one of the finest late ▷ Jacobean examples of this medium. The main plot is taken from *God's Revenge against Murther* by John Reynolds. The combination of death, sexual desire and madness makes *The Changeling* an important text for ▷ psychoanalytical criticism.

Chapbooks

The name for a kind of cheap literature which flourished from the 16th to the 18th centuries, after which they were replaced by other forms. They were so called because they were sold by 'chapmen' or travelling dealers. Their contents consisted commonly of traditional romances retold, often from the French, in crude form: ▷ *Bevis of Hampton, Guy of Warwick, Till Eulenspiegel,* ▷ *Doctor Faustus* are examples. Some of them, such as *Dick Whittington*, about the poor boy who ends up as Lord Mayor of London, have survived as children's stories to the present day, and are often the theme of Christmas ▷ pantomines.

Chapman, George (?1559–?1634)

Poet and dramatist. As a poet he is particularly famous for one of the best-known translations of ▷ Homer's ▷ *Odyssey* and ▷ *Iliad*. It is, however, a very free translation, expressing more of Chapman himself, as an Elizabethan intellectual with strong philosophical interests characteristic of his time, than of the spirit of the ancient Greek poet. He saw the epics as heroic exemplifications of moral greatness, in accordance with ▷ Stoic ethical categories much later than Homer. In his conception, the great man had strong passions but also strong pride which raised him above the corrupting influences of society; on the other hand, this passion and pride had to be tempered by philosophical fortitude and discipline if they were not to be self-destructive. The dramatic conflicts implied in this view of Homer dominate Chapman's tragedies (1603–31): ▷ *The Tragedy of Bussy d'Ambois*; *The Conspiracy and Tragedy of Charles Duke of Byron*; *The Revenge of Bussy d'Ambois*; and *Caesar and Pompey*. Of these the first is acknowledged to be the

finest. All of them contain fine passages, and none is without fairly serious imperfections. Bussy is a magnificent portrayal of the heroic man who dominates his morally mean environment but cannot control his passions; in *The Revenge*, Clermont, his brother, is a less successful example of the man of tempered passion and stoical calm. Chapman also wrote eight comedies, including ▷ *May Day*, and he completed the narrative poem ▷ *Hero and Leander*, left unfinished by ▷ Christopher Marlowe.

Bib: Bradbrook, M. C., *George Chapman*; Ide, R. S., *Possessed with Greatness*; Braunmuller, A. R., *National Fictions: George Chapman's Major Tragedies*.

Characters, Theophrastian

In the early 17th century a form of ▷ essay devoted to the description of human and social types grew up, and collections of such essays were known as 'Characters'. The origin of the fashion is in the brief sketches by one character of another in the comedies of the time – *eg* those of ▷ Dekker and ▷ Jonson – and in the verse satires of such writers as ▷ Donne and ▷ Joseph Hall. The tone was always light and often satirical; as a literary form, Characters displaced the satirical ▷ pamphlet popular in the last decade of the 16th century and written by such men as ▷ Greene and ▷ Nashe. The basic pattern of the form was the *Characters* of the ancient Greek writer ▷ Theophrastus (3rd century BC); hence the designation 'Theophrastian'.

The two most famous collections were that of ▷ Sir Thomas Overbury – partly by other hands – published in 1614, and *Microcosmographie* by John Earle, published in 1628. The short and witty pieces also made them attractive literary exercises for ladies of the court, and both ▷ Cecily Bulstrode and ▷ Lady Frances Southwell wrote such 'characters'. The fashion continued, though it became less popular, throughout the 17th century and into the 18th. It was eventually superseded by the more elaborate and individualized studies by Addison and Steele in the *Spectator*, especially the De Coverley papers, and by the growth of the 18th-century novel.

Charlemagne (742–814)

King of the Franks, son of Pepin the Short and crowned emperor of the western world by Pope Leo III on Christmas Day 800. The subject of heroic legends and romances, including ▷ epics by ▷ Boiardo, ▷ Ariosto and ▷ Tasso, and *chansons de geste*, epic poems in Old French, of which the best known is the early 12th-century *Chanson de Roland*. Off the battlefield, he reformed Frankish law, introduced jury-courts and a new coinage, and furthered missionary work and monastic reform. Most important to English literature was the 'Carolingian Renaissance' of learning he established at court, led by the Northumbrian Alcuin, and imitated a century later by King Alfred.

Charles I

King of Great Britain and Ireland (1625–49). He had limited intellectual abilities, and the causes of religious and economic conflict were so strong during his reign that it ended in civil war, his defeat and his execution. Together with his wife, ▷ Henrietta Maria, he created around him a court of taste, refinement and distinction. His connoisseurship led to a fine collection of pictures, later dispersed by ▷ Oliver Cromwell, who sold them to obtain international currency. His patronage of the Flemish artist Van Dyck resulted in some highly flattering portraits that have done the king much good with posterity. His personal qualities, his tragic end and his nobility in its endurance were the basis of a strong sentimental, sometimes even a religious, devotion to his memory. For example, there are churches dedicated to Charles the Martyr in a few places (*eg* Tunbridge Wells) in Britain.

▷ Civil Wars.
Bib: Carlton, C., *Charles I*.

Charles II

King of Great Britain and Ireland (1660–85). The Restoration of the monarchy brought him back from exile after the ▷ Interregnum following the execution of his father, ▷ Charles I, in 1649. Politically unscrupulous, he was nonetheless one of the most intelligent kings in English history. His court was a centre of culture and wit as well as of moral licentiousness. His lack of scruple enabled him to raise the monarchy to a new pitch of popularity, in spite of the growing strength of Parliament and its increasing independence of royal authority. His was the last royal court in England to be a centre of cultural vitality.

▷ Cavalier Poets.
Bib: Fraser, A., *King Charles II*.

Chaste Maid in Cheapside, A (1613)

A comedy by ▷ Thomas Middleton. It is one of the ▷ 'citizen comedies' of the ▷ Jacobean period, with a characteristic theme of a merchant (Yellowhammer) scheming against Sir Walter Whorehound, a dissolute landed gentleman, so as to secure marriage with his daughter and entry into the landowning class, while Whorehound in turn tries to marry off his mistress to Yellowhammer's son and thereby gain Yellowhammer's money. These intrigues of the gentry and the citizenry against each other were a common theme of the comedies of the time. The play makes mock of both classes, and has a characteristic robustness in the way in which it uses the social ▷ satire at a deeper level than the merely topical relationships, so as to bring out basic types of human greed, vanity and lust, in the tradition of ▷ Ben Jonson's 'comedy of humours'.

▷ Humours, Comedy of.

Chaucer, Geoffrey (c 1340–1400)

Influential poet of the 14th century who occupies a privileged place in the history of English literary traditions because his work has been continuously transcribed, published, read and commented upon since his death.

He was the son of a London vintner, John Chaucer (1312–68), and served in the court of ▷ Edward III's son Lionel (later Duke of Clarence). In 1359 he was taken prisoner while fighting in France with Edward III, and ransomed. His wife, Phillipa de Roet, whom he married perhaps in 1366, was the sister of John of Gaunt's third wife, Katherine Swynford. Substantial records exist of Chaucer's career in royal service, as a member of the court and diplomat. He is first recorded as a member of the royal household in 1367 and he made several diplomatic journeys in France and Italy, which perhaps gave him the opportunity to gain access to the work of important 14th-century Italian writers (▷ Dante, ▷ Petrarch, ▷ Boccaccio). He was appointed controller of customs in the Port of London in 1374, was 'knight of the shire' of Kent in 1386 (*ie* represented Kent in the House of Commons), and was appointed clerk of the king's works in 1389 and then deputy forester of the king's forest at Petherton in Somerset in 1391. He returned to London for the last years of his life and was buried in Westminster Abbey. His tomb, erected some time later (1555?) gives the date of his death as 25 October 1400.

The upward mobility of Chaucer's family is clear not only from the professional life of Chaucer himself but also from that of his son Thomas, who married into the nobility and became one of the richest men in England at the time. Thomas's daughter, Alice, married William de la Pole, Duke of Suffolk, and their

grandson, John, Earl of Lincoln, was heir
designate to the throne of ▷ Richard III. We
may only speculate about the part Chaucer's
literary activities played in advancing his social
status and that of his family. Although more
records survive of Chaucer's professional life
than any other English writer of the time,
the records do not contain any references to
his literary labours. Thus, dating Chaucer's
literary works is an exercise in hypothesis and
depends largely on information provided in
Chaucer's own list of works, notably in the
prologue to the *Legend of Good Women*, and in
the prologue to the *Man of Law's Tale*.

Chaucer's literary work is notable for
its range and diversity. It explores the
possibilities of a number of different literary
genres, and includes dream-vision poems
(the *Book of the Duchess*, the *House of Fame*,
the *Parliament of Foulys*, the *Legend of Good
Women*), a classical love-tragedy (▷ *Troilus
and Criseyde*), story-collections (the *Legend
of Good Women* and ▷ *The Canterbury Tales*,
which itself encompasses a great range and
variety of genres), as well as shorter lyrical
texts, ▷ translations (of Boethius's *Consolation
of Philosophy* and probably the first part of the
English translation of the *Roman de la Rose*)
and scientific treatises (on the Astrolabe,
and the *Equatorie of the Planets*, which is now
generally accepted as Chaucer's work).

A distinctive feature of Chaucer's literary
work is that it engages not only with French
and Latin literary traditions but also with
the work of earlier and contemporary Italian
writers (notably Boccaccio). His work became
a reference point for later poets in English,
and is frequently discussed in terms which
suggest it played a founding role in the
establishment of an English literary tradition
– a point neatly underlined by the subsequent
establishment of Poet's Corner around
Chaucer's tomb in Westminster Abbey.
Bib: Benson, L., et al. (eds.), *The Riverside
Chaucer*; Boitani, P. and Mann, J. (eds.), *The
Cambridge Chaucer Companion*; Crow, M. C.,
and Olsen, C. C. (eds.), *Chaucer Life Records*.

Cheshire Cheese, The
A tavern off Fleet Street in London, and a
favourite resort of ▷ Ben Jonson, and, after it
was rebuilt, of Samuel Johnson (1709–84) and
Yeats (1865–1939), who liked to claim it as a
haunt. It still exists.

Chettle, Henry (1560–1607)
An Elizabethan playwright and printer
who collaborated with a number of his
contemporaries such as ▷ Drayton, and

is the sole author of a ▷ revenge drama,
Hoffman (1602). He is best remembered for
printing ▷ Robert Greene's famous attack of
▷ Shakespeare and ▷ Marlowe, *A Groatsworth
of Wit* (1595). He subsequently apologized
to Shakespeare in his *Kind-Heart's Dream*,
praising Shakespeare's 'uprightness of dealing'
and his 'honesty'.
Bib: Jenkins, H., *The Life and Works of
Henry Chettle*.

Children in the Wood (Babes in the Wood)
A Ballad (1593) well known for its story,
which is often retold in books of children's
fairy tales (▷ Children's books). It concerns
the plot of a wicked uncle to murder his little
nephew and niece, whose property he means
to seize. The hired murderers abandon the
children in the forest, where they perish and
the birds cover them over with leaves. The
wicked uncle is then punished by God, with
the loss of his son, his wealth and eventually
his life.

Children of St Paul's
▷ Paul's, Children of St.

Children's books
Until the 19th century, children were not
regarded as beings with their own kind of
experience and values, and therefore did
not have books written specially for their
entertainment. The literature available
to them included popular versions of old
romances, such as ▷ *Bevis of Hampton*,
and magical folk-tales, such as *Jack the
Giant-Killer*, which appeared in ▷ chapbooks.
Children also read such works as ▷ John
Bunyan's ▷ *Pilgrim's Progress*.
Bib: Wooden, W. W., *Children's Literature of
the English Renaissance*.

Chronicle Plays
▷ History Plays.

Church of England
The history of the Church of England is
closely bound up with the political and social
history of England.

The Church of England became independent
in 1534, when ▷ Henry VIII caused Parliament
to pass the ▷ Act of Supremacy that declared
him to be the 'Supreme Head of the English
Church and Clergy'. This action was political
rather than religious; Henry was conservative
in his religious beliefs, and reaffirmed
the traditional Catholic doctrines by his

Act of the Six Articles (1539). However, a ▷ Protestant party, influenced by the German reformer ▷ Martin Luther, had long been growing in England and was favoured by the Archbishop of Canterbury, ▷ Thomas Cranmer, and towards the end of his reign, Henry was influenced by his ▷ Puritan sixth wife, ▷ Katherine Parr. Under the boy king ▷ Edward VI, the Protestants seized power, and Catholic doctrine was modified by Cranmer's two Books of Common Prayer (▷ Common Prayer, The Book of). These changes were accompanied by the destruction of images and the covering up of holy wall-paintings in village churches; such actions, combined with the rapacity of the nobles who seized church money, were unpopular, and partly reconciled the nation to a return to the Catholic Church under ▷ Mary I. She too became unpopular owing to her persecution of Protestants, and her successor, ▷ Elizabeth I, attempted a compromise Settlement, by means of which she hoped to keep in the Church of England both the Catholics and the more extreme Protestants. She succeeded, in so far as her Settlement prevented religious conflict breaking into civil war during her reign.

The Roman Catholics were and remained a small minority, but during the first half of the 17th century the extreme Protestants (now known as the Puritans) grew in strength, especially in London and in the south and east. Their hostility to the monarchy and their dislike of religious direction by bishops led in the end to the ▷ Civil War and the overthrow of ▷ Charles I. Under the Protectorship of the Puritan ▷ Oliver Cromwell, the Church of England ceased to exist as a state religious organization, but in 1660 the monarchy and Church of England were restored, and Puritans were excluded from the Church, from political rights and from attendance at the universities of Oxford and Cambridge. From this time, the Puritans (increasingly called ▷ Dissenters or Nonconformists) set up their own churches.

Churchyard, Thomas (c 1520–1604)
Poet. Churchyard's career combined a marginal position at court with a near-successful attempt at professional authorship, and although his work is not well known at the present time, he was acknowledged as important by the younger ▷ Elizabethan poets such as ▷ Spenser and ▷ Ralegh. Indeed, Spenser makes Churchyard 'Palemon' in his *Colin Clout*, characterized by his long career as a poet. Churchyard began his court associations as ▷ Surrey's page and then served in several battles on the continent; these exploits were later to form the basis of his *Generall Rehearsall of Warres* (1579). He wrote a considerable amount of panegyric poetry, probably in pursuit of a perpetually elusive preferment; for example, *The Worthiness of Wales* (1587) celebrates the mythic genealogy of the Tudor dynasty (▷ Tudor Myth). His poetry is included in ▷ *Tottel's Miscellany* (1557), while his most well received work, 'The Legend of Shore's Wife', appears in ▷ *A Mirror For Magistrates* (1563 edition).
Bib: Chalmers, G., *Churchyard's Chips*.

Cicero, Marcus Tullius (106–43 BC)
Roman statesman, and writer on rhetoric, politics and philosophy. Politically he is famous for his vigorous resistance to the conspiracy of Catiline against the government of the Republic. This is the theme of ▷ Ben Jonson's tragedy ▷ *Catiline*, of which Cicero is the hero. Cicero's mastery of eloquence in his various writings, and his prestige in ancient Rome, caused him to be much admired in the ▷ Middle Ages and afterwards. Cicero's *Somnium Scipionis* (*Dream of Scipio*) influenced ▷ Chaucer's *Parliament of Foulys*, and in the 16th century the growing body of English prose writers such as ▷ Roger Ascham tended to take as a model either the rolling, musical sentences of Cicero or, by contrast, the terse pointed sentences of ▷ Seneca.

Citizen comedies
Comedies, especially between 1600 and 1640, using contemporary London and its middle class as their setting, *eg* ▷ Ben Jonson's ▷ *Bartholomew Fair* (1614), ▷ Thomas Middleton's ▷ *A Chaste Maid in Cheapside* (1611), and ▷ Philip Massinger's ▷ *The City Madam* (1632). The energy and anarchic activity of these plays seem to align with ▷ Mikhail Bakhtin's later evocation of the carnivalesque.
Bib: Gibbons, B., *Jacobean City Comedy*; Leggatt, A., *Citizen Comedy in the Age of Shakespeare*.

City Madam, The (1632)
A comedy by ▷ Philip Massinger. It is about a London merchant whose wife and daughters grow outrageously extravagant in their tastes. To teach them a lesson, the father, Sir John Frugal, temporarily retires from the world and leaves his affairs in the hands of his hypocritically humble brother, Luke. Once he has power in his hands, Luke throws off his pretence, becomes arrogant and harsh, and

humiliates his nieces and sister-in-law. Like so many comedies of the age *The City Madam* ridicules the extravagance and pretentiousness of the new urban bourgeoisie.
▷ Capitalism.

City of Destruction, The
In ▷ Bunyan's ▷ *Pilgrim's Progress* the town from which the pilgrim, Christian, flees to the ▷ Celestial City, *ie* Heaven. The City of Destruction stands for the world divorced from spiritual values, doomed to the destruction that is to overcome all merely material creation.

City Wit, The (1629)
A fast-moving, intensely theatrical ▷ citizen comedy of manners by ▷ Richard Brome, in which the cash-nexus provides the driving force behind the plot. The play dramatizes the recovery of the fortunes and family ties of a resourceful young London prodigal, Crasy, assisted by his wily servant Jeremy.

Civil Wars, The
Enlgand has had two recognized periods of Civil War:

1 The more important, in the 17th century, is also called the Great Rebellion. It was fought between the king (▷ Charles I) and Parliament, and divided into the First Civil War (1642–6), ending with the Parliamentary victory at Naseby (1645) and the capitulation of Oxford (1646), the royalist capital. The Second Civil War (1648–51) also ended with Parliamentary victory, this time over the Scots, who had been the allies of Parliament in the First Civil War, but took the king's side in the Second. The issues were complicated; simplified, the economic interests of the urban middle classes coincided with their religious (▷ Puritan) ideology and conflicted with the traditional economic interests of the Crown, correspondingly allied with Anglican religious belief.

2 The other occurred in the 15th century and is usually known as the Wars of the Roses.

Clarendon, Edward Hyde, Earl of (1609–74)
Statesman and historian; author of *The True Historical Narrative of the Rebellion and Civil Wars in England* about the ▷ Civil War, during which he had supported ▷ King Charles I. The published history combines two separate manuscripts: a history written 1646–8 while the events were fresh in his mind, and an ▷ autobiography written

between 1668 and 1670 in exile and without the aid of documents. In consequence, Books I–VII are superior in accuracy to Books VIII–XV, with the exception of Book IX, containing material written in 1646. Clarendon's history is a literary classic because of its series of portraits of the participants in the war. His book is a notable contribution to the rise of the arts of ▷ biography and autobiography in England in the 17th century and contributed to the development which in the 18th century produced the first English novels.

As a statesman, Hyde was at first a leading opponent of Charles I, but his strongly Anglican faith led him to take the royalist side shortly before the war. He became one of the king's chief advisers. He followed the royal court into exile, and was Lord Chancellor and ▷ Charles II's chief minister at the Restoration (1660). The king's brother, the future James II, married his daughter, so that he became grandfather of Queen Mary II and Queen Anne. He was made the scapegoat for the unpopularity of Charles II's government in its early years, however, and was driven into exile in 1667. He lived the remainder of his life in France.
▷ Histories and Chronicles.
Bib: Huehns, G., *Selections from the History of the Rebellion and the Life*; Wormald, B. H. G., *Clarendon, Politics, History and Rebellion*; Firth, C., *Essays, Historical and Literary*.

Classical education and English literature
Classical education is based on the study of the 'classics', *ie* the literature of ancient Greece and Rome, principally from ▷ Homer to the great Latin poets and prose writers (*eg* ▷ Virgil, ▷ Ovid, ▷ Cicero) of the 1st century BC – 1st century AD. Latin is more closely bound up with western history and culture, and is the easier language for English speakers to study; consequently it has been more widely used in schools than Greek, and it has been studied at earlier stages of education. Roman literary culture was, however, based on that of the Greeks.

The movement known as the ▷ Renaissance started in Italy in the 14th century; it was, first of all, the enthusiastic rediscovery and collection by scholars of ancient classical texts, and the development of new and more accurate methods of studying them. It did not long remain merely a scholarly movement; the scholars influenced the writers and artists, and these in turn, in the 15th and 16th centuries, aroused enthusiasm in the upper classes of all western Europe. The Renaissance practice of studying the classics for their own sake and not under the direction of the Church brought the discovery of a new principle of growth in literature and the other arts. Knowledge of the classics became a principle of discrimination: those who did not have it were by implication more primitive in their development and often from a lower social class.

The Renaissance first seriously affected England early in the 16th century. The pattern for classical education in the national public schools and the more local grammar schools was formed by such men as John Colet (?1467–1519), High Master of St Paul's School. ▷ Sir Thomas More, author of *Utopia* and Chancellor to ▷ Henry VIII, gave prestige to ▷ humanist values in the royal court. ▷ Erasmus visited England from Holland and made friends among these and other English humanists.

But ancient Greece, and Rome in its greatest days, were pagan; their values were social rather than religious. Thus there was the possibility of divided loyalty between the Rome that was the starting-point of so much European art, thought and politics, and the later Rome that was the centre of the originally Hebrew and very unclassical religion of Christianity. The Roman Catholic Church in the 15th and early 16th centuries at first responded to the humanists favourably, even when they were critical of its traditions and practices. The thought and outlook of pagan Greece and Rome nevertheless did not agree well with the ancient Hebrew roots of Christianity as shown in the Old and New Testaments of the Bible. The 16th-century Protestant ▷ Reformation was partly the outcome of humanist criticism of the Church, but it was also a return to the Word of God as the Bible displayed it. Thus from 1560 to 1660, much English imaginative writing has two aspects: the poets ▷ Edmund Spenser and ▷ John Milton, for example, have a Protestant aspect, which is biblical and Hebraic, and a classical aspect, strongly inspired by the classical Renaissance. The poet ▷ Ben Jonson is much more classical than Protestant, while ▷ George Herbert is strongly religious in the moderately Protestant, Anglican tradition, and despises the kind of subject matter (*eg* 'classical pastoral') that Ben Jonson accepted. Both, however, had an equally classical education.

Another division arose from the difference between native literary traditions, which continued in their non-classical character, and the classical qualities and standards that many writers felt should permeate and regulate the native tradition. This division did not correspond to religious differences: the most Latin of all English poets is the ▷ Puritan John Milton. ▷ Shakespeare is well known for his indifference to the classical 'rules' that critics like ▷ Sir Philip Sidney thought necessary to good drama, while his contemporary, Ben Jonson, favoured them, though not slavishly.

Classical and native traditions of literature rivalled and nourished each other until the middle of the 17th century, and so did Protestant biblical and secular classical philosophies of life. But after the Restoration in 1660, religious passions declined and sceptical rationalism began to take their place.

Classical mythology

Ancient Greek mythology can be divided between the 'Divine Myths' and the 'Heroic Myths'.

The divine myths are known in differing versions from the works of various Greek poets, of whom the most notable are ▷ Homer and Hesiod. Hesiod explained the origin of the world in terms of a marriage between Earth (Ge or Gaea) and Sky (Uranus). Their children were the 12 Titans: Oceanus, Crius, Iapetus, Theia, Rhea, Mnemosyne, Phoebe, Tethys, Themis, Coeus, Hyperion, and Cronos. Cronos overthrew his father, and he and Rhea (or Cybele) became the parents of the 'Olympian gods', so called from their association with the sacred mountain Olympus. The Olympians, in their turn, overthrew Cronos and the other Titans.

The chief Olympians were Zeus and his queen Hera. The other gods and goddesses were the offspring of either, but as Zeus was usually at war with Hera, they were not the joint parents. They seem to have been seen as male and female aspects of the sky; their quarrels were the causes of bad weather and cosmic disturbances. The principal offspring of Zeus were Apollo, Artemis, Athene, Aphrodite (sometimes represented as a daughter of Uranus out of the sea), Dionysus, Hermes and Ares. Zeus had three sisters, Hestia, Demeter (the corn goddess) and Hera (also his wife), and two brothers, Poseidon who ruled the sea, and Hades who ruled the underworld. In the 3rd century BC the Olympian gods were adopted by the Romans, who used the Latin names more commonly known to later European writers. Uranus, Apollo and some others remained the same. Gaea became Tellus; Cronos = Saturn; Zeus = Jupiter (or Jove); Hera = Juno; Athene = Minerva; Artemis

= Diana; Hermes = Mercury; Ares = Mars; Hephaestus = Vulcan; Aphrodite = Venus (and her son Eros = Cupid); Demeter = Ceres; Poseidon = Neptune. There were numerous minor deities such as nymphs and satyrs in both Greek and Roman pantheons.

The Olympian deities mingled with men, and rivalled one another in deciding human destinies. They concerned themselves particularly with the destinies of the heroes, *ie* those men, sometimes partly divine by parentage, who were remarkable for the kinds of excellence that are especially valued in early societies, such as strength (Heracles), or cunning ($\triangleright$ Odysseus). Each region of Greece had its native heroes, though the greatest heroes were famous in legend all over Greece. The most famous of all was Heracles (in Latin, Hercules), who originated in Thebes. Other leading examples of the hero are: Theseus (Athens); Sisyphus and Bellerophon (Corinth); Perseus (Argolis); the Dioscuri, *ie* Castor and Pollux (Laconia); Oedipus (Thebes); Achilles (Thessaly); Jason (Thessaly); Orpheus (Thrace). Like the Greek gods and goddesses, the Greek heroes were adopted by Roman legend, sometimes with a change of name. The minor hero of Greek legend, $\triangleright$ Aeneas, was raised to be the great ancestral hero of the Romans, and they had other heroes of their own, such as Romulus, the founder of Rome, and his brother Remus.

After the downfall of the Roman Empire of the West, classical deities and heroes achieved a kind of popular reality through the plants and zodiacal signs which are named after them, and which, according to astrologers, influence human fates. Thus in $\triangleright$ Chaucer's *The Knight's Tale* (from $\triangleright$ *The Canterbury Tales*), Mars, Venus, Diana and Saturn occur, and owe their force in the poem as much to medieval astrology as to classical legend. Otherwise their survival has depended chiefly on their importance in the works of the classical poets, such as Homer, Hesiod, $\triangleright$ Virgil and $\triangleright$ Ovid, who have meant so much to European culture. In Britain, important poets translated and thus helped to 'naturalize' the Greek and Latin poems; *eg* $\triangleright$ Gavin Douglas in the 16th century and Dryden (1631–1700) in the 17th century translated Virgil's $\triangleright$ *Aeneid*; $\triangleright$ Chapman in the 16th century and Pope (1688–1744) in the 18th century translated Homer's epics. In the 16th and 17th centuries, poets used major and minor classical deities to adorn and elevate poems intended chiefly as gracious entertainment, and occasionally they added deities of their own invention.

Claudius
King of Denmark in $\triangleright$ Shakespeare's $\triangleright$ *Hamlet*. He mounts the throne after secretly murdering his brother, Hamlet's father, and he marries Hamlet's mother. At the opening of the play, Hamlet does not know that his father's sudden death was due to murder, but he is disgusted by the situation on three counts: Claudius's marriage with his sister-in-law is technically illegal according to the law of the time whilst indicating lack of due grief on the part of his mother, and Hamlet himself should naturally have succeeded to the throne, although the law of succession was elective in Denmark.

Claudius differs from most evil men portrayed by Shakespeare and his contemporaries. We hear of the murder at second hand, from the Ghost; Claudius's own confession of wickedness in the chapel (III. iii) excites the audience's compassion as well as their indignation, since his remorse appears so evident; his conspiracies against his nephew may be in self-defence, since he knows that Hamlet is plotting revenge. The fact that Claudius is not self-evidently a cruel tyrant is one of the features that differentiates *Hamlet* from other $\triangleright$ revenge tragedies of the period: dramatically, it helps to make intelligible Hamlet's doubt and hesitancy in carrying out his revenge.

Cleopatra of Egypt (51–30 BC)
The last of the dynasty of the Ptolemies. The chief authority for the facts of her life is the Greek historian $\triangleright$ Plutarch (1st century AD) in his life of Antony. She was joint sovereign of Egypt with her younger brother Ptolemy Dionysus. Driven out of Egypt, she withdrew to Syria, where she met the Roman general $\triangleright$ Julius Caesar while she was preparing to counter-attack. Caesar took her side, re-established her on the throne and made her his mistress. When Caesar was assassinated, she became the mistress of Caesar's ally Mark Antony, until they were jointly defeated by Caesar's nephew and adopted son, Octavianus. She then committed suicide. Cleopatra's relationship with Antony is the subject of $\triangleright$ Shakespeare's $\triangleright$ *Antony and Cleopatra*, while $\triangleright$ Samuel Daniel's verse tragedy, *Cleopatra* (1594), has as its subject her dealings with Octavian after Antony's death. A destroyed play on the same theme by $\triangleright$ Fulke Greville (*Antony and Cleopatra*) also existed.

Clifford, Lady Anne (1590–1676)
One of the most accomplished and fascinating diarists of her age. Lady Anne Clifford

was the only child of George Clifford,
third Earl of Cumberland and Margaret
Russell. However, on his death in 1605 it
was discovered that her father had left the
family estates to his nearest surviving male
relative. Much of Lady Anne's life was
devoted to regaining what she considered to
be her rightful inheritance, even though both
her husband and ▷ King James I opposed
her demands. This marriage, to Richard
Sackville, Earl of Dorset, was unhappy, but
she fared little better in her second attempt at
wedlock, to Philip Herbert, Earl of Pembroke
and Montgomery; she was widowed for a
second time in 1649. At last, in 1643, she
gained possession of her lands and began
systematically rebuilding and refurbishing
each of her six castles. During the ▷ Civil
War she was a staunch supporter of the
Royalist cause and continued to prove her
strength of character by resisting a three-year
siege by the Parliamentary forces. After 1653
she settled down to write her own and her
family's history, and this work, *Great Books*,
together with her diaries and letters, provides
us with one of the most lively and dramatic
▷ autobiographies by a Renaissance woman.
Lady Anne was a learned woman who had
been tutored by ▷ Samuel Daniel and
whose personal chaplain at Wilton had been
▷ George Herbert. She was celebrated in
verse by ▷ Aemilia Lanyer. When she died
at the age of 86 Lady Anne was a wealthy
matriarch, for not only had she inherited her
own estate, but she had also benefited from
the rich jointures acquired at the deaths of
her two detested husbands.
Bib: Sackville-West, V. (ed.), *The Diary of
Lady Anne Clifford*; Graham, E. et al. (eds.),
*Her Own Life: Autobiographical Writings by
Seventeenth-century Englishwomen*; Fraser, A.,
The Weaker Vessel.

**Clinton, Lady Elizabeth, Countess of
Lincoln (c 1574–1630)**
Writer on motherhood. One of the earliest
female exponents of breast-feeding. Lady
Elizabeth had not fed any of her own 18
children herself, but regretted this later and
wrote *The Countess of Lincoln's Nursery* (1622)
confessing her mistake. The treatise advises
all women, but especially the Countess's
daughter-in-law, to breast-feed so that they
might follow the 'Ordinance of God' and
strengthen the mother-baby bond. This
attitude should be seen not simply as an
impassioned plea by a mother denied her
'natural' rights, but as part of a theoretical
debate in which ▷ humanists and reformers

advocated the necessity of breast-feeding (for
example, ▷ Erasmus in 'The New Mother'
[1523]). Moreover, ▷ Thomas Lodge's
dedicatory poem reinforces the theoretical
nature of the work.
▷ Grymeston, Elizabeth; Leigh, Dorothy.
Bib: Travitsky, B. (ed.), *A Paradise of Women*.

Clout, Colin
▷ Colin Clout.

Colin Clout
The name adopted by ▷ Edmund Spenser
in his ▷ pastoral sequence ▷ *The Shepherd's
Calendar* and his ▷ allegorical work *Colin
Clout's Come Home Again* (1594), written to
describe his visit to London and the court
in 1589–91. The name became something of
a code-word amongst the Spenserian poets,
who, in emulation of Spenser, would refer to
'Colin' and adopt their own pastoral personae.

Collins, An
Devotional poet. Little is known about her
life except that which is revealed in her
one extant work, the ▷ autobiographical
Divine Songs and Meditations (1653). It can
therefore be assumed that she belonged to
a reasonably well-off family, that she had
suffered serious ill health since childhood
and had, consequently, not been engaged in
the usual female occupations or been able to
have children. She was certainly antagonistic
to the more radical forms of ▷ Puritantism,
but it is disputed as to whether she was pro- or
anti-Calvinist (see G. Greer (ed.), *Kissing the
Rod* (1988) and E. Graham et al. (eds.), *Her
Own Life* (1989)). Her poems are spiritual in
nature, drawing upon biblical imagery and
focusing upon the torments and respites of the
Christian soul on earth.
▷ Calvin, John.
Bib: Hobby, E., *Virtue of Necessity*.

Colonialism
Although it is known that colonies were
established in early history, the term is now
taken to refer to nationalistic appropriation
of land dating from the ▷ Renaissance
period in the west, and is usually understood
as perpetrated on black or coloured non-
Europeans in Asia, Africa, Australasia, the
Americas or the Caribbean by the white
western European powers. Colonialism does
not have to imply formal annexation, however.
Colonial status involves the imposition of
decisions by one people upon another, where
the economy or political structure has been
brought under the overwhelming influence
of another country. Western colonialism had

its heyday from 1450 to 1900. It began in the Renaissance with three voyages of discovery; the new territories were annexed for their material resources and for the scope they offered to missionary efforts to extend the power of the Church.

Works from ▷ Shakespeare's ▷ *The Tempest* to Joseph Conrad's (1857–1924) *Heart of Darkness* (1902) demonstrate the struggle to determine the meaning of colonial power.
▷ Race.
Bib: Memmi, A., *The Colonizer and the Colonized*; Said, E., *Orientalism*; Spivack, G. C., *In Other Worlds*.

Comedy
▷ Humours, Comedy of; Citizen Comedies; Commedia dell'Arte.

Comedy of Errors, The (1592)
An early comedy and ▷ Shakespeare's shortest play, based on ▷ Plautus's *Menaechmi*. The elements of ▷ farce and confusion in the original are enhanced in Shakespeare's taut play – it observes the neo-classical unities of time, place and action – by the addition of a second pair of twins, the Dromios, servants to the lost and separated Ephesian and Syracusan Antipholi. Shakespeare further departs from his source by foregrounding the marriage of Adriana and the Ephesian Antipholus with reference, imaginatively, to St Paul's view on marriage and sexual identity. The play is full of vitality and supersedes the reductive and mercenary view of society propounded in its classical source.

Commedia dell'Arte
A kind of Italian comedy, developed in the 16th century, in which the plot was written but the dialogue was improvised by the actors. Certain characters regularly recurred in these plays, and by the 18th century they were adopted in England (by the way of France) and became a part of the English puppet shows (*eg* ▷ Punch and Judy) and of the ▷ pantomime tradition. Such characters, anglicized, include Harlequin, his mistress Columbine, Pantaloon, Punch.

Common Prayer, The Book of
The first *Book of Common Prayer* was prepared under the supervision of ▷ Archbishop Cranmer and issued in 1549 to meet the needs of the ▷ Church of England for services and prayers in the vernacular. It is of great importance as a work of literature, for Cranmer succeeded in combining the plainness and directness of English with the dignity and sonority of Latin. Prayer Book language became a familiar and formative influence in speech and writing second only in importance to the Bible itself. There were revisions in 1552 and 1559. The Prayer Book authorized in 1662 was substantially the 1559 revision. A fairly extensive revision was blocked by Parliament in 1928. There are now alternative forms of the various services in use.

Communism
Communism may be interpreted in two ways: firstly, the older, imprecise sense covering various philosophies of the common ownership of property; and secondly, the relatively precise interpretation understood by the Marx-Leninist Communist Parties throughout the world. It is the first form which is relevant to ▷ Renaissance studies.

The older philosophies derive especially from the Greek philosopher ▷ Plato. His ▷ *Republic* proposes that society should be divided into classes according to differences of ability instead of differences of wealth and birth; the state is to provide for the needs of all and thereby abolish rivalries and inequalities between rich and poor; children are to be educated by the state, and women are to have equal rights, opportunities and training with men. In England, one of the most famous disciples of Plato is ▷ Sir Thomas More in his ▷ *Utopia* (1516). More's prescriptions are similar to Plato's in many respects, but though he also requires equal opportunity and training for men, he keeps the monogamous family intact, whereas Plato wanted a community of wives and children to be brought up by the state. Both Plato and More require for their schemes an all-powerful state in the charge of an intellectual aristocracy; what we would call 'enlightened totalitarianism'.

In practical experience, the vows of poverty taken by members of orders of monks and friars and the communal ownership of property in such communities may have kept alight for people in general the ideal of the freedom of the spirit attainable by the renunciation of selfish material ambitions and competition. Protestant sectarian beliefs emphasizing the equality of souls led to such an abortive communistic enterprise as that of the ▷ Levellers in the ▷ Interregnum.

Companies, Joint Stock
Companies whose profits are distributed among the shareholders. They began in the 16th century and largely superseded the older

'regulated company' whose members traded each on his own account and combined only for common protection. The greatest of the regulated companies was the Merchant Adventurers, founded in the 15th century; the greatest of the joint stock companies was the East India Company, founded in 1600.
▷ Capitalism; Colonialism.

Complaint
A term used to refer to poems (in a variety of forms), usually in the voice of a first-person speaker, which lament the vicissitudes of life, especially the pangs of disappointed or unrequited love. Used by medieval French poets, it appears to have been employed first by ▷ Chaucer, who intercalated complaints within larger narrative contexts, but who also produced a number of individual complaint poems. In Renaissance literature, ▷ Spenser's ▷ *The Shepherd's Calendar* provides a good example of a complaint.

Compleat Angler, The (1653)
A discourse on the sport of fishing (in full, *The Compleat Angler, or the Contemplative Man's Recreation*) by ▷ Izaak Walton, first published in 1653; its 5th edition has a continuation by Charles Cotton (1630–87) and came out in 1676. The book has been described as perhaps the only handbook of art and craft to rank as literature. This is because Walton combines his practical instruction with digressions about his personal tastes and opinions, and sets it in a direct, fresh description of the English countryside which may be contrasted with the artificial pastoralism that had hitherto been characteristic of natural description. The book has the form of a dialogue mainly between Piscator (Fisherman) and Venator (Hunter), which takes place on the banks of the River Lea near London. Cotton's continuation is transferred to the banks of the River Dove between Derbyshire and Staffordshire. Throughout the text, Walton also relates moral issues to the political events of his day and, while not strictly ▷ allegorical, *The Compleat Angler* does include numerous social references.
Bib: Bevan, J., *Izaak Walton's The Compleat Angler*.

Comus (1634)
The name now given to the ▷ masque written by ▷ John Milton and performed at Ludlow Castle in 1634. The work's original title was simply *A Maske, presented at Ludlow Castle, 1634, before the Earl of Bridgewater,* *Lord President of Wales.* This title stresses the important features of any masque – its occasional quality, and the names of those who either witnessed or took part in the masque. Music for the masque was composed by ▷ Henry Lawes and principal parts were taken by the children of the Earl of Bridgewater. The masque endeavours to demonstrate the triumph of virtue and chastity over luxury and sensual excess, although generations of readers and critics have found it easier to identify with the anti-hero Comus, rather than with the 'Lady' who opposes his arguments.
Bib: Editions include: Diekhoff, J. S. (ed.), *A Maske at Ludlow*.

Conceit
A conceit is a ▷ metaphor or simile that initially appears improbable, but which forces the reader to acknowledge the comparison even though it is exceedingly far-fetched. The classic example comes from ▷ John Donne's poem 'A Valediction: forbidding Mourning' where he compares himself and his mistress to 'stiff twin compasses'. Comparing two lovers to a mathematical instrument at first seems strange, but the aptness is derived from the fact that even when one partner (foot of the compasses/lover) moves away from the other, they are always joined together (at the hinge of the compasses/in their hearts). This intellectual delight in complicated parallels originates in the ▷ Petrarchan influence upon ▷ Elizabethan poetry and it became an important aspect of ▷ sonnets and of ▷ metaphysical verse.

Condell, Henry (d 1627)
▷ Heming, John.

Confessio Amantis
A story-collection about love and related subjects, in octosyllabic couplets, written by ▷ John Gower in the late 1380s. A confession of a lover (Amans) to Venus's priest (Genius) provides the occasion for the collection; the priest tells exemplary stories to help the lover analyze his own behaviour. Seven of the eight books of the *Confessio Amantis* are organized as illustrations of one of the Seven Deadly Sins: Book VII is devoted to advice about the government of self and society. The framework and contents of Gower's work draw together traditions of courtly love literature and of religious treatises on the processes of penitence. The collection concludes with the healing of the lover as the penitential process is completed.

The stories themselves are drawn largely from ▷ Ovid, from medieval versions of the Troy story and from the Old Testament, but large amounts of bookish lore (such as the history of religion, the history of culture) are encompassed in the confessional frame, thus giving the work an encyclopaedic quality. There is some overlap between the stories in the *Confessio Amantis* and those retold in various contexts in ▷ Chaucer's work (notably the stories of Florent, Ceyx and Alcione, Constance, Phoebus and the Crow, Pyramus and Thisbe), and the early version of the text contains complimentary references to Chaucer's work. Undoubtedly each writer knew and read the work of the other.

The Prologue and Epilogue of the *Confessio Amantis* place it in the context of universal and contemporary history. The narrator begins by suggesting that the work was commissioned by ▷ Richard II and concludes with remarks about its value for the English king and the English realm. Although the first version dates from the later 1380s, the opening and closing sections were revised to accommodate the changing political scene in England and the work was rededicated to Henry of Lancaster (later ▷ Henry IV). The *Confessio Amantis* was translated into Portuguese, probably in the late 14th century.

▷ Henry IV; Richard III; *Pericles*.
Bib: Macaulay, G. C. (ed.), *The English Works of John Gower*; Minnis, A. J. (ed.), *Gower's Confessio Amantis: Responses and Reassessments*.

Congregationalism
Congregationalists differ from other Christians not so much on credal beliefs as on their ordering of church life. For them, Christ rules primarily through the local congregation rather than through the Pope or bishops. In the 16th century, followers of this belief were called ▷ Brownists, after their founder, Robert Browne; by the mid-17th century they were known as Independents. It was in this period that the movement had special importance; it became widely influential amongst the Parliamentary opponents of ▷ Charles I and numbered ▷ Oliver Cromwell among its supporters. With other Dissenters they went through hard times after the Restoration but survived to be part of the Evangelical Revival.

Constable, Henry (1562–1613)
Poet. Constable's early career appeared to promise him the fruits of preferment at ▷ Elizabeth I's court; he received the ▷ patronage of ▷ Walsingham and ▷ the Earl of Essex, and was the friend of ▷ Sir Philip Sidney and Sir John Harington, as well as acquainted with two court ladies, ▷ Mary Sidney and Penelope Rich (to both of whom he dedicated sonnets). However, in the late 1580s he converted to ▷ Catholicism and left the English court for France, where he was to reside until the accession of ▷ James I in 1603. At first he was well received by the king, but on the discovery of incriminating letters he was imprisoned in the Tower in 1604. Constable was released the same year, but in 1610 he returned to the continent and died in Liège. He is mainly remembered for his sonnet sequence *Diana* (1592), which is spiritual in tone and stylistically influenced by ▷ Ronsard.
Bib: Grundy, J., *The Poems of Henry Constable*.

Cooper's Hill (1642)
▷ Denham, Sir John.

Copernicus (1473–1543)
This was the Latinized form of surname of Nicolas Koppérnik, a Polish astronomer. In *De Revolutionibus orbium coelestium* (*Concerning the Revolutions of the Heavenly Spheres*) (1543) he expounded for the first time since classical times the belief that the earth and other planets move around the sun. This was contrary to the hitherto accepted theory of the Egyptian astronomer ▷ Ptolemy, according to which the earth was the centre of the solar system. The Ptolemaic system suited the traditional Christian conception of the universe and the place of man within it – it is still assumed, for instance, in ▷ Milton's epic of the Creation, ▷ *Paradise Lost* – but the Copernican theory caused little scandal since at the time it was regarded merely as an ingenious hypothesis. Only when ▷ Galileo claimed its validity on demonstrable grounds after the invention of his new telescope, did the Church condemn the theory outright in 1616 and require Galileo to repudiate his findings.

Copyright, The law of
The right of writers, artists and musicians to refuse reproduction of their works. The right is now established law in every civilized country. The first copyright law in England was passed under Queen Anne in 1709. Before this, it was possible for publishers to publish books without the author's permission, and without allowing him or her any profits from sale, a practice very common during the lifetime of ▷ Shakespeare.
▷ Shakespeare's plays; Stationers' Register.

Coriolanus (?1608)
A ▷ tragedy by ▷ Shakespeare about a
legendary Roman hero (5th century BC).
Shakespeare took the story from the *Lives* by
▷ Plutarch translated into English by ▷ Sir
Thomas North. A war is being waged between
Rome and the neighbouring city of Corioli,
capital city of the Volscians. The hero of the
play, Caius Marcius, wins the title Coriolanus
for his heroism against the enemy. But Rome
is morally at war within herself: the arrogant
patricians (aristocrats) despise the plebs, or
common people, who in turn are factious and
disorderly. Coriolanus differs from his fellow
patricians only in being still prouder than they
are, in that he cannot stoop to flatter the plebs
for their votes. They succeed in expelling him
from the city, whereupon he allies himself
with the Volscians and returns to destroy it.
His mother, Volumnia, who embodies the
qualities of the arrogant patricians and has
herself bred her son to value his pride above
all, succeeds in deterring him; he is then
assassinated by the Volscians as a traitor.
The tragedy has peculiar interest for its study
of social influence on the individual, and it
is difficult to determine whether society, as
embodied by the mob/group, is unthinking or
reasonable. It is less popular than some other
tragedies by Shakespeare, but it is certainly
among the finest of his plays.

Corombona, Vittoria
The tragic female protagonist of ▷ *The White
Devil* by ▷ John Webster. Her resilience in
the face of adversity combined with her lack
of sexual and moral integrity render her a
fascinating and emancipated character. This is
evident particularly in the famous trial scene
when she emerges as morally no more guilty
than her accusers, who use the full panoply
of the law to pursue their spurious ends
against her.

Cortegiano, Il (The Courtier)
▷ Castiglione, Baldassare.

Cotton, Priscilla (d 1664)
Pamphleteer. Cotton was a ▷ Quaker,
who was imprisoned in Exeter gaol for
preaching with her compatriot, Mary Cole.
She is noteworthy as the first woman to
write in defence of women preaching in *To
the Priests and the People of England* (1655).
This represented a general trend amongst
▷ Puritan women to speak openly of their
faith, since the authority to preach (God's)
was higher than that which forbade them to
do so (man's). Cotton's other works provide

similar forthright defences of women and
Quakers (*As I was in the Prison House* (1656),
A Briefe Description (1659) and *A Visitation of
Love* (1661)).
Bib: H. Hinds in Cerasano, S. P. and
Wynne-Davies, M. (eds.), *Gloriana's Face*.

Counter-Reformation
A movement in the Catholic Church to
counter the ▷ Protestant ▷ Reformation. It
arose from the Council of Trent (1545–63)
composed of the ecclesiastical leaders of
the Catholic Church. The only important
English writer to be influenced by the
Counter-Reformation was the poet ▷ Richard
Crashaw.

Courtly Love
Since the 1950s there has been considerable
debate over the historical authenticity of
'courtly love', the term being coined in
the late 19th century to refer to a codified,
stylized expression of the experience of love
found in medieval European texts. Many of
the problems have arisen from the over-rigid
use of this term by literary critics. What is
clear from considering the literary culture
of the 12th century onwards is that the
stylized expression of the lover's experience
in texts cannot be assimilated and organized
into a single code of behaviour or set of
procedural 'rules': courtly love is a disparate
phenomenon, arising out of the confluence of
various literary and philosophical traditions,
and its definition would vary, to some extent,
depending on the provenance of the medieval
texts under discussion.
   The notion of a refined and ennobling
love experience is not a medieval invention;
scholars have traced Arabic influences in
the modes of expression employed by the
troubadour poets of 12th-century France,
whose work is often taken as the earliest
expression of courtly love sentiments in
medieval Europe. Classical Latin texts,
especially the treatises on the arts and
remedies of loving produced by ▷ Ovid, exert
a great influence on medieval attempts to
formalize and codify the lover's experience.
What is distinctive about medieval expressions
of courtly love is the development of a range
of terms and conventions which portray the
love experience in terms of feudal models
and ethics: the male lover serves his lady as
a member of a court might do his lord; the
relationship is one of love service, in which
the lady has the power to bestow gifts and
rewards to her faithful love-servant. This
love service is frequently represented as a

refining, disciplined experience that has its own protocol, and there may be a sense of contiguity between the quality of the love experience for the female object of desire and love of a transcendental, divine subject (indeed the first may lead to the second, as it does in ▷ Dante's ▷ *Divina Commedia* and in ▷ Petrarch's *Rime Sparse*). 'Fin'amor' is an important term within the more general conceptual framework signalled by 'courtly love': it derives from a tradition of moral philosophy and denotes a quality of loving which is not self-seeking, self-gratifying or possessive.

How far the conventionalized modes of representing love experience and ideals in medieval texts influenced and reflected courtly practice at the time is a controversial and complex area, and generalizations are of little profit here. However, the influence of economic and political factors in determining marital arrangements should not be underestimated and, in practice, there seems little room for the exercise of female choice in the arrangements for choosing a legally recognized partner. The conceptual framework offered by the phenomenon of courtly love perhaps served a powerful compensatory function. If this feudalized love ethic arose out of the social circumstances of a specific historic moment, its power to transcend those circumstances and be used as a register for expressing and shaping ideals about loving is demonstrated by its survival through the Renaissance period and beyond. Bib: Boase, R., *The Origin and Meaning of Courtly Love*.

Cowley, Abraham (1618–67)

Poet and essayist. Ever since Samuel Johnson's disparaging comments on Cowley in his *Lives of the Poets* (1779–81), Cowley's reputation has suffered, and yet Cowley is one of the most important and influential of the mid-17th-century poets. A Royalist in politics, he accompanied ▷ Queen Henrietta Maria into exile in Paris in 1644–6, returned to England in 1654, was imprisoned in 1655 and later released.

His chief works include: *Poeticall Blossoms* (written 1633), a collection of poetry published in 1656 which contained Pindaric ▷ odes and ▷ elegies on William Harvey among others, and an essay on the advancement of science: *A Proposition for the Advancement of Experimental Philosophy* (1661). Cowley's attachment, after the ▷ Civil War, to the figures associated with the early ▷ Royal Society is evidenced both in his important ode

celebrating the Royal Society (first published in Thomas Sprat's *History of the Royal Society*) and in his celebration of scientific figures and their works in his poetry.

As well as celebrating the advance of science, Cowley also composed an unfinished ▷ epic, *A Poem on the Late Civil War* (1679), which he abandoned at the point when the war began to turn against the Royalist forces. He also anticipated ▷ John Milton's ▷ *Paradise Lost* in attempting a biblical epic, *Davideis* ('A sacred poem of the Troubles of David', published in the *Poems* of 1656). In the 19th century and through much of the 20th, Cowley was read as a species of inferior ▷ John Donne or ▷ Thomas Carew, yet the range of his writing (which embraced science, ▷ translation and experiments in form and metre as well as critical statements on the nature of poetic discourse) make him an important figure in his own right. Bib: Hinman, R., *Abraham Cowley's World of Order*; Trotter, D., *The Poetry of Abraham Cowley*.

Cramond, Elizabeth (d1651)

Devotional writer. Cramond was the author of *A Ladies Legacie to her Daughters* (1645) which consists of three separate sets of prayers drawn from her own personal experiences. The first consoles her daughters for their lack of monetary inheritance, the second is a series of devotions written upon the death of her second husband, and the third was meant to bring private solace during a protracted illness.

Cranmer, Thomas (1489–1556)

Archbishop of Canterbury, and responsible for the *Book of Common Prayer* (1549 and 1552) containing the liturgy of the ▷ Church of England. He was made Archbishop of Canterbury by ▷ Henry VIII during the king's conflict with the Papacy, and supported his rejection of the Pope's authority (▷ Act of Supremacy, 1534), the starting-point of the Church of England. Under Henry's Roman Catholic daughter, ▷ Queen Mary I, Cranmer renounced his opinions, but repudiated his renunciation when he was burnt at the stake in 1556. He is especially important for the literary value of his Prayer Book.
▷ *Common Prayer, Book of.*
Bib: Ridley, J., *Thomas Cranmer*.

Crashaw, Richard (?1612–49)

Poet. He belongs to the ▷ Metaphysical school of English poets, but in a special sense. In 1645 he became a Roman ▷ Catholic,

despairing of the survival of the Church of England at that stage of the ▷ Civil War. He earlier came under the influence of the work of the Italian baroque poet Giovanni Battista Marino (1569–1625), whose extravagance of imagery to some extent resembled the drawing together of unlike ideas into a single image that typified the English metaphysicals. Although Crashaw was perhaps the most sensuous of the English poets of this tendency, his Catholicism and the influence of Marino give to Crashaw's ecstasy an impersonal quality quite different from the direct, very personal devotional poetry of ▷ Donne and ▷ George Herbert – the latter of whom had been Crashaw's first master. Crashaw's masterpiece is his *Hymn to Saint Theresa*; the one that shows his extravagances most obtrusively is *The Weeper*. His poems were published in 1646 in one volume under the titles *Steps to the Temple* and *The Delights of the Muses*.
Bib: Roberts, J. R. (ed.), *New Perspectives on the Life and Art of Richard Crashaw*; Warren, A., *Richard Crashaw*; White, H. C., *The Metaphysical Poets*; Williamson, G., *The Donne Tradition*.

Cressida
The lover of the Trojan prince Troilus in medieval and post-medieval versions of the Troy story, who is involuntarily separated from Troilus when forced to join her father Calchas in the Greek camp (Chalchas, a priest, has previously deserted the Trojan side). In the Greek camp she becomes the lover of Diomedes. She first appears in this role in the 12th-century text the *Roman de Troie*, composed by Benoît de Sainte-Maure (in which she is called 'Briseida') and it is possible that the figure of Briseis, a lover of Achilles, whose story features in one of ▷ Ovid's *Heroides*, provides a precedent for the development of the Briseida character. The form of her name changes as the story of her love affair with Troilus is amplified and reworked by a series of writers from Benoît onwards, notably ▷ Boccaccio (Criseida), ▷ Chaucer (Criseyde), Robert Henryson (Cresseid), and ▷ Shakespeare (Cressida).

Cromwell, Oliver (1599–1658)
Chief commander of the Parliamentarian forces in the ▷ Civil War against ▷ Charles I and Lord Protector of the Realm (1653–8) in place of a king. He belonged to the landowning class in the east of England and supported the Independents among the ▷ Puritans. It was his generalship that

defeated the forces of Charles I and the Scottish supporters of ▷ Charles II after the execution of Charles I. After his death, his son, Richard Cromwell, succeeded as Lord Protector for some months, after which Charles II was restored by the action of one of Oliver's generals, General Monk, in 1660. After 1660 he suffered the censure of his political opponents and it was not until Thomas Carlyle published *Oliver Cromwell's Letters and Speeches* (1845) that his stature was generally appreciated.
Bib: Fraser, A., *Cromwell Our Chief of Men*.

Cromwell, Thomas (1485–1540)
Chief minister of ▷ Henry VIII; organized the dissolution of the English monasteries in 1536 and 1539. His sister married Morgan Williams; their son adopted the name of Cromwell and was the direct ancestor of ▷ Oliver Cromwell.
Bib: Elton, G. R., *Thomas Cromwell*.

Cultural Materialism
The most important book in the formation of cultural materialism is Jonathan Dollimore and Alan Sinfield's *Political Shakespeare* (1985). The foreword to this collection of essays acts as a manifesto for this new radical ▷ Marxist criticism. The authors themselves trace the origins of the theory to general dissatisfaction in the British academic world with the traditional essentialist ▷ humanism of existing criticism and the rise of numerous approaches (▷ feminism, ▷ structuralism, ▷ psychoanalytical criticism) which challenge this premise. Apart from a debt to the political commitment to change, derived from Marxism, cultural materialism also draws upon Raymond Williams's cultural analysis, which 'seeks to describe the whole system of significations by which a society or a section of it understands itself and its relations with the world' (Dollimore and Sinfield). Thus, cultural materialism rejects any notion of 'high culture' and sets material values in the place of the idealism of conventional criticism, looking instead at texts in history. Cultural materialism also has links with ▷ new historicism (particularly the work of Stephen Greenblatt) in its emphasis upon the nature of subjectivity and the decentring of man, and with feminism, where the exploration of the gendered human subject is an overlapping interest.

Cunningham, Lady Margaret (?–c 1622)
Scottish author of letters and an ▷ autobiography, her work is not well known,

but her life story provides dramatic and romantic reading. Cunningham was married to Sir James Hamilton of Crawfordjohn in 1598, but her strong ▷ Protestant faith and moral values soon clashed with his ▷ Catholic convictions and boorish behaviour. When reconciled she wrote him passionate letters and verses in which she attempted to reform him, but after their final separation in 1608 she wrote of how he had denied her food and shut her out of their home. Cunningham had 11 children, five by Crawfordjohn and six by her second, happier marriage to Sir James Maxwell of Calderwood. Her autobiography was published in 1827 and is available at the National Library of Scotland.

Cymbeline (1609–10)

A late tragicomedy by Shakespeare; sometimes called a romance because of its avoidance of realism. Much of the play is set in the court of the ancient British king Cymbeline (1st century AD) and the climax is the defeat of a Roman invasion; on the other hand the love triangle of Posthumus, the British princess Imogen, and the Italian Iachimo is thoroughly ▷ Renaissance; Shakespeare has in fact combined a story of ancient British history from the chronicler ▷ Raphael Holinshed with a love-story from ▷ Boccaccio's ▷ *Decameron*. Thus a victory of British patriotism over Roman imperialism is fused with a more up-to-date victory of English single-minded devotion over Italian duplicity. *Cymbeline* has also been called a reconciliation play, because, like ▷ *Pericles* before it and ▷ *The Winter's Tale* and ▷ *The Tempest* after it, it steadily darkens with murderous conspiracy from the outset to the middle, and then lightens towards a general clarification in candour and love at the end. Also like the other three plays, *Cymbeline* has as a central theme the loss to the world and, except in *The Tempest*, to the father of a young girl whose recovery expresses the recovery of the qualities of youth, purity, beauty, trust and potentiality.

▷Romances of Shakespeare.

Damon

A shepherd poet in ▷ Virgil's eighth eclogue. Hence the name is sometimes used in English ▷ pastoral poetry for a shepherd and sometimes as a pseudonym for a real person.

Damon and Pythias

In Greek legend, symbols of loyal friendship. Pythias was condemned to death by Dionysius of Syracuse, and asked for temporary release from prison to arrange his affairs. Damon gave himself as pledge for Pythias's return to prison in time for his execution, and Pythias duly returned so that his friend should not be killed in his place. In admiration, Dionysius forgave him. The story is the subject of an early Elizabethan play, *Damon and Pithias* (1564) by ▷ Richard Edwards, parodied in ▷ Ben Jonson's ▷ *Bartholomew Fair*.

Daniel, Samuel (1562–1619)

Poet and dramatist. After returning from extensive travel in France and Italy (c 1586), he was employed as a tutor to the son of ▷ William Herbert, Earl of Pembroke (patron of ▷ Shakespeare) and to ▷ Mary Sidney's family, as well as to ▷ Lady Anne Clifford. His first publication was 28 sonnets included in the unauthorized edition of ▷ Sir Philip Sidney's ▷ *Astrophil and Stella* (1591). In 1592 he published his own collection of sonnets under the title of *Delia*. His dramatic work includes *The Tragedy of Cleopatra* (1594), and *Philotas* (1605), which deals with a trial, on a charge of treason, of an ambitious favourite of ▷ Alexander the Great – a theme which the authorities thought uncomfortably close to the events of the ▷ Essex rebellion of 1601 and which led to Daniel being summoned before the Privy Council to explain the play's intentions. His publications also included several ▷ masques, and a philosophical dialogue in verse form, entitled *Musophilus* (1599), which discusses the conflict between ▷ humanist theory and the value of practical arts. Daniel's masques are considered some of the most beautiful and, perhaps, challenging of the ▷ Jacobean court entertainments. Although never as scholarly as those of ▷ Ben Jonson, Daniel's shows, under the ▷ patronage of ▷ Queen Anne, presented gender roles in a disturbing light.

Daniel's major project, however, was his huge unfinished work *The Civil Wars*. This historical ▷ epic dealing with the Wars of the Roses first appeared in four books in 1592, and by 1609 eight books in all had been published, which brought his account to the marriage of ▷ Edward IV. After the project had been abandoned, Daniel turned to writing a prose history of England, which appeared in two parts between 1612 and 1617. In addition to his historical enterprises, Daniel published, in 1603, his answer to ▷ Thomas Campion's *Observations in the Art of English Poesy*.

Though Daniel's sonnets represent the major portion of his writings read in the 20th century, his attempt at creating a historical epic forms an important part of the late Elizabethan project (shared in by ▷ Edmund Spenser and ▷ Michael Drayton) to create a firmly realized sense of national identity.

▷ Histories and Chronicles.
Bib: Michel, L. (ed.), *The Civil Wars*; Rees, J., *Daniel: A Critical and Biographical Study*.

Dante Aligheri (1265–1321)

Poet and philosopher. Very little is known about the early life of Dante. He was born in Florence, a member of the Guelf family, and married Gemma Donati in 1285. His involvement in Florentine politics from 1294 led in 1300 to his exile from Florence, to which he never returned. He died at Ravenna in 1321. According to his own report, he was inspired throughout his life by his love for Beatrice, a woman who has been identified as Bice Portinari (d 1290).

It is difficult to date Dante's work with any degree of precision. The *Vita Nuova* (1290–4) is a lyric sequence celebrating his inspirational love for Beatrice, linked by prose narrative and commentary sections. His Latin treatise *De Vulgari Eloquentia*, perhaps begun in 1303–4 but left unfinished, is a pioneering work of literacy and linguistic commentary. Here Dante considers the state and status of Italian as a literary language, and assesses the achievements of earlier French and Provençal poets in elevating the status of their vernacular media. The *Convivio* (1304–7) is an unfinished philosophical work, a 'banquet of knowledge', composed of prose commentaries on allegorical poetic sequences. Dante's political ideas, specifically the relationship between the Pope, Emperor and the universal Empire, are explored in *De Monarchia* (c 1310). Dante may not have begun his principal work, the ▷ *Divina Commedia*, until as late as 1314. This is supremely encyclopaedic work, which encompasses a discussion of every aspect of human experience, knowledge and belief. Dante was read and admired by English poets in the 16th and 17th centuries.
Bib: Holmes, G., *Dante*.

D

D'Avenant (Davenant), Sir William (1606–68)

Theatrical innovator, impresario, dramatist and poet, D'Avenant's career spanned the reign of ▷ Charles I, the ▷ Interregnum and the Restoration. A pivotal figure in the history of the English theatre, he was involved in most of the developments of this transitional period, including the dissemination of theatrical techniques associated with the aristocratic cultural form of the ▷ masque to the public stage, the creation of new genres (he is credited with the first English ▷ opera), and the introduction of actresses to the professional English stage. He adapted some of ▷ Shakespeare's plays to the new theatrical conditions, including ▷ The Tempest with Dryden (1667) in a version that was the basis of English productions until 1838. During the 1650s, as official Interregnum disapproval of stage plays waned, he openly mounted several musical performances, including ▷ The Siege of Rhodes (1656), which is often considered to be the first English opera. When the theatres reopened in 1660 D'Avenant and ▷ Killigrew obtained the only two patents granted by ▷ Charles II allowing them to stage theatrical performances in London. D'Avenant formed the ▷ Duke's Company and began converting Lisle's Tennis Court at Lincoln's Inn Fields into a theatre. After his death D'Avenant's widow, ▷ Lady Mary D'Avenant, inherited his patent.
Bib: Blaydes, S. B. and Bordinat, P., *Sir William Davenant: An Annotated Bibliography, 1629–1985*.

D'Avenant Lady Henrietta Maria (d 1691)

Theatre proprietress, wife of ▷ Sir William D'Avenant: she took over management of the ▷ Duke's Company after his death in 1668, and saw his plans for a new theatre at Dorset Garden to completion. Lady D'Avenant was born in France, and met William during his stay there, probably in 1646. He returned about ten years later and brought her back to England as his wife in 1655. She had at least nine children by him, and also cared for some of his children by his earlier marriages. As theatre manager she operated effectively, delegating many artistic and technical problems, ensuring the publication of her husband's works, founding Nurseries for the training of young actors and actresses, and defending the interests of the actor-manager George Jolly after a campaign by ▷ Thomas Killigrew and Lady D'Avenant's late husband to cheat him and squeeze him out of the profession. In 1673 she ceded control of the company to her son Charles, but held on to her shares in the company and various rights, including income from a fruit concession at the playhouse.
Bib: Hotson, L., *The Commonwealth and Restoration Stage*.

Davies, Lady Eleanor (1590–1652)

Author of prophecies and spiritual revelations. Lady Eleanor's maiden name was Audeley, but she is more commonly known by Davies, the surname of her first husband, ▷ Sir John Davies, whom she married in 1609. Although always learned, it was not until 1625 that she received her first revelation and published *A Warning to the Dragon and All His Angels*, a work replete with the contemporary fashion for anagrams (for example, she reworks her own names as 'A Snare O Devil' (Davies) and 'Reveale O Daniele' (Audeley)). She prophesied her own husband's death when he threw *A Warning* onto the fire, and immediately commenced wearing mourning clothes; he died the following year. Her second marriage, to Sir Archibald Douglas, followed the same pattern, he burning her books and she predicting his spiritual downfall. Strangely, Lady Eleanor's prophecies often came true. She predicted the death of ▷ Buckingham in 1628, the outcome of ▷ Henrietta Maria's pregnancies and, more dangerously, the downfall of ▷ Charles I and the Archbishop of Canterbury ▷ William Laud. This last work, which she published in Amsterdam, resulted in her being summoned before the Court of High Commission in 1633 and accused of writing scandalous and fanatical pamphlets. It was suggested that she be committed to Bedlam, but in the event she was fined £3,000, imprisoned for two years, her books were burned, and she was humiliated by a mocking anagram of her name, 'Never So Mad A Ladie' (Dame Eleanor Davies). Undeterred, she continued to prophesy and was incarcerated in both Bedlam and the Tower of London before the ▷ Civil War heralded a more permissive age for women writers, preachers as well as prophetesses. In 1648 she presented her 1633 prophecies, newly entitled *The Armies Commission*, to ▷ Oliver Cromwell, and finally received benign recognition from the state. She also had the sweetness of revenge, since Laud had been executed in 1645, and she was able to write to Charles I before he was beheaded, reminding him of the accuracy of her predictions. Lady Eleanor's prophecies were finally published in an uncensored form

as *The Restitution of Prophecy* (1651) and she was honoured at her death, perhaps somewhat ironically, with the epitaph: 'In a woman's body, a man's spirit'.
Bib: Frazer, A., *The Weaker Vessel*.

Davies, John, of Hereford (?1565–1618)
Very little is known of this prolific writer, often confused with his better-known namesake, ▷ Sir John Davies. Davies was a writing master and the author of numerous ▷ epigrams on his poetic contemporaries. He also taught ▷ Prince Henry and became part of the young prince's court. Perhaps his most ambitious project, however, was a group of three long poems, which undertook to survey existing areas of human knowledge, and which cover a vast number of disparate topics, including English history, psychology, religion and human anatomy. These poems are: *Mirum in Modum* (1602), *Microcosmos* (1603), and *Summa Totalis* (1607).
Bib: Rope, H. E. G., 'John Davies of Hereford: Catholic and Rhymer,' *Anglo-Welsh Review* II (1961), pp. 20–36.

Davies, Sir John (1569–1626)
Poet, lawyer and attorney-general for ▷ Ireland (1606–19). Sir John Davies wrote virtually all his poetry in the years 1593–9. After 1603 Davies devoted his career to advancement within the Jacobean administration of Ireland, being one of the architects of the policy of 'plantation' in Ulster which brought Scots and English to the northern parts of Ireland, a source of friction ever since. In 1609 he married ▷ Lady Eleanor Davies, the author of prophecies and spiritual revelations. In 1612 Davies published an account of Ireland, entitled *A Discoverie of the True Causes why Ireland was never entirely Subdued nor brought under Obedience of the Crown of England Untill his Majesties Happie Raigne* – a work which can be compared in its delineation of English misunderstanding of Irish culture to ▷ Edmund Spenser's accounts of Ireland at the end of the previous century. Davies died in 1626 having had his death prophesied by his wife the previous year.
   Davies' chief poetic works are the two long poems *Orchestra* (1596) and *Nosce Teipsum* (1599), a series of epigrams and the 26 acrostic poems on the name of ▷ Elizabeth I, *Hymns of Astrea* (1599). Both *Orchestra* and *Nosce Teipsum* are, in their own ways, remarkable works. *Orchestra*, composed c 1594, announces itself as 'A Poem of Dauncing', and that, in essence, is what it is: a philosophical account of

the physical world in terms of a universal dance. *Nosce Teipsum*, on the other hand, develops no over-all ▷ conceit, but is instead a philosophical poem on human knowledge derived from Davies' reading in the works of ▷ Cicero, ▷ Montaigne and the two French philosophers Philippe de Mornay and Pierre de la Primaudaye. The end of the poem is to promote self-knowledge, as the title, which translates as 'Know Yourself', indicates.
Bib: Editions include: Kreuger, R. (ed.), *Poems*.

Day, John (1574–1640)
English dramatist contemporary with ▷ Shakespeare and ▷ Ben Jonson. In his plays he collaborated with a number of other dramatists such as ▷ Henry Chettle and ▷ Thomas Dekker. His *Isle of Gulls* (1606), played by the Children of the Queen's Revels, lost them royal favour at Court because of the play's satire on the impact in the country of the ▷ Jacobean accession. Day's most acclaimed work is his ▷ masque *The Parliament of Bees* (1609).
Bib: Oastler, C. L., *John Day, the Elizabethan Printer*.

Decameron, The
A collection of 100 stories in prose, compiled by ▷ Boccaccio in the years 1349–51. The fictional framework of the collection describes how the stories were told by a company of ten gentle-ladies and gentlemen who decide to retreat from plague-ridden Florence and spend two weeks in the country. They spend their weekdays telling short stories to pass the time, and the proceedings are organized by one member of the company who is elected anew every day. Many of the stories concern heterosexual relations of some kind, usually set in the contemporary world, and treated in a variety of serious and comic ways. Boccaccio's work undoubtedly provided many later writers and dramatists (including ▷ Shakespeare) with an important source of narratives. Many of Boccaccio's stories were incorporated into William Painter's ▷ *Palace of Pleasure*, and the first English translation of the *Decameron* itself appeared in 1621.
Bib: McWilliam, G. H. (trans.), *The Decameron*.

Deconstruction
A concept used in critical theory. It has a long philosophical pedigree, but is usually associated with the work of the French philosopher ▷ Jacques Derrida. It is a

strategy applied to writing generally, and to literature in particular, whereby systems of thought and concepts are dismantled in such a way as to expose the divisions that lie at the heart of meaning itself. If interpretation is a process designed to reduce a text to some sort of 'order', deconstruction seeks to undermine the basis upon which that order rests. Deconstruction challenges the notion that all forms of mental and linguistic activity are generated from within an autonomous 'centre', advancing the more disturbing proposition that such centres are themselves to be grasped textually only as rhetorical constructions.
Bib: Derrida, J., *Speech and Phenomena*; *Writing and Difference; Of Grammatology*; *Positions*; Norris, C., *Deconstruction: Theory and Practice*; Parker, P. and Hartman, G., *Shakespeare and the Question of Theory*.

Defence of Poesie, The
▷ *Apologie for Poetrie, An.*

De Flores
A tragic villain in ▷ Thomas Middleton's play ▷ *The Changeling* who has fallen in love with his master's daughter and blackmails her into a sexual encounter which leads to the destruction of them both.

Deism
A form of religious belief which developed in the 17th century as an outcome of the ▷ Reformation. ▷ Edward Herbert evolved the idea that, while the religion revealed in the Gospels was true, it was preceded by 'natural' religion, according to which by his own inner light a man could perceive all the essentials of religious truth.

Dekker, Thomas (?1570–1632)
Dramatist and pamphleteer. His best-known play is ▷ *The Shoemaker's Holiday*, based on ▷ Thomas Deloney's *The Gentle Craft* – a narrative about the London crafts. The play celebrates the proud traditions of the citizens, and the romantic zest of its plot and dialogue has kept it alive. His next best known play is *The Honest Whore*, Pt. I (1604). He was essentially a dramatist of middle life. He collaborated with ▷ Rowley in *The Witch of Edmonton* (1623); with ▷ Middleton in *The Roaring Girl* (1611); and with ▷ Massinger in *Virgin Martyr* (1622).

His pamphlets are as notable as his plays, especially *The Wonderful Year* (1603), a vivid account of an epidemic of plague in London, and *The Gull's Hornbook*, a satire on the manners of a fashionable young man. He was a master of the racy, vigorous, colloquial prose of his time. Dekker was immensely popular in his own time and, despite a falling off in esteem, has been critically reappraised, and it is now possible to perceive him as a politically aware and strongly ▷ Protestant dramatist.
Bib: Bowers, Fredson, *The Dramatic Works of Thomas Dekker* (4 vols.); Bose, T., *The Gentle Craft of Revision in Thomas Dekker's Last Plays*; Gasper, J., *The Dragon and the Dove*.

Deloney, Thomas (?1543–?1600)
Pamphleteer and balladeer. Little of Deloney's verse can be securely attributed to him, although in the 1590s he was the most popular ▷ ballad writer in England. It is, however, Deloney's prose narratives – *The Gentle Craft* (complete version ?1635), *Thomas of Reading* (1612, 12th edition) and *Jack of Newbery* (1619, 8th edition) – that have secured for him a reputation. These works anticipate the kind of novel which Daniel Defoe (1660–1731) was later to write. They mark the end of the tradition of producing courtly romance such as ▷ Sir Philip Sidney's ▷ *Arcadia*, and share, with the writings of ▷ Thomas Nashe, an interest in depicting the life led by those outside the elevated circles of the court.

As well as his fictional works, Deloney produced ▷ translations and ▷ anthologies, which include his *Strange Histories of Kings* (1600). Despite the diversity of his output, it is for the creation of a 'middle-class' fiction that Deloney is of importance.
Bib: Lawless, M. E., *Apology for the Middle Class: The Dramatic Novels of Thomas Deloney*.
▷ Elizabethan Novels; Pamphlet.

Denham, Sir John (1615–69)
Poet and playwright. He took the Royalist side in the ▷ Civil War, translated Book II of the ▷ *Aeneid* into pentameter couplets (*The Destruction of Troy*, 1656) and published a play in ▷ blank verse, *The Sophy* (1642). His *Cooper's Hill* (1642; enlarged version, 1655), a topographical poem describing the scenery around Windsor, was much admired and imitated. In it he abandons the *enjambements* of his Virgil translation, preferring a balanced, end-stopped couplet. The passage on the Thames was cited and imitated by poets from John Dryden (1631–1700) onwards as the perfection of heroic couplet writing:

O could I flow like thee, and make thy stream
My great example, as it is my theme!
Though deep, yet clear, though gentle, yet not dull,

Strong without rage, without o'er-flowing full.

The lines are comically parodied in Alexander Pope's (1688–1744) *Dunciad* (Bk. III, ii. 163–6). Samuel Johnson (1709–84), in his *Lives of the Poets* (1781), called Denham 'one of the fathers of English poetry'.
Bib: O'Hehir, B., *Harmony from Discords: a Life of Sir John Denham.*

Derrida, Jacques (b 1930)
Although he is primarily a philosopher, the influence of Derrida's work on the study of literature has been immense. He is the originator of a mode of reading known as ▷ 'deconstruction', the major stand in what is now regarded as the general area of ▷ post-structuralism. His main works are *Speech and Phenomena* (trans. 1973), *Of Gramatology* (trans. 1974), and *Writing and Difference* (trans. 1978). For Derrida, as for ▷ Saussure, language is composed of differences; that is, a series of non-identical elements that combine with each other to produce linguistic signs which are accorded meaning. Traditionally, this process is anchored to an organizing principle, a centre, but Derrida questions this concept and rejects the idea of a 'presence' in which authority resides, thereby lifting all restrictions upon the 'play' of differences. But, in addition to the idea that language is composed of 'differences', Derrida also deploys the term '*différance*' to indicate the continual postponement of 'presence' which is located in all signifiers. Thus, signs are produced through a relatively free play of linguistic elements (difference), but what they signify can never be fully present since meaning is constantly 'deferred' (*différance*). Derrida's influence has been greatest in the U.S.A., where after his visit to Johns Hopkins and his teaching at Yale, deconstruction has become the successor to American new criticism.

Descartes, René (1596–1650)
French philosopher, mathematician. In ethics and religious doctrine he was traditional, but in method of thought he was the starting-point of the total reliance on reason – rationalism - that was pre-eminent in the later 17th and 18th centuries. In his *Discours de la Méthode* (1637) he reduced knowledge to the basic principle of *Cogito, ergo sum* (I think, therefore I am), from which intuition he deduced the existence of God and thence the reality of the external world. He also distinguished mind and matter, finding their

source of combination again in God. It was the influence of Descartes' writings that drew the English philosopher John Locke, the dominant figure in English rationalism, to the study of philosophy.
▷ Hobbes, Thomas.

Devil is an Ass, The (1616)
A satirical comedy by ▷ Ben Jonson, attacking the speculators, financial tricksters, and their dupes, in contemporary London. The young dupe, Fitzdottrel, is cheated out of his land by the 'projector' Meercraft with elaborate projects of land reclamation; Pug, an inferior devil trying his hand at deceiving and betraying humanity, finds that he is not the equal in this to human beings themselves.

Didactic literature
Literature designed to teach or to propound in direct terms a doctrine or system of ideas. In practice, it is not always easy to identify; so much literature is didactic in intention but not in form; sometimes writers renounce didactic intentions but in practice use didactic forms. Thus ▷ Spenser declared that ▷ *The Faerie Queene* was meant to 'fashion a gentleman . . . in vertuous and gentle discipline', but the poem may be enjoyed for its imaginative vision without much regard to its didacticism, and the same it true of ▷ Bunyan's ▷ *Pilgrim's Progress*, ▷ Ben Jonson's ▷ masques, and the writings of ▷ Sir Philip Sidney.

Dido (Elissa)
In Roman legend, the daughter of a king of Tyre, and the reputed founder of the city of Carthage. ▷ Virgil brings her into his epic of the founding of Rome, the ▷ *Aeneid*; she falls in love with ▷ Aeneas when he is shipwrecked on the North African coast, and when he forsakes her to fulfil his destiny, she kills herself. The Romans identified her with the guardian goddess of Carthage.
   She is the subject of a tragedy, *Dido* (1594) by ▷ Christopher Marlowe and ▷ Thomas Nash.

Difference
A term introduced by ▷ Ferdinand de Saussure in his study of linguistics and used in literary theory. It is the means whereby value is established in any system of linguistic signs whether it be spoken or written. Saussure's *Course in General Linguistics* (1915) argues that in speech it is 'the phonetic contrasts', which permit us to distinguish

between one word and another, that constitute meaning. In writing, the letters used to form words are arbitrary signs, and their values are therefore 'purely negative and differential' (Saussure). The result is that the written sign becomes important only insofar as it is different from other signs within the overall system of language. The notion of difference as a principle of opposition has been extended beyond the limits of structuralist thinking laid down by Saussure. For example, the ▷ Marxist philosopher ▷ Mikhail Bakhtin in a critique of Saussurean ▷ structuralism argued that 'the forms of signs are conditioned above all by the social organization of the participants involved and also by the immediate conditions of their interaction' (*Marxism and the Philosophy of Language*, 1930). Thus the clash of opposites through which meaning and value emerge is determined by the social positions of those who use the language. This means that secreted at the very heart of the form of the linguistic sign is a series of dialectical opposites whose interaction refracts the struggle taking place within the larger framework of society itself. For Bakhtin these oppositions can be defined in terms of the struggle between social classes, but the dialectical structure of these conflicts makes the notion of difference suitable for any situation that can be analysed in terms of binary opposites. For example, for ▷ feminism this would be an opposition between 'masculine' and 'feminine' as the basis upon which sexual identity is constructed. ▷ Jacques Derrida has adapted the term to form the neologism '*différance*', which denotes the deferral of meaning whereby no sign can ever be brought into direct alignment with the object it purports to recall. Meaning is, therefore, always *deferred*, and can never be final.

Diomedes

A Greek hero in the Trojan war, and king of Argos. In ▷ Chaucer's ▷ *Troilus and Criseyde* and ▷ Shakespeare's ▷ *Troilus and Cressida*, he seduces ▷ Cressida (Criseyde) from her devotion to the Trojan prince, Troilus.

Discourse

A term used in critical theory. Especially in the writings of ▷ Michel Foucault, 'discourse' is the name given to the systems of linguistic representations through which power sustains itself. For Foucault discourse manifests itself only through concrete examples operating within specific areas of social and institutional practice. He argues that within individual discourses a series of mechanisms are used as a means of controlling desire and power, which facilitate 'classification . . . ordering [and] distribution' (Foucault). In this way a mastery is exerted over what appears to be the randomness of everyday reality. It is thus possible to investigate those discourses which have been used to master reality in the past, *eg* discourses concerned with questions of 'sexuality', criminality and judicial systems of punishment, or madness, as Foucault's own work demonstrates.
Bib: Foucault, M., *The Order of Things; Power/Knowledge: Selected Interviews and Other Writings* (ed. C. Gordon).

Dissenters

A term used for those ▷ Puritans who, owing to their 'dissent' from the established ▷ Church of England, were refused certain political, educational and (at first) religious rights from the second half of the 17th century. That is to say, they could not enter Parliament, they could not enter a university, and, until 1688, they could not join together in worship. Puritans were not thus formally restricted before 1660. They were released from their political restraints in 1828. In the 19th century it became more usual to call them Nonconformists or Free Churchmen. The term does not apply to Scotland, where the established Church is ▷ Presbyterian, not the episcopalian Church of England.

Dissociation of Sensibility

A critical expression made famous by T. S. Eliot (1888–1965) and used in his essay *The Metaphysical Poets* (1921, included in his *Selected Essays*). He states: 'In the seventeenth century a dissociation of sensibility set in, from which we have never recovered; and this dissociation . . . was aggravated by the influence of the two most powerful poets of the century, ▷ Milton and Dryden' (1631–1700). Eliot's argument is that before 1660 poets, in particular the ▷ Metaphysical poets, were 'engaged in the task of trying to find the verbal equivalent for states of mind and feeling', and that after that date 'while the language became more refined, the feeling became more crude'. Poetry, henceforward, is put to more specialized purposes: 'Tennyson (1809–92) and Browning (1812–89) are poets, and they think; but they do not feel their thought as immediately as the odour of a rose. A thought to ▷ Donne was an experience, it modified his sensibility.' The implication behind the argument is that poets (with exceptions) ceased to bring all their faculties to bear upon their art: 'Racine or Donne looked into a good deal more than the heart. One must look into the cerebral cortex, the nervous system, and the digestive tracts.'

The theory has had great influence. Those who uphold it support it with the evidence provided by the rise of modern prose after 1660, and the gradual displacement of poetry from its centrality in literature thereafter; poetry either subjected itself to the rational discipline of prose or, in the 19th century, it tended to cultivate areas of feeling to which this rational discipline was not relevant. However, the theory has been attacked for various reasons. Eliot himself felt that he had used the expression in too simplified a way ('Milton', 1974, in *Poets and Poetry*), and that the causes of the process were more complicated than his earlier essay had implied. Other writers have suggested that such a dissociation did not happen; or that it happened in different ways at different periods; or that, if it did happen, no deterioration in imaginative writing can be attributed to it. See Frank Kermode, *Romantic Image* and F. W. Bateson in *Essays in Criticism*, vol. 1.

Divina Commedia (Divine Comedy)
The principal work of the Italian poet ▷ Dante (1265–1321). For an account of its contents, see the entries under its major sections: ▷ *Inferno*, ▷ *Purgatorio*, ▷ *Paradiso*. Bib: Cunningham, G. F., *The Divine Comedy in English, 1290–1966*; Sinclair, J. N. (trans.), *The Divine Comedy*.

Doctor Faustus, The Tragical History of
A tragedy in ▷ blank verse, with comic episodes in prose, by ▷ Christopher Marlowe. The play resembles a medieval ▷ morality play in that its theme is Faustus's sacrifice of his soul to the devil (represented by Mephistophilis) for the sake of unlimited power, glory and enjoyment in this world. On the other hand, it is also thoroughly ▷ Renaissance in its treatment: the conflict of choice is made convincing as it would not have been in a medieval play, and the psychology, not only of Faustus but of Mephistophilis, is presented with moving insight. The medieval and the Renaissance outlooks fuse in *Doctor Faustus*, showing the very important continuity, as well as the contrast, between the two outlooks.

There are two uncertainties about the play. One is about its date. Marlowe uses the material of the German *Faustbuch* (*Faustbook*), which is about an early 16th-century scholar

who had claimed powers of black magic, and fuses this historical figure with medieval legends about a man selling his soul to the devil. The earliest surviving English version is dated 1592, and the maturity of the poetry also suggests a date for the play late in Marlowe's live. On the other hand, some critics have found good reason to date *Faustus* at least as early as 1588. The other uncertainty concerns the extent of Marlowe's authorship. Did he have a collaborator for the comic parts? And were some of these added after his death? The edition of 1616 has considerably extended comedy, as compared with the first edition of 1604. The main reason for suspecting a collaborator is that much of the comedy is superfluous as well as trivial. It is, however, a mistake to suppose that the mere presence of comedy is injurious to the highest tragedy; the combination is frequent in Elizabethan serious drama – tragedies and history plays – including ▷ Shakespeare's, and it is one of the inheritances from medieval mystery and morality plays, with which English Renaissance drama kept a close relationship. Some of the comedy in *Faustus* enriches the tragedy by extending its relevance to common life, *eg* in the parody in which Faustus's servant, Wagner, also tries his hand at summoning the devil.

▷ Faust; Mephistopheles.

Dogberry and Verges
Comic constables in ▷ Shakespeare's play ▷ *Much Ado About Nothing*. Dogberry is famous for his misuse of words.
▷ Malapropism.

Don Juan
The hero of legends from various European countries. His exploits were the subject of the Spanish play *El Burlador de Sevilla* by Tirso de Molina (1571–1641), who gave him his distinctive character of sensual adventurer. Plays and stories were woven round him in French and Italian, and he is the protagonist of an opera by Mozart (*Don Giovanni*).

Donne, John (1572–1631)
Poet, Dean of St Paul's and prose writer. John Donne is (and was) regarded as one of the most important writers of the ▷ Renaissance period. The early part of his life was spent at the margins of the Elizabethan court. He took part in the expeditions of the ▷ Earl of Essex to Cadiz in 1596 and the Azores in 1597, and became private secretary to the Lord Keeper, Sir Thomas Egerton, in 1598. He travelled

on the continent in 1605–6 and 1611–12. Originally a Roman ▷ Catholic, he was ordained into the Anglican Church in 1615, becoming Reader in Divinity at Lincoln's Inn in 1616, and Chaplain to Viscount Doncaster's embassy into Germany in 1619. In 1621 he was made Dean of St Paul's, and in the following year an Honorary Member of the Council of the Virginia Company.

Donne's works cover an enormous variety of genres and subjects. They include religious works such as the *Devotions on Emergent Occasions* published in 1624 and the *Essays in Divinity* (1651); anti-Catholic works such as *Pseudo-Martyr* (1610) and *Ignatius his Conclave* (1611); a considerable number of sermons (collections appearing in 1625, 1626, 1634 and 1640); a treatise on suicide entitled *Biathanatos* (1646); a collection of paradoxes (1633); and, in poetry, ▷ satires, ▷ lyrics, ▷ elegies, ▷ epigrams, verse letters and divine ▷ sonnets.

As a preacher, Donne was justly famous in an age of famous preachers, as ▷ Izaak Walton, his first biographer, recalled. His poetry, however, with the important exception of the two anniversary poems of 1611 and 1612, did not, for the most part, appear until after his death, when a collection was published in 1633. His poetry was, however, well known among his contemporaries, numerous manuscript versions of both his secular and his religious verse being in circulation. Donne's privileged status in the canon of English literature only came about in the first part of the 20th century (1920–50), when the highly-wrought and intellectual witticism of his verse fitted the critical tenor of the day, that is ▷ new criticism. Recent attempts have been made to see Donne as more anxious (J. Carey), but the pre-World War II image remains entrenched. The recent discovery of the *Dalhousie Manuscripts*, which provide us with contemporary transcriptions, implies that editions of Donne's work will change over the next decade.
Bib: Grierson, H. J. C. (ed.), *Poems* (2 vols.); Smith, A. J. (ed.), *John Donne: The Complete English Poems*; Patrides, C. A. (ed.), *The Complete English Poems of John Donne*; Bald, R. C., *Donne: A Life*; Carey, J., *John Donne: Life Mind Art*; Parfitt, G., *John Donne: A Literary Life*.
▷ *Songs and Sonnets*.

Don Quixote de la Mancha (1605–15)
A satirical romance by the Spanish writer Miguel de Cervantes (1547–1616). It begins as a satire on the medieval and ▷ Renaissance style of romance about wandering knights and their adventures in the pursuit of the rectification of injustices. It deepens into an image of idealism perpetually at odds with the pettinesss, vulgarity and meanness of the real world. Don Quixote is an impecunious gentleman whose mind has been turned by reading too many romances. He sets out on his wanderings accompanied by his servant, Sancho Panza, the embodiment of commonplace credulity and a shrewd sense of personal advantage. He takes as his patroness a peasant girl, Dulcinea del Toboso, whom he transfigures in his imagination and who is quite unaware of his devotion. The book was translated into English in 1612–20, and again a hundred years later in a more famous version by Peter Motteux. Its influence on our literature has been extensive. In the 17th century the burlesque element is emulated by ▷ Francis Beaumont in his play ▷ *The Knight of the Burning Pestle* and by ▷ Samuel Butler in his mock epic ▷ *Hudibras*.

Dorset, Lord
▷ Sackville, Thomas.

Doubting Castle
In Part I of ▷ John Bunyan's ▷ *Pilgrim's Progress*, the castle belonging to the Giant Despair, where Christian and Hopeful lie prisoners. In Part II the Castle is destroyed by the champion Greatheart.

Douglas, Gavin (?1475–1522)
Scottish poet and Bishop of Dunkeld. Unlike many of his contemporaries, he wrote only in the vernacular, and is most famous for his translation of ▷ Virgil's ▷ *Aeneid*, *Aeneados*, printed in 1533, which seems to have been used by the ▷ Earl of Surrey. His allegorical poem, the *Palice of Honor* (1501), was influenced by ▷ Chaucer's *House of Fame*. Douglas, who was heavily involved in ecclesiastical and secular politics, died in exile in England.
Bib: Small, J. (ed.), *Works*; Bawcutt, P., *Gavin Douglas: A Critical Study*.
▷ Classical Mythology.

Dowland, John (1563–1626)
Composer and lutenist. Refused the post of court lutenist by ▷ Elizabeth I, Dowland travelled on the continent from 1594 to 1606, becoming famous throughout Europe as a composer for the lute. He was finally given the post of court lutenist by ▷ James I, but does not appear to have composed any work

of note after this overdue royal recognition. He wrote three books of *Songs or Ayres* (1597, 1600 and 1603) while abroad, from which several songs are still known today.
Bib: Poulton, D., *John Dowland.*

Dowriche, Anne

Poet. Anne Edgecombe was married to Hugh Dowriche, the rector of Honiton, and in 1589 published her major work, *The French Historie, A Lamentable Discourse of Three of the Chiefe and Most Famous Bloodie Broiles That Have Happened in France for the Gospell Of Jesus Christ*, which recounts the suffering of the Protestant martyrs in France in a manner similar to that of ▷ John Foxe's *Acts and Monuments* (1563). The poem is written in ▷ alexandrines and includes many long heroic speeches by the major characters.
   ▷ Protestantism.

Drake, Sir Francis (?1549–96)

Built up at the end of the 19th and early 20th century as a national hero for his seafaring exploits. He engaged in numerous voyages in which he successfully raided Spain and her American colonies, and circumnavigated the world in his ship the *Golden Hind*, 1577–81. He was one of the commanders of the English fleet against the ▷ Armada during the attempted Spanish invasion of 1588.
Bib: Williams, N., *Francis Drake.*

Dramatic Irony

Dramatic irony occurs when a character in a play makes a statement in innocent assurance of its truth, while the audience is well aware that he or she is deceived.

Drayton, Michael (1563–1631)

Poet. Little is known of the life of this prolific writer, whose works encompassed a wide range of ▷ genres and subject matter. His collection of ▷ sonnets, gathered under the title *Idea's Mirror*, first appeared in 1594, and consists of 51 sonnets, mainly in the ▷ Petrarchan mode. The sequence was continuously revised, with additions appearing in the editions of 1602, 1605 and the final version of 1619.
   Apart from sonnets, however, Drayton wrote ▷ eclogues indebted to ▷ Edmund Spenser, ▷ Ovidian verses and historical poetry. Of his historical poetry, *Piers Gaveston* (1593, revised in 1596) is remarkable for its combination of the Ovidian and the homoerotic. In 1596, Drayton published the first version of a historical narrative – *Mortimeriados* – an ambitious account, in

verse, of the events which ▷ Christopher Marlowe was to dramatize in his play *Edward II.*
   In common with Spenser and ▷ Samuel Daniel, Drayton was alert to the importance of celebrating the idea of the nation-state. Drayton's contribution to this late Elizabethan project was the topographical verse description of England, *Poly-Olbion* (Part I, 1612; Part II, 1622). *Poly-Olbion* sets out to celebrate, in ▷ alexandrine verse, not only the geographical features of England, but the customs and histories of all the counties of the kingdom. It was an ambitious project which was never to reach completion. But *Poly-Olbion* was only one part of Drayton's desire to celebrate English history. Another aspect of his historiographical enterprise is revealed in the publication, in 1606, of his *Poems Lyric and Pastoral.* The collection contains two verse accounts on themes of considerable national importance – a version of ▷ Richard Hakluyt's 'First Voyage to Virginia', and an account of the battle of Agincourt based mainly on ▷ Raphael Holinshed's *Chronicles.* The creation of a national past and the formation of a national identity can thus be seen as merging in the work of this writer.
   ▷Histories and Chronicles.
Bib: Hebel, J. W., Tillotson, K. and Newdigate, B. H. (eds.), *Complete Works* (4 vols.); Brink, J. R., *Michael Drayton Revisited;* Hardin, R. F., *Drayton and the Passing of Elizabethan England.*

Drummond, William, of Hawthornden (1585–1649)

Scottish poet. Drummond's first publication was a eulogy on the death of Prince Henry, the eldest son of ▷ James I of England, published in 1613. A volume of poems was published in 1614, and then withdrawn, revised, and republished as *Poems: Amorous, Funeral, Divine, Pastoral, in Sonnets, Songs, Sextains, Madrigals*, whose title indicates the range of Drummond's interests. A large proportion of the verses contained in the 1616 collection are paraphrases and translations of continental writers. Other volumes of verse followed, including a celebration of the visit of James I to Edinburgh in 1618. Perhaps Drummond's most famous work is not poetic, however, but is instead his record of a series of remarkable conversations with Ben Jonson, who visited Drummond in 1618. Drummond was careful to keep a record of Jonson's conversation, though much of what was said is the product (one supposes) of a good deal of drink rather than critical insight.

Nevertheless, *Conversations with Drummond of Hawthornden*, first published in 1711, does suggest something of Jonson's wit.
Bib: MacDonald, R. H. (ed.), *Poems and Prose of William Drummond of Hawthornden*.

Du Bartas, Guillaume de Saluste, Sieurdu Bartas (1544–90)
Protestant poet and soldier. The major work for which Du Bartas became famous in England in the 17th century was his ▷ epic on the story of the creation entitled *La Semaine* (1578), which was followed by a continuation, *La Seconde Semaine* (1584). This enormous poem, which celebrates the first two weeks of the biblical creation of the world, was to have a considerable influence on English writers in the period, though it is now hardly read. The ▷ translation of Du Bartas's work into English became the major undertaking of Joshua Sylvester (1562/3–1618), though he was not the only English writer to attempt translations of the work. ▷ Philip Sidney is said to have produced a translation (now lost), and ▷ James I and ▷ Thomas Lodge both translated small parts of the text. In the 17th century Du Bartas's original and Sylvester's translation became inseparably associated with one another, and a considerable number of poets were to praise the work or write under its influence. 'Divine Bartas', as he became known, was praised by ▷ Edmund Spenser, ▷ Samuel Daniel, ▷ Michael Drayton and ▷ Edmund Campion. Perhaps the high point of the reputation of the work was in the influence that it had on ▷ John Milton's *Paradise Lost*. In the 18th century, however, Du Bartas's reputation underwent a decline from which it has never properly recovered.
Bib: Sylvester, J.(trans.), Snyder, S. (ed.), *The Divine Weeks and Works of Guillaume de Saluste, Sieur du Bartas* (2 vols.).

Du Bellay, Joachim (1522–60)
Together with ▷ Ronsard, one of the most prominent of the French Renaissance group known as the ▷ Pléiade. His *Deffence & Illustration de la langue francoyse* (1549) is often regarded as their manifesto. He was the nephew of Cardinal Jean du Bellay, the protector of ▷ Rabelais, and spent the years 1553–7 in Rome in the service of his uncle. It was here that he composed the sonnet collection *Les Regrets* (based on ▷ Ovid's *Tristia*) as well as *Les Antiquitez de Rome* and the *Songe* of which ▷ Spenser's versions, *Ruines of Rome* and *The Visions of Bellay*, appeared in the 1591 *Complaints*.
Bib: Keating, L. C., *Joachim du Bellay*.

Duchess of Malfi, The (1613)
With ▷ *The White Devil*, one of the two famous verse tragedies by ▷ John Webster. The plot is taken from a tale by the Italian writer Matteo Bandello in an English version included in William Painter's ▷ *Palace of Pleasure*. Set in Italy, the drama concerns the vengeance taken upon the young Duchess for marrying her steward, Antonio, against the commands of her brothers, the Cardinal, and Ferdinand Duke of Calabria, who is her twin. Ferdinand employs an impoverished malcontent soldier, ▷ Bosola, as his instrument for the mental torturing of the Duchess, but Bosola has a character of his own, and is filled with remorse. The Duchess is finally strangled, but Ferdinand goes mad with horror at his own deed, and ends by killing Bosola, who had already killed the Cardinal.

Two main problems arise in assessing the drama. The first is whether the Duchess is purely a guiltless victim. She is a young widow who marries a man of lower status for love: commentators argue that contemporary opinion was against the remarrying of widows, that the Duchess offends against the principle of degree by marrying beneath her, and that her deception of her brothers offends against the principle that a just life must be led in openness. None of these arguments is likely to have force with modern audiences, and those contemporary with the play must have been chiefly impressed by the proud dignity with which the Duchess sustains her cumulative afflictions. The more important problem is that of the brothers' motives. That of the Cardinal is intelligible: he is a cold ▷ Machiavellian who resents his sister's humiliation of the family, and no doubt the fact that by her second marriage she now has heirs to her estate. But Ferdinand's prolonged sadism, and his madness after her death, seem in excess of their ostensible causes. The natural explanation is that he is incestuously in love with his sister, and insanely jealous at her marriage; this is doubted by some critics who point out that incestuous passion is nowhere explicit in the play, which was written at a time when such motives were rarely left to the audience's inference. Webster may have preferred to leave the question open, since the bond between a twin sister and brother might itself sufficiently explain Ferdinand's extravagance. Another explanation, since the play is remarkable for its strikingly effective individual scenes, might be that Webster was more interested in opportunities for dramatizing situations than in the exposition of a dominant theme. Even this reductive judgement cannot obscure the grandeur with which Webster dramatizes extreme passion and the horror of its degradation, and, in contrast, the dignity with which an individual can outface suffering.

Duessa
Character in ▷ Edmund Spenser's ▷ *The Faerie Queen*. She is described as 'clad in scarlet red' (Book I. ii. 13), which associates her with the Catholic Church, Antichrist and the Whore of Babylon, as ▷ Protestant commentaries on *Revelation* XVII. 4 make clear. She may also be identified in the poem's contemporary political ▷ allegory as ▷ Mary Queen of Scots, and was so identified by her son ▷ James VI and I.
▷ Catholicism (Roman) in English literature.

Duke of Milan, The (1621)
A ▷ tragedy of court intrigue, possessive jealousy and murder by ▷ Philip Massinger.

Duke's Company, The
The Acting company formed by ▷ Sir William D'Avenant after the Restoration of ▷ Charles II. It performed from June 1661 at the former Lisle's Tennis Court in Lincoln's Inn Fields, which had been converted to a theatre. In November 1671 the company moved to a new playhouse at Dorset Garden, also known as the Duke's Theatre, where it remained until its union with the King's Company to form the United Company in 1682.

Dutch Courtesan, The (1605)
A punitive satirical comedy by ▷ John Marston about deceit and youthful recklessness.

Eagleton, Terry (b 1943)

The foremost ▷ Marxist critic writing in
Britain today. Until recently Eagleton was
a Fellow at Wadham College, Oxford, and
he has for some time been a leading force
in Marxism's encounter with a range of
intellectual movements from ▷ structuralism
onwards. His book *Criticism and Ideology*
(1976) laid the foundation for the introduction
into British literary criticism of the work of
the French critic Pierre Macherey, and is
a clear development of ▷ Louis Althusser's
understanding of culture. In later works, such
as *Walter Benjamin or Towards a Revolutionary
Criticism* (1981), *The Rape of Clarissa* (1982),
The Function of Criticism (1984), and ▷ *William
Shakespeare* (1986) he has sought to develop a
sophisticated ▷ materialist criticism which is
prepared to engage with, but which refuses to
be overawed by ▷ post-structuralism.
▷ Rhetoric.

Earle, John

▷ Characters, Theophrastian.

Eastward Hoe (1605)

A ▷ citizen comedy about London apprentices
and craftsmen written collaboratively by
▷ George Chapman, ▷ Ben Jonson and
▷ John Marston. Modern interest in this
play stems not primarily from its undeniable
imaginative vitality so much as from its
foolhardy satire of the Scots in Act III,
which led to the imprisoning and facial
disfigurement (ears and noses cut) of Jonson
and Chapman – Marston had decamped. The
play is one of several works of the period such
as ▷ Thomas Middleton's ▷ *A Game At Chess*
and ▷ John Day's *Isle of Gulls* to challenge
or parody the volatile contemporary political
order through the theatre.

Eclogue

A short pastoral dialogue, usually in verse.
The most famous example is the *Bucolics*
of the Latin poet ▷ Virgil. The word is
often used as an equivalent for ▷ idyll, or a
▷ pastoral poem without dialogue. One of the
most famous examples of a Renaissance poem
written in the tradition of Virgilian eclogues is
▷ Spenser's ▷ *The Shepherd's Calendar*.

Education

The 'discovery of learning' in the
▷ Renaissance was made partly through the
activity of the humanist scholars
(▷ humanism), beginning in Italy in the 14th
century, and extending gradually northwards
to the rest of Europe. The humanist use of
disinterested scholarship awakened men to
the importance and potentialities of acquiring
knowledge for its own sake. The medieval
aristocrat had long formed an image of
nobility that far excelled the primitive one of
the bloodthirsty warrior; he now began to see
that the cultivation of his mind was central to
his acquirement of courtly accomplishments
and to the aristocratic ideal of the perfected
man. The distinction between genders is
deliberate, as women of all classes would
have received little or no education in the
▷ Middle Ages.

Another cause of the changed attitude
to education was the invention of printing,
introduced into England late in the 15th
century by ▷ William Caxton. The major
obstacle to learning so far had been the lack
of material; books had to be copied by hand,
and most learning had been conducted by
discussion between teacher and student.
Printing, however, made books plentiful and
if they were not cheap, at least they were far
more accessible than they had been, to both
rich and poor.

The humanist passion for education began
in the universities and thence extended
gradually to the rest of society through the
scholarship and writings of such men as
▷ Grocyn, ▷ Linacre, Colet, ▷ More, and
above all, the Dutch humanist ▷ Erasmus,
who resided at Cambridge from 1511 to
1514. One of the chief objects of the scholars
was to clarify and enlarge Latin culture, out
of which the whole civilization of western
Europe had grown, but they also taught the
universities to extend their studies from Latin
to Greek and Hebrew texts, especially those
that had constituted the original texts of
the ▷ Bible, from which the medieval Latin
version, the ▷ Vulgate, had been translated.
The critical spirit of the Renaissance easily
led to the reforming spirit of ▷ Protestantism,
and Cambridge soon became and remained
a centre of ▷ Reformation ideas. As
in literature and philosophy, so, too, in
religious thought this enlargement of
understanding and activity of mind extended
from the universities throughout society.
The translations of the Bible into English,
encouraged by ▷ Henry VIII (1509–47), and
the ▷ Book of Common Prayer, compiled by
▷ Archbishop Cranmer under ▷ Edward VI
(1547–53), brought English laymen close to
the spiritual texts of Christianity; hitherto the
Bible and the liturgies had been mysteries in
the control of the priests.

The Reformation, however, was not

altogether helpful to the spread of education. Henry VIII dissolved the monasteries and friaries in 1536 and 1539, and since these made important contributions to the universities, Oxford and Cambridge suffered at least financially. A minor ill effect of Henry's action, but minor only because the numbers affected were small, was the closure of the nunnery schools, the only institutions for the education of girls. Much worse was the closing down of many grammar schools under Edward VI. Many of these, established by town guilds and chantries, had religious affiliations, and Edward VI's Protestant politicians gladly made this the excuse for seizing the funds with which they had been endowed. Some, indeed, were refounded with the title 'King Edward VI Grammar School', with the result that for three centuries this boy king enjoyed the reputation of being a great patron of education, but in fact far more schools were lost than refounded.

These setbacks were, however, temporary. Gradually, from 1560, new schools were opened, including some (for instance, Rugby) which later became famous as public schools. The universities also recovered from their difficulties, and it is in the reign of ▷ Elizabeth I (1558–1603) that we first find them attended by large numbers of the great men of the age, including the poets ▷ Ralegh, ▷ Spenser, ▷ Sidney and ▷ Marlowe, and the philosopher statesman, ▷ Francis Bacon. The college system was now strongly established; it imposed effective discipline and established the relationship between tutor and student as the principal method of instruction, as it is to the present day. Young men of the upper classes began to be sent to the universities as a regular practice to complete their education, unless they completed it in the London ▷ Inns of Court.

It was not until the 17th century that the well-known public schools – especially Winchester and Eton – became predominantly aristocratic. The young nobleman was more often educated, until he went to the university, by tutors in his home. Gentlemen, however, commonly went to grammar schools. At Repton, later a public school, the first 20 names on the list of pupils in 1564 include the sons of 5 gentlemen, 13 small farmers and 4 tradesmen. There were often entrance fees into the grammar schools, graduated according to the rank of the pupil, but some of the town schools, such as the one probably attended by ▷ Shakespeare in Stratford-upon-Avon, were free to the sons of burgesses, *ie* established citizens.

Boys received a predominantly classical education – chiefly in Latin literature – as they were to continue to do until late in the 19th century, though at the universities they might in addition acquire some knowledge of mathematics, the sciences and ▷ Aristotelian philosophy. The universities still followed the medieval pattern of the trivium and the quadrivium, though thinking was much freer and more varied, and no longer subjected to theology. Teaching continued to ignore what were known as the 'mechanical arts'. It was, however, beginning to be a practical age, and in 1597 Sir Thomas Gresham founded Gresham College in London for lectures which included physic (*ie* medicine), law and navigation, as well as the more 'liberal' subjects. Gresham College lasted until 1768, by which time other institutions of a similar kind existed. The Inns of Court were attended especially by young men who, like the poet ▷ John Donne, were ambitious but not wealthy, for a legal training was the most useful practical one for a public career in politics and administration as well as the law itself.

▷ Women, Education of.

Edward II (1307–27)

King of England. His reign is chiefly noted for his decisive defeat by the Scots in the Scottish War of Independence (battle of Bannockburn, 1314) and for his conflicts with the barons over his excessive indulgence of favourites, especially Piers Gaveston.

▷ Christopher Marlowe's play *Edward II* presents him as a decadent sensual prince in ▷ Renaissance style, but pitiable in his horrible death by assassination.

Edward III (1327–77)

The King of England under whom the Hundred Years' War with France began. Up to 1360 he was notably successful, and the English armies won the battles of Crécy (1346) and Poitiers (1356). He was succeeded on the throne by his grandson ▷ Richard II, his eldest son, the Black Prince, having died in 1376.

The play ▷ *Edward III* (1596) has sometimes been ascribed to ▷ Shakespeare, at least in part.

Edward III (1596)

An historical drama about the perverted courtship of the Countess of Salisbury by the king, and set during the French wars. It is one of the anonymous plays that, it has been argued (by Kenneth Muir, *Shakespeare as Collaborator*, and G. R. Proudfoot, *British Academy Shakespeare Lecture 1985*), on internal evidence should be attributed to ▷ Shakespeare.

Edward IV (1461–83)

First of the kings of England belonging to the House of York; he was victorious in the Wars of the Roses over the last King of the House of Lancaster, ▷ Henry VI.

Edward IV plays a prominent part in ▷ Shakespeare's ▷ *Henry VI, Part III*, where he first appears as the Earl of March, and in ▷ *Richard III*, in which he dies and his throne is seized from the rightful heir, his son, by Edward IV's brother, Richard, Duke of Gloucester.

Edward VI (1547–53)

The boy king who succeeded ▷ Henry VIII. Under the regency of the Protectors (the Duke of Somerset and, later, the Duke of Northumberland) Henry's essentially political ▷ Reformation became more ▷ Protestant in doctrine, though the new ▷ *Book of Common Prayer* was a wise compromise. Persecution of Roman Catholics in Edward's reign led to a reaction against Protestantism when his sister ▷ Mary succeeded him.

Edwards, Richard (1523–66)

Master of the children of the Chapel Royal and author of the popular courtly drama about ideal friendship, ▷ *Damon and Pithias* (1561), as well as of an influential, posthumously published collection of poets of the early ▷ Elizabethan period, *The Paradyse of Dainty Devises* (1576).

Elegy

An elegy is usually taken to be a poetic lament for one who has died, or at least a grave and reflective poem. In ancient Greek and Latin literature, however, an elegy was a poem written in a particular metre (line of six dactylic feet alternating with lines of five feet) and it had no necessary connection with death or gravity; the Latin poet ▷ Ovid used it for love poetry. Following his example, the English poet ▷ John Donne wrote a series of elegies with amorous or satirical themes. Most of the famous elegies in English, however, follow the narrower and more widely accepted definition: ▷ Milton's ▷ *Lycidas* is inspired by the death of his friend Edward King.

Elements, The (Four)

The 'four elements' are the ancient Greek and medieval conception of the basic components of matter; they are air, fire, earth and water. It was a division made by Empedocles of Sicily and adopted by ▷ Aristotle. Aristotle was writing before the beginnings of chemical analysis and considered matter in regard to the 'properties' or qualities that he believed all things to possess; these he found to be 'hotness', 'coldness', 'wetness' and 'dryness'. His four elements contained these properties in different combinations: air = hot and wet; fire = hot and dry; earth = cold and dry; water = cold and wet. These, therefore, were the basic constituents of nature. Aristotle's great prestige in the ▷ Middle Ages caused his theory to dominate the thought of the time. The medieval alchemists, forbears of the modern analytical chemist, noticed that the properties of various kinds of matter change, *eg* iron becomes rust, and they deduced from Aristotle's theory that materials could be changed provided that they retained the same basic properties, *eg* lead could be changed into gold. The theory dominated European thought until the 17th century, when the English 'natural philosopher' and chemist Robert Boyle (1627–91) taught that an element is to be regarded as a substance in itself and not as a substance with certain basic properties. Since Boyle, chemists have discovered that elements are very much more numerous than the original four, and that air, fire, earth and water are not in fact elements at all. Nonetheless, the pervasiveness of these so-called 'four elements' in our environment has caused them to keep their hold on the modern imagination, when it is not engaged in scientific thinking, so that they are still employed as symbols for the basic constituents of our experience of the world in some imaginative literature.

The theory of the 'four elements' was connected in classical and medieval times with the medical and psychological theory of the 'humours', or four basic liquid constituents of the body. The blood humour ('hot and wet') is linked to air; choler ('hot and dry') is associated with fire; phlegm ('cold and wet') corresponds to water and melancholy ('cold and dry') to earth. The preponderance of one or other of these humours in the make-up of a person's character was supposed to determine the temperament.
▷ Humour.

Elf

In old English myth, a tiny supernatural being, neither good nor bad in itself, but commonly responsible for mischief. It is of

Teutonic origin but it became increasingly associated with the fairy – of Latin origin – a less malicious kind of creature. ▷ Edmund Spenser, in the ▷ *Faerie Queene* uses the word in places for the Queen's knights. The more mischievous kind of fairy came to be called a goblin, *eg* ▷ Puck in ▷ Shakespeare's ▷ *A Midsummer Night's Dream*.
▷ Fairies.

Elizabeth I (1558–1603)

Queen of England. Her reign was an extremely critical one, in which the personal fate of the queen was unusually bound up with that of the nation and the national Church. As a ▷ Protestant, she broke ▷ Mary's ties with Rome and restored her father's independent ▷ Church of England, but tolerance and compromise won her the loyalty of ▷ Catholics and ▷ Puritans alike. For 30 years she successfully played off against each other the two great Catholic powers, France and Spain. While she remained single, there was always a chance that her Catholic cousin ▷ Mary, Queen of Scots and widow of a French king, might succeed her. Even when Mary, deposed by the Scots, took refuge in England and connived at plots to murder her, Elizabeth avoided reprisals for nearly 20 years. Mary's eventual execution was followed in 1588 by Philip of Spain's attempted invasion of England, which resulted in the defeat of his powerful fleet, the great ▷ Armada. This was represented as a great triumph for Elizabeth personally, and in her person the English nation saw its own triumph.

The reign saw an efflorescence of national spirit in other ways. It was the period of the first great achievements in English seamanship. Elizabeth's court was the focus of the real flowering of the English ▷ Renaissance, expressing itself through music and literature; especially, the age of English poetic drama began. Commerce expanded through the joint stock merchant companies and with it a wealthy upper class, partly landed and partly mercantile, who left their mark in the immense country mansions they built all over the land. It was also the period of nationalistic expansion and the founding of many colonies (▷ Colonialism) in the New World. The queen herself, though cautious in statesmanship, was spirited and highly cultivated. She is now recognized as an author of considerable skill and learning; her speeches and poetry are available in contemporary editions.
▷ Companies, Joint Stock; Drake, Sir

Francis; Elizabethan period of English literature; Ralegh, Sir Walter; Sidney, Sir Philip; Sixteenth-century literature.
Bib: Salter, R., *Elizabeth I and Her Reign*; Travitsky, B., *The Paradise of Women*.

Elizabeth, Queen of Bohemia (1595–1660)

Poet and patron. The daughter of ▷ James I, Princess Elizabeth was more influenced by her brother ▷ Henry than by her father. Her marriage to the Elector Palatine in 1613 and their acceptance of the crown of Bohemia in 1619 confirmed her early ▷ Protestant leanings. On the loss of Bohemia in 1620 and throughout the ensuing negotiations with Spain, Elizabeth crossed the continent in search of funds and support for the Protestant cause. In Britain she was seen as a tragic heroine in exile and called 'the winter queen', while her Protestantism identified her with the old queen, ▷ Elizabeth I, and there were angry requests for James to send aid to his daughter. She also wrote some poetry.
Bib: Greer, G. (ed.), *Kissing the Rod*.

Elizabethan novels

The events in a novel or novella are not drawn directly from traditional or legendary sources but are invented by the writer, so that they are new (or 'novel') to the reader. The 'novels' of the Elizabethan period are distinguishable from the long prose romances, such as Sir Philip Sidney's ▷ *Arcadia*, by their comparative brevity, but *Arcadia* is sometimes included among them.

The Italian novella began its history in the 13th century, and one of its best practitioners, ▷ Giovanni Boccaccio, was already well known in England, especially from ▷ Chaucer's adaptation of his work. In the first 20 years of ▷ Elizabeth I's reign, various Italian 'novelle', especially those of Bandello (?1480–1562), were ▷ translated into English, notably by William Painter in his collection ▷ *The Palace of Pleasure* (1566–7). These translations created a taste for the form, and led to the production of native English 'novels'. ▷John Lyly's ▷ *Euphues* (1578) was the first of these. Best known among those that followed are: Lyly's *Euphues and his England* (1580), Barnabe Rich's (1542–1617) collection *Farewell to the Military Profession* (1581), ▷ Robert Greene's ▷ *Pandosto* (1588) and *Menaphon* (1589), ▷ Thomas Lodge's *Rosalynde* (1590), ▷ Thomas Nashe's ▷ *Unfortunate Traveller* (1594), and ▷ Thomas Deloney's *Thomas of Reading, Jack of Newbury* and *The Gentle Craft* (all between 1596 and 1600). The style of these works varies greatly. Rich, Greene and Lodge wrote mannered and courtly tales in imitation of Lyly; Nashe's rambling narrative is sometimes strongly realistic, and his style parodies a wide range of contemporary prose styles; Deloney addressed a middle-class public and at his best (in *Thomas of Reading*) anticipates the sober vividness of Daniel Defoe (1660–1731). The taste for the form lapsed in the early 17th century. There is no continuous development between the Elizabethan novel and the novel form as we know it today: the latter has its beginnings in the work of Defoe in the early 18th century, though it had late 17th-century forerunners.

Both the Italian and the English novels were used as sources for plots by contemporary English dramatists. Shakespeare's ▷ *Twelfth Night* is drawn from *Apolonius and Silla* in Rich's collection, adapted from an Italian original; his ▷ *As You Like It* is based on Lodge's *Rosalynde*; his ▷ *Winter's Tale* draws on Greene's *Pandosto*.
Bib: Margolies, D., *Novel and Society in Elizabethan England*.

Elizabethan period of English literature
The term 'Elizabethan' is used confusingly in regard to literature.
1 It is generally applied accurately to the lyric poetry and prose (*eg* ▷Elizabethan novels) which flowered during the reign of ▷ Elizabeth I and especially during the last half of it.
2 On the other hand the term 'Elizabethan drama' is sometimes made to cover not only the beginnings of poetic drama (roughly 1588–1600), but also the period that succeeded this in the reign of ▷ James I and even the period of its final decline under ▷ Charles I, *ie* until the closing of the theatres in 1642. But critics usually distinguish the mature phase as ▷ Jacobean and the decline as ▷ Caroline. By this more accurate designation, an Elizabethan dramatist would be such as ▷ Marlowe, the early Shakespeare, ▷ Greene, ▷ Lyly, or ▷ Peele; the Jacobean drama would include mature and late Shakespeare, ▷ Jonson, ▷ Tourneur, ▷ Webster, ▷ Middleton; and the Caroline drama, the later work of ▷ Massinger, ▷ John Ford and ▷ James Shirley.
3 In literary terminology, 'Elizabethan' has further to be distinguished from Tudor. The queen was herself the last of the ▷ House of Tudor, but Tudor drama, the Tudor lyric, Tudor prose etc. commonly refer to work during the previous reigns, *ie* between the accession of

▷ Henry VII in 1485 and her own accession in 1558.

Elyot, Sir Thomas (?1499–1546)
Diplomat and scholar. A member of ▷ Sir Thomas More's circle, he was friendly with ▷ humanists such as ▷ Erasmus, ▷ Thomas Linacre and John Colet (1467–1519). His major publication was *A Book Named the Governor* (1531), dedicated to ▷ Henry VIII. The work is similar to educational and political conduct books such as ▷ Baldassare Castiglione's *Il Cortegiano* and ▷ Machiavelli's *Il Principe*, in that it sets out the humanist ideal of the educated and powerful monarch. Elyot also wrote two other works of political philosophy – *The Image of Governance* (1541) and *The Doctrinal of Princes* (composed c 1534).
Bib: Warren, L. C., *Humanistic Doctrines of the Prince from Petrarch to Sir Thomas Elyot*.

Emblem-books
Books, very popular in England in the 16th century, containing pictures of ordinary objects (compasses, bottles, flowers, etc.) together with short poems showing how the object could be used to teach a truth applicable to life or conduct. Probably the first English emblem-book was Thomas Palmer's *Two Hundred Poosees* (c 1565), created for the ▷ Earl of Leicester. The fashion influenced the imagery of the 17th-century ▷ Metaphysical poets who commonly used simple objects as more or less complex illustrations of human experience, as when the poet ▷ John Donne in 'Valediction Forbidding Mourning' compares the relationship of himself and his wife when he goes on a journey to a pair of geometrical compasses whose points can divide but which yet remain united. Poets such as ▷ Francis Quarles and ▷ George Wither wrote verses sometimes shaped like such objects – a bottle, wings, etc. George Wither's *A Collection of Emblems, Ancient and Modern* appeared in four volumes in 1635, Frances Quarles' *Emblems* also in 1635, and the slightly earlier collection by ▷ Henry Peachman entitled *Minerva Britannia* in 1612. Peacham's collection set out to proclaim not so much philosophical truths, but to celebrate English 'worthies' such as ▷ Francis Bacon. It has been argued that poets such as ▷ Richard Crashaw, ▷ George Herbert and ▷ Henry Vaughan were influenced by emblem-books. Such an influence might possibly be discerned not just in the imagery of individual poems, but in

the titles and organization of their collections of poetry.

Bib: *Emblematica: An Interdisciplinary Journal for Emblem Studies.*

Empson, William (1906–84)

Critic and poet. Empson was born in Yorkshire and worked under ▷ I. A. Richards at Cambridge. His main critical works are: *Seven Types of Ambiguity* (1930), *Some Versions of Pastoral* (1935), *The Structure of Complex Words* (1951) and *Milton's God* (1961). Volumes of his verse include: *Poems* (1940) and *Collected Poems* (1955).

As a critic, he was very influential, especially through his analysis of the nature of language when it is used in imaginative writing, particularly poetry. His approach was influenced by the attitudes to language of 20th-century linguistic philosophers, especially Bertrand Russell and Wittgenstein, who concentrated on the tendency of language, by the ambiguities inherent in it, to confuse clear thought. Empson's teacher, Richards, in his *Principles of Literary Criticism* (1924), discussed the kinds of truth that are to be found in poetic statements, and how these truths differ from, without being less valuable than, the truths of philosophical and scientific statement. Empson's first book (*Seven Types*) discusses the way in which various kinds of semantic ambiguity can be used by poets, and shows the relevance of this study to the assessment of poems. It has become a major text in what came to be known as ▷ new criticism. His later books develop the psychological (particularly ▷ Freudian) and philosophical aspects of this approach. More recently ▷ post-structuralist and ▷ psychoanalytic critics have become interested in *Seven Types of Ambiguity*. Empson's poetry is difficult, academic – heavily annotated by him – and itself highly ambiguous.

▷ *Paradise Lost.*

England's Helicon

An Elizabethan verse ▷ anthology, published in 1600 and possibly edited by one Nicholas Ling. The collection mainly comprises ▷ pastoral verse, and contains poems by ▷ Sir Philip Sidney, ▷ Edmund Spenser, ▷ Michael Drayton, ▷ Thomas Lodge and others, as well as 'The Passionate Sheepheards Song' by ▷ Shakespeare. This last was taken from Act IV of ▷ *Love's Labour's Lost*, first published in quarto in 1598. The poem was republished in ▷ *The Passionate Pilgrim* of 1599. In 1614 a second edition of *England's Helicon* appeared, which included additional verses by Sidney and a poem by ▷ William Browne.

Bib: Macdonald, H. (ed.), *England's Helicon.*

Epic

1 A narrative of heroic actions, often with a principal hero, usually mythical in its content, offering inspiration and ennoblement within a particular cultural or national tradition.

2 The word denotes qualities of heroism and grandeur, appropriate to epic but present in other literary or even non-literary forms.

Epics occur in almost all national cultures, and commonly give an account of national origins, or enshrine ancient, heroic myths central to the culture. For European culture at large, much the most influential epics are the ▷ *Iliad* and the *Odyssey* of ▷ Homer and the ▷ *Aeneid* by ▷ *Virgil.* ▷ C. S. Lewis in *Preface to Paradise Lost* makes a helpful distinction between primary and secondary epics: primary ones, such as Homer's, are composed for a society which is still fairly close to the conditions of society described in the narrative; secondary epics are based on the pattern of primary epics but written for a materially developed society more or less remote from the conditions described, *eg* Virgil's *Aeneid.* In English literature the Old English *Beowulf* may be counted as a primary epic. A number of attempts at secondary epic have been made since the 16th century, but ▷ John Milton's ▷ *Paradise Lost* is unique in its acknowledged greatness and its closeness to the Virgilian structure. ▷ Spenser's ▷ *The Faerie Queene* has many epic characteristics, but, in spite of the important classical influences upon it, the poem's structure is derived from the 'romantic epic' of the 16th-century Italian poets, ▷ Ariosto and ▷ Tasso; moreover, though ▷ allegory often plays a part in epics, the allegorical elements in *The Faerie Queene* are so pervasive as to present a different kind of imaginative vision from that normally found in them.

Bib: Merchant, P., *The Epic.*

Epicoene, or The Silent Woman (1609)

A comedy by ▷ Ben Jonson. Epicoene means having the characteristics of either sex. The main character, Morose, who has an extreme hatred of noise, wants to disinherit his nephew and marry a silent woman if she can be found. A completely silent one is found, but after marriage she finds the use of her tongue and is anything but silent. Morose promises to reinstate his nephew as his heir, with an additional reward, if he can free his uncle of

the wife who is now the opposite of what he hoped. The nephew then discloses that the wife is a boy disguised. Though not one of the greatest of Jonson's comedies, it has always been one of his most popular, owing to a large cast of lively comic characters. The play is given a close analysis in Dryden's (1631–1700) *Essay on Dramatic Poesy*.
    ▷ *Querelle des Femmes*.

Epic simile

Prolonged similes, commonly used in ▷ epic or heroic poetry, giving the subject described a spaciousness suited to its grandeur. Thus in ▷ *Paradise Lost* Bk. I, ▷ Milton wants to say that the fallen Satan is as big as a whale; this would be to use an ordinary simile. He expands it to an epic simile thus:

> As huge as . . .
>   . . . that Sea-beast
> *Leviathan, which God of all his works*
> *Created hugest that swim th'Ocean stream:*
> *Him haply slumbring on the Norway foam*
> *The Pilot of some small night-founder'd Skiff,*
> *Deeming some Island, oft, as Sea-men tell,*
> *With fixéd Anchor in his skaly rind*
> *Moors by his side under the Lee, while Night*
> *Invests the Sea, and wishéd Morn delayes:*
> *So stretcht out huge in length the Arch-fiend*
> *lay . . .*

Epigram

For the ancient Greeks the word meant 'inscription'. From this, the meaning extended to include very short poems notable for the terseness and elegance of their expression and the weight and wit of their meaning. The richest of the ancient Greek collections is the Greek ▷ *Anthology*; the greatest Latin masters were ▷ Catullus and Martial. ▷ Ben Jonson's *Epigrams* contains epigrams in their tradition. After him, epigrams became shorter and most commonly had satirical content.

Epitaph

An inscription on a tomb, or a short verse or prose inscription that might serve such a purpose. As literary compositions, epitaphs became popular in the ▷ Renaissance, and the requirement of brevity gives epitaphs a resemblance to ▷ epigrams.

Epithalamion (1594)

▷Edmund Spenser's ▷ ode written in 1594, and published at the end of the ▷ sonnet sequence ▷ *Amoretti* (1595). The poem celebrates the marriage of Spenser to Elizabeth Boyle at Cork on 11 July 1594.
    ▷ *Prothalamion*.

Epyllion

A term, now largely unused, to describe the short-lived but popular Elizabethan genre of the minor or brief ▷ epic. It often, though not exclusively, denoted narrative verse which took as its model not the epics of ▷ Homer or ▷ Virgil, but the writings of ▷ Ovid. The genre flourished in England in the late 16th century, and includes works such as ▷ Thomas Lodge's *Scilla's Metamorphosis* (1589), *Ovid's Banquet of Sence* (1595) by ▷ George Chapman (?1559–1634) and ▷ Francis Beaumont's *Salmacis and Hermaphroditus* (1602). The most famous examples of the genre are undoubtedly ▷ Christopher Marlowe's ▷ *Hero and Leander* of 1598, to which Chapman and Henry Petowe (fl 1598–1612) appended 'continuations', and ▷ Shakespeare's ▷ *Venus and Adonis* (1593). Invariably, the epyllion's subject matter was erotic myth, but unlike earlier translations of Ovid, there was no attempt at placing the erotic within ▷ allegorical or moral context.
Bib: Alexander, N. (ed.), *Elizabethan Narrative Verse*.

Erasmus, Desiderius (?1466–1536)

Dutch-born Augustinian monk, translator, ▷ humanist, educationalist, biblical scholar and linguist. Erasmus was one of the most important northern European scholars of the ▷ Renaissance period. The diversity of his interests, the range of his accomplishments, and the weight of his influence on European thought in the 16th century and later are almost impossible to quantify.
    Erasmus' chief works are: the *Adages* (first published in 1500), the *Enchiridion* (1503), the *Praise of Folly* (1509) and the *Colloquies* (first published in 1516). But to these popular successes can be added his editions of the Church Fathers, paraphrases, commentaries on the scripture, editions of the classics and a huge correspondence with other European scholars and thinkers, the most important of whom, in England, was his close friend ▷ Sir Thomas More. The *Praise of Folly*, a satirical work which ranges widely over all aspects of public life in the period, was conceived while Erasmus was travelling to England to see More – a circumstance preserved in the work's punning Latin title: *Encomium Moriae*.
    The *Enchiridion*, on the other hand, is a manual of the Christian life which encourages knowledge of pagan (that is ▷ classical)

literature as a preparative towards attaining Christian scriptural understanding. The *Adages* – a work which grew from some 800 'adages' or classical sayings into over 4,000 short essays by the time Erasmus died – provided an entry into classical literature, and into humanistic thought generally, for the public at large. Similarly, the *Colloquies* expanded as Erasmus worked at the project until they eventually formed a wide-ranging series of dialogues on a huge variety of topics, which were to include education, games, travel, parenthood, punishment and social and religious questions.

Bib: *The Collected Works of Erasmus*; Huizinga, J., *Erasmus of Rotterdam*.

Essay, The
'Essay' derives from the French *essai*, meaning 'experiment', 'attempt'. As a literary term it is used to cover an enormous range of composition, from students' exercises to thorough scientific and philosophical works, the only quality in common being the implied desire of the writer to reserve to him or herself some freedom of treatment. But the essay is also a recognized literary form in a more defined sense: it is understood to be a fairly short prose composition, in style often familiarly conversational and in subject either self-revelatory or illustrative (more or less humorously) of social manners and types. The originator of the form was the French writer ▷ Montaigne.

Montaigne's essays were published in completed form in 1595, and translated by ▷ John Florio into English (1603). His starting-point is 'Que sais-je?' ('What do I know?') and it leads him into a serious inquiry into his own nature as he feels it, and into investigations of facts, ideas and experiences as he responds to them. In 1597 the first important English essayist, ▷ Francis Bacon, published his first collection of essays, of a very different kind: they are impersonal and aphoristic, weightily sententious. The character writers ▷ Sir Thomas Overbury, John Earle (?1601–65), Cecily Bulstrode and ▷ Lady Frances Southwell use the classical model of the Greek writer ▷ Theophrastus, reminding one that with so indefinite a form it is impossible to be too precise about the dating of starting-points. ▷ Abraham Cowley published the first essays in English closely corresponding to what is now understood by the form, and perhaps shows the first sign of its degeneracy: easiness of tone, which in Montaigne is a graciousness of manner introducing a serious and interesting

personality, but which in less interesting writers may be an agreeable cover for saying nothing in particular.

Essays, Bacon's
▷ Bacon, Francis.

Essex, Robert Devereux, Earl of (1566–1601)
Patron, poet and favourite of ▷ Queen Elizabeth I. Robert Devereux, second Earl of Essex was the stepson of the ▷ Earl of Leicester and followed him into the intimate circle of the queen's favourites. He pursued a political and martial career which won him glory throughout the 1590s; however in 1599 he was sent to ▷ Ireland to suppress Tyrone's rebellion and returned unexpectedly without Elizabeth's permission having failed in his mission. He remained under house arrest until in 1601 he attempted to seize power from the queen in an ill-fated rebellion. He was executed on 25 February of the same year. Although Elizabeth had ordered his death, even in the face of final pleas for mercy, she never recovered her old vigour and the last 18 months of her reign seem to have been shrouded in a recognition of her own mortality. Some of Essex's fellow conspirators arranged for a special performance of what we believe to be ▷ Shakespeare's ▷ *Richard II* around the city of London on the day before the revolt. The play shows the abdication of an unpopular monarch and its enactment was supposedly to rouse the crowds into calling for a similar relinquishing of power on the part of Elizabeth. Shakespeare also refers to Essex in ▷ *Henry V*, where a successful return from the Irish campaign is hoped for.
Bib: Lacey, R., *An Elizabethan Icarus*.

Euphues (1578–80)
A prose romance by ▷ John Lyly, in two parts; the first, *Euphues, or the Anatomy of Wit* was published in 1578; the second, *Euphues and his England*, in 1580. The tales have very little story; they have been described as 'pattern books' for courtly behaviour, especially in love. Their most striking quality is their elaborate style: long sentences balance clause against clause and image against image, so as to produce an effect of ornament taking priority a long way over sense. ▷ Falstaff in ▷ *Henry IV Part I* (II.iv) parodies Euphues when he is burlesquing the king, *eg* 'for though the camomile, the more it is trodden on, the faster it grows, yet youth, the more it is wasted, the sooner it wears'. Though often parodied as the language of

fops, the style was much imitated, especially
by Elizabethan romance writers such as
▷ Robert Greene in *Menaphon* (1589) and
▷ Thomas Lodge in *Rosalynde* (1590). Even
▷ Beatrice and Benedick in ▷ Shakespeare's
▷ *Much Ado About Nothing* indulge in the
courtly verbal play characterized by Lyly. The
name 'Euphues' is from Greek, and means
generally, 'well endowed by nature'. ▷ Roger
Ascham in *The Schoolmaster* had already
used it to designate a man well endowed
for learning and able to put it to good use.
Ascham was an admirer of ▷ Castiglione's
The Courtier, and Lyly's cult of the courtly
virtues is in the same tradition. Basic to it
is the conception that nature is not to be
imitated but to be improved upon.

Euripides (480–406BC)

The last of the three great Athenian writers of
▷ tragedy, the other two being ▷ Aeschylus
and ▷ Sophocles. Like them, he had no direct
influence upon the Elizabethan period of
English drama, though ▷ Gascoigne's *Jocasta*
(1575) is a translation of an Italian adaptation
of Euripides' *Phoenissae*. Like Aeschylus and
Sophocles, however, Euripides was admired
by ▷ Milton, who emulated the Greeks
in ▷ *Samson Agonistes*. Among Euripides'
surviving plays are *Alcestis, Medea, Hippolytus,
Andromache, Hecuba, Bacchae, Electra, The
Trojan Women, Orestes, Heracles, Iphigenia at
Aulis, Iphigenia among the Tauri, Ion.*

Every Man in his Humour (1598)

The first important play by ▷ Ben Jonson. By
▷ 'humour' is to be understood as a passion
generated by irrational egotism and amounting

sometimes to a mania. The play – which is
better known in its revised form with English
characters than in the first
version of 1598 with Italian characters – is
a comedy of misunderstandings bred largely
through the deceitfulness of Brainworm, a
mischievous servant, acting on the absurd
humours of the other characters: the jealousy
of the merchant Kitely, the credulity of his
young wife, the susceptibility of her sister, the
bullying boastfulness of the cowardly soldier
Bobadill, etc.
▷Humours, Comedy of.

Every Man out of his Humour (1599)

The second of ▷ Ben Jonson's comedies of
▷ humours, with a range of satirical portraits:
Fastidious Brisk, the foppish courtier with the
sharp tongue; Sordido, the landowner who
delights in shortages because they increase
the price of his grain; Deliro, the infatuated
husband; Puntarvolo, the knight who takes
out an insurance on his pets; Fungoso, the
would-be courtier who is always behind the
fashion, etc. The method of satire is partly
through character sketches in the tradition
of ▷ Theophrastus and partly through
the method that Jonson developed from
▷ Marlowe (in ▷ *The Jew of Malta*) of making
a character carry his extravagance to the point
of self-caricature. This play is, however, too
narrow in the range and depth of its satire to
rank among Jonson's great ones. The opening
scene includes a speech (by Asper, lines
93–120) which contains an explicit account of
what Jonson meant by a ▷ 'Humour'.
▷ Characters, Theophrastian.

Faerie Queene, The (1590–6)
▷Edmund Spenser's unfinished ▷ allegorical romance. *The Faerie Queene* was first mentioned in correspondence by Spenser in 1580, and was probably circulating in manuscript form by 1588. Books I–III were published in 1590, and a second edition which contained Books IV–VI appeared in 1596. In 1609 a folio edition of the poem appeared, which contained the first six books of the poem, together with the ▷ 'Mutabilitie Cantos'. This is all of the work which has survived, though whether any more was written is doubtful.

The design of the poem, and Spenser's general conception of what the poem should set out to achieve, is recorded in a letter from Spenser to ▷ Sir Walter Ralegh that was published in the first edition of 1590. Here Spenser explains that his intention was to 'fashion a gentleman or noble person', and we can thus understand the poem as forming part of that ▷ Renaissance desire to create and sustain a personal identity. But the work is also a legendary history and celebration of the emergent British state and its monarch, ▷ Elizabeth I. The urgency of this project is understandable given Spenser's own residence in the unstable environment of ▷ Ireland for much of the period of the poem's composition.

In structure the poem follows the adventures of six knights, representing (Spenser claimed in his letter to Ralegh) the ▷ Aristotelian virtues. But the poem is episodic rather than possessed of a cumulative narrative structure. At the same time, to mention Aristotle is to mention only one of the poem's many progenitors, which include ▷ Plato, ▷ Ludovico Ariosto's *Orlando Furioso*, ▷ Torquato Tasso, ▷ Virgil and Arthurian romance.

The Faerie Queene is perhaps best thought of as a rich synthesis of ▷ Protestant and ▷ humanist ideals, and, at the same time, an anxious declaration of faith in the vision of national identity which it is the poem's task to display. Its influence on later writers, especially ▷ John Milton, was enormous.

▷ Arthur, King; Belphoebe; Duessa; Fidessa; Florimell; Gloriana; Orgoglio; Red Cross Knight.
Bib: Hamilton, A. C. (ed.), *The Faerie Queene*; Heale, E., *The Faerie Queene: A Reader's Guide*; Miller, D. L., *The Poem's Two Bodies*.

Fairies
Supernatural beings such as provide material for folk-tales all over the world. In Britain, as in many other countries, fairies have been regarded as neither good nor evil, but sometimes mischievous and sometimes beneficent, as human behaviour has given opportunity and invitation (see for instance Mercutio's speech on Queen Mab in ▷ Shakespeare's ▷ *Romeo and Juliet*, I. iv). Belief in them has been thought to be a vestige of pre-Christian beliefs in nature-spirits. Stories about them sometimes include elements of medieval romance and classical myth; thus in Shakespeare's ▷ *A Midsummer Night's Dream*, ▷ Oberon derives from a 13th-century French romance, *Huon de Bordeaux*, ▷ Titania is used as a version of Diana the huntress in ▷ Ovid's ▷ *Metamorphoses* and ▷ Puck, also called Robin Goodfellow, is from English folklore. ▷ Spenser's ▷ Faerie Queene Gloriana gives Queen Elizabeth I the allure of romance at the same time as identifying her with the Platonic ideal of Glory. Although ▷ witches play a part in fairy stories, witchcraft, as exemplified by 16th- and 17th-century belief and manifested in Shakespeare's ▷ *Macbeth*, is altogether more serious and sinister, and requires separate treatment.

Fair Maid of the West, The (1600/1630)
A romantic and ▷ picaresque comedy in two parts (1600 and 1630) by ▷ Thomas Heywood. It is set during ▷ Essex's expedition to the Azores in 1597 and dramatizes the adventures of the chivalrous Master Spencer and the beautiful Bess Bridges, whom he champions and who rescues him in turn after his capture by the Spaniards.

Faithful Shepherdess, The (1610)
A ▷ pastoral romance by ▷ John Fletcher which, in a short but influential preface about tragicomedy, acknowledges its indebtedness to the pastoral idiom of G. B. Guarini, the author of the seminal and famous pastoral play, *Il Pastor Fido* (1598); it thereby contributed to the vogue of English tragicomedies in the 1610s. But, whereas Fletcher's definition of tragicomedy specifically precluded death from its imaginative idiom, the English uses of the genre have tended to weld together the tragic and comic modes in a harsher manner and allowed death its full place in Arcadia.

Falstaff, Sir John
A character in ▷ Shakespeare's history plays, ▷ *Henry IV, Parts I and II*, and in the comedy

▷ *The Merry Wives of Windsor*. His death is described in ▷ *Henry V* (II. ii). In the history plays he is a very active comic character, embodying fleshly indulgence, and considered to be the chief injurious influence on Prince Hal (Henry), the heir to the throne. Though a fully realized character in his own right, he clearly carries also some force from medieval ▷ allegory, representing the temptations of physical indulgence or 'riot'. Accordingly Hal, once anointed as King Henry v, casts him off at the end of *Henry IV, Part II*. In *The Merry Wives* he is much less substantial, and plays the role of a comparatively commonplace buffoon.

▷Oldcastle, Sir John.

Fanshawe, Lady Ann (1625–80)

Biographer. Although her *Memoirs* (completed 1676) ostensibly tell the life of her beloved husband for the benefit of his son, in fact they are a vivid and lively account of her own experiences, as well as those of Sir Richard Fanshawe. Lady Ann's life after she married Sir Richard in 1644 was full of the poverty-stricken turmoils and disappointments that characterized the Royalist party during the ▷ Interregnum. She was almost shipwrecked, almost abducted by pirates (she saved herself by adopting the disguise of a cabin boy), trapped in Galway during an outbreak of the plague, and bore 14 live children. Although the Fanshawes shared in the triumphal return of the monarchy, at her husband's death in 1666 Lady Ann was again left without financial support and she remained poor until her death. *Memoirs* is a dramatic account of the life of the Fanshawe family, but it is also a deeply moving account of marital love, which despite numerous trials endured undiminished.

▷Biography; Autobiography.
Bib: Fraser, A., *The Weaker Vessel*; Wilcox, H., in Cerasano, S. P. and Wynne-Davies, M. (eds.), *Gloriana's Face*.

Farce

A term used for comedy in which realism is sacrificed for the sake of extravagant humour. Its derivation is from stuffing used in cookery, and as a literary term it was applied to light and frivolous material introduced by actors into the medieval mystery plays. By the time of the ▷ Renaissance it was usually applied to lightweight comedies, but still retained the earlier sense of anarchy and misrule.

▷Bakhtin, Mikhail.

Faust

The Faust myth is much older than those legends that crystallize round the historical figure of Faust and form a part of it. The myth of men seeking great earthly power from demons at the cost of their immortal souls goes back to the ancient Jews at about the time of Christ, and centres on several figures of medieval European Christendom. In the 16th century the myth received new vitality through the influence upon it of various bodies of ideas: ▷ Renaissance ▷ humanism, in its sceptical and critical spirit; neo-Platonic (▷ Platonism) mysticism, in its conception of the potentially immense reach of the human mind; and the Protestant ▷ Reformation, in its adherence to the pure Word of God as opposed to humanist claims for reason and Catholic claims for authority. The historical Faust was an early 16th-century German philosopher who was ridiculed by other intellectuals for his extravagant pretensions to magical powers. Nonetheless, pamphlets and plays built up a widespread, partly comic and partly serious image of him as the pattern of human arrogance eternally damned for his preference of human learning over the Holy Word. ▷ Mephistopheles, the devil with whom Faust made his bargain, was himself condemned to eternal suffering and regarded himself in this light. ▷ Christopher Marlowe's ▷ *Doctor Faustus* is much the most interesting product of this tradition.

Faustus

▷ *Doctor Faustus, The Tragical History of*.

Fell, Margaret (1614–1702)

Pamphleteer and autobiographer. Until her 38th year Margaret Fell led an unremarkable and conventional life, having married Thomas Fell, a judge, in 1632. But in 1652 she heard the ▷ Quaker ▷ George Fox preach and instantly converted. Most of her household converted and although her husband did not he remained tolerant of her faith, allowing her to use their house, Swarthmore Hall, as a centre for Quakerism. She was never an itinerant preacher like ▷ Priscilla Cotton, but formed the pivot of a strong Quaker community and wrote numerous pamphlets and letters, some to noted personages such as ▷ Henrietta Maria and ▷ Oliver Cromwell. When she refused to abstain from Quaker practices and meetings during her trial in 1664, Margaret was imprisoned, but she used the opportunity to write and produced an important text in women's history, *Women's Speaking Justified* (1666). She married George

Fox in 1669 and died within the warmth and admiration of her own family at the age of 88. Her writings were published posthumously as *A Brief Collection* (1710).

▷Autobiography.

Bib: Fraser, A., *The Weaker Vessel*.

Feminism

In literary criticism this term is used to describe a range of critical positions which argue that the distinction between 'masculine' and 'feminine' (▷ gender) is formative in the generation of all discursive practices. In its concern to bring to the fore the particular situation of women in society, 'feminism' as a focus for the raising of consciousness has a long history, and can be taken to embrace an interest in all forms of women's writing throughout history. In its essentialist guise, feminism proposes a range of experiences peculiar to women that are, by definition, denied to men, and which it seeks to emphasize in order to compensate for the oppressive nature of a society rooted in what it takes to be patriarchal authority; for example, the Renaissance texts about motherhood such as ▷ Dorothy Leigh's *The Mother's Blessing* and ▷ Lady Elizabeth Clinton's *The Countess of Lincoln's Nursery*. A more materialist (▷ Materialism) account would emphasize the extent to which gender difference is a cultural construction, and therefore amenable to change by concerted political action; here the defences of women may be cited, such as those by ▷ Jane Anger, ▷ Ester Sowernam and ▷ Rachel Speght. Traditional materialist accounts, especially those of ▷ Marx, have placed the issue of 'class' above that of 'gender', but contemporary feminism regards the issue of 'gender' as frequently cutting across 'class' divisions, and raising fundamental questions about the social role of women in relations of production and exchange. Insofar as all literature is 'gendered', then feminist literary criticism is concerned with the analysis of the social construction of 'femininity' and 'masculinity' in particular texts. One of its major objectives is to expose how hitherto 'masculine' criticism has sought to represent itself as a universal experience. As such it is essential that books include references to women writers, in order to redress the balance. Similarly, the focus is adjusted in order to enable literary works themselves to disclose the ways in which the experiences they communicate are determined by wider social assumptions about gender difference, which move beyond the formal boundaries of the text. To this

extent feminism is necessarily the focus of an interdisciplinary approach to literature, psychology, sociology and philosophy.

Psychoanalytic feminism, for example, often overlaps with socialist feminism. It approaches the concept of gender as a problem rather than a given, and draws on ▷ Freud's emphasis on the instability of sexual identities. The fact that femininity – and masculinity – are never fully acquired, once and for all, suggests a relative openness allowing for changes in the ways they are distributed. Literature's disturbance and exploration of ways of thinking about sexual difference have proved a rich source for feminist critics.

Bib: de Beauvoir, S., *The Second Sex*; Greene, G. and Kahn, C. (eds.), *Making a Difference: Feminist Literary Criticism*; Millett, K., *Sexual Politics*; Spender, D., *Feminist Theorists*; ▷ *Querelle des Femmes*.

Ferdinand

The most conspicuous characters bearing this name in English literature are:

1 the King of Navarre in ▷ Shakespeare's ▷ *Love's Labour's Lost*;

2 the son of King Alonso of Naples and lover of Prospero's daughter Miranda in Shakespeare's ▷ *The Tempest*;

3 the Duke of Calabria, villain of ▷ John Webster's play ▷ *The Duchess of Malfi*.

Ferrar, Nicholas

▷ *Little Gidding*.

Ferrers, George (c 1500–1579)

Poet. Ferrers was Master of the King's Pastimes at the court of ▷ Henry VIII and in this post was responsible for writing and producing several ▷ masques. He was still in the royal service during the reign of ▷ Elizabeth I and composed several verses to be recited during her visit to Kenilworth (▷ George Gascoigne). Ferrers is best known, however, for his part in the planning, with William Baldwin, of ▷ *A Mirror for Magistrates* (1559, 1563 and 1578), a work which recorded in verse the political successes and failures of historical persons.

Fidessa

A character in ▷ Edmund Spenser's ▷ *The Faerie Queene* (Book I). Though the name Fidessa implies fidelity, she is, in reality, the false ▷ Duessa, and her intention is to lead the ▷ Red Cross Knight, standing for the faith of ▷ Protestant ▷ Church of England, into captivity.

Field, Nathaniel (1587–1633)
Actor; he was one of the most famous
in the lifetime of ▷ Shakespeare. He is
mentioned in the First ▷ Folio edition of
Shakespeare's works as having played parts
in them, and he also took leading roles in
plays by ▷ Ben Jonson and the chief one
in ▷ George Chapman's most famous play,
▷ Bussy d' Ambois. He wrote two ▷ 'citizen
comedies' in the style of Jonson: *A Woman is a
Weathercock* and *Amends for Ladies*.
Bib: Perry, W. (ed.), *The Plays of Nathan Field*.

Field of Cloth of Gold
The name given to the meeting-place of the
English ▷ Henry VIII and the French Francis
I, in France. The object of the meeting
near Guisnes in 1520 was to arrange an
alliance, but the encounter is less memorable
politically than it is for its characteristically
▷ Renaissance splendour.

Fifth Monarchists
A sect of ▷ Puritans who believed, on the
basis of a prophecy in the Bible (*Daniel* 2),
that ▷ Oliver Cromwell's rise to power was a
preparation for the Second Coming of Christ
and the establishment of the great fifth and
last monarchy, the previous four having been
the Assyrian, the Persian, the Greek and the
Roman. In disillusionment, they began to turn
against Cromwell and after the Restoration
of the monarchy in 1660 they tried to raise a
rebellion in London. It was easily suppressed
and the leaders were executed.

Filostrato, Il
▷ Boccaccio's version of the love affair
between the Trojan prince Troilo and
Criseida, written in *ottava rima* in 1335, and
used by Chaucer as the principal source for
▷ *Troilus and Criseyde*.
Bib: Havely, N. R. (trans.), *Chaucer's Boccaccio*.

Flamineo
Brother, and ultimately pimp, of ▷ Vittoria
Corombona in ▷ *The White Devil* by ▷ John
Webster. Flamineo is presented as an
embittered and cynical villain who spurns
all the dictates of conscience and duty for
self-advancement.

Fletcher, Giles (the elder) (?1549–1611)
Author of a book on Russia (1591), suppressed
by the government at the request of the English
joint stock Russia Company (▷ Companies,
Joint Stock) as likely to offend the Russian
government and hinder trade. He also wrote

a sonnet sequence, *Licia, or Poems of Love*
(1593) in emulation of ▷ Sir Philip Sidney's
▷ *Astrophil and Stella*.
Bib: Barry, L. E., (ed.), *English Works*.

Fletcher, Giles (the younger) (1585–1623)
Poet; author of ▷ allegorical religious poems,
especially his ▷ epic in ▷ Spenserian stanzas,
Christ's Victorie and Triumph (1610). He
was the younger son of ▷ Giles, Fletcher
the elder.
Bib: Hunter, W. B. (ed.), *The English
Spenserians*.

Fletcher, John (1579–1625)
Dramatist; nephew of ▷ Giles Fletcher
the elder. The 1679 edition of his work
contains 57 plays – the largest of all the
Elizabethan collections – but most of them
were collaborations.
    Among the works probably by himself
alone are: *The Faithful Shepherdess* (1608), a
▷ pastoral; the tragedies *Bonduca*
(▷ Boadicea) and *Valentinian* (1614); the
tragicomedies, *The Loyal Subject* (1618) and
The Humorous Lieutenant (1619); the comedies,
The Wild Goose Chase, Monsieur Thomas and
The Pilgrim (1621).
    It was in collaboration with ▷ Beaumont
that Fletcher produced his most famous work;
their best plays are commonly held to be the
tragicomedy ▷ *Philaster* and the tragedy *The
Maid's Tragedy*. Another tragedy, *A King and
No King* (1611), was greatly admired by John
Dryden (1631–1700); the domestic comedy
The Scornful Lady (1610) has also been highly
praised.
    Fletcher seems to have ceased collaborating
with Beaumont in 1613, and to have joined
briefly with ▷ Shakespeare. ▷ *Henry VIII*,
formerly attributed to Shakespeare entirely, is
now thought to be partly Fletcher's work, and
Shakespeare is also thought to have written
part of ▷ *The Two Noble Kinsmen*.
    Fletcher's name has also been linked with
several other dramatists, including ▷ Ben
Jonson, but especially with ▷ Massinger
between 1619 and 1622. Among these
Massinger collaborations are *Thierry and
Theodoret* and *The False One*.
    Fletcher's reputation stood highest at
the Restoration, when he was ranked with
Shakespeare and Jonson. The opinion of
most 20th-century criticism is that he was an
extremely skilful theatrical craftsman, a master
of striking but superficial dramatic effects; his
verse, similarly, is admitted to be fluent and
musical, but is felt to lack authentic depth and
strength of feeling.

Bib: Waith, E. M., *The Pattern of Tragicomedy in Beaumont and Fletcher*; Bradbrook, M. C., *Elizabethan Tragedy*; Danby, J., *Poets on Fortune's Hill*; Finkelpearl, P. J., *Court and Country Politics in the Plays of Beaumont and Fletcher*; Maxwell, B., *Studies in Beaumont, Fletcher and Massinger*; Leech, C., *The John Fletcher Plays*.

Fletcher, Phineas (1582–1650)
Elder son of ▷ Giles Fletcher the elder; ▷ allegorical poet in the tradition of ▷ Edmund Spenser. Principal work: *The Purple Island, or the Isle of Man* (1633), an allegorical representation of the human mind and body.
Bib: Hunter, W. B. (ed.), *The English Spenserians*; Longdale, A. B., *Phineas Fletcher: Man of Letters, Science and Divinity*.

Florimell
A character in ▷ Edmund Spenser's ▷ *Faerie Queene* (Books III and IV). She is one of Spenser's representations of chaste love.

Florio, John (?1553–1625)
Translator, Florio published, in 1578 and 1591, two Italian phrase books, as well as an Italian–English dictionary, *A World of Words* (1598). His best-known work, however, was his ▷ translation of the *Essays* of ▷ Montaigne, which was published in 1603.
Bib: Yates, F. A., *John Florio*.

Fluellen
A character in ▷ Shakespeare's history play ▷ *Henry V*. He is a Welsh officer in the army of Henry, fighting in France. He is presented as a brave and fine soldier, but also as a comic character, with the weaknesses of emotional and irritable pride associated with the Welsh in the English mind of Shakespeare's time. The name is a corruption of Llewellyn.

Folio
As applied to books, a folio is one for which the paper has been folded once, and therefore of the largest size. The expression 'the first folio' commonly refers to the first collected edition of ▷ Shakespeare's plays (1623); there were three other folio editions of Shakespeare's plays in the 17th century.
The 1623 volume is edited by two fellow actors of the King's Men – Heming and Condell – and contains a preface by them and prefatory poems, notably one by ▷ Ben Jonson. Following the poems there is a list of the 'principal actors in all these plays'; the list includes Shakespeare himself, ▷ Richard Burbage, ▷ Nathaniel Field, and of course the editors. The edition opens with the print of a rather inferior engraved portrait of the poet by Martin Droeshout. Thirty-six plays are included; ▷ *Pericles*, included by modern editors, is omitted. Eighteen of the plays had already been published in small ▷ quarto editions (some of them close to the folio version and some differing substantially), and the remainder were being published for the first time. The plays are undated, and grouped into Comedies, Histories and Tragedies; some have divisions into ▷ acts and scenes, and some are without them.

Ford, John (1586–?1640)
The best of the ▷ Caroline dramatists. He is best known for two tragedies, ▷ *'Tis Pity She's a Whore* and *The Broken Heart* (1633), and a tragic history play, *Perkin Warbeck* (1634). Less well known are *Lover's Melancholy* (1629) and *Love's Sacrifice* (1633). He collaborated with other dramatists, notably with ▷ Dekker and ▷ Rowley in *The Witch of Edmonton* (1623). In spite of sensational themes and incidents (*eg 'Tis Pity* is about incestuous love), Ford's characteristic tone is the melancholy of private, frustrated passion; pathos rather than tragedy. Indeed, late 20th-century criticism has suggested that there are reasoned and serious themes in the plays and that far from being precious, Ford focuses on the moral judgements of his age.
Bib: Anderson, Donald K., *John Ford*; Neill, M. (ed.), *John Ford: Critical Re-Visions*.

Forest of Arden
▷ Arden, Forest of.

Formalism
School of literary thought which flourished in Russia after 1917. Its main exponents, particularly ▷ Roman Jakobson, focused on the differentiation between literary language and other forms of written expression. The insights of the formalists have influenced later critics.
▷ Deconstruction.

Forman, Simon (1552–1611)
Astrologer, physician and diarist. This unusual figure is of importance to us because of his casebook or diary and his *Book of Plaies*, where he recorded personal information about prominent ▷ Elizabethan figures, as well as recounted details from the performances of several plays. For example, he has provided us with material about ▷ Aemilia Lanyer's life, as well as comments about

▷ Shakespeare's ▷ *Macbeth*, ▷ *Cymbeline* and ▷ *The Winter's Tale*. It was Forman's casebook which first gave A. L. Rowse the idea that Lanyer was the dark lady of Shakespeare's sonnets. While this hypothesis has little or no verification, Forman's personal revelations and his wide acquaintance with contemporary gossip make his work an important source of ▷ Renaissance social history and biographical detail.
Bib: Rowse, A. L., *Simon Forman: Sex and Society in Shakespeare's Age*.

Foucault, Michel (1926–84)

Along with ▷ Louis Althusser and ▷ Jacques Derrida, Foucault is one of the most influential of French philosophers whose work has been taken up by the practitioners of other disciplines. Foucault rejects the totalizing explanations of human development in favour of a more detailed analysis of how power functions within particular ▷ discourses. In *Madness and Civilization* (1965) he explored the historical opposition between 'madness' and 'civilization', applying ▷ Ferdinand de Saussure's (1857–1913) notion of differential (▷ Difference) to the various ways in which society excludes the behaviour that threatens it. He later took up this issue in *Discipline and Punish* (1977), and *I Pierre Riviere* (1978). In *The Order of Things* (1971) and *The Archaeology of Knowledge* (1972) he investigated the ways in which human knowledge is organized, and the transition from discourses which rely upon a notion of 'self-presence', to those which operate differentially to produce the kind of linguistic self-consciousness characteristic of post-modernism. In essays such as those translated in *Language, Counter-memory, Practice* (1977), he sought to clarify specific areas of opposition through which discourse is constructed. At the time of his death he had embarked on an investigation of the discourses of sexuality through the ages, and the three volumes of *The History of Sexuality* (1978–87) have now been published. Towards the end of the 20th century Foucault has exerted a strong influence on Renaissance criticism, primarily in the fields of ▷ new historicism and ▷ cultural materialism.
▷ Archaeology.

Four P's, The (1568)

One of the amusing ▷ interludes written by ▷ John Heywood. It begins with a competition between a palmer, a pardoner and an apothecary, judged by a pedlar, to find the best liar.

Fox, George (1624–91)

Religious leader. He founded the Society of Friends (▷ Quakers), and left a journal of his spiritual experience, published in 1694. Apart from its religious importance, Fox's journal is one of the classics amongst the English diaries. In 1669 he married ▷ Margaret Fell, a Quaker pamphleteer.
Bib: Foulds, E. V., *George Fox and the Valiant Sixty*.

Foxe, John (1516–87)

Author of the *Book of Martyrs*; this was the title under which it was popularly known; the correct title of the 1st edition (1563) was *Acts and Monuments of these latter and perilous days*. Foxe was a ▷ Puritan who first set out to write a history of Christian martyrdom in Latin. The first outline dealt chiefly with the 14th-century reformers, the English John Wycliffe (?1320–84) and the Bohemian John Huss. In 1554 he went abroad to escape persecution under the Catholic ▷ Mary, and completed his book there. The English version is fierce and eloquent, and had immense sales; for generations it inspired hatred for ▷ Catholicism in Britain, and was read alongside the ▷ Bible by simple folk who read little else. It is a classic of popular prose in the ▷ Elizabethan period.
▷ Reformation.
Bib: Olsen, V. N., *John Foxe and the Elizabethan Church*.

French literature in England

The influence of ▷ Petrarch, felt early on both sides of the Channel, was prolonged by the Italian vogue prevalent in France in the 1550s–70s and compounded by the English admiration for ▷ Pierre de Ronsard. Ronsard's love poetry found favour with the ▷ Renaissance sonneteers, ▷ Henry Constable (1562–1613), ▷ Samuel Daniel and ▷ Thomas Lodge among them. ▷ Spenser's cultivation of the 16th-century French poet ▷ Joachim Du Bellay is untypical of his age. However, it is noticeable that poetry is the favoured genre for imitation, possibly because in France itself it is at once the most deeply exploited and the most cohesively organized. Of French drama there is no trace in England; and the fortunes of prose are the fortunes of translation, as represented most momentously in ▷ Shakespeare's recourse to ▷ John Florio for ▷ Montaigne's essay *Des Cannibales* for ▷ *The Tempest*. Yet while Montaigne can unquestionably be said to have had a hand in shaping the English ▷ essay form, ▷ Rabelais leaves more elusive traces and to discern his equivalent in English literature, one has to look as close to the Renaissance as Sir John Harington (?1560–1612), ▷ Thomas Nashe and ▷ Samuel Butler.

Florio and Sir Thomas Urquhart (1611–60) – Rabelais's 17th-century translator – are authors in their own right. At the same period, Joshua Sylvester's (c 1563–1618) translation of ▷ Guillaume de Salluste Du Bartas was no less influential.

Freud, Sigmund (1856–1939)

The founder of psychoanalysis, and one of the seminal figures of 20th-century thought. Born in Moravia, then part of the Austro-Hungarian Empire, he settled in Vienna. He began his career as a doctor specializing in the physiology of the nervous system and, after experimenting briefly with hypnosis, developed the technique of free association for the treatment of hysteria and neurosis. His work is based on a number of principles. The first is psychic determinism, the principle that all mental events, including dreams, fantasies, errors and neurotic symptoms, have meaning. The second is the primacy of the unconscious mind in mental life, the unconscious being regarded as a dynamic force drawing on the energy of instinctual drives, and as the location of desires which are repressed because they are socially unacceptable or a threat to the ego. The third is a developmental view of human life, which stresses the importance of infantile experience and accounts for personality in terms of the progressive channelling of an initially undifferentiated energy or libido. Important aspects of ▷ psychoanalytical theory and practice arising from these principles include the theory of infantile sexuality and its development, centred on the ▷ Oedipus complex, the techniques of free association and dream interpretation as means of analysing repressed material, and the beliefs that much behaviour is unconsciously motivated, that sexuality plays a major role in the personality, and that civilization has been created by the direction of libidinous impulses to symbolic ends (including the creation of art). Freud regarded neurotic and normal behaviour as differing in degree rather than kind.

Despite his scientific orientation, Freud's thought had affinities with that of the Romantic poets, and several features of modern literature which show his influence also have Romantic antecedents. These include a particular interest in the quality and significance of childhood experience, a fascination with memory and with what is buried in the adult personality, and a concern with disturbed states of consciousness. The stream of consciousness technique and other experimental narrative techniques which abandon external realism in favour of the rendering of consciousness, of dreams or of fantasies, owe much to Freud's belief in the significance of these areas of experience, which had been relatively neglected by scientific thought. Furthermore, the technique of free association revealed a tendency of the mind, when rational constraints were lessened, to move towards points of psychic conflict, and this discovery helped to validate new means of structuring literary works, through association, symbol and other forms of non-rationalistic patterning (for example in the work of T. S. Eliot (1888–1965)). The view that the individual's unconscious life is as important as his or her public and social self is crucial to much 20th-century literature, which rests on the assumption that human beings live through their unconscious, and that sexuality is central to the personality. The Freudian unconscious is in particular the realm of fantasy, and Freudian thought has encouraged the belief that fantasy is of profound significance in our lives, with considerable consequences for literary forms and modes.

Psychoanalysis has developed very considerably since Freud, and continues to interact with literary practice and theory. In the field of theory, those who have studied but radically revised Freud's ideas, such as ▷ Jacques Lacan and ▷ feminist theorists, have been especially important.
Bib: Brown, J. A. C., *Freud and the Post-Freudians*; Freud, S., *Introductory Lectures on Psychoanalysis*.

Friar

The friars were members of the mendicant orders of monasticism that originated in the 13th century. Whereas monks lived in ▷ monasteries that were corporate owners of property, friars were individually self-supporting either by their own labour or by begging – hence 'mendicant'. Friars answered important religious and social needs, since they were, unlike monks, free in their movements to go where they were most needed, working as poor men among the poor. Thus the orders spread rapidly throughout Europe after the deaths of their two main founders, St Dominic (d 1221), founder of the Dominicans, and St Francis of Assisi (d

1226), founder of the Franciscans. These remained the dominant orders, though many others were introduced (some including both men and women), such as the Carmelites, the Augustinian Hermits, and the Capuchins.

Like other institutions, the friars tended to degenerate from their ideal. Just as the Monk in ▷ Chaucer's ▷ *Canterbury Tales* is a bad monk because he refuses to remain bound to his monastery, so the Friar is a bad friar because as a 'limitor' or licensed beggar he abuses his spiritual functions for money, and the friar in Chaucer's *Summoner's Tale* is worse. The friars in Elizabethan plays, *eg* Friar Laurence in ▷ Shakespeare's ▷ *Romeo and Juliet*, are in general depicted from a distance, since England was by then a ▷ Protestant country with few friars; they represent 'wise men', often endowed with magical powers.

Friar Bacon and Friar Bungay

A romantic comedy by ▷ Robert Greene, first acted in 1592. The title characters are based on historical figures – Franciscan ▷ friars of the 13th century whom popular tradition had made into magicians – and the play is based on a pamphlet of anecdotes about them. It has a double plot: one action concerns Bacon's manufacture of a brass head endowed (with the help of the devil) with power of speech, and the other is a ▷ pastoral love-story about the rival loves of Prince Edward and Lord Lacy for Margaret, a village maiden. The play is Greene's best; his use of the double plot to present two aspects of a theme, and his treatment of romantic love, have relevance to the later development of ▷ Elizabethan drama, including ▷ Shakespeare's.

Froissart, Jean (c 1337–1410)

A French chronicler and poet who visited England on several occasions and recorded events at the courts of France and England from 1325–1400 in the form of a chronicle narrative, translated into English prose by Lord Berners in 1523–5. Froissart's lyric and dream-vision poetry influenced ▷ Chaucer's work.

Galileo Galilei (1564–1642)
Italian astronomer; he was able, by improving
the newly invented telescope, to confirm the
theory of ▷ Copernicus that the earth revolves
round the sun, contrary to the theory of
▷ Ptolemy that the earth is the centre of the
solar system. The observation was made in
1610; in 1611 the English poet ▷ John Donne
wrote the *Anatomy of the World*:

> *And new Philosophy calls all in doubt.*
> *The Element of fire is quite put out;*
> *The Sun is lost, and th'earth, and no man's wit*
> *Can well direct him where to look for it.*

In fact the Church was disturbed at the
implications of Galileo's discovery in regard
to acceptance of the Holy Scriptures, and
declared it a heresy. Nonetheless Galileo's
view slowly became accepted. ▷ Milton, in his
epic of the Creation of the World, ▷ *Paradise
Lost*, uses the Ptolemaic theory, though he had
met Galileo and alludes to him in the poem
('the Tuscan Artist' of Bk. 1, lines 288–91).
Bib: Drake, S., *Galileo*.

Gallathea (1585)
A lyrical and courtly transvestite comedy
by ▷ John Lyly about a virgin-sacrifice
to Neptune and the ensuing unwitting
love-affair of two disguised girls, one of
whom Venus promises to transform into a
boy. The play's heroine provides an early
model for ▷ Shakespeare's Viola in ▷ *Twelfth
Night*, and through its jewelled elegance and
mythopoeia Lyly's play took English comedy
to new heights in the crucial decade preceding
the 1590s.

Game at Chess, A (1624)
A bold political ▷ allegory by ▷ Thomas
Middleton. It enjoyed a short but highly
successful run in London, because of its
imaginative use of the pieces of chess and
its appeal to popular sentiment hostile to
the proposed Spanish marriage. In the play
England is represented by white and Spain
by black.

Gamelyn
An anonymous Middle English verse
romance, dating from the mid-14th century.
Gamelyn is the youngest of three brothers
who is deprived of his heritage and ill-treated
by his eldest brother. He takes to the forest
and leads the life of an outlaw with a band
of merry men. Eventually he succeeds in
overthrowing the forces of the law which
side with his unjust brother, retrieves his

heritage and is appointed Chief Justice. The
romance appears in some manuscripts of
the ▷ *Canterbury Tales* as the tale told by the
pilgrim Cook (which is evidently an attempt by
a 15th-century editor to fill out the unfinished
state of ▷ Chaucer's text). *Gamelyn* was used
by ▷ Thomas Lodge for his prose romance
Rosalynde (1590), which ▷ Shakespeare used
as a source for his comedy ▷ *As You Like It*.
Bib: Sands, D. (ed.), *Middle English Verse
Romances*.

Gammer Gurton's Needle
A slight but very lively verse comedy of
uncertain authorship, first acted in 1566, and
printed in 1575. Gammer = old woman. She
loses her needle, which she had been using to
mend her man's breeches. The whole village
is upset, until the needle is found in the seat
of the breeches.

Ganymede
In Greek myth, a beautiful youth who was
carried up to heaven on the back of an eagle
and became cup-bearer to the gods and
Zeus's lover.
 In ▷ Shakespeare's ▷ *As You Like It*,
Rosalind takes the name when she dresses as
a boy to go to the Forest of ▷ Arden.

Garden of Cyrus, The (1658)
A treatise on the quincunx (a shape or pattern
composed of five parts) by ▷ Sir Thomas
Browne. It was published together with ▷ *Urn
Burial*, or *Hydriotaphia*, and is characteristic of
Browne's delight in intellectual curiosity and
his interest in the relationship between science
and faith.

Gardens
By the 15th century the upper classes were
cultivating gardens in an ornamental style, but
it was in the later 16th century that the real
enthusiasm for gardening began. ▷ Francis
Bacon's essay *Of Gardens* (1625) is the best
known of many literary manifestations of it.
 The gardens of the period were formal,
with straight alleys; plentiful use was made
of hedges of box and yew for dividing
flowerbeds into ornamental geometrical
shapes ('knot-gardens') for flanking alleys, for
making 'mazes' such as the one that survives
at Hampton Court, for arbours (sheltered
places) in which seats could be placed and for
the topiary work (cutting hedges and bushes
into the shapes of birds, people, etc.) that
Bacon despised. Utility was not ignored by
rich gardeners and their travel overseas made
it possible for them to import new vegetables

such as the potato and the beetroot; these, however, were not cultivated as large crops until much later. Herbs such as marjoram, thyme, rosemary and others were valued both for adding savour to food and medicinally – as the Friar explains in ▷ Shakespeare's ▷ *Romeo and Juliet* II.ii. Rhubarb was also commonly used medicinally. Orchards were important; apples, pears, apricots, almonds, peaches, figs, cherries and currants were all cultivated. Botany and horticulture were studied enthusiastically.

The enthusiasm for gardening, especially during the period 1550–1650, coincided with widespread interest in the literary modes of ▷ pastoral. In these, the garden is commonly used as an emblem for the innocence and freedom of unspoilt nature, in contrast to the corruption and anxiety of life in the towns and at court. Two traditions combined in the literary pastoral: the ▷ Bible-nourished ▷ Puritans recalled the bliss of the original Garden of Eden before the Fall of Man; and poet-scholars like ▷ Edmund Spenser (the Garden of Adonis in ▷ *The Faerie Queene* III.6) recalled the golden ages of Greek and Latin pastoral myth. Shakespeare uses a garden as an emblem of society in ▷ *Richard II*, III.4 and as an emblem of innocence in ▷ *The Winter's Tale*, IV.3. ▷ Andrew Marvell wrote several of his best poems on gardens as emblems of lavish happiness; the most famous of these is *The Garden* (about 1650).
Bib: Strong, R., *The Renaissance Garden in England*.

Gargantua
A giant, chiefly known as the hero of ▷ François Rabelais's romances *Gargantua* and *Pantagruel*, though he had a previous existence in French folklore connected with the Arthurian (▷ Arthur, King) legends. He is mentioned in ▷ Shakespeare's ▷ *As You Like It* II.2 before Rabelais had been translated into English (1653), though Shakespeare may have read Rabelais in French.

Garter, The Order of the
An order of knighthood instituted by ▷ Edward III about 1344. The order was an imitation of the legendary one established by ▷ King Arthur, and Edward III built the great round tower of Windsor Castle as its meeting-place. In keeping with the ▷ Tudor myth, several panegyric poems link ▷ Elizabeth's courtiers to the chivalric idealism of Edward's and Arthur's reigns. More significantly, ▷ Spenser weaves the garter motif into his praise of Elizabethan knighthood in ▷ *The*

Faerie Queene. ▷ Shakespeare alludes heavily to the garter and its ceremonies in ▷ *The Merry Wives of Windsor*.

Gascoigne, George (1539–77)
Poet and playwright. His chief works include the unauthorized *A Hundreth Sundrie Flowers*, published in 1573; a collection of poems republished in 1575 as *The Posies*; some of the earliest ▷ satires, including including *Glasse of Government* (1575), *The Steel Glass* (1576); and a number of plays which include *Supposes* (1566), one of the earliest comedies in English and *Jocasta* (1573) the second English ▷ tragedy. Gascoigne's talents also encompassed fiction, a treatise on prosody and a ▷ masque held at Kenilworth for ▷ Elizabeth I. Gascoigne's verse grew increasingly out of favour as he could, or would, not imitate the court wits such as ▷ Lyly, and continued with the more old-fashioned ▷ lyrical style.
▷ Ferrers, George; Breton, Nicholas.
Bib: Johnson, R. C., *Gascoigne*.

Gender
Originally used to distinguish between the categories of 'masculine' and 'feminine'. In modern ▷ feminist criticism it denotes something more than the different physical characteristics of both sexes. Feminist criticism regards 'masculinity' and 'femininity' as primary social constructions, supported by a range of cultural phenomena. The relationship between men and women is seen in material terms as a process of domination and subordination which functions objectively in material relations, but also subjectively in the ways in which men and women think of themselves. The concept of gender draws attention to the objective and subjective constructions of sexual difference, making possible an understanding of the mechanisms by which they operate, and offering the possibility of change.

There is a difference between the more sociological accounts and those – sometimes psychoanalytically based – which suggest there is something irreducible and specific in the nature of sexual difference. Here 'gender' is not one cultural label among others, but a firmly established basis for identity, as masculine or feminine (and not necessarily according to biological sex).

Genre
In its use in the language of literary criticism the concept of 'genre' proposes that particular groups of texts can be seen as parts of a

system of representations agreed between writer and reader. For example, a work such as ▷ Aristotle's *Poetics* isolates those characteristics that are to be found in a group of dramatic texts given the generic label ▷ 'tragedy'. The pleasure an audience derives from watching a particular tragedy emanates in part from its fulfilling certain requirements stimulated by expectations arising from within the form itself. But each particular tragedy cannot be reduced simply to the sum of its generic parts. It is possible to distinguish between a tragedy by ▷ Sophocles, and one by ▷ Shakespeare, yet at the same time acknowledge that they conform in certain respects to the narrative and dramatic rules laid down by the category 'tragedy'. Each example, therefore, repeats certain characteristics which have come to be recognized as indispensable features of the genre, but each one also exists in a relationship of difference from the general rule. The same kind of argument may be advanced in relation to particular sorts of poetry or novels. The concept of genre helps to account for the particular pleasures which readers/spectators experience when confronted with a specific text. It also offers an insight into one of the many determining factors which contribute to the formation of the structure and coherence of any individual text.

Gentleman

By the 16th century the connection between the gentleman and the fighting man had already been established, and coats of arms, whose original function had been to distinguish a man for his followers and friends in battle, were regarded as indispensable. They could be obtained for money from the Heralds' College (as ▷ Shakespeare's father obtained his in 1596), and as soldiering was not a profession for which there was much opportunity in a peaceful country, they were freely granted. English society was anyway very mixed and the sons of long-established gentlemen became apprentices (▷ Apprenticeship) in the City. By the 17th century the feeling that a gentleman was known by his behaviour more than by his birth was thus more firmly established and James II is said to have remarked that he could turn a man into a nobleman but God Almighty could not turn him into a gentleman.

Geoffrey of Monmouth (d 1155)

Author of the highly influential account of British history in Latin prose, the ▷ *Historia*

Regum Britanniae (*History of the Kings of Britain*), completed c 1138, which opened up a new vision of insular history, revealing Britain to be a formerly great European power. Little is known for certain about Geoffrey of Monmouth himself. He was probably born in Monmouth, of Welsh or Breton extraction, and seems to have been a resident of Oxford, probably a canon of the college of St George's, for many years of his life (?1129–51). In 1151 he became Bishop Elect of St Asaph. Before finishing his history of Britain, he produced a version of Merlin's prophecies, which were then incorporated into the history itself. At a later stage he returned to the subject of Merlin and around 1150 produced a Latin poem, the *Vita Merlini* (*The Life of Merlin*).

His history of Britain is an accomplished and complex exercise in history writing. He claims to have access to a source of British history, 'an ancient book in the British language', which has not been used by his contemporary historiographers, nor their predecessors. His narrative seems less likely to be the product of a single unidentified source, and much more the result of a careful act of compilation (using the work of contemporaries such as William of Malmesbury and earlier authorities on the history of the island, notably Gildas, Bede, and Nennius) and fabrication. In Geoffrey's narrative, a shadowy period of the island's past – the period before and after the Roman conquest, up to the beginnings of Saxon control in the 6th century – was given relatively detailed documentation, and a rather startling revision of Roman/British and British/Saxon power relations was advanced which disrupted some of the accepted facts of insular history. Geoffrey not only suggested that at certain stages of British history the power of Britain was a major threat to that of Rome, but that Britain was a unified realm well into the 6th century. His history also presented a picture of Britain as a world-famous chivalric centre during the reign of ▷ King Arthur. A powerful argument for unified rule emerges from the history, which is a point of some relevance to the turbulent political context in which Geoffrey was writing.

The historical value of the *History of the Kings of Britain* was a controversial issue, debated and disputed by some historians of the 12th and later centuries. But Geoffrey's formulation of British history was widely used in chronicle histories of the island up to the 16th century and provided a historic foundation for the development of Arthurian

narrative during the medieval period. Approximately 200 manuscripts survive of the history, and in addition there are numerous vernacular translations and adaptations extant. Poetic and dramatic versions of early British history, such as ▷ *Gorboduc* (1565), ▷ Spenser's ▷ *Faerie Queene*, ▷ Shakespeare's ▷ *King Lear* and ▷ *Cymbeline*, all use material that derives ultimately from Geoffrey of Monmouth's *History of Britain*.
Bib: Thorpe, L. (trans.), *Geoffrey of Monmouth: The History of the Kings of Britain*.

German influence on English literature
There was little German influence on English literature before the late 18th century; however, there are a few isolated examples before that date, two of which are particularly interesting because they show clearly that the structural model of influencing and influenced literature falsifies what is a far more complex pattern of reciprocal interchange between two literary cultures. For many years it was a matter of debate whether the anonymous work *Der bestrafte Brudermord* was derived from one of the sources of ▷ Shakespeare's ▷ *Hamlet* or was merely a botched version of the play. It is now thought that the German play can teach us nothing about Shakespeare's sources, but another classic of the Elizabethan stage, ▷ Christopher Marlowe's ▷ *Doctor Faustus*, does draw upon a German source, a legend that did not give rise to a classic in its own language until the appearance of Johann Wolfgang von Goethe's (1749–1832) ▷ *Faust* over two centuries later.

Globe Theatre
The theatre used by the Lord ▷ Chamberlain's Men; ▷ Shakespeare's plays were performed there, he acted in it, and was one of the shareholders. It was built by ▷ Richard Burbage in 1599 out of the materials of 'The Theatre' erected in 1576; the new site was at ▷ Bankside on the south bank of the Thames in Southwark. It was built of wood, open in the centre, and the surrounding galleries ('this wooden O' – Prologue, ▷ *Henry V*) were roofed with thatch. It is thought to have held about 3,000 spectators. From the roof flew a flag depicting Atlas carrying a globe with a Latin inscription equivalent to 'All the world's a stage' (▷ *As You Like It* II. vii. 138). The theatre was burnt down in 1613 during a performance of ▷ *Henry VIII*, rebuilt, and finally pulled down in 1644. Much of the information about the Globe comes from the contract for the Fortune Theatre (built in 1599), the structure of which is specified as

resembling the Globe, except that the Fortune was square. A panoramic view of London dated 1616 gives a view of the Globe among other theatres. In the main, the structure of the Globe, like that of its contemporaries, derived from that of the typical inn-yard where plays were commonly performed when theatres were not available.
Under the inspired leadership of Sam Wannemaker and the auspices of the International Shakespeare Globe Centre, the Globe is about to rise again in Southwark, according to its original specifications and near to its old site. The original Globe's foundations have been discovered, but in the 1990s have been reconcealed within the foundations of a highrise office block. Wannemaker's Globe will be the first all-timber building licensed in London in the 20th century and will cater for international performances of Shakespeare, lectures and exhibitions. It is expected to open in 1992.
▷ Theatres.
Bib: Orrell, J., *The Quest for Shakespeare's Globe*.

Gloriana
The ▷ Faerie Queene of ▷ Edmund Spenser's poem; she represents ▷ Elizabeth I.

Glyndŵr, Owain (?1354–1416)
A Welsh chieftain who rebelled against ▷ Henry IV of England, and for a time ruled most of Wales. He was eventually defeated by Henry's son, the future ▷ Henry V. Glyndŵr is a character in Shakespeare's play ▷ *Henry IV, Part I* as an ally of the English rebel Hotspur. He is there presented as a boastful poet and mystic.

Golding, Arthur (?1536–1605)
Translator. Golding's chief work was an important translation of ▷ Ovid's *Metamorphoses* (1565–67) that was instrumental in promoting knowledge of Ovidian subjects and forms in England.

Gorboduc, or Ferrex and Porrex
A tragic drama by ▷ Thomas Norton (1552–84) and ▷ Thomas Sackville. The story is taken from British legendary history; the immediate source is Grafton's *Chronicle* (1556) but this in turn derives from the 12th-century ▷ *Historia Regum Britanniae* (*History of the Kings of Britain*) by ▷ Geoffrey of Monmouth. It is the first play to be written in ▷ blank verse, and is modelled on the tragedies of ▷ Seneca.
Gorboduc is a king of Britain. His reign

has been a prosperous one, when he decides to retire from government and divide his kingdom between his two sons, Ferrex and Porrex. He carries out the division against the advice of his wisest councillor. Jealousy and distrust between the two brothers break into civil war, which ends in the death of both and a rising of the whole people, who slay Gorboduc and his queen. The country is saved from final ruin only by Fergus, Duke of Albany, who, with the aid of other nobles, succeeds in restoring order under single sovereignty.

The drama has slight literary value of its own, but it has considerable historical significance. Sackville and Norton were eminent politicians who foresaw great dangers to the kingdom if ▷ Queen Elizabeth I should die without heirs. The play was first acted before the queen in 1562 and is plainly designed as a warning to her against leaving her kingdom exposed to disunity. The authors are thus using history (or legend, which was not clearly distinguished from history) as later and greater dramatists were to use it, notably ▷ Shakespeare: that is to say, as a storehouse of political lessons that could be applied to the politics of their own time. The theme of the divided kingdom resembles one of the greatest of Shakespeare's tragedies, ▷ *King Lear*, which deals with the situation in far profounder terms. The Senecan model also anticipates later Elizabethan taste, and the use of blank verse was the starting-point for the rich development of the medium by ▷ Marlowe and Shakespeare. Apart from Seneca, a literary influence upon the writers is the collection of tragic tales ▷ *A Mirror for Magistrates* (1559), to which Sackville made the most memorable contribution. This also used legend and history, recounted in a solemn style, to warn and edify contemporary courtiers and public men. The Senecan solemnity and formality of *Gorboduc* gave it peculiar dignity for the contemporary public, raising it above the (often much more lively) style of the familiar ▷ interludes and comedies of the day, and giving it the requisite impressiveness to influence the queen. It is not known what she thought of it, but ▷ Sir Philip Sidney excepted it from his general condemnation of the English drama of his day, and wrote in his *Apologie for Poetrie*: 'it is full of stately speeches, and well sounding phrases, climbing to the height of Seneca's style, and as full of notable morality . . . ' However, he goes on to complain of its failure to observe the so-called ▷ Aristotelian unities of space and time.

Gosson, Stephen (1554–1624)

Preacher and pamphleteer. Stephen Gosson's chief claim to a measure of literary fame is due to his being the author of *The Schoole of Abuse* (1579), a ▷ pamphlet attacking poetry and drama which is said to have occasioned ▷ Philip Sidney's ▷ *An Apologie for Poetrie*. Ironically, Gosson's career had begun as a dramatist, but he underwent a religious conversion and became a fierce ▷ Puritan critic of the drama. *The Schoole of Abuse*, if it has a somewhat nebulous relationship to the development of Sidney's critical text, nevertheless did call forth a response from ▷ Thomas Lodge, who replied to Gosson with his *A Reply to Stephen Gosson Touching Plays* (1579). Gosson, in turn, replied to Lodge with his *Plays Confuted in Five Actions* (1582). This interchange, though it added little of substance to dramatic criticism, is itself part of the continuing English debate in the 16th and 17th centuries concerning the corrupting or otherwise influence of drama. **Bib:** Ringer, W. A., *Stephen Gosson: A Biographical and Critical Study*.

Gower, John (?1330–1408)

Poet. Only a tentative outline can be established of Gower's life. His family had Yorkshire origins and Kent connections (Gower's language bears traces of Kentish influence and he bought lands there in 1378). A reference in one of his works suggests he had a training in law, a point confirmed by other documentary evidence. Gower seems to have been based in London for most of his life. By 1398, and perhaps for some time earlier, he was living in the priory of St Mary Overy (now Southwark Cathedral), where he was buried.

He wrote extensively in three languages, French, Latin and English. Before 1374 he composed his *Cinkante Balades* and some time between 1376 and 1378 he produced the *Mirour de l'Omme*, another French work, written in octosyllabic 12-line stanzas, tackling the subject of fallen man, his vices and virtues. His Latin poem, *Vox Clamantis (The Voice of One Crying)*, composed c 1379–81, addresses the subject of political governance and, more specifically, the disturbances of the reign of ▷ Richard II (notably the Peasant's Revolt). In his major English poem, the ▷ *Confessio Amantis*, Gower turned from overtly political and satirical subjects to take a middle way, 'somwhat of lust, somwhat of lore', recounting the experiences of a lover's confession and instruction. But here too Gower's concern with the ethics of government of self and society is very evident. His anti-war sentiments are clearly expressed in his later English poem, addressed to ▷ Henry IV, *In Praise of Peace*.

In the colophon added to the *Confessio Amantis*, Gower suggests that his major works should be seen as a triptych, as 'three books of instructive material'. His evident ambition to figure as a moral commentator and watchman of his times, and to be remembered as such, was fulfilled. His literary reputation in the century following his death was high, and his name frequently coupled with that of ▷ Chaucer as a founding figure of the English poetic tradition. He is represented as a figure of old poetic authority in ▷ Shakespeare's play ▷ *Pericles* (which reworks the story of Apollonius of Tyre, drawn from Gower's *Confessio Amantis*). However, from the 18th century onwards, there seems to have been a decline in interest in his work and his literary reputation has only revived in recent years. **Bib:** Fisher, J. H., *John Gower: moral philosopher and friend of Chaucer*; Macaulay, G. C. (ed.), *The Works of John Gower, The English Works of John Gower*.

Grace Abounding to the Chief of Sinners (1666)

The spiritual ▷ autobiography of ▷ John Bunyan, author of ▷ *The Pilgrim's Progress*. The torments undergone by Christian in the latter book are substantially those of Bunyan in the earlier one. Bunyan had a similar spiritual awakening to Christian's, being aroused by a book; he suffers the terrible conviction of sin, like Christian; he believes himself to commit the sin of blasphemy as Christian thinks he does in the Valley of the shadow of Death; at last he achieves confidence in God's mercy. Much of the narrative is an account of painful mental conflict; but Bunyan never lost the sanity of perception into the fanaticism and mental morbidity of others, such as the old man who told him that he had certainly committed the sin against the Holy Ghost (for which there is no forgiveness). The book records how he developed that compassionate understanding of other men's spiritual conflicts which makes *The Pilgrim's Progress* the antecedent of the great English novels.

Greek literature

Until Greece was conquered by the Romans in 146 BC, it was a country of small states, mixed racial stock and cultural origins from all round the eastern Mediterranean. These states attained a high level of self-conscious political and artistic culture, which later enriched the Roman Empire and was thence transmitted to medieval and modern Europe.

The beginnings of Greek literature cannot be dated but its first period ended about 500 BC. The period contains ▷ Homer's epics, the ▷ *Iliad* and the *Odyssey*, and the poems of Hesiod. Homer's epics are the real starting-point of European imaginative literature; Hesiod's *Theogony* is one of the principal sources of our knowledge of the Greek religious system. In English literature since the 18th century, the term ▷ elegy has implied narrower limits of subject and treatment than it had for the Greeks and the Romans, but the Greek evolution of the elegy and the ▷ lyric in this period has shaped our ideas of the character and resources of the short poem. An important variety of the lyric (whose principal characteristic was originally that it was intended to have musical accompaniment) was the 'Pindaric ▷ ode', so called after its most famous practitioner, Pindar; this was much imitated by English poets from the 17th to 19th centuries.

The second period (500–300 BC) is called the 'Attic Period' because it centred on the greatest of the Greek cities, Athens, capital of the state of Attica. The outstanding imaginative achievement of the Athenians was the creation of dramatic literature. The 'choral lyric', sung by choirs on religious occasions and especially on the festival of the wine-god Dionysus, was developed into a dialogue by Thespis in the 6th century. In the 5th century this was further developed into dramatic tragedy by three writers whose works have a fundamental influence on all our ideas of the theatre: ▷ Aeschylus, ▷ Sophocles and ▷ Euripides. The primitive religion of the Greeks, based on the worship of the gods as the all-powerful forces of nature, was the origin of Greek ▷ tragedy; it was also the origin of comedy, of which the greatest Greek writer was ▷ Aristophanes. Athens, in this period, also developed Greek prose literature in the works of the first of the historians, Herodotus, in the immensely influential philosophies of ▷ Plato and ▷ Aristotle, and in political oratory, especially that of Demosthenes.

Desmosthenes achieved fame by his efforts to sustain the Greeks in their wars (357–338 BC) against Philip of Macedon, a state to the north of Greece. The war ended with the Macedonians making themselves the dominant power in Greece. They did not actually destroy the independence of the states, but the intensity and many-sidedness of Greek city life diminished. However, Philip's son ▷ Alexander the Great (ruled 336–323 BC) took Greek culture with him in his rapid conquests round the eastern Mediterranean and as far east as north-west India. The result was the 'Hellenistic Period', lasting until the Roman conquest, after which it did not cease but went into a new phase. The culture of Greece now became a climate of civilization shared by many lands; it was no longer even centred in Greece but in the university city of Alexandria in Egypt. The price paid for this expansion was that without the sustenance of the vigorous Greek city life, the literature lost its force, depth and originality, though it retained its secondary qualities such as grace and sophistication. The best-known imaginative works of this period are the ▷ 'pastoral' poems by ▷ Theocritus and others; they influenced the Roman poet ▷ Virgil, and were extensively used as models by ▷ Renaissance poets in the 16th and 17th centuries.

In the Graeco-Roman period (146 BC– AD 500), the Greeks were the teachers and cultural allies of their conquerors, the Romans. ▷ Latin literature written under Greek influence now excelled what continued to be written in Greek. Yet Renaissance Europe felt so much closer to the Romans than to the Greeks that it was the Greek writers of this period who influenced it more deeply than the earlier Greeks did. The historian and biographer ▷ Plutarch, for instance, was widely read in England in the age of ▷ Shakespeare, who used him as a sourcebook for his plays. The Greek romances, the best known of which is *Daphnis and Chloe* by Longus (2nd century AD), were imitated by 16th-century writers such as Sir Philip Sidney in ▷ *Arcadia*. To this period also belongs one of the most influential pieces of Greek literary criticism, the treatise *On the Sublime* by Longinus.

In considering the influence of Greek literature on European, and in particular on English, literature, we have to distinguish between the influence of Greek philosophy and that of Greek imaginative writing. Plato and Aristotle had profound effects on Christian thought. Plato was made dominant by St Augustine of Hippo (4th–5th century), until St Thomas Aquinas replaced his influence by that of Aristotle. In the 16th century, Plato again became most important, but now as a source of ▷ humanist as well as of religious ideas. Aristotle remained dominant as the first philosopher of literature for three centuries, and together they are still regarded as the important starting-points of European philosophy. Greek imaginative writing, on the other hand, made its impression on European, and especially English, imaginative writing chiefly through its assimilation by Roman writers. It was not, for example, the unexcelled Greek dramatists who impressed themselves on the equally unexcelled English dramatists of the age of Shakespeare, but the comparatively inferior Roman ones, ▷ Plautus in ▷ comedy and ▷ Seneca in tragedy.

Greene, Robert (1558–92)

Dramatist and pamphleteer. He was one of the ▷ University Wits, having himself been at Cambridge. Four plays by Greene, apart from collaborations, have survived: *Alphonsus, King of Aragon* (?1587); ▷ *Friar Bacon and Friar Bungay* (1589); *History of Orlando Furioso* (acted 1592), *The Scottish History of James IV* (acted 1594). Of these the best known are the second and the fourth, and in them the melodious and fluent handling of the ▷ blank verse and the appealing portrayal of the heroines anticipate ▷ Shakespeare's romantic comedies of the 1590s.

Greene is more notable for his prose. This includes romances written in emulation of ▷ Lyly's ▷ *Euphues* and ▷ Sidney's ▷ *Arcadia*, including *Pandosto*, ▷ *The Triumph of Time*, from which Shakespeare derived ▷ *The Winter's Tale* (1610). More distinctive and very lively reading are his 'cony-catching pamphlets' (*ie* booklets about criminal practices in the London underworld), *A Notable Discovery of Cosenage* (*ie* 'cozenage' or criminal fraud, 1591) and *The Blacke Booke's Messenger* (1591) – both excellent examples of Elizabethan popular prose. A semi-fictional ▷ autobiography, *Greene's Groatsworth of Wit bought with a Million of Repentance* (1592) is notorious for containing the earliest reference to Shakespeare as a dramatist and actor, though it is an oblique one. The object of the pamphlet is ostensibly a warning to three others of the University Wits – probably ▷ Peele, ▷ Marlowe and ▷ Nashe – to amend their lives. The allusion to Shakespeare – 'an upstart crow beautified with our feathers . . . in his owne conceyt the onely shake-scene in a countrey' – comes by way of a charge of plagiarism. Thirty-five prose works, most of them short, and many containing lyrics of great charm, are ascribed to Greene.

▷ Elizabethan novels.
Bib: Provost, R., *Robert Greene et ses romans*; Crupi, C. W., *Robert Greene*.

Greville, Sir Fulke, 1st Baron Brooke (1554–1628)

Poet, courtier, dramatist, ▷ biographer. Almost all of Fulke Greville's poetic works were published after his death. They include a collection of ▷ sonnets, religious and philosophical poems, and songs gathered under the title *Caelica*, which appeared in the collection of his works published in 1633 as *Certaine Learned and Elegant Works*. A life-long friend of ▷ Philip Sidney, Greville wrote a life of Sidney which was published in 1652 as 'A Dedication to Sir Philip Sidney' in Greville's history of the Elizabethan era. A further volume of his work was published much later in the 17th century when *The Remains: Poems of Monarchy and Religion* was issued in 1670. His two plays – *Alaham* (written c 1600) and *Mustapha* (produced 1603–8) – though set in an exotic and remote world, are valuable attempts at dealing with the important contemporary issues of power and authority in the state. However, he also wrote a play now destroyed, *Antony and Cleopatra* (▷ Cleopatra). Greville was a member of the brilliant intellectual circle surrounding Sidney at court, and enjoyed considerable favour from both ▷ Elizabeth I and ▷ James I of England before his death in 1628 when he was murdered by an offended servant.
Bib: Rees, J. (ed.), *Selected Writings*; Rees, J., *Fulke Greville, First Lord Brooke, 1554–1628: A Critical Biography*; Gouws, J. (ed.), *The Prose Works of Fulke Greville*.

Grey, Lady Jane (1537–54)

Letter and prayer-writer as well as poet, the 'nine days' queen' of romantic legend and misty representation on canvas and celluloid is not often remembered for her small but impressive literary output. In life she became a pawn in the game of ▷ Tudor monarchy, manipulated by both her father, the Duke of Suffolk, and her father-in-law, the powerful Duke of Northumberland. Lady Jane was proclaimed queen on 10 June 1553, but when ▷ Mary Tudor entered London on 19 July, she and her husband were imprisoned in the Tower and beheaded six months later. Lady Jane was well educated and a staunch ▷ Protestant and her written work was, not surprisingly, preserved in ▷ John Foxe's *Acts and Monuments* (1563). The impassioned spiritual conviction and the acute political awareness of Lady Jane's writing suggests that conventional portrayals of her as quiet and submissive may have more to do with feminine stereotypes than with her actual character.

Bib: Travitsky, B. (ed.), *The Paradise of Women*.

Grindal, Edmund (?1519–83)

Archbishop of Canterbury. Grindal was educated at Cambridge and, as a staunch ▷ Protestant and ▷ Calvinist, received the patronage of ▷ Nicholas Ridley, but had to leave England during the ▷ Catholic reign of ▷ Mary I. At the accession of ▷ Elizabeth I he returned and became Bishop of London in 1559 and, with Cecil's support (▷ Burghley), Archbishop of Canterbury in 1575. As such Grindal should have been one of the shaping forces of Elizabethan Protestantism, but he failed to live up to his early promise. There are several reasons for this: firstly, he had little firm purpose, which he mitigated with bouts of severity, as, for example, when he denounced ▷ John Stow as a Papist; and secondly, he could not accept Elizabeth's political alliances with Catholic nations, nor curb his own zeal for prophesying and for the open discussing of scriptures, practices of which the queen disapproved. He is, however, celebrated in the 'May' and 'July' ▷ eclogues of ▷ Spenser's ▷ *The Shepherd's Calendar* (1579).
Bib: Collinson, P., *Archbishop Grindal, 1519–1583: the Struggle for a Reformed Church*.

Grocyn, William (?1446–1519)

English ▷ humanist, and one of the earliest propagators of the study of ancient Greek in England; taught at Oxford.

Grymeston, Elizabeth (1563–c 1602)

▷ Essayist. A ▷ Catholic, Grymeston had a difficult life with family feuds, ill health and the death of eight of her nine children. She found time and energy, however, to write and her work was published posthumously as *Miscelanea, Meditations and Memoratives* (1604). On the basis of this work Grymeston has become known as the first woman essayist writing in English. Her work is somewhat learned, including numerous classical references and intricate metaphors.
Bib: Beilin, E. V., *Redeeming Eve*.

Gunpowder Plot (1605)

A conspiracy by a section of English Roman ▷ Catholics to destroy the ▷ Protestant government of ▷ James I by blowing up the Houses of Parliament at a time when the king and the members of the Houses of Lords and Commons were all in the building. The plot was inspired by the ▷ Jesuits and led by Robert Catesby, but undertaken by Guy Fawkes. The date was fixed for 5 November and the explosives were all laid, but the plot was betrayed and Fawkes was arrested on the threshold of the cellar on 4 November. This 'discovery' was somewhat stage-managed by the government, which was possibly deeply implicated in the gestation of the plot through the use of double-agents. ▷ *Macbeth* and ▷ *Catiline* both seem to allude to the incident. 5 November has since been celebrated annually with fireworks and bonfires on which Guy Fawkes is burnt in effigy.

Bib: Dehuna, B., *Jonson's Romish Plot*.

H

Hakluyt, Richard (?1553–1616)
Geographer. In 1589 and 1598 he published his *Principal Navigations, Voyages and Discoveries of the English Nation*, being a record of English explorations, which had lagged behind those of the French, Spanish, Portuguese and Dutch until the middle of the century, and then made prodigious progress with the nationalistic energy characteristic of England in the reign of ▷ Elizabeth I.
Bib: Parks, G. B., *Richard Hakluyt and the English Voyages*.

Halkett, Lady Anne (1623–99)
Devotional writer and autobiographer.
Lady Anne had two unsuccessful romances before marrying Sir James Halkett in 1656, but this marriage was to last for only 14 years and, as a widow, she earned her own living by teaching and writing. Her religious meditations and ▷ autobiography ran to 50 volumes of manuscript material, but it is her life-story (edited in 1979 by J. Loftis as *The Memoirs of Anne, Lady Halkett and Ann, Lady Fanshawe* (▷ Ann Fanshawe)) that remains her most interesting work. Halkett's memoirs are practical, but carry an undercurrent of humour that allows for particularly feminine observations, as, for example, when she dresses the future James II in women's clothes to facilitate his escape in 1648.
   ▷ Scottish literature.
Bib: H. Wilcox in Cerasano, S. P. and Wynne-Davies, M. (eds.), *Gloriana's Face*.

Hall, Edward (?1498–1547)
Chronicler; author of *The Union of the Noble and Illustrious Families of Lancaster and York* (1542; enlarged 1548, 1550).
This tells of the bitter rivalries of the two branches of the House of Anjou (Plantagenets) from the death of the childless ▷ Richard II in 1400, and the accession of ▷ Henry IV, first of the House of Lancaster, to the death of the last of the House of York, ▷ Richard III, in 1485, and the accession of Henry Tudor as ▷ Henry VII. He idealizes Henry VII and ▷ Henry VIII, partly because they re-established dynastic harmony, and partly because, as a ▷ Protestant, Hall was strongly sympathetic to Henry VIII's reform of the Church. The Chronicle was one of ▷ Shakespeare's two main source-books for his English history plays, the other being ▷ Holinshed.
   ▷ Histories and Chronicles.
Bib: Kingsford, C. L., *English Historical Literature in the Fifteenth Century*.

Hall, Joseph (1574–1656)
▷ Satirist; 'character' (▷ Characters, Theophrastian) writer, religious controversialist; bishop, 1627–47. He published his *Virgidemiae* (or *Harvest of Rods*, ie for chastisement) in 1597–8; he claimed to be the first English satirist, but ▷ John Donne and ▷ John Marston were writing at the same time, not to mention ▷ Edmund Spenser's *Mother Hubberd's Tale*. He may have considered himself more truly a satirist than his rivals inasmuch as he was stricter in following classical ▷ Latin models, notably ▷ Juvenal. Like Juvenal, he attacked what he saw as contemporary vices. His *Characters of Virtues and Vices* (1608) was likewise in classical tradition, this time modelled on the Greek ▷ Theophrastus, and was also intended for the moral improvement of the age.
Bib: Davenport, A., *The Poems of Joseph Hall*; Huntley, F. L., *Bishop Joseph Hall*.

Hamlet (c 1601)
A ▷ tragedy by ▷ Shakespeare, written in about 1601. Three early versions of it exist: the imperfect ▷ quarto of 1603, the superior quarto of 1604, and the version in the First ▷ Folio of 1623, which omits some of the material in the 1604 quarto, but also contains authentic passages not in that text. The story was a widespread legend in northern Europe. Shakespeare's immediate source is likely to have been Belleforest's *Histoires Tragiques* (1559), and Belleforest's own version came from a 13th-century Danish chronicler, Saxo Grammaticus. But Shakespeare also had another source: a play of the same name already existed and is thought to have been a lost play by ▷ Thomas Kyd. It is referred to without mention of the author by ▷ Nashe in a letter accompanying ▷ Greene's *Menaphon* (1589), by ▷ Henslowe in his Diary (1594) and by ▷ Lodge in *Wit's Misery* (1596). There are also parallels between Shakespeare's play and Kyd's ▷ *Spanish Tragedy*: both have ghosts and a play within the play; Kyd's tragedy is about a father seeking vengeance for his son, and Shakespeare's is about a son avenging his father. In both plays there are obstacles to the vengeance: in Kyd's play, the obstacle is a straightforward one, of how to bring retribution upon an offender who is so powerful as to be beyond the law; in Shakespeare it is so subtle that Hamlet's hesitations have been among the most discussed subjects in criticism.
   Certain features of Shakespeare's play require special attention in assessing the play.
   1 The basic situation is that Hamlet's uncle

▷ Claudius, has married Hamlet's mother, Gertrude, only a month after the death of her husband, old Hamlet. Claudius has, moreover, ascended the throne ignoring the claim of his nephew and with the consent of the court. This thoroughly distasteful situation reflects badly not only on Claudius and Gertrude, but on the court as well, and it has already plunged Hamlet into disgust at the opening of the play. We need also to remember that marriage to a sister-in-law was of at least doubtful validity: it constituted ▷ Henry VIII's legal ground for divorce from Katharine of Aragon.

2 It is only later that Hamlet learns from his father's ghost that old Hamlet was murdered by Claudius. The revelation does not lead directly to action, but to Hamlet feigning madness, and to the 'play within the play', before which Claudius, in the audience, betrays his guilt.

3 Claudius's self-betrayal, however, is incriminating only to Hamlet and his friend Horatio, who have already learned the facts. Either Hamlet mistrusts the Ghost, who may not have been truly the spirit of his father, or it is part of his vengeance to inform Claudius that his guilt is known. One of the beliefs about ghosts current in Shakespeare's time was that they were sometimes evil spirits assuming the disguise of dead men.

4 Hamlet's hostility extends not merely to Claudius, but to the whole court, in so far as they are or may be subservient to Claudius. Thus Hamlet behaves brutally to Ophelia (the girl he loves) because he suspects (although she is entirely innocent) that she is being used as a kind of decoy by Claudius and by her father, Polonius.

5 Laertes, Ophelia's brother, is a contrast to Hamlet in being a straightforward revenger: he immediately seeks the death of Hamlet for causing the deaths of his father and sister. But his impetuosity puts him on the side of evil, for it causes him to connive with Claudius.

6 Claudius is an unusual villain for the drama of the time, for he is not *seen* to be evil on the stage; we know of his guilt indirectly. Even his conspiracy against Hamlet's life can be excused as action in self-defence.

These features of the play suggest that Shakespeare was exposing traditional beliefs about revenge as over-simplified. Revenge is difficult if we do not feel the guilty man to be guilty: 'One may smile, and smile and be a villain' (I. v. 108). Further, revenge does not solve evil, if evil lies in a complex situation: 'The time is out of joint; O cursed spite/That ever I was born to set it right' (V. i. 189–90).

Finally, revenge itself may be morally wrong: what *was* the Ghost?

Harington, Sir John (1561–1612)

Poet, translator, courtier and brother to the well-respected literary patron, ▷ Lucy Russell, Countess of Bedford. Harington's ▷ translation of ▷ Ludovico Ariosto's ▷ *Orlando Furioso* (published in 1591) was undertaken, so it is said, as a punishment exacted by ▷ Elizabeth I for his having translated part of the bawdy sections of that poem. Whatever the circumstances of its production, Harington's work established itself as one of the most important of Elizabethan translations. In addition to his work on Ariosto, Harington also wrote a humorous piece entitled *A New Discourse of a Stale Subject, called the Metamorphosis of Ajax* (1596). This work, with its punning title (Ajax = A 'Jakes' = a water closet) contains diagrams and instructions on the installation of a plumbing system. The queen suspected that the work contained a subtle allusion to the ▷ Earl of Leicester and banished Harington from court. During this banishment he put his hydraulic theories into practice, installing the first water closet in England at Richmond Palace. A tendency to overdo a joke is suggested by the publication, again in 1596, of *An Anatomy of the Metamorphosed Ajax*.
Bib: Haughey, R., *Harington of Stepney, Tudor Gentleman: His Life and Works.*

Harsnett, Samuel (1561–1631)

Bishop of York and religious writer. Harsnett's church career was somewhat varied in that he wrote ▷ satires against the ▷ Puritans and the ▷ Catholics (the latter, *A Declaration of Egregious Popish Impostures* (1603), being the source for Edgar's spirit names in ▷ *King Lear*), yet was himself charged with favouring Popery, which led to his resignation from the post of master at Pembroke Hall, Cambridge. In practice he was a somewhat domineering churchman, too concerned with ceremonies to be popular. Strangely, he is best known today as the censor who failed to read ▷ Sir John Hayward's *The First Part of the Life and Raigne of King Henrie the IIII* (1599) with its eulogistic dedication to ▷ Essex. Hayward was imprisoned for the offence this gave to ▷ Elizabeth I, but Harsnett managed to convince the Attorney-General of his innocence.

Harvey, Gabriel (?1545–1630)

Man of letters and scholar; friend of ▷ Edmund Spenser, who presents Harvey

as Hobbinol in ▷ *The Shepherd's Calendar*.
Harvey argued vigorously for substituting
Latin quantitative metres (based on length of
syllables) for the English accentual rhythms
which rely on accent. Otherwise he is chiefly
known for his violent quarrels (especially with
▷ Thomas Nashe and ▷ Robert Greene),
which caused his name to figure prominently
in the ▷ pamphlets of the time.
    ▷ Classical education and English
literature.
Bib: Stern, V. F., *Gabriel Harvey: His Life,
Marginalia and Library*.

Hatton, Sir Christopher (1540–91)
Courtier. One of the many apocryphal
stories about ▷ Elizabeth I concerns Sir
Christopher Hatton; who, it is said, attained
the queen's favour because she thought
him an accomplished dancer. Certainly he
promoted himself as ▷ Leicester's rival for
the queen's affections and was to remain
an ever-hopeful bachelor until his death.
This role ensured him political preferment
and several public posts: he was made a
Gentleman Pensioner in 1564, became Lord
Chancellor in 1587, and accepted the post
of Chancellor of Oxford University in 1588.
He was also given Ely Place in London,
now the site of Hatton Garden. Like most
of Elizabeth's favourites, Hatton was also
interested in the arts; he was the patron of
▷ Spenser and ▷ Churchyard, and wrote Act
IV of *Trancred and Gismund* (c 1567), a tragic
play based on a story by ▷ Boccaccio.
Bib: Williams, N., *All the Queen's Men*.

Hayward, Sir John (?1564–1627)
Historian. Hayward was the author of several
learned histories: *Lives of the III Normans,
Kings of England* (1613), *Life and Raigne of
Edward the Sixt* (1630), *The Beginning of the
Reign of Elizabeth* (1636), and *The First Part
of the Life and Raigne of King Henrie IIII*
(1599), and it is for this last work that he is
best known today. The history of Henry III
contained a eulogistic dedication in Latin to
the ▷ Earl of Essex, which severely angered
▷ Elizabeth I as it appeared to criticize her
own rule, and Hayward was subsequently
imprisoned.
    ▷ Harsnett, Samuel.

Hegemony
Originally used to denote political domination.
In its more modern meaning and in its use
in literary criticism it has come to refer to
that process of political control whereby the

interests of a dominant class in society are
shared by those subordinated to it. Hegemony
depends upon the consent of subordinate
classes to their social positions, but the
constraints within which that consent operates,
and the ways in which it is experienced, are
determined by the dominant class. This
concept also offers ways of understanding
the different kinds of social and personal
relationships represented in literary texts.
Along with a number of other concepts, it
opens the way for an analysis of the different
forms of negotiation that take place within
texts, and between text and reader, and serves
to emphasize the social context of experience,
consciousness and human interaction.
    ▷ Materialism.

**Heming, John (d 1630) and Condell,
    Henry (d 1627)**
Acting colleagues of ▷ Shakespeare and
editors of the first edition of his collected
plays, known as the First ▷ Folio, 1623.

Henrietta Maria, Queen (1609–99)
Patron and dramatist. ▷ Charles I's queen
had a significant impact upon the culture
of the ▷ Stuart court. As a French princess
she had had the benefit of experiencing the
greater freedom allowed women in France.
For example, they were able to write private
plays and ▷ masques, as well as to perform
in them. As a British queen she encouraged
the arts and was an ardent supporter of
drama, but created a scandal when she
attempted to compose her own plays and act
on stage, albeit only within the confines of
the court. It was probably the performances
of the queen and her ladies-in-waiting in
Walter Montague's *The Shepherd's Paradise*
that caused William Prynne's attack against
actresses in *Histrio-mastix* (1632). Henrietta
Maria's Catholic upbringing also brought
about censure from the increasingly ▷ Puritan
country, and her influence on the court was
seen to create a divide between the world
of London nobility and the rest of the
nation. Still, the religious air that invades the
▷ Platonic masques of the ▷ Caroline court
imbue them with an ethereal and delicate
quality lacking in the showy entertainments of
▷ James I's reign.
Bib: Veevers, E., *Images of Love and Religion*.

Henry IV (1399–1413)
King of England. He was called Bolingbroke
from the name of his birthplace. His father,
John of Gaunt, Duke of Lancaster, was a

younger son of ▷ Edward III; his cousin ▷ Richard II exiled Henry and confiscated his estates, in retaliation for which Henry succeeded in raising a rebellion and seizing the throne. Richard died mysteriously in prison. Henry thus became first of the three kings of the House of Lancaster, really a junior branch of the Plantagenet line. His reign was the subject of two plays by ▷ Shakespeare, ▷ *Henry IV, Parts I* and *II*.

Henry IV, Part I

A ▷ history play by ▷ Shakespeare, performed about 1597 and printed in a ▷ quarto edition, 1598. The central character is Prince Hal, the king's son and later ▷ Henry V. The king is grieved first by the opposition of some of his nobels led by the Percy family, notably Henry (Harry) Hotspur, son of the Earl of Northumberland, and secondly by the dissolute conduct of his own son, who wastes his life in taverns instead of emulating Hotspur in a career of military honour. Hal's tavern companion is ▷ Sir John Falstaff, one of the greatest of Shakespeare's comic characters. The contrast between Hotspur and Falstaff is the prominent feature of the play: Hotspur lives only for honour, without relating it to social responsibility; Falstaff, only for pleasure, in equal indifference to social consequences. Hotspur is thus passionate but inhuman, and Falstaff all too human in his passions. At the end of the play, Hal kills Hotspur at the battle of Shrewsbury, but Falstaff manages to steal the credit for Hotspur's death. The play is close to the ▷ morality tradition in its feeling and structure, Hotspur and Falstaff standing for 'honour' and 'riot' respectively; both in their different ways are rebels, the first in political terms against the state, and the second in spiritual terms against reason. Shakespeare's main sources were the chronicles of ▷ Hall and ▷ Holinshed.
▷ *Henry IV, Part II*.

Henry IV, Part II

▷ Quarto edition 1600. A continuation of ▷ Shakespeare's *Henry IV, Part I*, though independent in mood and dramatic structure. The Percy rebellion continues, though Hotspur is dead. A sick weariness is over the country, and the king is dying. Hal is still the central character, and again flanked by contrasting types: on the one side Falstaff, pleasure-loving still but now ageing and grasping for the power he expects when Hal becomes King Henry V; on the other side, the scrupulous and fearless Lord Chief Justice,

who has faced his responsibilities so far as to send the Prince himself to prison for riot. However, when Hal becomes king at the end of the play, he unexpectedly upholds the Lord Chief Justice and dismisses Falstaff from favour. Again, the ▷ morality drama tradition is a strong influence: the just king upholds the principle of justice, and sets his face against riot and self-indulgence. Some of the best scenes are still comedy, though the mood of *Part II* is grimmer than that of *Part I*; the comedy is chiefly in Mistress Quickly's Boar's Head Tavern in London, and on the country estate of Justice Shallow. Shakespeare's sources were again the 16th-century chronicles of ▷ Hall and ▷ Holinshed.
▷ History plays; ▷ *Henry IV, Part I*.

Henry V (1413–22)

King of England, and second of the House of Lancaster. His brief reign is memorable for his brilliant victory over the French at Agincourt. By the Treaty of Troyes (1420) he was recognized as heir to the throne of France, his claim to which had been the cause of the war. His dissolute youth (▷ Shakespeare's ▷ *Henry IV*) was a popular legend but is probably unfounded, though he was on bad terms with his father. He modelled himself on ▷ King Arthur, the heroes of the Crusades and the ideal of the Christian monarchy (the French war, in English eyes, was a just one) and in English tradition he became a national hero.

Henry V

A ▷ history play by ▷ Shakespeare performed in 1599; an imperfect version printed in 1600. It records the battle of Agincourt, Henry's great victory in France; this is the triumphal conclusion to the series that had so far dramatized national disaster: ▷ *Richard II*, ▷ *Henry IV, Parts I and II*. This play has been censured as too much a patriotic pageant with too little genuine dramatic interest. However, there is drama in the spectacle of a small national army, united in moral purpose under a Christian king, confronting a rich and massive array of selfishly disunited nobility. The disintegrative elements on the English side are still present in the traitors Scroop and Grey, and in ▷ Falstaff's former cronies, Pistol, Bardolph and Nym. The union of the British Isles is forecast by the presence not only of the prominent Welsh officer, ▷ Fluellen, but of Irish and Scottish officers as well, though Scotland was in fact an ally of France at the time. The play is indeed primarily a patriotic drama, but it is by no means an uncritical one. There is, for instance, the obvious element of conflict in Henry between his dual aspects as king and man, evident especially in his dialogue with Williams and his soliloquy in IV.i; modern critics (*eg* Traversi, *Approach to Shakespeare*) find many examples of irony at the expense of Henry in the play. It is interesting to note that *Henry V* has been filmed twice, each time with the director taking the eponymous lead: by Laurence Olivier (1907–89) in 1944, and by Kenneth Branagh in 1989.

Henry VI (1422–61)

King of England, and last of the House of Lancaster. He was strongly religious but no man of action, and his reign was darkened by the Wars of the Roses and by the final defeat of England in the Hundred Years' War.

Henry VI, Parts I, II and III

Three very early ▷ history plays by ▷ Shakespeare, perhaps written between 1590 and 1592. *Parts II* and *III* were published in 1594–5 under different titles, but *Part I* not until 1623; it was possibly written, or revised, after the other two. Together they make the first three parts of a tetralogy, ending with ▷ *Richard III*, in which the spreading feuds, hatreds, crimes and vengeances finally concentrate all their force in the wickedness of one man. *Part I*: the defeat of the English in the Hundred Years' War, and the beginning of aristocratic feuds; *Part II*: the marriage of Henry to the vigorous Margaret of Anjou, Jack Cade's popular rebellion, and the opening of the civil Wars of the Roses; *Part III*: Henry's final defeat and murder at the hands of the York branch of the Plantagenets, Edward Early of March (Edward IV, 1461–83) and his brother Richard of Gloucester (Richard III, 1483–5). The Henry VI plays have vivid and poignant episodes but are inferior to the masterly *Richard III*. The 16th-century chroniclers ▷ Hall and ▷ Holinshed are the sources of the plays.

Henry VII (1485–1509)

King of England. He was the first of the House of ▷ Tudor, of Welsh origin and related to the House of Lancaster; he defeated ▷ Richard III, last of the House of York, at the battle of Bosworth (1485), with a mainly Welsh army. Henry connected his Welsh background with ▷ King Arthur, and gave this name to his eldest son (d 1502). He was a notably able ruler, and was later paralleled with ▷ Henry V as a restorer of

national unity and order after civil war. At the end of ▷ Shakespeare's ▷ *Richard III* he makes an appearance as a national redeemer. ▷ Francis Bacon wrote a life of him (1622). **Bib:** Chrimes, S. B., *Henry VII*.

Henry VIII (1509–47)

King of England. He was a powerful and talented man, entitled Defender of the Faith by the Pope for his ▷ pamphlet against ▷ Martin Luther, but he replaced Papal authority with his own by the Act of ▷ Supremacy, 1534, an act important for the subsequent development of national identity and sovereign independence. He is notorious for having had six wives, two of whom he executed and two divorced. His personal power was great but he generally exerted it through Parliament.

▷ Tudor, House of; Parr, Katherine.
Bib: Smith, H. M., *Henry VIII and the Reformation*.

Henry VIII

A ▷ history play written (probably) by ▷ John Fletcher and ▷ Shakespeare in 1612–13. Its main episodes concern the divorce of Katharine of Aragon, the downfall of ▷ Cardinal Wolsey, and the triumph of ▷ Thomas Cranmer. The play ends with the triumphal christening of Henry's daughter, ▷ Princess Elizabeth, the future queen. In 1613 a performance of the play at the ▷ Globe Theatre caused the destruction of the building by fire.

Henry, Prince of Wales (1594–1612)

Patron. The brief, but enormously influential, period in which Henry governed his own household and cultivated his own cultural and political circles was seen by the ▷ Jacobean court as a rebirth of the ▷ Elizabethan golden age. The disillusionment that developed after the immediate glow of ▷ James I's coronation had faded, began to focus upon his son as a possible source of integrity, honour, cultural development and staunch ▷ Protestantism. Although the burden of expectation must have been great, Henry appeared to answer these demands. His early death (probably the earliest recorded case of typhoid) make it impossible to say how far he would have continued to extend his popularity, for it is easier to maintain an idealized value system from the margins of power than from the centralized role that kingship would have necessitated. Nevertheless, Henry cultivated those courtiers and writers who had been

popular in Elizabeth's day, such as the ▷ Earl of Southampton and ▷ Michael Drayton. He is also known for his participation in two of ▷ Jonson's ▷ masques, *Prince Henry's Barriers* (1610) and *Prince Oberon* (1611).
Bib: Strong, R., *Henry, Prince of Wales, and England's Lost Renaissance.*

Henslowe, Phillip (d 1616)

Theatre owner and builder. The ▷ Rose, the Hope, and the Fortune Theatres were all at least partly owned by him, and although an efficient businessman, he was also compassionate. His son-in-law was the famous actor ▷ Edward Alleyn of the ▷ Admiral's Men, whose finances he looked after. His *Diary*, 1592–1609, is a main source for the theatrical history of the age, but is not in itself very informative.
   ▷ Theatres.
Bib: Carson, N., *A Companion to Henslowe's Diary.*

Herbert, Edward, 1st Baron Herbert of Cherbury (1583–1648)

Poet, philosopher and diplomat. Edward Herbert (Lord Herbert of Cherbury) was elder brother of ▷ George Herbert. A friend of ▷ John Donne, ▷ Ben Jonson and ▷ Thomas Carew, and an ardent Royalist before the ▷ Civil War, Herbert's major works were his ▷ autobiographical *The Life of Lord Herbert Written by Himself* (published by Horace Walpole in 1765); his philosophical *De Veritate* (1624) and his volume of poems *Occasional Verses* (1665).

The *Life*, written when Herbert was in his 60s, recalls his earlier adventures as a younger man, prior to his return from Paris in 1624, where he had been ambassador. The *De Veritate*, which was of considerable influence in the 17th century, attempts to explore rationalist positions in the general field of religious experience. Herbert's own religious position was that of an orthodox Anglican, of a strongly anti-Calvinist persuasion. He is seen to be the father of ▷ Deism and a forerunner of the Enlightenment.

Although his poetry was not published until 1665, the major portion of his verses was written before 1631. His poetic contemporaries thus included both his brother and Donne, of whose verses Herbert's poetry is strongly reminiscent.
   ▷ Calvin, John.
Bib: Herbert, C. A., 'The Platonic Love Poetry of Lord Herbert of Cherbury', *Ball State University Forum* II; Hill, E. D., *Edward, Lord Herbert of Cherbury.*

Herbert, George (1593–1633)

Poet. Herbert shares, with ▷ John Donne, the distinction of being one of the most widely read of the 17th-century poets in modern times. Though he was not ordained as a priest until 1630, and though court connections ensured that the earlier part of his life was spent in cosmopolitan circles, all the extant poems are devotional in nature.

His poetry was first published posthumously, in 1633, when *The Temple: Sacred Poems and Private Ejaculations* appeared under the auspices of his friend Nicholas Ferrar shortly after Herbert's death. The collection met with enormous approval, and was a considerable influence on ▷ Richard Crashaw, amongst others. The poems in *The Temple* are deceptively simple at first glance. Yet in his exploitation of the speaking voice, and in the complexity of the complete structure of the volume of poems, Herbert rivals Donne for a fierce logical presence in his verse. Of considerable importance to Herbert's poetic undertaking is his espousal of a direct form of poetic discourse – one that, in many respects, looks forward to the reformist projects of later 17th-century theoreticians of language.

Herbert's other major work was the prose manual *A Priest to the Temple* (1652), which is a form of conduct-guide for the ideal Anglican priest. ▷ Izaac Walton published a *Life* of Herbert in 1651.
Bib: Hutchinson, F. E. (ed.), *The Works of George Herbert*; Vendler, H., *The Poetry of Herbert*; Summers, J. H., *George Herbert: His Religion and Art*; Strier, R., *Love Known: Theology and Experience in George Herbert's Poetry.*

Herbert, Sir Henry (1595–1673)

▷ Master of the Revels, 1623–42. He belonged to the literary Herbert family, which included his brothers ▷ Edward Herbert, ▷ George Herbert and Thomas Herbert, as well ▷ William Herbert in whose house, Wilton, Sir Henry met ▷ King James I and was awarded the post of Master of the Revels. Initially he seems to have been the deputy of Sir John Astley (who had succeeded ▷ Sir George Buc in 1622), but by 1623 Herbert was in full control. His influence was considerable as he was a conscientious reader of all plays and made careful excisions, for example, of all blasphemous language. He resumed his post on the Restoration of the monarchy in 1660, but had lost much of his fortune during the ▷ Interregnum and never fully recovered either his wealth or his position.

Bib: Adams, J. Q., *The Dramatic Records of Sir Henry Herbert*.

Herbert, William (1580–1630)

Poet, dramatist and courtier, William Herbert, third Earl of Pembroke is one of the candidates for 'W. H.', the young man to whom ▷ Shakespeare's ▷ sonnets are dedicated. The grounds for this identification, apart from the initials, are Herbert's noble rank, his status as a well-known patron, and the fact that the First ▷ Folio is partly dedicated to him. If Herbert is identified as the young man, then Mary Fitton his mistress could be linked to the dark lady of Shakespeare's work. When Herbert came to the court of ▷ Elizabeth I, he first attempted to join her coterie of favourites, but was too melancholy and scholarly for this somewhat chivalric group. He then fell out of favour completely when he got Fitton, a lady-in-waiting, pregnant and refused to marry her; he was later to have two illegitimate children by ▷ Lady Mary Wroth. Herbert was imprisoned in the Fleet and never really gained acceptance at court until the accession of ▷ James I. A supporter of ▷ Ralegh, he had interests in ▷ colonial investments. Herbert also wrote ▷ masques and poetry, which were published in 1660. He was one of the wealthiest men in England and became an increasingly significant political figure, helping to overthrow the Earl of Somerset (whom he replaced as Lord Chamberlain) and to promote another royal favourite, ▷ Buckingham. Later, however, he was central to the resistance to Buckingham's influence over James and their pro-Spanish policies. He was a major patron of the arts and literature, and was praised particularly for this by ▷ Ben Jonson.

Hermeneutics

Used in literary criticism to denote the science of interpretation as opposed to commentary. Hermeneutics is concerned primarily with the question of determining meaning, and is based upon the presupposition of a transcendental notion of understanding, and a conception of truth as being in some sense beyond language. Hermeneutics also postulates that there is one truth, and is therefore opposed on principle to the notion of 'pluralism' that is associated with ▷ deconstruction and ▷ materialist readings.

Hero and Leander

A poem left unfinished by ▷ Christopher Marlowe and completed by ▷ George Chapman (1598). Hero was a priestess of Aphrodite, and lived at Sestos on the European shore of the Hellespont. A youth called Leander, who loved her and lived at Abydos on the opposite shore, used to swim across to her at night, until he was drowned in a storm. Marlowe's poem is one of the finest narrative poems of this period.

Heroic, Mock

A literary mode in which large and important events are juxtaposed with small and insignificant ones for a variety of comic, satirical or more profoundly ironic effects. Although mock heroic is most closely associated with 18th-century literature, it is found in all periods. An early example is ▷ Chaucer's *Nun's Priest's Tale* (▷ *The Canterbury Tales*) in which the cock behaves like a prince, although he is merely the property of a poor widow. The 'most Lamentable Comedy' of Pyramus and Thisbe, performed by ▷ Bottom and the 'mechanicals' in ▷ *A Midsummer Night's Dream*, is a particularly complex example. The low social status and eager enthusiasm of the actors contrasts not only with the stilted nobility of the characters they impersonate, but also with the unimaginative condescension of the 'audience' within the play.

Herrick, Robert (1591–1674)

Poet. Robert Herrick's poetry was published in a collection entitled *Hesperides* (1648), which appeared together with a companion volume, *His Noble Numbers*. Numerous manuscript versions of his poetry circulated in the 17th century, but the vast majority of his verse is represented in the 1648 publication. As one of the few ▷ Renaissance poets to gather his work into a single volume, it is important to look at Herrick's poetry as a self-consciously coherent pattern.

He has long been associated with the ▷ Cavalier poets, although his writing is of a quite different kind. Indeed, Herrick's gently mocking tone shows up the ▷ Stuart ▷ utopianism as hollow dreams. Herrick's chief stylistic models were the ▷ epigrammatic Latin poetic styles to be discovered in the works of ▷ Catullus and ▷ Horace. His delight in the epigrammatic style contrasts with his other memorable poetic achievement – the creation of fantasies which combine ▷ pastoral motifs with minutely observed details of nature. The poem that opens the 1648 collection ('The Argument of His Book') sets out his poetic manifesto, which is revealed to be one of

nostalgic longing for a rural ideal, probably unobtainable.
Bib: Martin, L. C. (ed.), *Robert Herrick's Poetical Works*; Rollin, R. B. & Patrick, J. M. (eds.), *Trust to Good Verses: Herrick Tercentenary Essays.*

Heywood, John (?1497–?1580)
Dramatist. He wrote highly entertaining short plays of the kind known as ▷ interludes, *eg Play of the Weather* (1533), *A Play of Love* (1534), and ▷ *The Four P's* (1568).
Bib: Johnson R. C., *John Heywood.*

Heywood, Thomas (?1574–1641)
Dramatist, actor, poet, pamphleteer; Heywood was, by his own claims, immensely prolific. His field was especially the drama of sentiment with middle-class characters, and to this belong his best-known plays, ▷ *A Woman Killed with Kindness* and *The English Traveller.* His ▷ blank verse, though not great poetry, benefits by the influences of a great age, and though plain, sometimes achieves poignancy. His first play may have been *The Four Prentices of London*, obviously appealing to a citizen (as distinct from a court) audience by its combination of romance and idealization of the middle class. This was perhaps acted as early as 1592. His many plays include ▷ *The Fair Maid of the West; Edward II; The Wise Woman of Hogsdon.* However, Heywood had a more pervasive role in the theatre of the day, which he believed should be for public enjoyment and not as an attempt at 'literature'. He wrote several civic ▷ pageants, was a shareholder in ▷ Queen Anne's Men, and, most importantly, wrote a sharp defence of the theatre against ▷ Puritan condemnation, *An Apology for Actors* (pub. 1612).
Bib: Boas, F. S., *Thomas Heywood.*

Hilliard, Nicholas (c 1547–1619)
Miniaturist. One of the most well-known artists of the Elizabethan court, Hilliard somehow managed to capture the self-fashioning golden age of this world with his sumptuous detail, delicate brush strokes and abundant use of ▷ allegory and mythology. Even the size of the works contributes to the sense of the intimate and precocious coteries surrounding ▷ Elizabeth I. He was praised in verse by ▷ Donne and ▷ Constable, and he wrote his own work, the *Art of Limning* (1603), where he argues that painting is a suitable practice for a gentleman.
Bib: Murdoch, J. (ed.), *The English Miniature;*

Strong, R., *Nicholas Hilliard* and *The English Renaissance Miniature.*

Hippolyta
In Greek myth, the queen of the Amazons. Heracles conquers her and gives her in marriage to Theseus of Athens. She appears as the bride of Theseus in ▷ Shakespeare's ▷ *A Midsummer Night's Dream* and ▷ *Two Noble Kinsmen.*

Historia Regum Britanniae (History of the Kings of Britain)
Major work of ▷ Geoffrey of Monmouth completed around 1138, recounting the history of the kings of the island from its foundation by Brutus to the loss of British sovereignty in the reign of Cadwallader.
▷ Arthur, King.

Histories and Chronicles
Histories and chronicles are important in the study of literature in two ways: as sources for imaginative material and as literature in their own right. However, with the exception of the Venerable Bede, it was not until the 17th century that English historians began to achieve the status of major writers.
▷ Geoffrey of Monmouth (d 1154) is the most important amongst a number of medieval historians for originating two national myths in his ▷ *Historia Regum Britanniae*; the myth that Brutus, great-grandson of ▷ Aeneas, was the founder of the British race, and the myth of ▷ King Arthur as the great defender of British Christianity. Both had importance in nourishing nascent English patriotism. When England became a centralized state under the ▷ Tudor monarchs, ▷ Henry VII chose the name Arthur for his eldest son. It was the main task of Tudor chroniclers both to heighten patriotism and to identify it with loyalty to the ruling family. This was the purpose of the Latin history of England by the Italian Polydore Vergil, in the service of Henry VII and ▷ Henry VIII. More important was > Edward Hall's *The Union of the two Noble and Illustrious Families of Lancaster and York* (1548), which showed the House of Tudor to be the saviour of the nation after the civil Wars of the Roses in the 15th century. ▷ Raphael Holinshed's *Chronicles of England, Scotland and Ireland* (1578) was a compilation from various sources, including Geoffrey of Monmouth, and begins in ancient biblical times. The belief of the time was that history was useful as the means by which the present could learn from the past as a source of warnings, precepts and examples.

The imaginative writers used the material of the chronicles in this spirit. Geoffrey of Monmouth, Hall and Holinshed were sources for many of the historical dramas of the reign of ▷ Elizabeth, including those of ▷ Shakespeare, and also for narrative poets such as those who contributed to ▷ *A Mirror for Magistrates* (1559), ▷ Samuel Daniel (*Civil Wars*, 1595–1609) and ▷ Michael Drayton (*The Barons' Wars*, 1603). Much of this new interest in history arose from the ▷ Renaissance transference of attention from heavenly destinies to earthly ones; thus the period 1500–1650 also produced the first eminent antiquarians, notably William Camden (1551–1623), and the first historical ▷ biographies: ▷ Thomas More's *Richard III* (written 1513), George Cavendish's life of ▷ Cardinal Wolsey (written shortly after the Cardinal's death but not published in full until 1667), ▷ Francis Bacon's life of Henry VII (1622) and ▷ Lord Herbert's life of Henry VIII (1648).

History plays (chronicle plays)
These are especially a phenomenon of the last two decades of the 16th century, when they may have accounted for more than one-fifth of the plays written in a very prolific period of the drama. The history play is distinct from what is ordinarily called historical drama, which is a phenomenon of the 19th and 20th centuries, and, like the historical novel of the same period, involves reconstructing another period of history in awareness of its differences in customs, habits, outlook, etc. Absence of 'scientific' history in the 16th century debarred dramatists from a 'historical' sense. On the other hand, they were familiar with the dramatization of biblical events relevant to the Fall and Redemption of Man in the religious mystery plays: in a similar way history was to them and their audiences a collection of tales about the past, many of which were relevant to contemporary national predicaments. Thus in the 16th century the English Church and state had cut loose from the Roman Catholic Church, and there was consequent interest in the reign of ▷ King John (1199–1216) when there had been a comparable quarrel between king and pope; in the reign of ▷ Elizabeth I men were alarmed at the possible consequences of the queen's dying without a direct heir, and this caused them to be interested in the reign of ▷ Richard II, and so on. The ▷ morality plays also influenced the histories: until the 16th century, moralities had concerned themselves with the spiritual destinies of men in general,

but the growth of national consciousness, the splintering off of national churches in the 16th century and the increased importance of the national ruler in deciding human destinies, all caused morality dramatists to extend their interest to politics and to draw on history for their subject matter. Thus ▷ John Bale, supporter of Henry VIII in his emancipation of the English Church from Rome, wrote *King John* (?1547) to make his case for Henry's policy. The morality content of Bale's play gives it coherent structure, but the chronicles of the 1580s, *eg The Famous Victories of Henry V* (?1588), relied chiefly on the eventfulness of their episodes. It was ▷ Marlowe (*Edward II*, ?1593) and ▷ Shakespeare in his two great tetralogies (▷ *Henry VI, Parts I, II* and *III* and ▷ *Richard III;* ▷ *Richard II,* ▷ *Henry IV, Parts I* and *II* and ▷ *Henry V*) and ▷ *King John*, who gave psychological and intellectual substance to the history-play form. Marlowe did little more than bring his characters vividly to his audience, but Shakespeare brought deep insights to bear on the nature of political society and its problems. His two tetralogies have been called a great national dramatic epic covering the years 1377–1485; however, it is the second half of the period (from 1422 to 1485; the reigns of Henry VI, Edward IV and Richard III) which constitutes his earlier work (perhaps 1590–93) while the plays concerning the first half (Richard II, Henry IV, Henry V) are relatively mature work (perhaps 1596–99). *King John* (?1596) is between the tetralogies in regard to maturity of style.

It becomes difficult, in the maturer Shakespeare, to draw a clear line between history plays and tragedy. ▷ *Julius Caesar* follows the Greek historian ▷ Plutarch closely, but it is also a tragedy; and ▷ *King Lear* derives from the chronicler ▷ Holinshed as does ▷ *Henry V*, though the former is not history. The history plays and tragedies in fact merge into each other; both contain politics, and both present tragic catastrophe.

Hobbes, Thomas (1588–1679)
Philosopher. Together with the writings of ▷ Francis Bacon and ▷ René Descartes, the political and philosophical theories of Thomas Hobbes dominated thought in late 17th-century England. Yet, unlike Bacon's boundless optimism, Hobbes's philosophy appeared to be determined by an almost cynical view of human nature and society. In his great analysis of the individual and the individual's place in society, *Leviathan* (1651), Hobbes argued that human society was governed by two overwhelming individual

concerns: fear (of death, other individuals, etc.) and the desire for power. For Hobbes society is organized according to these two principles, and can be rationally analysed as a 'mechanism' (an important Hobbesian concept) governed by these two concerns.

Leviathan itself emerged out of the turmoil of revolutionary upheaval in England during the ▷ Civil War, and the figure of the 'Leviathan' – the sovereign power, though not necessarily the monarch – expresses a desire for stable government. But in addition to *Leviathan* Hobbes published in various fields of philosophical and social enquiry. His interest in language and the uses of ▷ rhetoric was to be influential amongst post-Restoration thinkers. But it was his analysis of the mechanical laws (as he saw them) of production, distribution and exchange that was to be of profound importance in British economic and philosophical thought in the 18th century and later.

Hobbes's chief works include: *The Elements of Law* (written by 1640, but published ten years later); *De Cive* (1642, translated into English in 1651); *De Corpore* (1655, translated in 1656); and *De Homine* (1658). Hobbes also undertook an analysis of the causes of the English Civil War in composing *Behemoth* (1682), as well as critical work – in particular his *Answer* to ▷ Sir William D'Avenant's *Preface to Gondibert* (1650).
Bib: Molesworth, Sir W. (ed.), *The English Works of Thomas Hobbes* (11 vols.); Mintz, S. I., *The Hunting of Leviathan*.

Hobbinol
▷ Harvey, Gabriel.

Hoby, Lady Margaret (1571–1633)
Diarist. Although Lady Margaret's diary is important in generic terms in that it is the earliest diary written by an Englishwoman to have survived, its contents are repetitive and mundane. She dutifully recounts her morning prayers and the day-to-day running of a Renaissance household. Sometimes humorous juxtapostionings occur, but it is difficult to ascertain whether the irony is intentional. She was married three times before she was 30: to Walter Devereux, the brother of the ▷ Earl of Essex; to Thomas Sidney, the brother of ▷ Mary Sidney, Countess of Pembroke; and to Thomas Hoby, son of ▷ Thomas Hoby and ▷ Elizabeth Russell. Her diary was published this century: *The Diary of Lady Hoby*, ed. Dorothy M. Meads (1930).

Hoby, Sir Thomas (1530–66)
Translator. Primarily known for his ▷ translation of ▷ Castiglione's *Il Cortegiano* as *The Courtier*, which he wrote in Paris in 1552–3, but which was not published until 1561. It was an immediate success and influenced both young noblemen and women who attempted to emulate the idealized characters in the text, as well as late Elizabethan writers who portrayed similar courtly debate in their own works (▷ Spenser, ▷ Jonson and ▷ Shakespeare). Hoby was the first husband of ▷ Lady Elizabeth Russell, who was also an accomplished translator.
▷ Hoby, Lady Margaret.
Bib: Crane, T. F., *Italian Social Customs of the Sixteenth Century*.

Holbein, Hans, the younger (c 1487–1543)
Painter. Born in Augsburg, Germany, Holbein came to England to the household of ▷ Sir Thomas More in 1526–8 on the recommendation of ▷ Erasmus, for whom he had illustrated *Praise of Folly* (1509). Several works of the More household remain, as well as sketches or paintings of ▷ Thomas Cromwell, ▷ Sir Thomas Wyatt and Henry Howard, ▷ Earl of Surrey, as well as his most famous portrait of ▷ Henry VIII. Holbein's meticulous and naturalistic style was a dramatic innovation in England and heralded the end of medieval symbolic representations in favour of the greater individuality of ▷ Renaissance art.
Bib: Robert J., *Holbein*.

Holinshed, Raphael (d ?1580)
Chronicler: *Chronicles of England, Scotland and Ireland* (1578). The history of England was written by Holinshed himself but a vivid *Description of England* added to the history is by William Harrison. The history of Scotland is a translation of a Scottish work written in Latin – *Scotorum historiae* (1527) by Hector Boece – and the account of Ireland is by Richard Stanyhurst, Edward Campion and others. ▷ Shakespeare and other Elizabethan dramatists used the *Chronicles* as a principal source book for history plays; Shakespeare also used them for ▷ *Macbeth*, ▷ *King Lear* and ▷ *Cymbeline*.
▷ Histories and Chronicles.

Holy War, The (1682)
An ▷ allegory by ▷ John Bunyan. Its subject is the fall and redemption of man. The city of Mansoul has fallen into the hands of Diabolus (the Devil) and has to be recaptured by Emmanuel (Jesus Christ), who besieges it.

Homer

Ancient Greek ▷ epic poet, author of the ▷ *Iliad* and the *Odyssey*, basic works for ▷ Greek literature. Ancient traditions exist about Homer, for instance that latterly he was blind and that seven cities claimed to be his birthplace, but nothing is conclusively known about him. Archaeological investigation has disclosed that the destruction of Troy, following the siege described in the *Iliad*, took place in the 12th century BC; linguistic, historical and literary analysis of the poems show them to date as artistic wholes from perhaps the 8th century BC. That they are artistic wholes is in fact the only evidence for the existence of Homer; efforts to show that they are compilations by a number of poets have proved unconvincing, though it is clear that Homer himself was using the work of other poets between the Trojan war and his own time.

Homosexuality

Accorded a marginal place in literary representation, and when it has been shown, usually hedged about with implications of the exotic, the abnormal or at least the exceptional. When Radcliffe Hall published her plea for the recognition and acceptance of lesbianism, *The Well of Loneliness* (1928), even though it had a sympathetic preface from the sexologist Havelock Ellis, testifying to its scientific accuracy, the book was condemned as obscene and banned. This is in line with official attempts to promote heterosexual activity within marriage as the healthy norm. In the 1950s and 1960s aversion therapy was used in an effort to impose or restore this norm in homosexuals. The Kinsey Reports on *Sexual Behaviour in the Human Male* (1948) and *Female* (1953), however, showed that what had been defined as deviant behaviour was far more widespread than had been believed, thus challenging the 'naturalness' of heterosexuality. Homosexual behaviour in certain circumstances defined as private was decriminalized, but not until ten years after the Wolfenden report recommended it. Meanwhile, criticism, which had often ignored the homoerotic elements in ▷ Renaissance literature, began to acknowledge the possibility of homosexual ▷ discourses within hitherto heterosexually romanticized texts. The practice of cross-dressing in ▷ Shakespeare's ▷ comedies and the universal use of boy-actors to play female roles have been recognized as ways in which sexuality and gender-roles were questioned and challenged. For example, ▷ Rosalind's final speech

in ▷ *As You Like It*, where the boy-actor acknowledges his sex while still disguised as the heroine, opens out a whole range of sexual interpretations. In poetry, ▷ Marlowe's ▷ *Hero and Leander* focuses on the male protagonist as the centre of male erotic attention, while ▷ Katherine Philips' stated love for her female friends has led to her inclusion in the lesbian canon.

Hooker, Richard (?1553–1600)

Theologian. His most significant work was *Laws of Ecclesiastical Polity* (1593–7). This was the first outstanding polemic expounding the ▷ Church of England viewpoint, and its main purpose was to defend the Church against attacks by ▷ Protestant reformers. Such reformers (the ▷ Puritans) trusted only the ▷ Bible as authority on matters of religion, since only the Bible was acknowledged to be inspired by God. They criticized the Church of England for being too near the Roman Catholic Church in its organization (*eg* in its retention of the authority of bishops) and for resembling the Roman Church in its excessive reliance on other kinds of authority. Hooker considered that the Puritans were making major issues out of inessentials, and that their attacks were dangerous both socially and religiously, since the state was indissolubly bound up with the Church, and it was essential for both to adapt themselves to historical change and requirement, and to draw upon the law of nature as well as upon the Holy Scriptures for guidance. Law he regarded as inherent in created nature and as the same principle, whether seen in the aspect of natural order, social order or divine order. In this view of law, Hooker is essentially a conservative thinker, inheriting from the ▷ Middle Ages the view of the universe as a system of related degrees ranging from God down to the four ▷ elements of hot, cold, moist and dry as the basis of matter. Though conservative, the outlook was not reactionary; it was the most widely accepted assumption of the time, implicit in the imaginative literature, see *eg* the speech of Ulysses in ▷ Shakespeare's ▷ *Troilus and Cressida* (I. iii. 75).

However, for all Hooker's conservatism, in the ▷ Civil War and post-Civil War period his works were widely read by radicals as well as by the more conservative-minded. Hooker's appeal to radicals was based on the posthumous publication, in 1648, of a further three books of his *Laws of Ecclesiastical Polity* – books whose authenticity has long been debated. What recommended Hooker to

radicals was the role he assigned to consent in religion, and the fact that, in the later parts of the *Laws*, he offered no defence of divine-right episcopacy.
Bib: Keble, J. (ed.), *The Laws of Ecclesiastical Polity*; Cargill-Thomson, W. D. J., *Studies in the Reformation: Luther to Hooker*.

Horace (Quintus Horatius Flaccus, 65–8 BC)

Roman poet of the Augustan age. His work divides into three classes; his ▷ Satires, ▷ Odes and Epistles. The last includes the *Ars Poetica* or *De Arte Poetica* (*Concerning the Art of Poetry*), which became an important critical document for Europe – for England particularly in the 18th century. It emphasizes the importance of cultivating art in poetry; he lays down the principle that if you do not understand poetry it is better to leave it alone. Art means above all the cultivation of alert judgement: expression and form must be appropriate to theme; characterization and form must be consistent with the subject and with themselves; conciseness is a virtue in didacticism; adaptation of a writer is allowed but plagiarism is not; the poet must study to be wise as a man, and he must be his own severest critic; a just critic is a severe one.
▷ Ben Jonson translated the *Ars Poetica* (pub. 1640) and depicted Horace sympathetically in *The Poetaster*; rivals regarded this as an affected self-portrait.
▷ Ariosto.

Hoskyns, John (1566–1638)

Poet and rhetorician. Hoskyns was educated at Winchester and New College, Oxford, but was expelled from the latter for writing ▷ satire. He was an eloquent lawyer and, finally, MP for Hereford. His poetic writing and contribution to style was for a long time unrecognized; however, it is now apparent that ▷ Jonson used Hoskyns' *Directions for Speech and Style* (1599) in *Timber*, and that several poems written by Hoskyns have been misattributed to others, such as ▷ Donne. His poetry is often witty and down-to-earth, the shorter pieces being amongst the best.

Hotspur (Sir Henry Percy) (1364–1403)

Eldest son of the first Earl of Northumberland. ▷ Shakespeare represented him in ▷ *Henry IV, Part I*, where he is shown as the generous, tempestuous warrior, devoted entirely to honour, but failing to relate it to any feeling for human good. He is thus, despite these qualities, a destructive force.

Hudibras (1663, 1664 and 1678)

A mock-heroic (▷ Heroic, Mock) ▷ satire in tetrameter couplets by ▷ Samuel Butler (1612–80). The Presbyterian Sir Hudibras and his Independent Squire Ralpho undergo various adventures designed to expose the hypocrisy of the ▷ Puritans, interspersed with satire on various scientific and intellectual follies. The poem's structure parodies the 16th-century ▷ epic romances of ▷ Ariosto and ▷ Spenser, and the hero takes his name from a knight in Spenser's ▷ *Faerie Queene*. In spirit it owes much to Cervantes' anti-romance satire ▷ *Don Quixote*. The poem's politics pleased ▷ Charles II, who gave Butler £300 and a pension of £100 a year. Though the work fails to sustain narrative interest it establishes its own distinctive vein of rollicking farce and homespun philosophizing:

> *Honour is, like a widow, won*
> *With brisk attempt, and putting on;*
> *With ent'ring manfully and urging;*
> *Not slow approaches, like a virgin.*
> (I. ii. 911–14)

Butler's loose tetrameters with their vigorous colloquial diction and crude rhymes became an established medium for broad satire, known as 'hudibrasticks'.

Humanism

The word has two distinct uses: 1 the intellectually liberating movements in western Europe in the 15th and 16th centuries, associated with new attitudes to ancient Greek and Latin literature; 2 a modern movement for the advancement of humanity without reliance on supernatural religious beliefs.

1 Humanism in its first sense had its beginnings in Italy as early as the 14th century, when its pioneer was the poet and scholar ▷ Petrarch (1304–74), and reached its height (greatly stimulated by the recovery of lost manuscripts after the fall of Constantinople in 1453) throughout western Europe in the 16th century, when it first reached England. Its outstanding characteristic was a new kind of critical power. In the previous thousand years European civilization had above all been dominated – even created – by the Church, which had put the literatures of the preceding Latin and Greek cultures to its own uses and had directed movements in thought and art through its authority over the religious orders and the universities. The humanists began by criticizing and evaluating the Latin

and Greek authors in the light of what they believed to be Roman and Greek standards of civilization. Some of the important consequences of humanism were these: the rediscovery of many ancient Greek and Latin works; the establishment of new standards in Greek and Latin scholarship; the assumption, which was to dominate English education until the present century, that a thorough basis in at least Latin literature was indispensable to the civilized man; the beginnings of what we nowadays regard as 'scientific thinking'; the introduction of the term ▷ Middle Ages for the period between the fall of the Roman Empire of the West (5th century AD) and the ▷ Renaissance, meaning by it a period of partial and inferior civilization. The most prominent of the European humanists was the Dutchman ▷ Erasmus, and the most prominent of the earlier English humanists was his friend ▷ Sir Thomas More. The Church was not at first hostile to humanism; indeed such a pope as Leo X (reigned 1513–21) was himself a humanist. When, in the second 30 years of the 16th century, the critical spirit became an increasingly aggressive weapon in the hands of the religious reformers – the Renaissance branching into the ▷ Reformation – the attitude of the Church hardened, and humanists in the later 16th century found themselves restricted by the religious quarrels of ▷ Protestants and Catholics, or obliged (like ▷ Montaigne) to adopt a retiring and circumspect policy. In the 17th and 18th centuries, humanism hardened into ▷ neo-classicism.

2 'Humanism' is also used as a general expression for any philosophy that proposes the full development of human potentiality. In this sense, 'Christian humanism', since the 16th century, has stood for the marriage of the humanist value attached to a conception of humanity based on reason with the Christian value based on Divine Revelation. An example of a Christian humanist movement is that of the Cambridge ▷ Platonists in the 17th century. 'Liberal humanism' values the dignity of the individual and their inalienable right to justice, liberty, freedom of thought and the pursuit of happiness; its weakness lies in its concentration on the single subject and its failure to recognize the power of institutions in determining the conditions of life.

▷ Intertextuality.
Bib: Kinney, A. F., *Continental Humanist Poetics*.

Humour
The original meaning was 'liquid'. Ancient Greek and Latin medicine passed on to the ▷ Middle Ages the theory of four liquids (humours) in the human body: phlegm, blood, yellow bile or choler, and black bile or melancholy. Individual temperaments derived their quality from the predominance of one or other 'humour'; thus we still speak of 'phlegmatic' or very calm temperaments, 'sanguine' or ardent temperaments, 'choleric' or easily angered ones, and 'melancholy' or depressive temperaments. In the later 16th century a man's humour was his characteristic disposition, whether or not related to the original four physical humours. It could also have other meanings: his mania or obsession; his caprice or whim; his passing mood.

All these uses can be found in ▷ Shakespeare and his contemporaries; *eg* in ▷ *Julius Caesar* II.i., Portia begs her husband Brutus not to risk his health in the 'humours' (moistures) 'of the dank morning', but in the same scene Decius has declared that he can induce Caesar to go to the Capitol by giving 'his humour the true bent', *ie* by exploiting Caesar's disposition to superstition. In ▷ *The Merchant of Venice* IV.i, Shylock suggests that if an explanation is required for his preferring a pound of Antonio's flesh to 3,000 ducats, it should be put down to his caprice – 'Say it is my humour'; in ▷ *As You Like It* IV.i, ▷ Rosalind speaks of being in a 'holiday humour', *ie* in a gay mood.

▷ Ben Jonson in ▷ *Every Man in His Humour* III.i, speaks of a humour as 'a monster bred in a man by self-love and affectation, and fed by folly', *ie* produced by egotism, encouraged by fashionable ostentation, and not restrained by good sense.

▷ Humours, Comedy of; Satire; Wit.

Humours, Comedy of
A form of drama especially associated with ▷ Ben Jonson. Starting from the traditional psychology that explained a temperament as the product of its physical constitution, Jonson treats ▷ humour as the monstrous distortion of human nature by egotism and the self-regarding appetites, notably some form of greed. Partly timeless satire on human nature, the comedy of humours is also social satire since such personal extravagances are nourished by social tendencies: new prospects of wealth let loose unbounded lusts, as with Sir Epicure Mammon (in Jonson's ▷ *The Alchemist*); the rush of speculation on often fantastic 'projects' (*ie* financial enterprises requiring investment) encourages unlimited

credulity in the foolish, *eg* Fitzdottrel in ▷ *The Devil is an Ass*; the prevalence of avarice causes adventurers to overreach themselves in their contempt for their victims and in their own megalomania (Volpone and Mosca in ▷ *Volpone*). Jonson's world is a jungle of predators and victims, free from the restraint of religion, reason or respect for tradition. But the passions which Jonson exposes in their excess arise from human energies that are themselves fine and belong to that exhilaration in the scope for human fulfilment which is characteristic of the ▷ Renaissance. Jonson's more massive characters, though they condemn themselves by the exorbitance of their language, make speeches of great poetic splendour and force. The hyperbole of ▷ Christopher Marlowe in ▷ *Tamburlaine* and ▷ *The Jew of Malta* provides the tradition for Jonson's eloquence. Jonson's great comedies are *Volpone* and *The Alchemist*. *The Devil is an Ass* is nearly as fine, and ▷ *Bartholomew Fair* and ▷ *Epicoene, or The Silent Woman* are memorable. The mode was first established by ▷ *Every Man in his Humour*. ▷ *Sejanus* is a satirical tragedy, with similarities to the great comedies.

Among Jonson's followers, ▷ Massinger (▷ *A New Way to pay Old Debts*, and ▷ *The City Madam*) and ▷ Middleton (▷ *A Chaste Maid in Cheapside*) are the best.

▷ Bakhtin, Mikhail.

Hutchinson, Lucy (1620–c 1675)
Prolific writer. Lucy Hutchinson displayed her immense intelligence as a child (she could read perfectly by the time she was four) and excelled her brothers at scholarly activity. Although her family thought this would repel any future husband, it was her quiet learning that attracted John Hutchinson and their marriage, which lasted from 1638 until his death in 1664 was a deeply romantic one. As a Parliamentarian, her husband was imprisoned at the Restoration, and her ▷ biography of him (*Memoirs of the Life of Colonel Hutchinson*, pub. 1806) was partly written to ensure that their children knew about and admired his life. However, she was also aware of the similar work by the Royalist ▷ Margaret Cavendish. Lucy Hutchinson also translated ▷ Lucretius and ▷ Virgil, wrote several Christian tracts (she became a ▷ Baptist in 1646), and an ▷ autobiography.
▷ Translation.
Bib: Fraser, A., *The Weaker Vessel*.

Hymns
The word 'hymn' is of ancient Greek origin; it meant a song of praise to the gods. Such songs have been important in all the religions that have lain behind European culture: Latin hymns were composed and sung in the Christian churches from the earliest days of Christianity, and the Jewish hymns, or ▷ Psalms, are shared by the Jewish and the Christian religions.

The English hymn began its history in the religious ▷ Reformation under ▷ Edward VI when the abandonment of the Latin form of service produced the need for hymns in English. The Psalms were the obvious resource, but they had been translated into English prose. Accordingly, in 1549, the first or 'Old Version' of metrical Psalms was published; the authors were Sternhold and Hopkins. The most famous of this collection, and the only one now generally known, is the 'Old Hundredth' (Psalm 100): 'All people that on earth do dwell'. The Old Version of the metrical Psalms was replaced by the 'New Version' (1696) by Tate and Brady. From this Book, two psalms are still familiar: 'Through all the changing scenes of life' and 'As pants the hart for cooling streams'.

The majority of hymns in English, however, were not metrical Psalms, but specially composed original poems. The great period of English hymn composition was the 17th and 18th centuries. However, it is necessary to distinguish between short religious poems which have been adopted as hymns, and poems which were composed as hymns. Some of the best religious poets of the 17th century, notably ▷ Herbert and ▷ Vaughan, produced work in the first group. But the first professional hymn-writer (as distinct from the composers of the metrical Psalms) was the Anglican bishop Thomas Ken (1637–1711). His best hymns, *eg* 'Awake my soul', and 'Glory to thee, my God, this night', are distinguished poetry.

It was, however, the ▷ Dissenters – the ▷ Puritan movements excluded from the ▷ Church of England by the Act of Uniformity (1662) – and their Evangelical sympathizers within the Church of England, rather than the orthodox Anglicans, who were at first most active in hymn-writing. The Church of England had a set form of worship in *The Book of Common Prayer* (▷ *Common Prayer, Book of*); hymns (in addition to the prose versions of the Psalms) were allowed in this service, but no special provision was made for them. But the Dissenting sects had no set form of worship; hymns for this reason alone were important to them. They were also important for three other reasons: Dissent was strong among classes in touch with traditions of ▷ ballad and folk-song; most forms of Dissenting faith demanded strong participation by the congregation in the act of worship; in the 17th century, Dissenters underwent persecution and communal militant hymn-singing encouraged their spirit of endurance. ▷ John Bunyan included hymns in his ▷ *Pilgrim's Progress*, written in prison; one of these – 'Who would true valour see' – is famous.

Idealism

In philosophy, any form of thought that finds reality not in the mind of the perceiver (the subject), nor in the thing experienced (the object), but in the idea in which they meet. In its earliest form idealism was developed by Socrates and his disciple ▷ Plato. Their influence was important in the 16th-century Europe of the ▷ Renaissance, *eg* on ▷ Edmund Spenser.

In ordinary usage, idealism means the ability to conceive perfection as a standard by which ordinary behaviour and achievement is to be judged. This view is really an inheritance from Plato, who believed that earthly realities were imperfect derivatives of heavenly perfections. To 'idealize' a thing or person is to present the image of what ought to be, rather than what experience knows in ordinary life. In imaginative art we have come to consider this as a fault, but to a 16th-century critic such as ▷ Sir Philip Sidney poetry existed for just such a purpose.

In modern critical theory idealism is associated with the anti-materialist (▷ Materialism) impulse to denigrate history and social context. The meaning of this term is complicated by its history within the discipline of philosophy, and by its common usage as a description of human behaviour not susceptible to the 'realistic' impulses of self-interest. The term is sometimes used in critical theory to denote the primacy of thought, and to indicate a particular kind of relationship between writer and text where it is a sequence of ideas that acts as the deep structure for events and relationships.

Ideology

This term is defined by ▷ Karl Marx and Friedrich Engels (1800–95) in *The German Ideology* as 'false consciousness'. A further meaning, which Raymond Williams (1921–87) traces to the usage initiated by Napoleon Bonaparte, denotes a fanatical commitment to a particular set of ideas, and this has remained a dominant meaning in the sphere of modern right-wing politics, especially in relation to the question of dogmatism. The term has come to the fore again in the ▷ post-structural Marxism of ▷ Louis Althusser, where it is distinguished from 'science'. Ideology here is defined as the means whereby, at the level of ideas, every social group produces and reproduces the conditions of its own existence. Althusser argues that 'Ideology is a "representation" of the imaginary relationship of individuals to their real conditions of existence' (*Lenin and Philosophy*, 1971). In order to ensure that political power remains the preserve of a dominant class, individual 'subjects' are assigned particular positions in society. A full range of social institutions, such as the Church, the family and the education system, are the means through which a particular hierarchy of values is disseminated. The point to emphasize, however, is that ideology disguises the real material relations between the different social classes, and this knowledge can only be retrieved through a theoretically aware analysis of the interrelationships that prevail within society at any one time. A ruling class sustains itself in power partly by coercion (repressive apparatuses), but also by negotiation with other subordinate classes (▷ hegemony; Althusser's ideological state of apparatuses).

Social change occurs when the ideology of the dominant class is no longer able to contain the contradictions existing in real social relations. The function of literary texts in this process is complex. In one sense they reproduce ideology, but they may also offer a critique of it by 'distancing' themselves from the ideology with which they are historically implicated. Since all language is by definition 'ideological', insofar as it is motivated by particular sorts of social relationship, the language of a literary text can very often be implicated in an ideology of which it is not aware. The text's implication in ideology can only be excavated through a critical process that seeks to uncover the assumptions upon which it is based.

Bib: Althusser, L., *For Marx*; Thomson J. B., *Studies in the Theory of Ideology*.

Idyll

In ancient Greek literature it originally meant a short poem. The Greek poet ▷ Theocritus called his poems about the rural life of Sicily 'idylls'. When the term was revived in the ▷ Renaissance, it was consequently used for a short ▷ pastoral poem, similar to an ▷ eclogue except that an eclogue was more likely to be in dialogue. As pastoral verse commonly presented happiness or virtue in pure and simplified terms, an idyll then came to be used loosely for any piece of writing presenting experience in such a way, often an episode from a longer work.

Iliad

An ▷ epic by the ancient Greek poet ▷ Homer. Its subject is the siege of Troy by an alliance of Greek states; the occasion of the war is the elopement of Helen, wife of Menelaus, king of the Greek state of Sparta,

with Paris, a son of Priam, king of Troy.
The poem is in 24 books; it begins with the
Greeks already besieging Troy. In Book I the
chief Greek hero, Achilles, quarrels with the
Greek commander-in-chief, Agamemnon, king
of Argos and brother to Menelaus. Achilles
withdraws from the fighting, and returns to
it only in Book XIX after the killing of his
friend Patroclus by the chief Trojan hero,
Hector. Achilles kills Hector in XXII, and
the poem ends with Hector's funeral in Troy.
Hector is the principal hero of the epic, much
of which is taken up with his exploits, along
with those of other Greek and Trojan heroes
and with the intervention of the gods on either
side. There is much speculation about the
respective dates of the historical events and
of the poem itself. Present opinion seems to
be that the historical city of Troy fell early in
the 12th century BC and that the poem was
written about 300 years later. The surviving
text dates from the 2nd century BC.

The *Iliad* has had an enormous influence
on the literature of Europe. With Homer's
Odyssey, it set the standard for epic poetry,
which until the 19th century was considered
the noblest poetic form. Its first successor
was the ▷ *Aeneid* (1st century BC) by
the Roman poet ▷ Virgil. The poem has
been several times translated into English
verse, the Renaissance version by ▷ George
Chapman (1611). ▷ Shakespeare presents a
dramatized version of events in ▷ *Troilus and
Cressida*.

Imitation, Renaissance Theories of

Renaissance, like medieval, theories of
imitation were of considerable importance to
writers and rhetoricians of the 16th and 17th
centuries. However, imitation did *not* mean
copying or plagiarism; nor was it suggestive
of ▷ translation. Instead, imitation was the
process by which Renaissance writers invested
their own discourse with authority, aesthetic
form and structure by assimilating texts
from the ▷ classical past and incorporating
them into their own work. A frequently
used ▷ metaphor to describe the process is
that of digestion. When ▷ Ben Jonson, for
example, sets out to describe an ideal of
rural life and aristocratic benevolence in his
poem 'To Penshurst', he not only evokes the
Kentish countryside and the family who dwell
at Penshurst, he organizes his description
according to models found in his reading in
▷ Virgil, ▷ Juvenal, Martial (c AD 40–104)
and other classical authors. Imitation is,
in this sense, much more than allusion or
reference. Rather, it is the means whereby the

Renaissance writer could place his/her own
work within a tradition of public or private
utterance.
Bib: Cave, T., *The Cornucopian Text: Problems
of Writing in the French Renaissance*; Greenes,
T. M., *The Light in Troy: Imitation and
Discovery in Renaissance Poetry*.

Imperialism

A desire to build up an empire, that is to
dominate politically and assimilate other
countries. It has a long history, from Rome
to the present day, although the main period
of imperialism began with the 17th-century
conquests of the Americas and reached its
height in the 1880s and 90s.

Inferno, The

The first part of ▷ Dante's great poem,
the ▷ *Divina Commedia*, which describes
the poet's journey through Hell, under the
guidance of ▷ Virgil, where he speaks to
various former friends and enemies. Hell is
conceived of as a conical funnel, reaching to
the centre of the earth. Various categories
of sinners are assigned to the nine gradated
circles, where they receive appropriate
punishments. The first circle is reserved
for pre-Christian pagans who have not had
the chance of knowing the true faith. Virgil
belongs to these, whose only punishment
is the hopeless desire for God. At the very
bottom is Satan (Lucifer) himself, and from
him Dante and Virgil pass through the
earth to its opposite surface, where they
arrive at the foot of the Mount of Purgatory
(▷ *Purgatorio*).

Inns of Court

Although London did not have a university, the
Inns of Court provided esteemed educational
facilities for the sons of the nobility and gentry
and were by no means considered inferior
to the institutions at Oxford and Cambridge.
Indeed, apart from law, history, music and
writing were all practised at the Inns, and many
of the most well-known writers and politicians
passed through their doors. To name but a
few: the historian ▷ Seldon was at the Inner
Temple; the poet ▷ Suckling at Gray's Inn;
▷ Carew at Middle Temple; and ▷ Donne at
Lincoln's Inn. The Inns were also important
for the development of Renaissance drama in
that many plays were first performed in their
central courtyards, for example, ▷ *Twelfth
Night* was performed in Middle Temple
in 1602.
Bib: Bland, D. S., *Three Revels from the*

Inns of Court; Prest, W. R., *The Inns of Court Under Elizabeth I and the Early Stuarts*.

Instauratio Magna (The Great Renewal)
The title of the great philosophical work projected by ▷ Francis Bacon and left incomplete. According to Bacon's plan of 1620 it was to have consisted of six parts: I. A review of existing sciences; *De Augmentis Scientiarum*, Latin translation of ▷ *The Advancement of Learning* (1605). II. Outline of a new inductive method; ▷ *Novum Organum (The New Instrument)*. This exists in a compressed form, unfinished. III. A Natural History to be used as a basis for inductive conclusions. The tract *Parasceve (Preparative)* and the *Historia Ventorum (History of the Winds)*; *Historia vitae et mortis (History of Life and Death)*; *Sylva Sylvarum (Forest of Forests)*, a collection of facts and observations. IV. Examples of investigations by the new method, of which there remains only a small fragment, *Filum Labyrinthi (The Thread of the Labyrinth)*. V. Hypotheses of Bacon's own, to be tested by inductive experiment, of which only a preface exists, though some other writings may have been intended to belong to it. VI. A synthesis of conclusions from the inductive method, none of which remains.

Interludes
Short plays of a kind popular especially in the 16th century before the great flowering of Elizabethan drama. In general they were more secular than ▷ morality plays, which were still being performed, but moralities and interludes are not always clearly distinguishable, and indeed the term 'interlude' was applied to religious plays as early as the 14th century. Nonetheless there is no other convenient term for such slight works as ▷ John Heywood's *Play of the Weather* (1533), in which an emissary of the gods tries to find out the ideal weather for humanity, only to discover that opinions conflict hopelessly. The function of such a play seems to have been entertainment after a banquet in a nobleman's hall or in a college, or during the intervals of business of a town council, etc. That it was a performance during intervals of business or other kinds of entertainment, or perhaps of long, serious plays to provide light relief, has been assumed from the usual meaning of 'interlude' in ordinary speech; however, the word has also been surmised to mean merely 'a play between' performers taking parts. One of the best-known examples is the interlude of *Pyramus and Thisbe* played before Theseus and his court in the last act of ▷ Shakespeare's ▷*A Midsummer Night's Dream*.

Interregnum
The term used for the period 1649–60, between the execution of ▷ Charles I and the accession of his son Charles II – the Restoration. It is divided into the period 1649–53, when England was ruled by the House of Commons and a Council of State, and the period 1553–8 when ▷ Oliver Cromwell and for a brief time his son Richard were Protectors.

Intertextuality
A term first introduced into critical theory by the French ▷ psychoanalytical writer Julia Kristeva (b 1941), relating specifically to the use she makes of the work of ▷ Mikhail Bakhtin. The concept of intertextuality implies that literary texts are composed of dialectically opposed utterances, and that it is the function of the critic to identify these different strands and to account for their oppositions within the text itself. Kristeva notes that Bakhtin's '"dialogism" does not strive towards transcendence . . . but rather towards harmony, all the while implying an idea of rupture (of opposition and analogy) as a modality of transformation' (*Desire and Language*; trans. 1980). Similarly, no text can be entirely free of other texts. No work is written or read in isolation, it is located, in Kristeva's words, 'within the totality of previous . . . texts'. This is a second important aspect of intertextuality, and is important in discussing pan-European movements in the ▷ Renaissance, such as ▷ humanism.
▷ Feminism.

Ireland
A brief sketch of the confused and tormented history of this country during the ▷ Renaissance period perforce has to concentrate on its relations with England; this account may conveniently be divided into phases.

1150–1600 – Period of Disorder
Henry II was the first English king to be acknowledged sovereign of Ireland, but at no time before 1600 did the English succeed in establishing an efficient central government. In the 12th century Ireland consisted of warring Celtic kingdoms, with a Norse settlement along the east coast. The conquest was not undertaken by Henry but by his Anglo-Norman nobility, notably Richard

Strongbow, Earl of Pembroke in alliance with the Irish king of Leinster. By 1500 Ireland was ruled by a mixed English and Irish aristocracy, the former regarded as English by the Irish and as Irish by the English. English law and speech were secure only in a narrow region known as the Pale, centred on the capital city of Dublin. The first real crisis in relations between England and Ireland arose in the 16th century, when the Irish refused to receive the English Protestant ▷ Reformation. Fierce wars against Spanish armies that landed in Ireland with a view to invading England were followed by fierce suppression under ▷ Elizabeth I, for instance under the governorship of Lord Grey de Wilton. The poet ▷ Edmund Spenser was appointed de Wilton's secretary (1580) and given a grant of land in the province of Munster as part of a plan to settle the country with Protestant overlords; his castle was burnt down in 1598, a year before his death. Spenser's singularly stern view of Justice in ▷ *The Faerie Queene* (Artegall, Bk. V) is a reflection of his Irish experiences as is his propagandistic prose treatise, *View of the Present State of Ireland* (1596). By 1600 Ireland was a nation of mixed English and Celtic people, with an English-speaking aristocracy, and firm identification with the Roman Catholic faith. The Ulster rebellion (1595) gathered force, with Spanish aid, until in 1599 a large English force under the command of the Earl of ▷ Essex was sent to crush the revolt. The expedition was, however, to fail miserably and English political losses were only recouped fully in 1602 under the command of Mountjoy. The problem as England saw it in the next two centuries was how to subdue a previously independent country to effective Protestant rule.

1600–1660 – Irish Protestant Ascendancy
The policy of settling Protestants in Ireland was notably successful in one of the four provinces under ▷ James I (1603–25) when Ulster became the Anglo-Scottish Protestant fortress which it has remained to this day. ▷ Oliver Cromwell was savage in the subjection of Catholic Ireland to his authority, and by extensive confiscations increased the class of Protestant landlords. This violent suppression was to recur until the formation of the Irish Free State in 1922. The Northern Protestant provinces, however, still remain part of the United Kingdom and the resulting division has led to a perpetuation of the troubles throughout the 20th century.

Irony
From the Greek = 'dissimulation'. A form of expression by which the writer intends his meaning to be understood differently and less favourably, in contrast to his overt statement.

Italian influence on English literature
Apart from the influence of Italian literature, Italy as a country was particularly important to England in the 16th and early 17th centuries. The English attitude to Italy was complicated – a mixture of admiration, envy, intense interest and disapproval amounting to abhorrence. The Italian cities were for Englishmen the centres and summits of civilization, and such centres in most periods are supposed to represent not only what is most advanced in thought and behaviour, but also what is most extravagant and corrupt.

Two Italian books of the 16th century were immensely fascinating to Englishmen, and the English response to them explains much of the contradiction in English feeling. The first was ▷ Castiglione's *Courtier* (1528, trans. 1561), which offered a model for the virtues and accomplishments of the perfect ▷ gentleman; this was greatly admired by English courtly figures such as the ▷ Earl of Surrey, ▷ Sir Thomas Wyatt, ▷ Sir Philip Sidney, ▷ Sir Walter Ralegh and ▷ Edmund Spenser, and was approved even by such an anti-Italian as ▷ Queen Elizabeth's private tutor, ▷ Roger Ascham. The other was ▷ Machiavelli's *Prince* (1513). This book was not translated into English until 1640, but many educated Englishmen knew Italian in the 16th century; in any case, Gentillet's *Contre Machiavel* (*Against Machiavelli*, 1576) was widely known in England and translated in 1602. Machiavelli's object was to develop a political science capable of uniting Italy; this did not interest Englishmen, but they were deeply horrified by Machiavelli's demonstration that for such politics to be effective they had to disregard ordinary morality and good faith. The work no doubt impressed English statesmen such as Elizabeth's minister Cecil (▷ Burghley), but it made 'politics' – 'politic' – 'politician' into evil words for those not occupied by statecraft, and a Machiavellian was synonymous with an atheist or with one who had taken the devil as his master. Such a man was ▷ Shakespeare's ▷ Richard III, and it is Machiavelli who speaks the prologue to ▷ Christopher Marlowe's play ▷ *The Jew of Malta*. When Sir Andrew in Shakespeare's ▷ *Twelfth Night* says (III. ii) 'for policy I hate: I had as lief [would as soon] be a ▷ Brownist as a politician' he is coupling a ▷ Puritan sect hated by dramatists and playgoers with Machiavellians hated by the Puritans and anti-Puritans alike. More superficially, travel in Italy was supposed to induce folly and affectation and to corrupt morals, as for example is stated in ▷ Nashe's ▷ *The Unfortunate Traveller*. As Roger Ascham put it in *The Scholemaster* (1570): 'what the Italian saith of the Englishman . . . *Englese Italianato, è un diavolo incarnato*, that is to say, you remain men in shape and fashion, but become devils in life and condition.' Italians were poisoners and seducers like Iachimo in Shakespeare's ▷ *Cymbeline*. It was not only because their fiction was popular that so many Elizabethan and Jacobean plays were based on Italian tales ('*novelle*'), but because Italy could be appealed to as the land where human nature was richest, darkest and brightest.

The fact that Rome was the centre of the ▷ Catholic Church was of course bad enough for Protestant Englishmen after 1540; before that date the image was brighter, and throughout the century Englishmen did not forget that Italy was the nation of such great scholars and philosophers as Pico della Mirandola (1463–94), whose works ▷ Sir Thomas More partly translated. It was the independence of the best Italian minds that attracted the best English minds of the 16th and 17th centuries. The free-thinking Italian philosopher Giordano Bruno (?1548–99) despised the stale traditions of the English universities on his visit (1583–5), but he admired Queen Elizabeth and made friends with men such as Sir Philip Sidney and Sir Walter Ralegh. The astronomer ▷ Galileo, who, like Bruno, came into conflict with the inquisition, was studied by the poet ▷ John Donne, and received visits from the sceptical philosopher ▷ Thomas Hobbes and the Puritan ▷ John Milton. Milton's visit to Italy (1638–9) enriched him with encounters with scholars and patrons of learning, while at the same time he felt in danger from the papal police because of his religious opinions; this is another example of the complicated relationships of Englishmen with Italy.

After 1650 Italy by no means lost its fascination for the English, but it was Italy as a storehouse of the past, rather than a challenging present, that drew Englishmen and -women.

J

Jack Horner

A nursery rhyme usually considered to derive from a study about one of the profiteers who acquired land from the monasteries when these were dissolved by ▷ Henry VIII. Another old rhyme goes:

> Hopton, Horner, Smyth and Thynne,
> When the abbots went out, they came in.

Jack Wilton

▷ Nashe, Thomas.

Jacobean

Used to indicate the period of ▷ James I (1603–25) and applied especially to the literature and style of architecture of his reign. In literature, it is most commonly a way of distinguishing the style of drama under James from the style that prevailed under ▷ Elizabeth. Strictly, Elizabethan drama is experimental, expansive, sometimes ingenuous, in fairly close touch with medieval tradition but energetic with ▷ Renaissance forces. It includes the work of the ▷ University wits – ▷ Christopher Marlowe, ▷ Thomas Kyd, ▷ Robert Greene, ▷ George Peele – and also early ▷ Shakespeare. Jacobean drama is thought of as critical, sombre, disillusioned. It includes mature and late Shakespeare, ▷ Ben Jonson, ▷ Cyril Tourneur, ▷ John Webster, ▷ Thomas Middleton, ▷ Francis Beaumont and ▷ John Fletcher. The ▷ Caroline period is associated with such figures as ▷ Philip Massinger, ▷ John Ford, and ▷ James Shirley. Courts were the centre of culture, and courts depended largely on the circumstances of monarchs: while the reign of Elizabeth was prosperous at home and (mainly) triumphant overseas, that of James saw increasing disagreement at home, and experience abroad was negative or even nationally humiliating. The reign of ▷ Charles I was yet more bitter in home dissensions but his court was one of distinction and refinement. The tone of the drama varied with these differences in national fortune and court conduct. However, the labelling of literary periods is always to some extent simplifying and even falsifying.

The Jacobean period was the first that was really rich in prose, with writers like ▷ Francis Bacon, ▷ John Donne and ▷ Lancelot Andrewes. Their work contrasts especially with Restoration prose, which sacrificed the poetic qualities of the Jacobean writing for the sake of grace and lucidity.

▷ Seventeenth-century literature.

Jakobson, Roman (1896–1982)

Born in Moscow, where he was educated. He worked in Czechoslovakia for almost 20 years, between 1920 and 1939, and after the German invasion he escaped to Scandinavia before going to the U. S. A. where he taught in a number of universities and became Professor of Russian Literature at the Massachusetts Institute of Technology. During his formative years he was heavily influenced by a number of avant-garde movements in the Arts, but in his own work he laid specific emphasis upon the formulation of a 'poetics' which took into account the findings of ▷ structuralism, and the work of the Russian formalists (▷ Formalism). He was an active member of the Society for the Study of Poetic Language (OPOYAZ), which was founded in St Petersburg in 1916, and in 1926 he founded the Prague Linguistic Circle. His wife Krystyna Pomorska notes, in a recent collection of his writings, that poetry and visual art became for Jakobson the fundamental spheres for observing how verbal phenomena work and for studying how to approach them (Roman Jakobson, *Language and Literature*, 1987).

▷ Metonymy.

Bib: Hawkes T., *Structuralism and Semiotics*; Jakobson, R., *Language and Literature* and *Verbal Art, Verbal Sign, Verbal Time*; Bennett, T., *Formalism and Marxism*; Erlich V., *Russian Formalism: History-Doctrine*.

James I of England and VI of Scotland

A member of the Scottish House of ▷ Stuart, he ruled over Scotland alone (1566–1603) and then over England as well (1603–25). He was the first sovereign ever to reign over the whole of the British Isles. His accession to the throne of England was due to the death without children of his cousin ▷ Elizabeth I, last of the House of ▷ Tudor. The literature and architecture of his era is known as ▷ Jacobean, a term transferred, especially in architecture, to the greater part of the 17th century. James was also an accomplished author in his own right. His works include *Basilikon Doron* (1599), an address to his son, ▷ Prince Henry, on the rules of good government; *True Law of Free Monarchies* (1598), which argues that the monarch's power is absolute and God-given; and several theological treatises.

Bib: Ashton, R., *James I By His Contemporaries*.

James IV (1590)

A romantic transvestite comedy by ▷ Robert Greene which dramatizes the loves of James IV and of his English wife Dorothea against whose life he conspires. The play's main action – which is the stuff of melodrama – is framed by the choric comments of Oberon and Bohan, a misanthropic Scot. In this respect Greene's practice accords with similar dramatic strategies adopted in ▷ Kyd's *The Spanish Tragedy*, and it also anticipates the Chinese-box structure of ▷ *A Midsummer Night's Dream* and, to a lesser extent, ▷ Shakespeare's use of an induction in ▷ *The Taming of the Shrew*.

Jesuit

A member of the Society of Jesus, a religious order founded by Ignatius Loyola, and approved by the Pope in 1540. The Jesuits were in the forefront of combating ▷ Protestantism. In the reign of ▷ Elizabeth I they led, or were reputed to lead, the various conspiracies against her on behalf of the ▷ Catholic claimant to the English throne, ▷ Mary Queen of Scots; they were therefore regarded as national as well as religious enemies. Their advanced training made them skilled debaters and subtle negotiators. Notable English Jesuits of the English Renaissance include ▷ Edmund Campion and ▷ Robert Southwell.

Jew of Malta, The

A ▷ blank-verse drama by ▷ Christopher Marlowe, written and performed about 1590; published 1633. An actor impersonating the Italian political philosopher ▷ Machiavelli speaks the prologue and thereby sets the tone of the play, since to the English of Marlowe's time Machiavelli, who had sought to conduct politics amorally by scientific methods, was a godless monster. We thus expect a play dominated by evil. However, a comic tradition for the presentation of godless monsters had come down to Marlowe from the medieval mystery plays, which had presented such figures as Herod and Satan as grotesque caricatures, frightening but funny at the same time. So the Machiavellian central character, Barabas the Jew, boasting that his wealth has been acquired iniquitously, is made too impressive to be taken lightly and yet too extravagant to be taken soberly. His only philosophy is the art of gaining advantage. In the first half of the play he tries to outwit the Christians of Malta, who, scarcely less Machiavellian than himself, try to deprive him of his wealth. He eventually betrays the island to the Turks, and proceeds to try to outwit them, but he falls victim to his own plot. In a famous essay on Marlowe (*Selected Essays*), T. S. Eliot (1888–1965) described the play as an example of 'the farce of the old English humour, the terribly serious, even savage comic humour'; in his essay on ▷ Ben Jonson, Eliot points to *The Jew of Malta* as the forebear of Jonson's Comedy of ▷ Humours.
▷ Race.

Joan of Arc (Jeanne d'Arc) (1412–31)

A French national heroine for the leading part she played in turning the Hundred Years' War finally against the English invaders of France.

For some time the English continued to remember her as a witch, and she is so represented in the early play by ▷ Shakespeare, ▷ *Henry VI, Part I*, where she appears under her French nickname of 'La Pucelle' – the Maid.

Joceline, Elizabeth (1596–1622)

Tract-writer. Elizabeth Brooke was brought up by her maternal grandfather, Bishop Caderton, who was Master of Queens' College, Cambridge, and she was educated in religion, languages, history and art. She married Tourell Joceline in 1616, and died in childbirth six years later. While she was pregnant she wrote a book of moral and religious instruction for her unborn child, which is especially interesting in its gender-specific teachings. While being aware that a son would traditionally be the preferred sex, Joceline is careful to point out that a daughter will be equally welcome to her. Her touching account was published as *The Mothers Legacie To Her Unborn Childe*, with a preface by her husband, in 1624.
Bib: Travitsky, B. (ed.), *The Paradise of Women*.

John

King of England, 1109–1216. His reign was particularly disturbed; he succeeded in raising against him both his own nobles and the Church, as well as losing his father's French possessions. In 1215 the alliance of nobles and Church successfully imposed on him the Magna Carta, by which he agreed not to infringe the rights of the Church or of his subjects.

His quarrel with the Church caused him to be regarded favourably in the 16th century when the Tudors were occupied in reducing the Church from a supranational into a national institution; thus he is idealized in the

play *King John* (1547) by ▷ Bishop Bale. In
Shakespeare's play ▷ *King John*, his crime is
the death of his nephew Arthur, and sympathy
is still with him against the Church; there
is no mention of Magna Carta. It was in
the 17th-century quarrels between the kings
and parliaments that this document became
important, as seeming to justify parliamentary
resistance to the Crown.

Jones, Inigo (1573–1651)

Architect and stage designer. He is sometimes
called 'the English ▷ Palladio' because he
was strongly influenced by the Italian architect
of that name, and he was in fact the first
important classical (Palladian) architect in
English architecture. Jones and his assistant
John Webb brought classical ideas into
the material and commercial worlds of
London architecture and the ▷ Renaissance
theatre. Outstanding buildings of his design
include the Banqueting Hall in Whitehall
and St Paul's church in Covent Garden,
both in London. He also designed sets for
▷ masques, to which words were contributed
by ▷ Ben Jonson, ▷ Samuel Daniel and other
poets among his contemporaries. Scenery
and music were as important in the masque
as poetry, and the fusion led to bitter rivalry
between Jones and Jonson, who satirized him
as In-and-In Medlay in *The Tale of a Tub*.
Bib: Orrell, J., *The Theatres of Inigo Jones
and John Webb*; Simpson, P. and Bell, C. F.,
*Designs by Inigo Jones for Masques and Plays at
Court*; Orgel, S. and Strong, R., *Inigo Jones:
The Theatre of the Stuart Masque*.

Jonson, Benjamin (1572–1637)

Dramatist and poet; always known as Ben
Jonson. In drama, he was ▷ Shakespeare's
most distinguished rival, but they differed
greatly in gifts and achievement. Sixteen of
his plays, not including ▷ masques, have
survived; 14 comedies and two tragedies.
Their merits vary greatly: his universally
acknowledged masterpieces are the comedies
▷ *Volpone* (1605 or 1606) and ▷ *The Alchemist*
(1610), to which some distinguished critics
add the satirical tragedy ▷ *Sejanus* (1603).
In the second rank of importance, the
following are usually included: ▷ *The Devil
is an Ass* (1616), of great satirical power but
less dramatic concentration; ▷ *Epicoene, or
The Silent Woman* (1609) and ▷ *Bartholomew
Fair* (1614), slighter in content but vigorous
entertainments; and ▷ *Every Man in his
Humour* (1598), the first of the comedies of
▷ humours with which his name is identified.
Although all of Jonson's work contains

passages of interest, his remaining plays
have faults (such as excessive academicism,
diffuseness of treatment or narrowness of
satirical range) that usually restrict their
interest to scholars. They are: *Every Man out
of his Humour* (1599); *Cynthia's Revels* (1600);
The Poetaster (1601); ▷ *Catiline* (a tragedy,
1611); *The Staple of News* (1625); ▷ *The New
Inn* (1629); *The Magnetic Lady* (1632); *The
Tale of a Tub* (1633); *The Case is Altered* (an
early work, before he had discovered his
characteristic comic medium; 1597). He
left unfinished a ▷ pastoral drama *The Sad
Shepherd*.

Jonson was very much a man of his age
and his personal life as well as his writing
both display a series of contradictions.
Society was undergoing radical changes; the
unsettlement of accustomed moral values
gave scope to extravagance and folly. He
himself was a man of strong appetites
and vitality, but he understood and deeply
cared for the restraining and directing
qualities of civilization. His conception of
civilization derived partly from his typically
▷ Renaissance admiration for ancient Roman
culture, which he thoroughly assimilated
through ▷ Latin literature, and partly from
the traditional virtues of English society,
which economic and religious changes were
challenging. He was thus a moral satirist
who delighted in animal vitality and human
aspiration, but who made it his business to
chasten the ▷ 'humours' (or, as we might say,
'manias') to which society was liable when it
escaped the control of civilized discipline and
reason. This made him a self-conscious artist
in matters of literary form, and his plays, his
prose miscellany (*Timber: or Discoveries made
upon Men and Matter*, published 1640), and
his conversations reported by the Scottish
poet ▷ Drummond, contain much critical
comment on the virtues of poetic and
dramatic discipline – often at the expense of
his contemporaries, including Shakespeare.
At the same time he was a highly independent
writer who showed no disposition to subject
his work to the restriction of a code of rules.

In his non-dramatic poetry, Jonson
produced a body of fine poetry which
influenced the form of later ▷ lyric verse.
His poems have neither the emotional
extravagance of the idealizing love poets of
the age, nor the rough texture of a realist like
▷ Donne; they combine the grace of manner
of the former with the masculine strength
of the latter, and fuse a vitality personal
to Jonson with an intellectual control he
learnt from Latin poets such as ▷ Catullus.

▷ Andrew Marvell was to learn from Jonson an incisiveness to temper the imaginative ingeniousness he learnt from Donne, and the school of ▷ Cavalier Poets of the reign of ▷ Charles I got from him much of their grace and poise.

Jonson had considerable importance as a personality who exercised influence by his talk. He was not born into the aristocratic circles of a poet like ▷ Philip Sidney, but fashioned his career himself from bricklayer's son to proto-poet laureate. His proud and independent attitude to his noble patrons helped to enhance respect for the independence of the literary profession. His meetings and discussions with other poets at the ▷ Mermaid Tavern were commemorated by ▷ Francis Beaumont in *Francis Beaumont to Ben Jonson* and much later by John Keats (1795–1821) in *Lines on the Mermaid Tavern* (1818), and in his old age he had a school of disciples who called themselves 'the sons of Ben'. They included such poets as ▷ Thomas Carew and ▷ Robert Herrick. The 1616 ▷ Folio of his *Works* contained a carefully edited self-presentation of his career to date, with two highly selective poetry sequences (*Epigrams, The Forest*), all the court masques but no civic commissions, and only those plays he wished to preserve. He was mocked for treating play-books as serious literature, but this marks a watershed in the reception of dramatic texts in English, and set the precedent for the ▷ Shakespeare First Folio. **Bib:** Knights, L. C., *Drama and Society in the Age of Jonson*; Eliot, T. S., in *Selected Essays*; Barish, J. A., on Jonson's dramatic prose and (ed.) critical essays; Partridge, E. B., *The Broken Compass: A Study of the Major Comedies*; Barton, A., *Ben Jonson, Dramatist*; Duncan, D., *Ben Jonson and the Lucianic Tradition*; Leggatt, A., *Ben Jonson: His Vision and His Art*; Miles, R., *Ben Jonson: His Life and Work*; Riggs, D., *Ben Jonson: A Life*; Evans, R., *Ben Jonson and the Poetics of Patronage*; Dutton, R., *Ben Jonson: Authority and Criticism*, Orgel, S., *The Jonsonian Masque*.

Journalism

The distinction between journalism and literature is not always clear, and before the rise of the modern newspaper with its mass circulation in the second half of the 19th century, the two forms of writing were even more difficult to distinguish than they are today. The most superficial but also the most observable difference has always been that journalism puts immediacy of interest before permanency of interest, and easy readability

before considered qualities of style. But of course what is written for the attention of the hour may prove to be of permanent value.

The ▷ 'pamphlets' of writers such as ▷ Thomas Nashe and ▷ Thomas Dekker in the 1590s, and those on the controversial religious matters of the day such as the Marprelate pamphlets, are no doubt the earliest work with the stamp of journalism in English.

Julius Caesar (c 1599)

A historical tragedy by ▷ Shakespeare based on the events of 44 BC, when Caesar was assassinated on suspicion of seeking to overthrow the Roman republic and make himself king. The conspiracy against him is led by Brutus, descendant of the Brutus who, according to legend, had first established the republic by throwing out the Tarquin line of kings in the 6th century. Brutus is a friend of Caesar, and his motive in organizing Caesar's assassination is his disinterested love of Rome; his chief associate, Cassius, on the other hand, is motivated by personal envy and resentment. The third outstanding character in the drama is Caesar's friend Mark Antony, who, after the assassination, treacherously but most successfully turns the Roman mob against Brutus and Cassius and drives them out of Rome. Acts IV and V show the defeat of Brutus and Cassius at the battle of Philippi (42 BC). Caesar himself plays a comparatively small part, although he is, alive and dead, the centre of the drama. The dramatic interest arises from the interplay between the characters of Brutus, Cassius and Antony, and from the conflicts in the mind of Brutus, who, as a good man, finds himself in the tragic dilemma of having to commit a horrible crime against a man he loves for the sake of the nation. Shakespeare based the events, with some interesting alterations, on ▷ Plutarch, whose *Lives* has been translated into English by ▷ Thomas North (1579). The play dates from about 1599.

▷ Caesar, Gaius Julius.

Juvenal (Decimus Junius Juvenalis) (AD ?60–?130)

Roman satirical poet. His 16 satires describe the society of his time and denounce its vices. ▷ Satire, as a literary form, is usually regarded as being a Roman invention, but Juvenal was the first of the Romans to associate it altogether with denunciation; his predecessor, ▷ Horace, had used it for ironic comment and discussion but was only intermittently denunciatory with the moral conviction associated with Juvenal. Like Horace, Juvenal had a strong influence on English poetry from 1590 until 1800; during these two centuries satire was increasingly practised, and Horace,

Juvenal, or Horace's disciple Perseus were taken as models. Both ▷ Thomas Nashe and John Oldham (1653–83) have been described as 'the English Juvenal'.

Kemp, William (fl.1593–1602)
A famous comic actor; contemporary with
▷ Shakespeare. He acted parts such as
Peter, the comic servant of the Nurse in
Shakespeare's ▷ *Romeo and Juliet*, and the
muddle-headed constable ▷ Dogberry in
▷ *Much Ado About Nothing*, and excelled at
jigs. His most famous exploit was dancing
from London to Norwich (more than a
hundred miles) for a bet. He and ▷ Richard
Tarlton established a national reputation for
themselves as comic actors, as ▷ Richard
Burbage and ▷ Edward Alleyn did as
tragic ones.
Bib: Wiles, D., *Shakespeare's Clown*.

Killigrew, Thomas (1612–83)
Dramatist, actor, manager. Born in London
to Sir Robert Killigrew, he became a page
of honour to ▷ Charles I, possibly from
1625. Killigrew wrote his first play, *The
Prisoners*, in 1635 and in the following year he
married one of ▷ Queen Henrietta Maria's
maids of honour, Cecilia Crofts, by whom
he had at least one son before she died in
1638. Killigrew remained loyal to the king
after the outbreak of the ▷ Civil War, and
was imprisoned for a time. He afterwards
travelled as an exile on the Continent during
the 1640s, serving first the Duke of York,
later James II, and then Prince Charles, later
▷ Charles II. His exploits during that period
are romanticized in his play *Thomaso; Or, The
Wanderer* (published 1664).

After the Restoration he was granted one
of the two royal patents to form a theatre
company which became known as the King's
Company. In 1667 Killigrew set up a nursery
to train young actors, in Hatton Garden, and
in 1673 he became Master of the ▷ Revels,
after the death of ▷ Sir Henry Herbert
(1596–1673). This made him responsible
for supervising theatrical entertainment and
licensing theatres and he held the post for
four years before resigning in favour of his
son Charles. In 1682 the King's Company,
having foundered for several seasons,
was effectively absorbed by the ▷ Duke's
Company, but by then Killigrew had little
to do with it. He was buried at Westminster
Abbey, near his first wife and a sister.
▷ D'Avenant, William.

King, Henry (1592–1669)
Poet and Bishop of Chichester. King, himself
the son of a bishop, was prebend of St Paul's
until his appointment as Bishop of Chichester

in 1642. A year later he was expelled from
his bishopric by the ▷ Puritans, but was
reinstated after the Restoration. The major
poetic influences on King were ▷ John
Donne (with whom he was friendly) and
▷ Ben Jonson. The majority of his poetry was
published in 1657, when his *Poems, Elegies,
Paradoxes and Sonnets* appeared. A large
proportion of King's poetic output consisted
of responses to public occasions, obituaries
and ▷ elegies: these included two separately
published elegies on ▷ Charles I (1648
and 1649).
Bib: Berman, R., *Henry King and the
Seventeenth Century*.

King and No King, A (1611)
A tense and melodramatic tragicomedy by
▷ Beaumont and ▷ Fletcher which explores
and tests the limits of courtly and romantic
psychology.

King John
A ▷ history play (*The Life and Death of King
John*) by ▷ Shakespeare, perhaps derived
from the anonymous *Troublesome Reign of King
John*, and written before the great history
plays ▷ *Henry IV, Parts I and II*, which first
exhibit his genius in maturity. Anticipations of
this maturity show themselves in the central
character, Philip Faulconbridge, illegitimate
son of the previous king, Richard I. The reign
of the historical ▷ King John (1199–1216) was
very unsettled: in the play, the disturbance
arises from John's having usurped the throne
from his nephew Arthur, whose cause is taken
up by the king of France, the Church, and
his nobles. Philip, 'the bastard', is excluded
by his illegitimacy from the privileges and
status of the class into which he is born,
and he at first enters the king's service in a
spirit of cynicism, like that of Shakespeare's
other ▷ bastard, Edmund in ▷ *King Lear*.
By degrees he takes to heart the dangers to
the nation of the disorderly passions among
the great men, and he acquires a political
conscience. He is presented substantially, and
stands out from the relatively flat background
of the rest of the characters. However the
theme that has given the play most of such
popularity as it possesses centres not on the
Bastard but on the child Arthur, whose pathos
persuades his gaoler Hubert to spare his life.
Arthur later dies from a fall in an attempt
to escape.

Historically, the best-known fact about
the reign of John is Magna Carta, the Great
Charter which the nobles and Stephen
Langton, Archbishop of Canterbury, forced

the king to accept as a guarantee against tyrannical interference with the rights of the subject. Shakespeare does not mention this; it came into prominence for the national imagination only in the next reign, during the quarrels between ▷ King James I and his Parliaments.

King Lear (1605)

A tragedy by ▷ Shakespeare. The play survives in two substantially different source texts: the 'Pied Bull' ▷ quarto of 1608 and the ▷ folio edition (1623). The quarto edition contains some 300 lines which are missing from the folio, and the folio has 100 lines not in the earlier text. Most modern editions of the play conflate the two sources to make them yield a composite text which contains all the missing lines. This accommodating editorial policy has been challenged persuasively by one of the most exciting Shakespearean ventures of the second half of the 20th century, the publication of a radical edition of the complete works by Oxford University Press under the general editors Gary Taylor and Stanley Wells. Their conclusion, that Shakespeare revised and shortened *King Lear* for the folio edition, can no longer be ignored in critical discussions of the play.

The main plot of *King Lear* proceeds from the division of the kingdom of England and Lear's ill-judged rejection of his daughter Cordelia, who refuses to conform to her father's demand for a public expression of her love for him. The subplot traces the rise and fall of Edmund, the bastard and ruthless son of the Earl of Gloucester who, at Edmund's instigation, wrongfully persecutes his loyal and legitimate heir, Edgar. The double plot of the play widens its imaginative treatment of parents and alienated children and portrays a society fallen from the bias of nature, in which the old, though guilty, are more sinned against than sinning. The play offers an almost unmitigated, dark and apocalyptic vision of a universe in which good characters, particularly Cordelia, perish as well as bad ones like Goneril, Regan and Edmund. For this reason, and because Shakespeare's play contravenes poetic justice, Samuel Johnson (1709–84) preferred it in its mutilated, rewritten version by Nahum Tate (1681), which ended happily as a tragicomedy with the marriage of Edgar and Cordelia. Modern audiences have responded with empathy to the play's bleak vision.
Bib: Elton, W. R., *King Lear and the Gods*; Taylor, G. and Warren, M. (eds.), *The*

Division of the Kingdoms: Shakespeare's Two Versions of King Lear.

King's Men, The

▷ Chamberlain's Men, The Lord.

Knevet, Ralph (1600–71)

Poet. Knevet was attached in a clerical capacity to the Paston family in Norfolk from 1628 until 1637, and wrote numerous religious poems, heavily indebted to ▷ George Herbert. Similarly, his attempt at political ▷ allegory is confined to a 'continuation' of ▷ Spenser's ▷ *The Faerie Queene*, entitled *A Supplement of the Faery Queene* (1635). He also wrote a parodic ▷ masque, *Rhodon and Iris* (1631), for the florists' guild at Norwich. Other extant works are: *Stratiotikon, or a Discourse of Militarie Discipline* (1628) and *Funerall Elegies* (1637).
Bib: Charles, A. M. (ed.), *The Shorter Poems of Ralph Knevett*.

Knight of the Burning Pestle, The (1607)

A comedy by ▷ Francis Beaumont. It mocks the London middle-class taste for extravagant romances in the Spanish tradition about the adventures of wandering knights ('knight-errantry'). It also parodies a contemporary play, *The Four Prentices of London* by ▷ Thomas Heywood, who flattered this taste. It seems to owe something to Cervantes' ▷ *Don Quixote* (Pt I, 1605), itself a parody of the Spanish romances; this, however, was not translated until 1612 (▷ Spanish influence on English literature).

The play at first purports to be called *The London Merchant* but a grocer and his wife, sitting in the audience, become worried that this may turn out to be a ▷ satire on London citizens. They are determined to have something to flatter their vanity, and force their apprentice, Ralph, up on to the stage to perform the role of a 'grocer errant'; he wears on his shield the sign of a burning pestle, *ie* an implement used by shopkeepers. The play of *The London Merchant* proceeds together with Ralph's Quixote-like adventures, and the grocer and his wife, still in the audience, interpose appreciative comments.

The comedy shows the great theatrical dexterity achieved by English dramatists at the height of the Shakespearean period. A main part of this dramatic skill is the intermingling of styles – song, comic rhyme, serious ▷ blank verse, and colloquial prose.

Knox, John (1505–72)

Scottish religious reformer. More than anyone else, he was responsible for the conversion

of Scotland from Catholic to ▷ Calvinist
Christianity, and the eventual establishment
of the national ▷ Presbyterian Church there.
This brought him into conflict with ▷ Mary
Queen of Scots, but he was out of the country
when rebellion forced her to abdicate in 1567
and seek the protection of ▷ Elizabeth I. His
*History of the Reformation of Religion within the
realme of Scotland* includes an account of his
celebrated controversy with the queen. Knox's
vehement antagonism towards the concept,
as well as the actuality, of female sovereign
power has recently been highlighted by
▷ feminist critics.
Bib: Ridley, J., *John Knox.*

Kyd, Thomas (1558–94)
Dramatist. He is associated with the group
known as the ▷ University Wits. His only
known and important contribution to the
output of the group is ▷ *The Spanish Tragedy*
(1587), extremely popular in its own time
and the first important ▷ revenge tragedy.
He was probably also the author of a lost
play on ▷ Hamlet, used by ▷ Shakespeare
as the basis of his own; even without this,
it is clear that Shakespeare developed the
revenge theme from Kyd's first handling of
it. Kyd's own starting-point was the tragedies
of the Roman dramatist ▷ Seneca, whose *Ten
Tragedies* had been published in translation
(1559–81). He was not interested in Senecan
form, but in Seneca's mingling of dramatic
horror and the stern restraints of ▷ Stoic
philosophy, both of which were congenial to

the Elizabethan age. Kyd's other surviving
tragedies are only attributed to him and are
much less important: *Soliman and Perseda*
(?1588) and *Cornelia* (?1593), an adaptation of
a Senecan tragedy by the French dramatist
Robert Garnier.
    Kyd was arrested in 1593 on suspicion of
being involved in anti-immigrant incitement;
the Socinian treatise on atheism was
raised as an issue later and he implicated
▷ Christopher Marlowe by saying that the
treatise really belonged to him. He was
released after Marlowe's mysterious death in
the same year, and seems to have died soon
afterwards in poverty.
Bib: Murray, P. B., *Thomas Kyd.*

Kynaston, Sir Francis (1587–1642)
Poet and translator. While at Lincoln's Inn,
Kynaston wrote several ▷ masques, and his
verse romance, *Leoline and Sydanis* (1642),
displays evidence of this early theatrical
involvement. The poem follows the structure
of a five-act play, similar to ▷ Shakespeare's
early comedies, and includes a complicated
Renaissance masque set in an ancient Irish
court. The language and style are reminiscent
of ▷ Spenser, showing quasi-medieval
influences, and indeed, Kynaston translated
▷ Chaucer's ▷ *Troilus and Criseyde* into
Latin. He also opened an academy for
the sons of the nobility called Museum
Minervae, where he hoped to teach them a
combination of languages, courtly skills and
the sciences.

L

Lacan, Jacques (1901–81)
French psychoanalyst whose re-readings
of ▷ Freud have become influential within
the area of literary criticism. Lacan's *The
Four Fundamental Concepts of Psychoanalysis*
(trans. 1977), and his *Ecrits: A Selection*
(1977) outline the nature of his revision of
Freudian psychoanalytic method. A further
selection of papers has appeared under the
title of *Feminine Sexuality* (trans. 1982). It is
to Lacan that we owe the terms 'imaginary'
and 'symbolic order'. Similarly, it is to
his investigation of the operations of the
unconscious according to the model of
language – 'the unconscious is structured
like a language' – that we owe the notion
of a 'split' human subject. For Lacan the
'imaginary' is associated with the pre-Oedipal
(▷ Oedipus complex) and pre-linguistic
relationship between mother and child (the
'mirror' stage) where there appears to be no
discrepancy between identity and its outward
reflection. This is succeeded by the entry
of the infant into the 'symbolic order', with
its rules and prohibitions centred around
the figure of the father (the phallus). The
'desire of the mother' is then repressed by the
child's entry into language and the 'symbolic
order'. The desire for 'imaginary' unity is also
repressed to form the unconscious, which the
interaction between analyst and patient aims
to unlock. Some of the fundamental divisions
that Lacan has located in the 'subject'
have proved highly adaptable for a range of
▷ materialist literary criticisms, including
(more controversially) ▷ feminism.

Lanyer, Aemilia (1569–1645)
Poet. Aemilia was the daughter of one
musician, Baptista Bassani, and wife to
another, Alfonso Lanyer, yet she seemed
to have provided for herself through the
system of ▷ patronage, being mistress to
Lord Hunsdon, ▷ Shakespeare's patron,
and later employed by Margaret Clifford,
Countess of Cumberland, the mother of
▷ Lady Anne Clifford. Many of the details
of her life come to us through the entries
in ▷ Simon Forman's casebook or diary, as
Lanyer consulted – and probably slept with
– this well-known Renaissance astrologer. In
1611 she published *Salve Deus Rex Judaeorum*
(*Hail God, King of the Jews*) in an attempt
to gain economic preferment. While the
poem is introduced with the usual variety
of panegyric verses (including one to the
Countess of Cumberland), it also contains
a proto-feminist prose address to women
readers, a defence of Eve and other female

characters in the biblical narrative, and the
earliest known English country-house poem,
about Cookham, the Cumberland residence.
As such, Lanyer may be read as innovative
both in form and content, and as participating
in the current debate about the vices and
virtues of women (▷ *Querelle des Femmes*). It is
also worth noting that, despite A. L. Rowse's
protestations, there is no evidence to support
the hypothesis that Lanyer was the dark lady
of Shakespeare's sonnets (▷ Shakespeare –
sonnets).
Bib: Travitsky, B. (ed.), *The Paradise of
Women*; Beilin, E. V., *Redeeming Eve*; Hannay,
M. P., *Silent But For The Word*.

Latimer, Hugh (?1490–1555)
One of the chief English ▷ Protestant
reformers. He was favoured by ▷ Henry VIII
and supported the king's separation of the
▷ Church of England from papal authority.
However, he went further than Henry in his
independence of thought, and in 1539 he
resigned the bishopric of Worcester because
he could not accept Henry's conservative
statement of doctrine, the Act of Six
Articles. Under the more Protestant regime
of ▷ Edward VI he became a very popular
preacher, but in 1555 he was burnt alive as a
heretic under the Catholic ▷ Mary I. Among
his memorable works is his letter to Henry VIII
(1530) urging the free circulation of the
▷ Bible in translation.
   ▷ Reformation.

Latin literature
Rome began as a small Italian city state,
and grew to an empire that surrounded the
Mediterranean and extended as far north
as the borderland between England and
Scotland. Politically, it established the
framework out of which modern Europe
grew. Culturally, in part by native force and
in part by its assimilation and transmission
of the older and richer culture of Greece,
its literature became the basis of European
values, and especially those values that arise
from the individual's relationship to his
society.
   Between 300 and 100 BC, Rome began to
produce literature, and at the same time, after
its conquest of the rich Greek colonies in
southern Italy, to expand its imaginative and
intellectual vision and to increase and refine
the expressiveness of the Latin language
through the study of ▷ Greek literature.
Primitive Roman literature had been of two
kinds, that of the recording and examination
of public life and conduct in annals of

eminent men and in oratory, and that of the distinctively Roman art of ▷ satirical comedy. These centuries saw the production of the comic dramas of ▷ Plautus and ▷ Terence. The orator and historian Cato the Censor upheld the virtues of Roman severity against Greek sophistication and luxury; the dominant figure, however, was the poet Ennius (239–169 BC), who preserved a balance between Greek and Latin values by emulating ▷ Homer in a patriotic ▷ epic in Latin idiom and Greek metre, the *Annales*.

The first half of the first century BC was the last great period of the Roman Republic. Active participation in politics was still one of the principal concerns of Roman aristocrats, and by this time Romans had studied and profited from lessons in depth and force of thinking from Greece. ▷ Cicero was the great persuasive orator of public debate; such was the power of his eloquence that the period is often known as the Ciceronian age. ▷ Julius Caesar's terse, practical account of his wars in Gaul and invasion of Britain shows a different kind of prose excellence, and the vividness of Sallust's histories of episodes in recent Roman history is different again. It was thus an age of prose, but it included one of the finest of all philosophical poems, the *De Rerum Natura* ('Concerning the Nature of Things') of ▷ Lucretius, who expounded the thought of the Greek philosopher Epicurus. It included also the passionate love poems of ▷ Catullus, who gave new vitality to Greek mythology.

Julius Caesar's great-nephew, ▷ Augustus Caesar, became the first Emperor in 27 BC, and he ruled until his death in AD 14. The Republic ended, and with it the kind of moral thought and eloquence which had made Cicero so famous. Roman literature, however, entered upon its most famous period – the Augustan Age. If the Empire had not quite reached its greatest extent, its power was nonetheless at its peak: the old traditions of austerity and energy were not yet extinct, and civilization, wealth and sophistication had not yet overbalanced into decadence resulting from excessive luxury. Augustus himself was a patron of letters. In prose, the outstanding writer was the historian Livy, but it was above all an age of poetry. The most famous of Roman poets, ▷ Virgil, celebrated great traditions, looked back to by a stable society, in which active political participation had become difficult or unimportant. His contemporary, ▷ Horace, celebrated the values of civilized private life. Tibullus, Propertius, and above all ▷ Ovid were poets of pleasure

appealing to the refined taste of an elegant society.

The last period of Roman literature lasted approximately a hundred years from the death of Augustus. The Emperors were bad, the idea of Rome was losing much of its force, society was showing symptoms of decadence. The best writers became more detached from and more critical of Roman society. In the philosophy and drama of ▷ Seneca, the heroic poetry of ▷ Lucan, the satire of Persius (34–62), the Greek philosophy of ▷ Stoicism seemed the strongest defence of human dignity against social oppression and distress. The most powerful work, however, was the savage satire of ▷ Juvenal and the sombre history of his time by Tacitus.

Literature in Latin did not of course end here, nor did it end with the Roman Empire in the 5th century AD. Latin became the language of the Roman Catholic Church, and therefore of the early medieval educated classes. It remained a living, growing language until its style was fixed by ▷ Renaissance scholars in the 16th century. Even in the 17th century, ▷ Francis Bacon wrote much of his philosophy in Latin, and ▷ Milton wrote Latin poetry. Classical Latin was read and admired in medieval England, but knowledge of it was incomplete and inaccurate; much of this knowledge was obtained (for instance by ▷ Chaucer) from contemporary French and Italian writers whose traditions were closer to classical Latin. Virgil retained great prestige, and Terence was studied in the monasteries for the purity of his style. After 1500, the Renaissance caused English writers to study and emulate the classical writers. Writers modelled themselves on styles of classical prose; the terse manner of Seneca and Tacitus was imitated by Bacon. More important than the study of styles was the way in which English writers again and again measured themselves against their own society by placing themselves in the position of Roman writers, and then assessed their society from a Roman standpoint. So, in the late 16th century ▷ Donne modelled his ▷ elegies on those of Ovid, and a little later ▷ Ben Jonson rewrote the lyrics of Catullus; in the 17th century Milton emulated Virgil as Virgil had once emulated Homer.

Laud, William (1573–1645)
Archbishop of Canterbury under ▷ Charles I. He firmly resisted the desire for further reform among the religious extremists, and even tried to impose religious uniformity upon Scotland. His rigour was partly responsible for

the discontent that led to the outbreak of the
▷ Civil War in 1642. Parliament, which had
already secured his imprisonment in 1641,
ordered his execution in 1645.
Bib: Carlton, C., *Archbishop William Laud*.

Lawes, Henry (1596–1662)
Composer. One of the most well-known
English Renaissance composers after
▷ Dowland, Lawes is primarily of concern
to literature students because of his close
collaboration with several distinguished poets
of his time. After being made a court musician
to ▷ Charles I in 1631, he collaborated with
▷ Carew, ▷ Herrick, ▷ Lovelace, ▷ Suckling
and ▷ Waller. But Lawes' most famous work
was with ▷ Milton, for whom he composed
musical accompaniments to ▷ *Arcades* and
▷ *Comus*, and he produced and acted in the
latter performance. The success of Lawes's
collaboration with the poets of his day
resided partly in his belief that there was an
indissoluble link between musical rhythms and
the metrical patterns of spoken language.
Bib: Evans, W. M., *Henry Lawes: Musician and
Friend of Poets*.

Leavis, Frank Raymond (1895–1978)
Critic. From 1932 till 1953 he edited
Scrutiny, a literary review with high critical
standards and pervaded by his personality.
It maintained that the values of a society
in all its activities derive from its culture,
and that central to British culture is English
literature; that a literature can be sustained
only by discriminating readers, and therefore
by a body of highly trained critics working
together, especially in the collaborative
circumstances of a university (*Education
and the University*, 1943). The need for
the testing of judgements by collaborative
discussion is important in Leavis's view of
criticism. Unfortunately, collaboration may
become uncritical discipleship, and this was
one of the two unfortunate consequences of
the exceptional force of Leavis's personality.
The other unfortunate consequence was
the hostility that this force of personality
aroused in many critics who were not
among his collaborators and followers. He
maintained that true critical discernment
can be achieved only by a total response
of the mind – intellectual, imaginative and
moral. Thus a critical judgement reflects
not only the work of literature being judged,
but the worth of the personality making
the judgement, so that Leavis's censure
of critics with whom he strongly disagreed
was sometimes extraordinarily vehement,

as in his *Two Cultures?: The Significance of
C. P. Snow* (1962). However this vehemence
was a price he paid for his determination
to sustain a living tradition of literature not
only by assessing contemporary writers with
the utmost rigour, but also by reassessing
the writers of the past, distinguishing those
he thought had a vital relevance for the
modern sensibility from those that stand as
mere monuments in academic museums.
Such evaluative treatments caused him to be
widely regarded as a destructive critic; his
attack on the three-centuries-long prestige
of ▷ Milton (*Revaluation* 1936 and *The
Common Pursuit* 1952) gave particular offence.
Although still influential, Leavis must now be
considered together with more contemporary
literary theories, such as ▷ post-structuralism
and ▷ materialism, which have tended to
challenge radically and contradict vehemently
his criticism.

**Leicester, Robert Dudley, Earl of
(?1531–88)**
One of the principal favourites of ▷ Elizabeth I
and for some time expected to become her
husband. The *Kenilworth Festivities* were
organized by Leicester in an attempt to
woo the queen. This is also one example
of his role as a major patron of the arts and
literature in the Elizabethan period. He was
also the uncle of ▷ Sir Philip Sidney, killed at
Zutphen during Leicester's campaign to assist
the Netherlands in their resistance to Spain.
Like his nephew Essex, he showed staunch
▷ Protestant leanings through his support of
the ▷ Puritans in the Privy Council during
the 1570s. Leicester had the brilliance which
Elizabeth liked in her personal favourites,
although for her statesmen she preferred
more sober types such as Cecil (▷ Burghley)
and ▷ Walsingham. Scandalous stories were
rumoured about his relationships with women,
and in particular about his early marriage with
Amy Robsart.
▷ Essex, Robert Devereux, Earl of;
Gascoigne, George.
Bib: Rosenberg, E., *Leicester, Patron of Letters*.

Leigh, Dorothy (no date)
Writer on motherhood. Leigh was a widow
who chose to write a book of instruction for
her three young sons and their future wives
that was published as *The Mother's Blessing*
(1616). The book consists of four parts: a
dedication to ▷ Elizabeth of Bohemia asking,
from the precarious position of a woman
writer, for the queen's protection; a letter
to her sons explaining her intentions; an

allegorical poem about bees; and the main body of the advice, which covers personal behaviour and spiritual practice.

▷ Elizabeth Grymeston, Lady Elizabeth Clinton.
Bib: Travitsky, B. (ed.), *A Paradise of Women.*

Letter-writing

This is clearly an important branch of literature even when the interest of the letters is essentially historical or ▷ biographical. Letters may also be, by intention or by consequence of genius, works of intrinsic literary value. Because of the restrictions imposed upon Renaissance women writers, their canon often exists in the form of letters rather than published works. See, for example, ▷ Ann Bacon's letters to her son ▷ Francis Bacon, ▷ Lady Margaret Cunningham, ▷ Lady Jane Grey and the correspondence between ▷ Joan and Maria Thynne.

Levellers, The

An important political party during the period of the ▷ Civil War and the Commonwealth. It first became prominent in 1647; the term was first found in a letter of November of that year, describing them as people who wanted to 'rayse a parity and community in the kingdom'. Mainly found among soldiers and opposed to kingship, the Levellers feared that the Parliamentary leaders were insufficiently firm. Two documents were composed by them, *The Case of the Army Truly Stated* and *The Agreement of the People*, asking for a dissolution of Parliament and change in its future constitution. They were at odds with ▷ Oliver Cromwell, who suppressed the mutinies they engineered. Parliament declared other Leveller writings by John Liburne treasonable and in March 1649 their leaders were arrested. A public meeting in London in their support and risings at Burford and Banbury were suppressed. Associated with them were the 'True Levellers' or 'Diggers' of April 1649, who took possession of some unoccupied ground at Oatlands in Surrey and began to cultivate it. The leaders, arrested and brought before Fairfax, denounced landowners.

▷ Utopianism.

Leviathan (1651)

▷ Hobbes, Thomas.

Lewis, C. S. (Clive Staples) (1898–1963)

Novelist, critic, poet and writer on religion. Born in Belfast, Lewis served in France during the World War I. From 1925 until 1954 he was a Fellow of Magdalen College, Oxford and tutor in English, and from 1954 was Professor of Medieval and Renaissance Literature at Cambridge. His fiction reflects an interest in fantasy, myth and fairy tale with an underlying Christian message. He wrote a science-fiction trilogy: *Out of the Silent Planet* (1938); *Perelandra* (1943) (as *Voyage to Venus*, 1953); *That Hideous Strength* (1945). *The Lion, The Witch, and The Wardrobe* (1950) was the first of seven fantasy stories for children. His popular theological works include: *The Problem of Pain* (1940); *Miracles* (1947) and *The Screwtape Letters* (1942), which takes the form of letters from an experienced devil to a novice devil. *A Grief Observed* (1961) is a powerful autobiographical work, an account of his grief at the death of his wife. He also wrote such classics of literary history as *The Allegory of Love* (1936) and *A Preface to Paradise Lost* (1942)

▷ *Paradise Lost.*

Lily, William (?1468–1522)

Scholar; a pioneer of Greek studies, and part-author with Colet of a famous textbook on Latin that was still in use in the 19th century.

Linacre, Thomas (?1460–1524)

Physician, and a pioneer in Greek and Latin scholarship. He was chiefly responsible for founding the College of Physicians in 1518, and translated into excellent Latin some of the works of the Greek physician Galen. He is, however, less famous for his literary work than for the nobility of his character and for his zeal in promoting the study of medicine at Oxford and Cambridge.

Lindsay (Lyndsay), Sir David (c 1490–1555)

Scottish poet, courtier to James IV and 'Usher' of the infant James V. He was entrusted with various overseas diplomatic missions and knighted in 1542. He is most famous for his satirical work, especially his verse ▷ morality play, the *Satyre of the Thrie Estates* (1540), which analyses the corruption of Church and State. His other works include 'The Dream' (1528), an allegorical lament on the mismanagement of the realm; *The Complaynt and Testament of the Papyngo* (Parrot) (1530), in which a parrot is used as the mouthpiece for advice to the king and warnings to courtiers; and his two-part narrative about a Scottish laird, the *Historie of ane Nobil and Vailzeand Squyer, William Meldrum* (1550).
Bib: Hamer, D. (ed.), *Poetical Works*; Kinsley, J. (ed.), *A Satire of the Three Estates.*

Little Gidding

A small religious community founded
by the Anglican theologian Nicholas
Ferrar (1592–1637) at a manor house in
Huntingdonshire in 1625. It was dispersed,
and the buildings destroyed, by Parliamentary
soldiers at the end of the ▷ Civil War (1646).
▷ Charles I visited the community in 1633
and according to tradition he came again after
his final defeat at the battle of Naseby (1645).

Lodge, Thomas (1558–1625)

Poet and man of letters. He was one of
the group now known as the ▷ University
Wits – university scholars who used their
learning to make a career as professional
writers for the expanding reading public
of the late 16th century. In many ways his
career is representative of this new kind of
▷ Elizabethan professional writer.

He was the son of Sir Thomas Lodge, a
Lord Mayor of London, and was educated
at Merchant Taylors School and Trinity
College, Oxford. He then became a student
of law at Lincoln's Inn, London, in 1578.
The law students of the ▷ Inns of Court in
the reign of Elizabeth were a leading element
of the literary public, and others besides
Lodge found these law colleges a nursery
for literary rather than legal talent. During
the next 20 years he practised all the kinds
of writing popular at the time. His first work
(1580) was a ▷ pamphlet entitled *A Defence
of Plays*, written in answer to ▷ Stephen
Gosson's attack on theatrical literature, *Schoole
of Abuse* (1580). Besides other pamphlets,
he wrote prose romances interspersed with
lyrics (*eg Rosalynde, Euphues Golden Legacy*,
1590, and *A Marguerite of America*, 1596),
verse romances (*eg Scilla's Metamorphosis*,
1589, reissued as *Glaucus and Scilla*, 1610),
a ▷ sonnet sequence (*Phillis*, 1593), and a
collection of epistles and ▷ satires in imitation
of the Roman poet ▷ Horace, *A Fig for
Momus* (1595). He also wrote plays, or at least
collaborated with playwrights, *eg* a chronicle
play *The Wounds of Civil War* (printed 1594),
and, probably with ▷ Robert Greene, *A
Looking Glass for London and England* (1594).
Besides this writing activity, he joined two
piratical expeditions against Spain, the first
to the Canary Isles in 1588, and the second
to Brazil in 1591. It was on the first that he
wrote his most famous work, the romance
Rosalynde, later used by Shakespeare as the
story for ▷ *As You Like It*, and on the second
that he wrote *A Marguerite of America*. After
1596, when he published the penitential
and satirical pamphlets (*Wit's Misery* and

World's Madness), he became converted to
Roman Catholicism and took to the study of
medicine, receiving the degree of M. D. from
Oxford University in 1603. His literary works
during the remainder of his life were serious
and chiefly translations (*eg* of Josephus (1602)
and ▷ Seneca (1614)), and religious and
medical treatises.
Bib: Sisson, C. J., *Lodge and Other Elizabethans*.

Long Parliament, The

A parliament which was summoned by
▷ Charles I in 1640 and which continued
until 1653, when it was dissolved by ▷ Oliver
Cromwell. It was this parliament that broke
with the king and started the ▷ Civil War
in 1642. In 1648 those of its members who
were disposed to come to terms with the
king were expelled by Colonel Pride ('Pride's
Purge') and the remainder continued to sit
under the nickname of 'the Rump'. After
dissolving it, Cromwell called parliaments
of his own but after his death in 1658 it
reassembled and in 1660, the year of the
Restoration of the monarchy, it dissolved
itself to make way for a new parliament
under the restored king, ▷ Charles II. His
government did not recognize the legality of
Cromwell's parliaments, so that in law the
Long Parliament was considered to have sat
continuously from 1640 to 1660.

Lord Chamberlain's Men, The
▷ Chamberlain's Men, The Lord.

Lovelace, Richard (1618–58)

Poet. One of the so-called ▷ 'Cavalier poets',
Lovelace fought on behalf of the king during
the ▷ Civil War. The majority of his poetry
was written before 1649, when his collection
of poems entitled *Lucasta* appeared. *Lucasta*
is prefaced with a commendatory poem by
▷ Andrew Marvell, and his work might be
thought of as anticipating themes expressed
in Marvell's poetry, in particular the search
for a form of disengagement from the world.
It is not, however, with the more republican
Marvell that Lovelace is associated, but
with aristocratic codes of love and honour
embraced by the literary and military circles
in which Lovelace moved. Of special note are
the series of 'bestiary poems' (*eg* 'The Snail'
or 'The Grasshopper'), which often seem to
offer themselves as a form of disguised, or
encoded, commentary on the political crisis of
the pre-Civil War period.
Bib: Wilkinson, C. H. (ed.), *The Poems
of Richard Lovelace*; Weidhorn, M., *Richard
Lovelace*.

Love's Labour's Lost (1594–5)
A comedy by ▷ Shakespeare, published in a
▷ quarto edition in 1598. It is a play for court
taste, recalling the comedies of ▷ John Lyly;
the plot is light and fantastic, and a pretext for
dextrously witty dialogue and poetic flights of
fancy. But the graceful artificiality is enriched
by a freshness that arises from elements of
rural life, both in imagery employed by the
courtiers and in some of the characters. As
in later comedies written by Shakespeare
in the decade 1590–1600 (▷ *A Midsummer
Night's Dream*, ▷ *As You Like It*, ▷ *Twelfth
Night*), the witty courtiers end by making
fools of themselves in their own way, much as
the clowns and simple-minded pedants do –
predictably – in theirs.

The King of Navarre and three of his lords
vow to shut themselves away from pleasure
and ladies in order to devote themselves to
study. They quickly find excuses to break
the vow when the king is visited by the
Princess of France and three of her ladies
on an embassy. A subplot concerns a group
of ludicrous characters – the proud but
seedy Spaniard, Don Armado; the pedantic
schoolmaster Holofernes; Sir Nathaniel, the
country clergyman, and Costard the rustic –
who attempts to entertain the lords and ladies
with a performance of the ▷ interlude of
the ▷ 'Nine Worthies'. The courting of the
princess and her ladies by the king and his
lords is abruptly ended by the announcement
of the death of the princess's father. The play
ends with the ladies imposing a year's ordeal
on their suitors.

Some scholars have seen in the play
a light satire on the ▷ School of Night.
Some of the characters are identified with
living contemporaries, for instance Armado
with ▷ Sir Walter Ralegh, who is said to
have been one of the key members of the
School.

Lucan (Marcus Annaeus Lucanus)
(AD 39–65)
A Roman poet: author of the poem *Pharsalia*
about the struggle for power between ▷ Julius
Caesar and Pompey. ▷ Christopher Marlowe
translated the first book (1600). In ancient
times Lucan was noted for his florid style, and
for his gift for ▷ epigram.

Lucian (2nd century AD)
Greek ▷ satirist. He is especially known
for his satirical dialogues and for his
True History, an account of imaginary
voyages.
    ▷ *Timon of Athens*.

**Lucretius (Titus Lucretius Carus) (1st
century BC)**
Roman poet; author of the great didactic
poem *De Rerum Natura* ('Concerning the
Nature of Things'). It outlines the philosophy
of the Greek thinker Epicurus, which is based
on the atomic theory of Democritus. The poet
seeks to expound that all reality is material.
The gods exist but they also are material,
though immortal, and they are not concerned
with the affairs of men; the soul exists but
it, too, is material and mortal like the body,
dissolving into its original atoms after death.
Lucretius is not, however, a cynical poet; he
testifies to the beauty of the natural world and
the poem opens with an eloquent invocation
to Venus, the conception of whom is followed
by ▷ Edmund Spenser in ▷ *Faerie Queene* Bk.
IV, x, stanza 44 onwards. Lucretius' love of
the natural world and his reverence for reason
caused him to be greatly admired during
the ▷ Renaissance and the succeeding two
centuries.

Lumley, Lady Joanna (1537–76)
Translator and dramatist. Lumley is
interesting in that she is one of only three
Renaissance Englishwomen to translate or
compose complete dramas, the other two
being ▷ Elizabeth Cary and ▷ Mary Sidney.
Like her cousin ▷ Lady Jane Grey she was
well educated, and had access to one of the
finest libraries in England, owned by her
father, Henry Fitzalan, Earl of Arundel. Her
prose ▷ translation of ▷ Euripides' tragedy
Iphigenia at Aulis was transcribed into a
notebook, together with several Latin pieces
(a modern edition was published in 1909,
ed. Harold H. Child). The work is notable
in several ways: it is the first known attempt
to translate a Greek drama into English;
it adopts a strongly pro-women stance and
reveals the possible abuses of women within
a patriarchal society; and, finally, it is all the
more remarkable an achievement since she
could only have been 15 or 16 when she
undertook the translation.
Bib: Travitsky, B. (ed.), *The Paradise of
Women*.

Luther, Martin (1483–1546)
German religious reformer, and the chief
figure in the European movement known as
the ▷ Reformation. The beginning of this is
often dated from 1517, when Luther fixed
on the church door at Wittenberg his 95
'Theses' against the sale of 'indulgences'; a
consequence of this was his condemnation by
the Pope at the Diet of Worms (1521).

Luther's influence on the English Reformation is a matter of dispute. Before he separated the English church from the authority of the Pope, ▷ Henry VIII wrote a treatise against Luther, for which the Pope awarded him the title Defender of the Faith (*Fidei Defensor*), still used by English monarchs. Lutheran influences were felt by humanists such as John Colet and ▷ Sir Thomas More, and inspired ▷ William Tyndale's translation of the ▷ Bible, the first of several in the 16th century. They certainly operated on the doctrines represented by the second Prayer Book, introduced by ▷ Archbishop Cranmer under ▷ Edward VI. However, reformist influences had been current in England since ▷ John Wycliffe in the 14th century.
Bib: Brecht, M., *Martin Luther*.

Lycidas (1637)

A ▷ pastoral ▷ elegy by ▷ John Milton, written in 1637. It is in the form of a monody, *ie* modelled on the ▷ odes sung by a single actor in ancient Greek ▷ tragedy. Line lengths vary between three and five feet, and the rhymes follow no regular pattern, but the mournful, majestic sonority is consistently sustained. Milton is lamenting the death of his college friend Edward King, a gifted young man who was drowned at sea, but it is not a poem of personal loss. The theme is the tragic loss of promise: King is seen as a young man of talent and serious endeavour in an age whose spiritual laxity requires the reforming zeal of such a spirit. Greek pastoral imagery is used – gods, muses, nymphs, including Camus, invented for the occasion as the god of the river that flows through Cambridge where Milton and King had studied. More important, however, is the pastoralism of the ▷ Bible: King was a good shepherd; the clergy are spiritual shepherds by their function, but mostly bad ones.

Lydgate, John (c 1370–1449/50)

A prolific 15th-century writer who seems to have enjoyed a higher contemporary literary reputation than he does now. He was born in Lydgate, Suffolk, and entered the famous and well-endowed monastery of Bury St Edmunds c 1385. He successfully aspired to noble and royal patronage, and his vast literary output provides a cultural 'barometer' of his time. He translated a number of key texts on classical, historical and moralizing subjects, including his monumental *Troy Book* (composed over eight years, 1412–20), which is a translation of Guido de Columnis's Troy

story; the *Siege of Thebes* (1420–2), which he presents as a contribution to the ▷ *Canterbury Tales*; the *Pilgrimage of the Life of Man* (1426–30); and the *Fall of Princes* (1431–8), which is a translation of a French version of ▷ Boccaccio's compilation of tragedies (*De Casibus Virorum Illustrium*). He also composed dream-vision poems (including the *Temple of Glass*, modelled on ▷ Chaucer's *House of Fame*), large numbers of lyric poems and a selection of dramatic pieces (including ▷ Mummings), designed for performance on various ceremonial occasions or to mark court festivities. His development of a Latinate, aureate poetic register influenced the style of court poetry in the 15th century.

Lydgate styled himself as a follower of Chaucer, and his reputation as a leading man of letters was evidently established during and after his lifetime: from the later 15th century onwards, his name is coupled with that of Chaucer's as a founding figure of the English literary tradition. Although his enormous output finds less favour with modern readers, he is undoubtedly a writer of monumental dimensions, who assimilated some of the important, authoritative narratives of medieval European court culture and made them available to a prestigious English audience. The scale of his work is daunting but that is also his strength.
Bib: Norton-Smith, J. (ed.), *Poems*; Pearsall, D., *John Lydgate*.

Lyly, John (1554–1606)

Poet, writer of romances, dramatist. He was a popular writer for the cultivated society of court and university circles.

His prose romances, ▷ *Euphues, or the Anatomy of Wit* (1578) and *Euphues and his England* (1580), contain little story and are mainly pretexts for sophisticated discussion of contemporary manners and modes in a style whose graceful ornateness is really an end in itself. Its artificiality, now regarded as its fault, was at the time regarded as a virtue of high cultivation. It was much imitated in the last 20 years of the 16th century, and it was also parodied, *eg* by ▷ Shakespeare in his early comedies and, through ▷ Falstaff, here and there in ▷ *Henry IV, Part I*.

Lyly's comedies are in the same elaborately sophisticated style, and are in fact the first *socially* sophisticated comedies in English. The plays were performed by boy-actors in private theatres; they were not intended for the socially mixed audiences of public theatres such as the ▷ Globe. *The Woman in the Moon* (before 1584) was the only one of these in verse. He followed it with prose plays interspersed with graceful lyrics: *Sapho and Phao* (1584); *Alexander and Campaspe* (1584); ▷ *Gallathea* (1585); *Endimion* (1588); *Midas* (1589); *Mother Bombie* (1594); and *Love's Metamorphosis* (published 1601). The best known of these are *Alexander and Campaspe*, *Endimion* and *Mother Bombie*. They have grace and wit, and were closer to popular taste than was Restoration comedy a century later. Lyly's writing was an adjunct to his search for preferment from his early patron, the Earl of Oxford, and from the queen; he was given hope of becoming Master of the ▷ Revels, but died a disappointed man.

▷ Theatres.

Bib: Hunter, G. K., *John Lyly*.

Lyric

In ancient Greece the name given to verse sung to a lyre (from the Greek '*lurikos*' = 'for the lyre'), whether as a solo performance or by a choir. In English usage, the term has had different associations in different historical literary periods. Elizabethan critics first used the term in England: ▷ George Puttenham, for example, describes a lyric poet as someone who composes 'songs or ballads of pleasure to be sung with the voice, and to the harpe'. From the illustrative quotations in the O. E. D. (s.v. lyric), it is clear that in later usage musical accompaniment was no longer considered essential to the definition of the form.

Bib: Lindley, D., *Lyric*.

M

Macbeth (1605–6)

A ▷ tragedy by ▷ Shakespeare; it probably dates from 1605–6, and was first printed in the First ▷ Folio edition of Shakespeare's collected works, 1623.

The material for the tragedy comes from ▷ Raphael Holinshed's *Chronicle of Scottish History* (1578). Macbeth was an historical king of Scotland who reigned approximately 1040–58. He seems to have been a capable and beneficent sovereign in spite of his usurpation of the throne and sundry acts of cruelty, and Holinshed so records him. Shakespeare blackens his character, elevates his predecessor Duncan into a kind of saint, and makes a virtuous figure out of Macbeth's associate Banquo. Banquo was the legendary ancestor of James VI of Scotland, who ascended the English throne as ▷ James I in 1603. The relative idealization of Banquo, the prominence of witchcraft – a subject that was one of King James's hobbies – and other indications show that the play was written to appeal to the king's interest. They are all put to artistic purpose by Shakespeare, however, and enhance rather than deflect from his imaginative intention.

The tragedy is the conversion of a good man into a wholly evil one. Macbeth begins as the heroic warrior who defends Scotland against a triple enemy: the king of Norway has invaded Scotland in alliance with the open rebel Macdonwald and the secret rebel Cawdor. After his victory, Macbeth is confronted by a triple enemy assailing his own soul: the witches; his own evil desires; and his wife, who reinforces these desires. He first encounters the witches, who predict that he is to be king of Scotland, after being made Thane (Lord) of Cawdor. As Macbeth knows nothing of Cawdor's part in the rebellion and invasion, both prophecies are to him equally incredible. The second is, however, immediately confirmed by emissaries from Duncan, king of Scotland. Macbeth is now lord of Cawdor and finds himself haunted by thoughts of bloodthirsty ambition: he becomes his soul's own secret enemy. The witches and his own desire would not in the end have been sufficient to cause him to murder the king, but Lady Macbeth dedicates herself to reinforcing his ambition. Macbeth is thus brought to murder Duncan, though in a state of horror at the deed, and becomes king on the flight of Duncan's son Malcolm. After the murder, however, he becomes a hardened man, though a restless and desperate one; he proceeds to the murder of Banquo, whose children the witches have predicted will succeed him on the throne, and then degenerates into massacre and tyranny. The play exemplifies one of the beliefs of Shakespeare's time, that the soul of man is the pattern of the state, and that where evil breaks into the soul of a king it will extend over the state he rules.

Macbeth was written in Shakespeare's maturest period; together with *Othello*, ▷ *King Lear*, and ▷ *Antony and Cleopatra*, it is accounted one of his finest tragedies.

Machiavelli, Nicolo di Bernardo dei (1469–1527)

Italian political theorist and historian. Machiavelli can be thought of as having two discrete existences. One is that of the Florentine diplomat, author of the comedy *La Mandragola* (1518) and of a series of important treatises on politics and statecraft: *The Prince* (1513), *Art of War* (1520) and *The Discourses* (1531). The other existence, however, is that which haunted the imagination of English writers in the 16th century and later, when Machiavelli's reputation as a cynical, cunning and diabolic figure emerges. In fact, Machiavelli's own works were very little known in England (other than by unreliable report) until a translation of *The Prince* appeared in 1640, though translations of his *Art of War* and portions of his historical works had been translated and published in 1560 and 1593 respectively. Nevertheless, it is this image of Machiavelli which became influential in England, as is evidenced by ▷ Christopher Marlowe's creation of the stage-figure Machevill in his play ▷ *The Jew of Malta*. We can perhaps best understand this image of the Italian thinker in England as the embodiment, or focus, of a network of anxieties experienced within the emergent ▷ Protestant state, and directed outwards on the threatening presence of continental (and Catholic) Europe.
Bib: Gilmore, M. P. (ed.), *Studies on Machiavelli*.

McKerrow, R. B. (Ronald Brownlees) (1872–1940)

Editor and bibliographer who was co-founder of the Malone Society (1906), dedicated to the study and editing of early and often neglected English drama. He wrote the seminal *An Introduction to Bibliography for Literary Students* (1927). He was one of the driving forces behind the 'New Bibliography' and is the author of the important *Prolegomena* (1939) for an Oxford edition of ▷ Shakespeare's works. This latter, which aimed at discovering an editorial methodology from ten selected texts, has proved an important milestone on the road to the new and revisionary Oxford University Press Shakespeare edited by Gary Taylor and Stanley Wells.

▷ Shakespeare – history of textual study.

Madrigal

A poem composed to be sung, with or without instrumental accompaniment. It derived from the Italian '*canzone*', and flourished in England especially between 1580 and 1630; one of its main practitioners is said to be ▷ William Byrd, although he himself did not consider his songs to be madrigals. It was sung chorally, and had three forms:

1 The Ayre. This had a melody composed for the top voice, which was accompanied by the other voices to the same melody.

2 The Ballet. This resembled the ayre, but was distinguished by its dance-like melody and refrain.

3 The Madrigal proper. This had different 'parts', *ie* melodies, for the individual voices, and was so composed that the melodies interwove. The parts were sometimes composed with the effect of dramatic contrast, *eg* by Thomas Weelkes (?1575–1623). Great attention was paid by composers to bringing out the meaning of the words, so that poets and musicians worked in close collaboration. Only ▷ Thomas Campion is known to have composed music for his own words, but others are believed to have done so. Ayres and madrigals are common in the plays of the period, and most of the poets wrote them.

Makin, Bathsua (1612–c 1680)

Educationalist and poet. Her poetry, *Musa Virginea* (1616), is a multilingual collection dedicated to various members of the royal family, but it is for her role as a teacher of women that Makin is best known. In the early 1640s she was appointed tutor to Princess Elizabeth, the sister of ▷ Charles II, and following the Restoration of the monarchy she opened a school at Tottenham High Cross and advertised it with the publication of *An Essay to Revive the Antient Education of Gentlewomen* (1673). Dedicated to the princesses Anne and Mary (somewhat inappropriately, since their father opposed the education of women), this treatise sets out the benefits of a scholarly education for women and cites numerous examples, including ▷ Elizabeth I, ▷ Ann Bradstreet and ▷ Katherine Philips, to prove her argument. Oddly, Makin takes on a male persona in the book and is very careful to

assert that schooling for girls will not make them equal with boys, but better wives. Rather than dismiss Makin as simply accepting the renewed repression of women in Restoration monarchist circles, it is important to realize that she was attempting to win custom for her school and was, within certain confines, offering women the education necessary for independent and fulfilled lives.

Bib: Hobby, E., *Virtue of Necessity*; Fraser, A., *The Weaker Vessel*.

Malapropism

A comic misuse of language, usually by a person who is both pretentious and ignorant. The term derives from the character Mrs Malaprop in Richard Brinsley Sheridan's (1751–1816) play *The Rivals* (1775). This comic device had in fact been used by earlier writers, such as ▷ Shakespeare in the portrayal of ▷ Dogberry in ▷ *Much Ado About Nothing*.

Malcontent, The (1604)

A ▷ tragicomedy by ▷ John Marston, with additions by ▷ John Webster. An intrigue engineered by the villainous Lord Mendoza has caused the deposition of Giovanni Altofronto, the noble Duke of Genoa, and substituted the weak Pietro Jacomo, who is married to Aurelia, daughter of the Duke of Florence. Altofronto, however, has returned to his own court in disguise as Malevole (the 'malcontent'). He is tolerated as a witty though sour court jester and commentator on the times and its corrupt manners. Meanwhile he awaits his chance for revenge and the recovery of his dukedom. Mendoza continues to conspire against the new duke, whose wife is Mendoza's mistress, and Malevole in turn conspires against Mendoza. In the end, Mendoza is exposed, and Pietro and Aurelia penitently resign the duchy back to the rightful duke.

The play is part ▷ satire and part ▷ revenge play, midway between ▷ Ben Jonson's comedies of ▷ humours (*eg* ▷ *Volpone*) and ▷ Tourneur's ▷ *Revenger's Tragedy*. The malcontent role of bitter commentator on society is a common one in ▷ Jacobean drama; ▷ Bosola in ▷ Webster's ▷ *Duchess of Malfi* is a well-known example, but ▷ Hamlet, Iago (in ▷ *Othello*) and Thersites in ▷ *Troilus and Cressida* all have some aspects of the malcontent in their parts. The essence of the role is that the malcontent is somehow frustrated from satisfying his ambitions or being accepted by the rest of society; such exclusion gives him the motives (morally acceptable or otherwise) and the detachment for his satire.

Malone, Edmund (1741–1812)
The most well-known early editor of ▷ Shakespeare's works, many of whose textual emendations and editorial principles are still widely used. His greatest work remains his posthumously published edition of the complete Shakespeare (1821) and his research on the order in which Shakespeare's plays were written. He was also the first to denounce the Shakespearean forgeries of William Henry Ireland (1775–1835), one of whose fake plays, *Vortigern and Rowena*, was performed as Shakespeare's at Drury Lane.

Malory, Thomas
Identifying which Thomas Malory produced the work known as the ▷ *Morte d' Arthur* in around 1469/70 remains a controversial issue. Sir Thomas Malory of Newbold Revel (c 1446–71) is the most generally accepted candidate for the role. He was in the service of the Earl of Warwick in the French wars (c 1414), and by 1440 was established as a country gentleman, being knighted in 1442. After 1450 his public standing seems to have radically declined. His extensive spells in prison (on a range of charges including rape) after 1450 may have provided the opportunity for his literary labour. Although it is possible to recreate the public life of this Sir Thomas Malory, there is no documentation that sheds any light on his literary career.
▷ Caxton, William.
Bib: Lacy, N. et al. (eds.), *The Arthurian Encyclopaedia*; Takimiya, T. and Brewer, D. (eds.), *Aspects of Malory*.

Mariana
A character in ▷ Shakespeare's ▷ *Measure for Measure*; she was betrothed to Angelo, the deputy of the Duke of Vienna, and after being cast off by him she lives forsaken in 'the moated grange' until the Duke compels Angelo to marry her. She is the subject of one of the most famous poems by Alfred Tennyson (1809–92) – *Mariana*.

Marina
A character in ▷ *Pericles, Prince of Tyre*, a play written wholly or in part by ▷ Shakespeare. She is the daughter of King Pericles, who loses her at sea and later recovers her (V. i) in a scene described by T. S. Eliot (1888–1965) as one of the most beautiful by Shakespeare. She is the subject of one of Eliot's Ariel Poems, *Marina*.

Marlowe, Christopher (1564–93)
Dramatist and poet. Son of a Canterbury shoemaker; educated at King's School, Canterbury, and Corpus Christi College, Cambridge. He most likely began writing plays on leaving Cambridge. Most of them eventually entered the repertoire of the Lord ▷ Admiral's Men, with ▷ Edward Alleyn taking leading roles such as Tamburlaine and Faustus. Marlowe probably became a government agent, and his mysterious death in a fight in a tavern at Deptford – nominally about who should pay the bill – may have had a political cause. When he died, he was under shadow of charges of atheism on the evidence of his fellow dramatist, ▷ Thomas Kyd.

His four major plays were written between 1585 and 1593; ▷ *Tamburlaine the Great, Parts I and II*; ▷ *The Jew of Malta*; *The Tragical History of* ▷ *Doctor Faustus*; *Edward II*. *Dido, Queen of Carthage* (with ▷ Nashe 1594) and *The Massacre at Paris* (1593) are attributed to him. His non-dramatic poetry is famous for the narrative ▷ *Hero and Leander*, based on the Greek of Musaeus (5th century AD) and completed by ▷ Chapman, and the lyric *The Passionate Shepherd*. Little else has survived, apart from his translation of ▷ Ovid's *Amores* (printed 1596) and of *The First Book of Lucan* (printed 1600). It has been suggested, without evidence, that he had a share in the writing of a number of other plays, including ▷ Shakespeare's ▷ *Henry VI*, ▷ *Titus Andronicus*, and ▷ *Richard III*.

Marlowe was much the most innovative dramatic writer in the 16th century after Shakespeare, and much the most important influence upon Shakespeare. His importance is due to the energy with which he endowed the ▷ blank-verse line, which in his hands developed an unprecedented suppleness and power. His plays have great intensity, but they show a genius that is ▷ epic rather than dramatic – at least in *Tamburlaine* and *Doctor Faustus*, his acknowledged masterpieces; his best-constructed piece of theatre, *Edward II*, is also the least typical of his poetic genius. On the other hand the final scene of *Doctor Faustus* is one of the most intensely dramatic in English literature. In the musical handling and control of the ten-syllable line, he learned from ▷ Spenser and contributed to ▷ Milton as well as to Shakespeare.
▷ Faust.
Bib: Boas, F. S., *Christopher Marlowe*; Levin, H., *The Overreacher*; Steane, J. B., *Marlowe: a critical study*; Leech, C. (ed.), *Essays on Marlowe*; Eliot, T. S., in *Selected Essays*; Kelsall, M., *Christopher Marlowe*;

Masington C. G., *Christopher Marlowe's Tragic Vision*; Robinson, J. H., *Marlowe, Tamburlaine and Magic*; Shepherd, S., *Marlowe and the Politics of Elizabethan Theatre*.

Marprelate, Martin
The pen-name for an anonymous author or authors of a series of ▷ pamphlets that appeared 1588–90. They were written from a ▷ Presbyterian standpoint denying the validity of bishops, and they attacked the religious establishment, by which the Church was governed by crown-appointed bishops. The bishops were satirized so vigorously in such expressive, popular prose that the authorities were alarmed into commissioning such gifted writers as ▷ Thomas Nashe, ▷ John Lyly and ▷ Robert Greene to reply to them. The leaders of the movement were arrested in 1593, and the government of ▷ Elizabeth I imposed severe restrictions on sermons and on the press. (Marprelate: mar = damage, ruin; prelate = bishop.)

Marriage
According to Laurence Stone, in England marriage only gradually acquired its function of regulating sexual chastity in wedlock: up to the 11th century polygamy and concubinage were widespread and divorce was casual. In 1439 weddings in church were declared a sacrament and after 1563 in the Roman ▷ Catholic Church the presence of a priest was required to make the contract valid. In this way, what had been a private contract between two families concerning property exchange – in 1948 Claude Lévi-Strauss was the first to point out women's universal role in such transactions between men – became regulated. Ecclesiastical law always recognized the formal exchange of oral promises (spousals) between the parties as a legally binding contract; as the Church got more powerful it exerted greater control over the circumstances in which those promises were made. In 1604 the hours, place and conditions of church weddings were defined and restricted; notice and publicity (the calling of the banns) were required as a guard against bigamy and other abuses. One effect of this was to create a demand for clergymen willing to perform weddings outside the specified conditions.
   ▷ Women, Status of.
Bib: Stone, L., *Family, Sex and Marriage in England, 1500–1800*.

Marston, John (?1575–1634)
Satirist and dramatist. His father was a lawyer. John Marston was educated at Brasenose College, Oxford; lectured in the Middle Temple (one of the ▷ Inns of Court); entered the Church in 1609. His writing life runs from 1598 to 1607. During this period he engaged in literary warfare with ▷ Ben Jonson ('the war of the theatres') who satirized Marston and ▷ Dekker in *The Poetaster* (1601) and elsewhere. The two men were, however, intermittently friends, and collaborated (with Chapman) in writing ▷ *Eastward Hoe* (1605), for which they were imprisoned for offending the king's Scottish friends.
   In 1598 Marston published *The Metamorphosis of Pygmalion's Image* and, under the pen-name of W. Kinsayder, a collection of ▷ satires entitled *Scourge of Villainie*. The satires are modelled on those of the Roman poet Persius. Their language is coarse and vigorous, and the violence and disgust they exhibit become a feature of Marston's dramatic writing. His plays are his most successful work, but they are very uneven. ▷ *Antonio and Mellida* and *Antonio's Revenge* (1599 – *Antonio*) are ▷ revenge plays in the tradition of Kyd's ▷ *The Spanish Tragedy*, and exhibit a mixture of ▷ Stoic idealism and melodramatic sensationalism, with passages of intense poetry. ▷ *The Malcontent* is a tragicomedy and usually considered to be Marston's most effective work; its satirical qualities and the role of the central character suggest comparisons with ▷ Shakespeare's ▷ *Measure for Measure* and ▷ *Hamlet*. ▷ *The Dutch Courtesan* (1605), *The Parasitaster, or the Fawne* (1606) and *What You Will* (1607) are comedies; *Sophonisba, Wonder of Women* (1605) and *The Insatiate Countess* (?1606) are tragedies.
   It was Marston's lack of critical control and the bad taste of his extravagance which caused the satirical attacks on him by Jonson. His violent revulsion from sensuality and worldly vice inspired some of his best passages as well as his worst ones.
Bib: Ellis-Fermor, U. M., *The Jacobean Drama*; Caputi, A., *John Marston, Satirist*; Finkelpearl, P., *John Marston of the Middle Temple*.

Marvell, Andrew (1621–78)
Poet. He was educated at Hull Grammar School (where his father was master) and Trinity College, Cambridge. He travelled in Europe, and in 1650 became tutor to the daughter of Lord Fairfax, the ▷ Civil War Parliamentary general. In 1653 he became

tutor to ▷ Cromwell's ward, and in 1657 ▷ John Milton's assistant in the foreign secretaryship. In 1659 he became Member of Parliament for Hull, which he continued to represent after the Restoration of the monarchy in 1660, apart from a period in which he was secretary to Lord Carlisle.

The main body of Marvell's ▷ lyric poetry is to be found in *Miscellaneous Poems* of 1681, which contains his best-known verse. He published, in addition to the lyric poetry for which he is famous, a number of ▷ satirical works and, in 1672–3, the curious amalgam of theological controversy and prose satire which is *The Rehearsal Transprosed* – the work for which he was most famous in the 17th century. But it is the lyric poetry that has attracted most modern critical attention. Of enduring fascination to modern criticism has been the question of the relation of Marvell's poems of the 1650s to the poet's own political sympathies. Is, for example, his celebration of the return of Cromwell from Ireland ('An Horatian Ode upon Cromwell's Return from Ireland') enlisting sympathy for Cromwell, or ▷ Charles I? Or is it, as some modern critics have argued, simply disinterested? Similarly, to what extent does his poetry represent a struggle to escape out of the turmoil of civil war? More radically, does the poetry dramatize the impossibility of any such retreat?

Together with the poetry of ▷ John Donne and ▷ George Herbert, Marvell's poetry has come to be appreciated as some of the most important to have been written in the 17th century. But modern criticism has, itself, not been disinterested in championing Marvell's work. For ▷ F. R. Leavis, Marvell became an ideological touchstone, while for ▷ Marxist literary historians Marvell's work represents a continually fascinating test-case of the relationship between literature and history.
Bib: Legouis, P. (ed.), *The Poems and Letters of Andrew Marvell*; Patterson, A., *Marvell and the Civic Crown*; Chernaik, W., *The Poet's Time*; Stocker, M., *Apocalyptic Marvell*.

Marx, Karl (1818–83)
Born in Trier of German-Jewish parentage, and attended university in Berlin and Bonn, where he first encountered Hegelian dialectic. He met Friedrich Engels (1820–95) in Paris in 1844, and in 1848, the Year of Revolutions, they published *The Communist Manifesto* together. In that year Marx returned to Germany and took part in the unsuccessful revolution there before fleeing to Britain, where he was to remain until his death in 1883. In 1867 he published *Capital*, the voluminous work for which he is best known. Marx is justly renowned for his adaptation of the Hegelian dialectic for a ▷ materialist account of social formations, which is based upon an analysis of the opposition between different social classes. He is arguably the most prolific thinker and social commentator of the 19th century whose work has had far-reaching effects on subsequent generations of scholars, philosophers, politicians and analysts of human culture. In the political ferment of the 1960s, and especially in France, his work has been subject to a series of extraordinarily productive re-readings, especially by philosophers such as ▷ Louis Althusser, which continue to affect the understanding of all aspects of cultural life. In Britain Marx's work is what lies behind a very powerful literary and historical tradition of commentary and analysis, and has informed much work in the areas of sociology and the study of the mass media. *Capital* and a range of earlier texts have come to form the basis of the materialist analysis of culture.
▷ New Historicism; Feminism.

Mary I (1553–58)
Queen of England. She was the eldest child of ▷ Henry VIII, who had used his divorce from her mother, Katharine of Aragon, as a pretext for taking the control of the English Church out of the hands of the Pope and into his own. Under her brother ▷ Edward VI England had swung further into ▷ Protestantism but Mary restored the Roman ▷ Catholic religion of her mother. In 1554 she married the most fanatically Catholic sovereign in Europe, Philip II of Spain; this involved her in wars with France and the loss of the last English possession there – the town of Calais. Her reign, not bloodthirsty by comparison with that of Philip in his own dominions, was nonetheless severely repressive of Protestantism, and some 300 English Protestants were burnt alive, including ▷ Cranmer and the eloquent ▷ Bishop Latimer. ▷ John Foxe's *Book of Martyrs* (1563) consigned her memory to national hatred, and she has come down in school books as 'Bloody Mary'. Her sister and successor ▷ Elizabeth I restored a moderate form of Protestantism.
▷ Tudor, House of.
Bib: Loades D., *Mary Tudor: A Life*.

Mary Queen of Scots (1542–67)
Queen of Scotland. She was born a few days before the death of her father, James V. In

1548, when she was five years old, she was betrothed to Francis, heir to the French throne, and was sent to France. She returned to Scotland only after the death of her husband in 1560; she was Catholic, but in the meantime the Scottish Protestants had with English help overthrown the Catholic establishment in their country. Mary in consequence found herself opposed to her people, led by the reformer ▷ John Knox. She was dangerously involved in English politics not only because she would be heir to the English throne should ▷ Elizabeth of England die childless, but because in the eyes of Catholics she was already legitimate Queen of England, since the Catholic Church did not recognize the legality of the marriage between Elizabeth's father, ▷ Henry VIII, and her mother. For diplomatic reasons, Mary married her cousin, Lord Darnley, a worthless young man who treated her abominably. In 1567 Darnley was murdered. The evidence for Mary's complicity in the murder is in the so-called 'casket letters', but their authenticity is uncertain. However, three months later she married his murderer, Lord Bothwell. Her subjects rebelled, and Mary was imprisoned but escaped and fled to England. Elizabeth gave her shelter, but the succession of plots against her on Mary's behalf eventually drove the English queen to authorize the Scottish queen's execution. Her son, already recognized as James VI in Scotland, became in 1603, on the death of Elizabeth, ▷ James I of England as well.

Owing to her charm, beauty, intelligence and misfortune, Mary became a legend in Europe. The greatest imaginative work about her is the tragedy *Maria Stuart* by the German poet Schiller; in English literature she is the subject of a dramatic trilogy by ▷ Algernon Swinburne (1837–1909) and of ▷ Walter Scott's (1771–1832) novel, *The Abbot* (1820). **Bib:** Fraser, A., *Mary Queen of Scots*.

Masque

A form of dramatic entertainment which combined verse, music, dancing and scenic effect in about equal proportions. In England it flourished between 1580 and 1630, and was essentially an aristocratic style of entertainment, especially popular at the royal court. The performers were commonly professional actors, while the masquers themselves, who remained silent, were played by ladies and gentlemen of the court. The subject was often symbolic – a conflict between virtue and vice (as in ▷ John Milton's ▷ *Comus*) – or ceremonial, celebrating a great personage, *eg* Milton's ▷ *Arcades* in honour of the Countess of Derby. The masque was often preceded by an anti-masque, the content of which was comic and often satirical; the anti-masque was always performed by professionals.

Masques were sophisticated entertainments for carefully selected audiences. They were in keeping with many forms of imaginative expression of the age, and may be regarded as a synthesis of them. First of all, the visual sense had been highly developed by the great ▷ Renaissance schools of painting and architecture in Italy and France, and a favourite activity of artists was to translate into visual terms the allegorical vision that the Renaissance had inherited from the ▷ Middle Ages. This visual ▷ allegory influenced the poets; much of the best of ▷ Edmund Spenser's ▷ *The Faerie Queene* consists of brilliantly visualized allegorical scenes such as the House of Busirane (Book III, canto 12). Secondly, the age attached great importance to spectacles such as ▷ pageants (*ie* ceremonial processions), which often contained symbolic, masque-like features; a famous example (which still survives) was the annual Lord Mayor's Pageant in the City of London, for which the dramatist ▷ George Peele was more than once employed as designer. Thirdly, masques appealed to the contemporary taste for imaginative extravagance, delighting in the fairy tales of English folklore and in classical mythology as well as in grand pageantry. Fourthly, the fantastical styles of many Elizabethan plays – attributable partly to popular taste and partly to the explorations of ▷ humanist scholars – made them either akin to masques (*eg* ▷ Robert Greene's *James IV*, Peele's *The Old Wives' Tale*, ▷ John Lyly's *Mother Bombie*), or capable of including masques as part of the dramatic ingredient, *eg* ▷ Shakespeare's ▷ *Love's Labour's Lost* and ▷ *The Tempest*. Finally, it was an age of close musical and literary collaboration, and masques provided opportunities for musicians and poets to collaborate on a large scale, just as they already did on a small scale in the ▷ madrigal.

Dramatists who were eminent for their composition of masques included ▷ George Chapman, ▷ John Fletcher and ▷ James Shirley, but the greatest of them – in his own estimation and probably that of others – was ▷ Ben Jonson. He collaborated with the composer Alfonso Ferrabosco the younger, and the great architect ▷ Inigo Jones; with the latter he had bitter quarrels as to which of them had artistic control of the production.

Amongst Jonson's most celebrated masques are those performed under the authority of ▷ Queen Anne: *Masque of Blackness* (1606), *Masque of Beauty* (1608) and *Masque of Queens* (1609). The most famous of all masques, however, is Milton's *Comus*, composed for the Earl of Bridgewater, whose children acted the main parts, when he was installed as Lord President of Wales. Part of the fame of *Comus* is due to its untypical quality of containing much larger speaking parts than most masques did; thus Milton allowed himself more poetic scope than was usual. For this reason, some critics prefer to call *Comus* a ▷ pastoral drama, like Jonson's *The Sad Shepherd* (1637) and Fletcher's *The Faithful Shepherdess* (1610). However, pastoral dramas and masques had much in common; both were spectacular and symbolic rather than dramatic.

Though designed as a form of lavish court entertainment, it is true that, in the 1630s especially, the masque also played a significant political role in the culture of the court. It existed to legitimize, through spectacle and pageantry, the authority of the monarch and the central position of the court in the affairs of the nation. At the same time, however, the masque form is implicated in the cultural breakdown that preceded the ▷ Civil War. Not only were masques extravagantly expensive to produce (as critics of the court pointed out), but they may also have served to suggest to the monarch and those around him that a harmony pertained in the affairs of the nation, and in the court's relationship to the world outside, when no such harmony in fact existed.
Bib: Lindley, D. (ed.), *The Court Masque*; Orgel, S. and Strong, R., *Inigo Jones: The Theatre of the Stuart Masque*.

Massinger, Philip (1583–1640)
Dramatist. His father was in the service of the great Herbert family. He left Oxford University without a degree in 1607. He has been suspected of ▷ Catholic sympathies, largely on the strength of four plays: *The Virgin Martyr* (1620), ▷ *The Duke of Milan* (1621), *The Maid of Honour* (1621), and *The Renegado* (1624). He collaborated extensively with other dramatists, especially ▷ Fletcher, but 16 or 18 plays are attributed to him alone; of these, the two usually regarded as being of the most enduring value are the comedies, ▷ *A New Way to Pay Old Debts* (1625) and ▷ *The City Madam* (1632). He himself regarded his tragedy ▷ *The Roman Actor* (1626) as his masterpiece. The dates of these plays show them to belong to the last, or ▷ Caroline, phase of what is commonly called Elizabethan drama because it started in the reign of ▷ Elizabeth 1. Two plays by Massinger are central to our understanding of the ▷ censorship of drama in the period: *Sir John Von Olden Barnavelt* (with ▷ Fletcher, 1619) and *Believe as you List*, both of which survive in manuscript. The latter was only allowed a licence after changes to disguise contemporary applications. The comedies mentioned still show a lively influence from ▷ Ben Jonson; they deal with contemporary politics and theatre and detail the latest scandals of the time. On the other hand, Massinger's tragedies have been accused of a lack of that intensity which gave grandeur to the work not only of ▷ Shakespeare but of ▷ Chapman, ▷ Tourneur and ▷ Webster. Massinger's ▷ blank verse is in the late Shakespeare tradition, but grown so flexible as almost to have lost its rhythms into prose. However, he handled his sustained periods skilfully and sometimes impressively, anticipating ▷ Milton.
Bib: Eliot, T. S., in *Selected Essays*; Knights, L. C., *Drama and Society in the Age of Jonson*; Dutton, R., *Mastering the Revels: The Regulation and Censorship of English Renaissance Drama*.

Master of the Revels
▷ Revels, Master of the.

Materialism
The philosophical theory that only physical matter is real and that all phenomena and processes can be explained by reference to it. Related to this is the doctrine that political and social change is triggered by change in the material and economic basis of society.
▷ Marx, Karl; Cultural Materialism; New Historicism.

May Day (1611)
A complex, multiple-plot comedy by ▷ George Chapman which skilfully interweaves a wealth of romance and native ▷ pastoral motifs with stock characters from Plautine (▷ Plautus) and Terentian (▷ Terence) comedy. Unlike Chapman's tragedies, *May Day* is unimpeded by an overly inflated and abstract rhetoric.

Measure for Measure (1603–4)
A play by ▷ Shakespeare. It was probably written in 1603–4, and was first printed in the First ▷ Folio of 1623. Its plot derives from *Promos and Cassandra* (1578), the translation by ▷ George Whetstone of a tale by the Italian Cinthio. In the Folio it is grouped

with the comedies, but modern critics are inclined to call it a ▷ problem play, a modern classification that includes ▷ *Troilus and Cressida*, ▷ *All's Well that Ends Well*, and sometimes ▷ *Hamlet*.

Vincentio, Duke of Vienna, is faced with the difficulty of enforcing severe laws against unchastity after they have fallen into disuse; he finds that the claims of justice and virtue conflict with those of mercy and compassion. He makes the experiment of pretending to leave the country so as to depute the task to Angelo, a man of austere life and rigid principle. In fact, the Duke remains on the scene, disguised as a friar, to watch the experiment. Angelo condemns Claudio to death for seducing his betrothed before marriage. Claudio's sister Isabella, a novitiate nun, comes to plead for her brother's life, urged on by Lucio, a man of loose life but a friend of Claudio's. Angelo is appalled to find that his lust is aroused for Isabella. His strict principle is transformed into brutal hypocrisy when he attempts to blackmail Isabella into surrendering herself in return for her brother's life. The disguised Duke induces her to pretend to consent, while he substitutes for her ▷ Mariana, whom Angelo has cold-heartedly discarded in spite of his engagement to her. Even after Isabella's apparent consent, Angelo orders Claudio's execution in order that no witness of his brutal conspiracy shall survive. Finally the Duke reveals himself, and exposes his deputy, but spares his life on the appeals of Isabella and Mariana.

It is necessary to remember the biblical text (*Matthew* 7:1) from which the title is taken: 'Judge not that ye be not judged: For with what judgement ye judge, ye shall be judged: and with what measure ye mete, it shall be measured to you again.' The three main problems that perplex critics are:

1 The Duke is evidently intended to be a virtuous ruler, who even plays the role of God, the invisible witness of our most secret thoughts and actions. Viewed realistically, however, he escapes from his duty and then plays the role of a mean spy on Angelo's actions. The mistake here is to confuse the conventions of modern, realistic drama with the conventions of Shakespeare's drama. The latter saw character in terms of role, or social function, first, and in terms of individual psychology only second. Vincentio is a ruler as God is the Ruler; by taking on the role of the omnipresent witness who has ultimate power of judgement, he is extending his function, not escaping from it. Recently, connections between the Duke and ▷ James I, who also

pursued pacifist policies, have been asserted, adding a historicist approach.

2 Isabella is presented as a virtuous woman, and yet she seems inexcusably callous in her refusal to put her brother's life before her own chastity. This is not a problem if we understand that Isabella's religious vocation is the meaning of life to her (I. iv); she has to be educated into seeing that virtue can never retain its value if it is segregated from life, just as law can never operate widely if it is isolated from knowledge of the human heart; this is Angelo's mistake.

3 Although the death penalty on Claudio is cruel, no one disputes that he has committed an offence, and yet later Angelo (by the contrivance of the Duke) is made to commit the same offence with Mariana, for which neither of them is held guilty. An answer to this is the difference between Claudio's and Angelo's actions. Claudio had offended against the law, but not against his betrothed, Juliet, whereas Angelo had previously offended against Mariana by renouncing his engagement to her, though not against the law. Morally, the play shows that Angelo's offence is the worse, and is in fact made good by his 'sin' of the Duke's contrivance.

For an adverse view of the play, see A. P. Rossiter in *Angel with Horns*; for favourable ones, see F. R. Leavis in *The Common Pursuit* and Wilson Knight in *The Wheel of Fire*; for a historical approach, see L. Marcus, *Puzzling Shakespeare*.
Bib: Hawkins, H., *Measure for Measure*.

Melville, Lady Elizabeth Culross (no dates)
Poet. Her poem, *Ane Godly Dreame* (1603), is a Calvinist account of the horrors of hell in store for all those except God's anointed. It is a first-person dream vision of a pilgrimage through smoking pits and damned souls, which combines strong imagery with graceful eight-line stanzas. It belongs to the Scottish tradition of ▷ Presbyterian texts in which individual prophesying and personal interpretations of the ▷ Bible were increasingly encouraged.
▷ Calvin, John; Scottish literature in English.
Bib: Greer, G. (ed.), *Kissing the Rod*.

Menander (342–293 BC)
An Athenian comic poet whose plays were popular in the classical world and provided the characteristic matrix of ▷ New Comedy, which became the model for both ▷ Plautus and ▷ Terence. Menander is widely acknowledged by the Roman dramatists

as their mentor, but it was not until the 20th century (1905) that substantial parts of manuscripts of his plays and one complete work (*Dyskolos*, 1955) were discovered. These confirmed the high regard in which Menander was held by his contemporaries.

Mephistopheles

An evil spirit whose name first occurs in the German *Faustbuch* (1587), a collection of tales about the necromancer ▷ Johann Faust. He is one of the seven great princes of hell. As Mephostophilis he is best known in English through Marlowe's ▷ *Doctor Faustus* (1592).

Merchant of Venice, The (1596–7)

A comedy by ▷ Shakespeare. It is dated by external evidence 1596–7. Its two outstanding incidents – the winning of a bride by undergoing a test, and the demanding of a pound of human flesh by the usurer – occur in a number of earlier narratives, but Shakespeare seems to have depended principally on a collection of Italian novels called *Il Pecorone* (*The Blockhead*) and the *Gesta Romanorum* (*Tales of the Romans*). ▷ Quarto edition, 1600; included in the First ▷ Folio (1623).

The play has a double plot.

1 An impoverished young Venetian, Bassanio, seeks to marry a wealthy heiress, Portia of Belmont. For the expense of the courtship he has to borrow 3,000 ducats from his friend, the merchant Antonio. When Bassanio and Portia meet, they fall in love at first sight, but before she can surrender herself, Bassanio has to pass the test of the caskets, ordained by her dead father. The test is to choose between a gold, a silver, and a lead casket; the right casket contains her portrait. He passes the test, but their rejoicing is interrupted by the arrival of a letter from Antonio.

2 Antonio's money is all invested in mercantile expeditions, so that to help Bassanio he has had to borrow from the Jewish usurer, Shylock. Shylock has made the strange stipulation that Antonio will have to surrender a pound of flesh in default of repayment. Antonio's letter now relates that his voyaging ships have all been lost, he is penniless, and will have to pay the pound of flesh. The two plots join in the trial scene of IV. i. The issue has come before a court of law at which Portia appears disguised as a young lawyer instructed to judge the case. She appeals to Shylock to show mercy, but when he insists on the letter of the law she lets him have it: he may take his pound of flesh, but

there is no mention of blood in the bond; if he sheds any, the law of Venice is clear: his lands and goods are to become the property of the state. Antonio is saved, and Shylock has to undergo certain severe penalties, including compulsory conversion to Christianity. Act V concludes the play with light comedy and the lyrical union of several pairs of lovers.

Like others of Shakespeare's earlier comedies, the play is a mixture of courtly sophistication, light fantasy, and moving realism. The plot belongs to fable and fairy story, and the love affairs to the tradition of courtly romance. On the other hand, Shylock is a very powerful, sombre figure and brings a sharp criticism to bear on the otherwise glibly accepted value judgements of the court. His bond, however, is counterbalanced by Antonio's arrogant treatment of him and the eloquent irony with which Shylock protests against it. The trial scene is one of the elements of fable in the play: in real terms, Shylock is being treated with gross unjustice, but the real theme is the contrast between Mercy and the Law. It is the function of mere Law to be merciless; he who refuses mercy and insists on law must abide by the consequences.
▷ Race.
Bib: Danson, L., *The Harmonies of Merchant of Venice*.

Mercutio

The friend of Romeo and related to the Prince in ▷ Shakespeare's tragedy ▷ *Romeo and Juliet*. He makes the celebrated speech about Queen Mab in I. iv. His quarrelsomeness leads to his death at the hands of Tybalt, the cousin of Juliet, followed by Romeo's fatal duel with Tybalt.

Meres, Francis (1565–1647)

Author of *Pallados Tamia, Wit's Treasury* (1598), a book of moral and critical reflections. One chapter is an account of English writers, and his comments are interesting for estimating their reputations at the time.
Bib: Smith, G. G., *Elizabethan Critical Essays*.

Mermaid Tavern

A 16th-century tavern in London's Bread Street. According to legend the Bread Street, or Friday Night, Club was founded by ▷ Sir Walter Ralegh, and was one of the earliest English clubs and meeting-places of writers.

Merry Wives of Windsor, The (1597)

A comedy by ▷ Shakespeare, probably written 1597 in connection with the celebrations

of the ▷ Garter Knights, to whose order
the younger Lord Hunsdon, patron of
Shakespeare's acting company, was elected
that year; an imperfect edition came out in
1602 and a corrected version was published
in the First ▷ Folio of 1623. The critic John
Dennis (1657–1734) states that it was written
at the request of ▷ Queen Elizabeth 1, who
wanted a play about ▷ Sir John Falstaff in
love. Falstaff had been a great popular success
in the two ▷ *Henry IV* plays. It has also been
suggested that Shakespeare was emulating
the realistic comedy of ▷ Thomas Dekker
(▷*Shoemaker's Holiday*, 1600) and ▷ Ben
Jonson (▷ *Every Man in his Humour*, 1598;
▷ *Every Man out of his Humour*, 1599). *The
Merry Wives* is the only play by Shakespeare to
be written mainly in prose.

Falstaff makes love to two married women,
the wives of Ford and Page; but the wives and
their husbands finally expose him in Windsor
Forest, after he has been beset by neighbours
disguised as fairies. A subordinate plot
concerns the wooing of Anne Page by three
suitors, and how she and Fenton, the suitor
she prefers, contrive their elopement.

Apart from Falstaff, other characters recur
from the *Henry IV* and *V* plays: Nym, Pistol,
Slender, Mistress Quickly. Falstaff in *The
Merry Wives* bears little resemblance to the
creation of the earlier plays.

Metamorphoses

Poems in Latin by ▷ Ovid. They are a series
of mythological tales whose common subject is
miraculous transformation of shape, beginning
with Chaos into Cosmos, ending with ▷ Julius
Caesar into a star, and including such tales
as Baucis and Philemon, the peasants who
unawares gave hospitality to the gods, who
granted them immortality as a pair of trees.
They were popular in medieval Europe and
afterwards, up till the 19th century, and have
often been translated, in whole or in part, into
English *eg* by ▷ Arthur Golding in the 16th
century and by George Sandys in the 17th.

Metaphor

A figure of speech by which unlike objects
are identified with each other for the purpose
of emphasizing one or more aspects of
resemblance between them. An example is
▷ George Herbert's linking of his heart and
blood with a book and ink in 'Good Friday':

> *Since bloud is fittest, Lord, to write
> Thy sorrows in, and bloudie fight;
> My heart hath store, write there, where in
> One box doth lie both ink and sinne.*

▷ Metonymy.

Metaphysical conceit
▷ Metaphysical Poets; Conceit.

Metaphysical Poets
The accepted designation of a succession of
17th-century poets, of whom the following
are the principal names: ▷ John Donne,
▷ George Herbert, ▷ Richard Crashaw,
▷ Andrew Marvell, ▷ Henry Vaughan,
▷ Abraham Cowley. The term came to be
applied to them in a special sense; that is to
say, they were not so described because their
subject was the relationship of spirit to matter
or the ultimate nature of reality; this is true
of ▷ Lucretius, ▷ Milton and ▷ Dante, who
have little else in common. It is true that some
of them – Donne, Herbert, Vaughan and
Crashaw especially – were metaphysical in this
generally accepted sense, but the adjective is
applied to them to indicate not merely subject
matter, but qualities of expression in relation
to subject matter.

Samuel Johnson (1709–84) was the first
so to classify these poets: 'The metaphysical
poets were men of learning, and to show
their learning was their whole endeavour'
(essay on Cowley in *Lives of the Poets*). The
sentence shows that he is using the term
disparagingly, and this disparagement had
already been expressed by John Dryden
(1631–1700): 'Donne affects the metaphysics
not only in his satires but in his amorous
verses . . . [he] perplexes the mind of the
fair sex with nice speculations of philosophy'
(*Discourse concerning the Original and Progress
of Satire*, 1693). Dryden and Johnson were
antagonistic to Donne and his followers
because they valued above all the assurance,
clarity, restraint and shapeliness of the major
Augustan poets of ancient Rome. Critics and
poets of the 20th century have on the other
hand immensely admired Donne, Herbert
and Marvell, but they still use 'Metaphysical'
as the term under which to group them.
H. J. C. Grierson (Introduction, *Metaphysical
Poetry: Donne to Butler*) justifies it because it
indicates 'the peculiar blend of passion and
thought, feeling and ratiocination which is
their greatest achievement.' However, they
have also been labelled '*The Fantasticks*'
(an anthology edited by W. S. Scott) and
L. B. Martz has suggested *The Poetry of
Meditation* (the title of his book). The first
of these alternative designations suggests a
resemblance between the English poets and
their so-called 'baroque' contemporaries in
Italy (Marino), Spain (Góngora) and France

(Théophile de Viau and Saint-Amant); the
second emphasizes the difference – the
greater balance and control among the English
poets; it may be said that Crashaw, at one
extreme, belongs more to the former, and
Herbert, at the other extreme, is much better
described as 'meditative'.

The distinctiveness of the Metaphysicals
was their use of the so-called 'metaphysical
▷ conceit' – *ie* paradoxical metaphor causing
a shock to the mind by the unlikeness of the
association, *eg* Donne's

> *her pure and eloquent blood*
> *Spoke in her cheeks, and so distinctly wrought,*
> *That one might almost say her body*
> *thought.*
>> (*Second Anniversary*)

or Herbert's

> *Only a sweet and virtuous soul*
> *Like season'd timber, never gives;*
> *But though the whole world turn to coal*
>> *Then chiefly lives.*
>>> (*Virtue*)

In most respects, therefore the term is so
broad, and embraces poetic styles and forms
so disparate, that its use is nearly meaningless,
being little more than an anthologist's
convenience.
Bib: Smith, A. J., *The Wit of Love*.

Metonymy

The naming of a person, institution or
human characteristic by some object or
attribute with which it is clearly associated,
as when a Christian heart is referred to as a
marble floor:

> *Hither sometimes sinne steals, and stains*
> *The marbles neat and curious veins:*
> *But all is cleansed when the marble weeps.*
>> ▷ George Herbert, 'The Church-floore'

Metonomy has taken on additional meanings
since the advent of ▷ structuralism. One
of the originators of Russian ▷ Formalism,
▷ Roman Jakobson, draws a distinction
between ▷ 'metaphor' – the linguistic
relationship between two different objects
on the grounds of their similarity – and
'metonymy' as a means of establishing a
relationship between two objects in terms
of their continuity. Where metaphor is
regarded as a major rhetorical device in *poetry*,
metonymy is more usually associated with
prose. The critic and novelist David Lodge
takes up this distinction in his book *The
Modes of Modern Writing* (1977), and suggests

that 'metaphor' and 'metonymy' constitute
a structurally significant binary opposition
that enables the distinction to be made
between poetry and drama on the one hand,
and prose on the other. Lodge emphasizes,
however, that these terms are not mutually
exclusive, but rather contribute to 'a theory
of dominance of one quality over another'.
Hence it is possible for a novel to contain
'poetic' effects and vice versa.

Microcosmographie
▷ Characters, Theophrastian.

Middle Ages, The
A term used by historians to cover the
period between the fall of the Roman
Empire of the West (end of the 5th century)
and the beginning of the ▷ Renaissance,
conventionally dated from the extinction of
the Roman Empire of the East (Byzantine
Empire) in 1453. The expression dates from
the 16th century when it is found in the Latin
writings of a number of ▷ humanists – '*media
aetas*', '*medium aevum*'. The conception in
the 16th century was that civilization was
renewing itself by rediscovery of the ancient
civilizations of Greece and Rome; scholars
considered that the centuries between the
5th and 15th were a relatively dark period of
ignorance and cultural backwardness. For long
after the 16th century modern history was
commonly assumed to have begun with the
15th-century Renaissance. Some scholars are
inclined to think this view mistaken; many of
them also consider that the so-called Middle
Ages had much more continuity with classical
history than the men of the Renaissance
supposed. The term Middle Ages is thus a
misleading and erroneous one but its use has
become habitual and cannot be dispensed
with. Moreover the Renaissance of the
15th–16th centuries did herald an important
change, however one interprets it, and it is
still useful to have a term to designate the
centuries which preceded it.

In English history, it is common to think
of the Middle Ages as extending from the
Norman Conquest of 1066 until the end of
the Wars of the Roses and the accession of
▷ Henry VII (first of the House of ▷ Tudor)
in 1485. The period from the 5th to the
11th century is called loosely the Old English
period. The term Middle Ages was first used
by ▷ John Donne in a sermon in 1621.

Middleton, Elizabeth (no date)
Poet. Little is known about Elizabeth
Middleton, although G. Greer in *Kissing the*

Rod (1988) suggests that she might belong to the Myddleton family of Denbighshire and includes detailed genealogical material to that effect. We know of her existence through one extant devotional poem, 'The Death and passion of Our Lord Jesus Christ' (1637). It has 173 six-line stanzas which take the form of an oratorio, the biblical narrative event being followed by a passionate statement of one speaker's emotional response. Her imagery is simple, but strong, and her language is clearly influenced by other religious writers such as ▷ Robert Southwell.

Middleton, Thomas (1580–1627)

Dramatist. Little is known about his life; he may have been a student of law in London and in the 1590s he was at Oxford University. Later he was often employed to write ▷ pageants to celebrate civic occasions, and in 1620 he was appointed city chronologer (historian).

His masterpieces were two tragedies: ▷ *Women Beware Women* (1614) and ▷ *The Changeling* (1622), with a subplot by ▷ William Rowley. The latter play is one of the finest tragedies in English since ▷ Shakespeare. In his comedies he was one of the two notable successors to ▷ Ben Jonson, the other being ▷ Philip Massinger. His best are probably: *A Trick to Catch the Old-one* (1604), ▷ *The Roaring Girl* (with ▷ Dekker, 1606), and above all ▷ *A Chaste Maid in Cheapside* (1611). These, like others of his comedies, are ▷ citizen comedies, *ie* about London middle-class life, like the comedies of Dekker, but presented with more substantial realism. ▷ *A Game at Chess* (1624) was a political satire provoked by the king's failure to marry his son to a Spanish princess; its performance was stopped by the protest of the Spanish ambassador. *The Witch*, a ▷ revenge play of uncertain date, may have influenced Shakespeare's ▷ *Macbeth* but was more probably influenced by it, and Middleton has been thought by some to have contributed Act III, Sc. v in *Macbeth*.

With Rowley, Middleton also wrote *A Fair Quarrel* (1614); *The World Tost at Tennis* (1620); *The Spanish Gipsy* (1623). Plays ascribed to Middleton alone: *The Old Law* (1599); *Blurt, Master-Constable* (1601–2); *The Family of Love* (1602); *Michaelmas Term* (1605); *The Phoenix* (1607); *A Mad World, my Masters* (1606); *Your Five Gallants* (?1607); ▷ *No Wit, No Help like a Woman's* (?1613); *Anything for a Quiet Life* (?1617); *More Dissemblers besides Women* (before 1622); *The Widow* (uncertain date). Eleven of his ▷ masques have survived.

He also wrote some minor poetry and prose ▷ pamphlets.
Bib: Bradbrook, M. C., *Elizabethan Tragedy*; Knights, L. C., *Drama and Society in the Age of Jonson*; Barker, R. H., *Thomas Middleton*; Heinemann, M., *Puritanism and Theatre*; Mulryne, J. R., *Thomas Middleton*.

Midsummer Night's Dream, A (1595)

A comedy by Shakespeare. From internal evidence it has been dated about 1595; it was printed in 1600. The title refers to the fantastic quality of events, resembling a dream on Midsummer night, when fantastic dreams were supposed to be commonly experienced.

The characters are in four distinct groups. The background is the court of a character from Greek mythology, King Theseus of Athens, on the eve of his marriage to ▷ Hippolyta, queen of the Amazons. The four lovers whose confusions form the bulk of the action, Helena and Demetrius, Hermia and Lysander (as they are eventually paired), have classical names, but their story is a typical comedy of ▷ Renaissance romantic love, in which they are all victims of blind passion. The third group is made from the Athenian artisans whose names – ▷ Bottom, Quince, Snout, Flute and Starveling – show them to be English types of Shakespeare's own day. They celebrate Theseus' wedding night (and that of the other lovers) by performing the interlude ▷ 'Pyramus and Thisbe' – intended to be tragic but, as they carry it out, decidedly comic. The fourth group is the ▷ fairies. In general (especially ▷ Puck, or Robin Goodfellow) these are drawn from English folklore, but their king, ▷ Oberon, comes from *Huon de Bordeaux* (a medieval French romance) and Titania from ▷ Ovid's ▷ *Metamorphoses*. Oberon, through Puck, confuses the lovers as they wander through the wood near Athens, and causes Titania to fall in love with Bottom, who, for the night, is given an ass's head. The fantasy is deftly contrived.

Mildmay, Grace (1552–1620)

Autobiographer. Despite an extremely strict upbringing, during which she was regularly beaten, Mildmay gained confidence in her writing and educational capabilities through her tutoring by a poor relation. At 15 she married Anthony Mildmay and later in life ran the large estates at Apethorpe. It was not until she became a grandmother that she attempted to record her life for the benefit of her daughter, Mary Fane, so that the younger woman could learn from the example of her mother. The ▷ autobiographical diary focuses mainly upon the bringing up of children and how to educate the young, its ultimate end being a preparation for the eternal life in heaven. The work exists in manuscript at Northants public library, but extracts are published in 'An Elizabethan Gentlewoman', ed. R. Wiegall, in *Quarterly Review* (1911). **Bib:** Travitsky, B. (ed.), *The Paradise of Women.*

Milton, John (1608–74)

Poet and prose polemicist. Milton was born in London, the son of a scrivener and musician, and educated at St Paul's School and Christ's College, Cambridge. After leaving Cambridge in 1632, Milton lived for the next five years at his father's house in Horton. During this, his early poetic career, he wrote the companion pieces ▷ *L'Allegro* and ▷ *Il Penseroso*, two ▷ masques, ▷ *Arcades* and ▷ *Comus*, and the ▷ elegy ▷ *Lycidas*. From 1638 to 1639 Milton travelled abroad, chiefly in Italy. His Italian journey was to have a lasting influence on his later development, not least in the contact he established among Florentine intellectuals. But more than that, it reaffirmed his distaste – loathing even – for Roman ▷ Catholicism, and focused his intense opposition to the Laudian (▷ Laud, William) regime in England.

Milton's continental journey was interrupted early in 1639 at Naples, where he claims to have first heard news of the political crisis in England. He was later to claim that he thought it 'base that I should travel abroad at my ease for the cultivation of my mind while my fellow citizens at home were fighting for liberty' (*Defensio secunda*). Returning to England, Milton embarked upon what has now come to be seen as the second phase of his career – that of a political prose writer and propagandist for the anti-Royalist cause in the English ▷ Civil War. Between 1640 and 1655, Milton was to write little poetry. His energies and his sympathies were now to be engaged fully on the side of the republican forces in England – though he was not an uncritical supporter of the new experiment in government. From this period can be dated the series of great prose declarations dealing with political and religious questions – *Of Reformation* (1641), his attack on episcopacy in the *Apology for Smectymnuus* (1642), his statement on personal liberty contained in *The Doctrine and Discipline of Divorce* (1643). These works were followed by ▷ *Areopagitica* (1644), *Tenure of Kings and Magistrates* (1649), *Eikonoklastes* (1649), the two 'defences' of the

English people (1651 and 1654), *A Treatise of Civil Power* (1659) and, almost at the moment when ▷ Charles II returned to England to re-establish the claims of monarchy, *A Readie and Easie Way to Establish a Free Commonwealth* (1660). The list of topics upon which Milton wrote in this period is bewildering, but running through all his prose writings is a stable belief that the English people have been chosen, by God, to perform a necessary political act – the establishment of a state based on principles of choice and, within certain bounds, freedom.

▷ *Paradise Lost*, Milton's great religious and political poem, was begun at some point in the mid-1650s – perhaps in the growing awareness that although there had been political choices in England, the wrong choice had been made. The poem was not published, however, until 1667, with a second (revised) edition appearing in 1674, shortly before Milton's death in November of that year. But the period after 1660 is usually recognized as the third and final phase of Milton's career. It is the period of the publication of ▷ *Paradise Regained* and ▷ *Samson Agonistes*. Though it has long been claimed that Milton's absorption in the task of writing these works marked an end to his career of political engagement, it is probably truer to say that these works signal a renewed, and possibly deeper, investigation of the themes which had occupied him for most of his life – the questions of political and religious liberty, the problems associated with choice and rule, and the problematic nature of government and obedience.
Bib: Carey, J. and Fowler, A. (eds.), *The Complete Poems of John Milton*; Wolfe, D. M. (ed.), *Complete Prose Works of John Milton*; Parker, W. R., *Milton: A Biography*; Hill, C., *Milton and the English Revolution*; Nyquist, M. and Ferguson, M. (eds.), *Re-membering Milton*.

Mimesis

In ▷ Plato's *Republic* 'mimesis' is used to designate 'imitation', but in a derogatory way. The term is given a rigorous, positive meaning in ▷ Aristotle's *Poetics*, where it is used to describe a process of selection and representation appropriate to tragedy: 'the imitation of an action'. Literary criticism from ▷ Sir Philip Sidney onwards has wrestled with the problem of the imitative function of literary texts, but after ▷ structuralism, with its questioning of the referential function of all language, the term has taken on a new and problematic dimension. Mimesis has frequently been associated with the term 'realism', and with the capacity of language to reflect reality. At particular historical moments, *eg* the ▷ Renaissance, or the present time, when reality itself appears to be in question, then the capacity of language to represent reality is brought to the fore. The issue becomes even more complex when we realize that 'reality' may be something other than our experience of it.

Mirror for Magistrates, A (1559)

A collection of verse monologues spoken by characters in English history and legend. The collection was inspired by ▷ John Lydgate's *The Fall of Princes* (1494), and written by William Baldwin, ▷ George Ferrers and others. Nineteen verse monologues are spoken by historical figures from the reigns of ▷ Richard II to ▷ Edward IV, and in the main the intention of these verse accounts is to warn rulers and subjects against (respectively) tyranny and rebellion. After the first edition of 1559, numerous editions appeared throughout the 16th century and well into the 17th. With each edition, the work expanded, though the edition of 1563 (with contributions by ▷ Thomas Sackville) is claimed to be, artistically, the most satisfactory. The edition of 1610 (the last, though there were reissues of 1619, 1620 and 1621) is the largest of what had become a series rather than a sequence of editions.

Though the *Mirror* was perhaps not an artistically distinguished enterprise, it nevertheless exerted a considerable thematic influence on the writing of history plays in the period, and on the conception of ▷ tragedy pursued by ▷ Elizabethan and ▷ Jacobean writers. It partakes, too, in that Elizabethan attempt at creating a sustained account of national history of which the work of ▷ Samuel Daniel, ▷ Michael Drayton and ▷ Edmund Spenser is also, in part, representative.

▷ Histories and Chronicles.
Bib: Campbell, L. B. (ed.), *A Mirror for Magistrates*.

Misrule, Lord of

Title given to the master of revels for the 12 days of the Christmas festivities, which mark a licensed period of disorder and which may be celebrated in medieval noble and royal households.

▷ New Historicism.

Monasteries and Monasticism

The practice of monasticism arose in the lands about the eastern Mediterranean in the early centuries of Christianity, and was inspired by the belief that the holy life could be lived only in isolation from the practical interests of worldly society. By the 14th century monasteries were losing their value, and monks were often useless parasites like the Monk in ▷ Chaucer's ▷ *The Canterbury Tales*. When ▷ Henry VIII dissolved the monasteries (1536–9) the measure met with no resistance in the south-east but it provoked the rebellion known as the ▷ Pilgrimage of Grace in the north.

There were no monasteries in Britain after the middle of the 16th century, but since the second half of the 19th century some have been re-established.

Montague

The family of which Romeo is a member, and the sworn enemies of Juliet's family, the ▷ Capulets, in ▷ Shakespeare's play ▷ *Romeo and Juliet*.

Montaigne, Michel de (1533–92)

French essayist, and inventor of the ▷ essay form. His life was lived partly at court, or performing the office of magistrate in the city of Bordeaux, and partly in retirement. During retirement, he wrote his *Essais* ('experiments'), the first two volumes of which were published in 1580, and the third in 1588. He was a scholar, well read in ▷ humanist literature and in the works of the ancient Greeks and Romans. His favourite author was ▷ Plutarch.

The *Essays* seem to have been begun as commentaries on his reading, perhaps to assist his exceptionally bad memory. From this grew a desire to arrive at a complete image of man; as a means to this, he tried to develop a portrait of himself, since 'each man bears the complete stamp of the human condition'. The sentence shows the still-prevailing view of his time, that human beings followed general principles in the structure of their personalities – a view quite unlike the view that grew up in the 18th century and came to predominate in the 19th, that each individual is unique. He recognized, however, the difficulties in arriving at conclusive ideas about human nature, and the essays are characterized by the scepticism with which he weighs contradictions and opposing views.

Montaigne was translated into English by ▷ Florio in 1603. The essays had an extensive influence upon English literature. Whether the long essay entitled *Apologie de Raimond de Sebond* had an important influence on ▷ Shakespeare's ▷ *Hamlet* is a controversial question; but Gonzalo

in Shakespeare's ▷ *Tempest* quotes from
Montaigne's *Des Cannibales* in II. i. 143–60
('I' th' commonwealth . . . '). More important
were the emulators of Montaigne in the
essay form. Montaigne's sceptical, searching,
flexible mind resembles those of ▷ Robert
Burton (▷ *Anatomy of Melancholy*) and ▷ Sir
Thomas Browne (▷ *Religio Medici*). These,
however, were not essayists; the Montaigne
tradition of essay writing was taken up later in
the century by ▷ Abraham Cowley (*Essays in
Verse and Prose*, 1668).
Bib: Friedrich, H., *Montaigne.*

Montgomerie, Alexander (c 1545–98)
Poet. Montgomerie was a ▷ Scottish court
official, man of action and writer; he was
admired by ▷ James II (James VI of Scotland)
and was granted a pension in 1583. After
having been suspected of involvement in a
▷ Catholic plot, he left Scotland in 1586
to travel in Europe. His most well-known
work is *The Cherrie and the Slae* (1597), an
▷ allegorical work contrasting the cherry's
elevated and valued position with the sloe's
lowly and despised growth. It is meant to
be sung aloud. He also wrote ▷ sonnets
in which a ▷ Petrarchan influence is clear,
Flyting of Montgomery and Polwart (published
posthumously in 1621), and a general output
of ▷ lyrics and songs.
Bib: Jack, R. D. S., *Alexander Montgomerie.*

Morality plays
A term used by modern critics to distinguish
plays expounding points of moral doctrine,
extant from the 15th century, from other
kinds of contemporary vernacular drama that
commemorate the events of Christian history
(such as the cycle plays or saints' plays).
The plots of morality plays are ▷ allegorical
narratives of one kind or another; the human
protagonists tend not to be individualized
or given an historical identity. The scope
of the plays may vary: whereas the *Castle
of Perseverance* dramatizes the epic story of
'Humankind's' life from birth to beyond the
grave, and requires great dramatic resources,
Mankind focuses on an exemplary episode
in Mankind's life, and seems designed as an
itinerant production by a smaller acting group.
Generally, however, the genre is associated
with plays like *Mankind*, which can be
performed in halls by smaller acting groups.
Behind plays such as *Castle of Perseverance*,
Mankind and *Everyman* is a long tradition of
Christian instruction and teaching: sermons
addressed to lay audiences and manuals of
instruction may employ similar devices of

analysis and instruction to those dramatized
in these morality plays, which endow
abstract notions, concepts, processes, with a
tangible form.
But this kind of drama is not confined to
expounding points of religious doctrine. In
the morality plays dating from the late 15th
century (such as Henry Medwall's *Fulgens
and Lucres*), or from the 16th century (such
as John Rastall's *Of Gentilness and Nobility*),
issues of social order (in these cases the
relationship between social rank and moral
virtue) come under scrutiny. The instructional
impetus of this kind of drama can be used
for secular as well as religious ends. This
dramatic form has had more impact on the
drama of the Renaissance than the cycle plays,
due to the flexibility of its form and the use of
allegory for ethical and moral analysis.
Although the term 'morality' play is useful
for locating a distinctive dramatic form
popular in the 15th and 16th centuries,
it should not be regarded as a fixed and
wholly distinctive dramatic genre. Allegorical
personages appear in the cycle drama, and
saints' plays too, and many plays confound
rigid generic categories: ▷ John Bale's play
King John (c 1536), for example, presents
a historical narrative and an allegorical
commentary on the action at the same time.
Bib: Cawley, A. C. et al., *The Revels History
of Drama in English: Vol. I Medieval Drama*;
Davenport, W. A., *Fifteenth-Century English
Drama: the Early Moral Plays and their Literary
Relations.*

**More, Sir Thomas (St Thomas More)
(1478–1535)**
Scholar, thinker and statesman. He was the
leading ▷ humanist of his day, and a friend of
▷ Erasmus. For some time he was a particular
favourite of ▷ Henry VIII, who raised him to
the Lord Chancellorship, the highest office
in the state. However, More firmly refused
to recognize the king's divorce from Queen
Katharine and the ▷ Act of Supremacy
(1534). For this the king executed him, and
the Catholic Church canonized him exactly
400 years later.
More's *History of King Richard III* (1513)
has been called the first masterpiece of
▷ history and ▷ biography in English, but his
principal work, ▷ *Utopia* (1516), was in Latin,
translated into English in 1551. While More's
idealized characteristics have often been
emphasized, recent criticism has detected a
darker side to his writing, which may be seen
in his intemperate tone, detailing of extreme
forms of conduct, and biting irony. Famous as

a ▷ patron of letters and arts, he invited the painter ▷ Holbein to England.

▷ Catholicism (Roman) in English literature; Roper, Margaret More.
Bib: Surtz, E. (ed.), *Selected Works*; Sylvester, R. S. and Harding, D. P. (eds.), *The Life of Sir Thomas More*; Hexter, J. H., *More's Utopia: The Biography of an Idea*; Greenblatt, S., *Renaissance Self-fashioning*; Martz, L. L., *Thomas More: the Search for the Inner Man*.

Morte D'Arthur

The *Morte D'Arthur* is the conventional title for a highly influential prose narrative, completed in 1469/70 by a Sir Thomas ▷ Malory, which recounts the foundation, history and destruction of ▷ King Arthur's court and the knights of the Round Table. Until 1934 Malory's narrative was known only through ▷ Caxton's edition (first printed in 1485) entitled the *Morte D'Arthur*, but the discovery of a manuscript version of the text in 1934, and its publication in 1947 as Malory's *Works*, revealed the extent of Caxton's editorial intervention. Whereas Caxton's text is divided into 21 books, the *Works* is composed of eight narratives (called 'Tales', or 'Books'), which are relatively self-contained, but taken together form an overall history of Arthur's reign. The first recounts the founding of Arthur's kingdom and the Round Table; the second concerns Arthur's campaign for Rome; the third is devoted to the adventures of Lancelot; the fourth is taken up with the romance of Gareth; the fifth is predominantly concerned with a version of Tristan's history; the sixth recounts the Quest of the Holy Grail; the seventh relates the events that follow Lancelot's return to court and his love affair with Guinevere; the eighth recounts events leading up to the break-up of the Round Table and the end of all Arthur's knights. This organization into eight Tales/Books helps point up Malory's narrative strategy: he has not chosen to present events in a continuous narrative sequence, organized chronologically. Rather he has cultivated a looser structure that enables his reader to follow a number of narrative lines which make up the sequence of Arthurian history.

Malory drew material for his work principally from the massive cycles of Arthurian narrative that had been compiled in France in the 13th century and in which accounts of the adventures at Arthur's court were organized in interlaced narrative forms. Malory has abbreviated and reorganized this material, drawing out some of the narrative threads from the interlaced sequences, and reordering some of the adventures. His narrative is structured as an investigation into the meaning of the codes and ethos of that world. The institution of the Round Table is meant to introduce a civilizing code of behaviour to Arthur's kingdom, but the stories of the knights' adventures reveal the difficulty of working out a chivalric ethos in practice. The narrative explores and celebrates chivalric values, but it does not present a narrow moralizing account of Arthurian history, nor a simple explanation of why the brave new world of Arthur's court eventually collapses in such disarray. Malory's narrative is structured in such a way that no single chain of actions 'causes' the breakdown of the Round Table: the relationships between events and actions are more mysterious than in the Old French sources.
Bib: Vinaver, E. (ed.), *Malory: Works*; Cowen, J. (ed.), *The Morte D'Arthur*.

Mother Hubberd's Tale, or Prosopopeia (c 1579)

A verse ▷ satire by ▷ Edmund Spenser, in ten-syllable couplets, presented in the form of a fable; 'Prosopopeia' means 'endowing things or animals with personalities'. It was published with other poems in *Complaints* (1591) but written at about the same time as ▷ *The Shepherd's Calendar* (1579). It was written at a time when ▷ Elizabeth I seemed inclined to marry the Duke of Anjou, brother of Henry III of France. He was hated by the more convinced ▷ Protestants in England (of whom Spenser was one) because he was a Catholic and a member of the family responsible for the Massacre of St Bartholomew, 1572, in which French Protestants had been slaughtered. The fable tells how the ape and the fox steal the lion's crown while he sleeps. The ape is Anjou, and the fox is William Cecil, Lord Burghley, Spenser's enemy.

Much Ado about Nothing (1598)

A comedy by ▷ Shakespeare. It was acted in 1598, and printed in 1600. The main plot is drawn from ▷ *Orlando Furioso* (Bk V) and from a novel by Bandello. The scene is Messina, at the court of the governor, Leonato, who receives a visit from the Prince of Aragon, his evil-minded brother, Don John, and the Prince's friend, Claudio. The main plot concerns Claudio's indirect courtship of Hero, Leonato's daughter, the frustration of their marriage plans by Don John, who plants a slander on Hero, the eventual exposure of the slander, and the reconciliation. A subplot concerns the relationship between Benedick and Beatrice, who are famous in the court for their war of wits in which they declare mutual detestation; a plot is devised which enables each to recognize that their war is really a mask disguising their real love, and they acknowledge this to each other. The subplot joins the main plot when Beatrice tests Benedick's feelings for her by demanding that he challenge Claudio (his friend) to a duel for slandering Hero. The play is more famous for its subplot (and for ▷ Dogberry and Verges, the comic constables) than for its main plot, owing to the vividness of the characters in the former and the comparative colourlessness of those in the latter. However the comedy has unity and impressiveness once the reader sees in it a strong current of satire. The court, like other ▷ Renaissance courts, is an environment in which witticism is valued without regard to true feeling, disguise of some sort is normal, artifice has more prestige than nature, and carefully cultivated appearances take the place of reality. In such a world, it is natural that Claudio should be a superficial lover easily deceived by a stratagem and that a mere game played in mockery of Beatrice and Benedick should lead to their stumbling on the truth. Their moment of truth stands out with dramatic poignancy. Similarly, Dogberry's naïve stumbling over language is a contrast to the courtiers' artificial perversion of it.

Mulcaster, Richard (c 1530–1611)

Educationalist. Mulcaster was the first headmaster of Merchant Taylors School, London, where he taught ▷ Andrewes, ▷ Kyd, ▷ Lodge and ▷ Spenser, and in 1596 he became the high master at St Paul's School. His views on education were ▷ humanist; he believed, for example, that girls should be educated to as high a standard as boys. Mulcaster wrote two books on education, *Positions* (1581) and *The Elementarie* (1582), and he also contributed ▷ masques, entertainments and commemorative verses to state and city occasions, such as the funeral orations on ▷ Elizabeth I in 1603.
Bib: Elsky, M., *Authorizing Words*.

Mummers' Plays/Mumming

Although many Mummers' plays survive from various parts of the country, all of the texts date from the 18th century or later. Characteristically they take the form of a fight between a Champion (often St George) and an Antagonist who is killed but resurrected at the end through the agency of a Doctor. The plays often conclude with a Dance and

the opportunity for a collection of money. Archetypal patterns are ritually enacted within these plays, though the texts as we have them may themselves be the product of folkloric revivals. Access to folk-drama and rituals of the past is necessarily difficult because by its very definition this kind of cultural activity does not depend on written records or texts. Information about medieval folk-drama is derived from the records of attempts by ecclesiastical authorities to ban, curb or suppress it.

Mummings, as their name suggests, are dumb-shows, particularly masquerades and disguisings associated with the festivities of the New Year and Shrove-Tide. Again, though there are records of prohibitions on mummings from the early medieval period, the texts that survive from the 15th century are of mummings contrived as occasions of civic and aristocratic entertainment, such as those composed by ▷ John Lydgate (in which a dumb-show is accompanied by a verse commentary). They were the precursors to ▷ masques.

▷ Misrule, Lord of; Bakhtin, Mikhail.
Bib: Brody, A., *The English Mummers and their Plays*.

Munda, Constantia (no date)

Polemical tract-writer in the debate about women. 'Constantia Munda' is a pseudonym for a female response to Joseph Swetnam's attack upon women (▷ *Querelle des Femmes*), which was published as *The Worming of a Mad Dogge* (1617). The treatise begins with a poem thanking her mother for setting an example of virtue and piety, and continues with a prose defence of women asserting them to be valued equally with men by God. It also accuses Swetnam of praising only masculine virtues and of classifying all women as the same when there are many different levels of moral virtue to be found.

▷ Sowernam, Ester; Speght, Rachel.
Bib: Henderson, K. U. and McManus, B. F. (eds.), *Half Humankind*.

Munday, Anthony (1553–1633)

Poet, dramatist, translator and ▷ pamphlet writer. Munday's somewhat prolific career is marked by a keen interest in narrative, but little imaginative skill in his use of language. Of his life outside the theatre we know little, and can only speculate about his being a boy-actor and a double agent (moving between the ▷ Protestant state and ▷ Catholic insurgents). Of his many pamphlets, several are staunchly Protestant, and the contents of the others

are general, appealing to popular rather than specific tastes. He also wrote poetry, some of which is included in ▷ *England's Helicon*, and while employed as London's official poet (1592–1623), he composed several civic entertainments. However, Munday is better known for his dramatic collaborations and his ▷ translations of prose romances. He was one of the revisers of ▷ *Sir Thomas More* (c 1596) and collaborated with ▷ Henry Chettle on two plays about ▷ Robin Hood, *The Downfall of Robert, Earle of Huntington* and *The Death of Robert, Earle of Huntington* (both 1598). Munday may now be seen as an important contributor to the ▷ Elizabethan novel through his translations of the prose romances *Palladine of England* (1588) and *Amadis of Gaule* (c 1590). He is satirized by ▷ Jonson as Antonio Balladino in *The Case is Altered.*
Bib: Hayes, G. R., *Anthony Munday's Romances of Chivalry*; Turner, C., *Anthony Munday: An Elizabethan Man of Letters.*

'Mutabilitie Cantos', The (1609)
When the 1609 ▷ folio edition of ▷ Edmund Spenser's ▷ *The Faerie Queene* was published, two further cantos of the poem, and two stanzas of a fragmentary third canto, were printed. These, the putative cantos vi, vii, and a fragment of viii of Book VII of the poem, were described in the 1609 edition in the following way: 'TWO CANTOS of *Mutabilitie*: Which, both for Forme and Matter, appeare to be parcell of some following Booke of the *FAERIE QUEENE* under the legend of Constancie'. The precise relationship between these cantos and the main body of the poem has been a subject of dispute ever since their first appearance. The fragmentary nature of the material, together with the theme of the verses (not simply constancy, but a dispute between mutability or 'change' and nature) might, it has often been thought, provide a key to the interpretation of Spenser's complete project, *The Faerie Queene*. Whatever the theological or artistic nature of these final cantos, in reading them after the main body of the poem many modern readers have concluded that they are evidence for the resistance of Spenser's text to any form of 'closure'.

N

Nashe, Thomas (1567–1601)

Pamphleteer, poet and playwright. He spent six years at St John's College, Cambridge, and is numbered among the ▷ University Wits who made the decade 1590–1600 an unusually lively period in literature. Two features of this liveliness were ▷ satire and prose romance (sometimes misleadingly called ▷ 'the Elizabethan novel'). Nashe contributed to both: his best-known work, ▷ *The Unfortunate Traveller, or the Life of Jack Wilton* (1594), is one of the outstanding romances of the decade, and it includes some of his best satire, often in the form of a ▷ parody of some of the contemporary styles of fine writing. Most of the rest of his satire was also in prose. *Pierce Penniless, His Supplication to the Devil* (1592) is a satire in the tradition of the allegorical ▷ morality plays, an attack on the qualities that made for success in the London of his day, and a denunciation of them as new versions of the ▷ Seven Deadly Sins; the method looks forward to ▷ Ben Jonson's comedy of humours (▷ Humours, Comedy of). His last work, *Lenten Stuff* (1599), is a comic extravaganza on Yarmouth, a fishing town, and the red herring. Other prose work includes his early ▷ pamphlets attacking the ▷ Puritan side in the ▷ Marprelate controversy amd vigorous disagreement with ▷ Gabriel Harvey on literary and moral questions between 1593 and 1596. His *Christ's Tears over Jerusalem* (1593) records his repentance for religious doubts.

Nashe escaped being sent to prison in 1597 for an attack on abuses in his play *The Isle of Dogs*, which has been lost. His co-author Jonson and the other actors were imprisoned – Nashe fled. The only play of his sole authorship which survives is *Summer's Last Will and Testament* (1592). This defends the traditional festivities of the countryside against Puritan condemnation of them, and at the same time attacks the useless extravagance of courtiers. It includes some very fine lyrics especially *In Plague Time* and *Autumn*.

Nashe is chiefly known as a prose-writer; his prose is notable for the abundance of its energy and its carnivalesque spirit, which compensate for the confusion of its organization. His gift for parody and the rapidity and vividness of his expression show that the greater coherence and lucidity which English prose was to achieve in the 17th century was not all gain. The freedom and zest of his comic writing owe something to earlier ▷ Renaissance writers – the Italian poet and comedian ▷ Pietro Aretino and the great French satirist ▷ François Rabelais.

However, recent criticism has suggested that there is a clear ideological centre to Nashe's works, and this revival of interest must be set alongside the idea of his writing being incoherent and uncontrolled.
Bib: McKerrow, R. B. (rev.), *The Works of Thomas Nashe* (5 vols); Hibbard, G. R., *Nashe: A Critical Introduction*; Hutson, L., *Thomas Nashe in Context*; Nicholl, C., *A Cup of News*.

Nationalism

The emotion or the doctrine according to which human egotism and its passions are expanded so as to become identical with the nation state. As a widespread phenomenon it is usually dated from the American War of Independence (1775–83) and from the French Revolution and the wars that followed it. However, an intense national self-consciousness existed among the older European nations before, though without the fanaticism which has been characteristic of it since 1790. Thus strong national feeling arose in England and France in consequence of the Hundred Years' War in the 15th century; it arose again in the 16th and 17th centuries under the English queen ▷ Elizabeth I and the French king Louis XIV respectively. Possibly these earlier emotions should be distinguished as patriotism, but the distinction is vague, especially in plays such as ▷ Shakespeare's ▷ *Henry V*.

Natural Law

According to theologians (*eg* ▷ Richard Hooker), that part of the Divine Will that manifests itself in the order of the material world, distinguishable from but of a piece with human and divine law. Modern scientists define it as the principles of uniformity discernible in the behaviour of phenomena, making such behaviour predictable. For the 18th century, the existence of Natural Law was important as the basis for ▷ Natural Religion.

Natural Religion

A belief first taught by ▷ Lord Herbert of Cherbury; according to him, belief in God and right conduct are planted in human instincts. This Christian doctrine was the basis for deistic thought (▷ Deism) in the later 17th and 18th centuries, and contributed to the growth of religious toleration, though also to passivity of religious feeling and hence to indifference. Herbert's aim was to resolve the doubts arising out of the religious conflicts of his time – see *eg* ▷ Donne's *Third Satire*.

Nature

The word is used throughout English literature with meanings that vary constantly according to period or to mode of expression, eg philosophic, religious or personal. This note is intended to guide the student by showing some of the basic approaches to the idea.

1 *Creation and the Fall*. Fundamental to all conceptions of Nature is traditional Christian doctrine. This influences English writers even when they are using a more or less agnostic or atheistic approach. The doctrine is that Nature is God's creation, but by the fall of man, symbolized by the story of Adam's disobedience in the book of *Genesis*, earthly nature is self-willed and destructive, though not to the extent that the Divine Will and Order is obliterated in it.

2 *All-embracing Nature*. Nature is sometimes seen as the whole of reality so far as earthly experience goes. For instance, the opening 18 lines of ▷ Chaucer's *Prologue to* ▷ *The Canterbury Tales* show Nature as the great reviver of life.

3 *Nature and God*. In line with traditional Christian doctrine, ▷ Natural Law is linked to Human Law and Divine Law as a manifestation of the Divine Will in such works as ▷ Hooker's *Laws of Ecclesiastical Polity* (1597). However, from the beginning of the 17th century, there was a new interest in the function of human reason as an instrument for the acquisition of knowledge independently of religious feeling. Men like ▷ Ralegh (*History of the World*, 1614) and ▷ Bacon (▷ *The Advancement of Learning*) began to ask what, given that God was the Primary Cause of Nature, were the Secondary, or Immediate Causes of natural phenomena.

4 *Nature as Moral Paradox*. The Christian conception of Nature as both God-created and spoilt by the fall of man led at various times to the problem that Nature is both good and evil. According to the medieval conception, maintained until the middle of the 17th century, human society was itself the outcome of the Divine Natural Order, so that it was by Natural Law that children should honour their parents, subjects their sovereigns, etc. On the other hand, the natural passions of men and beasts, unrestrained by reason, were the source of rapacity and ruin. Thus ▷ Shakespeare's ▷ King Lear begins by relying on the former conception of Nature, but is exposed to the reality of the latter.

5 *Nature for Man's Use*. Implicit in Christian doctrine was the belief that Nature was created *for* man; that it was his birthright to exploit and use it. This begins with the conception of Nature as the Great Mother, originating in pre-Christian times but pervasive in medieval verse and later, eg in much Elizabethan ▷ pastoral poetry. It took a more active significance when the 17th- and 18th-century 'natural philosophers' from ▷ Bacon onwards sought methods by which man could increase his power over Nature.

6 *Nature and Art*. 'Art' in earlier contexts often includes technology, eg in Polixenes' remarks on cultivation to Perdita in ▷ *The Winter's Tale* IV. iii; here art is seen as itself a product of nature. But art was often set against nature in Shakespeare's time and afterwards, eg in ▷ Sidney's ▷ *Apology for Poetry*: 'Her [*ie* Nature's] world is brazen; the Poets only deliver a golden'; here the function of imaginative art seems to be the opposite of the 18th-century poets' and novelists' conception of 'truth to nature', but Sidney meant that poetry should improve on Nature, not falsify it; the creation must be ideal but consistent with Nature.

7 *Nature opposed to Court and City*. 'Art', however, was not necessarily an improvement. The city and the court, in Shakespeare's time, were the centres of new financial forces generating intrigue and 'unnatural' (*ie* inhuman) behaviour. There was also a kind of pastoral made by idealizing the life of the great country houses, eg ▷ Ben Jonson's *Penshurst* and ▷ Aemilia Lanyer's *Salve Deus Rex Judaeorum*.

Neo-classicism

This term can be understood for the purposes of English literary culture as that which refers to the ▷ Renaissance of classical culture and its influence on English literature down to the end of the 18th century. This influence operated mainly by the cultivation of Latin culture, and was mediated first by Italy and later by France. In the 16th century England developed a fine school of classical scholars, of whom the best known was ▷ Thomas More. Through travellers and scholars such as ▷ Sir Thomas Wyatt and Henry Howard, ▷ Earl of Surrey, poetry and prose received strong influences from Italian writers such as ▷ Petrarch and French ones such as ▷ Ronsard who already belonged to the classical revival. A critic like ▷ Sidney showed the influence of Italian critics who in their turn were developing 'rules' out of classical writers for dramatic construction, etc. All these influences matured in the last decade of the 16th century but their effect was uneven; the greatest of the rising dramatists, ▷ Shakespeare, ignored the neo-classical rules for dramatic construction, whereas ▷ Ben Jonson, his chief rival in the theatre by 1600, was deeply affected by classical principles and classical culture generally. ▷ Pastoral poems, deriving from Italian influences and more directly from Virgil, were numerous from ▷ Spenser's ▷ *The Shepherd's Calendar* (1579) onwards, and in the 1590s there was a widespread production of ▷ sonnets under the influence of Petrarch. Much of the classical influence was on the level of ornament, however, as it was in English architecture in the same period. Jonson was outstanding in his absorption of classical influence to a deep level, and it was deeper in his lyrical work than in his drama. He is, in fact, an important link with the next phase of English neo-classicism – that which began in 1660 and lasted throughout the 18th century.

Neo-Platonism
▷ Platonism.

New Atlantis, The (1626)
A philosophical tale by ▷ Francis Bacon, in the tradition of ▷ Sir Thomas More's ▷ *Utopia* (1615). It was left unfinished at Bacon's death, and published in 1626. The title is an allusion to the mythical island described by ▷ Plato in his dialogue *Timaeus*. Bacon's island is called Bensalem (*ie* an analogous place to Salem or Jerusalem, the holy city) and its chief glory is its university, 'Solomon's House'. Unlike the English universities of Bacon's day, this is devoted to scientific research – 'the knowledge of causes, and secret motions of things; and the enlarging of the bounds of human empire, to the effecting of all things possible'. The boundless optimism of this Baconian ideal was to be reflected in the work of 17th-century science in general.

New Comedy
Unlike ▷ Aristophanes's Old Comedy, New Comedy as extant in the writings of ▷ Menander, ▷ Plautus and ▷ Terence does not address specific and topical issues so much as focus on general moral and imaginative motifs. Its formulae consist of stock characters such as the young rake, the wily servant (*servus dolosus*), the courtesan, the braggart soldier (*miles gloriosus*) and the irascible old man (*senex*). The plays are populated by lost children and siblings. The genre of New Comedy proved highly influential for English literature. It could more readily accommodate the

▷ neo-classical ▷ Horatian moral stance that distinguishes much Elizabethan drama, and its generalized approach proved politically safe in a theatre where every play needed a licence for performance from the Lord Chamberlain's office.

New Criticism
This term is given to a movement which developed in the late 1940s in the U.S.A., and which dedicated itself to opposing the kind of criticism that is associated with Romanticism and 19th-century realism. The 'practical criticism' of ▷ I. A. Richards was an influential stimulus to this movement, in which emphasis was placed upon the self-contained nature of the literary text. In the work of 'new' critics such as Cleanth Brooks, W. K. Wimsatt, John Crowe Ransom, Allen Tate and R. P. Blackmur, concern with the 'intention' of the writer was replaced by close reading of particular texts, and depended upon the assumption that any literary work was self-contained. New Criticism placed a particular emphasis upon poetry, and asserted that the individual poem 'must not mean but be'.

New Historicism
A theoretical movement which developed in America in the 1980s and which has had an enormous influence on ▷ Renaissance studies, especially in the field of ▷ Shakespeare criticism. It developed its identity partly against the historical approaches of ▷ New Criticism and the unselfconscious historicism of earlier critics. New historicism draws upon ▷ Marxist criticism in its emphasis upon political and social context and rejection of individual aspiration and universalism, but at the same time it insists that historical context can never be recovered objectively. It is essential to understand that new historicists do not assume that literature reflects reality and that these 'reflections' enable the reader to recover without distortion the past presented in the texts. Rather, they look for an interplay between text and society, which can never be presented neutrally. Moreover, the reader must be aware of his or her *own* historical context: we read texts from the perspective of our own age and can never perfectly recreate history. For example, while ▷ race is a contentious issue for Renaissance dramatists, 20th-century political sensibilities make us aware of different issues when watching plays such as ▷ *The Merchant of Venice* and ▷ *Titus Andronicus*. The Marxist approach of the new historicists has also been influenced by

▷ post-structuralism, and by the blending of these two theories in the works of ▷ Althusser and ▷ Foucault.

▷ Cultural materialism; Materialism; Poetics.
Bib: Greenblatt, S., *Renaissance Self-fashioning*; Howard, J. E. and O'Connor, M. F., *Shakespeare Reproduced*; Tennenhouse, L., *Power on Display*; Veeser, H. A., *The New Historicism*; Dutton, R. and Wilson, R. (eds.), *The New Historicism and Renaissance Drama*.

New Inn, The (1629)
A late play by ▷ Ben Jonson which attempts to work native romance motifs into the fabric of a contemporary ▷ citizen comedy. More than any Jonson play, *The New Inn* has been the particular discovery of the 1970s, when several leading Jonson scholars championed its claim to being a masterpiece of mixed genre and a Jonsonian tribute to ▷ Shakespeare.

New Learning, The
Study of the Bible and the Greek classics in the original languages instead of through Latin versions (▷ Greek literature; classical education). This study in the 15th–16th centuries was an important influence in the ▷ Renaissance and the ▷ Reformation.

New Model Army, The
Formed by Parliament in 1645 towards the end of the ▷ Civil War between itself and ▷ King Charles I. The war had so far been indecisive owing to the amateurish soldiering on both sides. Parliament now ensured that its own army should be highly professional. The result was the decisive victory of Naseby in June 1645. The commander was Sir Thomas Fairfax, but its most gifted general was ▷ Oliver Cromwell, who between 1646 and 1660 made the English army one of the most formidable in Europe. Cromwell's special contribution was his highly trained force of cavalry, the Ironsides.

New Science
The term 'New Science' or 'New Philosophy' is something of a catch-all phrase, but one which is usually used to suggest the revolution in scientific understanding in Europe generally in the 16th and 17th centuries. On the continent, the work of ▷ Galileo in the field of astronomy and Andreas Vesalius (1514–64) in the area of human anatomy signalled a reassessment of the study of the natural world. In England the influence of ▷ Francis Bacon in the area of scientific methodology was to

be of considerable importance. However, English science in the 16th century lagged behind the work that was taking place on the continent. But, with the publication of William Harvey's discovery of the circulation of the blood (1628), an age of remarkable scientific innovation began in the British Isles.

The influence of the 'New Science' of the age on literature is a much-debated topic. Certainly poets such as ▷ John Donne and ▷ Henry Vaughan were aware of the changes taking place in the ordering and understanding of the natural world, and this awareness is reflected in their writings. Others, such as ▷ Abraham Cowley, were enthusiastic in promulgating ideas and experimental attitudes associated with new scientific methodology. ▷ Thomas Traherne, on the other hand, found himself in the paradoxical situation of being fascinated with the products of scientific enquiry while being deeply suspicious of the anti-fideistic tendency of much of the work that was undertaken.
Bib: Debus, A. G., *Man and Nature in the Renaissance*.

Newspapers
Periodicals resembling newspapers began in a small way in the reign of ▷ James I; in the decades of the ▷ Civil War and the ▷ Interregnum they increased in number owing to the need of both sides to engage in propaganda. From 1695 press ▷ censorship was abandoned; newspapers and weekly periodicals began to flourish.

New Way to Pay Old Debts, A (1625)
The best-known comedy by ▷ Philip Massinger. The main character is Sir Giles Overreach, a man of powerful energy and unlimited rapacity, who has no scruples in his schemes to increase his own wealth and social greatness. He is, however, outwitted by those very social superiors, Lord Lovell and Lady Allworth, whom he attempts to flatter and use; they take the side of the young people whom he tries to victimize, his nephew Wellborn and his daughter Margaret. Overreach thus 'overreaches' himself, in the manner of ▷ Ben Jonson's characters, and he is in fact the last vigorous representative of the comedy of ▷ humours tradition. The weakness of the play is that Overreach's opponents are colourless characters, so that the play is artistically unbalanced in Overreach's favour. Massinger's use of ▷ blank verse is extremely flexible to the point sometimes of insipidity, although in the best passages it regains much of the concentrated force of Jonson himself.

Overreach is based on a contemporary profiteer, Sir Giles Mompesson.

Nine Worthies

The subject of literary, artistic and dramatic representation from the later medieval period onwards, the so-called 'Nine Worthies' is a group representing the best knights of all time, made up of three figures each from the periods of pagan, Old Testament and Christian history. Composition of the list, especially the Christian representatives, may vary somewhat but most of the versions found in England include Hector, ▷ Alexander, ▷ Julius Caesar, Joshua, David, Judas Maccabeus, ▷ King Arthur, ▷ Charlemagne, Godfrey of Bouillon. The 'Nine Worthies' theme promotes the notion of chivalry as a transhistorical phenomenon and is part of the developing mythology of knighthood, in evidence throughout the medieval period (and after). The list of Nine Worthies is first recorded in an Old French Alexander narrative of the early 14th century, and a dramatized pageant of the 'Nine Worthies' is included in ▷ Shakespeare's ▷ *Love's Labour's Lost*.

North, Sir Thomas (?1535–?1601)

▷ Translator. He is especially known as the translator of ▷ Plutarch's *Lives* of the ancient Greek and Roman heroes. The translation was from the French of Amyot, and was published in 1579. It was not close, but very clear and vigorous, and constituted one of the masterpieces of English prose. It was widely read in ▷ Shakespeare's day, and was used by Shakespeare himself as the basis for his plays ▷ *Julius Caesar*, ▷ *Antony and Cleopatra* and ▷ *Coriolanus*. Other translations by North were the *Dial of Princes* (from *Reloj de Principes* by Guevara) published in 1557, which set the fashion for ornate writing culminating in ▷ Lyly's ▷ *Euphues*; and *The Moral Philosophy of Doni* (1570), an Italian collection of eastern fables.
Bib: Cowley, C. H., *The First English Translators of the Classics*.

Norton, Sir Thomas (1532–84)

Poet and dramatist. A staunchly ▷ Protestant barrister, Norton participated in the questioning of ▷ Catholics during ▷ Elizabeth I's reign, as well as translating ▷ Calvin's *Institutes* (1561). He is best known to literature students, however, for his collaboration with ▷ Thomas Sackville in the composition of ▷ *Gorboduc* (1561), which is assumed to be the first 'English' ▷ tragedy. Written in ▷ blank verse, it was enormously influential. Norton's poetry was included in ▷ *Tottel's Miscellany*.

Novum Organum (1620)

A philosophical treatise by Francis Bacon, the *Novum Organum* (*New Instrument*) was written in Latin and published in the ▷ *Instauratio Magna* (1620) in an incomplete form. His aim was to describe a method of gaining power over nature through a complete and correctly founded system of knowledge. Knowledge must be acquired by experience and experiment, *ie* inductively. The obstacles to true knowledge are false assumptions, which Bacon calls 'Idols'. These are of four kinds: the Idols of the Tribe are common human weaknesses such as allowing the emotions to interfere with the reason; the Idols of the Cave are individual weaknesses arising from individual upbringing; Idols of the Market-place arise from erroneous uses of language, such as using names for non-existent things, or for concepts which have been inadequately defined; Idols of the Theatre are caused by false philosophical principles and by incorrect reasoning. The object of speculative science must be to discover the true 'forms' of things, beginning with the forms of 'simple natures', *ie* the true manifestations of the most elemental phenomena such as heat and light. By inductive experiment certain axioms will be made of increasing generality and abstractness. Thus Bacon sought a method of recognizing what he called 'an alphabet of nature' so that a reliable language could be built up from it. The method of discovery proved too slow to be scientifically useful in the coming centuries, but his approach was a development from the too exclusively deductive methods of medieval thought towards the modern scientific combination of deduction and experiment.

No Wit, No Help Like a Woman (1613)

A high-spirited comedy by ▷ Thomas Middleton which evolves on a complex double-plot level and reworks material from ▷ Ben Jonson's ▷ *Epicoene* and ▷ Shakespeare's ▷ *Twelfth Night*. The play's heroine, Kate Low-water, a disguised married woman intent on recovering her lost fortune, is one of the most charismatic female characters in the drama of the period. The extent to which the play's idiom of mercenary ▷ citizen comedy becomes submerged in Shakespearean romance depends largely on Kate's magnetic personality.

Nut-Brown Maid, The

A 15th-century anonymous poem, first printed
in 1502. It is in 30 12-line stanzas, spoken
by a young man and woman alternately, with
the respective refrains 'Alone a banished
man' and 'I love but you alone', and
their debate focuses on the faithfulness
of women. Although the woman believes
her lover to be an outlaw, she remains
true.

O

Oberon

In Germanic myth, king of the elves, or fairies. A French 13th-century romance, *Huon of Bordeaux*, in which he occurs, was translated into English in 1534. From this ▷ Robert Greene introduced him into his romantic play ▷ *James IV* (1594), and ▷ Shakespeare into his comedy ▷ *A Midsummer Night's Dream*. He was used thereafter in a number of works, including a ▷ masque by ▷ Ben Jonson (in which ▷ Prince Henry is identified with Oberon) and the poem *Nymphidia* by ▷ Michael Drayton.
▷ Fairies.

Objective correlative

An expression first used by the critic and poet T. S. Eliot (1888–1965) in his essay on ▷ *Hamlet* (1919). Eliot describes ▷ Shakespeare's play as an artistic failure because it 'is full of some stuff that the writer could not drag to life, contemplate, or manipulate into art'. He goes on: 'The only way of expressing emotion in the form of art is by finding an "objective correlative"; in other words, a set of objects, a situation, a chain of events which shall be the formula of that *particular* emotion; such that when the external facts . . . are given, the emotion is immediately evoked.' He then instances the sleep-walking scene in ▷ *Macbeth* as a successful 'objective correlative', and adds: 'The artistic "inevitability" lies in this complete adequacy of the external [*ie* the event on the stage is witnessed by the audience] to the emotion; and this is precisely what is deficient in *Hamlet*.'
Eliot's adverse judgement of *Hamlet* has not been widely accepted, but the term 'objective correlative' has passed into critical currency.

Ode

The Pindaric Ode is modelled on the works of Pindar, a Greek poet of the 5th century BC, best known for his odes celebrating the victors at the Olympic games. These were accompanied by music and dance, and were disposed in a threefold pattern corresponding to the movements of the Greek dramatic chorus (*strophe, antistrophe, epode*). From the 17th century onwards English poets took Pindar as a model for lyric and declamatory verse expressive of highly wrought emotion. ▷ Jonson's 'Cary/Morrison Ode' is the first successful Pindaric ode in English. ▷ Abraham Cowley established the 'irregular ode', which sanctions unpredictable variations in line-length, rhyme and metre within each stanza.

The Roman poet ▷ Horace imitated Pindar, but his odes employ unvarying stanza forms. The 'regular' Horatian ode was imitated by ▷ Andrew Marvell in his *Horatian Ode upon Cromwell's Return from Ireland*.

Odysseus

The Greek hero and king of Ithaca in the *Odyssey*, an epic by ▷ Homer. In Latin he was known as Ulixes, which has been converted into Ulysses. He also occurs in Homer's ▷ *Iliad*, where he is famous among the Greek leaders for his wise advice. In the dramas of ▷ Sophocles and ▷ Euripides his wisdom shows as mere cunning, but ▷ Shakespeare (in ▷ *Troilus and Cressida*) shows him as the sane politician, making the best of a bad world.

Oedipus complex

In ▷ Freudian psychoanalysis ▷ Sophocles' story of Oedipus, who killed his father and married his mother, is used as a model of the way in which human desires and feelings are structured during the passage from infancy to adulthood. The triangular relationship modelled on Sophocles' text can be used to explain relationships within the family, which is the model of socialization available to the child. In order for successful socialization to occur, the child must emerge from the position of desiring an incestuous relationship with individual parents – for which in the case of the male, the penalty would be castration – and to transfer the affections for the mother onto another. The most commonly cited instance of this in Renaissance literature is ▷ Hamlet's tortuous relationship with his mother. The Oedipus complex, and the model of triangulated desire upon which it is built, must be overcome in order for individual gendered human subjects to take their place in a world of which they are not the centre. This process of 'decentring' is explained by ▷ Jacques Lacan as an acceptance of the repression of desire imposed upon the subject by the father, an acceptance of a 'symbolic castration'. This raises a number of difficulties in the case of the gendered *female* subject who can never break free of the castration complex imposed upon her by a phallocentric ▷ symbolic order. This, for example, could be used to explain ▷ Beatrice's tragic fate in ▷ *The Changeling*. Basically the Oedipus complex is used to account for a particular hierarchy of relationships within the family unit. It is a process through which the male is expected to pass in order to reach mature adulthood, and it seeks to offer an explanation of the ways in which authority operates as a system of constraints and laws.

Oldcastle, Sir John (1378–1417)

Sir John Oldcastle became Lord Cobham and died a martyr for Wycliffite (▷ Wycliffe, John) heresy, which rejected transubstantiation. There is cogent evidence to suggest that ▷ Falstaff in ▷ *Henry IV* was originally called Oldcastle, notwithstanding ▷ Shakespeare's explicit disclaimer of this in the 'Epilogue' to *Henry IV, Part II*. The complete works of Shakespeare edited by Gary Taylor and Stanley Wells retains (uniquely) Oldcastle for Falstaff in *Henry IV, Part I*, on the basis that the name was changed for reasons of political accommodation, not for aesthetic ones.

Old Comedy

▷ Aristophanes.

Open field system

That system of land use especially typical of medieval English agriculture. Land under cultivation was divided into strips, and distributed among the peasants of the village or manor. The strips were not surrounded by hedges or fences, so that good farmers suffered from the effects of the bad farming of their immediate neighbours. The system began to be replaced in the 16th century, when landowners preferred sheep-farming.

Orlando Furioso (1532)

A romance epic by the Italian poet ▷ Ludovico Ariosto. It is in the tradition of Italian developments of the legends centring on the French hero Roland, who in the reign of ▷ Charlemagne (768–814) repelled the Muslim invasion of Europe. Ariosto invents fantastic episodes and complicated romantic intrigues and adventures. Orlando goes mad because his lady, Angelica, marries a Moorish youth, but he is cured in time to defeat Agramante, king of Africa, who has been besieging Paris. Many linked tales and episodes accompany this central theme, as is usual in the 16th-century romantic ▷ epic, of which Ariosto is the master and ▷ Edmund Spenser (▷ *The Faerie Queene*) one of his chief emulators.

Othello (1604)

A ▷ tragedy by ▷ Shakespeare, first acted in 1604. It was based on an Italian tale in *Hecatommithi* by Giraldi Cinthio (1565; translated into French 1584).

The full title of the play is *Othello, the Moor of Venice*: the extended title emphasizes Othello's position as commander of Venetian forces against the Turks and his ▷ race, both clues to the understanding of his tragedy. Othello is highly valued by the Venetians for his military prowess, but he is not a member of Venetian society; he is first and last a soldier, a member of a military community, trusting and trusted by his brother officers. Consequently it is as astonishing to him when Desdemona, a conventional Venetian aristocratic girl, leaves her home to marry him, as it is outrageous to her indignant father, Brabantio. Venice urgently needs Othello to defend Cyprus against the Turks, so Brabantio is forced to accept the match; however he warns Othello that a girl who has behaved so unpredictably once may prove as unreliable a wife as she has been a daughter. Othello is in rapture; his bliss is the greater for its incredibility, so that he naïvely imagines himself transported into a heaven on earth. But his junior officer, Iago, has motives of resentment against him; the most concrete of these is that the Florentine, Cassio, has been promoted over his head. Moreover, he is himself a cynic who has a low opinion of human nature and of the scope for genuine happiness. Partly as a double revenge against Othello and Cassio, partly as a cynical game the object of which is to bring Othello down to his own level of reality, he contrives first to disgrace Cassio temporarily, and then to insinuate into Othello's mind the suspicion, mounting by degrees to certainty, that Cassio and Desdemona are conducting a secret love affair. In Othello's mind the circumstances make this affair more than plausible: he has the habit of trusting Iago as his confidential officer; Desdemona has come to him out of a foreign society; Cassio is the sort of man who would have been considered an eligible husband for her. Until their marriage, Othello had had a single-minded dedication to his military vocation. The marriage has enriched this dedication, since it was Desdemona's admiration for him as a soldier that attracted her to him, but he now finds that his jealousy has divided his single-mindedness and is destroying his integrity. Accordingly he murders her, in the belief that heavenly justice is on his side. Desdemona, however, has been presented as one of the most innocent of all Shakespeare's heroines, for whom adultery is unimaginable, and her innocent goodness has won the heart of her lady companion, Emilia, who is Iago's wife. Emilia, who has been ignorant of Iago's plot but has unintentionally assisted him in it, realizes his guilt and publicly exposes him; Othello, restored to his dignity, makes a final speech of self-assessment, and kills himself.

Othello follows ▷ Hamlet in the sequence of Shakespeare's tragedies and is another masterpiece in the tradition of ▷ revenge tragedy. It is psychologically much more lucid, though perhaps not a more sophisticated play, than Hamlet, and is one of the most eloquent of Shakespeare's dramas.

Opera in England
Opera, in the sense of a staged drama in which the words and music are of equal importance, began in Italy at the end of the 16th century. It was an integral part of the ▷ Renaissance, arising out of the attempt to revive what were thought to be the performance practices of Greek drama. Subjects, therefore, were tragedies drawn from classical mythology and the words were set to a declamatory style of singing known as recitative. The first English opera was The Siege of Rhodes, with a libretto by ▷ William D'Avenant and music (now lost) by Matthew Locke and others. It was first produced in 1642, at a time when the ▷ Puritans had closed the theatres, and seems to have been an attempt to circumvent the ban on plays. After the theatres reopened in 1660, many plays were given with musical interludes, ▷ Shakespeare being adapted for this purpose, for example, by D'Avenant.

Orgoglio
A character representing Arrogance in ▷ Edmund Spenser's ▷ Faerie Queene. He occurs in Book I. cantos vii and viii; he captures the ▷ Red Cross Knight and is slain by Prince Arthur (▷ Arthur, King). The name derives from the Italian for pride.

Oriana
A name sometimes used for ▷ Elizabeth I by Elizabethan poets. It comes from the 15th-century Spanish-Portuguese romance Amadis de Gaula, in which Oriana is a British princess beloved by the hero, Amadis.
▷ Spanish influence on English literature.

Orlando
The Italian form of the name Roland, hero of the Old French Chanson de Roland (Song of Roland). From the Italian 16th-century romantic epics by ▷ Ariosto, the name passed into English romance narratives, being used, for example, for the hero of ▷ Shakespeare's romantic drama ▷ As You Like It.

Ottava rima
An Italian stanza of eight lines rhyming a b a b a b c c. It was used by ▷ Boccaccio in the 14th century. Pulci in the 15th century used it for the mock-heroic (▷ Heroic, Mock), ironic style with which the stanza is chiefly associated in English.

Overbury, Sir Thomas (1581–1613)
Essayist and poet; as a writer he is chiefly remembered as the author of one of the most widely read collections of 'Theophrastian' character sketches (▷ Characters, Theophrastian), published in 1614. ▷ John Webster, ▷ Thomas Dekker, ▷ John Donne, ▷ Cecily Bulstrode, ▷ Lady Frances Southwell and others made additions to subsequent issues of the collection between 1614 and 1622.

Overbury was also the victim of one of the most sensational murders in English history. He tried to oppose a love intrigue between ▷ James I's royal favourite, Thomas Carr, Earl of Somerset, and the young Countess of Essex. The lovers conspired to have Overbury poisoned; the crime came to light, and the prosecution was conducted by ▷ Francis Bacon. Carr and the Countess were convicted and disgraced, but their agents who actually administered the poison were hanged.

Ovid (Publius Ovidius Naso) (43BC–AD 17)
Roman poet, and the last of the greatest period of Latin poetry, the Augustan Age. He wrote for the sophisticated and elegant society of the capital of the Empire, but the immorality of his Ars Amatoria ('Art of Love') offended the Emperor ▷ Augustus who (for this and some other more mysterious offence) exiled him to the Black Sea about AD 9. The works by which Ovid is principally known are: the Amores, love poems in what is called the 'elegiac' couplet; the Ars Amatoria; the Remedia Amoris, in which he tries to redeem himself for the offence he caused by the Ars Amatoria; the Heroides, in which he makes the heroines of myth give tongue to their misfortunes; the ▷ Metamorphoses, a collection of tales about miraculous transformations of shape; the Fasti, a poetic account of the Roman calendar; and the Tristia, verse epistles lamenting his exile.

Ovid was one of the most read and influential poets in later centuries; in England this is especially true from the 16th to 18th centuries. His most popular work was the Metamorphoses; these were repeatedly imitated and translated, memorably by ▷ Golding in the 16th century and by Sandys in the 17th.

In 1598 ▷ Shakespeare was called 'the English Ovid' because the source of his ▷ *Venus and Adonis* was the *Metamorphoses*, whilst that of *The Rape of Lucrece* was the *Fasti*; moreover the quality of these two poems was felt to be Ovidian. ▷ Marlowe translated Ovid's love elegies, and the freedom and vigour of his kind of love poem influenced ▷ Donne in his elegies. As early as the 14th century ▷ Chaucer got the tales in his *Legend of Good Women* from the *Heroides*, and these poems set a tradition in 'Heroic Epistles' which began with ▷ Drayton in the early 17th century and culminated in

Alexander Pope's (1688–1744) *Eloisa to Abelard*. Ovid's influence is traceable repeatedly in the work of ▷ Spenser and touched ▷ Milton. Thus he may be said to have affected, either in subject matter or in style, almost all the major poets from Chaucer to Pope, and his influence was equally extensive among lesser figures. The influence was not always deep, however, and it can be ascribed partly to his being the liveliest and most beguiling of the Roman poets regarded as the basis of a cultured understanding of literature.

▷ Elegy; Latin literature.

P

Pageant

The word drives from the name of a kind of stage used in medieval mystery plays that moved in procession to prearranged positions in the town and exhibited scenes from the Bible dramatizing the fall of man and his redemption by Christ. In modern England, a pageant is a display, commonly in the form of a procession, celebrating a historical or legendary event, usually with patriotic significance. This sense of the word 'pageant' has a clear relationship with the mystery plays, and illustrates a particular dramatic viewpoint. The mysteries were dramatic inasmuch as they represented conflicts between good and evil, but the stories and their outcome were fully known to the audience, so that there was small place for the unexpected. The modern pageant is an undramatic spectacle, and such pageants existed in the 16th century, symbolizing non-biblical legends of patriotic significance like the story of St George and the Dragon. Thus the traditions of the pageant are twofold: in one sense it is purely spectacle, but in another it may be a spectacle combined with the narrative of a conflict, which is dramatic only because the conflict is seen as symbolic of human experience. This second sense of the pageant tradition is important for understanding ▷ Elizabethan ▷ history plays, especially those of ▷ Shakespeare. Thus, in ▷ *Henry IV, Part I* the modern audience is inclined to see the drama as a conflict for the identity of Prince Hal, who on the one hand is faced with the temptations of self-indulgence through ▷ Falstaff, and on the other with the task of winning 'honour' from ▷ Hotspur. Yet the audience is misled by this approach, since in I. ii Prince Hal declares that he is in no danger of yielding to Falstaff, and his acquisition of honour is also foreknown through the historical fact of the battle of Agincourt; Hal is thus not the hero of an inner moral and an outer physical conflict, at least in the sense that there is the smallest uncertainty in the audience's mind about the outcome. On the other hand, Falstaff and Hotspur – the self-indulgent favourite and the self-centred politician – are dangers to which any nation is everlastingly exposed. Thus the dramatic interest of the play is not Hal but the nation, and the play is essentially the re-enactment of a conflict to which the nation is perpetually exposed – a dramatic pageant in the mystery and ▷ morality tradition.

Palace of Pleasure, The

An anthology of tales translated from the Italian and Latin, compiled by William Painter (?1540–94) and published 1566–7. Writers include Bandello, ▷ Boccaccio, Herodotus and Livy. It was used as a source book for plots by ▷ Elizabethan dramatists, including ▷ Shakespeare who drew on it, at least to some extent, for ▷ *All's Well that Ends Well*, and perhaps some other plays.

Palladio, Andrea (1508–80)

Italian architect. Palladio's villas, public buildings and churches – built between 1540 and 1580, and to be found in Venice, Vicenza and the countryside around these two important Italian ▷ Renaissance cities – were to have a lasting effect on English and American architectural styles. The first great English classical architect ▷ Inigo Jones was strongly influenced by Palladian ideals of design. These ideals – usually manifested in symmetrical fronts and applied half-columns topped by a pediment – were themselves derived from Palladio's intense study of architectural styles to be found in the surviving antiquities of ancient Rome. Indeed, Palladio was himself the author of one of the earliest guidebooks to the city's remains when he published his *Le Antichita di Roma* in 1554. This work, together with his *Quattro Libri dell' Architettura* (1570), served to publicize the classical forms of architecture that came to dominate design in the 17th and 18th centuries.

The 'Palladian' style expresses key Renaissance aesthetic ideas. Those ideas, which encompass proportion, harmony and balance, were to become of great importance during the 18th century when Palladio's designs, and studies of his works, were much in vogue.

Bib: Wittkower, R., *Architectural Principles in the Age of Humanism*; Ackerman, J. S., *Palladio*.

Pamphlet

Any short treatise published separately, usually without hard covers. It is usually polemical, *ie* written to defend or attack some body of ideas, especially religious or political ones. In the 16th century and especially towards the end of the reign of ▷ Elizabeth I pamphleteering became a widespread literary industry, the beginning of journalism. ▷ Thomas Nashe and ▷ Thomas Dekker were amongst the most famous pamphleteers, and the ▷ Marprelate controversy was the most famous of the 'pamphlet wars'. In the

17th century ▷ Milton was the most famous writer of pamphlets, and ▷ *Areopagitica* is his masterpiece.

Pandosto, The Triumph of Time (1588)
A prose romance by ▷ Robert Greene, used by ▷ Shakespeare as the basis for his late play, ▷ *The Winter's Tale*.

Pantagruel
A comic romance by ▷ François Rabelais, published in its first version in 1532. Pantagruel is the son of ▷ Gargantua.

Pantaloon
A character in old Italian popular comedy. He represented a Venetian, and the name derived from the Venetian saint San Pantaleone. He became a popular figure in international ▷ pantomime, and appears as a stupid old man wearing spectacles, slippers and clumsy trousers or pantaloons, from which comes 'pants'. Pantaloon used also to be a term for any feeble-minded old man, *eg* in ▷ Shakespeare's ▷ *As You Like It*.

Pantheism
A term used to cover a variety of religious and philosophical beliefs which have in common that God is present in Nature and not separable from it in the sense in which a cause is separable from its effect, or a creator from his creation. Pantheism is implicit in doctrines derived from ▷ Plato, *eg* in some of the neo-Platonists of the 16th century, and in some poetry inspired by the natural environment.

Pantomime
Originally, in ancient Rome, a representation by masked actors, using gestures and dance, of religious or warlike episodes. One actor played many parts, male and female, with changes of mask and costume. It was often accompanied by music. It was used for episodes in medieval religious drama, and as the 16th-century Italian ▷ *commedia dell' arte* it became a form of popular drama that spread all over Europe together with a number of traditional characters such as Harlequin and the Clown.
Bib: Bakhtin, M., *Rabelais and his World*.

Paradise Lost (1667)
An ▷ epic poem by ▷ John Milton, first published in ten books in 1667, but reorganized and published in 12 books in a second edition of 1674. The composition of *Paradise Lost* was possibly begun in the mid-1650s, but the idea for an epic based on scriptural sources had, in all probability, occurred to Milton at least as early as 1640, when the four drafts of an outline ▷ tragedy were composed. These drafts, contained in a Trinity College, Cambridge manuscript, indicate that in its original conception, *Paradise Lost* (or, to give the poem its draft title, *Adam Unparadized*) was to have been a sacred drama, rather than an epic. This hint at a dramatic origin, on the lines of classical Greek tragedy, helps to explain the undoubtedly dramatic qualities to be found in the poem – for example the soliloquizing habits of Satan, and the *perepeteias*, or discoveries, where new ▷ ironies in the narrative are allowed to unfold.

The chief source of the poem is the ▷ Bible, but the Bible as glossed and commented upon by the Patristic (early Christian) authorities, and by ▷ Protestant theologians. But also important to Milton's project were the classical writers – ▷ Homer and ▷ Virgil – from whom Milton's conception of 'epic' was principally inherited. ▷ Edmund Spenser's ▷ *The Faerie Queene* was also vital to Milton's handling of language and imagery. To these principle sources can be added the epics of ▷ Ludovico Ariosto and ▷ Torquato Tasso, ▷ Ovid's *Metamorphoses*, the *De rerum natura* of ▷ Lucretius, and the once popular, though now little read, *La Semaine* by ▷ Guillaume de Saluste Du Bartas. Once these sources have been remarked upon, however, the possible progenitors of Milton's poem still remain numberless, since *Paradise Lost* draws upon the whole field of intellectual endeavour open to a classically trained European scholar in the 17th century.

For all that it is a poem rooted in Milton's literary experience, it is also a poem of, and for, its times. The poem's chief theme is rebellion – the rebellion of Satan and his followers against God, and the rebellion of Adam and Eve against divine law. Within this sacred context, Milton sets himself the task of justifying God's creational will to his 17th-century readers. But, in confronting questions such as choice, obedience and forms of government, Milton also raises the issues of freedom, social relationships and the quality and definition of power – whether almighty, satanic or human. We can thus understand the poem as confronting political questions that, in the moment of its composition and eventual publication following the English ▷ Civil War and the Restoration of the monarchy, were of real urgency to both the republican Milton and his readers. This is not to say that, as some of Milton's commentators have claimed, the poem operates as a veiled ▷ allegory of events in mid-17th-century England. But the issues faced by the protagonists in *Paradise Lost* are also issues that were at the heart of contemporary political debate. To entwine matters of theology and political theory was by no means a strange grafting to Milton's contemporaries. Religion and politics were inseparably twinned, and *Paradise Lost* confronts that conjunction at every point.

The history of the poem's critical reception since the date of its publication is itself a commentary on the history of English literary 'taste'. For all that 18th-century writers admired Milton's grand scheme, their admiration was tinged by a certain uneasiness. Both Joseph Addison (1672–1719) and Samuel Johnson (1709–84) felt that Milton's achievement was undoubtedly immense, but that it was also an achievement which could not and should not be replicated. For the poets of the Romantic period – William Blake (1757–1827), Percy Bysshe Shelley (1792–1822), John Keats (1795–1821) and the William Wordsworth (1770–1850) of *The Prelude* – *Paradise Lost* was read as a significant text in the history of the individual's struggle to identify him or herself within the political and social sphere. But rather than understand the poem as a theological epic, they tended to read it as a text of human liberty, with Satan, rather than God, as the focus of the poem's meaning. In the 20th century, following the re-evaluation in poetic taste prompted by W. B. Yeats (1865–1939), T. S. Eliot (1888–1965) and ▷ F. R. Leavis, *Paradise Lost* was seen, once more, as a masterpiece of questionable stature. Was it, perhaps, removed from what Eliot and Leavis in particular cared to identify as the 'English tradition'? The debate initiated by Leavis and his followers was to be answered in a series of important accounts of the poem by ▷ C. S. Lewis, ▷ William Empson and Christopher Ricks. In the 1970s and 1980s attention has been refocused, by ▷ Marxist and ▷ feminist critics especially, on what have long been unexamined aspects of the poem: its treatment of patriarchal authority and its relationship to the continuing historical debate on the intellectual culture of the revolutionary period. At the same time, Milton's themes of language and identity have rendered the poem a fruitful text for ▷ psychoanalytical criticism. We might conclude, then, that whilst perhaps the greatest achievement of the English literary ▷ Renaissance, *Paradise Lost* is also a text open to continuous re-reading and revision. **Bib:** Carey, J. and Fowler, A. (eds.), *The Complete Poems of John Milton*.

Paradise Regained (1671)

An ▷ epic poem by ▷ John Milton in four books, it was first published (together with ▷ *Samson Agonistes*) in 1671. Begun after the publication of ▷ *Paradise Lost* in 1667, the poem can, in some sense, be thought of as a sequel to *Paradise Lost*. In particular, the poem's treatment of Christ, his resistance to temptation, and the redeeming nature of his ministry on earth, cast him in the theologically traditional role of the 'Second Adam' – a regenerative and redeeming force in the world.

Where *Paradise Lost*, however, was conceived of along lines inherited from classical epic, *Paradise Regained* is in the form of the 'brief epic' in the style of the book of *Job*. The chief subject matter of the poem is the temptation of Christ in the wilderness, described in the gospel of *St Luke*.

Paradiso

The third and final section of ▷ Dante's great poem, the ▷ *Divina Commedia*. Dante has been led through the Inferno and the Purgatorio by the spirit of the Roman poet ▷ Virgil. Now his guide is Beatrice, the woman who had inspired Dante's love. As the Inferno was divided into circles, so Paradise is divided into spheres: the sphere of the Moon, of Mercury, Venus, the Sun, Mars, Jupiter, Saturn, the Fixed Stars, and the Primum Mobile, or First Mover. Each sphere contains the kind of spirit the ancient Greek and Roman myths had caused to be associated with it: Mars, the Christian warriors and martyrs; Jupiter, the just rulers; Saturn, the holy contemplatives, etc. The spheres are in ascending order of merit, and culminate in Dante's remote, ecstatic vision of God Himself. In each, Dante has conversations on philosophical and spiritual matters with the men and women from history whom he conceives to have been assigned there.
▷ *Inferno; Purgatorio.*

Parker, Matthew (1504–75)

Became Archbishop of Canterbury on the accession of ▷ Elizabeth I, and was her main ally in her policy of keeping the ▷ Church of England on its unique midway course between the Roman Catholic Church and the more decidedly ▷ Protestant sects such as the

▷ Lutherans and ▷ Calvinists, represented in England by the ▷ Puritans. He was a notable scholar, and promoted the 'Bishop's Bible' (1568), which became the basis for the 'Authorized Version' of 1611.

▷ Bible in England; Reformation; Catholicism (Roman) in English literature.

Parody

Parody consists of mocking a style of literary production through an exaggerated imitation. It is close to ▷ satire in its criticism of eccentricities, but it must always refer to literature or a way of writing, rather than satire's more open scope. For example, Cervantes' ▷ Don Quixote is a parody of chivalric romance and ▷ Shakespeare includes some parody of ▷ Lyly's ▷ Euphues in ▷ Much Ado about Nothing.

Parr, Queen Katherine (1512–48)

Devotional writer. Last of ▷ Henry VIII's six wives, Katherine was widowed twice before she married the aging king. She immediately influenced the court towards a more contemplative and ▷ Protestant character, while initiating religious debate with Henry himself. Katherine was especially concerned with education and was a known protector and patron of the new Protestant universities; moreover, she personally directed the education of the future ▷ Edward VI and ▷ Elizabeth I. Her religious activities became somewhat radical and she was in danger of being executed over the ▷ Anne Askew affair, but being forewarned of the plot against her she skilfully manipulated the king into supporting her. Katherine Parr's two works are devotional in nature: *Prayers and Medytacions* (1545) and *Lamentacion of a Sinner* (1547).
Bib: Travitsky, B. (ed.), *The Paradise of Women*.

Parr, Susanna (no dates)

Religious writer and autobiographer. Known for one work, *Susanna's Apologie Against the Elders* (1659), we may deduce that Susanna Parr was attacked by the elders of her ▷ Baptist church in Exeter when she left, and that they tried to have her excommunicated. She was angered by their attack and, rather than accept the more conventional female role of victim, decided to defend herself in print. Interestingly, she attributes the more radical position to the minister who opposed her, Lewis Stuckley, but even though she appears to position herself within the main body of Baptist beliefs, her views on the rights of women to speak in church are clearly not conventional. She uses biting irony to ridicule her attackers, but also includes detailed descriptions of church practices and contemporary theological arguments.

▷ Autobiography.
Bib: Graham, E. et al. (eds.), *Her Own Life*.

Passionate Pilgrim (1599)

An anthology of poetry containing odes by ▷ Richard Barnfield (1564–1627) formerly attributed to ▷ Shakespeare.

Pastoral

A form of literature originally developed by the ancient Greeks and Romans in the ▷ idylls of the former (*eg* ▷ Theocritus's) and the ▷ eclogues of the latter (*eg* ▷ Virgil's). Ancient pastoral idealized the Greek state of ▷ Arcadia, which had a rustic population of shepherds and herdsmen. The ▷ Renaissance of the 16th century, deeply interested in the literature of the Greeks and Romans, revived the pastoral mode; the earliest forms of it date back in Italian literature to the 15th century, but it was the romance *Arcadia* (1504), by the Italian poet Sannazaro, which was particularly influential throughout Europe. The appeal of the pastoral kind of literature was partly to human wishfulness – the desire to conceive of circumstances in which the complexity of human problems could be reduced to its simplest elements: the shepherds and shepherdesses of pastoral are imagined as having no worries, and they live in an ideal climate with no serious physical calamities; love and death, and making songs and music about these experiences, are their only preoccupations. Another function of pastoral, however, was as a vehicle of moral and social criticism; the shepherds and shepherdesses sought the pleasures of nature and despised or were innocent of the corrupting luxury of courts and cities. This allowed the pastoral to be used for political ends and for the self-presentation of the author. Finally, pastoral presented a means of offering, allegorically, thinly disguised tributes of praise and flattery to real people whom the poet admired or wanted to please. The satirical, moral and eulogistic functions of Renaissance pastoral all tended to make it allegorical, since it was through allegory that the poet could most safely make his criticisms felt, and could most eloquently convey his praise. Allegory also suited the neo-Platonic (▷ Platonism), idealizing cast of mind so characteristic of 16th-century writers. When we remember that the tradition of romantic love was one of the most ardently pursued inheritances from the ▷ Middle Ages, and that the circumstances of pastoral lent themselves to its expression, it is not surprising that the pastoral mode was so extensively cultivated in 16th-century Europe. To England it came late, by way of influences from France, Spain and Italy, but it lasted longer; it was especially pervasive in the last quarter of the 16th century, and continued till the mid-17th; there was a minor revival early in the 18th century.

The first important English pastoral poem is ▷ Edmund Spenser's ▷ *The Shepherd's Calendar*, which consists of an eclogue for each month of the year; the tone is morally didactic in some, satirical in others, and eulogistic of the queen in a third group. ▷ Philip Sidney's ▷ *The Arcadia* is a pastoral romance whose purpose is entertainment, but it idealizes the courtly virtues, as does Book VI of Spenser's ▷ *The Faerie Queene*, about Sir Calidore, the Knight of Courtesy. ▷ The University Wits, ▷ Peele, ▷ Lyly, ▷ Greene and ▷ Lodge, wrote pastoral dramas in verse and romances in prose, and one of the best pastoral works of the 1590s is ▷ Shakespeare's ▷ *As You Like It*, based on Lodge's romance *Rosalynde* (1590). Shakespeare dramatized the pastoral mode with a difference, however: the fanciful world of pastoral romance is contrasted with the world of common sense, and the fairyland pastoral country of shepherds and shepherdesses with Greek names is juxtaposed to the real English countryside and its commonplace peasants, so that his pastoral romance is also anti-pastoral. It was not unusual, however, to salt pastoral with elements from real country life – Spenser does it in *The Shepherd's Calendar*, and Shakespeare does it most skilfully in ▷ *The Winter's Tale* IV. iii. More conventional pastoral dramas were ▷ John Fletcher's *Faithful Shepherdess* (1610) and ▷ Ben Jonson's *The Sad Shepherd* (1635). The artificiality of pastoral lent itself to the ▷ masque form, which combined music, poetry, dancing and decor in equal proportions; Jonson, the master of masque, wrote a number of pastorals for it, but by far the most famous pastoral masque is ▷ Milton's ▷ *Comus*.

Of the various forms of pastoral, the prose romance had the shortest life, and ended with the 16th century; the last pastoral drama was Elkanah Settle's *Pastor Fido* (1677). In non-dramatic poetry, pastoral lasted much longer. ▷ Michael Drayton is the next pastoral poet of note after Spenser with *Idea:*

The Shepherd's Garland (1593) and *Endimion and Phoebe* (1595); ▷ Marlowe's famous pastoral ▷ lyric *Come Live With Me* was first printed in 1599, and pastoral lyric writers in the tradition of Spenser were numerous from 1590 up to 1650; they included Nicholas Breton (?1545–?1626), ▷ George Wither (1588–1667), ▷ William Browne (1591–1643), and above all ▷ Robert Herrick. However, the most famous poems in 17th-century pastoral are Milton's ▷ *L'Allegro* and ▷ *Il Penseroso* and his ▷ elegy ▷ *Lycidas*.

Classical pastoral has not been practised notably since the first half of the 18th century. However, William Empson (*Some Versions of Pastoral*, 1935) sometimes uses the term more widely than classical pastoral denotes.
Bib: Patterson, A., *Pastoral and Ideology*; Chaudhuri, S., *Renaissance Pastoral and its English Developments*.

Patronage in literature

A system by which the monarch or nobility afforded protection and livelihood to an artist, in return for which the artist paid him special honour, or returned him service in the form of entertaining his household and his guests. The great period for this system was the 16th century, but patronage continued to be an important cultural and social institution until the end of the 18th century. In the ▷ Middle Ages the writer or scholar might work under the protection of a religious order, but already ▷ Chaucer was dependent on the patronage of John of Gaunt. After the 18th century, through circulating libraries and wide circulation of periodicals, writers could rely on support from the general public; but from the 16th to 18th centuries failure to secure a patron might mean oblivion, or at least starvation. In the 16th century patronage was a commonly found institution since noblemen and women still kept large households and it was assumed that these would include entertainers (such as a band of actors) and scholars who performed educational and secretarial functions. Since women interested in literature were actively discouraged from writing and publishing their own work, patronage of a male author was a way in which they could participate in literary productivity. In this century actors ('players') who were not attached to some household were regarded as vagabonds liable to punishment or shutting up in houses of correction by the public authorities; by the end of the century, however, the Lord ▷ Chamberlain's Men, the Lord ▷ Admiral's Men, etc. were attached to their patrons

only in name, and they performed in public theatres or at court. The ▷ Earl of Essex (patron of ▷ George Gascoigne), the ▷ Earl of Southampton (patron of ▷ Shakespeare), and ▷ Sidney's sister, ▷ Mary Sidney, were among the great patrons in the reign of ▷ Elizabeth I, but the most valuable patron was the sovereign. Disagreeable necessities of patronage were the flattering 'dedications' that commonly preceded works of literature, and poems written specially to honour or gratify the patron, such as ▷ Donne's *First* and *Second Anniversary* commemorating the death of Elizabeth Drury, daughter of his patron Sir Robert Drury – though Donne's poems are evidence that such work was by no means necessarily bad or insincere. The status of men of letters steadily gained in esteem, however, freeing the writer of the necessity of servility, and ▷ Ben Jonson was one of the most vigorous in upholding its dignity and independence. Nonetheless, it tended to be true under Elizabeth and her successor, ▷ James I, that writers were either 'gentlemen amateurs' like Sidney and ▷ Ralegh, able to work independently, or professional writers like Jonson and Shakespeare, for whom patronage was important if not indispensable.
Bib: Brennan, M., *Literary Patronage in the English Renaissance*; Lytle, G. F., and Orgel, S., *Patronage in the Renaissance*; Rosenberg, E., *Leicester, Patron of Letters*.

Paul's, Children of St

A company of boy-actors, chosen from the choirboys of St Paul's Cathedral, who were very popular with audiences at the end of the 16th century. Their chief rivals among boy-actors were the Children of the Chapel Royal. Both were to some extent serious rivals of the adult actors (see ▷ Shakespeare's ▷ *Hamlet* II. ii). The boy companies were used especially for ▷ pastoral plays, such as those of ▷ John Lyly and ▷ George Peele.
▷ Acting, The profession of.
Bib: Gair, R., *The Children of Paul's*.

Peacham, Henry (c 1576–1643)

Author and artist. Although Peacham was interested in writing, he may be seen as an example of the ideal 'Renaissance man' whose interests and skills covered a wide range of topics and fields, for he was also proficient at music, drawing and mathematics. It is perhaps no surprise that one of his most popular works, *The Complete Gentleman* (1622), is a manual for young ▷ gentlemen on how to behave and on what scholarly accomplishments they should set out to

achieve. He combined his own literary and artistic skills in *Minerva Britanna* (1612), an ▷ emblem-book, and wrote a treatise on the practical skills of artistry, *Graphice* (1606). He was well connected at the court of ▷ James I, being associated with ▷ Jonson and ▷ Byrd; however, his own aesthetic leanings brought him closer to ▷ Henry, Prince of Wales, the king's elder son. Peacham has left the only contemporary picture of a ▷ Shakespeare play in performance, a scene from ▷ *Titus Andronicus*.
Bib: Cawley, R. R., *Henry Peacham: his contribution to English poetry*.

Peele, George (1556–96)

Poet and dramatist and one of ▷ University Wits, Peele was educated at Christ's Hospital and Oxford University. His work comprised various forms of dramatic entertainment characteristic of the taste of the time. His best-known plays are the ▷ pastoral play *The Arraignment of Paris* (?1584), acted by the Children of the Royal Chapel, and *The Old Wives' Tale* (1590), which is something like a dramatized folk-tale. He also wrote a biblical play, *The Love of King David and Fair Bethsabe* (1587), and patriotic ▷ history plays, *The Famous Chronicle of King Edward I* (printed 1593) and *The Battle of Alcazar with the Death of Captain Stukeley* (?1588), and a number of other plays have been attributed to him. In 1585 and 1591 he designed ▷ pageants for London's Lord Mayor's Show. As a precursor of ▷ Shakespeare he has a similar importance to ▷ Robert Greene; he helped to give greater smoothness and flexibility to the use of the ▷ blank-verse line, and combined elements appealing to popular taste with qualities of courtly refinement. He can thus be regarded as a contributor to the rich variety of tone that is unique to the best Elizabethan drama.
Bib: Prouty, C. T., *Life and Works*; Cheffaud, P. H., *George Peele*.

Pembroke, Countess of

▷ Sidney, Mary.

Penseroso, Il (c 1631)

A poem by ▷ John Milton, published in 1645 though composed c 1631. The poem is a companion piece to ▷ *L'Allegro*. The title can be translated from the Italian as signifying the thoughtful or reflective individual. The poem celebrates the retired life of thought and contemplation.

Pericles, Prince of Tyre (1608–9)

A play, acts III–V of which are considered to be by ▷ Shakespeare; acts I–II are mainly or entirely by another writer. The play was published in 1609 in an untrustworthy edition, but it was not included in a collected edition of Shakespeare's works until (in the same version) the Third ▷ Folio of 1664. The story is based on a well-known late classical romance, Apollonius of Tyre, used by John Gower in his 14th-century cycle of poems, ▷ *Confessio Amantis* (Book VIII). Gower appears in the play to speak the chorus, but the play does not follow his version in all respects; another source book was Lawrence Twine's *The Pattern of Painful Adventures*, first published in 1576.

In the first two acts, the play has a very rambling structure, but from Act III it follows a pattern characteristic of Shakespeare's last four plays. Although in each of these the pattern is varied, they have in common a central relationship between a prince and his daughter – in this case Pericles and ▷ Marina. Pericles is separated from her and is led to believe that both she and her mother, Thaisa, are dead. By the end of the play, however, he recovers them both, and the recovery restores him to happiness and health. The scene (V. i) in which Marina, at first unrecognizing of and unrecognized by her father, restores him from his stupor of sorrow, is of remarkable beauty, and recalls the scene in ▷ *King Lear* (IV. vii) in which Cordelia restores her father.

Petition of Right
A demand leading to a law forced on ▷ King Charles I by Parliament in 1628; it ended imprisonment without trial, the raising of taxes without Parliamentary authorization, martial law (*ie* legal judgements enforced under military authority), and the billeting of troops in private houses as an indirect means of forcing political obedience. It was the first major clash between Charles and Parliament in the conflict that ended in the ▷ Civil War of 1642–6.

Petrarch (Francesco Petrarca) (1304–74)
Italian poet and scholar. Petrarch's influence on English ▷ Renaissance poetry is incalculable. Petrarch's early years were spent in the Papal court at Avignon, but his life was one of constant movement – he described himself as *peregrinus ubique*, a wanderer everywhere. He travelled throughout Provence and Italy, living for eight years in Milan (1353–61), but visited in that time centres as far afield as Prague and Paris.

Travelling was to become a central metaphor in Petrarch's writing. The idea of the journey in his own life seemed to imitate great journeys of the past – those of the Apostles, St Augustine of Hippo (345–430), and the ▷ Homeric heroes. Life itself could be represented as a journey, or pilgrimage or, on occasion, a flight. This ▷ metaphor of transience was to be one of the many 'Petrarchan' motifs that English poets were to assimilate with such delight (cf ▷ Sir Thomas Wyatt's sonnet 'My galley charged with forgetfulness').

Petrarch's chief works are his *Africa* (a Latin ▷ epic on *Scipio Africanus*), the *Secretum* (a self-analytical dialogue), and his collection of poetry, the *Canzoniere*. The *Canzoniere* (also known as the *Rime* or *Rime sparse*) contained, by the end of his life, some 366 poems in all, the majority of which deal with the poet's love for 'Laura' – the unobtainable ideal of womanhood – whom Petrarch claimed to have first seen in church on 6 April 1327. In addition to the *Canzoniere*, he composed imitations of ▷ Virgil's *Eclogues* and the six *Trionfi* (*Triumphs*) poems – the triumphs of Love, Chastity, Death, Fame, Time and Eternity.

The *Trionfi* and the *Canzoniere* were medieval best-sellers. Both circulated widely in manuscript form before their first publication in 1470. The *Trionfi* were to have a huge influence upon all forms of Renaissance representation – poetry, painting, tapestry, medals, emblems, ▷ pageants and theatre. At the same time, the introspective self-analysis, and the depiction of a female ideal who is both mistress and saint in the *Canzoniere*, were to influence European poets of the 16th and 17th centuries. The ▷ sonnet sequences of ▷ Sir Philip Sidney, ▷ Samuel Daniel, ▷ Michael Drayton and others, as well as the poetry, in an earlier period, of Sir Thomas Wyatt and ▷ Henry Howard, Earl of Surrey, all took Petrarch as a starting-point. Similarly the anti-Petrarchism of some of ▷ Shakespeare's sonnets or ▷ Donne's poetry, is, in its vigorous denial of Petrarchan modes, a tribute to the pervasive influence on the Renaissance sensibility of the Italian poet's work.
Bib: Durling, R. M., (ed.), *Petrarch's Lyric Poems*; Minta, S., *Petrarch and Petrarchism*.

***Philaster, or Love lies a-bleeding* (1611)**
A romantic play by ▷ Francis Beaumont and ▷ John Fletcher; it was produced in 1611, and is in ▷ blank verse. It is the first in a style of ▷ tragicomedy that became characteristic of the English theatre during the next 30 years. Of all Beaumont and Fletcher's

collaborations, it is perhaps the most famous; it derives from the prose romances of chivalry popular in France and Spain, and to some extent (*eg* ▷ Philip Sidney's ▷ *The Arcadia*) in England. The plot is characteristic: Philaster is rightful king of Sicily, but his throne has been usurped by the king of Calabria, with whose daughter, Arethusa, he is in love. He keeps communication with her through his page, Bellario. Her father wants her to marry Pharamond of Spain, and to avoid this she reveals to him the love affair between Pharamond and Megra, a lady of her father's court. In revenge Megra makes out that Arethusa has been having an affair with Bellario, whom Philaster accordingly dismisses. It then turns out that Bellario is a girl disguised as a page for love of Philaster. This situation seems to be borrowed from ▷ Shakespeare's ▷ *Twelfth Night*, but Shakespeare combined poignant truth to natural feelings with the romantic extravagance of the plot. Beaumont and Fletcher's emotion is obviously 'poetic' but not convincing.

Philips, Katherine (1632–64)

Poet, translator and letter-writer. Katherine Philips is best known today for her poetic advocation of ▷ Platonic friendship between women; although she herself specified that this affection be free of bodily passions, she is often listed as an early lesbian poet. Married at the age of 17 to a man 38 years older than herself, she concentrated on her female friends, who are given appropriate names in her poems, 'Rosania' and 'Lucasia' to her own 'matchless Orinda'. Her poetry was first published in a pirated edition in 1663, although the official *Poems, By the Incomparable, Mrs K. P.* (1664) differed very little from the supposedly corrupt text. She also translated Corneille's *La Mort de Pompée* (1663) and her letters to Sir Charles Cotterell were published in 1705 as *Letters from Orinda to Poliarchus*. Unfortunately, just at the point when Orinda began to receive the public acclaim she had so long desired, she contracted smallpox and died.
Bib: Greet, G. (ed.), *Kissing the Rod*; Hobby, E., *Virtue of Necessity*.

Picaresque

From the Spanish *picaro*, 'rogue'. The term is especially applied to a form of prose fiction originating in Spain in the 16th century, dealing with the adventures of rogues. The first distinctive example in English is ▷ Thomas Nashe's ▷ *Unfortunate Traveller*.

Other traditions combine with the picaresque: the mock romance in the tradition of ▷ *Don Quixote*, and the tradition of religious pilgrimage (cf. ▷ *The Pilgrim's Progress*).

Pilgrimage of Grace, The

A rebellion provoked by the closing of the ▷ monasteries in 1536. It arose in and was chiefly supported by the north of England, and this fact shows that it had a social and political basis as well as a religious one. The south of England was economically and socially much more advanced as well as more closely in touch with movements of religious reform on the continent of Europe; in consequence, monasteries were not only becoming redundant there in their social functions, but were to some extent actively resented. In the north of England they were more respected on religious grounds, and still served social functions of poor relief and large employment of labour. In addition to these causes directly related to monastic institutions, there were other social causes bound up with the resentment of the old landed nobility of the north for the newer nobility of the south, who were encouraged and advanced in public service by ▷ King Henry VIII. The closing of the monasteries was a pretext for rebellion such as the northern nobility had been looking for. The rebellion was formidable, and the government, through its representative the Duke of Norfolk, had to come to terms; the terms, however, were not kept, and once the rebel army had dispersed, its leaders were executed.

Pilgrim's Progress, The

A prose ▷ allegory by ▷ John Bunyan. *The Pilgrim's Progress from this World to that which is to come* is in two parts: Part I (1678) tells of the religious conversion of Christian, and of his religious life – conceived as a pilgrimage – in this world, until he comes to the River of Death and the Heavenly City which lies beyond it; Part II (1684) describes the subsequent conversion of his wife Christiana and their children and their similar journey with a group of friends.

Both parts contain episodes that symbolize real-life experiences: thus, Christian, soon after the way has been pointed out to him, falls into the Slough of Despond – a bog representing the depression that overcomes the new convert when he has passed the stage of first enthusiasm. Later he has to pass through phases of spiritual despair and terror, symbolized by the Valleys of Humiliation and the Shadow of Death; he has to face the derision and anger of public opinion in the town of Vanity Fair, and so on. Christiana and the children have an easier time; perhaps Bunyan wished to show that God in his mercy shields the weaker pilgrims, or perhaps that public opinion is harsher to pioneers than to those who follow them.

Like Bunyan himself the 'pioneer pilgrims' – Christian and his associates – belong to the ▷ Puritan sects who were undergoing persecution in the reign of ▷ Charles ii, especially during the earlier years, when English society was in strong reaction against the previous Puritan regime of ▷ Oliver Cromwell. Yet *The Pilgrim's Progress* is much more than merely a dramatization of the Puritan spirit. By its allegorical content, it is related to the tradition of the allegorical sermon, which in village churches survived the ▷ Reformation of the 16th century, and some of the adventures (Christian's fight with Apollyon, the Castle of Giant Despair, the character of Greatheart) are related in spirit to popular versions of medieval and 16th-century romances, surviving in the ▷ chapbooks. These aspects give it a close relation with popular traditions of culture to an extent unequalled by any other major literary work. Another element of popular culture shows in Bunyan's assimilation of the English translation of the ▷ Bible, and this reminds us that for many households the Bible was the only book constantly read, and that during the next century Bunyan's allegory took its place beside it. Still more important than these links with the past is Bunyan's anticipation of the kind of vision of human nature that in the 18th and 19th centuries was to find its scope in the novel: his allegorized characters do not, as in past allegories, merely simplify human virtues and vices, but reveal how an individual destiny can be shaped by the predominance in a personality of an outstanding quality, good or bad; the adventures of the pilgrims are conditioned by the differences of these qualities. Thus, Christian and Faithful, fellow pilgrims, have radically different temperaments and correspondingly different experiences.

▷ Celestial City; City of Destruction; Doubting Castle.

Plague, The

A particularly severe epidemic of bubonic plague that struck London in 1664–5, although epidemics, either of the bubonic plague or of equally deadly diseases, had been frequent ever since the Black Death of the 14th century. The plague several times caused the compulsory closing of theatres (for fear of infection) during the lifetime of ▷ Shakespeare.

Plato (?428–?348 BC)

Greek philosopher. He was a follower of the Athenian philosopher Socrates, and his dialogues represent conversations in which Socrates takes the lead. The most famous of these 'Socratic' dialogues are *Protagoras, Gorgias, Phaedo, Symposium,* ▷ *Republic, Phaedrus, Timaeus.* His longest work, the *Laws,* does not include Socrates as a character. His central conception is that beyond the world of transient material phenomena lies another eternal world of ideal forms which the material world represents in the form of imitations. His figure for this in the *Republic* is that men in the material world are like people watching shadows moving on the wall of a cave; they see only these shadows and not the realities which cast the shadows. Plato is one of the two most influential philosophers in European thought, the other one being ▷ Aristotle, who was at first his pupil.
▷ Platonism.

Platonic Love

A term that has come to possess three distinct, if related, senses: 1 A love between individuals which transcends sexual desire and attains spiritual heights. This is the most popularly understood sense of the term. 2 The complex doctrine of love which embraces sexuality, but which is directed towards an ideal end, to be found discussed in ▷ Plato's *Symposium.* ▷ John Donne's poem 'The Extasy' explores this form of love. 3 A reference to homosexual love (cf. ▷ Katherine Philips). This third sense is derived from the praise of homosexual love to be found in the *Symposium.*

Platonism and Neo-Platonism

The term 'Platonism' is applied to the school of thought derived immediately from the Greek philosopher ▷ Plato. 'Neo-Platonism' names schools of thought that adapted his philosophy by adding to or modifying it. Two main periods of revival of Plato's thought are described as neo-Platonism: 1 that initiated by the pagan Plotinus (3rd century AD) in Rome, and at first a revival of Christianity, into which it was to some extent carried by St Augustine of Hippo (345–430) when he was converted; 2 that which Marsilio Ficino initiated by his studies of Platonic philosophy in Florence (15th century). The 17th-century group known as the Cambridge Platonists

(▷ Platonists, Cambridge) were true Platonists rather than Neo-Platonists.

1 Plato taught that beyond the world of transient phenomena surrounding us is one of permanent and imperishable ideas, but he relied on logical reason for the development of his philosophy. Neo-Platonism added a religious aspect that depended on revelation; it derived this influence from other philosophies and from eastern religions. The elements that St Augustine transferred to Christianity remained dominant until the 13th century, when Platonic influence was succeeded by that of ▷ Aristotle.

2 16th-century neo-Platonism in Italy revived the ancient neo-Platonist conception that the universe is peopled by many supernatural beings, and maintained that these existed in addition to the angels and devils allowed by Christian doctrine. It also taught that men, being essentially spirits, could, by the acquisition of wisdom and virtue, immensely increase their power and knowledge, and could control for their good and wise purposes the non-human supernatural spirits. Thus arose the idea of 'the Mage', or master of high magic: in ▷ Shakespeare's ▷ The Tempest, Prospero is such a neo-Platonic Mage, and Ariel is a spirit such as the neo-Platonists believed could be controlled and used. Neo-Platonism also influenced poetic conceptions, whereby the beloved lady of a sonnet sequence (eg ▷ Sir Philip Sidney's ▷ Astrophil and Stella) was a sublime image of her ideal soul, and virtues (eg those allegorized by ▷ Edmund Spenser in ▷ The Faerie Queene) could exist as ideal realities. In criticism, Sidney shows neo-Platonic influence in his conception that poetry should not merely represent but improve on nature, in accordance with the Platonic idea that the world of ordinary realities is an inferior imitation of the eternal idealities. This outlook emphasized the importance of the imagination as the faculty that could create ideal images and not merely imitate the general qualities common to classes of actual objects, in accordance with Aristotle's critical theory.

Platonists, The Cambridge

A group of thinkers at Cambridge University in the mid-17th century. Their aim was to combine reason with revealed religion, and to counteract the religiously destructive tendencies of the thought of ▷ René Descartes and ▷ Thomas Hobbes. Their concern with true religion was combined with a care for both clarity of thought and religious tolerance. Their chief representatives were Henry More (1614–87), Ralph Cudworth (1617–88), Benjamin Whichcote (1609–83) and John Smith (1618–52).
▷ Platonism and Neo-Platonism.
Bib: Patrides, C. A. (ed.), *The Cambridge Platonists*.

Plautus, Titus Maccius (?254–184 BC)

Roman comic dramatist. His comedies are based on situation and intrigue; they had a high reputation in his own time, but unlike the other outstanding Roman comedian, ▷ Terence, he was ignored during the Middle Ages. In the 16th century his reputation revived, and his style of comedy was emulated throughout western Europe. The play which is often called the first English comedy, Nicholas Udall's ▷ Ralph Roister Doister, is based on Plautus' *Miles Gloriosus* (*The Boastful Soldier*) and ▷ Shakespeare's ▷ Comedy of Errors on Plautus' *Menaechmi*, which, using a confusion between twins, may also have influenced Shakespeare's ▷ Twelfth Night. Again, Shakespeare's ▷ Taming of the Shrew may be partly based on Plautus' *Mostellaria*, and the last act of ▷ Jonson's ▷ The Alchemist is also indebted to it. Certain of Plautus' comic characters, such as that of the boastful soldier, as in Udall's play, started a tradition, exemplified by Captain Bobadill in Jonson's ▷ Every Man in his Humour and Parolles in Shakespeare's ▷ All's Well that Ends Well. These are the most important examples, but traces, at least, of Plautus in the background of English plays can be found in other works of Ben Jonson, and in plays by ▷ Thomas Heywood.

Play on words

A use of a word with more than one meaning, or of two words that sound the same in such a way that both meanings are called to mind. In its simplest form, as the modern pun, this is merely a joke. In the 16th and 17th centuries poets frequently played upon words seriously; this is especially true of ▷ Shakespeare and dramatists contemporary with him, and of the ▷ Metaphysical poets, such as ▷ John Donne and ▷ George Herbert.

Pléiade

The name given to the group of 16th-century poets led by ▷ Ronsard and ▷ Du Bellay, supposedly seven in total, although early mentions of poet comrades are far in excess of this number. Du Bellay's *Deffence & Illustration de la langue francoyse* (1549) sets out a credo common to the group as a whole: wholehearted promotion of the vernacular, imitation of the Ancients, rejection of medieval forms of ▷ lyric verse such as the *ballade* or *rondeau*, establishment of the 12-syllable ▷ alexandrine as the staple of French verse. Their cultivation of the ▷ sonnet stimulated the major English writers of the last decade of the 16th century such as ▷ Sidney, ▷ Spenser and ▷ Shakespeare.

Plutarch (AD 46–?120)

Greek biographer and moralist. He is chiefly famous for his 46 *Parallel Lives* in which he matches 23 famous men from Greek history with 23 famous Romans. The *Lives* were presented in an English version by ▷ Sir Thomas North in 1579; North did not translate them from the original Greek but from the French version by Jacques Amyot. North's book was as popular and influential in England as Amyot's was in France; Plutarch's conception of the great and many-sided man was in harmony with the 16th-century conception of the public virtues and personal accomplishments that should go to make the full man and the perfect courtier. The *Lives*, in North's version, were used as a source book by dramatists – notably by ▷ Shakespeare in ▷ *Julius Caesar*, ▷ *Antony and Cleopatra* and ▷ *Coriolanus*. Plutarch also wrote a number of treatises on moral and physical subjects known as the *Moralia* – a precedent for the ▷ essays of ▷ Bacon as well as the very different ones of the renowned French essayist, ▷ Montaigne.

▷ Translation.

Poetics

In ▷ Aristotle's ▷ *Poetics* the rules of ▷ 'tragedy' are abstracted from a collection of specific instances to form a theoretical model. The function of 'poetics', therefore, has always been to organize formally details of poetic structures, and to this extent it is both prescriptive and descriptive. This Aristotelian usage persists, though in considerably extended form, in the titles of works of critical theory, such as Jonathan Culler's *Structuralist Poetics* (1975). The theoretical works also address the issue of an organized system of analytical methods, as well as the aesthetics of artistic construction. More recently, for example in the work of ▷ new historicist critics such as Stephen Greenblatt, the phrase 'cultural poetics' is used to designate an investigation into 'how the boundaries were marked between cultural practices understood to be art forms and other, contiguous, forms of expression' (*Shakespearean Negotiations*, 1988). Such investigations seek to explain how

particular aspects of general cultural life are given artistic expression. Whereas Aristotle's poetic can be said to have a formalist bent, one of the ways in which the term has come to be used today locates the formal aspects of literary texts within a social context.

Poetics

A treatise on poetry by the Greek philosopher ▷ Aristotle. He had already written a dialogue *On the Poets*, which has only survived in fragments, and a treatise on ▷ rhetoric; knowledge of both is to some extent assumed in the *Poetics*. The *Poetics* is considered to have been an unpublished work, resembling notes for lectures addressed to students rather than a fully worked-up treatise for the general public like the *Rhetoric*. This accounts for its fragmentary character. Thus Aristotle distinguishes ▷ Tragedy, ▷ Epic and Comedy as the chief kinds of poetry, but Comedy is practically omitted from fuller discussion. ▷ Lyric, though it is referred to, is not included among the chief kinds, either because Aristotle considered it to be part of music or because he considered it to be taken up in Tragedy. The main part of the work is therefore concerned with Tragedy and Epic – the former more extensively than the latter. Aristotle's method is essentially descriptive rather than prescriptive; that is to say, he is more concerned with what had been done by acknowledged masters such as ▷ Homer and ▷ Sophocles than with what ought to be done according to so-called 'rules'.

Nonetheless, the *Poetics* became the most authoritatively influential of all critical works. Its dominance in European critical thought from the 16th to the 18th centuries was partly due to its influence on the most widely read of the Roman critics, ▷ Horace, and partly because it was rediscovered at the end of the 15th century when the ▷ Renaissance was at its height and the spirit of the Greek and Latin writers was felt to be civilization itself. Critics such as the 16th-century Italian Scaliger took what are mere hints in Aristotle and erected them into important rules of art, such as the 'neo-Aristotelian' unities of time and place. In England, important critics such as ▷ Jonson regarded Aristotle and neo-Aristotelianism with strong respect rather than total reverence, but the complete submission of minor critics such as Thomas Rymer (1641–1713) is exemplified by his obtuse treatment of ▷ Shakespeare's ▷ *Othello* in the essay *Short View of Tragedy* (1692).

Today the *Poetics* remains one of the most outstanding works of European thought.

Critics still use Aristotle's terminology in classifying poetic forms; his theory of art as imitation (different from ▷ Plato's) is still the starting-point of much aesthetic discussion; such terms as 'harmatia', for the element in human nature which makes it vulnerable to tragedy, 'peripeteia' for the reversal of fortunes common in tragic narrative, and 'katharsis' for the effect of tragedy on the mind of the audience, have been useful for a long time.

Poet Laureate
The laurel, also known as the bay (*Laurus nobilis*), was sacred to Apollo, the god most associated with the arts. The Greeks honoured Olympic victors and triumphant generals by crowning them with a wreath of laurel leaves. In the 15th century the universities of Oxford and Cambridge gave the title 'laureate', meaning worthy of laurels, to various poets including ▷ John Skelton and it was later given to court poets such as ▷ Ben Jonson. In 1668 the title gained its modern status when John Dryden (1631–1700) was granted a stipend as a member of the royal household charged with writing court odes and celebrating state occasions in verse.

Pollard, A. W. (1859–1944)
Influential bibliographer and ▷ Shakespearean scholar who is best known for his work on the *Short-Title Catalogue of Books Printed in England . . . 1475–1640* (1926), which was revised by Katharine Pantzer and others in 1976 (Vol. II) and 1985 (Vol. I).

Poor Laws
Laws which gave public relief to those among the poor who could not earn their own living and were not supported by others. The first great Poor Law was that of 1601, under ▷ Elizabeth I. The dissolution of the ▷ monasteries and other Church institutions that had undertaken the care of the destitute, together with a number of causes of unemployment (*eg* enclosures), caused a series of poor laws to be passed in the 16th century, of which the law of 1601 was the climax. Every parish was required to appoint overseers, whose task it was to provide work for the able-bodied unemployed, and relief (through a local tax called a 'poor rate') for those who were unable to work.

Porter, Endymion (1587–1649)
Poet and patron. No published writing survives, if it existed at all, but Endymion Porter was recognized as one of the influential figures in the cultural world of his day. He was known and respected by ▷ D'Avenant, ▷ Donne and ▷ Herrick, and would have been made a member of the proposed ▷ Royal Society. Some work has survived, a commemoration for D'Avenant, an epitaph for Donne, and several manuscript poems and letters to his wife. Although politically influential under the reign of ▷ Charles I (he was part of the ▷ Buckingham faction), during the ▷ Interregnum Porter and his ▷ Catholic wife were exiled and lived abroad in poverty.
Bib: Huxley, G., *Endymion Porter: the life of a courtier, 1587–1649*.

Post-structuralism
At first glance, the term post-structuralism seems to imply that the post-structuralists came after the structuralists and that post-structuralism was the heir of ▷ structuralism. In practice, however, there is not a clear-cut division between structuralism and post-structuralism. Although the two have different focuses of interest and preoccupations, many of their concerns bind them together. Structuralism encompasses approaches to criticism that use linguistic models to enable critics to focus not on the inherent meaning of a work but on the structures which *produce* or generate meaning. Post-structuralism focuses on the ways in which the texts themselves subvert this enterprise. For an example of a post-structuralist treatment of ▷ Renaissance literature, see J. Goldberg, *Voice Terminal Echo*.
Bib: Culler, J., *On Deconstruction*.

Poulter's Measure
A verse metre used by some 16th-century poets, it consisted of a 12-syllable line (▷ Alexandrine) alternating with a 14-syllable one. 'Poulter' = 'poulterer' – an allusion to variations in the number making up a dozen in the poultry trade. It was used by ▷ Thomas Wyatt, ▷ Henry Howard, Earl of Surrey and less distinguished poets.

> When Dido feasted first the wand'ring
>   Trojan knight,
> Whom Juno's wrath with storms did force
>   in Lybic sands to light,
> That mighty Atlas did teach, the supper
>   lasted long
> With crispéd locks, on golden harp, Jopas
>   sang in his song.
>
> (Wyatt, 'Jopas' Song')

Presbyterianism
A doctrine of church organization maintained by an important group of ▷ Protestants.

'Presbyter' comes from a Greek word meaning 'elder', and Presbyterianism is a system of church government by councils of elders. The system was devised by ▷ Calvin; it became dominant in Scotland under the leadership of ▷ John Knox and had wide support in England from about 1570. It is still the national Church of Scotland, but in England it seceded extensively to ▷ Unitarianism during the 18th century. In 1972 The English Presbyterians joined with the ▷ Congregationalists to form the United Reformed Church.

Preston, Thomas (1537–98)
Author of the early Elizabethan ▷ tragicomedy *Cambyses, King of Persia* (1569). He may also have written the popular and influential romance *Sir Cryomon and Sir Clamydes*.

Primose, Diana (no dates)
Poet. The only reference extant to this writer is on the title-page of her book *A Chaine of Pearls* (1630), ostensibly a panegyric to ▷ Elizabeth I. The queen, however, had been dead for 27 years and the poem is more likely an attack on ▷ Charles I, whose shortcomings are shown up by contrast with Elizabeth's virtues. Her narrative source is ▷ William Camden's *Annals of Queen Elizabeth* (1615; published in English in 1625), while the list of virtues are commonplace, such as chastity, temperance, justice and fortitude.
Bib: Greet, G. (ed.), *Kissing the Rod.*

Problem plays (of Shakespeare)
A term first used in the late 19th century by critics of ▷ Shakespeare to designate a group of his plays written between 1600 and 1604. These are: ▷ *Troilus and Cressida,* ▷ *All's Well that End's Well* and ▷ *Measure for Measure.* What makes these all 'problem plays' in the view of some critics is that it is difficult to discern the individual play's overall thematic direction. *Troilus and Cressida* is regarded as a problem because, while the Trojans are shown to be intrinsically nobler than the Greeks, they are also shown to be wrong, although the Greeks are not conclusively shown to be right in their outlook. Thus no positive value is preached by the play, nor does it seem to be light-hearted enough to be simply a comedy. *All's Well*, the slightest of the three, is a problem because the noble heroine uses means that nowadays we would despise to gain her lover, who does not, in any case, seem to be worth her trouble. The play is thus a 'romantic comedy', but one in which the romance has gone sour. *Measure for Measure* is a comedy which, in the opinion of some critics, is both too serious and too cynical in some of its characteristics to be successful either as a comedy or as a serious critique of society. Not every critic agrees that all these plays, or any of them, are really 'problematic'.
Bib: Tillyard, E. M. W., *Shakespeare's Problem Plays.*

Protestantism
A term used for all varieties of Christian belief which broke away from Roman Catholicism during the ▷ Reformation in the 16th century, or for religious communities not in agreement with Roman Catholicism but originating since the Reformation. It was first used in regard to those who protested against the Emperor Charles V's condemnation of the reformers in Germany at the Diet of Spires, 1529.

Prothalamion (1596)
A wedding song, written by ▷ Edmund Spenser and published in 1596. *Prothalamion* is roughly half the length of Spenser's other wedding song – ▷ *Epithalamion.* The ▷ ode celebrates the double wedding of two sisters – Lady Elizabeth and Lady Katherine Somerset in August 1596.

Psalms, The
A book of the Old Testament composed of the sacred songs of the ancient Jewish religion. In ancient Hebrew they were called 'praise-songs', indicating the predominant function of the collection, though other functions – lament, meditation, imprecation, etc. – were included. Authorship was traditionally attributed to King David, but it is evident that the psalms either date from after the Babylonian Captivity (6th century BC) or were re-edited then; in any case they originated at different periods.

In the 16th century, under the inspiration of the ▷ Protestant Reformation, the psalms were translated into English. There are two prose versions in official use in the ▷ Church of England: that of the Authorized Version of the ▷ Bible of 1611, and the older translation in *The Book of* ▷ *Common Prayer* dating from 1549. Both include some of the well-known masterpieces of English prose of the ▷ Renaissance. In addition, there are the metrical and rhymed versions especially favoured by the more extreme Protestants. The so-called 'Old Version' by Sternhold and Hopkins was published in its complete form in 1562. More distinguished attempts to versify the prose psalms were made in the 16th

century by ▷ Sir Philip Sidney and his sister
▷ Mary Sidney, the Countess of Pembroke,
and in the 17th by George Sandys, ▷ George
Wither and ▷ John Milton.
　　▷ Bible in England.

Psychoanalytical criticism

Psychoanalysis and literary criticism both seek
to interpret their respective objects of enquiry,
and both involve the analysis of language.
In its early manifestations psychoanalytical
criticism (*eg* Ernest Jones's *Hamlet and
Oedipus*, 1949) sought to apply the methods of
psychoanalysis to particular texts, in order to
uncover their 'unconscious'. Jones's claim was
to reveal the causes of ▷ Hamlet's behaviour
beginning from the assumption that 'current
response is always compounded partly of a
response to the actual situation and partly
of past responses to older situations that are
unconsciously felt to be similar'. The French
psychoanalyst ▷ Jacques Lacan's rereading of
▷ Freud has sought to render problematical
this relationship between patient and analyst,
and, by implication, between text and reader.
Lacan's description of the unconscious as
being structured 'like a language' raises
fundamental questions for the authoritative
role usually ascribed to the literary critic. To
this extent the 'unconscious' of the literary
text is brought into confrontation with the
unconscious of the critic.
　　Many of the terms taken from psychology
that are associated with Lacan's reading
of Freud have been incorporated into the
language of literary criticism; for example,
the decentred subject of psychoanalysis,
condensation, displacement, the realm of the
'imaginary', the ▷ symbolic order, all refer in
some way to textual mechanisms.
Bib: Laplanche, J. and Pontalis, J-B., *The
Language of Psychoanalysis*; Lacan, J., *The Four
Fundamental Concepts of Psychoanalysis*; Wright,
E., *Psychoanalytic Criticism*.

Ptolemy (Claudius Ptolemaeus) (2nd
　　century AD)

Astronomer, geographer and mathematician.
He was a native of the Egyptian city of
Alexandria, and may have been of Greek
origin. His theory of the structure of the
universe, according to which the planets,
sun and stars all revolved around the earth,
remained the accepted opinion until replaced
by the theory of ▷ Copernicus in the 16th
century and the observations of ▷ Galileo
in the 17th. This is the Ptolemaic System
summarized in the *Almagest*, his treatise on
astronomy.

Puck

In Old English, an evil spirit; from the
16th century a mischievous fairy, as in
▷ Shakespeare's ▷ *A Midsummer Night's
Dream*.
　　▷ Fairies.

Purgatorio

The second book of the ▷ *Divina Commedia*
by ▷ Dante. Having emerged from the
Inferno, the poet, still accompanied by
▷ Virgil, follows a spiral up to the Mount
of Purgatory, where the souls of the dead
are purged of the stains of their sins as they
await release into Heaven. They encounter
various groups of repentant sinners on the
seven circular ledges of the mountain, who
suffer punishments and pain, but do so more
willingly, knowing the suffering will pass in
the end. On its summit is the Earthly Paradise
where the poet meets Beatrice, who is to
guide him through the spheres of Heaven.
　　▷ *Inferno; Paradiso*.

Puritanism

The term is used in a narrow sense of
religious practice and attitudes, and in a broad
sense of an ethical outlook that is much less
easy to define.
　　1 In its strict sense, 'Puritan' was applied
to those Protestant reformers who rejected
Queen Elizabeth's religious settlement of
1560. This settlement sought a middle way
between Roman Catholicism and the extreme
spirit of reform of Geneva. The Puritans,
influenced by Geneva, Zurich and other
continental centres, objected to the retention
of bishops and to any appearance of what
they regarded as superstition in church
worship – the wearing of vestments by the
priests, and any kind of religious image.
Apart from their united opposition to Roman
Catholicism and their insistence on simplicity
in religious forms, Puritans disagreed among
themselves on questions of doctrine and
church organization. The principal sects were:
▷ Presbyterians, Independents (at first called
▷ Brownists, and later ▷ Congregationalists),
▷ Baptists, and (later) ▷ Quakers. They were
strong in the towns, especially in London,
and in the University of Cambridge, and
socially they were widespread and included
members of the aristocracy and the working
classes as well as the middle, commercial
classes where they had their chief strength.
Puritanism was very strong in the first half
of the 17th century and reached its peak of
power after the ▷ Civil War of 1642–6 – a
war which was ostensibly religious, although

it was also political. Matters of church government were much involved with matters of state government, since Presbyterians and Independents, who believed in popular control of the church, were not likely to tolerate royal control of Parliament's political affairs. Puritanism was both religiously and politically supreme in the decade 1650–60, but on the Restoration of the monarchy Puritans were denied participation in the ▷ Church of England, and refused rights of free religious worship. The last was granted them by the Toleration Act of 1689, and during the 18th century both Puritanism and the official attitude to it were modified under the influence of Rationalism.

2 In the broader sense of a whole way of life, puritanism has always represented strict obedience to the dictates of conscience and strong emphasis on the virtue of self-denial. In this sense individuals can be described as 'puritan' whether or not they belong to one of the recognized Puritan sects, or even if they are atheists.

The word 'Puritan' is often thought to imply hostility to the arts, but this is not necessarily true. In the reign of ▷ Elizabeth I poets such as ▷ Spenser and ▷ Sidney combined a strong puritan moral tone (without any Puritan doctrine in the sectarian sense) with an intense delight in artistic form; in the 17th century John Milton was an ardent Puritan, but his poetry is one of the climaxes of English ▷ Renaissance art. However, it is true that the strict Puritans of the age of ▷ Shakespeare were commonly opponents of the art of the theatre; this was partly because the theatres were sometimes scenes of moral licentiousness and disorder, and partly because the strict Puritan, in his intense love of truth, was very inclined to confuse fiction with lying. Thus in the later 17th century ▷ Bunyan was criticized by some of his Puritan comrades for writing fiction in his ▷ allegory ▷ Pilgrim's Progress.

What is called the 'Puritan conscience', on the other hand, had an important influence on one kind of art form – the novel. Puritans believed that the good life could only be lived by 'the inner light' – the voice of God in the heart – and to discern this light it was necessary to conduct the most scrupulous self-enquiry. This produced the kind of spiritual ▷ autobiography that was common

in the mid-17th century, and of which the best example is Bunyan's ▷ Grace Abounding. Such self-knowledge had two important consequences: it increased interest in, and understanding of, the human heart in others as well as the self, and the first results of this are apparent in Bunyan's Pilgrim's Progress; but it also encouraged a sense of the loneliness of the individual – a sense supported by the growing economic individualism of the later 17th century.

▷ Reformation.

Bib: Smith, N., Perfection Proclaimed.

Puttenham, George (d 1590)

The reputed author of The Arte of English Poesie (1589). The book is a thorough treatise on English poetic technique at the time, on the threshold of one of the great decades of English short poems. It discusses the various forms of metrical verse, discusses – without deciding between them – the rival merits of metrical and non-metrical forms and presents an enlightened review of English verse. With ▷ Sidney's ▷ Apologie for Poetrie, Puttenham's book is one of the two most important critical works of the ▷ Elizabethan period. It is more scholarly, if less eloquent, than Sidney's essay, but like Sidney, Puttenham is trying to establish civilized standards for the composition of poetry, and is opposed to the 'vulgar', popular traditions of a poet such as ▷ Skelton.

Bib: Willcock, G. D. and Walker, A. (eds.), The Arte of English Poesie.

Pyramus and Thisbe

The hero and heroine of a love story by the Roman poet ▷ Ovid (▷ Metamorphoses iv). The lovers are forbidden marriage by their parents, but they exchange vows through a hole in the wall that separates their respective houses. They agree to meet outside Babylon at the tomb of Ninus, but Thisbe, who arrives first, is frightened by a lion and hides in a cave, the lion meanwhile covering her dropped veil with blood. When Pyramus arrives and finds the bloody veil, he supposes Thisbe to be dead, and kills himself; Thisbe follows his example. In Shakespeare's play ▷ A Midsummer Night's Dream the artisans give a comically bungled performance of the tragedy before King Theseus of Athens.

Quakers

Originally a derisive name for the members of a religious society properly called the Society of Friends; the Friends are still known as Quakers, but the term has lost its contemptuous significance. The Society was founded by ▷ George Fox, who began his preaching career in 1647 and was aided by his wife ▷ Margaret Fell. He preached that the truth came from an inner spiritual light, and declared that no special class of men (*ie* priests) or buildings (*ie* churches) should be set apart for religious purposes. This individualism at first attracted a number of mentally disturbed followers whose ecstasies are perhaps responsible for the nickname 'Quaker', though Fox himself declared that it was first used in 1650 because he taught his followers to 'Tremble at the Word of the Lord'. They held a view, unusual among ▷ Puritans, that it was possible to gain complete victory over sin in this life. Such a doctrine, in addition to their refusal to accept those religious institutions that the other Puritans accepted, made them intensely unpopular for the first ten years of their existence. Later they became influential far beyond their numbers, which have remained comparatively few. Owing to the freedom of mind which is the essence of the movement, it is difficult to define their doctrine, which seems to vary greatly among individuals. On the other hand they are well known for a range of characteristic virtues: humanitarianism (they were amongst the first to protest against slavery – 1688); non-resistance to violence; respect for individuals regardless of race, sex, or religion; sobriety of conduct and tranquillity of mind. Because of their belief in equal respect for men and women, many of the published women writers of the mid-17th century were Quakers. One of the most important of their early members was William Penn (1644–1718), founder of the American colony of Pennsylvania. Like other Puritans, they were prominent in commerce, but took care to engage in activities that were not harmful; in consequence Quaker names are particularly well known in connection with the manufacture of chocolate.
Bib: Vann, R. T., *The Social Development of English Quakerism*.

Quarles, Francis (1592–1644)

Poet, emblematist, pamphleteer, Francis Quarles was a prolific author, producing not only a number of verse collections, but also a play, biblical paraphrases, a romance and two remarkable ▷ emblem-books: *Emblems* (1635) and *Hieroglyphics of the Life of Man* (1638). His earlier verse publications, such as *A Feast for Worms* (1620), *Hadasa: or, The History of Queen Esther* (1621) and *Sion's Elegies* (1624), were, in the main, adaptations of biblical themes. In the 1630s his attention was devoted to the production of his emblem-books and to occasional pieces. With the outbreak of the ▷ Civil War, Quarles published a series of anti-Puritan ▷ pamphlets. But it is for his emblematic work that Quarles is chiefly remembered; indeed, *Emblems* is said to have been the most popular book published in the 17th century.
Bib: Grosart, A. B. (ed.), *Complete Works in Verse and Proses* (3 vols); Hasan, M., *Quarles: A Study of His Life and Poetry*.

Quarto

A term used in publishing to designate a size of volume, made by folding the standard paper twice instead of only once (▷ folio size). The quarto editions of ▷ Shakespeare's plays are those published in his lifetime, as distinct from the folio collected editions after his death. Eighteen of his plays appear in separate quarto editions.

Queen Mab

A name for the queen of the fairies used in ▷ Shakespeare's ▷ *Romeo and Juliet* (I. iv) and ▷ Drayton's *Nymphidia*.

Querelle des Femmes

The ▷ Renaissance debate about the virtues and vices of women ('the quarrel about women') was a continuation of a medieval argument which in literary terms may be dated from Jean de Meun's attack on women in his section of *Roman de la Rose* (c 1277) and Christine de Pisan's response, *The Book of the City of Ladies* (1405), in which she defends women. The 'woman question' became a focus of attention again in the late 16th and early 17th centuries, commencing with the publication of Joseph Swetnam's *The Arraignment of Lewd, idle, froward, and unconstant women* (1615). ▷ Rachel Speght, who was primarily a devotional writer, challenged his arguments in a serious and theoretical manner, basing her own arguments upon God's, rather than man's, law. Two other women wrote more angry ripostes to Swetnam's vituperative outpourings: ▷ Constantia

Munda and ▷ Ester Sowernam, who adopted pseudonyms to protect their reputation, and, one suspects, to ensure their physical safety in a society hardly renowned for its championing of women's rights. An earlier defence of women occurs in ▷ Jane Anger's *Jane Anger, Her Protection for Women* (1588–9).

Bib: Henderson, K. U. and McManus, B. F. (eds.), *Half Humankind.*

Rabelais, François (?1495–1553)

French comic writer. He was successively
a Franciscan friar, then Benedictine monk,
before abandoning the religious life and
turning to the study of medicine (he became
a Bachelor Medicine at Montpellier in 1535).
He was protected by the powerful ▷ Du
Bellay family in his censorship disputes with
the Sorbonne. His famous works are all in
prose, but difficult to classify because of their
kaleidoscopic forms of narrative and plot.
▷ *Pantagruel* (1533) and ▷ *Gargantua* (1535)
were later reversed in sequence, Gargantua
being the father of Pantagruel. Ten years
and more later come *Tiers Livre (Third
Book*, 1545) and *Quart Livre (Fourth Book*,
first version 1548, expanded version 1552).
The authenticity of the *Cinquiesme Livre*
(1564) remains disputed, though the opening
section, *L'Isle Sonnante* ('Ringing Island'), was
published separately in Rabelais' lifetime and
is accepted by some as his work.

There is in Rabelais an exuberant
command of linguistic mechanisms that
underpins the entire range of comedy he
deploys, from simple pun to obscenity, and
from slapstick and absurdity to invective and
▷ satire. Among English writers consciously
indebted to Rabelais, ▷ Sir John Harington's
Metamorphosis of Ajax and *Anatomy* follow his
style, using coprological humour and mock
encomia; the Elizabethan journalist ▷ Thomas
Nashe has much of Rabelais' vitality;
▷ Robert Burton's ▷ *Anatomy of Melancholy*
has a comparable amplitude of language; and
▷ Samuel Butler's attack on the Puritans
(▷ Puritanism), the mock-epic ▷ *Hudibras*, is
more than Rabelaisian in its bitter humour.
Rabelais was notably translated by the
Scotsman Sir Thomas Urquhart (c 1611–60)
(Books I–II, 1653; Book III, 1693), with
continuations by Peter Motteux (1663–1718)
(Books IV–V, 1693–94).
Bib: Bakhtin, M., *Rabelais and his World.*

Race

There are few non-white or non-European
characters in ▷ Renaissance literature,
and when they do appear the portraits are
depressingly negative. Perhaps one of the
most difficult points to recognize and accept
is that writers otherwise classed as liberal
or radical often expressed racist views,
and it is essential that differences between
Renaissance and present-day cultures should
be acknowledged in relation to race. The
two groups most commonly isolated for
stereotypical treatment and prejudice are
blacks or moors and Jews. Black characters,
including Muly Mahamet in ▷ George
Peele's *The Batter of Alcazar* and Aaron in
▷ Shakespeare's ▷ *Titus Andronicus*, are
seen to personify lust, evil, alienation and
otherness. Their source is partly in the
demonic black-faced figures of folk-culture,
but also in the stories of the late 16th-century
Moor, Abdul-el-Malek. Jewish characters
had, for religious and economic reasons, long
been seen as merciless and miserly, the classic
examples being Shylock in ▷ Shakespeare's
▷ *The Merchant of Venice*, and Barabas in
▷ Christopher Marlowe's ▷ *The Jew of Malta.*
More complex black characters such as the
tragic hero of ▷ *Othello*, do exist, but they are
few and far between.
Bib: Jones, E., *Othello's Countrymen*;
Barthelemy, A. G., *Black Face, Maligned Race.*

Ralegh (Raleigh), Sir Walter (1552–1618)

Poet, historian, courtier, explorer, colonist.
The career of Sir Walter Ralegh has been
taken as almost symbolic of the 'Renaissance
ideal' of the complete individual – one
who, with an easy grace, excels in all forms
of endeavour. In addition to the pursuits
listed above, for example, one might add:
seaman, soldier, chemist, philosopher,
theologian, even pioneer in naval medicine
and dietetics, diplomat and (somewhat
unsuccessful) politician. Ralegh's military
experience included soldiering in France
(1569) and ▷ Ireland (1580). While in Ireland
Ralegh met ▷ Spenser, who approved of
his slaughter of Spanish troops at Smerwick.
As an explorer and colonist (▷ Colonialism)
Ralegh was the driving force behind the
project to found a colony on the eastern
seaboard of the North American continent
in 1585. The project was abandoned in 1586
and, after several unsuccessful expeditions,
the patent for what had become the Virginia
settlement lapsed to the Crown in 1603. In
1595, following a period of imprisonment in
the Tower due to Elizabeth I's displeasure at
his relationship with a member of her court,
Ralegh led an expedition to South America
– an enterprise which was to be repeated
in a further unsuccessful expedition to the
Orinoco in 1616. Ralegh's South American
exploits were directed chiefly towards gaining
treasure at the expense of the Spaniards,
and it was as a member of the expeditions to
Cadiz (1596) and the Azores (1597) that his
military reputation in fighting the Spanish was
established. With the accession of ▷ James I
in 1603, however, Ralegh's brand of vigorous
expansionism became unfavourable. With
the exception of the Orinoco expedition, the

R

period between 1603 and his execution in
1618 was spent in confinement in the Tower,
to which he had been committed following
his being found guilty of conspiring against
the king in November 1603. His execution on
the charge for which he had been sentenced
in 1603, was in fact due to his pursuit of an
anti-Spanish policy when such attitudes were
no longer favourably perceived at court.

Ralegh's life was, in some measure, his
greatest achievement, for it became one
of the foundation stones of the myth of
Elizabethan accomplishment. The fact
that almost every project in which he was
involved (exceptions being the Cadiz and
Azores expeditions) failed was conveniently
ignored. As a myth-maker, however, Ralegh
was a potent force: not only his own life, but
his earlier written works served to underline
the Elizabethan self-image. In particular *A
Report of the Fight about the Azores* (1591)
and *The Discovery of the Large, Rich, and
Beautiful Empire of Guiana* (1596) can both
be read as attempts at promoting an ideal
of national endeavour. Ralegh's poetry also
contributed to the romantic legend, tinged
as it is with a melancholic awareness of the
transitory nature of existence. Perhaps his
most significant poetic achievement, though,
is the fragmentary 'Ocean's Love to Cynthia'
– a brooding, obscure and allusive text of loss
and longing. A rather different proposition
is his *History of the World* (1614), which,
in its all-inclusiveness, might stand as an
apt commentary on its author. The *History*,
though it draws veiled comparisons between
the present and the past, concludes at the date
130 BC. It is yet another unfinished enterprise.
▷ School of Night.
Bib: Oldys, W. and Birch, T. (eds.),
Works (8 vols); Greenblatt, S., *Ralegh: The
Renaissance Man and His Roles*; May, S. W.,
Sir Walter Ralegh.

Ralph Roister Doister (1552)

A comedy by Nicholas Udall, printed in 1566,
and written in about 1552. It is sometimes
called 'the first English comedy', presumably
because the earlier 'comic interludes' notably
by ▷ John Heywood (*eg The Play of the
Weather* and *The Four P's*) were too slight to
count, whereas Udall's play, which may have
been written for the boys of Westminster
School, is an adaptation of the *Miles Gloriosus*
(*The Boastful Soldier*) by ▷ Plautus. The basic
situation is the same in both plays: vain but
foolish and boastful soldier makes love to a
respectable woman (Christian Custance in
Udall's play), who is betrothed to a merchant,

Gawin Goodluck, and Ralph is encouraged
in his misguided enterprise by a mischievous
associate, Matthew Merygreek. But the play
has a kind of farcical humour which has more
in common with the popular ▷ interludes and
even the May Games of English country life,
and it reads as a thoroughly native product.
The rhymed verse is rather primitive, but the
dialogue has realistic freshness. The comedy
is an example of humanistic learning married
to popular entertainment.

Randolph, Thomas (1605–35)

Poet and dramatist. Randolph revealed his
literary skills early on, writing poetry at the
age of ten, and then becoming renowned
for his Latin and English verses while a
student at Cambridge. The plays do not live
up to his early promise, however, and he is
most successful at short satiric pieces. For
example, although *The Jealous Lovers* (1632)
was performed before ▷ Charles I and
▷ Henrietta Maria, it is an uninspired and
glib romance. He is more skilful with country
scenes: the ▷ pastoral poems are beautifully
lyrical and his pastoral play, *Amyntas* (1630),
has some good rustic comedy pieces.
Randolph's most interesting work, *The Muse's
Looking Glass*, was written while he was still at
university, although only published in 1638;
it contains an actor who defeats a ▷ Puritan's
anti-theatre arguments and it is gratifyingly
▷ Jonsonian in tone.
Bib: Smith, G. C. M., *Thomas Randolph*.

Reader-response criticism

▷ Reception theory.

Reception theory

This movement is associated pre-eminently
with the German contemporary literary
theorists Wolfgang Iser and Hans-Robert
Jauss, and is often linked with reader-response
criticism. Reception theory emphasizes the
reader's consumption of the literary text
over and above the question of the sum total
of rhetorical devices that contribute to its
structure as a piece of literature. The work of
reception (*Rezeptionästhetik*) causes the reader
constantly to rethink the canonical value of
texts, since it involves noting the history of a
text's reception as well as the current value it
may possess for the critic. Insofar as reception
theory concerns itself with larger historical
questions, it emphasizes histories of response
which help to account for the reception of
particular texts in the present. The approach
to 'history' outlined here is pragmatic, and the
emphasis is laid firmly on the matter of the

interaction between text and reader and on the way cultural context is required to make sense of literature.

Recusancy

A term used under ▷ Elizabeth I for refusal, usually by Roman Catholics, to attend religious worship in the ▷ Church of England. The recusancy law continued to exist until the Toleration Act (1689), which permitted freedom of worship.

Red Cross Knight, The

The central figure of Book I of ▷ Edmund Spenser's ▷ The Faerie Queene. He represents Holiness, the ▷ Church of England and St George, whose red cross on a white ground is the national emblem of England. His adventures are connected with two women: Una, the true religion from which he is separated, and ▷ Duessa, the Roman Catholic Church which beguiles him. He is eventually united to Una with the assistance of Prince Arthur (▷ Arthur, King), who rescues him from the House of Pride.

Reformation

An important religious movement in the 16th century; its aim was to protest in a variety of ways against the conduct of the Catholic Church, which had hitherto remained undivided. The outcome was division: the Roman Catholics remained dominant in the countries bordering on the western Mediterranean and in south Germany; the new ▷ Protestant churches became supreme in northern Europe. The causes of the movement were political (the rise of the new nation-state); moral (resentment at the low example set by many of the clergy); and doctrinal (disagreement, stimulated by the new critical spirit of the ▷ Renaissance, over points of doctrine hitherto imposed by the authority of the Church).

The Reformation in England proceeded in three phases.

1 ▷ Henry VIII carried out the first in merely political terms. His desire to divorce Katharine of Aragon was merely a pretext; he himself sought complete control of the ▷ Church of England, and needed money; he resented the authority of the Pope in Rome and the internationalism of the monastic orders; he welcomed the opportunity to increase his wealth by confiscating their property. He declared himself Supreme Head of the Church of England by the ▷ Act of Supremacy, supported by Parliament and passed by it in 1533; he dissolved the monasteries in 1536–39. On the other hand his ▷ Six Articles of 1539 tried to keep the Church fully Catholic on all points except that of papal sovereignty. As the support by Parliament showed, he had popular opinion behind him, at least in southern England; the English Church had long been restive against the sovereignty of the Pope, particularly when, in the 14th century, he had reigned from Avignon in France, the home of the national enemy.

2 The second phase, under his son ▷ Edward VI, went further and aroused more national disagreement. The clergy were permitted to marry, and ▷ The Book of Common Prayer included 42 articles of faith (later reduced to 39) which defined the doctrine of the Church of England in Protestant terms. There was also extensive destruction of religious images in churches throughout the country. Henry's daughter ▷ Mary I undertook a complete reaction back to Catholicism, but her persecution of the Protestants and her subservience to her husband, Philip II of Spain, the most fanatical of the Catholic sovereigns, confirmed the country in a Protestant direction.

3 Henry's remaining daughter ▷ Elizabeth I contrived a religious settlement that was a compromise between the reforms of her father and those of her brother. The intention was to be inclusive: Catholics were not to be driven out of the Church of England if she could help it, and she wanted to keep as many of her Protestant subjects within it as possible. The result, however, was disunion: Catholics could not subscribe to the Church of England after the Pope had excommunicated the queen in 1571, and the more extreme Protestants were constantly pressing for further reforms, especially in the structure of church government (they mostly wanted the abolition of rule through bishops) and in the conduct of worship, which they wanted in full austerity. These ▷ Puritans, as they were called by their enemies, eventually established their own religious organizations, but not until after 1660. The vagueness of the Elizabethan settlement also gave rise to disagreement within the Church of England, and this has lasted until the present day: the High Church is the section which emphasizes the more Catholic interpretation of the settlement (ie more in keeping with Henry VIII's intentions), and the Low Church is the section which insists that the Church of England is essentially Protestant. This disagreement, however, has never disrupted the organization of the Church, which, under the headship

of the sovereign, is still that of the Catholic church of medieval England.

The Reformation in Scotland proceeded side by side with the Elizabethan phase in England, and helped to bring about a reconciliation of the two nations, who had been hostile to each other for three centuries. The Scottish Reformation, however, was extreme, under the leadership of ▷ John Knox, a disciple of the French reformer ▷ Calvin. The national Church of Scotland has remained Calvinist (▷ Presbyterian) to this day. Ireland remained Catholic, and in consequence suffered severe persecution by its English rulers in the 16th and 17th centuries. The only excuse for this tyranny was the real danger that Ireland might become a base for one of England's more powerful Catholic enemies – France or Spain.

Religio Medici (1635)

(*The Religion of a Physician*.) A work of spiritual and autobiographical reflection by ▷ Sir Thomas Browne. It was written c 1635, and seems not to have been intended for publication but for circulation among the author's friends. After its publication without Browne's permission in 1642, however, an authorized text was issued in 1643 that was subsequently translated into Dutch, German, Latin and French. As a form of ▷ autobiography, the work presents the image of a relaxed, sceptical, philosophic and endlessly self-intrigued author. Informed by a desire to reconcile religious belief with the kind of scepticism associated with the ▷ 'New Science' of the mid-17th century, Browne's work became something of a best-seller. Stylistically, in its engaging enjoyment of digressive, curious and highly intellectualized speculation, the work can be compared to the poetry of ▷ John Donne or, later, ▷ Henry Vaughan. But it also forms part of the trend towards sceptical enquiry that was to be fostered by ▷ Thomas Hobbes.

Renaissance in England, The

'Renaissance' (or 'Renascence') derives from Latin 'renascentia' = 'rebirth'. The word was first used by Italian scholars in the mid-16th century to express the rediscovery of ancient Roman and Greek culture, which was now studied for its own sake and not used merely to enhance the authority of the Church. Modern scholars are more inclined to use the term to express a great variety of interdependent changes which Europe underwent politically, economically and culturally between 1450 (although the

starting-points were much earlier) and 1600. The religious outcome of these changes is expressed through the terms ▷ Reformation and ▷ Counter-Reformation, a sequence of events closely bound up with the Renaissance.

In England, the Renaissance is usually thought of as beginning with the accession of the House of ▷ Tudor to the throne in 1485. Politically, this marks the end of the period of civil war amongst the old feudal aristocracy (the Wars of the Roses) in the mid-15th century, and the establishment of something like a modern, efficient, centralized state; technically, the date is close to that of the introduction of printing into England – an invention without which the great cultural changes of the Renaissance could not have occurred. Culturally, the first important period in England was the reign of the second Tudor monarch, ▷ Henry VIII. This was the period of the English ▷ humanists ▷ More, ▷ Grocyn, ▷ Linacre and the poet ▷ Sir Thomas Wyatt.

Several distinctive features characterize the English Renaissance. The first is the lateness of its impact. Italian, French, German, Dutch and Spanish scholars had already worked on the ancient Greek and Latin writers, and had produced works of their own inspired by the classics; in consequence, English culture was revitalized not so much directly by the classics as by contemporary Europeans under the influence of the classics. ▷ Castiglione's *The Courtier*, ▷ Machiavelli's *The Prince*, ▷ Ariosto's *Orlando*, were as important in the English Renaissance as ▷ Virgil's ▷ *Aeneid* or the plays of ▷ Seneca, and it was characteristic that ▷ North translated ▷ Plutarch's *Lives* not from the original Greek but from a French version. Such an influx of foreign influences, both contemporary and ancient, might have overwhelmed the native English literary tradition but for two more distinctive features: England as an insular country followed a course of social and political history that was to a great extent independent of the course of history elsewhere in Europe, for example in the peculiarity of the English Reformation, and this assisted the country in preserving its cultural independence; and owing to the example of the works of the 14th-century poet ▷ Chaucer, the native literature was sufficiently vigorous and experienced in assimilating foreign influences without being subjected by them. A fourth characteristic of English Renaissance literature is that it is primarily artistic, rather than philosophical and scholarly, and a fifth is the coinciding of the Renaissance and the Reformation in

England, in contrast to the rest of Europe, where the Reformation (or, in countries that remained Roman Catholic, the Counter-Reformation) succeeded the Renaissance.

The English Renaissance was largely literary, and achieved its finest expression in the so-called Elizabethan drama, which began to excel only in the last decade of the 16th century and reached its height in the first 15 years of the 17th; its finest exponents were ▷ Christopher Marlowe, ▷ Ben Jonson and ▷ William Shakespeare. Non-dramatic poetry was also extremely rich, and reached its peak in the same period in the work of ▷ Edmund Spenser, ▷ Philip Sidney, Shakespeare and ▷ John Donne, but it is typical of the lateness of the Renaissance in England that its most ambitious product, John Milton's ▷ epic ▷ *Paradise Lost*, was published as late as 1667. Native English prose shaped itself more slowly than poetry; More wrote his ▷ *Utopia* in Latin, which was the vehicle of some other writers, including ▷ Francis Bacon (in much of his work), owing to its advantages (for international circulation) over English at a time when the latter was little learned in other countries. Nonetheless English prose developed with vigour in native English writers such as ▷ Roger Ascham, Thomas North, ▷ Richard Hooker, in the English works of Francis Bacon, and in the translators of the ▷ Bible.
Bib: Braden, G. and Kerrigan, W., *The Idea of the Renaissance*.

Republic, The
A philosophical dialogue by the Greek philosopher ▷ Plato. Socrates discusses with his friends the nature of justice, and the conversation leads to an outline of the ideal state. Public life must exhibit the highest virtues of private life, and justice is achieved if the classes work together to contribute to society the virtues in which each excels. Democracy (the rule of the people), oligarchy (the rule of a small powerful group), and timocracy (the rule of men of property) are in turn rejected in favour of aristocracy – the rule of the best, trained by an exacting system of education. The aristocrat will seek wisdom, whereas the man of action seeks honour, and the merchant gratifies his appetites. Wisdom is a direct apprehension of the good conceived as a system of ideal forms; Book VII contains the famous parable of men sitting with their backs to these forms (the only substantial reality) watching the shadows on the wall of the cavern – *ie* phenomena apprehended by the senses – and supposing these shadows to be the only reality. Book X contains Plato's notorious rejection of poetry: poets must be expelled, though with honour, because they frustrate the pursuit of true wisdom by extolling the illusory phenomena of this world, and weaken the mind by stimulating wasteful sympathy with the misfortunes of men.

Revels, Master of the
An official at the royal court in the 16th and 17th centuries; his function was responsibility for court entertainments, *eg* ▷ masques, cf. Philostrate in ▷ *A Midsummer Night's Dream*. This function later involved the ▷ censorship of plays and licensing of theatres in the London region.
Bib: Dutton, R., *Mastering the Revels: the Regulation and Censorship of English Renaissance Drama*.

Revenger's Tragedy, The (1607)
A drama in ▷ blank verse attributed to ▷ Cyril Tourneur, although modern scholars incline increasingly to attribute it to ▷ Thomas Middleton. The scene is a dissolute ▷ Renaissance court in Italy. The sensual Duke has a vicious legitimate son, Lussurioso, by his first wife; the Duchess, his second wife, is in love with his illegitimate son, Spurio, who uses his bastardy as a pretext for general sensual rapacity; her own sons, Ambitioso and Supervacuo, are consumed with envy, and she herself is totally without moral restraint. This evil family is not so much a group of characters in the ordinary, realistic sense as an array of allegorical representations of the fleshly vices; their Italianate names suggest their ▷ allegories – Lussurioso = Luxury, Spurio = Falseness, etc. They are predatory on one another, and the downfall of the whole family is plotted by Vindice (= Revenger), whose betrothed has been poisoned by the Duke; he is assisted by his brother Hippolito. Disguised, Vindice enters the service of Lussorioso, and pretends to procure his own sister, Castiza (= Chastity) as mistress for his master; he finds to his horror that their own mother is prepared to sell her for the price of becoming a court lady. Vindice carries out his revenge on the Duke in a scene of great emblematic ferocity, and eventually contrives the bloodthirsty destruction of the whole family. He himself, however, is sent to his death by the Duke's virtuous successor: a Revenger, in however just a cause, is a criminal too dangerous to leave alive.

The violence of the action is redeemed from crudity by the energy, compression

and conviction of the language, and by the way in which Tourneur fuses three modes of feeling into original art. One of these is the tradition of medieval allegory, which was becoming diluted and abstract in much Renaissance poetry, but which in this play keeps its old power of condensing emotion into powerful images. Tourneur uses the allegorical form to substantiate ▷ Puritan detestation of sensual vice, which was the evil extreme of the Renaissance liberation of the physical appetites. At the same time, both these vices and Vindice's vindictiveness are expressed with an energy that is itself a rich manifestation of Renaissance feeling. In uniting these disparate resources, the play is one of the masterpieces of ▷ Jacobean drama.
▷ Revenge tragedy.

Revenge tragedy

A kind of tragedy that was particularly popular during and just after the lifetime of ▷ Shakespeare, *ie* 1590–1620. The plot of such plays was commonly the murder by a person in power of a near relative, wife, or husband of the central character, who is then faced with the problem of how, or sometimes whether, to carry out revenge against a murderer who, because of his social importance, is out of reach of ordinary justice. The literary inspiration for this kind of play came from the plays of the Roman poet ▷ Seneca, whose *Ten Tragedies* were translated into English between 1559 and 1581. Seneca's plays would doubtless have been insufficient in themselves, however, to get going the great English series of revenge tragedies, if the theme had not been relevant to English society. This society was in a stage midway between primitive lawlessness, in which justice is beyond the reach of the weak and unprivileged, and the modern state, in which justice is impartial and police are numerous and efficient. The tradition that revenge for an injury to a member of his or her family was a duty for the individual was still widely maintained; against it, the state maintained that revenge not carried out as due punishment through a court of law was a crime, and the Church taught that it was a sin. On the other hand, the law was unreliable, though not helpless, against the powerful and the powerfully protected, and in the face of the religious prohibition the revenger might consider himself to be the instrument of Divine Vengeance.

This state of conflict in the Elizabethan conscience made for different styles of revenge play. The first of those offering

straightforward treatment of the theme was ▷ Thomas Kyd's ▷ *The Spanish Tragedy*; Shakespeare's early ▷ history plays ▷ *Henry VI, Parts I, II* and *III* and ▷ *Richard III* are revenge plays as well, and another early example by Shakespeare is his ▷ *Titus Andronicus*. Later examples: ▷ *The Revenger's Tragedy* by ▷ Cyril Tourneur (or perhaps ▷ Thomas Middleton) and Thomas Middleton's ▷ *Women Beware Women*, to mention only plays of distinction. Another style might be called the 'anti-revenge' drama, in which the hero is too enlightened to seek revenge – examples are Tourneur's ▷ *The Atheist's Tragedy* and ▷ Chapman's *Revenge of Bussy d' Ambois*, both about 1611. The finest of all tragedies of revenge, Shakespeare's ▷ *Hamlet*, is between the two styles, inasmuch as the hero both accepts the obligation to revenge and has to fight against his revulsion from it. A third style might rather be called the tragedy of retribution, inasmuch as a crime is avenged but the drama is not centred on a specific avenger; such plays include ▷ Webster's ▷ *The White Devil* and ▷ *The Duchess of Malfi* and Middleton's masterpiece ▷ *The Changeling*. Revenge and retribution are of course akin, and the importance of revenge tragedy, apart from its intrinsic interest, is that it is the starting-point for the development of some of Shakespeare's greatest tragic themes, *eg* his ▷ *Othello* and ▷ *Macbeth*, though these are not usually placed in the same category.
Bib: Mercer, P., *Hamlet and the Acting of Revenge*.

Rhetoric

Rhetoric in the medieval period was a formal skill of considerable importance. It was taken to mean the effective presentation of ideas with a set of rules or style, and was founded in the classical tradition of ▷ Aristotle and ▷ Cicero. It was taught in monastic (▷ Monasteries) schools as part of the *trivium*, Rhetoric, Logic and Grammar, which used as its basic text Geoffrey de Vinsauf's *Poetria Nova* (1200). Rhetoric not only formed patterns in which texts should be written, but also governed how the works should be received and allocated them to particular categories, *eg* ▷ epic, debate or sermon. The system of rhetoric was paramount to the operation of literature in the medieval period.

Similarly, almost all of the practice or theory of writing in the ▷ Renaissance period was touched by what became known as the 'Art of Rhetoric'. Rhetorical theory formed an important part of the educational syllabus at the universities, and almost every major writer of the 16th and 17th centuries would have undergone some training in rhetoric. Rhetoric was learned first through reading the classical textbooks on rhetoric, in particular the works of Quintilian (especially the *Institutio Oratore*) and Cicero. Secondly, practical rhetorical exercises were performed by the student in which a particular topic was debated. In these debates, the student was expected to be able to organize an argument according to set formulae, producing examples with which to sustain the analysis that would themselves be derived from a suitable store of words, images, fables and ▷ metaphors discovered in reading classical texts.

But the production of arguments was only one part of the rhetoricians' skills. Rhetoric also involved the classification of language – in particular the classification and analysis of figures of speech. Further, it was understood as an enabling tool by which ▷ discourse could be reproduced. In essence, therefore, it offered a system for producing both speech and writing. This system can be considered under five distinct parts: 1 'invention', which signifies the discovery of arguments applicable to a given case; 2 'arrangement' or 'disposition', which governed the ordering of the arguments to be used; 3 'style' or the actual choice of words and units of expression; 4 the important area of 'memory', which helped the rhetorician develop skills in recalling the order and substance of the argument being deployed; 5 'delivery', which was applicable mainly to spoken discourse but which governed such details as the appropriate facial expressions or gestures that might be used.

Whilst rhetoric was understood as a way of facilitating the classification of the various parts of an argument, it was also a powerful tool in the analysis of discourse and it can thus be understood as a form of literary criticism. It was, however, in its abiding influence on stylistic forms that it was of most importance to the Renaissance writer. Numerous textbooks on rhetoric were published throughout the 16th century in England. Perhaps the most important were: Leonard Cox, *The Art or Craft of Rhetoric* (1624); Richard Sherry, *A Treatise of Schemes and Tropes* (1550); ▷ Thomas Wilson, *Art of Rhetoric* (1553); ▷ Henry Peacham, *The Garden of Eloquence* (1577); and Abraham Fraunce, *Arcadian Rhetoric* (1584). But many other texts were written with the art of rhetoric either governing the structure or informing the language. ▷ Sir Philip Sidney's ▷ *An Apologie for Poetrie*, for example, is

structured according to rhetorical principles of organization.

Recent developments in critical theory have sought to re-emphasize rhetoric as a form of critical practice, particularly in relation to the *effects* that any verbal construction may have on those to whom it is addressed. In this respect rhetoric is closely associated with some of the larger issues that surface in relation to the theory of 'discourse'. The recent emphasis upon the *structure* of discourse draws attention away from language as a means of *classifying* to one of examining the way discourses are constructed in order to achieve certain effects. Here the emphasis would be on the different *ways* in which particular figures are presented in language, and what that presentation may involve. This form of rhetorical analysis has been undertaken by ▷ Jacques Derrida in volumes such as *Of Grammatology* (1974), by Paul De Man in his *Blindness and Insight* (1971), by ▷ Terry Eagleton in *Criticism and Ideology* (1976), and in a whole range of texts by ▷ Michel Foucault.

Richard II (1377–99)

King of England, and last of the direct line in the House of Plantagenet (Anjou). He was the son of the Black Prince and the grandson of his predecessor, ▷ Edward III. His neglect of the war against France, his youthfulness (he came to the throne at the age of 11), and his capricious, inconsistent character all helped to make his reign a period of disorder; the throne was eventually usurped by his cousin, Henry Bolingbroke, who became first king of the House of Lancaster as ▷ Henry IV. Richard had an expensive court, and was a patron of the arts in so far as he intermittently showed favour to the poets ▷ Chaucer and ▷ Gower.

Richard II, King

An historical drama in ▷ blank verse by ▷ Shakespeare, based on the Chronicles of ▷ Holinshed. First performed in 1595, and published in a first ▷ quarto in 1597, it is the first of the second tetralogy of ▷ history plays by Shakespeare, the other three being ▷ *Henry IV, Parts I* and *II* and ▷ *Henry V*.

The theme of all four is kingship; ▷ Richard II is treated as a king whose sacred claim to the throne is beyond doubt, but is tragically unaccompanied by any capacity to rule. The leading story is about his relationship with his cousin, Henry Bolingbroke (▷ Henry IV); he drives Henry (not altogether without justification) into exile, and then quite unlawfully confiscates

Henry's land. Henry returns to England to defend his right, and receives so much support that he is driven to making himself king. Usurpers, however, were considered to be opposing God, since kings held the throne by God's authority, and so Henry does his best to persuade Richard to abdicate publicly. Richard does so, but he skilfully makes it clear to all the witnesses that his abdication is involuntary (IV. i), so that the public abdication only emphasizes, instead of relieves, Henry's guilt. Concerned as it is with the ritualistic aspect of monarchy – the ceremonies that are the signs of the sacredness of the office – the whole play has been observed by critics to have a ritualistic style in the formal patterning of much of the verse and the pageant-like ceremony of a number of the important scenes. Richard is imprisoned in the Tower, and is later assassinated; thus the effect of criminality in Henry's action in seizing the throne is confirmed.

▷ Earl of Essex.

Richard III (1483–85)

Last king of England in the House of York, which seized the throne from the House of Lancaster in 1461. The first of the short line was Edward IV (1461–83), Richard's brother; he was succeeded by his son, the boy king Edward V, whose throne Richard usurped. He was himself defeated and killed at the Battle of Bosworth (1485) by Henry Tudor, who succeeded as ▷ Henry VII, the first sovereign of the ▷ Tudor line. It was very much in the Tudor interest to blacken the character of Richard III, and 16th-century historians (Polydore Vergil, ▷ Thomas More, ▷ Holinshed) depict him as satanically evil. Modern historians have found it difficult to discover whether this account is just, and there have been some attempts to rehabilitate his character. One of the chief charges against him is the murder of his two nephews Edward V and Richard of York, the 'princes in the Tower'. That they were murdered is almost certain, but there is no proof that Richard was guilty.

▷ Histories and Chronicles.

Richard III (?1593)

An historical drama in ▷ blank verse by ▷ Shakespeare based on ▷ Holinshed's Chronicles, and the last of Shakespeare's first historical tetralogy, the other plays being the three parts of ▷ Henry VI. The ▷ Henry VI plays are about the Wars of the Roses, and the accumulation of hatred,

vengefulness and crime that those wars brought about. Richard III opens in the reign of Edward IV, Richard's brother, and shows the attempts of the king to induce his nobles to be reconciled. Fear and war-weariness make them comply, but Richard is still filled with ambition and cold-blooded cruelty. In spite of his appearance – he is a hunchback and has a withered arm – he has a magnetic personality and manages to win friends to help him in his conspiracies. By consistent treachery and ruthlessness he acquires the throne, but is shortly after defeated and killed by Henry Tudor (▷ Henry VII), who is shown in the play to have right and divine aid on his side. Though totally evil, Richard is presented as a character of energy and wit, the source of much sardonic comedy. Dramatically he is in the tradition of both ▷ Machiavelli's The Prince – a treatise of evil for Englishmen of Shakespeare's day – and of Herod in the medieval mystery plays. The play is the masterpiece of the earliest group of Shakespeare's plays, ie those probably written before 1594.

▷ History plays.

Richards, I. A. (1893–1979)

Critic. His approach to poetry was philosophic, linguistic and psychological. One of his important insights was that we are inevitably influenced by some kind of 'poetry', even if it is only that of bad films and magazine covers, or advertisements. In Principles of Literary Criticism (1924) and Science and Poetry (1926) he discusses what kind of truth is the subject-matter of poetry, the place of poetry in the context of the rest of life, and what is the nature of critical judgements of poetry. He worked to his conclusion on Benthamite lines, asking what is 'the use' of poetry; his conclusion was that poetry's function in the modern world is that formerly provided by religion – to provide a 'touchstone' of value, and hence, if only indirectly, a guide to living. This view resembles the judgements of other writers of the 1920s and 30s, though they arrived at this judgement by a different approach. Richard's Practical Criticism (1929) is a teaching manual for the study of poetry with the aim of training students to judge poems presented anonymously, without being influenced by the author's reputation; its ideas have been extensively followed in English and American schools and universities. Much of his later work has been purely linguistic, eg Basic English and its Uses (1943). Other works: The Meaning of Meaning (with Ogden, 1923); Coleridge on Imagination (1934); The Philosophy *of Rhetoric* (1936); *Speculative Instruments* (1955); *Goodbye Earth and other poems* (1959); *The Screens* (1961).

▷ New Criticism.

Bib: Hyman, S., *The Armed Vision*.

Ridley, Nicholas (?1500–55)
One of the leading religious reformers in the reign of ▷ Henry VIII and, with ▷ Cranmer and ▷ Latimer, one of the three principal martyrs in 1555 under the Roman Catholic reaction of ▷ Mary I. He helped Cranmer compile ▷ *The Book of Common Prayer* of 1549 and 1552, and thus contributed to one of the first English prose masterpieces. He became Bishop of London in 1549.

Ridolfi plot (1570)
Organized by the Italian Roberto di Ridolfi against ▷ Elizabeth I. He planned to marry the Catholic ▷ Mary Queen of Scots to the Duke of Norfolk and place her on the throne of England with Spanish help. The plot was discovered by Elizabeth's spies, but Ridolfi was himself in safety in Paris.

Roaring Girl, The, or Moll Cut-Purse (1606)
A buoyant and big-hearted comedy of gender ambiguity by ▷ Thomas Middleton, structured around the benevolent figure of Moll Cutpurse whose function in the play it is to smooth the course of true love. She is described by her detractors as a 'woman more than man, / Man more than woman,' and becomes the play's moral centre of reference. More than anything Middleton's Moll Cutpurse seems to be conceived of as a ▷ Jacobean ▷ citizen comedy version of ▷ Shakespeare's ▷ Rosalind from ▷ *As You Like It*.

Robin Hood
The hero of popular ▷ ballads from the 14th to 16th centuries. As a popular hero, he was to some extent the counterpart of ▷ King Arthur, the ideal of the noble class. Robin Hood lived in the forest of Sherwood near Nottingham in the Midlands; he was an expert archer and huntsman, stole from the rich in order to give to the poor, was the enemy of the rich churchmen but not a pagan. He is sometimes represented as a Saxon hero resisting the Norman-French aristocracy, but the period at which he was supposed to live varies from the 12th to 14th centuries.

The ballads about him do not have great literary merit, and the surviving texts do not date further back than the 15th century; the most important is *A Lytell Geste of Robyn Hode* (1510). ▷ Anthony Munday collaborated with ▷ Henry Chettle on two plays about the folk-hero, *The Downfall of Robert, Earle of Huntington* and *The Death of Robert, Earle of Huntington* (both 1598).

Roman Actor, The (1626)
A bloody ▷ tragedy by ▷ Philip Massinger set at the time of the emperor Domitian. The play dramatizes Domitian's marriage to the resourceful Domitia, whose husband he has executed. During a play-within-the-play he kills the actor Paris with whom she has fallen in love, which leads to her conspiring against him and his assassination.

Romances of Shakespeare
A term often used to express the character of four of the last plays by Shakespeare: ▷ *Pericles* (1608–9); ▷ *Cymbeline* (1609–10); ▷ *The Winter's Tale* (1610–11); ▷ *The Tempest* (1611).

The following are some of the qualities that distinguish these plays:

1 Extravagance of incident. Shakespeare abandons the comparatively realistic presentation characteristic of his tragic period, 1604–8. Events are extraordinary, and in *Pericles* and *The Winter's Tale* they are widespread in place and time; in *Pericles* and *Cymbeline* they are loosely related in plot. In *Cymbeline* and *The Winter's Tale* there is no consistency of period, and classical history mingles with 16th-century social settings. In *The Tempest* Shakespeare makes a freer use of magic than in any of his other plays, but in its strict unity of time and place this play is otherwise in contrast to the other three plays of the group.

2 Although *The Tempest* is again here to some extent a contrast to the others, the group belongs to a category known as ▷ 'tragicomedy'; that is to say *Pericles*, *Cymbeline* and *The Winter's Tale* each deepen into tragedy, which reaches a climax midway in the story, and then lighten towards a happy conclusion. *The Tempest* is different in that the tragedy has all taken place before the play has begun; the whole play is thus devoted to restoring happiness out of tragedy already accomplished.

3 In each play the theme concerns an ordeal undergone by the main character; in this respect, however, the plays show a progression. Pericles does no wrong; he is a passive sufferer, with no power of his own to relieve his suffering. Cymbeline commits errors, and the tragedy arises from

them, but he is not called on to act in order that the errors shall be redeemed. In *The Winter's Tale* Leontes' error amounts to a terrible crime, and this has to be expiated by a long period of unremitting repentance. Prospero, in *The Tempest*, has committed no error beyond severing himself from his worldly responsibilities; he is a powerful and virtuous man who could wreak vengeance on his enemies but chooses instead to reconcile himself to them by acts of godlike mercy.

4 In the first three plays, the ordeal of the hero is characterized by the loss of his family, and in each of them it is a daughter who is chiefly instrumental in bringing about the reunion which constitutes the happy ending. *The Tempest* is again somewhat different from the others. Here father and daughter remain together, but they are both cast off from the rest of the world; it is again the daughter who is instrumental in the final reunion.

In the romances the imaginative emphasis is on reconciliation. Prospero's statement in *The Tempest* that 'the rarer action is/In virtue than in vengeance' epitomizes the distance Shakespeare has travelled since ▷ *Hamlet* and the other tragedies, all of which are to some extent reworked in the late plays.

Romeo and Juliet (1597)

A romantic ▷ tragedy by ▷ Shakespeare. It was published in ▷ quarto in a corrupt form in 1597, and in a better edition in 1599. The story is an old one; Shakespeare's version is based on the poem *Romeus and Juliet* (1562) by Arthur Brooke, itself based on a French version of an Italian tale by Bandello (1554). The story is of the romantic love of Romeo, belonging to the family of ▷ Montague, and Juliet, of the ▷ Capulet family, both living in the Italian city of Verona. The affair has to be kept secret owing to the bitter hostility of the two families, and only Juliet's nurse and Friar Laurence, who marries them, know of it. Even so the affair is not allowed to continue peacefully; Juliet's cousin Tybalt provokes an affray that leads not only to his own death but to that of Mercutio, friend of Romeo and relative of the Prince of Verona, with the result that Romeo is exiled from the city. Moreover, Juliet's father, in ignorance of his daughter's secret marriage, proposes to marry her off in haste to a young nobleman, Paris. To enable her to escape this, Friar Laurence gives Juliet a potion that sends her into a profound sleep and causes her family to suppose her dead; the Friar's design is that she shall be placed in the family burial vault, and that meanwhile a message is to be sent

to Romeo directing him to come by night and steal her away. However, by an accident the message is not sent, and Romeo hears only of her death; he returns to Verona, but only to take poison and die by her side. A moment later, the effect of the potion wears off and Juliet recovers; she sees her lover dead beside her, and kills herself in turn.

The play is one of Shakespeare's early masterpieces, and is famous for its exquisite poetry and the dramatic excellence of some of its scenes (*eg* II. i where the lovers declare their love to each other in the 'balcony scene'), and of three of its characters, namely Juliet, her nurse, and Romeo's friend Mercutio. It is not, however, a tragedy in the sense in which we understand the term 'Shakespearian tragedy', in regard to the plays written after 1600. In these plays, tragedy is the outcome of the nature and situation of the central character (*eg* ▷ *Othello*), whereas in *Romeo and Juliet* the unhappy ending is more the result of accident – notably the failure to send the message to Romeo. On the other hand, it is possible that the usual response to the play is more sentimental than Shakespeare intended: Brooke's poem is puritanical and reproves the lovers for their passion; Shakespeare presents them sympathetically, but there are signs – *eg* the Friar's soliloquy opening II. iii – that he intended the passion to be regarded as a misfortune in itself. Whatever one's views on this, the excellence of the play arises above all from the actuality with which Shakespeare presents Juliet: the tradition of courtly romance is brought, as in ▷ Chaucer's ▷ *Troilus and Criseyde*, closely into relationship with real life.

▷ Courtly love.

Ronsard, Pierre de (1524–1585)

French poet, leader of the ▷ Renaissance group known as the ▷ 'Pléiade'. His output was wide-ranging (▷ odes, ▷ hymns, ▷ epic, ▷ elegies), but he is particularly famous for his love ▷ sonnets, Petrarchan (▷ Petrarch) in style, and it was in this form that Ronsard was influential among English sonneteers of the Renaissance, *eg* ▷ Henry Constable (1562–1613) and ▷ Samuel Daniel.
Bib: Langer, V., *Invention, Death and Self-definitions in the Poetry of Pierre de Ronsard.*

Roper, Margaret More (1505–44)

Margaret Roper, the daughter of ▷ Thomas More, became renowned in England for her learning. As a member of More's household, her education was of great importance, indeed she was perhaps the intellectual star of what

has been sometimes termed the 'School of More', which included More's children, wards, relatives and friends. In a letter written in 1521, ▷ Erasmus records that it was the education and intellectual capacities of Margaret Roper that convinced him of the value of education for women in general. Indeed, Margaret Roper may well have formed the basis for Erasmus's sympathetic portrait of the learned woman in one of his *Colloquies*. Many of Margaret Roper's works are now lost, but what is known of her is derived mainly from the letters she and her father exchanged while he was in prison prior to his execution, and from her husband's account of More's life, which is also an account of his wife. Her major surviving published work is her ▷ translation of Erasmus's commentary on The Lord's Prayer, which was published (though its translator was not acknowledged) as *A Devout Treatise Upon the 'Pater Noster'*, probably in 1524. Her daughter, ▷ Mary Basset, was also a learned translator.
Bib: McCutcheon, E., 'Margaret More Roper: The Learned Woman in Tudor England', *Women Writers of the Renaissance and Reformation* (ed.) K. M. Wilson.

Rosalind, Rosalynde
1 The central character in ▷ Shakespeare's comedy ▷ *As You Like It*. She is based on the heroine of ▷ Thomas Lodge's romance *Rosalynde, Euphues Golden Legacy* (1590)
2 A character in *January*, the first month of Spenser's ▷ *Shepherd's Calendar*; she has been thought to represent Rosa Daniel, the sister of the poet ▷ Samuel Daniel, and wife of ▷ John Florio, translator of the *Essays* of ▷ Montaigne.

Roscius (Quintus Roscius Gallus) (?126-62 BC)
A famous Roman comic actor. He wrote a treatise comparing acting and oratory, and the great orator ▷ Cicero took lessons from him. It became a habit to praise actors by comparing them to Roscius; thus ▷ Ben Jonson compared ▷ Edward Alleyn to him.

Rose Theatre
Opened by the theatre manager, ▷ Philip Henslowe, in 1587 on Bankside in Southwark. ▷ Shakespeare may have been a member of his company at the time. Henslowe managed the theatre together with his son-in-law, ▷ Edward Alleyn, until 1603. The foundations of the Rose were uncovered in 1990.
▷ Theatres.

Roundheads
A name for ▷ Puritan supporters of the Parliamentary party in the ▷ Civil Wars of 1642–51. They were so called because they habitually cut their hair close to their heads, whereas the Royalists (▷ Cavaliers) wore their hair ornamentally long. This Cavalier habit was regarded by the Puritans as a symptom of worldliness. The word has been traced back to 1641, when a Cavalier officer was quoted as declaring that he would 'cut the throats of those round-headed dogs that bawled against bishops'. Earlier than this, a ▷ pamphlet against long hair was published under the title of 'The unloveliness of lovelocks'.

Rowley, William (1585–1637)
English actor and dramatist who collaborated with ▷ Thomas Middleton on several plays, including ▷ *The Changeling* to which he almost certainly contributed the subplot. He also collaborated with ▷ Thomas Heywood and ▷ John Webster, among others, on *The Witch of Edmonton* (1608). However, Rowley's work is uneven and he is often thought to have produced the weakest portions of those plays he worked on.
Bib: Stork, C. W., *William Rowley*.

Royal Society, The
Founded with the authority of ▷ Charles II in 1662; its full name was 'The Royal Society of London for Promoting Natural Knowledge'. It grew out of a philosophical society started in 1645 and was composed of 'divers worthy persons, inquisitive into natural philosophy and other parts of human learning, and particularly of what hath been called the New Philosophy or Experimental Philosophy', in other words of men whose minds were moving in the way opened up by ▷ Francis Bacon. The Society took the whole field of knowledge for exploration; one of its aims was to encourage the virtue of intellectual lucidity in the writing of prose, and Thomas Sprat, writing the *History of the Royal Society* in 1667, defined the standards which writers were to emulate. The Royal Society was thus central in the culture of its time; it was promoted not only by scientists such as the chemist Boyle, but by writers as well.
▷ Porter, Endymion.

Russell, Lady Elizabeth (1528–1609)
Translator, letter-writer and poet. Lady Russell was sister to ▷ Ann Bacon and wife to ▷ Sir Thomas Hoby, themselves both learned translators. After Hoby's death, she

married Lord John Russell, but continued the supervision of her Hoby children, and her ▷ translation of John Poynet's *A Way of Reconciliation of a Good and Learned Man* (1605) is dedicated to her daughter. She wrote verse epitaphs, some in Greek and Latin, for her family, and corresponded with Sir William Cecil (▷ Burghley).

Bib: Travitsky, B. (ed.), *A Paradise of Women.*

Russell, Lucy, Countess of Bedford (d 1627)

Together with ▷ Mary Sidney, Countess of Pembroke and ▷ Mary Wroth (Lady Wroth), Lucy, Countess of Bedford was one of the most important ▷ patrons of poetry in the early 17th century. However, since her husband, Edward, third Earl of Bedford, came rarely to court (he had been exiled from court for his part in the ▷ Essex rebellion and later, in 1612, suffered partial paralysis from a fall), this role was based entirely upon her own talents and upon her Harington family connections – she was the sister of ▷ Sir John Harington. Herself a poet, she was also the patron of ▷ Ben Jonson, ▷ George Chapman, ▷ Samuel Daniel and ▷ Michael Drayton. Perhaps the poet who benefited most from her interest, however, was ▷ John Donne. Donne addressed seven of his verse letters (published in 1633) to the Countess, who was godmother to Donne's second daughter, Elizabeth.

Bib: Byard, M. M., 'The Trade of Courtiership: The Countess of Bedford and the Bedford Memorials – A Family History from 1585 to 1607', *History Today* (January, 1979), pp. 20–28; Hannay, M. P., *Silent But for the Word: Tudor Women as Patrons, Translators, and Writers of Religious Works.*

Russian Formalism

▷ Formalism.

Sackville, Thomas, first Earl of Dorset (1536–1608)

Poet, statesman, diplomat; created first Earl of Dorset in 1604. He contributed the *Induction* and the *Complaint of Buckingham* in the verse compilation ▷ *Mirror for Magistrates*; the *Induction* is the main basis for his fame as a poet. He also collaborated with Thomas Norton in writing the first ▷ tragedy in ▷ blank verse, ▷ *Gorboduc*.
Bib: Berlin, N., *Thomas Sackville*.

Salisbury, Sir Thomas (d 1643)

Poet. Salisbury studied at Oxford and the Inner Temple (▷ Inns of Court), but then left London at the death of his father to look after his family estates. He later became a Member of Parliament for his local constituency, Denbigh. A staunch Royalist, he was imprisoned for supporting ▷ Charles I at Edge Hill. Although he was a prolific poet, all that remains is *The History of Joseph* (pub. 1636).

Samson Agonistes (1671)

A ▷ tragedy in ▷ blank verse by ▷ John Milton, published (with ▷ *Paradise Regained*) in 1671. It is an example of Milton's blended ▷ Puritan-biblical and ▷ Renaissance-classical inspiration; the subject is drawn from the Old Testament (*Judges* 16) and the form from the ancient Greek tragedies of ▷ Aeschylus and ▷ Sophocles.

Samson, the Jewish hero, has been betrayed by his Philistine wife Dalila (spelt Delilah in the Authorized Version of the ▷ Bible, where she is not his wife) to her people, who are the foes of the Jews. His hair, on which depended his exceptional God-given strength, has been cut off; he has been blinded and cast into prison in Gaza, where his hair is allowed to recover its former length and he is subjected to slavery by his enemies. The play opens while he is resting from his enormous labours and he is approached by a chorus of lamenting Jews. In his mood of extreme despair, he is visited by his father Manoa, who hopes to negotiate his release from the Philistines; Samson, however, has the moral strength to refuse Manoa's suggestions, on the grounds that his lot is a consequence of his own moral weakness in betraying the secret of his strength to his wife. His next visitor is Dalila herself, who seeks his forgiveness in return for alleviation of his sufferings; he replies, however, that if he cannot pardon himself, her crime is still more unpardonable. This double moral victory heartens him enough to enable him to frighten away his third visitor, the Philistine giant Harapha, who comes to mock at him. Next a messenger arrives with an order that he is to come before the Philistine lords in order to entertain them with feats of his strength. To the dismay of the chorus, he accepts the order, but we learn from a messenger that it is only to destroy the entire assembly (including himself) by rooting up the two pillars which support the roof of the building. The chorus is left to chant praise of the hero and of the wisdom of God, who sustains his people.

It has long been assumed that *Samson Agonistes* was written after Milton had finished ▷ *Paradise Lost* (*ie* between 1667 and 1671). This traditional dating reinforces the connection between the blind and defeated hero of the work, and the blind and (ideologically) defeated figure of Milton after the Restoration. However, strong reasons have now been advanced for dating Milton's drama to a much earlier period of his career between 1647 and 1653. The two principle themes of modern criticism of the work have centred on the question of 'structure', and the question of whether the guiding spirit of the play is 'Hellenic', 'Hebraic' or 'Christian'. In essence, both of these questions address a problem that *Samson Agonistes* has long posed to readers – that interpretation of the work rests on locating it in relation to other texts (Greek tragedy or the Old Testament, for example) and to a specific historical moment.

Sandys, George (1578–1644)

Translator and travel writer. Son of the Archbishop of York, Sandys travelled extensively and published accounts of his journeys to Italy and the Near East in *A Relation of a Journey* (1615). He then moved to America as treasurer of the Virginia Company (1621) and began translating ▷ Ovid's ▷ *Metamorphoses*, the work for which he is best known. This text was published in 1626, with the first book of the ▷ *Aeneid* added at its reissue in 1632. He also translated Grotius's *Christ's Passion; A Tragedy* (1640) and rendered several parts of the ▷ Bible into verse. Sandys's Ovid was immensely influential on the Augustan writers (it had reached eight editions by 1690), and it was an important factor in establishing the heroic couplet as their preferred poetic metre.
▷ Turberville, George; Translation.
Bib: Davis, R. B., *George Sandys: Poet Adventurer*.

Sappho of Lesbos
Greek woman poet of the 6th century BC.
The fragments that have survived are famous
for their passion and simplicity. The term
'lesbian' for homosexual love among women
derived from her passionate poems referring
to her women friends. The poet ▷ Katherine
Philips was known as the 'English Sappho'
partly because of the many poems she
addressed to women.

Satire
A form of attack through mockery; it may exist
in any literary medium, but is often regarded
as a medium in itself. The origins of the word
help to explain the manifestations of satire.
It derives from the Latin 'satura' = a vessel
filled with the earliest agricultural produce of
the year, used in seasonal festivals to celebrate
harvest; a secondary meaning is 'miscellany of
entertainment', implying merry-making at such
festivals, probably including verbal warfare.
This primitive humour gave rise to a highly
cultivated form of literary attack in the poetry
of ▷ Horace, Persius (1st century AD) and
▷ Juvenal. Thus from ancient Roman culture
two ideas of satire have come down to us:
the first expresses a basic instinct for comedy
through mockery in human beings, and was
not invented by the Romans; the second is a
self-conscious medium, implying standards of
civilized and moral rightness in the mind of
the poet and hence a desire on his or her part
to instruct readers so as to reform their moral
failings and absurdities. The two kinds of
satire are interrelated, so that it is not possible
to distinguish them sharply. Moreover, it is
not easy to distinguish strict satire in either of
its original forms from other kinds of comedy.
Strict satire, *ie* satire emulating the
Roman poets, was one of the outcomes of
▷ Renaissance cultivation of ancient Latin
literature. Between 1590 and 1625 several
poets wrote deliberate satires with Juvenal,
Persius and Horace in mind: the most
important of these were ▷ Donne and ▷ Ben
Jonson, but ▷ Joseph Hall claimed to be the
first, and another was ▷ Marston.
Comedy of Humours (▷ Humours,
Comedy of) is one of the most easily
distinguishable forms of dramatic satire. It
is associated chiefly with Ben Jonson, and
has its roots in the older ▷ morality drama,
which was only intermittently satirical. The
'humours' in Jonson's conception are the
obsessions and manias to which the nature
of human beings invites them to abandon
themselves; they have a close relation to the

medieval ▷ Seven Deadly Sins, such as lust,
avarice and gluttony.
Bib: Kernan, A., *The Cankered Muse.*

Saussure, Ferdinand de (1857–1913)
Swiss linguist, generally regarded as the
founder of ▷ structuralism. Saussure's
Course in General Linguistics was published
two years after his death, in 1915, and
represents a reconstruction of three series
of lectures which he gave at the University
of Geneva during the years 1906–7, 1908–9,
and 1910–11. It was Saussure who pioneered
the distinction between 'langue' and
'parole', and who sought to define the
operations of language according to the
principles of combination and ▷ difference.
Although ▷ deconstruction has done much to
undermine the structuralist base of Saussure's
thinking, the concept of 'difference' as a
determining principle in establishing meaning
('signification') remains one of the key
concepts in modern critical theory. Moreover,
Saussure's work provided the foundation for
the methodological analysis of sign systems,
and the types of linguistic investigation he
undertook have been successfully appropriated
by literary critics.

Savonarola, Fra Girolamo (1452–98)
In Italian history a Florentine monk who led
a revolt against the worldly excesses of the
▷ Renaissance. His own reforms went to
excess, and he was eventually condemned and
executed as a heretic.

School of Night
A term used to designate a circle of
intellectuals that centred on ▷ Sir Walter
Ralegh in the early 1590s. It derives from
▷ Shakespeare's play ▷ *Love's Labour's Lost*
(IV. 3. 251–2). The courtier Berowne has
just been praising the lady Rosaline who has
a dark complexion: 'No face is fair that is not
full so black', whereupon the king breaks in:

O paradox! Black is the badge of hell,
The hue of dungeons and the School of Night.

'School of Night' has puzzled editors, who
have variously amended it to 'scowl' and
'stole'. Some modern scholars, however
(see especially the Cambridge Shakespeare
edition and M. C. Bradbrook's *The School
of Night*), consider that Shakespeare was
alluding to Ralegh's dark complexion and
to the reputation of himself and his circle
for atheism. At about the time the play was

written (1594–5), Ralegh, in disgrace at court, had retired to his country house and declared his preference for a life of study over the active and public life. The rival claims of the studious and retired and the active and public life is the theme of *Love's Labour's Lost*.

Ralegh's circle seems to have consisted of himself, the famous mathematician Thomas Harriot, the poets ▷ Christopher Marlowe and ▷ George Chapman, the Earls of Northumberland and Derby, and a few others. Marlowe and Harriot shared Ralegh's atheistic reputation, Chapman had highly developed philosophical interests, and Northumberland and Derby had esoteric interests in alchemy. **Bib:** Bradbrook, M. C., *The School of Night*.

Scottish literature in English
This belongs above all to the Lowlands; it is a distinctive branch of literature in the English language, the Lowland Scottish form of which had originally a close resemblance to that spoken in the north of England. Racially, linguistically and culturally, Lowland Scottish ties with England were close, despite the constant wars between the two countries between the late 13th and mid-16th centuries. In contrast, until the 18th-century destruction of Highland culture, the Lowlanders had little more than the political bond of a common sovereign with their Gaelic-speaking fellow countrymen of the north. While it is wrong to say that Scottish literature is a branch of English literature, the two literatures have been closely related. During the medieval period and through to the 15th century, Scottish poetry flowered, but this was halted by the Scottish religious ▷ Reformation, and all the political troubles attendant on it from 1550 till 1700. Such poets in this period as deserve attention (*eg* ▷ Drummond of Hawthornden, 1585–1649) were thoroughly anglicized. The native culture remained alive at popular level, however, especially in its fine ▷ ballad and folksong tradition, of which ▷ *Sir Patrick Spens* is one of the most notable examples.

Sejanus (1603)
A satirical tragedy by ▷ Ben Jonson. The central character is an historical figure, a favourite of the Roman emperor Tiberius (reigned AD 14–37). The play is a study of a man driven by extreme ambition; he first eliminates all his rivals to power in the Senate, and then, exploiting the emperor's love of luxurious indolence and inclination for retirement, he conspires to murder Tiberius' heirs in order to occupy the throne himself.

Tiberius, however, is too cunning for him; he employs Macro, a new favourite, to bring about the downfall of the old, and Sejanus ends up being torn to pieces by the Roman mob, leaving Macro, equally ambitious and unscrupulous, in his former seat of power. The sensuality of Tiberius and his court, and the violence of the politicians, are contrasted with a group of grim commentators led by Arruntius, remnants of the old stoical (▷ Stoics) Romans whose austere virtues had made Rome great. Ben Jonson presents through Sejanus one of the ▷ Renaissance 'men of power', glorying in the consciousness of unlimited resources, the pattern for whom is ▷ Christopher Marlowe's ▷ Tamburlaine. Sejanus is also the diabolical ▷ Machiavellian politician, without conscience and capable of any crime, such as recurs in many ▷ Elizabethan and ▷ Jacobean dramas. Yet in his unbounded appetites, he is almost a grotesque figure, like the ludicrous sensualists in Jonson's great comedies, ▷ *Volpone* and ▷ *The Alchemist*. The play may have been an attempt to rival ▷ Shakespeare's ▷ *Julius Caesar* of a few years before; it is much more learned in its use of ancient authors, and dramatically it is perhaps the more impressive work. The play was not liked at its first performance, and offended the Earl of Northampton; Jonson had to answer for it before the Privy Council.

Selden, John (1584–1654)
Historian and antiquary. Selden was educated at Oxford and the ▷ Inns of Court and became a Member of Parliament in 1623, in which capacity he voiced sharp criticism of the crown, withdrawing, however, before the execution of ▷ Charles I. His main works include the *History of Tithes* (1618), which attacked the clergy and was suppressed, and *Table Talk*, which was gathered together by his secretary Richard Milward and published in 1689. Selden was also a friend of ▷ Ben Jonson and ▷ Michael Drayton; indeed, he provided the 'illustrations' or notes for the latter's *Poly-Olbion* (1612 and 1622). He was also admired by ▷ John Milton for his interest in historical facts and authenticity, rather than relying upon myth and popular custom.
▷ Camden, William.
Bib: Fletcher, E. G. M., Sir, *John Selden, 1584–1654*.

Seneca, Lucius Annaeus (?4 BC–AD 65)
Roman philosopher and dramatist. He belonged to the ▷ Stoic school of philosophy, which taught that men should seek virtue,

not happiness, and that they should be superior to the influences of pleasure and pain. As an orator, he was famous for the weight and terseness of his expression – the 'Senecan style'. He was tutor to the emperor Nero during the latter's boyhood, but was later suspected of being involved in a conspiracy against him; Nero accordingly ordered him to end his life, which he did with true stoical dignity. His nine tragedies were modelled on those of ▷ Aeschylus, ▷ Sophocles and ▷ Euripides, but there is much doubt about whether they were ever intended to be performed in a theatre; they seem to be designed for declamation to small circles. They contain no action, though the subjects are of bloodthirsty revenge. Their titles: *Hercules Furens; Thyestes; Phoenissae; Phaedra (Hippolytus); Oedipus; Troades (Hecuba); Medea; Agamemnon; Hercules Oetaeus*. A tenth, *Octavia*, has proved to be by another author.

Neither as a philosopher nor as a dramatist was Seneca one of the most important figures of the ancient Mediterranean world, but he had great importance for the 16th-century ▷ Renaissance in Europe, and particularly for English poetic drama between 1560 and 1620. This influence was of three kinds: 1 Seneca's dramas provided inspiration for Elizabethan ▷ revenge tragedy or 'tragedy of blood'; 2 at a time of English literature when there was keen interest in modes of expression but no settled standards about them, Senecan style was one of the favourite modes, both inside and outside the drama; 3 at a time when inherited ideas about the ordering of society and the ethical systems that should control it were undergoing alarming transformations, Senecan stoicism had an appeal for thoughtful men that harmonized with ▷ Protestant strictness and individualism of conduct. The three influences were more related than might appear. The translator of Seneca's *Ten Tragedies* (1559–81) declares in his preface that their effect was 'to beat down sin', and Protestants were familiar with the vengefulness of Old Testament religion. Sensational drama could unite with serious social purpose, and thus mingle learned, sober conceptions of drama (*eg* ▷ *Gorboduc*) with the demands of popular taste. Outside the drama, the terse sententiousness of Senecan style is best found in the *Essays* of ▷ Francis Bacon.

Sermons

The word 'sermon' is used in English to denote a speech from a church pulpit for the edification of the audience, always in this context called a 'congregation'. The sermon

considered as a means of communication had a central importance in English life until the 19th century, when universal literacy and the rise of the mass-circulation newspaper tended to eclipse it. At a popular level, it reached a larger audience than any other form of public communication. ▷ Chaucer's Pardoner in the ▷ *Canterbury Tales* demonstrates the power that a medieval preacher felt he had over an ignorant and superstitious audience, but *The Pardoner's Tale* is partly a ▷ satire about how the sermon could be abused. The sermon was a means of religious and governmental (*eg* Elizabethan *Book of Homilies*) propaganda. Doctrine, speculative philosophy, social criticism and ethical problems of daily life were all within the sphere of the sermon, and interested all ranks of society in one way or another.

The sermons of ▷ Hugh Latimer, who lived through the most dramatic phase of the English ▷ Reformation, are some of the earliest examples in English of vivid prose in the popular and spoken idiom. Three famous preachers of the golden age of Anglicanism in the first half of the 17th century have left sermons addressed to the court or to other highly educated audiences. The best known of these is the poet ▷ John Donne, who became Dean of St Paul's in 1621. His sermons have massive learning, but his style is richly personal and persuasive, with a depth of feeling comparable to that of his great religious verse. ▷ Lancelot Andrewes was a subtle and elaborate analyst in language, and appealed more exclusively to the intellect.

The change that came over English in the middle of the century emphasized flexibility, control and lucidity at the expense of poetic emotive power. It is heralded by John Wilkins's book on preaching, *Ecclesiastes* (1646), which teaches the virtue of strict method in organizing a sermon. The main Anglican preachers of the next hundred years were Robert South (1634–1716), notable for his succinctness and satire, Isaac Barrow (1630–77), whom ▷ Charles II called 'the best scholar in England', John Tillotson (1630–94), famous for the elegance of his prose, and Joseph Butler (1692–1752), an acute thinker. The best of the ▷ Puritan preachers followed a similar course in a more popular idiom, for instance the Presbyterian Richard Baxter (1615–91), who declared 'The Plainest words are the profitablest oratory in the weightiest matters', and this is a criterion which ▷ Bunyan exemplifies at its noblest. The preaching by women began to be accepted in Puritan circles, and ▷ Priscilla Cotton, a ▷ Quaker, wrote the first work defending women's rights to preach, *To the Priests and People of England*.

Seven Deadly Sins

The sins for which, as the Church taught, the punishment was spiritual death (*ie* not a venial sin for which it was possible to obtain forgiveness). The list usually given is: Pride; Envy; Sloth; Gluttony (or intemperance); Avarice (or covetousness); Anger (ire, wrath); Lust. These sins were frequently personified, *eg* in the medieval ▷ morality plays, the Parson's Tale in Chaucer's ▷ *Canterbury Tales*, ▷ Spenser's ▷ *The Faerie Queene* and ▷ Marlowe's ▷ *Doctor Faustus*.

Seventeenth-century literature

The 17th century was one of the richest periods in the history of English literature, both for achievement and for variety. It also saw a revolution in the human mind, not only in Britain but elsewhere in Europe – a revolution that constitutes the birth of the modern outlook. The century begins with writers like ▷ William Shakespeare and ▷ John Donne, whose language fused thought and feeling in both poetry and prose; it ends with John Dryden (1631–1700) and John Locke (1632–1704), writers whose language was shaped by a new ideal of prose and who opposed 'judgement' to 'wit' – that is to say, the analytic to the synthetic powers of the mind. Another way of putting it is to say that the century opens with one of the most exciting periods of poetic drama in the whole history of Europe, and it closes with the most influential period of English ▷ satire, and the prose of fact which in the next century was to find its most ample form of expression in the novel.

We are in the habit of using the term 'Elizabethan drama' for this period of the English theatre, but in fact it was in the reign of ▷ James I, the ▷ Jacobean period, that this type of drama came to fruition. By 1600, Shakespeare was only approaching his best work, ▷ Ben Jonson was just beginning his career, and the plays of the other important dramatists – ▷ Chapman, ▷ Webster, ▷ Tourneur and ▷ Middleton – were as yet unwritten. The finest of this drama was the result of a precarious balance that kept the long medieval past in mind together with the social and intellectual changes of the present, and communicated with the populace as well as with the court. Already by 1610 this balance was being upset; the elegant but superficial taste of the younger dramatists

such as ▷ Beaumont and ▷ Fletcher was turning a national drama into an upper- and middle-class London theatre, which has remained dominant to the present day. By the time of the ▷ Caroline drama of the reign of ▷ Charles I, this transformation was nearing completeness in the plays of ▷ Massinger, ▷ Ford and ▷ Shirley. But in the meantime, the peculiar genius of the best dramatists, especially Shakespeare, had helped to produce among the lyric poets the school now so much admired under the name of the ▷ Metaphysicals. The Metaphysical poets (notably John Donne, ▷ George Herbert, and ▷ Andrew Marvell) owe their name to the possession of a quality that is central to Shakespeare's genius: the capacity to unite oppositions of thought and feeling under the control of a flexible, open, but poised intelligence; their poetry, like Shakespeare's work, thus expresses a peculiarly rich body of experience, united from different levels of the mind.

But the Metaphysicals were not the only fertile school of poets in the first half of the century, nor was Shakespearean drama the only kind from which poets could learn. Shakespeare's rival, Ben Jonson, was, as a dramatist, in isolated opposition to the Shakespearean drama. The difference lay partly in conceptions of form. Jonson imposed his form upon his matter; the confusion and violence of experience is shaped by a selective process which is a disciplining of the mind as well as a critical analysis of the subject. In his lyric poetry as well as in his dramas, this discipline shows itself in irony, proportion, and a union of strength with elegance. Jonson's example influenced the later Metaphysicals, notably Marvell, but it also led to a different school, not always to be sharply distinguished, which we know as the ▷ Cavalier Poets, such as ▷ Carew, ▷ Herrick and ▷ Lovelace. Above all, Jonson's criteria anticipated the 'classicists' of the later part of the century, especially Dryden.

But yet another poet left an important legacy to the 17th century. This was ▷ Edmund Spenser, who had perfected those qualities of musical cadence and sensuous imagery that many readers think of as essentially 'poetic'. He had his followers in the first 30 years of the 17th century, though none of note, but it is to him that ▷ John Milton owes most among his predecessors. In Milton, we have two very different 17th-century outlooks uneasily united: the love of all that is implied by the ▷ Renaissance, that is to say the revaluation of classical literature and the discovery of the glories of earthly civilization as opposed to those of a heavenly destiny, and devotion to ▷ Puritanism, implying the extreme Protestant belief that not only is all truth God's truth, but that the sole ultimate source of it is the Bible. This uneasy union produced in Milton the determination to impose on his society a Judaic-Christian conception of human destiny so grand that it compelled acceptance, and to use as his medium what was considered to be the grandest of all the ancient artistic forms, the ▷ epic. ▷ Paradise Lost (1667) was so impressive as an attempt to realize this impossible ambition, and so imposing in its union of the classical form and the biblical subject, that it has won the reverence of three centuries. But Milton's sonorous eloquence, like Spenser's sensuous music, was a kind of magic that subdued the intellect rather than persuaded it. The unfortunate consequence was the common belief among 18th- and 19th-century poets that 'sublime' poetry should elevate the emotions while passing by the intellect. This Miltonic influence no doubt encouraged exponents of reason such as Locke (Essay concerning Human Understanding, 1690) to believe that poetry belongs to an immature stage of mental development, before the mind has acquired reason and respect for facts, the best medium for which is prose.

From the beginning of the century, prose writers showed signs of seeing their function as clarifying the reason as opposed to enlarging the imagination. This turning away from the imagination went naturally with a gradual relegation of religion. ▷ Francis Bacon, in his ▷ Advancement of Learning (1605), treats religion with respect and then ignores it, and he ends his few remarks on poetry with the sentence, 'But it is not good to stay too long in the theatre'. The vivid imagery which strikes out of his terse style is more functional than that of earlier prose writers. Bacon's main theme is the inductive method of acquiring knowledge through experiment, and all his prose, including his Essays, is essentially practical. Although the imaginative connotations are preserved, the dominant tendency in the first half of the century (eg in the ▷ 'character' writers such as John Earle, and ▷ Robert Burton's treatise on psychology, ▷ The Anatomy of Melancholy) is to use prose descriptively and analytically. ▷ Thomas Browne's ▷ Religio Medici is written, like his other works, in the most sonorous prose in the English language, but Browne is defending his religious faith just because it exceeds his reason, and his poetic

style (in contrast to that of the great ▷ sermon writers like John Donne) is partly a conscious contrivance.

In the middle of the century, ▷ Thomas Hobbes published his treatise on political philosophy, ▷ Leviathan (1651), in which, with pungent ruthlessness, he forced his readers to face the 'facts' of human nature in their grimmest interpretation. After the Restoration of the monarchy (1660), the historian of the ▷ Royal Society, Bishop Sprat, laid down the new standards that were to guide the prose writer: 'a close, naked, natural way of speaking; positive expressions; clear senses; a native easiness'. However, the spiritual life of the middle and lower classes was not yet permeated by this rationalism. The spirit of Puritanism, still biblical and poetic, is expressed in the spiritual ▷ autobiographies of the Puritan leaders such as the ▷ Quaker ▷ George Fox (Journal, 1694), and, at its most impressive, that imaginative work ▷ The Pilgrim's Progress, by the ▷ Baptist tinsmith ▷ John Bunyan. In this work, the old ▷ allegories of the ▷ Middle Ages reach forward into the field of the novel, the new form which was to come into being in the 18th century.

▷ Dissociation of Sensibility; Humours, Comedy of; Elizabethan period of English literature.

Shakespeare, William (1564–1616) – biography

Dramatist and poet. He was baptized on 26 April 1564; his birth is commemorated on 23 April, which happens also to be St George's Day, the festival of the patron saint of England. His father, John Shakespeare, was a Stratford-on-Avon merchant who dealt in gloves and probably other goods; his grandfather, Richard Shakespeare, was a yeoman, ie small farmer, and his mother, Mary Arden, was the daughter of a local farmer who belonged to the local noble family of Arden, after whom the forest to the north of Stratford was named. John Shakespeare's affairs prospered at first, and in 1568 he was appointed to the highest office in the town – High Bailiff, equivalent to Mayor. A grammar school existed in Stratford, and since it was free to the sons of burgesses, it is generally assumed that William attended it. If he did, he probably received a good education in the Latin language; there is evidence that the sons of Stratford merchants were, or could be, well read and well educated. He married Anne Hathaway in 1582, and they had three children: Suzanna, born 1583, and the twin son and daughter, Hamnet and Judith, born in 1585.

Thereafter Shakespeare's life is a blank, until we meet a reference to him in *A Groatsworth of Wit* (1592), an autobiographical pamphlet by the London playwright ▷ Robert Greene, who accuses him of plagiarism. By 1592, therefore, Shakespeare was already successfully embarked as a dramatist in London, but there is no clear evidence of when he went there. From 1592 to 1594 the London theatres were closed owing to epidemics of plague, and Shakespeare seems to have used the opportunity to make a reputation for himself as a narrative poet: his ▷ *Venus and Adonis* was published in 1593, and *The Rape of Lucrece* a year later. Both were dedicated to Henry Wriothesley, ▷ Earl of Southampton. He continued to prosper as a dramatist, and in the winter of 1594 was a leading member of the Lord ▷ Chamberlain's Men, with whom he remained for the rest of his career. In 1596 his father acquired a coat of arms – the sign of a ▷ gentleman – and in 1597 William bought New Place, the largest house in Stratford. There he probably established his father, who had been in financial difficulties since 1577. In 1592, John Shakespeare had been registered as a recusant (▷ Recusancy); this might mean that he was a Catholic, but may equally show that he was trying to escape arrest for debt.

In 1598, ▷ Francis Meres, in his literary commentary *Palladis Tamia, Wit's Treasury*, mentions Shakespeare as one of the leading writers of the time, lists 12 of his plays, and mentions his ▷ sonnets as circulating privately; they were published in 1609. The Lord Chamberlain's Men opened the ▷ Globe Theatre in 1599, and Shakespeare became a shareholder in it. After the accession of ▷ James I the company came under royal patronage, and was called the King's Men; this gave Shakespeare a status in the royal household. He is known to have been an actor as well as a playwright, but tradition associates him with small parts: Adam in ▷ *As You Like It*, and the Ghost in ▷ *Hamlet*. He may have retired to New Place in Stratford in 1610, but he continued his connections with London, and purchased a house in ▷ Blackfriars in 1613. In the same year, the Globe theatre was burnt down during a performance of the last play with which Shakespeare's name is associated, ▷ *Henry VIII*. His will is dated less than a month before his death. The fact that he left his 'second-best bed' to his wife is no evidence that he was on bad terms with her;

the best one would naturally go with his main property to his elder daughter, who had married John Hall; his younger daughter, who had married Thomas Quiney, was also provided for, but his son, Hamnet, had died in childhood. His last direct descendant, Lady Barnard, died in 1670.

Owing to the fact that the subject-matter of ▷ biography was restricted until mid-17th century to princes, statesmen and great soldiers, the documentary evidence of Shakespeare's life is, apart from the above facts, slight. His contemporaries ▷ Christopher Marlowe and ▷ Ben Jonson are in some respects better documented because they involved themselves more with political events. Many legends and traditions have grown up about Shakespeare since near his own day, but they are untrustworthy. He was certainly one of the most successful English writers of his time; his income has been estimated at about £200 a year, considerable earnings for those days. After the death of Marlowe in 1593, his greatest rival was Ben Jonson, who criticized his want of art (in *Discoveries*, 1640), admired his character, and paid a noble tribute to him in the prefatory poem to the First ▷ Folio collection of his plays (1623).

Bib: Chambers, E. K., *William Shakespeare: A Study of Facts and Problems* (2 vols); Dutton, R., *William Shakespeare: A Literary Life*; Schoenbaum, S., *Shakespeare's Lives; William Shakespeare: A Documentary Life*.

Shakespeare – criticism
As with any exceptionally popular author, different ages have appreciated different aspects of Shakespeare. In his own day, popular taste, according to ▷ Ben Jonson, particularly enjoyed ▷ *Titus Andronicus*, now regarded as one of the least interesting of his plays. John Dryden (1631–1700) (*Essay on Dramatic Poesy*), picked out ▷ *Richard II*; Samuel Johnson (1709–84) (*Preface to Shakespeare*, 1765) admired the comedies. It is possible to understand these preferences: *Titus* is the most bloodthirsty of all the plays, and suited the more vulgar tastes of an age in which executions were popular spectacles. Dryden and Johnson both belonged to ▷ neo-classical periods. Johnson, like Dryden, was troubled by the differences in Shakespeare's tragedies from the formalism of ancient Greek and 17th-century tragedy that the spirit of their period encouraged them to admire, and Johnson's warm humanity caused him to respond to the plays which displayed wide human appeal

while their mode permitted some licence of form. Both Johnson and Dryden rose superior to the limitations of their period in according Shakespeare such greatness. The 19th-century inheritor of Johnson's mantle as the most perceptive critic of Shakespeare is S. T. Coleridge (1772–1834), whose seminal lectures on Shakespeare were inspired by German Romanticism. In his letters John Keats (1795–1821) offers some of the most enduringly valuable comments on Shakespeare's works before A. C. Bradley published *Shakespearean Tragedy* in 1904, which was to prove the most influential text on Shakespeare for two generations.

In the 20th century Wilson Knight (*The Imperial Theme, The Crown of Life*), Harley Granville-Barker (*Preface to Shakespeare*) and others such as D. A. Traversi (*An Approach to Shakespeare*) and H. C. Goddard (*The Meaning of Shakespeare*) have all contributed to our understanding of the plays and poetry. Shakespeare's education has been closely scrutinized by T. W. Baldwin in two volumes, *Shakespeare's Smalle Latin and Lesse Greeke*, and Geoffrey Bullough's eight volumes on Shakespeare's sources, *Narrative and Dramatic Sources of Shakespeare*, are indispensable to Shakespearean critics. Increasingly the critical debate has been conducted in a number of specialized journals, particularly the long-established *Shakespeare Jahrbuch, Shakespeare Survey, Shakespeare Studies*, and *Shakespeare Quarterly*. A few books are outstanding in their focus on particular aspects of Shakespeare, such as C. L. Barber's influential essay on Shakespearean comedy and the rituals of English folklore and country customs, *Shakespeare's Festive Comedy*, and Northrop Fry's archetypal study of comedy and romance, *A Natural Perspective*. Howard Felperin's distinguished book on Shakespeare's last plays, *Shakespearean Romance*, and Janet Adelman's thought-provoking study of *Antony and Cleopatra* and its mythopoeic imagery in *The Common Liar*, both reflect the influence of Frye in their sober and formally predicated approaches.

Of a more radical bent is Jan Kott's famous essay on ▷ *King Lear* in '*King Lear, or Endgame*' (1964), which argued the case for Shakespeare as our contemporary, with his finger imaginatively on the pulse of a dark, modern human predicament. On the same lines Peter Brook's famous production of ▷ *A Midsummer Night's Dream* in 1970 emancipated the play from its putative operatic and conformist frame and irretrievably altered our perception of it. By thus indicating the extent to which the theatre can influence interpretation of plays, Brook materially contributed to redirecting critical attention back to the stage.

Modern social and critical movements have made their impact felt in the field of Shakespeare studies: ▷ deconstruction, in the guise of a creative disintegration of the texts' organic status, and ▷ feminism provide the impetus for some of the most controversial writing on Shakespeare at the end of the 20th century, as do ▷ 'cultural materialism', particularly ▷ 'new historicism' and ▷ psychoanalytical theory. New historicism in particular seems set to command a wide audience in the works of Stephen Greenblatt and Louis Montrose, whose work combines the scholarly scruples of the older tradition with an acute sceptical and self-critical awareness of the historical and epistemological contexts of literary criticism in society.

Bib: Bradley, A. C., *Shakespearean Tragedy*; Barber, C. L., *Shakespeare's Festive Comedy*; Coleridge, S. T., *Shakespearean Criticism*; Dollimore, J., *Radical Tragedy*; Dryden, J., *Essays*; Frye, N., *A Natural Perspective*; Greenblatt, S., *Renaissance Self-Fashioning*; Jardine, L., *Still Harping on Daughters*; Johnson, S., *On Shakespeare*; Parker, P. and Hartman, G., *Shakespeare and the Question of Theory*, Ryan, K., *Shakespeare*.

Shakespeare – history of textual study
Apart from a scene sometimes ascribed to Shakespeare in the play ▷ *Sir Thomas More* (c 1596), none of Shakespeare's work has survived in manuscript. In his own lifetime, 18 of his plays were published in separate volumes (the ▷ Quartos), but this was probably without the author's permission, and therefore without his revisions and textual corrections. His non-dramatic poems, including the ▷ sonnets, were also published during his lifetime. After his death, his fellow actors Heming and Condell published his collected plays (except ▷ *Pericles*) in the large, single volume known as the First ▷ Folio, and this was succeeded by the Second Folio (1632), and the Third (two editions) and Fourth in 1663, 1664 and 1685. The Second Folio regularized the division of the plays into ▷ Acts and Scenes, and the second issue of the Third added *Pericles*, as well as other plays certainly not by Shakespeare. In several important respects the Folio editions were unsatisfactory:

1 The texts of some (though not all) of the smaller quarto volumes of the plays published

during the poet's lifetime differed materially from the text of even the First Folio, which in turn differed from the later folios.

2 The First Folio arranged the plays according to their kinds (Comedies, Histories or Tragedies) and gave no indication of the order in which the plays were written.

3 There was no evidence that even the first editors had had access to the best manuscript texts, and there were evident errors in some passages, the fault of either the editors or their printers, and editors of the later Folios made alterations of their own. Consequently, there was plenty of work during the next two centuries for scholars to re-establish, as nearly as possible, Shakespeare's original text. Work also had to be done on the chronological order of the plays, discovery of the sources of their plots, philological investigations of linguistic peculiarities, and research into the conditions in which the plays were originally acted.

Two of the most eminent 18th-century writers published editions of the plays; these were Alexander Pope (in 1725 and 1728), and Samuel Johnson (in 1765). Neither, however, was a sound scholarly edition, though Johnson's was important for its critical Preface and annotations. Lewis Theobald (1688–1744) attacked Pope's poor scholarship in his *Shakespeare Restored* (1726), and published his own edition in 1734. He was the first enlightened editor, and did permanently useful work both in removing post-Shakespearean additions and alterations and in suggesting emendations of corrupt passages. After him came Steevens and Capell, who compared the original Quarto texts with the Folio ones, and ▷ Edmond Malone (1741–1812), the most eminent of the 18th-century Shakespeare scholars. In 1778 he made the first serious attempt to establish the chronological order of the plays, and in 1790 he brought out the best edition of them yet established.

Shakespearean scholarship in the 18th century was more the work of individuals than a collaborative enterprise. They saw many of the problems involved in estimating the relative values of the early texts, the possibilities of scholarly emendation of corrupt passages, and the necessity of eliminating the errors of unscholarly 17th- and 18th-century editors. This work culminated in the publication of 'Variorum' editions of the plays, 1803–21. But the establishment of a really sound text required the study of wider subject-matter. Shakespeare's work had to be estimated as a whole so that his development

could be understood; philological study of the state of the language in his time was needed; historical events had to be examined for their possible relevance; many sources for the plots remained to be discovered; theatrical conditions and the relationship of Shakespeare to dramatists contemporary with him needed exploration; even handwriting was important, for the detection of possible misprinting. All this was the work of the collaborative scholarship of the 19th century. It was carried out by German scholars, by the English Shakespeare Societies led by Halliwell and Furnivall, and by the universities.

In the later 18th century Shakespeare became an inspiration to the movement in Germany for the emancipation of German culture from its long subjection to French culture. A. W. Schlegel's remarkable translations (1797–1810) were fine enough to enable Germans to adopt Shakespeare as something like a national poet. German scholars such as Tieck, Ulrici, Gervinus and Franz adopted Shakespearean studies with thoroughness and enthusiasm. They stimulated the foundation of Shakespeare Societies in England, and in 1863–6 the Cambridge University Press was able to publish an edition of Shakespeare's works, which, in its revised form (1891–93), is substantially the text now generally in use.

There has been considerable editorial activity in the 20th century, and it was to be expected that the 'New Bibliography', spearheaded by ▷ A. W. Pollard, ▷ R. B. McKerrow and W. W. Greg would produce a major reconsideration of the Shakespearean text. In the end the fruit of their research, and particularly of McKerrow's brilliant *Prolegomena for the Oxford Shakespeare* (1939), needed to wait for nearly 40 years before they were put to use by the editors of the *Oxford Shakespeare*, Gary Taylor and Stanley Wells. In the meantime Charlton Hinman produced two seminal volumes on the collations of the extant Folios in *The Printing and Proof-Reading of the First Folio*, and incorporated his findings in *The Norton Facsimile: The First Folio of Shakespeare*, which remains a standard work of reference. All the major university and other presses turned their attention to re-editing Shakespeare in the late 1960s and early 1970s. At a time when Oxford University Press were printing two complete one-volume Shakespeares (one old spelling and another modern spelling) as well as a huge textual companion and the entire works in separate editions for the Oxford English Texts, Cambridge University

Press published the first volume of Peter Blayney's exhaustive survey of the 'origins' of the First Quarto of ▷ *King Lear: The Texts of 'King Lear' and their Origins*. Cambridge, Methuen (New Arden), Macmillan and Longman have pursued similar goals, updating and editing afresh Shakespeare's works, each bringing to the canon a different approach. Whereas most of the editions have followed basically conservative principles, most have embraced to a greater or lesser degree the Oxford view of the plays as primarily works for the theatre. Increasingly, Oxford's view of Shakespeare as a dramatist who regularly reshaped his plays in line with theatrical and aesthetic demands is gaining ground. The particular focus for this hypothesis has become the two-text (Quarto and Folio) *King Lear*, which most editors now agree reflects two different versions of the play. The same editorial principles are being applied to other texts reflecting similar source situations, such as ▷ *Richard III*, ▷ *Hamlet* and ▷ *Othello*. Among Oxford's most radical proposals are the printing of two versions of *King Lear*, the calling of ▷ Falstaff ▷ 'Oldcastle' in ▷ *Henry IV, Part I*, as well as boldly recreating the text of ▷ *Pericles*.

The history of Shakespeare editing in Britain towards the end of the 20th century is ultimately one of the creative disintegration of the shibboleths of traditional editorial policy, even if all the changes proposed by contemporary scholars do not find favour with posterity.

Bib: Bowers, F., *On Editing Shakespeare*; Greg, W. W., *The Shakespeare First Folio: Its Bibliographical and Textual History*; Honigmann, E. A. J., *The Stability of Shakespeare's Text*; McKerrow, R. B., *Prolegomena for the Oxford Shakespeare*;Wells, S., *Re-Editing Shakespeare for the Modern Reader*.

Shakespeare's plays
Earliest publications. The first collected edition was the volume known as the First ▷ Folio (1623). This included all the plays now acknowledged to be by Shakespeare with the exception of *Pericles*. It also includes *Henry VIII*. Stationers (the profession then combining bookselling and publishing) were glad to bring out individual plays in ▷ quarto editions in his lifetime, however, and since there was no law of copyright these were often 'pirated', *ie* published without the permission of the author. On the whole, Shakespeare's company (the Lord ▷ Chamberlain's Men) did not want such publication, since printed editions enabled other acting companies to perform the plays in competition. Eighteen of Shakespeare's plays were published in this way, sometimes in more than one edition, and occasionally in editions that varied considerably. Since none of the plays has survived in the original manuscript, the task of modern editors is often to reconcile different quartos (where they exist) with each other, and any quartos that exist with corresponding versions in the First Folio. The following is a list of the separate editions of the plays, published while Shakespeare was alive or soon after his death, with dates of different editions where they substantially disagree with one another:

Titus Andronicus (1594)
Henry VI, Part II (1594)
Henry VI, Part III (1595)
Richard II (1597, 1608)
Richard III (1597)
Romeo and Juliet (1597, 1599)
Love's Labour's Lost (1598)
Henry IV, Part I (1598)
Henry IV, Part II (1600)
Henry V (1600)
A Midsummer Night's Dream (1600)
The Merchant of Venice (1600)
Much Ado About Nothing (1600)
The Merry Wives of Windsor (1602)
Hamlet (1603, 1604)
King Lear (1608)
Troilus and Cressida (1609)
Pericles (1609)
Othello (1622)

Order of composition. The First Folio does not print the plays in the order in which they were written. Scholars have had to work out their chronological order on three main kinds of evidence: 1 external evidence (*eg* records of production, publication); 2 internal evidence (*eg* allusions to contemporary events); 3 stylistic evidence. The following is an approximate chronological arrangement, though in some instances there is no certainty:

1590–91	Henry VI, Parts II and III
1591–92	Henry VI, Part I
1592–93	Richard III
	The Comedy of Errors
1593–94	Titus Andronicus
	The Taming of the Shrew
	Two Gentlemen of Verona
1594–95	Love's Labour's Lost
	Romeo and Juliet
1595–96	Richard II
	A Midsummer Night's Dream

1596–97	King John
	The Merchant of Venice
	The Merry Wives of Windsor
1597–98	Henry IV, Parts I and II
1598–99	Much Ado about Nothing
	Henry V
1599–1600	Julius Caesar
	As You Like It
	Twelfth Night
1600–1	Hamlet
	Measure for Measure
1601–2	Troilus and Cressida
1602–3	All's Well that Ends Well
1604–5	Othello
	King Lear
1605–6	Macbeth
1606–7	Antony and Cleopatra
1607–8	Coriolanus
	Timon of Athens
1608–9	Pericles
1609–10	Cymbeline
1610–11	The Winter's Tale
1611–12	The Tempest

Shakespeare is now believed to have written all of *Henry VIII* and to have collaborated with ▷ Fletcher on *Two Noble Kinsmen*. ▷ Romances of Shakespeare; Problem plays (of Shakespeare).

Shakespeare – Sonnets
First published in 1609, but there is no clear evidence for when they were written. They are commonly thought to date from 1595–9; ▷ Francis Meres in *Palladis Tamia* (1598) mentions that Shakespeare wrote ▷ sonnets. There are 154 sonnets; numbers 1–126 are addressed to a man (126 is in fact not a sonnet but a 12-line poem) and the remainder are addressed to a woman – the so-called 'dark lady of the sonnets', since it is made clear that she is dark in hair and complexion. There has been much speculation about the dedication: 'To the only begetter of these ensuing sonnets Mr. W. H. all happiness and that eternity promised by our everliving poet Wisheth the well-wishing adventurer in setting forth T. T.' 'T. T.' stands for Thomas Thorpe, the stationer (*ie* bookseller and publisher of the sonnets); speculation centres on what is meant by 'begetter' and who is meant by 'W. H.' W. H. may stand for the man (William Hughes?) who *procured* the manuscript of the sonnets for Thorpe, if that is what 'begetter' means. But if 'begetter' means 'inspirer', it has been conjectured that W. H. may be the inverted initials of Henry Wriothesley, ▷ third Earl of Southampton, to whom Shakespeare had dedicated his

▷ *Venus and Adonis* and *The Rape of Lucrece*, or they may stand for ▷ William Herbert, Earl of Pembroke or for someone else. Guesses have also been made as to the identity of the 'dark lady', who has been thought by some to be Mary Fitton, a maid of honour at court and mistress of William Herbert, or by A. L. Rowse to be ▷ Aemelia Lanyer. There is too little evidence for profitable conjecture on either subject.

Critics and scholars disagree about the extent to which the sonnets are autobiographical (and if so what they express), or whether they are 'literary exercises' without a personal theme. A middle view is that they are exploratory of personal relations in friendship and in love, and that some of them rehearse themes later dramatized in the plays – for instance 94 suggests the character of Angelo in ▷ *Measure for Measure*, and the recurrent concern with the destructiveness of time seems to look forward to ▷ *Troilus and Cressida* and the great tragedies. Since it is unknown whether the edition of 1609 is a reliable version, there is also some doubt whether the order of the sonnets in it is that intended by Shakespeare; most scholars see little reason to question it.

One of the most valuable recent editions of the *Sonnets* is Stephen Booth's, which uses the 1609 text, rightly accepting its ordering of the poetry as binding. Booth's edition compares the modern text with the ▷ Quarto versions at each stage. But if his extensive notes are instructive, they also tend to be too comprehensive in their suggestions of infinite and ultimately meaningless ambiguities in the text. John Kerrigan's edition of *The Sonnets and A Lover's Complaint* provides a sensitive text, informative notes and does justice to the often neglected *A Lover's Complaint*. Kerrigan authoritatively attributes the poem to Shakespeare and offers the best commentary on it to date.
Bib: Leishman, J. B., *Themes and Variations in Shakespeare's Sonnets*; Schaar, C., *Elizabethan Sonnet Themes and the Dating of Shakespeare's Sonnets*; Smith, H., *The Tension of the Lyre: Poetry in Shakespeare's Sonnets*; Fineman, J., *Shakespeare's Perjured Eye*.

Shepherd's Calendar, The (1579)
A pastoral poem by ▷ Edmund Spenser in 12 parts, one for each month of the year, published in 1579. The series is written in the tradition of the ▷ 'eclogues' of ▷ Virgil, *ie* verse dialogues in a rural setting, with shepherds and shepherdesses with classical, French or (more frequently)

English peasant names, *eg* ▷ Colin Clout (for Spenser himself) and Hobbinol (for his friend ▷ Gabriel Harvey). The intention is not that of 19th-century nature poetry to give a description of the countryside as it actually is at any particular time of the year, but to use the simplified conditions of an ideal rural setting as a standpoint for commenting on life, often that of the court. Four of the dialogues ('January', 'June', 'November' and 'December') are ▷ complaints, *ie* laments for such things as lost love ('January') or advancing age ('December'). Three of them are cheerful: 'March' in praise of love; 'April' in praise of ▷ Elizabeth I, and 'August', a shepherds' song competition, again in praise of love. 'February', 'May', 'July', 'September' and 'October' are 'moral' eclogues on such topics as respect for age ('February') or a ▷ Protestant attack on Roman Catholicism ('May'). The three main themes are love, poetry and religion. The verse is sophisticated and varied, owing much to the examples of Virgil and ▷ Theocritus, and also to the French 16th-century pastoralist Clement Marot, but paying tribute to ▷ Chaucer as well and following the free rhythms of medieval English poetry. The poem set a fashion for pastoral in England, and inaugurated the great lyrical period of the last 20 years of the 16th century.

Ship Money

An ancient tax for providing ships to defend the country in time of war. ▷ Charles I revived it in 1634 in time of peace and without the consent of Parliament. His action caused great resentment, but 12 judges gave their verdict that it was legal. Nonetheless, repeated revivals of the tax aroused positive resistance, notably from John Hampden, and it was one of the contributory causes of the ▷ Civil War, which broke out in 1642. In 1641 Parliament passed a law declaring Ship Money an illegal tax.

Shirley, James (1596–1666)

Dramatist. He was one of the last dramatists of the great Elizabethan–Jacobean–Caroline period of English drama, a period which lasted from 1580 to 1640 and included the career of ▷ Shakespeare. Shirley wrote fluent, graceful ▷ blank verse and is at his best in social comedy; in many ways he anticipates the Restoration writers of comedies of manners after 1660. His audience, as in Restoration comedy, was that of the elegant, refined court; it was not drawn from all social classes like the audiences for Shakespeare

and ▷ Ben Jonson, so that his plays have a comparatively narrow, though sophisticated, range of interests. He wrote over 40 plays, of which the best known are the tragedies *The Traitor* (1631) and *The Cardinal* (1641), and the comedies *The Lady of Pleasure* (1631) and *Hyde Park* (1632).

Bib: Butler, M., *Theatre and Crisis, 1632–42*; Burner, S., *James Shirley: A Study of Literary Coteries and Patronage in Seventeenth-Century England*.

Shoemaker's Holiday, The

A comedy by ▷ Thomas Dekker, published in 1600. It is a ▷ citizen comedy, *ie* designed to appeal to the taste and sentiment of the London merchant class, with a strong romantic flavour. The time of the story is mid-15th century, and the principal character is Simon Eyre, shoemaker and, at the end of the play, Lord Mayor of London. The story concerns the courtship by the young nobleman, Rowland Lacy, of Rose, the daughter of the existing Lord Mayor. The courtship is opposed both by his uncle, the Earl of Lincoln, and by Rose's father. Lacy disguises himself as a shoemaker, takes employment with Simon Eyre, and eventually, with the support of the king, they are successfully married. The play is mainly in prose, with blank verse interspersed; it has no profundity but its happy mood has kept it popular.

Sidney, Mary, Countess of Pembroke (1561–1621)

Writer, translator and literary patron. Mary was born Mary Sidney, and was a member of the remarkable family which included ▷ Sir Philip Sidney, her eldest brother. Her early years were spent at Penshurst Place, in Kent (later to be celebrated in ▷ Ben Jonson's 'To Penshurst') and at Ludlow Castle, the setting for ▷ John Milton's ▷ masque ▷ *Comus*. In 1577 she married Henry Herbert, Earl of Pembroke, and took up residence in her husband's great estate of Wilton Place. Wilton was to become, in the words of ▷ John Aubrey, '... like a college, there were so many learned and ingenious persons. She was the greatest patroness of wit and learning of any lady in her time.' Amongst her protégés were ▷ Edmund Spenser, ▷ Sir Fulke Greville, ▷ Thomas Nashe, ▷ Gabriel Harvey, ▷ Samuel Daniel, ▷ Michael Drayton, ▷ John Davies of Hereford, ▷ Ben Jonson and ▷ John Donne.

So great was her influence on the writers of the late 16th century that it is easy to forget that she was an accomplished author and translator in her own right, and one, moreover, who used her own literary efforts as well as the reworkings of her brother's texts to advance her own Protestant and political causes. She revised and published an altered version of her brother's ▷ *Arcadia*, completed his translations of the ▷ Psalms and translated the French Protestant thinker Philippe de Mornay's *Discourse of Life and Death*, ▷ Petrarch's *Trionfo della Morte*, and Robert Garnier's French ▷ neo-classical tragedy *Marc Antoine*.

▷ Patronage in literature; Cary, Elizabeth; Lumley, Lady Joanna.

Bib: Hannay, M. P., *Philip's Phoenix: Mary Sidney, Countess of Pembroke;* Waller, G. F., *Mary Sidney, Countess of Pembroke: A Critical Study of Her Writings and Literary Milieu.*

Sidney, Sir Philip (1554–86)

Poet, courtier, soldier and statesman. A member of a distinguished noble family, he was a fine example of the ▷ Renaissance ideal of aristocracy in his ability to excel in all that was regarded as fitting for a nobleman. He thus became a pattern for his age, as is shown by the numerous ▷ elegies to him, including one by ▷ Edmund Spenser (*Astrophel*) and one by ▷ James I of England. He was wounded at the battle of Zutphen in Flanders in characteristic circumstances, having discarded leg armour on finding that a comrade in arms had neglected to wear any; as he lay mortally wounded in the leg, he is reputed to have passed a cup of water to a dying soldier with the words, 'Thy need is greater than mine.'

Sidney's writings date mostly from the period 1580–83, when he was temporarily out of favour with ▷ Elizabeth I for political reasons, and was living with his sister ▷ Mary Sidney, Countess of Pembroke, at Wilton House near Salisbury; they were published after his death. Indeed, his work is permeated with political material and, as such, has become a focus of interest for ▷ cultural materialist and ▷ new historicist critics. His most famous poetry, the ▷ sonnet sequence ▷ *Astrophil and Stella*, was published in 1591, and inspired the numerous other sonnet sequences of the 1590s including ▷ Shakespeare's.

Apart from his sonnets, Sidney's poetic reputation rests on the verse interludes in ▷ *The Arcadia*, his prose romance, started in 1580 and published in 1590. His prose work also includes the most famous piece of Elizabethan criticism, ▷ *An Apologie*

for Poetrie, published in 1595. A collaboration with his sister, the verse paraphrase of the Psalms, was not published until 1823. He also wrote two ▷ pastoral poems published in Davison's *Poetical Rhapsody* (1602) and partly translated from the French Du Plessis Mornay's *A Work Concerning the Trueness of the Christian Religion* (1587).

Bib: McCoy, R. C., *Sir Philip Sidney: Rebellion in Arcadia;* Hamilton, A. C., *Sir Philip Sidney;* Waller, G. F. and Moore, M. D. (eds.), *Sir Philip Sidney and the Interpretation of Renaissance Culture.*

Seige of Rhodes, The (1656, revised in 1661)

▷ Opera-cum-heroic drama by ▷ Sir William D'Avenant, thought to have been written originally as a play, with music added later in order to circumvent the Commonwealth law against purely dramatic entertainment and gain the Government's permission to mount it at Rutland House. The performance helped pave the way for the reopening of the theatres, and for D'Avenant's own receipt of one of the monopoly patents as theatre manager. The action concerns the siege of Rhodes by Soleyman the Magnificent, and Duke Alphonso's unreasonable jealousy of his wife, the virtuous Ianthe, who eventually saves her husband and the island. D'Avenant said he wrote it partly to illustrate 'the Characters of Vertue in the shapes of Valor and Conjugal Love'. The staging, as with the earlier court ▷ masque, was accompanied by lavish spectacle.

Sir Patrick Spens

An old Scottish ▷ ballad describing the loss at sea of a Scottish ship, its commander Sir Patrick and all the crew. It exists in several versions; in the shortest, the ship puts to sea in bad weather at the order of the king and Sir Patrick foresees the disaster – brought about, apparently, by royal vanity. In the longest version, the ship goes to Norway to bring back a princess possibly based on the Maid of Norway who died at sea in 1290, or possibly the Scandinavian queen of James VI (16th century); the Norwegian lords complain about the behaviour of the Scottish nobility, who leave suddenly, in bad weather, having taken offence. Both versions are fine examples of the art of the ballad, but the shortest exhibits that form at its most economical and dramatic.

Sir Thomas More (c 1596)

Although the play has been roughly dated to 1596, there is no actual record of production and it exists in manuscript in the British Library, London. It follows the story of ▷ Sir Thomas More's life from his rise to favour in the court of ▷ Henry VIII to his friendship with ▷ Erasmus, his political downfall, and his execution. It is interesting primarily to students of English literature because ▷ Shakespeare may have been one of the contributors to the play, together with ▷ Henry Chettle, ▷ Thomas Dekker, ▷ Thomas Heywood, and ▷ Anthony Munday. The manuscript contains additions and revisions, possibly in response to heavy ▷ censorship of the original text by the Master of the Revels (▷ Revels, Master of the), and these may be as late as 1601.

Six Articles

A law passed through Parliament on the authority of ▷ Henry VIII in 1539. Having removed the English Church from the authority of the Pope and abolished the ▷ monasteries, Henry was concerned to prove himself a true Catholic 'without the Pope'. He therefore ordained that the traditional doctrines should be reaffirmed, especially 'the real presence' of Christ in the bread and wine taken in Holy Communion. ▷ Protestants, by then numerous in southern England, disliked the law, which they called 'the whip with six strings'.
▷ Reformation.

Sixteenth-century literature

In the 16th century changes in English society produced an extraordinary release of radical energies, particularly in the last decade. The powerful feudal system gave place to a new aristocracy and the growth of a new class, that of the country gentlefolk and the city merchants. The Church ceased to be part of an international organization and became part of the national polity, under the authority of the Crown. The ▷ Renaissance secularized learning and after a struggle for survival, the nation became succinctly nationalistic.

Yet in some respects the ▷ Middle Ages died slowly in England. Lord Berners' translation (1525) of the 14th-century *Chronicles* of ▷ Froissart belongs with the prose of ▷ Malory's ▷ *Morte d' Arthur*, and ▷ Sir Thomas More's principal work in English, *The History of King Richard III* (written 1513?), is medieval in spirit.

The language of prose made notable advances in the 16th century. It is significant that much of the finest prose was about education, such as ▷ Sir Thomas Elyot's *Governor* (1531) and ▷ Roger Ascham's *The Schoolmaster* (pub. 1570), and some of it arose out of the religious changes, notably ▷ William Tyndale's version of the New Testament, the Sermons of ▷ Latimer, and ▷ Cranmer's noble ▷ *Book of Common Prayer*.

In poetry, the same tentative movement away from the Middle Ages occurred. ▷ John Skelton has more vitality than the English (as distinct from Scottish) poets of the 15th century. ▷ Thomas Wyatt's poetry has a strong individuality and his rhythms, though often subtle, seem to be suspended between the roughness of the 15th century and the smoothness which ▷ Chaucer had introduced, thereby creating a tension redolent of the changing social position of the Tudor courtier. Henry Howard, ▷ Earl of Surrey and ▷ Thomas Sackville are less interesting than Wyatt, but their work is moving closer to the smooth handling of language which the Elizabethans prized so much in the ▷ sonnets of ▷ Sir Philip Sidney (pub. 1591) and in ▷ Spenser from ▷ *The Shepherd's Calendar* (1579) to ▷ *The Faerie Queene* (1596).

The ▷ morality play style of drama continued into the 16th century, although its content became less religious and more secular, as in Skelton's *Magnificence* (1516?) and the *Satire of the Three Estates* (1540) by the Scots poet ▷ David Lindsay. A lighter kind of play called the ▷ interlude (*eg* the plays of ▷ John Heywood) moved towards the first pure comedies, ▷ *Ralph Roister Doister* (written 1551?) and ▷ *Gammer Gurton's Needle* (1556). Meanwhile the morality play could be said to have become secular and (often) political, and tended to evolve into the historical drama, such as ▷ *Gorboduc* (1561) by Sackville and Norton, and *Cambyses* (1569) by Preston. Preston was a scholar; Sackville was an aristocrat. Now that the drama had lost its roots in the Church and the town rituals, it needed thoroughly professional writers to give it a fully developed form and life of its own. A group of just such writers – ▷ Thomas Kyd, ▷ John Lyly, ▷ George Peele, ▷ Robert Greene and ▷ Christopher Marlowe, collectively known as the ▷ University Wits – began work in the 1580s. They evolved among them a self-confident art of the theatre, and ▷ Shakespeare in his first decade (from ▷ *Henry VI* to *Hamlet*) was indebted to them.

These new writers, including Shakespeare himself, formed a new social phenomenon: the professional man of letters, who was not a nobleman like Wyatt, Surrey or Sidney, practising literature as part of the aristocratic life, nor a scholar or churchman like Ascham or Tyndale, practising it as a by-product of his profession, nor a court poet as Chaucer had been and Spenser was, practising it partly with a view to receiving court emoluments, but a writer who depended on monetary 'takings' from the public theatre. They contributed to the extraordinary vitality of the 1590s, not only in the drama but in prose pamphleteering and the kind of romance known as the ▷ Elizabethan novel, in which ▷ Thomas Nashe, ▷ Thomas Lodge and ▷ Thomas Deloney were among the foremost practitioners.

In the 1590s, drama, non-dramatic poetry of all kinds but notably the ▷ sonnet and the ▷ lyric, and prose including not only pamphleteers but the great philosophical writing of ▷ Richard Hooker (*Laws of Ecclesiastical Polity*) developed in new ways. The poetry has an extraordinary range of style, from the highly wrought music of Spenser's *Faerie Queene* to the involved and complex thought of ▷ Donne's ▷ *Songs and Sonnets*. Literary criticism has also made its beginnings with ▷ Puttenham's *Art of English Poetry* (pub. 1589) and Sydney's ▷ *Apologie for Poetrie* (pub. 1598). There were also a number of ▷ translations in the period; ▷ Italian and ▷ French writing and thought as well as the ancient classics (above all the philosophy of ▷ Plato and the critical theory of ▷ Horace, and, through the Italians, ▷ Aristotle) contributed a large part of the English literary Renaissance.

Skelton, John (c 1460–1529)
Poet; awarded the title of ▷ 'poet laureate' by the universities of Oxford and Cambridge; tutor to Prince Henry, later ▷ Henry VIII (1494–1502); ordained in 1498 and Rector of Diss from 1502. Skelton composed poetry in Latin but is most famous for his satirical English poetry, in which the corruption and corrupting influence of ▷ Cardinal Wolsey are frequent targets. He is a brilliant stylist, who seems to delight in the juxtaposition of learned and popular registers (often inserting Latin verses or tags into his work). He developed the 'skeltonic' verse form: lines containing 2/3 accented syllables which often alliterate, linked in couplets or sometimes longer rhyme runs of up to 14 lines. His work is highly self-conscious, playful, sometimes parodic, and reveals a wide acquaintance with the work of late 14th- and earlier 15th-century court poets. The *Bowge of Court* (1498) is a barely veiled attack on court corruption

through a reworking of the 'ship of fools' convention.

His *Phyllype Sparrow* (c 1505) is in two parts: the first represents an attempt by a young convent girl to compose a fitting memorial for her dead sparrow, using the resources of classical and Christian culture, which includes a parodic bird Mass; the second is a lengthy praise poem outlining the attractions of Jane herself, and the fantasies she arouses in the speaker. The *Tunnyng of Elinour Rummyng* (c 1517) is an exercise in creating the female grotesque which describes the establishment and the female patrons of Elinour's ale house. Skelton's later satires, *Speke Parrot, Colin Clout, Why Come Ye Nat to Court*, (all written c 1521–2) attack Wolsey's abuse of power in particular, and state and ecclesiastical corruption in general. Indeed, recent criticism suggests that his early vocation as a priest constantly affects his literary work, but towards social criticism and not inward contemplation like later spiritual writers (eg ▷ George Herbert). The *Garlande or Chapelet of Laurell*, heavily indebted to ▷ Chaucer's *House of Fame*, is Skelton's witty projection of his place, as a poet laureate, in the Hall of Fame. He is also the author of a ▷ morality play, *Magnyfycence* (c 1515–16), which examines the dangers of materialistic corruption at court.
▷ Catullus.
Bib: Carpenter, N., *John Skelton*; Fish, S., *John Skelton's Poetry*; Kinney, A. F., *John Skelton, Priest as Poet*; Scattergood, J. (ed.), *John Skelton: The Complete Poems*.

Smectymnuus
A name under which five ▷ Presbyterian writers wrote against episcopacy – rule of the Church by bishops – in the 17th century. The name was suggested by the initial letters of the names of the writers: Stephen Marshall, Edward Calamy, Thomas Young, Matthew Newcomen, and William Spurstow. Their ▷ pamphlet was attacked by ▷ Bishop Joseph Hall, and was defended in two pamphlets by ▷ John Milton in 1641 and 1642. ▷ Samuel Butler, in his poetic satire *Hudibras*, written against the ▷ Puritans, calls the Presbyterians the 'Legion of Smec'.

Songs and Sonnets (Donne) (c 1633–5)
A heading given to 55 love poems by ▷ John Donne. Though the poems themselves first appeared in the 1633 edition of Donne's *Poems* (with the exception of 'Breake of Day' and 'The Expiration', which had been published earlier), the category of 'Songs and

Sonnets' did not appear until the publication of the second edition of Donne's poetry in 1635. Despite the title, very few of the poems gathered under the heading are songs, or, in the technical sense, ▷ sonnets. Modern editors have questioned the authorship of two of the poems attributed to Donne (though not published either in 1633 or 1635), these being 'The Token' and the poem known as 'Self-Love'. Again, some modern editors have felt the need to add to the category by transferring other poems of Donne's into the group. Various attempts at arranging the poems into a sequence according to their presumed date of composition have been made, but with little real success.

Songs and Sonnets (Tottel)
▷ *Tottel's Miscellany*.

Sonnet
A short poem of 14 lines and a rhyme scheme restricted by one or other of a variety of principles. The most famous pattern is called the 'Petrarchan sonnet', from its masterly use by the Italian poet ▷ Petrarch. This divides naturally into an eight-line stanza (octave) rhyming *abba abba*, and a six-line stanza in which two or three rhymes may occur; the two stanzas provide also for contrast in attitude to the theme. The origin of the sonnet is unknown, but its earliest examples date from the 13th century in Europe, although it did not reach England until the 16th century. The immense popularity of the form perhaps derives from its combination of discipline, musicality and amplitude. The subject-matter is commonly love, but after the 16th century it becomes, at least in England, much more varied.

The first writers of sonnets in England were ▷ Sir Thomas Wyatt, and Henry Howard, ▷ Earl of Surrey; the popular anthology, ▷ *Tottel's Miscellany* (1559), made their experiments widely known. The first really fine sonnet sequence was ▷ Sir Philip Sidney's ▷ *Astrophil and Stella*. Its publication in 1591 set an eagerly followed fashion for its distinctively English form. This consisted of a single stanza of 14 lines concluding in a couplet; it is thought that the comparative scarcity of rhyming words in the English language may be the explanation of the greater number of rhymes and the freedom in the rhyming scheme in contrast to the Petrarchan form. The greatest of the succeeding sequences was undoubtedly ▷ Shakespeare's (▷ Shakespeare – Sonnets), but notable ones were produced by ▷ Samuel

Daniel, ▷ Michael Drayton, and ▷ Edmund Spenser.

The sonnet form continued to be used after 1600, notably by ▷ John Donne and ▷ John Milton, but much less for amorous themes and more for religious ones (*eg* Donne's *Holy Sonnets*), or, by Milton, for expressions of other forms of personal experience (*eg On his Blindness*) or political declamation (*On the Late Massacre in Piedmont*). Milton used the Petrarchan rhyme scheme, but he kept the English form of using a single stanza.
Bib: Lever, J. W., *The Elizabethan Love Sonnet*; Wuller, G., *English Poetry of the Sixteenth Century*.

Sonnets, Shakespeare's
▷ Shakespeare – Sonnets.

Sophocles (495–406 BC)
One of the three foremost ancient Greek dramatists, the other two being ▷ Aeschylus and ▷ Euripides. He wrote about 100 dramas, of which only seven survive: *Oedipus the King; Oedipus at Colonus; Antigone; Electra; Trachiniae; Ajax; Philoctetes*. His poetic language shows more flexibility than that of Aeschylus – their relationship in this respect has been compared to that of ▷ Shakespeare and ▷ Marlowe – and he used three actors on the stage instead of only two (not counting the Chorus). In his relationship to Euripides, he is quoted by ▷ Aristotle as saying that he depicted men as they ought to be whereas Euripides depicted them as they were.

Southampton, Henry Wriothesley, third Earl of (1573–1625)
Chiefly famous as a ▷ patron of letters, and particularly as a patron of ▷ Shakespeare. He was educated at St John's College, Cambridge from 1585 to 1589, where he made friends with the chief favourite of ▷ Elizabeth 1, the ▷ Earl of Essex, and was shown special favour by the queen herself. Shakespeare dedicated to him his poems ▷ *Venus and Adonis* (1593) and (in terms of warm devotion) *The Rape of Lucrece* (1594). There has long been much speculation about whether the young man in the sonnets (▷ Shakespeare – Sonnets) is Southampton, and whether the initials of 'Mr W. H.' in the dedication ('To the Onlie Begetter of These Insuing Sonnets') stand for 'Henry Wriothesley' reversed. Southampton accompanied Essex on his two naval expeditions against Spain in 1596 (to Cadiz) and 1597 (to the Azores), and distinguished himself by his daring on the

second of them. In 1598 he had to make a
hasty marriage with Essex's cousin Elizabeth
Vernon, and this angered the queen against
him. He was later concerned in Essex's
conspiracy against Elizabeth, and is thought
to have arranged a special performance of
Shakespeare's ▷ *Richard II* on the eve of the
rebellion. In 1601 he was sentenced to death;
however the sentence was commuted to life
imprisonment and when ▷ James I acceded
in 1603, Southampton returned to court. He
died of a fever when serving, with his son, as
a volunteer on the side of the Dutch in their
war with Spain. Other writers with whom
he was associated as patron included ▷ John
Florio, the translator of ▷ Montaigne, and
▷ Thomas Nashe, who dedicated ▷ *The
Unfortunate Traveller* to him.
Bib: Akrigg, G. P. V., *Shakespeare and the Earl
of Southampton*.

Southwell, Lady Frances (no dates)
Essay-writer. Lady Frances, like her friend
▷ Cecily Bulstrode, wrote Theophrastian
▷ character sketches which consisted
of short satirical essays on exaggerated
personality 'types'. Her 'Certain Edicts from
a Parliament in Eutopia' were published
with ▷ Sir Thomas Overbury's *The Wife*
(1615) – Overbury was one of the foremost
writers of such 'characters'. 'Certain Edicts'
reveals a sharp appreciation for some of the
artifices and mannerisms of the day, especially
those adopted by women wishing to seem
'feminine' at the expense of their intelligence.
Lady Frances was also central to the court
world, being a favoured lady-in-waiting to
▷ Queen Anne and a friend of ▷ Lady Anne
Clifford.

Southwell, Robert (?1561–95)
Poet and Roman Catholic priest. He worked
in England as a member of the ▷ Jesuit
order at a time when this was illegal; in
1592 he was arrested and tortured for
evidence of other priests, which he did
not disclose. He was executed after three
years in prison, where he wrote some
fine religious poems (*St Peter's Complaint
with Other Poems* and *Maconiae*, 1595).
His most famous poem is *The Burning
Babe*. He also wrote a long poem, *Fourfold
Meditation of the Four Last Things* (1606), and
a number of religious tracts, one of which,
Mary Magdalen's Tears, was imitated by
▷ Thomas Nashe in his *Christ's Tears over
Jerusalem*.
Bib: Devlin, C., *The Life of Robert Southwell:
Poet and Martyr*.

Sowernam, Ester (fl. 1617)
Tract-writer. One of the defenders of
women in the ▷ *Querelle des Femmes*, who
answered the attacks in Joseph Swetnam's
*The Arraignment of Lewd, idle, froward,
and unconstant women* (1615). 'Sowernam'
is a pseudonym that plays partly upon
Swet*nam*'s name, and partly upon one of his
catch-phrases – 'every sweet hath his sowre'
(meaning every good man has his wicked
female counterpart). 'Ester' is taken from
the fearless character in the ▷ Bible who, to
protect the Jews, hanged Haman, the man
who attacked them. Her work, *Ester Hath
hanged Haman* (1617), is written in a lively
style and sets out to prove the nobility of
women with erudition and humour. Today
it is assumed that this anonymous author
was female, since we are now aware that
middle-class women could have had an
education that would equip them with the
classical and scholarly allusions evident in the
text. Sowernam's defence should be compared
with that of ▷ Rachel Speght's, since she
herself draws parallels between the works,
saying that Speght's work 'doth rather charge
and condemn women'.
▷ Anger, Jane; Munda, Constantia.
Bib: Henderson, K. U. and McManus,
B. F. (eds.), *Half Humankind*; Travitsky, B.
(ed.), *The Paradise of Women*; Beilin, E. V.,
Redeeming Eve.

Spanish influence on English literature
The earliest translation of a Spanish
masterpiece into any language was that of
Cervantes' ▷ *Don Quixote* (1605–15) by
Thomas Shelton in 1612 (Part I) and 1620
(Part II). Of all Spanish texts, *Don Quixote*
was to have the most profound influence
on English literature: in the 17th century
▷ Francis Beaumont's ▷ *The Knight of the
Burning Pestle* (1607) and ▷ Samuel Butler's
▷ *Hudibras* (1663) utilize the comic elements
of the novel, while ▷ Philip Massinger's *The
Renegado* (1624) combines material from *Don
Quixote* together with Cervantes' play, *Los
Baños de Argel* (1615).

    The 16th and 17th centuries in Spain are
known as the Golden Age, which paralleled
in quality, but greatly exceeded in abundance
of texts, the creativity of the ▷ Elizabethan
and ▷ Jacobean ages in England. The plays
of Pedro Calderón de la Barca (1600–81)
have often been compared to those of
▷ Shakespeare. Spanish Golden Age
influence on contemporary English drama
can be seen in ▷ James Shirley's *The Young
Admiral* (1633) and *The Opportunity* (1634), as

well as in Beaumont and ▷ Fletcher's *Love's Cure* (1629) (▷ Spanish intrigue comedy).

The 17th-century translations of James Mabbe further facilitated Spanish literary influence in England; works translated by Mabbe include Cervantes' *Novelas ejemplares* (1613; *Exemplary Novels*, trans. 1640); the late medieval novelesque play *La Celestina* (c 1499) by Fernando de Rojas (c 1465–1541); and Mateo Alemán's (1547–?1614) ▷ picaresque novel, *Guzmán de Alfarache* (trans. 1622). The latter text, with *Don Quixote*, formed part of the broader, generic development of the picaresque novel in Spain, England and elsewhere in Europe, while *La Celestina* was one of the earliest medieval texts to be translated into English.
Bib: Loftis, J., *Renaissance Drama in England and Spain*; Cohen, W., *Drama of a Nation*.

Spanish intrigue comedy
English comedy influenced by, or using as its source, a type of Spanish play known as the '*comedia de capa y espada*' (comedy of cape and sword). The originals include works by Pedro Calderón de la Barca (1600–81), Lope de Vega (1562–1635), and Tirso de Molina (1571–1648). The plays frequently turn on conflicts of love and honour and are dominated by busy intrigue plots involving problems of mistaken identity, duelling, and concealment. One of the first of this variety was Sir Samuel Tuke's *The Adventures of Five Hours* (1663), based on a play by Calderón, and commissioned by ▷ Charles II. Other elements of the type include rigid fathers, brothers and uncles attempting to force young relatives into unwelcome marriages, and high-spirited women active in determining their own fates.
▷ Spanish influence on English literature.
Bib: Loftis, J., *The Spanish Plays of Neoclassical England*.

Spanish Tragedy, The
A drama by ▷ Thomas Kyd, probably written around 1587. It is the earliest important ▷ revenge tragedy, and both by date and by influence it is one of the principal starting-points of the great age of ▷ Elizabethan drama. The plot has no known source and is presumably Kyd's invention. The scene is Spain, just after the Spanish-Portuguese war of 1580. Andrea, a Spanish nobleman, has been unchivalrously killed in a battle by Balthazar, a Portuguese prince, who in turn is captured by Lorenzo, nephew of the King of Spain, and Horatio, son of Hieronimo, Marshal of Spain. The ghost of Andrea

and the spirit of Revenge sit above stage and watch the action throughout: Andrea is to witness how his death is to be avenged. This process is most intricate, and centres on Bel-imperia, Lorenzo's sister. She and Andrea have been lovers, and in consequence she detests Balthazar, who nonetheless seeks her in marriage with Lorenzo's support. She deliberately slights Balthazar by cultivating the affections of Horatio, who is in consequence murdered by Lorenzo and Balthazar.
Hieronimo – hitherto a background figure – discovers the identity of his son's murderers; half crazed with grief, he seeks justice, but his pleading is brushed aside by the king. He eventually secures it by contriving a play (within the play) in which the guilty parties suffer real deaths instead of simulated ones. Hieronimo then takes his own life after biting out his tongue. Thus Andrea (after displaying some impatience) watches how his own death is avenged. The audience sees how justice is brought about when it is left to mere human motives: not as Heaven would bring it, cleanly and economically, but wastefully and brutally, hatred breeding hatred, and callous contrivance countered by contrivance still more ruthless. Only Lorenzo can be described as an evil character – a ▷ Machiavellian schemer – the other characters are driven out of their natural virtue by vindictive bitterness. Hieronimo himself is momentarily checked by biblical authority – '*Vindicta mihi*': 'Justice is mine, saith the Lord' (*Romans* 12:19) – but he is driven on by the energy of his grief.

Kyd's poetry is undistinguished, but the play is theatrically so effective that it remained popular for a generation. In 1602 the play was expanded by some more effective verse, probably by ▷ Ben Jonson, whom the theatre manager ▷ Philip Henslowe paid for additions. However, these obscure rather than enhance Kyd's essential drama.

Kyd was certainly influenced by the plays of ▷ Seneca, for instance in his use of ▷ stichomythia and in the role of the ghost. Kyd's own influence was great, and can be seen in ▷ *Hamlet*. The dilemma of revenge, in one aspect seen to be a duty and in another an acknowledged sin, deeply preoccupied the Elizabethans. At the lowest level it was a pretext for the violence that appealed to them in the theatre – the 'tragedy of blood' – at a higher level it presented the problem of how it could be executed against evil-doers who were men of power or who were protected by such men; at a higher level still it was a natural vehicle for dramatizing the theme of the corrupted conscience, which both

▷ Renaissance and ▷ Reformation ideas brought to the forefront of social attention. *The Spanish Tragedy* was effective on all these planes.

Speght, Rachel (c 1598–1630)
Devotional and tract-writer. One of the respondents to Joseph Swetnam's attack on women (the other two being ▷ Constantia Munda and ▷ Ester Sowernam). Speght came from a learned family – her father edited ▷ Chaucer – and her ▷ pamphlet *A Mouzell for Malastomus* ('a muzzle for Black-Mouth'), published in 1617, is a serious and theoretical defence. It is divided into two sections, the first being a well-organized refutation of Swetnam's arguments, and the second a livelier and more wide-ranging disputation. To 20th-century readers Speght's hesitancy over asserting female virtues appears to defeat her own argument, and, indeed, she was accused of being irresolute by her contemporary, Sowernam. It is interesting to note, however, that Speght chose to write under her own name ('Sowernam' is a pseudonym) and that she was prepared to face any repercussions her open argument should incur. Primarily, Speght should be seen as a devotional writer and she is concerned with the plight and salvation of all humankind, rather than either sex in isolation. Her later work, the devotional poem *Mortalities Memorandum* (1621), is probably more representative of her true beliefs.
▷ *Querelle des Femmes*.
Bib: Beilin, E. V., *Redeeming Eve*; Travitsky, B. (ed.), *The Paradise of Women*; Nyquist, M. and Ferguson, M. (eds.), *Re-membering Milton*.

Spens, Sir Patrick
▷ *Sir Patrick Spens*.

Spenser, Edmund (?1552–99)
Poet. Spenser's poetry, and in particular ▷ *The Faerie Queene*, was possibly the single most influential body of writing to appear in the ▷ Renaissance period in England. Throughout the 17th century his influence was immense, not least on ▷ John Milton. In the 20th century, however, his reputation began to decline – readers preferring the so-called ▷ 'metaphysical' school of writing represented by ▷ John Donne. Yet, in recent years, there has been a revival of interest in Spenser, particularly among ▷ 'new historicist' and ▷ psychoanalytical critics for whom *The Faerie Queene* has become an endlessly fascinating text.
Spenser was born in London, but lived for most of his adult life in ▷ Ireland. He first visited Ireland in 1577, becoming in 1580 private secretary to Lord Grey, the newly appointed lord deputy of Ireland. From 1580 onwards Spenser's fortunes were connected with his progress through the ranks of the colonial administration of Ireland, and by 1588 Spenser had occupied the forfeited estate of the Earl of Desmond. The estate, at Kilcolman in County Cork, Spenser developed as a small 'colony' of six English householders and their families. Kilcolman was to be Spenser's home until 1598, when, in October of that year, the castle of Kilcolman was destroyed in the course of 'Tyrone's Rebellion'. Following the upheaval, Spenser returned to London for the last time, where he died, according to ▷ Ben Jonson, 'for lack of bread' in 1599.
Spenser's first published works were anonymous translations from ▷ Petrarch and the French poet ▷ du Bellay which appeared in a violently anti-Catholic collection in 1569. It was not, however, until the publication of ▷ *The Shepherd's Calendar* (1579 with five editions by 1597) that Spenser's poetic reputation became established. In 1580 he published a correspondence with ▷ Gabriel Harvey, an old friend from his Cambridge days, which set out his views on metrics and prosody. The correspondence is not, perhaps, of startling critical force. Further collections of poetry appeared in 1591, followed by his ▷ sonnet sequence ▷ *Amoretti* together with ▷ *Epithalamion* in a single volume in 1595. The ▷ autobiographical *Colin Clout's Come Home Again* (1594) (▷ Colin Clout) was followed by the ▷ Platonic *Fowre Hymnes* of 1596 and his celebration of the marriage of the daughters of the Earl of Worcester, ▷ *Prothalamion*, also in 1596. Spenser's major poetic work, *The Faerie Queene*, begun prior to 1579, appeared first in 1590 when the first three books of the poem were published. The second edition of Books I–III appeared together with Books IV–VI in 1596, and the final version (as we have it) of the poem after Spenser's death, when a ▷ folio edition including the ▷ 'Mutabilitie Cantos' was published in 1609.
In the late 16th century, Spenser was the dominating literary intellect of the period, and his reputation was sustained throughout the 18th century, reaching an apotheosis amongst the Romantic poets. To the modern reader he presents a complex set of problems and responses. As a 'source' for wide areas of Renaissance intellectual culture he has been continuously explicated and re-explicated,

his texts being examined for their Platonist, numerological, Lucretian ($\triangleright$ Lucretius) and $\triangleright$ Calvinist elements. But he is also a writer whose engagement with the creation of a national myth of identity was part of a vital Elizabethan project.
Bib: Greenlaw, E. et al. (eds.), *Works of Edmund Spenser* (10 vols.); Nohrnberg, J., *The Analogy of 'The Faerie Queene'*; Sale, R., *Reading Spenser*; Goldberg, J., *Endlesse Worke: Spenser and the Structures of Discourse*; Shepherd, S., *Spenser*.

Spenserian stanza

A verse form devised by $\triangleright$ Edmund Spenser for his poem $\triangleright$ *The Faerie Queene*. It consists of eight ten-syllable lines, plus a ninth line of 12 syllables ($\triangleright$ alexandrine), an iambic rhythm and a rhyme scheme as follows: *a b a b b c b c c*. Example from *The Faerie Queene*:

> *And as she looked about, she did behold,*
> *How over that same door was likewise writ,*
> *'Be bold, be bold,' and everywhere 'Be bold',*
> *That much she mused, yet could not construe it*
> *By any riddling skill, or common wit.*
> *At last she spied at that room's upper end,*
> *Another iron door, on which was writ,*
> *'Be not too bold'; whereto though she did bend*
> *Her earnest mind, yet wist not what it might*
> *intend.*
>
> (Book III, Canto xi, 54)

The stanza was used by Spenser's poetic disciples $\triangleright$ Giles and $\triangleright$ Phineas Fletcher early in the 17th century.

Stationers

In modern English, sellers of writing materials. In the $\triangleright$ Middle Ages and until the mid-17th century, however, they were booksellers, and were so called from their practice of taking up stalls or 'stations' at suitable places in cathedral towns (*eg* against the walls of St Paul's Cathedral in London) and universities. In the 16th and early 17th centuries they not only sold books, but printed and published them as well. The absence of a law of copyright (until 1709) made it lawful for stationers to publish authors' manuscripts whenever and however they could procure them, without the authors' permission. This kind of unauthorized publishing is now called 'pirating'. Eighteen of Shakespeare's plays were possibly pirated before the publication of the first collected edition of his plays in the First $\triangleright$ Folio of 1623, and the fact has caused some difficulties to scholars; there is no assurance that their publication was authorized by the poet, that he had revised the

plays for publication, or even that the stationer had procured a reliable version.

The Stationers' Company was formed in 1557 by royal charter; by this charter, no one not a member was entitled to publish a book except by special privilege, and all stationers had to record the titles of books they published; the Company's record of books is thus an important source of information for the literary historian, and particularly valuable evidence in dating many Elizabethan plays. The Company gradually lost its publishing monopoly in the 17th century.

The modern institution, Her Majesty's Stationery Office, publishes official government documents.
$\triangleright$ Stationers' Register.

Stationers' Register

An important source of bibliographical information for the 16th and 17th centuries. In 1557, $\triangleright$ Mary I granted the Worshipful Company of $\triangleright$ Stationers and Papermakers of London the monopoly of printing. Under the charter granted to the company, all printers were enjoined to record the titles of any works intended for publication for the first time in a register. Once a title had been recorded, no other member of the company was allowed to publish the book. The Stationers' Register thus *should* include the titles of all books intended for publication between 1554 and 1709. In practice, however, the record is incomplete. First, records for the years 1571–6 have been lost. Secondly, titles were sometimes entered but the book never published. Thirdly, on occasion a book was published without being entered. Finally, though titles were usually entered shortly before the actual publication of a book, there are cases where a period of years elapsed between the entering of a title and the final publication of a work. Nevertheless, the Stationers' Register is an important record of the English book trade in the period. Not least, it provides a valuable indication of what works were being considered for publication at a particular moment.
Bib: Arber, E. (ed.), *A Transcript of the Register of the Company of Stationers of London, 1554–1640* (5 vols); Eyre, G. E. B. (ed.), *A Transcript of the Register of the Worshipful Company of Stationers from 1640 to 1709* (3 vols).

Stichomythia

A terse but artificial style of dramatic dialogue, used in disputes between two characters, each speaking in turn a single line of verse. It originated in ancient Greek tragedies; from them it passed to ▷ Seneca, whose influence caused it to be used by some of the early Elizabethans.

Stoics
A school of philosophy founded by the Greek Zeno of Citium in the 4th century BC. It later extended to Rome, where its leaders became Epictetus and ▷ Seneca (both 1st century AD) and the Roman Emperor Marcus Aurelius (2nd century AD). They reasoned that all being is material, and therefore the soul is, and so are the virtues. The soul, however, is an active principle which sustains the body and proceeds from God; only the active principle has significance, and the wise person is therefore indifferent to material suffering and cares only for virtue governed by judgement that is in accordance with the principles of wisdom. Some of the ethical principles of Stoicism were in accordance with Christianity (which Marcus Aurelius nevertheless persecuted) and, abstracted from religious doctrine, they appealed to the ▷ Renaissance ideal of the noble soul; hence the recurrence of Stoic attitudes in the drama of ▷ Shakespeare and his contemporaries.

Stow, John (1515–1605)
Historian and antiquary. Stow's first interest was in literature rather than history, and he produced an edited version of ▷ Chaucer's poetry, *The Workes of Geoffrey Chaucer* (1561). His historical texts include the detailed and authoritative *Chronicles of England* (1580; later known as *Annales*) and *A Survey of London*, which is an invaluable account of the capital city during the ▷ Elizabethan period. He was suspected of ▷ recusancy and charged with owning Popish documents (▷ Edmund Grindal), but managed to convince the ecclesiastical commission of his innocence.

Strafford, Sir Thomas Wentworth, first Earl of (1593–1641)
Statesman, and one of ▷ Charles I's chief ministers. He began his career as an opponent of the king; as Member of Parliament for Yorkshire in 1625, he opposed the attempt of Charles's minister, The Earl of Buckingham, to raise taxes for war against Spain, and in 1627 he was imprisoned for refusing to contribute a forced loan to the king. His opposition to Charles was different in motive from that of other members; theirs was based on the desire to assert the power of Parliament, whereas Wentworth's motive was to secure efficient government. Consequently,

when in 1628 Parliament asserted itself by forcing on the king the ▷ Petition of Right, he changed sides. In 1632 Charles sent him to Ireland to reform the administration there. He was never consulted on English affairs until the major crisis brought about by the defeat of the royal troops by the Scots in 1639. Wentworth was then recalled, and made Earl of Strafford in 1640. Events, however, had gone so far that he could no longer help the king, and merely focused public hostility upon himself. Parliament condemned him to death by an Act of Attainder (*ie* a law effecting death of a subject without using the normal judicial process), and he was executed accordingly.

Structuralism
A form of critical theory chiefly derived from the work of ▷ Ferdinand de Saussure and from Russian ▷ formalism. Structuralism rejects the notion that the text expresses an author's meaning or that it reflects society, and treats it instead as an independent unit that activates various objective relationships with other texts. Structuralism, then, concentrates upon the relationship between cultural elements, especially those in binary oppositions, without which, it is claimed, meaning cannot exist. Thus for structuralists, texts remain within a self-contained and closeted world, ignoring author, reader and any form of external reality.
▷ Mimesis.
Bib: Culler, J., *Structuralist Poetics*.

Stuart (Stewart), House of
The family from which came the sovereigns of Scotland between 1371 and 1603, and the sovereigns of Scotland, England and Ireland between 1603 and 1714. The family originated in Brittany, from where they migrated to England in the 11th century and to Scotland in the 12th, where they acquired the surname 'Stuart' (variously spelt) by serving the kings of Scotland as Stewards. They came to the Scottish throne by intermarriage with the Bruce family, and the reigns until 1603 were as follows: Robert II (1371–90); Robert III (1390–1406); James I (1406–37); James II (1437–60); James III (1460–88); James IV (1488–1513); James V (1513–42); Mary (1542, deposed 1567); James VI (1567–1603). In 1603 ▷ Elizabeth I of England died childless, and James VI inherited the crown of England by virtue of his descent from Elizabeth's aunt Margaret, who had married James IV. James VI thus became also ▷ James I of England, and ruled over the two countries until 1625.

The succession during the ▷ Renaissance period continued as follows: Charles I (1625–49), after whom there was an ▷ Interregnum until 1660 when the monarchy was restored in his son, Charles II (1660–85).

Stubbes, Philip (?1555–?1611)

▷Puritan author of *The Anatomie of Abuses* (1583) who censured stage plays and wrote a strong and colourful prose. He may have been involved in the ▷ Martin Marprelate controversy, and was attacked in pamphlets by both ▷ John Lyly and ▷ Thomas Nashe. He is most valued now for his contribution to our understanding of the popular customs and festivals of the time.

Subjectivity

In its use in the language of literary criticism this concept is not to be confused with the notion of 'individual response' with which it has customarily been associated. ▷ Louis Althusser and ▷ Jacques Lacan developed the notion of human beings as 'subjects', that is points at which all of those social, cultural, and psychic forces which contribute to the construction of the individual come together. Implicit in the concept of the 'subject' is the idea of the grammatical positioning of the personal pronoun in a sentence, the 'I' being referred to as 'the subject of discourse'. Also implicit in the concept of 'subjectivity' is the notion of 'subjection', which raises fundamental questions about the ways in which the behaviour of individual 'subjects' is conditioned by external forces. Within the boundaries of critical theory the 'subject' is never unified (except through the functioning of an ▷ ideology that is designed to efface contradiction), but is, in reality, split or 'decentred'. This is part of a movement away from the kind of philosophical ▷ humanism which would place the individual at the centre of attention. It would attribute to him or her an autonomy of action as well as an authority arising out of the suggestion that he or she is the origin and source of all meaning. 'Subjectivity' is an indispensable category of analysis for ▷ feminism, ▷ psychoanalytical criticism and for the various kinds of ▷ materialist analyses of texts.
Bib: Belsey, C., *The Subject of Tragedy*.

Suckling, Sir John (1609–41)

Poet and dramatist. Suckling has been grouped with the ▷ 'Cavalier' poets associated with the Royalist cause during the ▷ Civil War. Closely associated with the court, his military career was marked by an ostentatious delight in the appearance rather than the reality of a campaign: he is said to have paid £12,000 from his own pocket to have 100 cavalrymen decked out in striking uniforms for the war against the Scots in 1639. The king's army, of which Suckling and his troops were a part, were routed. Following the abortive attempt to rescue the king's favourite, the ▷ Earl of Strafford, from the Tower, Suckling, who took part in the plot, fled abroad, where he died, possibly committing suicide and probably in the autumn of 1641.

Although the author of four plays, the most successful of which was *Aglaura* (first produced in 1637 as a ▷ tragedy, and revised and produced as a comedy in 1638), Suckling's reputation rests on his short ▷ lyric poems, written in an anti-Petrarchan style and calculated to strike the pose of a cynical rake.
Bib: Berry H. (ed.), *Sir John Suckling's Poems and Letters from Manuscript*.

Summer's Last Will and Testament (1592)

A lyrical ▷ allegory and ▷ pageant by ▷ Thomas Nashe, and his only surviving dramatic work.

Supremacy, Acts of

1 The law passed through Parliament on the initiative of ▷ King Henry VIII in 1534; it established the king as Supreme Head of the Church of England, and thus displaced the sovereignty of the Pope. The Act was the immediate consequence of Henry's dispute with the Pope over his attempt to divorce his queen, Katharine of Aragon; however, this immediate cause was insufficient by itself to bring about the break. Deeper causes include the growth of national feeling; longstanding resentment against some forms of papal taxation; distrust of Roman Catholic doctrine, first roused by ▷ Wycliffe and now reawakened by the German reformer, ▷ Luther; growing dislike of the international religious orders of monks and friars who were ultimately subject to the Pope. Nonetheless, Henry was a conservative in doctrine, and the act did not entail doctrinal reformation.
2 The similar law passed through Parliament on the initiative of ▷ Elizabeth I in 1559. Since the act of 1534, the English nation had undergone ▷ Protestant doctrinal ▷ reformation in the reign of ▷ Edward VI and had reverted to full Roman Catholicism under headship of the Pope in the reign of ▷ Mary I. In consequence, Elizabeth's Act of Supremacy was deliberately vague, so as to gain the widest possible national support from both Protestant and Roman Catholic

sympathizers. Elizabeth abandoned the title 'Supreme Head' and adopted that of 'Supreme Governor'.

Surrey, Henry Howard, Earl of (?1517–47)
Poet. He was the son of the Duke of Norfolk, the senior nobleman of England. Surrey and his father were both arrested by ▷ Henry VIII on a ridiculous charge of high treason. Surrey was executed, Henry's last victim; his father, also condemned to death, survived Henry and was reprieved. In character Surrey was a man of the ▷ Renaissance, with the Renaissance conception of the courtier as the complete man in all worthy things – art, learning and action. His poetry was thus a cultivation of poetic ideals on the model of the poets of the Italian Renaissance, and he shares with his older contemporary ▷ Sir Thomas Wyatt the distinction of being the first poet to naturalize Renaissance poetic modes in English; their work was published by ▷ Tottel in his *Miscellany* of 1557. Like Wyatt, Surrey cultivated the ▷ sonnet, and he was the first poet to use ▷ blank verse, in his translation of ▷ Virgil's *Aeneid*, Books 2 and 3. However, Surrey was respected for these contributions more by modern critics who have in the past pointed out that the merit of his poetry is much slighter than Wyatt's and that the flowering of the English short poem in the 1590s owed more to the sonnets of ▷ Sir Philip Sidney (▷ *Astrophil and Stella*) and to ▷ Edmund Spenser's pastorals (▷ *The Shepherd's Calendar*) than to the work of either Wyatt or Surrey.
Bib: Jones, E. (ed.), *Poems*.

Sutcliffe, Alice (no dates)
Poet. Alice Sutcliffe published only one work that we know of, *Meditations of Man's Mortalitie* (1633); it includes several panegyric poems written by men praising the extraordinary skill of the author – extraordinary in that she is a woman. Two of these were written by ▷ Ben Jonson and ▷ George Wither, and these, together with her dedication to Katherine, Duchess of Buckingham, reveal Sutcliffe's court

associations. Her husband, John Sutcliffe, was Groom of the royal chamber. The poems stand for themselves, however, regardless of any social connections, since they combine religious allusions with deeply passionate, grotesque and overtly physical language. Their admonition against sin and their warning of the Day of Judgement reside uneasily with a gothic sensuality.
Bib: Greer, G. (ed.), *Kissing the Rod*.

Symbolic order
A psychoanalytical term now frequently used in literary criticism. 'Symbolic' in this context refers initially to the notion that language itself is comprised of symbols which stand for things. But the French psychoanalyst ▷ Jacques Lacan observes that: 'It is the world of words that creates the world of things', and in so doing introduces an 'order' into what would otherwise be disparate units. That process of ordering is motivated by a series of impulses and desires which are not usually available to the conscious mind. Thus, the symbolic order is that order of representations through whose organization the child enters into language and the social order as a gendered human 'subject'. In the case of ▷ Freudian psychoanalysis, each symbol refers back to an Oedipal stage (▷ Oedipus complex) which the infant passes through on the way to maturity. In Lacan, the 'unconscious' is said to be structured like a language, already a system of representations through which the individual gendered subject realizes his or her identity. In some respect all literary texts traverse the realm of the symbolic order in that they represent and articulate those images through which reality is grasped discursively.

Syrinx
In Greek myth, a maiden pursued by the god Pan; she threw herself into the river Ladon, where she was changed into a reed, from which Pan made his pipe. In ▷ Spenser's ▷ *Shepherd's Calendar* for the month of April, Syrinx represents Anne Boleyn, mother of ▷ Elizabeth I.

T

Tamburlaine the Great, Parts I and II

Two dramas in ▷ blank verse by ▷ Christopher Marlowe, published in 1590. The subject is the life of the 14th-century central Asian Timur, who by his conquests rose from obscurity to become one of the most powerful men in Asia. A life of Timur by Pedro Mazia was translated into English and published in 1571.

Part I is a drama of conquest. Tamburlaine is an obscure shepherd chieftain who defeats Mycetes, king of Persia, and subsequently the king's brother, Cosroe, as well. He is next victorious over Bajazet, Emperor of Turkey, and finally captures Damascus from the Soldan (Sultan) of Egypt. His victories are a triumph of immense natural energy and ruthlessness over equally cruel but weak and decadent civilizations. However, Tamburlaine's barbarity is not merely brutish – he worships the potentialities of the human mind, and he falls passionately in love with his bride, Zenocrate, the daughter of the Soldan. Tamburlaine is, in fact, a product of Marlowe's characteristically ▷ Renaissance imagination, fascinated by the earthly magnificence available to men of imaginative power who have the energy of their convictions. The play is essentially non-moral; Tamburlaine is not judged, but presented as though he were a natural force.

Part II was probably written in consequence of the success of Part I, rather than foreseen as a sequel, though critics differ in their opinions about this. Tamburlaine is forced to face the truth that although he feels his energies to be inexhaustible, he cannot triumph over death – first that of Zenocrate, and then his own. This play is, therefore, a tragedy, that man feels himself to be infinite but is nonetheless mortal.

The plays are a most important advance in the use of blank verse as a medium of drama. Hitherto it had been used stiffly and unimaginatively; Marlowe, in these plays, made blank verse eloquent for the first time.

Taming of the Shrew, The

An early comedy by ▷ Shakespeare; probably written 1593–4, and first published in the First ▷ Folio of 1623. It may be partly a recasting of an anonymous play, The Taming of a Shrew (of uncertain date), and both are based on ▷ George Gascoigne's comedy Supposes (1566), itself a translation from the Italian of Ariosto's Suppositi (1509).

In a prologue of 'induction', a drunken tinker, Chistopher Sly, is subjected to a practical joke: a nobleman picks him up in his stupor, brings him to his mansion, and causes his servants to explain to him that he is himself a great lord who has for some time been out of his wits. The play is then performed by the nobleman's actors for Sly's benefit. The scene is Verona, and the plot concerns the successful attempts of a gentleman, Petruchio, to tame into obedience and love the wilful and ferocious Katharina, thought to be unmarriageable because of her shrewishness. A subplot concerns the courting of Katharina's sister, Bianca, by Lucentio (who is successful) and by Hortensio, who marries a widow instead. At a feast that concludes the play, Petruchio proves that he has, after all, the most affectionate and docile wife of the three. The play is essentially a comedy of situation, and may be regarded as one of several experiments in different kinds of comic form by Shakespeare in the years 1592–95. However, due to Katharina's complete submission in the closing scene, it has become problematic in 20th-century stage productions and for ▷ feminist criticism.

▷ Querelle des Femmes.

Tarlton, Richard (d 1588)

A famous comic actor, mentioned in 1583 as one of the Queen's Players, and a favourite clown of ▷ Elizabeth I. He dressed as a rustic ('a clown' was originally a term for a simple-witted country peasant) and was gifted at composing the rough, comic kind of verse known as 'doggerel'; he popularized on the London stage the mixture of song and dance, something like light opera, called country jigs. He wrote a comedy, The Seven Deadly Sins, for the Queen's Players, and after his death a number of volumes of popular humour – not necessarily his – were published under the title of Tarlton's Jests. He was one of the first actors to become a national figure. He was probably an innkeeper before he became an actor.

▷ Acting, The profession of; Yorick.
Bib: Levi, P., The Life and Times of William Shakespeare.

Tasso, Torquato (1544–95)

Italian poet. He continued the tradition of the romance ▷ epic, already made famous by ▷ Ludovico Ariosto's ▷ Orlando Furioso (1532), in his two major works, Rinaldo (1562) and Jerusalem Delivered (1581). Tasso's imagination was romantic but in his literary ideal he was ▷ classical, and the thought of the second poem is elevated by the high seriousness of the Catholic ▷ Counter-Reformation. His seriousness made his work very attractive to the English romance epic poet ▷ Edmund Spenser, whose very ▷ Protestant ▷ *The Faerie Queene* is also an attempt to rival Ariosto by a poem of similar form but imbued with strong religious feeling. Tasso's impress is strong on parts of *The Faerie Queene*, especially in its ▷ Platonism. *Jerusalem Delivered* was finely translated by Sir Edward Fairfax and published under the title of *Godfrey of Bulloigne or the Recovery of Jerusalem* in 1600.

Tasso was locked up for insanity by Alphonso II, Prince of Ferrara, between 1579–86; subsequent legend attributed his imprisonment to a love affair with the Princess Leonara d'Este.

▷ Translation; Italian influence on English literature.
Bib: Brand, C. P., *Torquato Tasso: a study of the poet and of his contribution to English literature.*

Taylor, Jeremy (1613–67)

Clergyman and religious writer. He was one of the representatives of Anglicanism in its most flourishing period, and his career shows the vicissitudes of the ▷ Church of England in the 17th century. The son of a barber, he was educated at a Cambridge grammar school and in the University of Cambridge. His talent for preaching attracted the favour of ▷ Archbishop Laud, to whom (and to ▷ King Charles I) he became chaplain. In 1645 he was captured by Parliamentary troops, and until 1660, while the Church of England was in abeyance, he was private chaplain to the Earl of Carbery. It was during this period that he wrote much of his best work. Later, he was made Bishop of Dromore in ▷ Ireland, where, contrary to his inclination, he was obliged to discipline clergy hostile to the Anglican establishment. He thus stands in contrast to his former patron, the authoritarian Archbishop Laud, and the change marks not merely a difference in personalities but the growth of the spirit of Anglican tolerance in the later 17th century. His *A Discourse of the Liberty of Prophesying* (1646) was a plea for religious toleration; his other outstanding works were his *The Rule and Exercises of Holy Living* (1650) and *The Rule and Exercises of Holy Dying* (1651).

▷ Sermons.
Bib: Stranks, C. J., *Jeremy Taylor*; Gosse, E., *Jeremy Taylor*; Smith, L. P., *The Golden Grove: Selected Passages from Jeremy Taylor.*

Taylor, John (c 1580–1653)

Poet and miscellanist. John Taylor was apprenticed, in early life, to a London waterman (ferryman). He enlisted in the Navy, making several voyages, and then returned to London to ply his trade as a waterman. Hence he became known as 'The Water Poet'. Taylor was an extraordinarily prolific writer. His large collected edition – *All the Works of John Taylor the Water Poet* (1630) – though it contains over 60 separate works, does not begin to represent his complete *oeuvre*. Almost any topic attracted his attention, and almost every topic did. He was famous for proposing preposterously difficult travel-projects, such as travelling from London to Edinburgh and back without spending any money, or rowing a paper boat. On the strength of these proposals, he would solicit subscriptions from the curious, who would then read his accounts of his difficulties and dangers. His death followed his last trip from London to Gravesend and back: a journey made all the more difficult by the fact of his being lame.
Bib: Notestein, W., *Four Worthies.*

Tempest, The (1611)

A play by ▷ Shakespeare probably written in 1611, and regarded by some as the last completely by his own hand. The plot does not derive from any known principal source. The setting of the island with its aboriginal inhabitant Caliban, and the shipwreck with which the play opens, owe details to travel books of the time, especially a ▷ pamphlet by Sir George Somers (1609) about his voyage to and shipwreck on the Bermudas.

Prospero, Duke of Milan, with his daughter Miranda, has been expelled from his duchy, where he had avoided the task of government for the sake of devoting himself to secret learning, by his wicked brother, Antonio. At the opening of the play Prospero and Miranda have lived on a lonely island for many years, served by the brutish savage Caliban and the sprite Ariel. By his magic powers, Prospero contrives the shipwreck on the island of his enemies – his brother Antonio, Alonso, King of Naples, who had conspired with Antonio, Alonso's wicked brother Sebastian and a few courtiers. Also shipwrecked, but separated from the others, is Ferdinand, the virtuous son of Alonso; each believes the other to be drowned. The situation is such that Prospero, if he wishes, can use his supernatural powers to execute vengeance on his enemies; instead he uses it to bring about reconciliation and forgiveness. Ferdinand, after a brief trial in which he is subjected to austere labours, is united with Miranda. Alonso's company is also subjected to trials, but finally reunited with Ferdinand and reconciled to Prospero, who discloses himself. A subplot concerns the farcical attempt of Trinculo and Stephano, Alonso's servants, to rob Prospero of his instruments of magic, with the aid of Caliban.

The play is the most symbolic of Sheakespeare's plays. Prospero is in the tradition of the ▷ Platonic mage, who, according to one line of ▷ Renaissance thought, could achieve extraordinary power by uniting exceptional wisdom with exceptional virtue. Miranda unites the innocence of nature with the nobility of high breed; her union with Ferdinand and their restoration to a corrupt world symbolize the renewal of vital forces. Caliban, on the other hand, represents the unredeemably brutal side of nature, and also the inherently vicious propensities of the body: he can be forced to serve, but he cannot be elevated. The other characters represent degrees of redeemability: the 'good old lord' Gonzalo has always been virtuous though he has been made to serve evil ends; Alonso has done evil but is capable of repentance; Antonio and Sebastian do not repent and can only be intimidated; the rest are merely passive and, in Antonio's words, 'take suggestion as a cat laps milk'.

The Tempest is the last of the four plays sometimes called ▷ romances, the others being ▷ *Pericles*, ▷ *Cymbeline*, ▷ *The Winter's Tale*. An interesting feature of it is that while the other plays in the group are very loosely constructed in terms of time and place, *The Tempest* has the greatest unity in these respects of all Shakespeare's plays: the action is restricted to the island, and occupies only three hours.

▷ Colonialism.

Terence (Publius Terentius Afer), ?190–?159 BC)

Latin dramatist. His six comedies are adaptations of older Greek comedies, especially those of ▷ Menander. They have been praised for the purity of their Latin and criticized for their deficiency of comic power. They were known, read and imitated throughout the ▷ Middle Ages and afterwards, *eg* his *Heautontimorumenos* (163) was adapted by ▷ Chapman into *All Fools* (1605). Other dramatists, including ▷ Ben Jonson, used some of his themes and comic devices, such as the role of the crafty slave (*eg* in ▷ *Volpone*). The five-act structure apparent in Terence's comedies eventually came to be

the model for publication of plays in England, though it is debatable how much influence it ever had on their composition and production.

Terza rima

The pattern used by the Italian poet ▷ Dante in his long poem the ▷ *Divina Commedia*. Each line is of 11 syllables, the last syllable unaccented, and the rhyme scheme follows the pattern *aba bcb cdc ded*, etc. Examples in English are rare and consist of 10-syllable lines. One reason for the scarce use of *terza rima* in English is the paucity of rhyming words in the language in comparison with Italian. The form was first used in English by ▷ Thomas Wyatt in his *Satires* and paraphrases of the ▷ Psalms.

Theatres

No special buildings were erected in England for dramatic performances until late in the 16th century. The earliest form of regular drama in England was the mystery plays, which began as interpolations in religious ritual in the churches. By the 15th century these plays were being performed at religious festivals in towns on movable stages or ▷ pageants, conveyed from point to point on wagons. In country districts at seasonal festivals such as May Day, primitive dramas of pagan origin – jigs, May games, Morris dances – were performed in the open air. The absence of theatres did not indicate scarcity of drama, but its wide pervasion of ordinary life.

Secular dramas of entertainment, such as we know today, grew up in the 16th century; they were performed in the courtyards of inns and in the great halls of country mansions, royal palaces, Oxford and Cambridge colleges, and the ▷ Inns of Court of London. The performers were professional actors who were usually incorporated in companies attached to noble or royal households, but by degrees this attachment became increasingly nominal, and actors required places where they could work independently and permanently. Hence the first playhouse, known as The Theatre, was erected by ▷ James Burbage in Shoreditch, outside the City of London, in 1576–7. It was followed by many others, including the ▷ Globe (1599), which is the most famous owing to its association with ▷ Shakespeare. None of these theatres survived the middle of the 17th century, but a contemporary sketch of one of them (the Swan) exists, and there is a detailed description in the contract for the Fortune (1600).

It is possible that their design reflected, however indirectly, that of the theatres of

ancient Greece and Rome (foreign visitors
certainly commented on the analogy), though
they certainly also incorporated features
of the typical inn-yard and the bear-pits, *ie*
the arenas for fights between animals. The
structures were usually of wood, and were
round or hexagonal, though they might
be rectangular. The centre was an arena
exposed to the open air, where the poorer
spectators stood; the richer ones sat in
galleries surrounding the arena. The stage was
probably divided into two or three parts; the
main ('apron') stage projected into the arena,
so that spectators surrounded it on three
sides. The wall at the back of this stage was
flanked by doors for exits and entries, between
which there was probably a rear stage, though
the sketch of the Swan does not include this.
Above the rear stage there was probably an
upper stage (to represent *eg* a castle wall);
above this again possibly a musicians' gallery.
A canopy may have extended partly across the
apron stage. The projection of the apron stage
– upon which spectators sometimes actually
sat – shows that the theatre of Shakespeare's
day was not adapted to convey illusion like the
typically modern theatre; scenery was scarcely
used, though 'props' (*ie* thrones, objects
representing flowery banks, etc.) were brought
on and off.

Such were the 'public theatres': there
were also 'private theatres', such as the
▷ Blackfriars which came into the hands of
Shakespeare's company in 1608. Pictures or
accounts of these do not survive, but they
were roofed, probably used some kind of
artificial lighting, and may have provided
more opportunity for scenery, though there
is no evidence of this in any commercial
playhouse before the 1630s. Scenic spectacle
was certainly not unknown or despised by
Shakespeare's contemporaries, but its use
was expensive and largely confined to the
courts. In the reign of ▷ James I there was a
pronounced fashion for ▷ masques, an early
form of opera, in which a poet, such as ▷ Ben
Jonson, and a designer, such as ▷ Inigo Jones,
collaborated.

The playgoers of the ▷ Renaissance
came from all social categories and appear
to have been particularly responsive to
political changes appearing before them in
theatrical guise. There are several excellent
works collating the evidence we have
about playgoers: A. Harbage, *Shakespeare's
Audience*; A. J. Cook, *The Privileged Playgoer in
Shakespeare's London*; and A. Gurr, *Playgoing
in Shakespeare's London*.
Bib: Berry, H., *Shakespeare's Playhouses*.

Theocritus

A Greek poet of the 3rd century BC. Little
is known about him, but his importance is
that he originated ▷ pastoral poetry in his
▷ 'idylls' or short poems about shepherds and
shepherdesses living in primitive simplicity in
the rural parts of Sicily. He may have written
these in the Egyptian city of Alexandria for
urban readers; one of the characteristics of
pastoral has been that it has expressed the
town-dwellers' fantasy of the beauty of country
surroundings, the simplicity of country living
and the purity of country air. Theocritus was
emulated by the Roman poet ▷ Virgil, and
both Theocritus and Virgil were taken as
models by the 16th-century ▷ Renaissance
poets in western Europe, of whom the most
notable English example is ▷ Edmund
Spenser.

Theophrastus

A Greek philosopher, follower of ▷ Aristotle,
of the 4th century BC. Amongst other writings,
he composed a series of descriptions of moral
types called *Ethical Characters*. These were the
original pattern for the minor literary form of
character-writing, widely practised in England
in the early 17th century. The most notable
example is John Earle's *Microcosmography*
(1628). Other examples: ▷ Joseph Hall's
Characters of Virtues and Vices (1608);
▷ Thomas Overbury's *Characters* (1614).
▷ Characters, Theophrastian.

Thirty-nine Articles

The code of religious doctrine which all clergy
of the ▷ Church of England have to accept.
In 1553, 42 articles were laid down; these
were reduced to 39 in 1571.

Thirty Years' War

A European religious war, lasting from 1618
to 1648, between nearly all the Catholic
and ▷ Protestant nations of Europe. It was
fought principally in Germany, to the ruin
of that country, and was concluded by the
Peace of Westphalia. Britain was one of the
few important countries that took hardly any
part in it.

Thynne, Joan (1558–1612) and Maria (c 1578–1611)

Letter-writers. Joan Thynne was the first
mistress of Longleat and Maria was her
daughter-in-law. Unfortunately, in personal
terms, the two women were never reconciled
to one another, but fortunately for present-day
readers, they left a collection of dramatic,
complex and intimate letters written over

a period of 30 years (their correspondence is available in a modern version, edited by A. D. Wall). Joan is much cooler and more reticent, both to her daughter-in-law and her husband, but Maria ranges from conventional submissiveness to angry diatribe and writes tender, sometimes erotic, letters to her spouse.

Tilney (Tylney), Edmund (d 1610)

Master of the ▷ Revels, 1579–1608. Tilney was appointed to the post of Master of the Revels after his prose tract, *A Briefe and Pleasant Discourse of Duties in Mariage called the Flower of Friendshippe* (1568), which was dedicated to ▷ Elizabeth I, was well received. Tilney's influence on court and public drama of the ▷ Elizabethan period was immense: he chose the works to be performed before the queen, and, more importantly, read every play composed for publication or public presentation that needed a licence. Thus, he was on familiar terms with ▷ Philip Henslowe and the other theatrical managers of the day, and he would have examined critically the manuscripts of a number of ▷ Shakespeare's plays in order to license them. At the accession of ▷ James I, Tilney seems to have given over many of his duties to ▷ Sir George Buc (possibly his nephew), and he retired fully in 1608.

Timber

A collection of commentary, paraphrase and ▷ translation by ▷ Ben Jonson, *Timber* was first published in the two-volume edition of Jonson's works that appeared after his death. As a record of Jonson's reading in the classics, it is invaluable. More than this, however, is the insight it provides into questions which inform Jonson's own aesthetic theories, in particular his use of ▷ 'Imitation'.

Timon

A rich citizen of Athens of the 5th century BC; he was celebrated for his hatred of mankind. He is referred to by a number of ancient Greek writers, including ▷ Aristophanes, and notably by ▷ Plutarch in his life of Mark Antony, and ▷ Lucian in his dialogue *Misanthropos*. ▷ Shakespeare (▷ *Timon of Athens*) makes him a rich, ostentatious philanthropist who becomes a misanthropist through disillusionment at men's ingratitude.

Timon of Athens (1607)

A tragedy by ▷ Shakespeare, written about 1607 and concerning ▷ Jacobean ▷ patronage and material power. The material is probably taken from ▷ Plutarch's life of Mark Antony (written 1st century AD), ▷ Lucian's dialogue *Misanthropos* (2nd century AD), and an anonymous play of Shakespeare's own day.

Timon is an Athenian nobleman who delights in the prodigal entertainment of his guests. In spite of his great wealth, he presently finds himself in debt; he is then outraged to discover that none of those to whom he has been so generous is prepared to help him. He invites his friends to one more banquet, but the steaming dishes, uncovered, contain only hot water; throwing the dishes and water at them, he drives his guests out of the house. In a frenzy of hatred, he then takes to a life of solitude in the wilderness, where he is visited by the cynical philosopher Apemantus, his devoted steward Flavius, the general Alcibiades, who is rebelling against the meanness of the Athenian government, and other characters from his past life of opulence. This part of the play consists of a series of dialogues that leave Timon resolute in his hatred of humanity, though he is obliged to make an exception of his disinterestedly loyal steward. The dialogue with Apemantus is the most striking. Apemantus has always forseen that Timon would be deceived by his friends, since he has a low opinion of human nature; Timon, however, retorts that Apemantus's cynicism is groundless except for the mean motive of jealousy, whereas he, Timon, has proved that humanity is inferior after testing it on the opposite hypothesis. Alcibiades is afflicted by the public meanness of the Athenian state, as Timon has been afflicted by private ingratitude; thus he regards Timon as an ally, though he cannot persuade him to join forces with the rebels. The rebellion of Alcibiades is successful, and when Timon dies, the Athenian rulers penitently acknowledge their ill-treatment of him.

▷ Timon.

'Tis Pity She's a Whore (1632)

▷ John Ford's greatest ▷ tragedy, which treats the passionate and incestuous love-affair between the siblings Giovanni and Annabella – and their relationship's inevitable progress towards destruction – with remarkable empathy and tact. When Annabella finds she is pregnant by her brother she marries a suitor, Soranzo, who discovers the truth about the child's paternity and conspires to revenge his own humiliation. The play concludes in a mass killing after a grotesque scene during which Giovanni enters with his sister's heart on the point of his dagger.

Titania
In ▷ Shakespeare's ▷ *A Midsummer Night's Dream*, the Queen of the Fairies and wife of ▷ Oberon, the king. The name derives from ▷ Ovid, who used it in his ▷ *Metamorphoses* for a variety of female deities, especially woodland ones.

Titus Andronicus (1594)
A tragedy by ▷ Shakespeare, published in 1594. The origin of the plot is not known; it may owe something to ▷ Ovid's Procne and Tereus, one of his ▷ *Metamorphoses* translated by Golding, 1565–7, and to ▷ Seneca's drama *Thyestes*, translated between 1559 and 1581. It is in any case a violent ▷ revenge tragedy of the kind that Shakespeare and his contemporaries derived from Seneca. The setting is imperial Rome; the plot concerns the revenge of Titus, a Roman general, for the atrocities committed by Tamora, the Queen of the Goths, against his family. She is aided by a villainous slave, Aaron the Moor. Much doubt has been expressed by scholars as to whether the play is entirely by Shakespeare, by Shakespeare in collaboration, or not by Shakespeare at all; the last opinion arises partly from the low esteem in which the play is usually held, although, according to ▷ Ben Jonson, it was popular among the contemporary public.

Tottel's Miscellany (1557)
An influential ▷ anthology of verse published by Richard Tottel, a bookseller, and Nicholas Grimald, a translator and scholar. It was originally entitled *Songs and Sonnets*, and included the work of the ▷ Earl of Surrey and ▷ Sir Thomas Wyatt. Their poems, the first of any distinction in English to show characteristics of ▷ Renaissance style, had never before been printed, though they had circulated in manuscript, and the great popularity of the anthology helped to shape the short poem so much cultivated in the last 20 years of the century; their success led to the publication of many similar anthologies.

Tourneur, Cyril (?1575–1626)
Dramatist. Not much is known of his life, except that he was employed abroad in military and diplomatic service, and died in ▷ Ireland on the return of the unsuccessful naval expedition under ▷ Buckingham to capture Cadiz. He is well known for two plays, one of which, ▷ *The Revenger's Tragedy* (1606–7), is regarded as one of the finest achievements of the period, and is attributed by most scholars to another

dramatist, ▷ Thomas Middleton. The other, ▷ *The Atheist's Tragedy* (1611), an interesting anti-revenge play, is much less esteemed. The case for Tourneur being the author of the more admired of the two plays is partly based on the resemblance to an obscure religious poem by him, *The Transformed Metamorphosis* (1600). He also wrote a number of ▷ elegies.
▷ Revenge tragedy.
Bib: Murray, P. B., *Tourneur*; Eliot, T. S., in *Selected Essays*; Bradbrook, M. C., in *Themes and Conventions of Elizabethan Tragedy*.

Tragedy
Tragedy as it is understood in western Europe has it origins in the Greek dramas by the Athenian dramatists ▷ Aeschylus, ▷ Sophocles and ▷ Euripides, in the 6th–5th centuries BC. Essentially the spirit of this writing was that inevitable suffering overwhelms the characters, and yet the characters maintain their dignity in the face of this suffering, and prove their greatness (and the capacity of human beings for greatness) by doing so. Greek tragedy arose out of their religious interpretation of the nature of human destiny. When Christianity prevailed over western Europe, a much more hopeful interpretation of human destiny dominated the thought of writers, and tragedy, in the Greek sense, became difficult to imagine and unnatural: if good men and women suffer in this world, they are rewarded in Heaven, and this is not tragic; wicked men and women who happen to suffer in this world may be damned in the next, but this is also not tragic because they are wicked. Hence medieval tragedy was on the whole reduced to the conception of the Wheel of Fortune – that chance in this world is apt to take men and women from prosperity to misfortune, whatever their spiritual merits.
In the late 16th century the tragic vision of human experience was rediscovered by some English dramatists, notably by ▷ Marlowe and ▷ Shakespeare. Insofar as it had a literary ancestry, this was not the tragedy of the ancient Greeks, which was scarcely known, but the comparatively debased imitation of it by the Roman poet ▷ Seneca, which helped to give rise to Elizabethan ▷ revenge tragedy or 'Tragedy of Blood'. More interesting was the growth of conceptions of human destiny which did not usurp the Christian conception, but existed side by side with it, as an alternative or perhaps complementary vision. Although, as C. Belsey points out, 'human tragedy' more often than not means male, English, middle-class tragedy.
The first important English tragedy is

Marlowe's ▷ *Doctor Faustus* in which the
hero forgoes eternal happiness after death
for the sake of earthly ecstasy; Marlowe sets
in opposition the Christian doctrine of the
soul and ▷ Renaissance delight in earthly
experience. ▷ *Hamlet*, in which Shakespeare
for the first time makes the task of revenge a
genuine moral dilemma, is perhaps the next.
The best-known achievements of English
tragic drama are Shakespeare's ▷ *Othello*,
▷ *Macbeth*, ▷ *King Lear*, ▷ *Antony and
Cleopatra* and ▷ *Coriolanus*. These cannot
be summed up in a phrase, but they have in
common that the hero's hope of some form
of supreme earthly happiness collapses into
terrible misery, brought about less by the
hero's character than through the nature
of earthly reality of which his character
forms a part. Among Shakespeare's later
contemporaries and successors, several
dramatists wrote distinguished plays in
the tragic style, *eg* ▷ Middleton's ▷ *The
Changeling* and ▷ Webster's ▷ *The Duchess of
Malfi* and ▷ *The White Devil*.

This period, from 1590 till about 1625, was
the only one in English literature in which
there were more than isolated examples of
distinguished theatrical tragedy. The single
important example of a work written in the
Greek style is ▷ Milton's ▷ *Samson Agonistes*,
but critics disagree as to whether it can be
called truly dramatic.
Bib: Belsey, C., *The Subject of Tragedy*;
Callaghan, D., *Women and Gender in
Renaissance Tragedy*; Dollimore, J., *Radical
Tragedy*; McAlindon, T., *English Renaissance
Tragedy*.

Tragedy of Arden of Faversham, The
   ▷ *Arden of Faversham, The Tragedy of.*

Tragical History of Doctor Faustus, The
   ▷ *Doctor Faustus, The Tragical History of.*

Tragicomedy
Drama in which the elements of both
▷ tragedy and comedy are present. Examples
are the ▷ romances of ▷ Shakespeare,
particularly ▷ *Pericles*, ▷ *Cymbeline*, and ▷ *The
Winter's Tale*, each of which reaches a tragic
climax halfway through and then lightens
towards a happy conclusion. A peculiarly
English form of tragicomedy developed in the
years 1610 to 1640, particularly in the works
of ▷ Beaumont and ▷ Fletcher.

Traherne, Thomas (c 1638–74)
Poet and religious writer. In the 17th century,
the only works published by Traherne were

three religious pieces, all of them in prose.
In 1896, however, the Victorian editor
A. B. Grosart discovered a collection of
manuscripts in a London bookshop which
he believed to be by ▷ Henry Vaughan. The
manuscripts were identified as being those
of Traherne, and comprised religious poems
and the remarkable mystical prose work
Centuries of Meditation. The latter constitutes
a spiritual ▷ autobiography, tracing the
author's progress towards 'felicity' (a key
term for Traherne). Criticism of Traherne's
poetry has in the 20th century concentrated
on his affinity with ▷ George Herbert, and
on his visionary delineation of childlike
experience. Understsood as a mystic and an
intellectual conservative in comparison to the
rationalism of 17th-century science, Traherne
has been closely linked with the Cambridge
▷ Platonists – almost as though he were
the poetic 'voice' of that group. Yet for all
Traherne's concern with 'the inward eye', in
fact his approach to language, his undoubted
fascination with the possibilities of rational
science (particularly as it had unfolded a new
perspective in which to understand the human
body) and his experimental verse forms make
him one of the most remarkable of later
17th-century writers.
Bib: Margoliouth, H. M. (ed.), *Traherne's
Centuries, Poems, and Thanksgivings*; Clements,
A. L., *The Mystical Poetry of Thomas Traherne*.

Translation
The life of English literature has always
issued from a combination of strong insular
traditions and participation in wider European
traditions. Translation has always been the
principal means of assimilating European
literatures into the English idiom, and it was
particularly important before the 18th century,
when the main streams of European cultural
life were flowing through other languages.
The aim of translators was then less to
make an accurate rendering than to make
the substance of foreign work thoroughly
intelligible to the English spirit; the character
of the translation thus proceeded as much
from the mind of the translator as from the
mind of the original writer. If the translator
had a strong personality, the translation often
became a distinguished work of English
literature in its own right. Translators with
less individuality often produced work
of historical importance because of its
contemporary influence on English writing.

From the 14th to the 18th centuries,
English writers were constantly absorbing
the ancient and contemporary Mediterranean

cultures of Europe, and worked on the literatures of France, ancient Rome, Italy, ancient Greece and Spain. There is no distinct boundary between translation and adaptation; ▷ Chaucer brought English poetry into accord with French and Italian poetry partly by freely adapting work in those languages. His outstanding work of translation is his version of Guillaume de Lorris's *Roman de la Rose*. French ceased to be the first language of the English upper classes in Chaucer's lifetime, but the English nobility continued to have strong ties with French aristocratic culture, and thus translations from French prose were in demand in the 15th and 16th centuries. ▷ Caxton, the first English printer, published many English versions of French romances. The outstanding 15th-century work of English prose was ▷ Malory's ▷ *Morte d'Arthur*, which Caxton published and which is partly a translation and partly an adaptation. The work of translation was an important influence on the development of a fluent English prose medium, and this is evident in the difference between ▷ Wycliffe's 14th-century translation of the Latin Bible and ▷ Tyndale's version of the New Testament from the Greek (1525). Lord Berner's translation of ▷ Froissart's *Chronicles* is another distinguished example of English prose development in the 15th and early 16th centuries.

Printing, the ▷ Renaissance, and the rise of new educated classes, all helped to expand translation in the 16th century, which was the first major period for translation of classical writers. These had been of central importance in the ▷ Middle Ages too (King Alfred and later Chaucer had translated Boethius's *De Consolatione Philosophiae*) but knowledge of them had now widened and standards of scholarship had advanced. The first important rendering in English of a great classical poem is that of ▷ Virgil's ▷ *Aeneid* by the Scots poet, ▷ Gavin Douglas (1553).

▷ Chapman's ▷ *Iliad* (1611) and *Odyssey* (1615) are impressive, but have less intrinsic merit as English literature. ▷ Ovid had long been a favourite poet, and translations were made of his poems by ▷ Arthur Golding (1565–67) and ▷ Christopher Marlowe (pub. 1597). But in the 17th and 18th centuries the best-known English version of Ovid was George Sandys's version of ▷ *Metamorphoses*, completed in 1626. Ovid had an extensive influence on poets, including ▷ Shakespeare; ▷ Seneca's influence on the poetic drama, both as a philosopher and as a dramatist, was equally conspicuous, and it was no

doubt helped by the historically important but otherwise undistinguished *Ten Tragedies*, translated by various hands and published between 1559 and 1581. Among the most distinguished prose translators of ancient literature in this period was Philemon Holland, remembered especially for his version of Pliny's *Natural History*, which he published in 1601. The best known of all, especially for his value to Shakespeare but also for the quality of his writing, is ▷ Thomas North, whose version (1579) of Plutarch's *Lives* was made not from the original Greek but from the French of Jacques Amyot. Several women also produced excellent translations in this period, perhaps because of a reluctance to face the censure inevitable upon the production of their own writing. These female translators include ▷ Ann Bacon; ▷ Mary Basset; ▷ Lady Elizabeth Cary; ▷ Katherine Philips; and ▷ Margaret Tyler.

Translations from the contemporary European languages were also numerous in the 16th and early 17th centuries, and indicate the constant interest of English writers in foreign literatures. ▷ Sir John Harington translated ▷ Ariosto's ▷ *Orlando Furioso* in 1591. ▷ Tasso's *Jerusalem Delivered* was translated as *Godfrey of Bulloigne* or *The Recovery of Jerusalem* (1600); ▷ Castiglione's very influential *Il Cortegiano* was translated by ▷ Sir Thomas Hoby (1561). The best known of all these contemporary works is ▷ John Florio's rendering of the *Essays* of ▷ Montaigne, published in 1603. Part I of Cervantes' ▷ *Don Quixote* was translated in 1612, before Part II was written. The first three books of ▷ Rabelais's ▷ *Gargantua* and ▷ *Pantagruel* were translated notably by Thomas Urquhart; two were published in 1653, and the third in 1694.

Many of the translations made before 1660, especially those in prose, were marked by a super-abundance of words, characteristic of much English writing in the 16th and 17th centuries; the originals tended to be amplified rather than closely rendered.
Bib: Cowley, C. M., *The First English Translators of the Classics*.

Trapnel, Anna (c 1622–c 1660)

Devotional and prophetic writer. Trapnel is one of the most well-known ▷ Baptist and ▷ Fifth Monarchist writers. She discovered her vocation in 1654, when she fell into an 11-day trance at the examination of Vavasor Powell, a fellow Fifth Monarchist. During this time she sang, chanted and spoke in tongues,

and upon her recovery her prophecies were published in *Strange and Wonderful Newes* and *The Cry of a Stone* (both 1654). Her writings take the form of verse and prose prophecies, which also contain a fair amount of ▷ autobiographical material, such as her being accused of witchcraft. Although Trapnel asserts that she is simply the mouthpiece of God, her prophecies, given in a dramatic, trance-like state, clearly satisfied her own desire to be the centre of attention. Her other two works, also published in 1654 (*Report and Plea* and *A Legacy for Saints*), carry a similar mixture of self-dramatization and Fifth Monarchist propaganda.
Bib: Graham E. et al. (eds.), *Her Own Life*; Hobby, E., *The Virtue of Necessity*; Greer, G. (ed.), *Kissing the Rod*.

Travel literature
This relatively large branch of ▷ Renaissance English literature may be conveniently discussed under two headings: 1 fantasy purporting to be fact; 2 factual accounts.
   1 *Literature of fantasy purporting to be fact.* So long as extensive travel was rarely undertaken, it was possible for writers to present accounts of fantasy journeys and to pass them off as fact without much fear of being accused of lying. Thus a 14th-century French writer produced the *Travels of Sir John de Mandeville*, a work of fiction or compilation from narratives by other travellers, but purporting to be an account of genuine journeys written by Mandeville himself. The work was translated into English in 1377, became extremely popular, and was long regarded as genuine. Long after the extravagances of the story were seen to be falsehoods, Mandeville, a purely fictional English knight, was thought to be the genuine author.
   2 *Literature of fact.* By the second half of the 16th century, the great Portuguese, Spanish and Italian explorers had discovered the Americas and greatly extended knowledge of eastern Asia. Liars could still find large, credulous audiences, but the facts were marvellous enough to require no distortion. Writers also began to feel strong motives for publishing truthful accounts. Thus ▷ Richard Hakluyt published his *Principal Navigations, Voyages and Discoveries of the English Nation* in 1589, partly for patriotic reasons. The English had been slow to start on exploratory enterprises, although by this time they were extremely active. Hakluyt, finding that the reputation of his nation stood low among foreigners in this field, wanted to demonstrate the reality of the English achievement, and

at the same time to stimulate his fellow countrymen to further endeavours. His book is really a compilation of accounts by English explorers; an enlarged edition came out in 1598, and a still further enlarged edition was published under the title of *Hakluytus Posthumus, or Purchas his Pilgrims* by Samuel Purchas in 1625. The accounts vary from those by accomplished writers like ▷ Sir Walter Ralegh to others by writers with little or no experience of writing; they constitute an anthology of early English descriptive writing in which the writers are concerned with the truthfulness of their accounts rather than with entertaining or deceiving the reader. Another example of this new kind of honest and truthful handling of the descriptive language is Captain John Smith's history of the founding of the colony of Virginia, *General History of Virginia, New England, and the Summer Isles* (1624). The contrast between this newer, plainer style and the extravagant and whimsical style more characteristic of the ▷ pamphleteers can be seen in accounts of travels in Europe by Thomas Coryate (?1577–1617), author of *Coryate's Crudities*, and Fynes Morison (1556–1630), author of *Itinerary*; Coryate is deliberately strange and fanciful, though an acute observer, but Morison is much more straightforward.

Troilus and Cressida (1601–2)
A play by ▷ Shakespeare, written 1601–2, and first printed in 1609. Its position in the first collected edition of Shakespeare's plays, the ▷ folio of 1623, is curious, inasmuch as it was placed by itself and not in one of the three groups of histories, tragedies and comedies. Shakespeare used as sources ▷ Caxton's *Recuyell of the Histories of Troy* (1474), translated from the French of Raoul le Febvre; ▷ Chaucer's ▷ *Troilus and Criseyde*, especially for Pandarus and the love story; ▷ Chapman's translation of the ▷ *Iliad* (for Thersites); and possibly ▷ Lydgate's *Troy-book*.
   Troilus, son of King Priam of Troy, woos Cressida, with the help of her uncle, Pandarus. Meanwhile the war continues between the Trojans and the Greeks; the latter are doing badly, because their chief warrior, Achilles, is sulking in his tent. The subtle Ulysses contrives a plan to rouse Achilles by provoking his vanity; he chooses the brutishly stupid Ajax to fight the Trojan champion, Hector; the ruse is successful. A pact is made of an exchange of prisoners, and the Trojans consent to hand over Cressida, whose father has deserted to the Greeks;

she and Troilus part, with many promises of
fidelity, but she quickly becomes the mistress
of the Greek Diomed, to the bewildered
disillusionment of Troilus, who sees her in
Diomed's arms during a truce. The end of the
play is a chaos of fighting, in which all higher
emotions are lost in a rage of murderous
hatred, and Hector, the noblest character
in the play, is treacherously murdered by
Achilles.

What bewilders critics is the hopelessness
of the play. Two of the finest episodes are
debating scenes, during the first of which
(I. iii) the Greeks discuss their failure in the
cold light of reason; in the second (II. ii) the
Trojans defy reason for the sake of emotional
dedication to 'honour'. But the play shows
that reason alone conduces to ignobility and
treachery, while honour alone is defeated by
the facts of human nature. The voice of truth
seems to be the mocking one of the Greek
clown Thersites, who despises everybody and
respects nothing. A possible view is that the
much-prized virtue of honour, so cultivated
by ▷ Renaissance courtiers, is an idealistic
value, a literary growth in terms of which real
life cannot be evaluated, whereas the 'reason'
of politicians by itself destroys the value of
living. This interpretation makes the play
more an affair of light-hearted mockery than
it is commonly taken to be; it is frequently
interpreted as a grim and despairing ▷ satire.

▷ Problem plays (of Shakespeare).
Bib: Adamson, J., *Troilus and Cressida*.

Troilus and Criseyde
▷ Chaucer composed *Troilus and Criseyde*
some time in the 1380s (before 1388). His
contribution to the medieval Troy story was
not to produce an English version of the
history of Troy, from beginning to end (in
the tradition of Benoît de Sainte-Maure and
Guido de Columnis), but to refract the Troy
story through that of the relationship between
Troilus ('little Troy') and Criseyde, organized
as an epic love-tragedy, with a five-book
division and elaborate apostrophes and a
palinode. The siege of Troy and past Trojan
and Greek history form a significant backdrop
to, and determining influence on, the conduct
and outcome of their affair.

The outline of Chaucer's narrative is taken
from ▷ Boccaccio's ▷ *Il Filostrato*, but in
addition to developing the background to
their story, Chaucer changes some aspects
of the presentation of its key characters, not
least in the role of the narrator himself, who
no longer presents Troilus's experience as
a cipher for his own but adopts the familiar

'ineffectual' Chaucerian role. Pandaro, the
go-between figure in Boccaccio's version, is
a cousin of Criseida and a peer of Troilus;
in Chaucer's version, Pandarus is Criseyde's
uncle and, though still a lover himself, plays
the role of an avuncular confessor to Troilus.
His engineering power is increased on a local
domestic scale and his role as stage-manager
of their affair is enhanced, but his controlling
powers are markedly circumscribed at the
same time: he may be on hand literally to
help Troilus into bed with Criseyde, but his
resources diminish as the larger context of the
siege intervenes in the lovers' lives. Criseyde
is more vulnerable, naïve and sensitive to the
pressures around her than her counterpart
in Boccaccio; there is no precedent for her
presentation as a woman under siege within
a siege. In Chaucer's version, Troilus is a
more bookish lover, who has a lyrical tradition
of love sentiments at his command, and his
songs and monologues in Book III celebrate
his relationship with Creseyde in metaphysical
terms. However, Chaucer is not presenting a
Divine Comedy in this narrative but a pagan
history, and one in which human love is
subject to the forces of time and change.

The organization of the poem into five
books reflects the progress of the love
affair: the broad opening panorama of Book
I gives Troilus and Criseyde a place in the
wider history of Troy; the focus narrows in
Books II and III, which chart the increasing
self-involvement of the lovers as they create
their own private world within Troy. Book IV
marks the interruption of the historical world
into their affairs, with the plan to exchange
Criseyde; and the final Book sketches the
'changing' of Criseyde, her transferral to the
Greek camp and engagement with Diomedes,
Troilus's reluctant perception of her change,
and his final change as he ascends the spheres
after his death and laughs at the behaviour
of mortals, their loves and longings, on
little earth. The book ends with its 'maker'
committing it to the care of his peers 'Moral
▷ Gower', and 'philosophical Strode'.
Bib: Windeatt, B. (ed.), *Troilus and Criseyde*;
Salu, M. (ed.), *Essays on Troilus and Criseyde*.

Troilus and Criseyde: the legend
The love affair between the Trojan Prince,
Troilus, and Criseyde, the daughter of the
Trojan priest Calchas, is not included in
classical versions of the Troy story, but first
appears in the work of the 12th-century
French writer Benoît de Saint-Maure. In
his *Roman de Troie*, details of the love-affair
emerge as the Criseyde figure (Briseida) is

handed over to join the Greeks at the request of her father (who deserts the Trojan side at the beginning of the war). Following the separation of the lovers, Troilus learns that Briseida has taken the Greek prince Diomedes for her lover, and denounces her infidelity, publicly, on the battlefield.

Boccaccio considerably amplified details of the early stages of the love-affair in his poem ▷ Il Filostrato, which is ▷ Chaucer's principal source for ▷ Troilus and Criseyde. In Chaucer's text, the relationship between the lovers and their wider historical context is more developed, and larger philosophical issues about the historical determination of their lives are opened up (notably by the injection of material derived from Boethius). By Chaucer's time, the Criseyde figure had become a proverbial figure of infidelity, but his text works against this proverbial grain and makes her betrayal a much more interesting and complicated phenomenon. Robert Henryson (c 1425–?1500) took up the opportunity to go beyond Chaucer's text (and pick up a loose thread of the narrative) by pursuing the end of Criseyde in his Testament of Cresseid: it is here that the notion of Cresseid's end as a leper is developed, though the 'cause' of her final state is a topic of debate and speculation within the poem.

▷ Shakespeare used both Troilus and Criseyde and the Testament of Cresseid in the composition of ▷ Troilus and Cressida, in addition to other medieval versions of the full-scale Troy story (descending from Benoît de Saint-Maure) and ▷ Homer's version of events.

Tudor, House of
The name of a family that ruled over England and Wales from 1485 until 1603. The succession was as follows: ▷ Henry VII; his son, ▷ Henry VIII; Henry VIII's three children, ▷ Edward VI, ▷ Mary I and ▷ Elizabeth I. Elizabeth died childless, and the throne passed to the Scottish family of ▷ Stuart, one of whom (James IV) had married a daughter of Henry VII.

The Tudors were of Welsh origin; Henry VII was the grandson of Owen Tudor, who married a member of the Lancastrian branch of the royal Plantagenet family. Henry thus acquired the claim of the House of Lancaster to the English throne, which he won at the Battle of Bosworth, the concluding battle of the Wars of the Roses, where he defeated ▷ Richard III of the House of York.

The Tudor family was notable for its abilities. Henry VII was a cautious ruler, who

reconstructed the government's finances. Henry VIII started the ▷ Reformation in England by founding the ▷ Church of England, and this became distinctively ▷ Protestant under the boy king Edward VI. Mary I was a Catholic, married Philip II of Spain, and re-established Catholicism in England, but she died childless, and Protestantism was restored by her sister Elizabeth, possibly the most successful sovereign ever to sit on the English throne. The last ten years of Elizabeth's reign saw the beginnings of the literary flowering known as the 'Elizabethan age'. Her reign was also remarkable for victory over Spain and the beginnings of English overseas enterprise.

Tudor myth
A term used by historians to express the 16th-century belief, encouraged by the royal House of ▷ Tudor, that the Tudors were national saviours from the horrors of the Wars of the Roses and restorers of legendary national greatness. The first Tudor, ▷ Henry VII, took the throne from ▷ Richard III in 1485 by force of conquest, and since usurpation of a kingdom from its rightful king was a deadly sin, it was important for the Tudors to prove that they had not been guilty of it. Henry maintained that his was the rightful claim, but this was too clearly open to doubt; however, if Richard III was a proved tyrant, the usurpation was justified. Sixteenth-century historians made it their business to blacken Richard's character, not only to please the Tudors, but in reflection of national relief that they had brought the civil wars to an end, with the consequence that Richard is the legendary evil man of English history. Such is the picture given by ▷ Thomas More's Richard III (1513), ▷ Edward Hall's Union of the Noble and Illustrious Families of Lancaster and York (1548), and ▷ Holinshed's Chronicles (1578). The Tudors also encouraged the belief that, as a Welsh line of princes, they could trace themselves back to King ▷ Arthur, the hero of the mythical British golden age. Henry VII called his eldest son Arthur, but he did not live to succeed to the throne. The impress of the Tudor myth is strong on ▷ Shakespeare's ▷ history plays.
Bib: Anglo, S., Spectacle, Pageantry, and Early Tudor Policy.

Turberville, George (c 1540–1610)
Poet and translator. Turberville was secretary to ▷ Thomas Randolph, and during 1568–9 went with him on a political mission to Russia, where he met Ivan the Terrible. An account

of this journey was reprinted by ▷ Hakluyt. He also knew ▷ Drummond, ▷ Gascoigne and ▷ Harington. Turberville is chiefly known for his translations of ▷ Ovid, early experiments with ▷ blank verse (*Epitaphes, Epigrams, Songs and Sonets* (1567)), and a book on hunting (*The Noble Art of Venerie or Hunting* (1575)).

▷ Sandys, George; Translation.
Bib: Hiller, G. (ed.), *Poems of the Elizabethan Age.*

Twelfth Night, or What You Will (1599–1600)

A comedy by ▷ Shakespeare, probably written 1599–1600 or possibly a little later. Its main source is a prose tale, *Apolonius and Silla* (1581) by Barnabe Rich, an English version of an Italian tale by Cinthio (▷ Elizabethan Novels). The comic situations arising from confusion between twins come down from *Menaechmi* by the Roman playwright ▷ Plautus; Shakespeare had already adapted this play into ▷ *The Comedy of Errors.* Two 16th-century Italian plays, *Inganni* (*Deceits*) and *Gl'Ingannati* (*The Deceived*) have also been suggested as possible sources.

The setting is the court of Orsino, Duke of Illyria, and the house of the wealthy Countess Olivia, whom he is courting. He uses as a go-between his page Cesario, really a girl, Viola, disguised as a boy. The page has already fallen in love with Orsino, and expresses sentiments on love so elequently to Olivia that the Countess believes herself in love, but with the page, not with the Duke. Meanwhile, Viola's twin brother, Sebastian, turns up, wearing the same style of clothes that his sister has chosen to wear as Cesario; he has been rescued from shipwreck by a sea-captain, Antonio, who feels a deep affection for him. The possibility of confusion is clearly various and great, and every possible confusion occurs. A subplot centres on Olivia's drunken kinsman, Sir Toby Belch, and her conceited steward, Malvolio; Sir Toby takes revenge on Malvolio for an insult, and incidentally gets mixed up in the confusions occurring round Viola and Sebastian by playing a trick on his friend, Sir Andrew Aguecheek, who is also courting Olivia. Sir Toby's interference ends in a clearing-up of the confusions of identity, and a subsequent suitable pairing off of Orsino and Viola, Sebastian and Olivia.

The comedy can be regarded as being about different forms of love, or imagining oneself to have fallen in love, and though the plot is bewildering in summary, it is deftly worked out theatrically and beautifully balanced, with finely cadenced poetry and a more unifying theme than any earlier comedy by Shakespeare. The title, like ▷ *A Midsummer Night's Dream* and ▷ *The Winter's Tale*, indicates the sort of occasion for which the story is suitable: Twelfth Night was the last night of the Christmas festival and a time of licensed disorder presided over by a Lord of ▷ Misrule, such as Sir Toby Belch. Although this title has often been seen to have little to do with the thematic content of the play, recent criticism suggests that the sense of misrule may be seen in attempts to cross class barriers (Malvolio), success at so doing (Maria), and the general economic self-sufficiency of Feste (▷ New Historicism).

Two Gentlemen of Verona, The (1594)

An early romantic comedy by ▷ Shakespeare, probably written about 1594.

Shakespeare's source seems to have been a Spanish tale, Montemayor's *Diana.* The plot is a double love-affair with complications: Proteus is in love with Julia, and Valentine with Silvia, but Proteus plays both Valentine and Julia false in his efforts to win Silvia. Julia follows Proteus, disguised as a page, while Valentine, by the contrivance of Proteus, has to flee and takes refuge as the captain of a band of robbers. Proteus in the end is confronted by both Valentine and Julia, and happiness is restored by his suitable repentance. In plot, poetry and characterization the play is clearly very immature, though it has a limpid charm. There is an element of low-life comedy in the role of Launce, servant to Proteus, accompanied by his dog. Julia's disguise and the sentiment of the play look forward to the much more interesting ▷ *Twelfth Night.*

Two Noble Kinsmen, The

A play of romantic love chiefly by ▷ John Fletcher, perhaps in collaboration with ▷ Shakespeare. It was probably written in 1612–13, and was printed in 1634. The plot derives from ▷ Chaucer's *Knight's Tale* (▷ *The Canterbury Tales*) about the tragic rivalry in love of Palamon and Arcite.

Tyler, Margaret (no dates)

Translator. Little is known of Margaret Tyler's life, the only biographical information coming from the dedicatory letter to her *A Mirrour of Princely Deedes and Knighthood* (1578), where she states that she belongs to the rich, ▷ Catholic Howard household. The preface to *A Mirrour* is important for students of women's history since it forthrightly states that women may write imaginative literature as well as men: 'my perswasion hath bene thus, that it is all one for a woman to pen a story, as for a man to addresse his story to a woman'. She also deals with the importance of female ▷ patronage.

Bib: Travitsky, B. (ed.), *The Paradise of Women*.

Tyndale, William (?1492–1536)

A translator of the Bible; his version was a principal basis for the Authorized Version of 1611. He was a convinced ▷ Protestant. His other works include: *Parable of the Wicked Mammon* (1528), *Obedience of a Christian Man* (1528), and *Practice of Prelates* (1530). These works influenced the forms that the extreme Protestantism of ▷ Puritanism took in England. In 1535, while on a visit to the Netherlands, he was arrested and later burned as a heretic.

▷ Bible in England; Reformation.
Bib: Daniell, D. (ed.), *The New Testament, translated by William Tyndale*.

Tyrwhit, Elizabeth (c 1530–78)

Devotional writer. Lady-in-waiting to ▷ Katherine Parr, she belonged to the queen's circle of ▷ Puritan women and only narrowly escaped being arrested for her outspoken ▷ Protestantism. Her *Morning and Evening Praiers, with divers Psalms, Himnes and Meditations* (1574) were published in Thomas Bently's collection of works by pious women, *The Monument of Matrones* (1582). The work consists of several unimaginative verses and a series of prose meditations; overall Tyrwhit's concern is more with the plain presentation and interpretation of female piety and spiritual learning than with literary skill or finesse. She was governess to ▷ Elizabeth I and the queen's own copy of *Morning and Evening Praiers* survives (in the British Library); it is bound with gold, has enamelled portraits of Solomon and Moses on the covers, and is furnished with rings to attach it to a woman's girdle.

Bib: Beilin, E. V., *Redeeming Eve*; Blain, V. et al. (eds.), *The Feminist Companion to Literature in English*.

Udall, Nicholas (1505–56)
The writer of ▷ *Ralph Roister Doister*.

Underwoods (1640–1)
Title of a collection of poems by ▷ Ben
Jonson, published in the second ▷ folio
edition of his *Works* in 1640–1. In the first
edition of his works (1616) a collection of
his poems had been given the title 'The
Forest'.

**Unfortunate Traveller, or the Life of Jack
   Wilton, The (1594)**
A romance by ▷ Thomas Nashe, published
in 1594. Wilton begins as a page in the
court of ▷ Henry VIII, and then travels
through Europe as adventurer, soldier of
fortune, and hanger-on of the poet Henry
Howard, ▷ Earl of Surrey. It is one of
the first notable ▷ picaresque tales in
English. Among other historical figures,
apart from Surrey, Wilton meets ▷ Sir
Thomas More, ▷ Erasmus and ▷ Pietro
Aretino; he witnesses historical events, such
as the struggle between the Anabaptists of
Munster and the Emperor Charles V, and
describes a plague in Rome. The book is
extremely episodic, and Jack himself has no
consistent character. The narrative begins
as a sequence of mischievous pranks in
the manner of the popular 'jest-books' of
Nashe's time, and at the other extreme
goes into brutally realistic descriptions of
rape and of the plague in Rome. Nashe's
story is remarkable for its creation of a
self-conscious narrative voice, and in its
awareness of its status as a text that is
created by the activity of a reader. At the
same time, its delight in the grotesque, and
in a constantly re-iterated ▷ discourse of
bodily distortion and pain, serves to make
the work one of the most vivid attempts
at linguistic refashioning in the 16th
century.
Bib: Rhodes, N., *Elizabethan Grotesque*.

Uniformity, Acts of
Laws passed by Parliament during and
after the ▷ Reformation to secure religious
union in England. The first was that of 1549
(under ▷ Edward VI) and the second and
more important in 1559, under ▷ Elizabeth I.
Both required the common use in church
worship of ▷ *The Book of Common Prayer*.
In 1662, under ▷ Charles II, another Act of
Uniformity insisted on its use by all clergy
and schoolmasters, and marks the beginning
of the ▷ dissenting sects as formally separate
religious bodies, distinct from the ▷ Church
of England.

Unitarianism
A doctrine of religion that rejects the usual
Christian doctrine of the Trinity, or three
Persons in one God (the Father, the Son,
and the Holy Ghost), in favour of a belief
in the single person of God the Father. It
originated in Britain in the 18th century and
was in accord with that century's rationalistic
approach to religion. The first Unitarian
church opened in London in 1774; many
English ▷ Presbyterians (in the 16th and 17th
centuries one of the largest sects outside the
▷ Church of England) became Unitarians.

University Wits
A group of young men in the reign of
▷ Elizabeth I who were educated at either
Oxford or Cambridge Universities, and
then embarked on careers as men of letters.
Their names were ▷ John Lyly, dramatist
and writer of the kind of romance known as
the ▷ Elizabethan novel; ▷ George Peele,
dramatist; ▷ Robert Greene, dramatist;
▷ Thomas Lodge, who tried most of the
branches of contemporary literature;
▷ Thomas Nashe, novelist and ▷
pamphleteer; ▷ Christopher Marlowe,
dramatist. To these, the name of ▷ Thomas
Kyd is sometimes added, although he is
not known to have attended a university.
Lyly was a writer for court circles, but the
others were representative of a new kind
of writer (of which ▷ Shakespeare was
also an example) who sought his fortune
with the general public. Most of them had
some kind of influence on, or relationship
with, Shakespeare: Lyly used the kind of
sophisticated diction which Shakespeare partly
emulated and partly parodied in ▷ *Love's
Labour's Lost* and elsewhere; Green wrote
a mellifluous ▷ blank verse that anticipates
some qualities in the earlier verse of
Shakespeare, and was the author of the 'novel'
Pandosto, source of ▷ *The Winter's Tale*; Lodge
wrote *Rosalynde*, the source of ▷ *As You Like
It*; Marlowe was the architect of the dramatic
blank-verse medium; Kyd possibly wrote the
first version of ▷ *Hamlet*.

Urn Burial, or Hydriotaphia (1658)
A treatise by ▷ Sir Thomas Browne,
published in 1658. Its starting-point is the
discovery of ancient burial urns in Norfolk;
this leads to an account of various ways of
disposing of the dead, and meditations on
death itself.

Utopia (1516)
A political and philosophical treatise by ▷ Sir Thomas More, in the form of an account of an imaginary, newly discovered country. It was written in Latin, and translated into English (after More's death) in 1551; it had already been translated into French (1530), and such was the European fame of the book that Italian, Spanish and German versions also appeared.

The idea of a fictional country was no doubt stimulated by recent Italian, Portuguese, and Spanish exploration, and in particular by ▷ travel literature such as Amerigo Vespucci's account of his travels (1507). Philosophically, the book is a pure product of ▷ Renaissance ▷ humanisim, and like other products of that movement, it was inspired by the ancient Greek philosopher ▷ Plato. The land of Utopia is the Platonic ideal of a country, only to be realized on the assumption that man is basically good. Private property is replaced by communal ownership; there is complete freedom of thought; war is regarded as abominable, and to be used only in the last resort, when it should be waged as effectively as possible, even, if

necessary, by unscrupulous means. Earthly happiness is glorified; the good life is the life of mental and physical fulfilment, rather than the medieval Christian life of self-denial and asceticism, but the Utopians are humane and benevolent, not self-indulgent. There is perfect mutual respect, and women receive the same education as men.

Utopian literature
▷ More's ▷ *Utopia* introduced into the English language the word 'utopian' = 'imaginary and ideal', and started a succession of 'utopias' in English literature. The idea of inventing an imaginary country to be used as a 'model' by which to judge earthly societies did not, however, originate with More, but with his master, the Greek philosopher ▷ Plato, who did the same in his dialogues *Timaeus* and the ▷ *Republic*. *Utopia*'s most notable successors in the 17th century were ▷ Bacon's unfinished ▷ *New Atlantis* (1626), in which science is offered as the solution for humanity, and James Harington's *Oceana* (1656), which put forward political ideas that were to have a powerful influence in America.

Vagabonds and vagrants
Generally known today as 'tramps'; men and women who have no settled residence or work, but live by begging or 'casual labour', wandering from place to place, finding shelter where they can. The 16th century was a period when vagrancy was a critical problem, for special causes: the dissolution of the ▷ monasteries (1536–9) caused unemployment among monastic servants and tradesmen, and ▷ enclosures of land for sheep-farming and parks evicted peasants from their farms. Some of the vagabonds (also called 'rogues') were wandering entertainers, including actors ('players') unattached to noble households; some were pedlars (like Autolycus in ▷ Shakespeare's ▷ The Winter's Tale) with goods for sale; a special class were the gipsies who appeared in England early in the 16th century. Many, more or less inevitably, became part of the underworld of crime, for which a large slang language of 'cant' grew up: Abraham men = pretended lunatics (Mad Tom, in Shakespeare's ▷ King Lear); 'hookers' or 'anglers' = thieves who extracted goods from houses with a hooked stick; 'rufflers' = highway robbers; 'priggers of prancers' = horse thieves. 'Prig' was at this time a common word for thief. This underworld was the subject of a class of popular literature known as 'rogue pamphlets', the most notable examples of which are ▷ Robert Greene's 'cony-catching' ▷ pamphlets, 1591–2.

The government tried to deal with the problem of vagrancy by constructive legislation (eg the ▷ Poor Law of 1601) and by severity – imprisonment, whipping, and, in the 17th century, branding.
Bib: Beier, A. L., Masterless Men: The Vagrancy Problem in England 1560–1640.

Vaughan, Henry (1622–95)
Poet. Henry Vaughan, together with his brother Thomas Vaughan (1622–66) the alchemist and poet, was born at Newton-by-Usk in Wales. Vaughan's Welsh roots were to feature prominently in his writing. He termed himself 'The Silurist' after a local Welsh tribe termed the Silures by Tacitus, and his third published collection of poems was entitled Olor Iscanus (1651), which can be translated as 'The Swan of Usk', a reference to Vaughan's native river. In addition to Olor Iscanus, three collections of Vaughan's poetry appeared in his lifetime: Poems with the Tenth Satire of Juvenal Englished (1646), Silex Scintillans (1650, revised ed. 1655), and Thalia Rediviva (1678).

Silex Scintillans perhaps provides a clue as to Vaughan's intellectual identity. The title means 'The Flashing Flint' – an image which was given emblematic significance on the title-page of the collection where a hand, issuing from a cloud, is shown striking fire from a flintstone, fashioned in the shape of a heart. The image, which signifies a 'stony' heart surrendering flames of divine love when struck by God's spiritual force, suggests ▷ George Herbert's influence on Vaughan. But the image, with its conjunction of stone and fire suggestive of a religious awakening (a theme explored in the collection of poems as a whole), also alerts us to another side of Vaughan's writing. In 1655 Vaughan published a translation of an 'Hermetic' work entitled Hermetical Physick and in 1657 appeared his The Chymists Key. Hermeticism – the linking of alchemy, magic and science – might also be thought of as represented in the physical image of the flint flashing with fire. These two elements in Vaughan's intellectual life combine in his poetry in a way reminiscent of ▷ Thomas Traherne's concern for expressing the physical and spiritual worlds.
Bib: Martin, L. C. (ed.), Works; Hutchinson, F. E., Henry Vaughan: A Life and Interpretation; Post, J., Henry Vaughan: The Unfolding Vision.

Venus and Adonis (1593)
A narrative poem in six-lined stanzas by ▷ William Shakespeare. It is dedicated to Henry Wriothesley, ▷ Earl of Southampton. It is based on the Romano-Greek myth of the love of Venus, the goddess of sexual beauty, for the beautiful youth ▷ Adonis. The poem probably emulates the love poem ▷ Hero and Leander by ▷ Marlowe (completed by ▷ Chapman) and is Shakespeare's earliest published work. The poem reflects the extent to which Shakespeare was indebted to ▷ Ovid, particularly to the ▷ Metamorphoses.

Verges
▷ Dogberry and Verges.

Vergil, Polydore
▷ Histories and Chronicles.

Vice, The
A 16th-century term for a type of tempter found in 16th-century ▷ interludes, used for the first time in ▷ John Heywood's Play of the Weather (1533), in which Merry-report is called the 'vice of the play'. The figure has precedents in the devil-tempters which appear in earlier medieval drama, and

descendants in the individualized tempters in Elizabethan drama.

Virgil (Publius Vergilius Maro) (70–19 BC)

Roman poet. He was born on a farm not far from Mantua in northern Italy, and is often referred to as 'the Mantuan'. He greatly esteemed the farming section of society to which he belonged, and valued the farming way of life. He was not, from the place of his origin, of Roman descent, but belonged to the first generation of Italians who felt a consciousness of nationhood, with Rome as their capital. By 40 BC he was in Rome, under the patronage of the wealthy Roman patrician (nobleman), Maecenas. He wrote the first work for which he is famous, the *Eclogues* or *Bucolics* (▷ Eclogue), between 42 and 37 BC; their title merely means short, selected pieces, and his intention was to praise the Italian countryside as the Greek poet ▷ Theocritus had praised the countryside of Sicily. The *Georgics* (37–30 BC), written at the instigation of Maecenas to encourage a sense of the value of a stable and productive society, is devoted to the praise of the farming way of life. The ▷ *Aeneid*, written during the remainder of his life, is an ▷ epic about the travels of ▷ Aeneas the Trojan, and emulates ▷ Homer's ▷ *Odyssey*. Its purpose is not merely this, but to relate the Romans to the great civilization of the Greeks, on which their own civilization was so much based, by making Aeneas the ancestor of the Roman nation. The *Aeneid*, with the epics of Homer, is one of the basic poems in the culture of Europe and is taken as a standard for what was, perhaps until the 19th century, regarded as the noblest form of literature.

Not even Homer exceeds Virgil in the extent of his influence and prestige in the 20 centuries of European culture. He did not, like all the Greek poets and many of the Roman ones, have to wait for the ▷ Renaissance to 'discover' him, for he was esteemed in the ▷ Middle Ages, when, indeed, he became a legend. This was partly owing to his *Fourth Eclogue*, which celebrated the birth of a child who was to restore the Golden Age (▷ Ages, Golden, Silver), a poem that in the Christian centuries was supposed to be a prophetic vision of the birth of Christ. He was thus regarded as more than merely a pagan poet, and ▷ Dante chose him as his guide through Hell and Purgatory in his 13th-century Christian epic, the *Divine Comedy* (▷ *Divina Commedia*). In direct literary influence, he was, even more than Theocritus, the pattern

for ▷ pastoral poetry, and even more than Homer, for the epic, although he was himself a student of both.

▷ Tudor myth.

Virgin Queen

A name for ▷ Elizabeth I of England, on account of the fact that she never married. The title enabled poets and other writers to associate her with Diana, the Roman goddess of chastity. The first English colony in America was called Virginia by ▷ Sir Walter Ralegh in her honour. The iconography associated with the public persona of Elizabeth is elaborate: see Frances Yates, *Astraea: The Imperial Theme in the Sixteenth Century*, and Roy Strong, *Gloriana: the Portraits of Elizabeth I* and *The Cult of Elizabeth I*.

Volpone

A comedy in ▷ blank verse by ▷ Ben Jonson. First acted in 1605 or 1606 and printed in 1607, it is often considered Jonson's masterpiece. The names of the principal characters signify their roles in the comedy: Volpone = fox; his servant Mosca = fly, since he is a parasite who tries to take advantage of the vicious natures of everyone; the lawyer Voltore = vulture, Corbaccio = crow, and Corvino = raven, because all three birds feed on dead bodies, and all three men hope to gain from Volpone's will when he dies. Volpone is well aware of this, and pretends to be very ill in order to extract gifts from his so-called friends; Corvino, a jealous husband, is even prepared to sacrifice his wife, the pure-hearted Celia. Mosca tries to outdo his master by blackmailing Corvino, and this leads Voltore the lawyer to bring them both to judgement. A subplot concerns an absurd Englishman and his wife, Sir Politick and Lady Would-Be, who are on a visit to Venice (the scene of the play) and are ▷ satires on the contemporary English enthusiasm for financial speculation through fantastic 'projects'. The concentrated satire in the ▷ morality tradition of the main plot rises to heights of great poetry: the play is not, as it first seems, a piece of savage cynicism, because the characters, especially Volpone, have a vivid zest for living which is morally condemned only because they carry it to the point of mania.

▷ Humours, Comedy of.

Vulgate, The

From the Latin 'vulgatus' = 'made public or common'. The name of St Jerome's Latin version of the ▷ Bible, completed in AD 405. For a long time it was the only authorized text for the Catholic Church. The ▷ Protestants in the 16th century insisted on extending Jerome's principle of making the Word of

God common to all, by translating it into other languages, a principle now accepted by the Catholic Church itself.

▷ Catholicism (Roman) in English literature.

W

Waller, Edmund (1606–87)

Poet. As with so many of his contemporaries, Waller's career reflects the vicissitudes of public life in the revolutionary period of the mid-17th century. As a member of Parliament prior to the ▷ Civil War, he opposed the bishops, but, on the outbreak of hostilities, he was on the Royalist side. In 1643 he was found guilty of plotting to surrender London to the Royalist armies, and was banished. In exile in Paris he became friendly with ▷ Thomas Hobbes, before returning to England (having secured permission) in 1651. On his return he wrote a 'Panegyric to my Lord Protector' (1655) addressed to ▷ Oliver Cromwell, but with the Restoration in 1660 Waller was fully restored to the king's favour, and proceeded to write a second panegyric, this time to ▷ Charles II.

Waller's chief verse collections were his *Poems* of 1645 (a second part being published in 1690) and his collection of religious verse, *Divine Poems* (1685). After 1660 he produced numerous occasional verses, including *To the King, Upon His Majesty's Happy Return* (1660) and *To the Queen, Upon Her Majesty's Birthday* (1663). But it is as a transitional figure that he has attracted critical comment. Waller's poetry can be seen as marking the transition from the 'witty' ▷ conceits of poets such as ▷ John Donne to the smoother ▷ neo-classicism of 18th-century poetry. Indeed, John Dryden (1631–1700), ignoring figures such as ▷ Robert Herrick and ▷ Ben Jonson, claimed that if Waller had not written, 'none of us could write'.
Bib: Thorn-Drury, G. (ed.), *Poems*, (2 vols.); Chernaik, W. L., *The Poetry of Limitation: A Study of Waller*.

Walsingham, Sir Francis (?1530–90)

Statesman. Walsingham was educated at the ▷ Inns of Court and, as a ▷ Protestant, was forced to leave the country during the ▷ Catholic reign of ▷ Mary I. He returned under ▷ Elizabeth I and acted as the queen's principal secretary, as well as being an excellent foreign diplomat. He was, however, too blunt for Elizabeth and she never treated him with the respect he deserved, although she did knight him in 1577. He was the main force behind the execution of ▷ Mary Queen of Scots for her implication in the Babington plot. His letters and papers remain extant and are an invaluable source for the history of Elizabethan politics.

Walton, Izaac (1593–1683)

Biographer. Izaac Walton's popular reputation has rested on his ▷ *The Compleat Angler* (1653, with revised editions in 1658 and 1661) – ostensibly a fishing manual. The comprehensive nature of the work is, however, hinted at in its subtitle: *The Contemplative Man's Recreation* – an evocation of an idyllic, reflective, ▷ pastoral nostalgia. As a biographer Walton was the author of a series of important 'lives' of 17th-century poets and divines. His *Life of John Donne* was published in 1658, and was followd by lives of ▷ Richard Hooker (1665), ▷ George Herbert (1670) and Robert Sanderson (1678). *The Life of Sir Henry Wotton* (▷ Henry Wotton) first appeared appended to a posthumous edition of Wotton's poetry in 1640 and was published separately in 1651. The two biographies of ▷ Donne and Herbert are the most renowned. Walton is concerned with recording his subjects' piously Anglican Christian virtue, but they are, nevertheless, important statements concerning the contemporary perception of these major writers and instances of a 17th-century art of hagiographic ▷ biography.
Bib: Keynes, G. L. (ed.), *The Compleat Walton*; Novarr, D., *The Making of Walton's Lives*.

Ward, Mary (1558–1645)

Religious writer and educationalist. Mary Ward's name has become associated with the history of female education. She set up a ▷ Catholic boarding school for girls at St Omer in the Netherlands (1609) and in 1639, under the auspices of ▷ Henrietta Maria, she returned to Britain, where she hoped to promote scholarly studies for young women. During the intervening years abroad, Mary Ward had frequently visited her home country on 'recruiting drives' for pupils, and such was her skill and that of her companions at evading arrest as Catholics that they were nicknamed the 'Galloping Girls'. Born into a ▷ recusant family, Ward eventually became a nun (1606) and established several religious communities in connection with her schools. Persecuted in Britain for her faith, on the continent she was attacked and even imprisoned for her radical views on the equality of women by the Catholic Church she gave her allegiance to. Her hopes for reform in Britain were crushed by the Civil War, and she died in a safe house outside York. Throughout her trials, which were made worse by ill health, Mary Ward retained her strong religious and educational convictions

together with a seemingly indomitable sense
of humour. These qualities come through
in her writings and in her last recorded
words, 'it matters not the who, but the what'.
Extracts from her work may be found in
M. C. Chambers, *The Life of Mary Ward*
(1882–7).
Bib: Fraser, A., *The Weaker Vessel*; Prior, M.
(ed.), *Women in English Society 1500–1800*.

Webster, John (1578–1632)
English dramatist about whom little is
known, although his father's life is well
documented. He is the author of two of the
most famous ▷Jacobean tragedies, ▷ *The
White Devil* (1612) and ▷ *The Duchess of Malfi*
(1613), and collaborated with ▷ Dekker,
▷ Fletcher, ▷ Ford and others on a number
of plays. Webster excels in constructing richly
metaphorical passages and iconographic
scenes, but he is less satisfactory on form and
in overall conception. His works have been
accused of lacking moral fibre in their pursuit
of grotesque and titillating images of death.
Bib: Morris, B. (ed.), *John Webster*.

Wheathill, Anne (no dates)
Devotional writer. Little is known about
Wheathill's life except that she was an
unmarried gentlewoman at the time she
composed her one known work, *A Handfull
of Holesome (though homelie) Hearbs Gathered
Out of the Goodlie Garden of Gods Most Holie
Word* (1584). This text consists of 49 prayers
arranged symbolically in accordance with
the title; their concerns are conventional, for
example how to avoid the sin of pride, how to
evade the temptations of the devil, and prayers
for faith and repentance. The book itself has
an attractive title-page, but the contents are
not exceptional.
Bib: Travitsky, B. (ed.), *A Paradise for Women*.

Whetstone, George (1550–87)
English poet and dramatist who is mostly
remembered for the comedy *Promos and
Cassandra* (1578), which ▷ Shakespeare used
in ▷ *Measure for Measure*.

White Devil, The (1608–9)
A tragedy by ▷ John Webster, published in
1612 with the subtitle ▷ *Vittoria Corrombona*,
written in 1608–9. It is based on the story of
the actual murder of Vittoria Accoromboni
(1585) as told in William Painter's ▷ *Palace
of Pleasure*. Vittoria is the wife of Camillo.
The Duke of Brachiano, husband to Isabella,
the sister of the Duke of Florence and of
Cardinal Montecelso, falls in love with her
and is assisted in winning her by her brother,

Flamineo. Flamineo causes the death of
Camillo, and Brachiano poisons his own
wife. In Act III, Vittoria is on trial before
Cardinal Montecelso for adultery and murder;
she is proudly defiant, and condemned to
confinement in a convent, where Brachiano
continues to visit her, and whence he
eventually steals her away and marries her. In
Act V, Flamineo kills his brother, Marcello,
who is upbraiding him for his wickedness,
and their mother sings over her dead son the
lovely dirge 'Call for the robin redbreast and
the wren'. The Duke of Florence's hireling,
Lodovico, avenges the death of Isabella by
killing Flamineo and Vittoria. 'My soul, like
to a ship in a black storm, is driven, I know
not whither'; the spirit of the stormy play is
expressed by this line spoken by the dying
Vittoria. The play contains many passages of
intense poetry, no virtuous characters among
the outstanding ones, and a number of fine
theatrical episodes which are difficult to
perform because they are long drawn out. The
unifying tone is of desperation produced by
destructive and self-destroying passions.

Whitgift, John (c 1530–1610)
Archbishop of Canterbury. Whitgift rose
to prominence at Cambridge University,
where he was appointed Regius Professor
of Divinity in 1567, and in the same year
he became chaplain to ▷ Elizabeth 1. He
was Bishop of Worcester (1577–83) before
being made Archbishop in 1583, after the
death of ▷ Edmund Grindal. Whitgift's
firm Anglican policy and his belief in
conformity – he reversed his predecessor's
policy of conciliation with the ▷ Puritan
sects – brought him into close alliance with
the queen, who appointed him to her Privy
Council and insisted that he attend her at
her deathbed. Subsequently, Whitgift was
responsible for ▷ James 1's ready acceptance
of the Anglican church at his accession in
1603. Whitgift's most well-known work is an
attack against ▷ Presbyterianism, *An Answere
to a Certen Libel Intituled, An Admonition to the
Parliament* (1572).
Bib: Dawley, P. M., *John Whitgift and the
Reformation*.

Whitney, Isabella (no dates)
Poet. The first known professional woman
poet writing in English, her two extant books,
Copy of a Letter . . . (c 1567) and *A Sweet
Nosegay* (1573), both contain moralizing
poetry which is primarily secular in tone.
Thematically, Whitney concentrates upon
the constancy of women and the fickleness

of men, using classical allusion to back up her light-hearted arguments and following the tradition of ▷ Ovid's *Heroides*. In *A Sweet Nosegay* she is indebted especially to Sir Hugh Platt's *Flours of Philosophie* whose maxims she translates into verse, although she also participates in the contemporary vogue for 'flower poetry', for example ▷ George Gascoigne's *A Hundreth Sundrie Flowres*. Her work also includes interesting material that is assumed to be ▷ autobiographical and is useful as such, since little about Whitney's life is known. It is probable that she was the sister of Geoffrey Whitney, the author of *A Choice of Emblemes* (1586), and that she had several sisters in service in London to whom she dedicated poems. She clearly knew London intimately since her last poem, 'Wyll and Testament', consists of a mock bequest to all the streets and buildings of London; it is entirely secular in tone and is reminiscent of the travel pieces in ▷ Thomas Nashe's ▷ *The Unfortunate Traveller* (1594).

▷ Emblem-books.
Bib: Travitsky, B. (ed.), *The Paradise of Women*; Beilin, E. V., *Redeeming Eve*.

Wilson, Robert (d 1600)

Dramatist and actor. We know little of Wilson's life, except that he joined the acting companies of the Earl of Leicester's Men after 1572 and of Queen Elizabeth's Men after 1583; he is also known for his brilliant extemporizing during dramatic performances. His dramatic writing includes *The Ladies of London* (c 1581), *The Three Lords and Ladies of London* (c 1589), and *The Cobbler's Prophecy* (c 1594). Wilson's dramatic output represents the bridge between writing for the medieval ▷ morality tradition and for the ▷ Renaissance public theatres.

Wilson, Thomas (c 1525–81)

Theorist and politician. Thomas Wilson had a successful public career as well as writing one of the most important ▷ Renaissance books on literary style, *Arte of Rhetorique* (1553 and 1560). An ardent supporter of ▷ Elizabeth I, he was appointed as Privy Councillor (1572) and Secretary of State (1578), and was involved in the successful prosecution of the Duke of Norfolk and ▷ Mary Queen of Scots. He was also a confirmed ▷ Protestant and spent most of ▷ Mary I's reign on the continent. His two most noted works are *Arte* and *Rule of Reason* (1551), the latter concerning itself with logic, rather than focusing on ▷ rhetoric as his later writing does. Wilson's *Arte* gives a series of epistles

and orations in different styles, some are meant to be copied, others are more akin to parodies, so that the whole text conforms to the Renaissance doctrine of both teaching and amusing – 'pleasure reconciled to virtue'.
Bib: Medine, P., *Thomas Wilson*.

Winter's Tale, The (1610–11)

A play by ▷ Shakespeare; one of his ▷ romances, dated 1610–11, and based on ▷ Robert Greene's *Pandosto*. Leontes, king of Sicilia, is married to Hermione, whom he deeply loves, and at the opening of the play is receiving a visit from Polixenes, king of Bohemia and the intimate friend of his childhood. Leontes becomes consumed by an insane jealousy, and is convinced that the child with which Hermione is pregnant has been fathered by Polixenes. He orders Camillo, a courtier, to poison Polixenes, but instead Camillo and Polixenes flee the country together. Leontes orders the trial of Hermione for adultery and, to appease his indignant courtiers, he sends to the oracle of Delphi in order to obtain what he believes will be confirmation of her guilt. The baby is born, but Leontes orders another courtier, Antigonus, to leave it in a desolate place to perish. At this point a succession of catastrophes is heaped on Leontes: he learns from the oracle that his wife is innocent, from Paulina, wife of Antigonus, that Hermione has died, and that his little son has also died, of grief at the suffering of his mother. The last scene of Act III shows Antigonus depositing the baby on the coast of Bohemia and her discovery by two shepherds. Thus far the play is tragic; Acts IV and V show recovery. The baby grows up into a beautiful girl, Perdita, who believes herself to be a shepherd's daughter. Florizel, son of Polixenes, courts her at the shepherds' sheep-shearing feast, but they have to flee to Sicilia to escape the anger of his father. Polixenes follows them, and at Leontes' court once more a great reconciliation takes place. Paulina discloses that Hermione is not dead, but has been kept in hiding until the return of Perdita, in accordance with the prediction of the oracle; in the last scene she is shown to Leontes as a statue of her supposedly dead self, but at the command of Paulina the statue gradually comes to life to the sound of music.

The summary shows that the play has no pretence to external realism; it is a fable about the destructiveness of the passions and the healing power of time. The symbolism is especially of the seasons: 'a winter's tale' is about deprivation, but the play ends in autumn, the season of recovered fulfilment, while the sheep-shearing scene (IV. 3) has springlike qualities, with Perdita reminding one of Persephone in her lines about the spring flowers. The ▷ pastoral aspect of the play shows pastoralism in a new light – not as an escape from change and decay into day-dream, but as a phase of development which must be outgrown if capacity for growth is to be fulfilled. The process of growth implies desire, fear and possessiveness, which form the state of mind of the jealous Leontes at the beginning of the play when he finds that he has outgrown his pastorally innocent friendship with Polixenes. From this false development, he can recover only by repentance.

Wit
This word has a number of distinct, though related, meanings. 1 The oldest meaning is identical with 'mind', as in ▷ Wycliffe's 14th-century translation of the Bible: 'Who knew the wit of the Lord?' (*Romans* 11:34). This use of 'wit' rarely occurs in the literature of the last hundred years. 2 Another long-established meaning is 'a faculty of the mind'. This is still in use today, as when we speak of someone having 'lost his wits', *ie* lost the use of his mental faculties. 3 A common meaning in the 17th and 18th centuries was the capacity to relate unlike ideas, as in Locke's definition: 'Wit lying in the assemblage of ideas, and putting these together with quickness and variety wherein can be found any resemblance or congruity, thereby to make up pleasant pictures in the fancy' (*Essay concerning Human Understanding*, 1690). ▷ Cowley, in his poem *Of Wit* (1656), wrote 'In a true piece of wit all things must be. Yet all things there agree.'
▷ Lyly, John; University Wits, The.

Witches
People supposed to be in league with the Devil, who gives them supernatural powers. The name 'witch' was sometimes used for both sexes, though those accused of being witches were usually women. They commonly had 'familiars' in the form of spirits disguised as animals of bad or sinister reputation – toads or cats of certain colours. To work their magic, witches uttered 'spells' or specially devised words, or they used objects ('charms') supposed to have magical properties; witches used to gather in small communities known as 'covens', and they assembled on one day of the year (a 'witches' Sabbath') to worship the Devil.

The common explanation of witchcraft is that, in Europe at least, it represents the long survival of pre-Christian pagan religions in which the gods were the embodiments of the powers of nature, usually in the forms of animals, often a goat, but in Britain commonly the bull, the dog, or the cat. More recently witchcraft, or the accusation of witchcraft, has been regarded as a 17th-century mechanism of social control, used to discourage women from living alone outside the authority of a male-dominated household.

That witchcraft was common in the ▷ Middle Ages is not surprising; it is at first sight surprising that it was conspicuous in the later 16th and early 17th centuries, and that not merely the ignorant and uneducated but some of the learned believed in it. ▷ James VI of Scotland and I of England, who has been called 'the greatest scholar who ever sat on the English throne', was himself deeply interested in it and wrote a denunciation of it – his *Daemonologie* (1599). The pamphlet *News from Scotland* (1591) describes his conversion from scepticism to belief in it, and seems to have been used by Shakespeare in the portrayal of the witches in ▷ *Macbeth*. James later, however, moved to a more sceptical position again. The first law in England making witchcraft an offence punishable by death was passed in 1603 (though causing death by witchcraft had been so punishable since 1563) and it was not repealed until 1736. ▷ Sir Thomas Browne declares his firm belief in it in ▷ *Religio Medici* (1643). The belief seems to have been particularly strong among ▷ Puritans and in Puritan countries, for instance in Scotland, 17th-century New England, and England under the ▷ Long Parliament. Rare survivals of it have been found in 20th-century England. It has been suggested that the prevalence of the belief in the 17th century and among Puritans is that their superstitious impulses were no longer satisfied by the ▷ Catholic system of mysteries (miracles, lives of the saints, etc.) that they had expelled from their faith by its 'purification'.

In the reign of James I, a number of plays besides *Macbeth* dealt with witchcraft, *eg* ▷ Dekker and ▷ Ford's *Witches of Edmonton* (1623) and ▷ Middleton's *The Witch* (1615).
Bib: Briggs, K. M., *Pale Hecate's Team*; Hester, M., *Lewd Women and Wicked Witches*.

Wither, George (1588–1667)
Poet. Between 1612, when Wither's first publication appeared, and the poet's death in 1667, there were very few years that

were not marked by the publication of at least one volume of verse or prose from this prolific author. Wither was possibly the most imprisoned writer in the history of English literature. In 1613 his ▷ satiric work *Abuses Stripped and Whipped* earned him a period of imprisonment, a punishment he earned once more in 1621, when *Wither's Motto* appeared, and which was to befall him again in 1646 (on publication of his ▷ pamphlet *Justiarius Justificatus*) and in 1660 (appearance of unpublished satire: *Vox Vulgi: A Poem in Censure of Parliament*). His later works were written in the belief that he was God's prophet. Of note, however, are several volumes of earlier verse, and his collection of emblems (▷ Emblem-books), which appeared in four volumes in 1635.
Bib: Hunter, W. B., *The English Spenserians*.

Wolsey, Thomas (?1475–1530)
Statesman and churchman. He was born of comparatively humble parents in Ipswich, but with the aid of various patrons he received rapid promotion in the Church. In 1507 he became chaplain to ▷ King Henry VII, who employed him on diplomatic affairs. In the next reign he was for 20 years practically the sole ruler of the country, having the full confidence of ▷ Henry VIII. He became Bishop of Lincoln, Bishop of Tournai in France, Archbishop of York, Cardinal, within reach of becoming Pope. At home he was a firm and able administrator. His foreign policy was skilful, but his personal ambitions led to its ultimate failure. In his anxiety to become Pope, he sought the favour of Emperor Charles V and allowed him to become too powerful in Europe. Charles was nephew to Henry VIII's queen, Katharine of Aragon, whom in 1528 Henry wanted to divorce. Since Charles had Rome in his hands, the Pope could not consent, and in 1529 Wolsey lost the favour of the king; his downfall was the more complete because he had no other powerful supporters in the country. His life was written by a member of his household, George Cavendish, but it was not published until 1641. His downfall was dramatized by ▷ Fletcher and ▷ Shakespeare in ▷ *Henry VIII*.
Bib: Ridley, J., *The Statesman and the Fanatic: Thomas Wolsey and Thomas More*.

Woman Killed with Kindness, A (1603)
A powerful domestic ▷ tragedy by ▷ Thomas Heywood, which explores the marriage, adultery and death of Anne Frankford, the wife of a gentle and upright man, who kills

her with his 'kindness' by refusing her his and her children's company. The seduction of Anne by Frankford's friend Wendoll and the husband's subsequent discovery of the lovers are presented with great sympathy and understanding. The play's subplot is informed by a similar range of domestic detail and is not without tenderness.

Women Beware Women (1614)
A baroque and vindictive ▷ tragedy of misdirected desire which ends in a bloodbath, by ▷ Thomas Middleton. Like ▷ *The Changeling* the play features a skilfully integrated subplot, which here dramatizes the incestuous love of Hippolito for his brother's daughter Isabella, whom he hopes to seduce with the help of her aunt. The most famous scene in the play concerns the seduction of Bianca by the Duke of Florence in a series of moves that parallel those of a game of chess played simultaneously between Bianca's mother-in-law and a corrupt go-between, Livia. Like ▷ Webster's ▷ *The White Devil*, *Women Beware Women* evinces a cynical and erotic awareness of the role of power and money in human relationships, and their ability to destroy even marriage.

Women, Education of
In medieval convents, nuns often learned and received the same education as monks. Thereafter, women's intellectual education was not widely provided for until the later 19th century, though much would depend on their social rank, their parents, or their husbands. ▷ Thomas More in ▷ *Utopia* advocated equal education for both sexes, and in the 16th century the enthusiasm for education caused some highly born women to be very highly educated; this is true of the two queens, ▷ Mary I and ▷ Elizabeth I, of the 'ten-days' queen' ▷ Lady Jane Grey (whose education is described in ▷ Ascham's *Schoolmaster*, 1570), and of the Countess of Pembroke (▷ Mary Sidney), Sidney's sister.
Bib: Fraser, A., *The Weaker Vessel*; Prior, M. (ed.), *Women in English Society 1500–1800*.

Women, Status of
Unmarried women had few prospects in Britain until the second half of the 19th century. In the ▷ Middle Ages they could enter convents and become nuns, but when in 1536–9 ▷ Henry VIII closed the convents and the monasteries, no alternative opened to them. Widows like ▷ Chaucer's Wife of Bath in ▷ *The Canterbury Tales* might inherit a business (in her case that of a clothier) and

run it efficiently, or like Mistress Quickly in Shakespeare's ▷ *Henry IV, Part II* they might run inns. Wives and their property were entirely in the power of their husbands according to the law, though in practice they might take the management of both into their own hands, like the Wife of Bath. A Dutch observer (1575) stated that England was called the 'Paradise of married women' because they took their lives more easily than continental wives. Nonetheless, a middle-class wife worked hard, as her husband's assistant (probably his accountant) in his business, and as a mistress of baking, brewing, household management and amateur medicine.
Bib: Fraser, A., *The Weaker Vessel*; Prior, M. (ed.), *Women in English Society 1500–1800*.

Wotton, Sir Henry (1566–1639)
Poet and courtier. Wotton was educated at Oxford, where he became acquainted with ▷ Donne, whose biography he wished to write (the task actually fell to ▷ Izaak Walton, who also wrote a memoir of Wotton himself). At court Walton became attached to the ▷ Essex faction and performed several intelligence-gathering tasks for the earl. He was welcomed by ▷ James I at his accession, since Wotton had carried secret messages to James when he was king of Scotland. He was given a diplomatic role by the king, and, among other duties, was ambassador to Venice. Although well known, it is worth recording Wotton's definition of an ambassador as an honest man who has to lie when abroad for the sake of his country. In 1624 he became Provost of Eton. The only work to be published during his lifetime was *The Elements of Architecture* (1624), but his many poems were gathered together after his death, together with Walton's memoir, as *Reliquiae Wottoniae* (1651). The lyrical pieces are characterized by a searching for honest, spiritual truth, and his panegyric poems – one to his patron, ▷ Elizabeth of Bohemia, is particularly fine – appear more honest than many of their kind.

Wriothesley, Henry
▷ Southampton, Henry Wriothesley, third Earl of.

Wroth, Mary (Lady Wroth) (?1586–?1652)
The niece of ▷ Philip Sidney and ▷ Mary Sidney, Countess of Pembroke, Mary Wroth was a member of court, where she danced with ▷ Queen Anne in ▷ Ben Jonson's ▷ masque, *The Masque of Blackness*. Jonson was a particular admirer of her talents, dedicating his play ▷ *The Alchemist* to her

and enthusiastically acclaiming her poetry. In 1614, following the death of her husband, Sir Robert Wroth, Mary Wroth was left with over £20,000 in debts, which she undertook to pay off. Financial difficulties stalked her for most of her life, a factor which may have induced her to publish the first part of her work *Urania* in 1621. The second part of this work, together with a ▷ pastoral ▷ tragicomedy entitled *Loves Victorie*, circulated in manuscript. *Urania* is the first prose romance written in English by a woman. Soon after its publication it was withdrawn, because various passages touched upon court intrigues. Like Philip Sidney's ▷ *Arcadia*, *Urania* contains poetry, including a sequence of songs and ▷ sonnets entitled *Pamphilia to Amphilanthus*, the title being derived from the names of the two protagonists of *Urania*. The sequence is important because, while participating in the ▷ Petrarchan tradition, it is also written from the perspective of a woman.
Bib: Roberts, J. A. (ed.), *The Poems of Lady Mary Wroth*; Hannay, M. P., 'Mary Sidney: Lady Wroth' in *Women Writers of the Renaissance and Reformation*, (ed.) Wilson, K. M.

Wyatt, Sir Thomas (1503–42)
Poet, courtier, diplomat. Wyatt's life, with its changes in fortune, perfectly represents the uncertain conditions of existence in the court of ▷ Henry VIII. Imprisoned several times (once because he was suspected of being the lover of Anne Boleyn), he brought to his writing an awareness of continental European styles and manner to which his life as a diplomat exposed him. His best-known poems appeared in ▷ *Tottel's Miscellany* (1557) together with poems by Henry Howard, ▷ Earl of Surrey, though his first printed works were his translations and adaptations of the ▷ Psalms (1549). His complex, ambiguous lyrics, with their development of ▷ Petrarchan motifs and images, are not only some of the earliest attempts at writing in a recognizably 'modern' (that is, non-medieval) style, but are important statements in their own right on the uncertain quality of life in the ▷ Renaissance polity.
Bib: Daalder, J. (ed.), *Collected Poems*; Foley, S., *Sir Thomas Wyatt*; Greenblatt, S., *Renaissance Self-Fashioning*.

Wycliffe, John (?1320–84)
Religious reformer. He was distinguished at Oxford for his ability in disputes; in 1374, he became Rector of Lutterworth, and soon

afterwards he started attacking the Pope and the papal court, at first chiefly on political grounds. He attacked the wealth of the senior clergy, and contrasted it with the poverty of the parish priests. This suited a party of the nobility headed by John of Gaunt, who became Wycliffe's patron and protector; they hated the rivalry of the upper clergy, and the powers possessed by the Pope to interfere in national affairs. His opposition to the papacy grew and was accompanied by opposition to international religious orders such as those of the ▷ friars; this divided Oxford into rival camps. He then went on to attack some of the central doctrines of the Church such as transubstantiation, *ie* the conversion of the bread and wine of the Sacrament into the actual body and blood of Christ. He also preached direct communion between the individual and God, and wanted an English ▷ translation of the ▷ Bible; in fact he made one, which is regarded as one of the foundation works of English prose. In all this he anticipated the ▷ Reformation, which divided the Church across Europe in the 16th century, yet such was the power of his protectors that he died safely in his bed. Although Wycliffe thus anticipated the 16th-century reformers, no independence could come to the ▷ Church of England until it suited the interests of the kings. The cause of Wycliffe's success was partly that ▷ Richard II was little more than a boy, and unable to decide on religious policy.

▷ Bible in England; Oldcastle, Sir John.

Wynkyn de Worde (d 1534)

Jan van Wynkyn moved to England with ▷ Caxton in 1476, and in 1491 took over Caxton's press, which he ran until his death c 1534. He published the first illustrated edition of ▷ Malory's ▷ *Morte D'Arthur* in 1498.

▷ Carol.

Yorick

In ▷ Shakespeare's ▷ *Hamlet*, the former king's jester whose skull the gravedigger turns up in V. i, giving Hamlet a subject for meditation. It has been conjectured that Shakespeare may have been alluding to ▷ Tarlton, or some other famous jester of the time.

Yorkshire Tragedy, A

A domestic ▷ tragedy published in 1608, and based on actual murders occurring in 1605. The play was ascribed to ▷ Shakespeare on its publication, but he is not now thought to have had any hand in it and ▷ Middleton is now the leading candidate for authorship. It is a forceful work, in a tradition of domestic tragedy that is an important subordinate line of the drama of Shakespeare's time: ▷ *Arden of Faversham*; *Warning for Fair Women* (Anon., 1599), and ▷ Thomas Heywood's ▷ *A Woman Killed with Kindness* (1603). They have in common that they deal with men and women of the middle classes (not, like the grand tragedy of the age, with the courts of princes), that they are realistic, and that they convey a strong moral warning.
Bib: Cawley, A. C. and Gaines, B. (eds.), *A Yorkshire Tragedy*.

Y

Zany

A court fool or jester, from the Italian 'zani' for actors or clowns in the ▷ Commedia dell'Arte.

Zeal-of-the-land Busy

A hypocritical ▷ Puritan in ▷ Ben Jonson's comedy ▷ *Bartholomew Fair*. It was common for Puritans of the period to give themselves names that were phrases derived from biblical texts.

Z

Chronology

This chronology gives a breakdown of important dates, both literary and historical. The literary dates are listed in the left-hand column and the historical events in the right-hand column. The listing is necessarily selective

Literary Dates	Historical Events
	1295 Edward I forms the Model Parliament **1337** Beginning of the Hundred Years' War **1349** The Black Death
c 1360 *Gawain and the Green Knight, Patience* and *Pearl* *Morte Arthure* **c 1367** *Piers Plowman* (A Text) **c 1369** Chaucer: *Book of the Duchess*	
1375–99 Chaucer: *Canterbury Tales* (? 1373–93) *House of Fame* *Legend of Good Women* *Trolius and Criseyde* Gower: *Confessio Amantis* Langland: *Piers Plowman* (B Text, 1377–79) Wycliffe: trans. of the Bible (1380) *Piers Plowman* (C Text, 1385–86)	**1377** Richard II **1381** The Peasants' Revolt: Wat Tyler's rebellion **1399** Henry IV
1400–24 James I of Scotland: *King's Quair* Paston Letters (1422–1507) Townley Mystery Plays Lydgate: *Fall of Princes* Caxton: *Recuyell of the Histories of Troy* (? printed 1474) Malory: *Morte d'Arthur* (printed 1485) Caxton: trans. of Aesop's *Fables* Henryson: *Moral Fables of Aesop* Skelton: *The Tunning of Elynor Rummyng*	**1413** Henry V **1415** Battle of Agincourt **1422** Henry VI
	1429 Joan of Arc raises the Siege of Orléans **1461** Edward IV **1475** Richard III **1476/7** Establishment of Caxton's printing press in England **1485** Henry VII **1492** Columbus discovers America **1498** Erasmus in England

1507
Dunbar: *Dance of the Seven Deadly Sins*
Skelton: *Book of Philip Sparrow* (? written)

1509
Henry VIII succeeds as king of England on death of
Henry VII

1513
Gavin Douglas: trans. of Virgil's *Aeneid* (written;
printed 1553)
1514
Barclay: *Eclogues* (completed)
1516
Sir Thomas More: *Utopia*

1517
Luther's 95 'Theses'; start of the Reformation
1520
Meeting at the Field of Cloth of Gold between Henry
VIII and Francis I
1521
Henry VIII Defender of the Faith
Luther appears before the Diet of Worms

1525
Tyndale: trans. of the New Testament

1526
Burning of Tyndale's trans. of the New Testament
1531
Henry VIII declared Head of the Church in England
1532
Submission of the clergy (to Henry VIII; begins
English Reformation)

1533
Skelton: *Magnificence* (posthumous)

1533
Jan. Henry VIII secretly married to Anne Boleyn
Apr. Divorce of Henry from Catharine of Aragon
June Coronation of Anne Boleyn
July. Henry VIII excommunicated by the Pope
Sept. Birth of Princess Elizabeth to Anne Boleyn
1534
England's final break with Rome
More's refusal to take oath to the succession
Parliament passes Act of Supremacy: Pope's powers
in England taken over by Henry VIII

1535
Coverdale: trans. of the Bible

1535
Henry VIII named 'Supreme Head of Church'
Trial and execution of Sir Thomas More
1536
Execution of Anne Boleyn
1539
Act of the Six Articles passed, 'abolishing diversity of
opinions'
Marriage treaty between Anne of Cleves and Henry
VIII
1540
Annulment of Henry VIII's marriage to Anne of
Cleves
Marriage between Henry VIII and Katharine
Howard
1542
Execution of Katharine Howard
Mary Queen of Scots accedes on the death of James V
of Scotland
1543
Marriage of Katherine Parr and Henry VIII
1545
Sir Thomas Elyot: *Defence of Good Women*

1545
The Council of Trent: beginning of the Counter-
reformation

1548
Book of Common Prayer

1547
Death of Henry VIII: succeeded by Edward VI
  (aged 4)
Repeal of the Six Articles (1539

1549
New *Book of Common Prayer* to be used from
  this date

1553
Gavin Douglas: trans. of Virgil's *Aeneid* (written 1513)
Wilson: *Art of Rhetoric*

1553
Death of Edward VI
Lady Jane Grey proclaimed queen, later executed
Mary I proclaimed queen in place of Lady Jane Grey
1554
Roman Catholicism re-established in England by
  Parliament
1556
Stationers' Company gains monopoly of English
  printing

1557
Earl of Surrey: trans. of Virgil's *Aeneid* (Books II
  and IV)
Tottel's Miscellany (poems by Surrey, Wyatt, et al.)
1558
Knox: *First Blast of the Trumpet*
1559
Mirror for Magistrates (first edition)

1558
Death of Mary I; accession of Elizabeth I
1559
Coronation of Elizabeth I
Act of Supremacy and Act of Uniformity

1561
Thomas Sackville (and Norton): *Gorboduc* (acted)
1563
Foxe: *Acts and Monuments* (Foxe's Book of Martyrs)
1565
Golding: trans. of Ovid's *Metamorphoses* (Books
  I–IV)

1563
The Plague in London kills many thousands

1566
Birth of James VI of Scotland
1567
Abdication of Mary Queen of Scots

1570
Ascham: *The Schoolmaster*

1572
St Bartholomew's Day massacre in Paris
1577
Francis Drake begins his circumnavigation of the
  globe
1578
James VI takes over government of Scotland

1577
Holinshed: *Chronicles*

1578
Lyly: *Euphues, the Anatomy of Wit* Part One
1579
North: trans. of Plutarch's *Lives* (from French)
Spenser: *Shepherd's Calendar*
1580
Lyly: *Euphues and his England*
Sidney: *Apologie for Poetrie*
1581
Joseph Hall: *Ten Books of Homer's Iliads*

1580
Performance of plays on Sunday forbidden
Francis Drake returns to England
1581
Laws against Roman Catholics passed
1583
Discovery of the Somerville plot to assassinate
  Elizabeth I
Discovery of the Throgmorton plot for Spanish
  invasion of England

1584
Greene: *Mirror of Modesty*
Knox: *History of the Reformation in Scotland*
Peele: *Arraignment of Paris*

1585
Ralegh establishes his first colony at Roanoke,
  Virginia

1586
Camden: *Britannia*

1586
The Star Chamber condemns Mary Queen of
  Scots to death

1587
Marlowe: *Doctor Faustus* (acted; published 1604)

1587
Mary Queen of Scots executed
1588
19 July. Spanish Armada sighted off the Cornish coast
29 July. The Battle of Gravelines: The Armada
  defeated

1589
Puttenham: *Art of English Poesie*
1590
Marlowe: *Tamburlaine* Parts I and II printed: Part I
  acted 1586–7
Sidney: *Arcadia*
Spenser: *Faerie Queene* (Books I–III)
1591
Sir John Harington: trans. of Ariosto's *Orlando
  Furioso*
Shakespeare: *Henry VI* (Parts II and III)
           The Two Gentlemen of Verona
Sidney: *Astrophil and Stella* (posthumous)
Spenser: *Complaints*
1592
Shakespeare: *Henry VI* (Part I)
Lyly: *Galatea*
Marlowe: *Edward II* (acted)

1592
Establishment of the Presbyterian Church
  in Scotland

1593
Henryson: *The Testament of Cresseid* (published)
Shakespeare: *Comedy of Errors*
           Richard II
           Venus and Adonis
1594
Hooker: *Ecclesiastical Polity* (Books I–IV)
Shakespeare: *Lucrece*
           Titus Andronicus
1595
Shakespeare: *Love's Labour's Lost*
           Midsummer Night's Dream
           Richard II
           Romeo and Juliet
Spenser: *Amoretti*
         Epithalamion
         Colin Clout's Come Home Again

1595
Death of Sir Francis Drake

1596
Jonson: *Every Man in his Humour* (acted)
Shakespeare: *Merchant of Venice*
           King John
Spenser: *Faerie Queene* (Books IV–VI)
         Four Hymns
1597
Bacon: *Essays*
Joseph Hall: *Virgidemiarum* (Books I–III)
Shakespeare: *Richard II*
1598
Chapman: trans. of Homer's *Iliad* (Books I–II;
  VII–XI)
Marlowe: *Hero and Leander*
Shakespeare: *Henry IV* Parts I and II
1599
Jonson: *Every Man out of his Humour*
Shakespeare: *Julius Caesar* (acted 21 Sept.)
           Henry V
           Much Ado About Nothing

1599
Birth of Oliver Cromwell

1600
Dekker: *The Shoemaker's Holiday* (first quarto)
Fairfax: trans. of Tasso's *Jerusalem Delivered*
Shakespeare: *The Merry Wives of Windsor*
 As You Like It
 Twelfth Night

1601
Shakespeare: *Hamlet*
1602
Marston: *Antonio's Revenge*
Shakespeare: *Troilus and Cressida*
1603
Jonson: *Sejanus*
Shakespeare: *All's Well that Ends Well*

1604
Marlowe: *Doctor Faustus* (earliest surviving edition)
Shakespeare: *Hamlet* (second quarto)
 Othello (acted)

1605
Drayton: *Poems*
Jonson: *Volpone* (acted; published 1607)
1606
Shakespeare: *King Lear* (acted)
 Macbeth (probably written by this date)
1607
Shakespeare: *Anthony and Cleopatra* (probably
 written; Stationers' Register 20 May 1608)
Tourneur: *Revenger's Tragedy*
1608
Thomas Heywood: *Rape of Lucrece*
Shakespeare: *Coriolanus* (probably written)
 King Lear (two quartos)
 Timon of Athens (probably written)
1609
Jonson: *Epicoene, or the Silent Woman* (Stationers'
 Register 20 Sept. 1610)
Shakespeare: *Pericles* (Stationers' Register 20
 May 1608)
 Sonnets
 Trolius and Cressida (two quartos)
1610
Beaumont and Fletcher: *Knights of the Burning
 Pestle* (? acted)
 The Maid's Tragedy (probably written)
Chapman: trans. of the *Iliad* (Books I–VII)
Jonson: *The Alchemist* (Stationers' Register 3 Oct.)
Shakespeare: *Cymbeline* (perhaps written)
 Winter's Tale (perhaps written)
1611
Authorized Version of the Bible
Chapman: trans. of the *Iliad* Books XIII–XXIV
Dekker and Middleton: *Roaring Girl* (printed)
Shakespeare: *Macbeth* (first recorded performance
 20 Apr.)
 The Tempest (perhaps written)
 Winter's Tale (acted by 15 May)
1612
Drayton: *Poly-Olbion* Part One
Webster: *The White Devil* (printed)
1613
Shakespeare: *Henry VIII* (acted 2 July)

1601
The execution of the Earl of Essex
1602
Bodleian Library founded
Re-conquest of Ireland begun
1603
Queen Elizabeth dies and is succeeded by James VI
 of Scotland as King James I of England
 and Ireland
1604
The Hampton Court Conference: James supports
 new translation of the Bible
James VI and I proclaimed king of 'Great Britain,
 France and Ireland'

1605
The Gunpowder plot

1606
Suppression of Roman Catholics by English
 Parliament
1607
English colony founded in Virginia

1611
The colonization of Ulster

1613
Globe Theatre burns down
Poisoning of Sir Thomas Overbury

1614
Chapman: trans. of the *Odyssey* Books I–XII
Jonson: *Bartholomew Fair* (acted; published 1631)
1615
Chapman: trans. of the *Odyssey* Books XIII–XXIV
1616
Jonson: *The Devil is an Ass* (acted)
          Underwoods
Webster: *The Duchess of Malfi* (acted; printed 1623)

1619
Drummond of Hawthornden: *Conversations with Ben Jonson*

1621
Burton: *Anatomy of Melancholy*
1622
Drayton: *Poly-Olbion* Part Two
Middleton and Rowley: *The Changeling*
1623
Shakespeare: *Comedies, Histiories and Tragedies* ('The First Folio')
Webster: *The Duchess of Malfi* (printed)
1624
Middleton: *A Game at Chess* (acted 6 Aug.)

1626
Sandys: trans. of Ovid's *Metamorphoses*
1631
Herbert: *The Temple*
Jonson: *The Devil is an Ass* (printed)
          The Staple of News (printed)
1633
Donne: *Poems* (posthumous (d. 1631))
Ford: *'Tis Pity She's a Whore* (printed)
1634
Thomas Carew: *Coelum Britannicum*
Milton: *Comus* (acted)
1637
Milton: *Lycidas*
1641
Milton: *Of Reformation Touching Church Discipline in England*
1642
Sir Thomas Browne: *Religio Medici*
Denham: *Cooper's Hill*
Milton: *Apology for Smectymnuus*
1644
Milton: *Areopagitica*

1646
Vaughan: *Poems*

1614
'The Addled Parliament'

1618
Start of the Thirty Years' War
Execution of Sir Walter Ralegh

1620
Freedom of worship granted to Roman Catholics in England in terms of marriage treaty between England and Spain
Pilgrim Fathers depart from Plymouth, England, in *Mayflower*

1625
Accession of Charles I
Marriage of Charles I and Henrietta Maria

1633
William Laud appointed Archbishop of Canterbury

1642
Civil War begins
Battle of Edgehill

1645
Prohibition of the Prayer Book by Parliament
Execution of Archbishop Laud

1648
Herrick: *Hesperides and Noble Numbers*

1649
Execution of Charles I
Abolition of the monarchy
Declaration of the Commonwealth

1651
Cleveland: *Poems*
D'Avenant: *Leviathan*

1651
Battle of Worcester

1653
Izzak Walton: *Compleat Angler*

1653
Long Parliament expelled by Cromwell
Establishment of Protectorate: Oliver Cromwell Lord
    High Protector

1654
Union of England, Scotland and Ireland

1656
Cowley: *Works* (includes 'Davideis' and 'Pindaric
    Odes')

1657
Middleton: *No Wit, No Help Like a Woman's*
            Two New Plays (includes *Women,*
                Beware Women)

1658
3 Sept. Death of Oliver Cromwell: succeeded by
    Richard Cromwell, his son, as Lord Protector 1660
16 Mar. Dissolution of the Long Parliament
Charles II invited to return to England by Convention
    Parliament

1661
Corporation Act: magistrates' oath of allegiance.

1662
Act of uniformity: revises Prayer Book: Licensing Act
    forbids import of anti-Christian literature

1665
The Great Plague

1666
2 Sept. Great Fire of London

1667
Milton: *Paradise Lost*

1671
Milton: *Paradise Regained*
        Samson Agonistes

1674
Rebuilding of the Theatre Royal, Drury Lane

1678
The Popish Plot: the Pope, France and Spain are
    accused of conspiracy to defeat Charles

1678
Bunyan: *Pilgrim's Progress* (Part One)

1681
Marvell: *Miscellaneous Poems* (posthumous)

1683
Rye House plot to kill Charles II and his brother,
    James, Duke of York

1684
Bunyan: *Pilgrim's Progress* (full text, including Part
    Two)

1685
Death of Charles II; succeeded by James II